THE
ENCYCLOPEDIA
OF ALBUMS

This edition published by Parragon 1999
Parragon
Queen Street House
4 Queen Street
Bath BA1 1HE, UK

Paperback ISBN   0-75253-336-3
Hardback ISBN   0-75253-323-1

Produced for Parragon by Foundry Design & Production,
Crabtree Hall, Crabtree Lane, Fulham, London SW6 6TY, UK.

All correspondence concerning the content of this book should
be addressed to The Encyclopedia of Albums, Parragon
Publishing, Queen Street House,
4 Queen Street, Bath, BA1 1HE, UK.

A copy of the CIP data for this book is available from the British Library.

AUTHORS

PAUL DU NOYER
Paul Du Noyer is a former editor of *Q* magazine, which he helped
to launch, and of *Mojo*, which he founded. He remains
Contributing Editor on both titles, as well as writing for a wide
range of other publications. In 1997 he wrote the widely
acclaimed book about John Lennon's solo songs, *We All Shine
On*.

MICHAEL HEATLEY
Michael Heatley was editor of *The History Of Rock*, a ten volume
series on popular music (1981–84). Since then, he's written over
50 music, sport and TV books, contributed to *Music Week*, *Gold
Mine (US)*, *Record Collector*, *RadioTimes* and many other
magazines. He is the founder of Northdown Publishing,
producers of quality music books.

PAUL LESTER
Paul Lester was features editor of *Melody Maker* from 1993 to
1997 and is now Associate Editor of the film and music monthly,
Uncut. He has written books on Pulp, Blur, Oasis, Björk, The
Prodigy and The Verve, freelances for *The Guardian*, pens a
column for Tower Records' *Top* magazine and is the pop reviewer
for BBC *News 24*.

CHRIS ROBERTS
Chris Roberts has written about music, cinema, books and
theatre for a wide range of publications. His book *Idle Worship*
was described by *The New York Times* as 'the most original music
book ever'. He has released records with the bands Catwalk and
Scalaland and lives in London.

Additional contributions by: Graham Betts, Nigel Cross, Philip
Dodd, Alan Kinsman, Andrea Thorn, Suresh Tolat, Ian Welch.

ACKNOWLEDGMENTS

We particularly acknowledge the assistance of Dave Bates who kindly
gave us access to his research database; he is currently working on a book
about the world's top music producers. Special thanks are due to Sean
and all the staff at Helter Skelter music bookshop in London's Denmark
Street; John Stickland; Valerie Pavett at St Martin's School of Art in
London; Alastair Blaazar, Jim Brittain and Lorne Murdoch at MCPS;
Jackie Da Costa at Re-Pro, The Guild of Recording Producers, Directors
and Engineers; Bob Shannon, co-author of *Behind the Hits*; and Bill
Pitzonka.

With grateful thanks to Frances Banfield, Kirsten Bradbury, Josephine
Cutts, Claire Dashwood, Philip Dodd, Grant Duffort, Dawn Eden,
Lucinda Hawksley, Sarah Henry, Helen Johnson, Penny Lane, Keeley
Lawrence, Dylan Lobo, Lesley Malkin, Lee Matthews, Ezra Nathan,
Brian Nevill, Martin Noble, Adrian Pay, Andrea Power, Ian Powling,
Miguel Rosales, Chris de Selincourt, Mike de Selincourt, James Smith,
Nigel Soper, Neil Spencer, Amanda-Jane Tomlins and the many record
companies who patiently supplied us with information.

We would like to acknowledge the following sources which proved
invaluable in cross-checking our research and would recommend to
readers interested in further reading: M. C. Strong, *The Great Rock
Discography*, Canongate, 1995; Paul Gambaccini, Jonathan Rice and Tim
Rice, *Guinness British Hit Albums*, Guinness, 1994; Colin Larkin (ed.),
The Guinness Encyclopedia of Popular Music, Guinness, 1994; Patricia
Romanowski and Holly George-Warren (eds), *The New Rolling Stone
Encyclopedia of Rock & Roll*, Fireside, 1995; Dafydd Rees and Luke
Crampton, *Q Encyclopedia of Rock Stars*, Dorling Kindersley, 1996;
Anthony DeCurtis and James Henke with Holly George-Warren (eds),
The Rolling Stone Album Guide, Virgin, 1992; and Dave McAleer, *The
Warner Guide To UK & US Hit Albums*, Carlton/Little Brown, 1995.

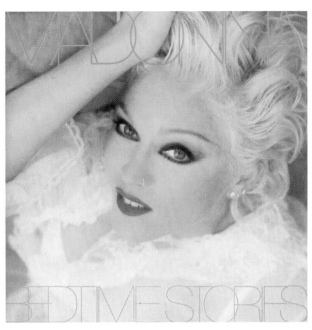

THE
ENCYCLOPEDIA
OF ALBUMS

Michael Heatley, Paul Lester, Chris Roberts

General Editor: Paul Du Noyer

Introduction

We move houses. We lose books. We replace our clothes when fashion shames us into it. Girlfriends, boyfriends, husbands and wives, are somehow not the fixtures that they used to be. Times change and people move on. But here's the weird thing. If there's one core value, just one constant in the flux of our lives, it's often our prized collection of albums. Burglars and borrowers and burst pipes all conspire against us sometimes, but, if we can, we keep those precious albums intact. Hopefully the hoard will grow a little all the time, like children do. Stacked together, on a shelf, the records become a lone symbol of continuity in our dislocated existences. They are, in some strange sense, who we are. As current marketing speak might put it: Albums R Us.

A song may bring to mind a moment of our past, but an album can summon up a whole chapter. Particular albums become entwined with our identities, permeating our minds, merging with our emotions. They become, in effect, a personal soundtrack to the epic, autobiographical movie that we each carry in our heads. Maybe it's because an album is so often heard alone, and usually listened to on the premises we call our own. They're rarely shared with a wider world (as singles are) and, often as not, we listen to albums with the 'phones clamped to our ears, lost to the planet and the rest of its inhabitants. And we form meaningful relationships with albums because they represent a colossal effort on the part of their creators. Far more than the average single song, an album is a prolonged expression of personality, in which the artist shares so much that he, or she, or they, can burn themselves out in the process. Albums R Them, too.

Albums carry such a heavy freight of psychic significance, both for their makers and their recipients, that it might require the innocence of a fool or the arrogance of a dictator to name the best 1000 of the species. The compilers of this book, however, seem to belong to neither of those categories – they have merely attempted an honest assessment of those works which have meant the most to the greatest number of

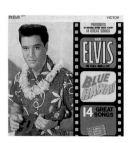

people. The only complication is that 'meant the most' can be measured either in breadth or in depth. Do we record the quantity of sales, or gauge the quality of appreciation? I think what has happened in the quest to bring you

this book is a shrewd compromise between the two. You cannot possibly agree with the finished list in its entirety: human beings are probably not made that way. And yet, after it has confirmed your impeccable taste and outraged your sense of natural justice, this book may have a third effect that is even more important. We hope that it might nudge you, in the most agreeably persuasive way, towards some beautiful music that you might not know as yet, and will in time come to love.

To compile this list we have surveyed the album from its very beginnings. The word itself is a legacy of the 10-inch 78. Those shellac discs could handle only one track per side; and so, to accommodate a long orchestral work or a collection of songs, the manufacturers would package the 78s together, in 'albums'. A great leap forward occurred in 1948 when Dr Peter Goldmark, at New York's CBS Laboratories, perfected 'Microgroove' vinyl records that played at 33 rpm and could house an entire symphony or soundtrack. Movie musicals and theatre cast recordings were the staple of 'long-playing' (LP) releases at first. In the 1950s Frank Sinatra popularized LPs as sets of thematically coherent, but otherwise unconnected, songs: **In The Wee Small Hours** and **Songs For Swingin' Lovers** are classics of the form. Rock 'n' roll took up the LP, too, although it remained an expensive item to the juvenile market, strictly secondary to the all-important single.

It's with the 1960s, and acts like Bob Dylan and The Beatles, that the album story starts to hot up. The former's **Blonde On Blonde** (1966) and the latter's **Sgt. Pepper's Lonely Hearts Club Band** (1967) transformed the LP's status, from a rag-bag of recycled singles and second-grade ballast, into A Major Statement. All of a sudden the LP was an 'album' once more, and it was Art. Outstripping the single in prestige and profitability, the album became the ultimate artefact of the rock

era. Eric Clapton was moved to
announce, in 1967: 'I'm a great
believer that singles will become
obsolete and LPs will take their
place. Singles are an anachronism.'
(Luckily for him, and his royalties
from *Layla* five years later, he was
wrong.) Liberated by the possibilities it offered, many artists
rose to the challenge. Van Morrison's **Astral Weeks** (1968)
and The Rolling Stones' **Exile On Main Street** (1972) are two
classic examples of rock albums which work as a unified whole,
becoming more than the sum of their parts. Rock had acquired
a mature and educated audience, who liked the respectability
that albums conferred, the sense of substance and permanence.

The elevation of the album, and the acceleration of industry
competition, encouraged the use of elaborate packaging,
turning sleeves into an art form to rival the music itself. Until
the eventual triumph of the compact disc in the late 1980s, 12-
inch LP covers were a broad canvas for the boldest graphic
experiments (and one reason why vinyl was preferred to its up-
and-coming rival, the cassette tape). By general consent the
album sleeve reached a peak of grandeur during the 1970s,
especially in the work of British design team Hipgnosis, whose
clients included Pink Floyd and Led Zeppelin. Covers portrayed
the power and mystique attributed to the artist, often produced
with an extravagant disregard for cost. The Rolling Stones
toyed with a Warhol trouser zipper (**Sticky Fingers**) and Alice
Cooper experimented with knickers (**School's Out**). A
specialist in elaborate fantasia, the painter Roger Dean
decorated some progressive rock albums that are now better-
known for their wrapping than their content.

Of course, punk rendered much of this indulgence
unfashionable. If the album encouraged musicians to raise their
aspirations, it also flattered their pretensions. Like pop, disco
and the dance styles that have thrived in the 1990s, punk was
essentially singles-driven: but the album has thrived anyway.
In time even new wave performers found a natural home there.
It was, and remains, the supreme medium for singer/songwriters
such as Elvis Costello. The reconstruction of George Michael

from Wham!'s teen dream to serious solo artist meant a parallel
shift in his priorities from hit songs to fully rounded collections.
Above all there was the phenomenon of Michael Jackson,
transcending his singles-bound past to create a series of the
biggest selling albums in history. Singles are periodically, if
prematurely, predicted to disappear, but no-one has questioned
the viability of albums. The only question has been, in what
form will we buy them? The real revolution of recent years has
not been one of music, but of technology.

Developed in the early 1980s, CDs have risen remorselessly,
originally at the expense of vinyl and now of cassettes as well.
Ever since Thomas Edison's wax cylinders were displaced by
shellac discs, audio formats have fought a Darwinian struggle
for existence. The eight-track cartridge led a brief, uncertain
life until its demise in 1979. Its natural predator, the cassette,
was a niftier offspring of the bulky reel-to-reel tape medium; it
may have lacked the romance of vinyl but scored for
practicality in the car or on the personal stereo. Now the
analogue formats of tape and vinyl are being superseded by
digital CD, favoured for its greater playing time, its clarity and
hardiness, and the convenience of track-surfing. Thanks to CD,
classical masterpieces can be heard without interruption, but
so can flatulent instrumental noodlings. The discipline of the
edit is a quality that musicians must rediscover. The CD now
enjoys almost universal acceptance, but it too has its
challengers.

Digital Audio Tape (DAT) was an early contender, which
has subsequently found its niche among professional users
rather than ordinary consumers. Mini Discs (scaled-down CDs
that you can also record over) and Digital Compact Cassettes
(DCC) joined battle in 1992, and seemed, if anything, to
cancel one another out. But the market will soon be ready for

a new recordable medium and the
Mini Disc looks like being the one
we'll take to. Along with its
probable counterpart the DVD (or
Digital Versatile Disc, which comes
with video capability), the MD will
continue to serve up music by the

album's worth. Perhaps it is only the Internet that threatens the album as our basic unit of musical consumption. If we are allowed to download individual tracks, to our own pick 'n' mix agenda, then the nagging suspicion that most modern albums are 'just too long' will find a way to assert itself. If that ever happens, the album will need to fight for its right to our time.

Of course the compilation, whether of one artist's work or several, is a mainstay of the album market. But, apart from very few notable exceptions such as **Woodstock, The Album**, it's a genre we've resisted in this book, preferring to focus on the 'album-as-album' – namely the purposeful effort to produce one body of work, integral and sustained. In the earliest years of pop, especially, album tracks were stockpiled haphazardly; they were corralled on to an LP as soon as there were sufficient in the can. But even then they represented a time and a place, and they hang together as much as the most ponderous 'concept album' ever has. So, no 'Best Of' sets in here, nor the so-called 'soundtrack' albums which are no more than Hollywood marketing ploys, nor anything of the 'Now That's What I Call Music Volume 182' variety.

What's left over is more than enough. The invention of the album was a catalyst that inspired an awesome outpouring of talent. It probably changed the face of the late twentieth century. Who could imagine life without it? Here, then, is a book of 1000 possibilities. Each great album is a world unto itself, so how did we arrive at such a list? The short answer is: with extreme difficulty. People, as we've noted, are passionate about their favourite albums, and cannot be reasoned out of loving what they love. Arguments abound, along with opportunities for resentment. Whole wars have been fought for causes that are less contentious. But in this case, we hope, there will be only limited bloodshed. We've tried to make our choices rational, using the following criteria.

Commercial success is quite obviously important. Nobody pretends that best-selling is always best, but you can do a lot worse than trust to market forces when it comes to popular

music. Think of **Thriller**, or **Bridge Over Troubled Water**, or **(What's The Story) Morning Glory?**. The charts have always failed to accommodate some records of undisputed genius, but they rarely put up with absolute rubbish for more than a couple of weeks. So we've taken close account of UK and US Top 5 positions since 1955. We've also looked out for those 'slow-burning' albums which have never taken the top honours but have nevertheless sold in steady amounts across a period of time. In a turtle-and-hare kind of fashion such records can often be the ultimate star performers: Pink Floyd's **Dark Side Of The Moon** has sold about 30 million copies, rising each day, but it never made Number 1 (while Derek & The Dominos' **Layla** LP never charted in Britain at all). As well as tracking the British and American charts we've assessed each album's international appeal, noting its success in key overseas markets such as Germany, Spain and Japan.

Critical acclaim, industry awards and general popularity polls also played a vital part in our selection. All-time and annual lists are a regular feature of magazines including *Rolling Stone*, *Q*, *NME* and *Mojo*; these publications occasionally invite their readerships to vote as well. We've reflected those preferences. Within the music industry are several well-established honours, like the Grammy Awards, the Brit Awards and the Mercury Music Prize, and these too are added to our reckoning. Of course, there will still be some excellent albums which slip through any number of nets, so we've also found room for some personal choices that might otherwise not qualify, but which simply demand to be recognized. So that explains Jackie Leven's **The Mystery Of Love (Is Greater Than The Mystery Of Death)** – in case you were wondering…Now read on. Dip in, dip out, explore and enjoy. There is always one more brilliant album to discover.

Paul Du Noyer

How to use this book

The encyclopedia is organized alphabetically by album name. To locate entries for a particular artist or group, refer to the Index of Artists at the back of the book. As part of the extensive research in the compilation of this encyclopedia, we consulted and cross-checked using a wide range of print, digital and microfiche sources. The following notes offer some background information, where appropriate, on our approach.

Release date: gives the date of a record's 'debut' – its first appearance in the world. According to sources used, this may be date of release or date of chart entry. Where the information was available we have given dates for both UK and US releases, otherwise we have provided a single date. Label: we provide the label of initial release, or both UK and US labels, where known. A list of abbreviations for instruments played is given below.

Wherever possible, we have endeavoured to provide a quote from the music press that helps to put the album in context. Ranging from adulatory to downright dismissive, these excerpts frequently offer an insight to an album's initial critical reception and work as a counterpoint to the contributors' entries. A small number of quotes compiled were written at the time of a record's re-release. For ease of reference, we have presented **Album Names** in bold and *Singles, songs or tracks* in italicized bold.

Instrument Abbreviations

ad	Accordian	dbb	Double Bass	lg	Lead Guitar	syb	Synth Bass
ag	Acoustic Guitar	dj	Disc Jockey	ls	Lap Steel	syh	Synth Horns
arr	Arranger	dm	Drum Machine	lv	Lead Vocals	t	Trumpet
as	Alto Sax	dp	Drum Programming	mba	Marimba	ta	Tuba
asg	Acoustic Slide Guitar	du	Dulcimar	md	Mandolin	tab	Tabla
b	Bass	e	Electronics	mh	Mouth Harp	tb	Timbales
bc	Bass Clarinet	ep	Electric Piano	mln	Mellotron	tg	Triangle
bg	Bongos	es	Electric Sax	mo	Mellodica	tm	Tambourine
br	Bodhran	est	Electric Sitar	o	Organ	tp	Tiompan
brs	Brass	fd	Fiddle	ob	Oboe	tr	Trombone
bs	Baritone Sax	fh	Flugelhorn	orc	Orchestration	ts	Tenor Sax
bt	Baritone	fl	Flute	p	Piano	tt	Turntables
bv	Backing Vocals	frh	French Horn	pc	Percussion	ty	Tympani
bz	Bellzouki	g	Guitar	pc	Piccalo	up	Uillean Pipes
c	Cello	ga	Groove Activator	pp	Pipes	v	Vocals
cb	Cowbell	gl	Glockenspiel	ps	Pedal Steel	va	Viola
ce	Celeste	gst	Guest (artist)	r	Reeds	var	Various Instruments
cg	Congas	gsy	Guitar Synthesizer	rap	RAP Artist	vl	Violin
cl	Clarinet	h	Harmonica	rc	Recorder	vp	Vibraphone
con	Conductor	hc	Handclapping	rg	Rhythm Guitar	vpc	Vocal Percussion
cp	Composer	hd	Harpsichord	s	Sax	w	Whistle
ct	Concertina	hn	Horn	sg	Slide Guitar	wa	Washboard
ctte	Clavinette	hp	Harp	ss	Soprano Sax	wor	Words
d	Drums	k	Keyboards	st	Strings	ww	Woodwind
db	Dobro	kp	Keyboard Programming	stg	Steel Guitar		
				sy	Synthesizer		

Abandoned Luncheonette

ARTIST Hall And Oates **RELEASE DATE** January 1974 (UK & US) **LABEL** Atlantic (UK & US) **PRODUCER** Arif Mardin **UK CHART** peak/weeks 0/0 **US CHART** peak/weeks 33/38 **TRACK LISTING** I'm Just A Kid (Don't Make Me Feel Like A Man)/Laughing Boy/She's Gone/Las Vegas Turnaround (The Stewardess Song)/Had I Known You Better Then/Lady Rain/When The Morning Comes/Abandoned Luncheonette/Everytime I Look At You **PERSONNEL** Daryl Hall (v, g), John Oates (v, g), and session musicians

Few acts have released such a diverse first trio of albums as Daryl Hall and John Oates: folk (**Whole Oats**), deep soul (this album) and warped but wonderful sci-fi rock (the Todd Rundgren-produced follow-up, **War Babies**). The jewel in this crown was *She's Gone*, taken to the top of the R&B chart by black vocal group Tavares some six months later. Producer Arif Mardin went on to turn the Bee Gees into disco kings. H&O made it later in the decade too – they were ahead of their time.

Abandoned Luncheonette *has a strong urban certainty in both writing and performing.* G. B., Melody Maker, April 1974

Abbey Road

ARTIST The Beatles **RELEASE DATE** September 1969 (UK & US) **LABEL** Apple (UK & US) **PRODUCER** George Martin **UK CHART** peak/weeks 1/81 **US CHART** peak/weeks 1/129 **TRACK LISTING** Come Together/Something/Maxwell's Silver Hammer/Oh! Darling/Octopus's Garden/I Want You/Here Comes The Sun/Because/You Never Give Me Your Money/Sun King/Mean Mr Mustard/Polythene Pam/She Came In Through The Bathroom Window/Golden Slumbers/Carry That Weight/The End **PERSONNEL** John Lennon (v, rg), Paul McCartney (v, b), George Harrison (v, lg), Ringo Starr (d)

Their last full recording (though the **Let It Be** shambles dragged on till it was released as the farewell album, in name at least), even George Martin was staggered by the productiveness of these sessions. One of the best-selling Beatles albums, it finds Harrison delivering two exquisite contributions in *Something*, and *Here Comes The Sun*, Lennon getting his teeth into *Come Together*, and the ever ambitious and prolific McCartney choreographing most of the second side's panoramic-long medley. The cover shot, with the four tackling a St John's Wood zebra crossing opposite the studio, has become perhaps one of the decade's most hilariously over-analysed and imitated icons.

Simply, side two does more for me than the whole of **Sgt. Pepper.** John Mendelsohn, Rolling Stone, November 1969

Abraxas

ARTIST Santana **RELEASE DATE** November 1970 (UK)/October 1970 (US) **LABEL** CBS (UK)/Columbia (US) **PRODUCER** Fred Catero, Santana **UK CHART** peak/weeks 7/52 **US CHART** peak/weeks 1/88 **TRACK LISTING** Singing Winds/Crying Beasts/Black Magic Woman/Gypsy Queen/Oye Como Va/Incident At Neshabur/Se A Cabo/Mother's Daughter/Samba Pa Ti/Hope You're Feeling Better/El Nicoya **PERSONNEL** Carlos Santana (lg, v), Gregg Rolie (k, v), David Brown (b), Mike Shrieve (d), Jose 'Chepito' Areas (pc), Mike Carabello (g)

The second album from Santana, the band formed by Mexican guitarist Carlos Santana, brought their Latin-influenced rock to a wide audience. Although they incorporated samba and salsa sounds, there were also hard rock and complex Afro-jazzy polyrhythms in the mix, gaining the admiration of the acid heads during the psychedelic era (Santana were one of only three bands to appear at both Woodstock festivals). With its cover of Fleetwood Mac's *Black Magic Woman* and reinterpretation of Tito Puente's *Oye Como Va*, the four-million selling **Abraxas** remains a classic of Seventies fusion.

He (Carlos Santana) has perfected a style associated with blues and cool jazz and crossed it with Latin music. It works well because the band is one of the tightest ever to walk into a recording studio. Jim Nash, Rolling Stone, December 1974

Absolutely Live

ARTIST The Doors **RELEASE DATE** September 1970 (UK)/August 1970 (US) **LABEL** Electra (UK & US) **PRODUCER** Paul A. Rothchild **UK CHART** peak/weeks 69/1 **US CHART** peak/weeks 8/20 **TRACK LISTING** Who Do You Love/Medley: Alabama Song/Backdoor Man/Love Hides/Five To One/Build Me A Woman/When The Music's Over/Close To You/Universal Mind/Break On Thru #2/The Celebration Of The Lizard/Soul Kitchen **PERSONNEL** Jim Morrison (lv), Ray Manzarek (o, b, v), Robbie Krieger (g), John Densmore (d)

Doors concerts were often described as rituals with Jim Morrison as the shaman conducting a religious communion between audience and band. It was something the studio albums could only subconsciously convey and, in the pre-video age, the next best thing to being there was a live album. Seen by Jim as 'a true document of our good concerts', though in reality culled from three live appearances in Philadelphia, LA and New York, it ultimately failed to deliver the goods as powerfully as other key live albums from the era, such as those by The Who.

A tight little band, excellent on building funky riffs, they create atmosphere for Jim's poetical outpourings. They can rock even if Ray Manzarek does sound a little hurdy-gurdy on organ... here is never a dull moment... C. W., Melody Maker, September 1970

According To My Heart

ARTIST Jim Reeves **RELEASE DATE** July 1969 (UK)/1965 (US) **LABEL** RCA Int (UK & US) **PRODUCER** – **UK CHART** peak/weeks 1/14 **US CHART** peak/weeks 0/0 **TRACK LISTING** – **PERSONNEL** Jim Reeves (v, g)

Like Patsy Cline, who had perished in similar circumstances the previous year, country star Jim Reeves's legend did not die when his plane went down in 1964 – and that was proved when, after two Number 2 albums (both posthumous chart entries), this

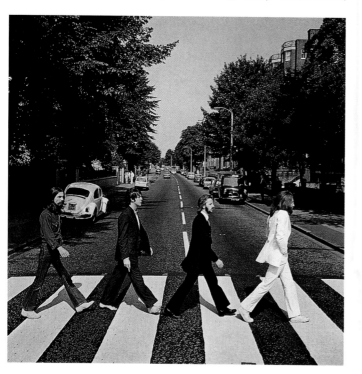

became his first UK Number 1 long-player and remained at the top until days after the fifth anniversary of the crash. In truth it was a very conservative chart, Ray Conniff and The Seekers being among the other Number 1s. But Reeves, who two decades after this album would sing with Cline new 'studio-produced' songs, remains suspended in time.

Jim's country roots shine through this set which must be another big commercial success. **Melody Maker, August 1969**

Achtung Baby

ARTIST U2 RELEASE DATE November 1991 (UK)/December 1991 (US) LABEL Island (UK & US) PRODUCER David Lanois, Brian Eno UK CHART peak/weeks 2/77 US CHART peak/weeks 1/9 TRACK LISTING Zoo Station/Even Better Than The Real Thing/One/Until The End Of The World/Who's Gonna Ride Your Wild Horses/So Cruel/The Fly/Mysterious Ways/Tryin' To Throw Your Arms Around The World/Ultra Violet (Light My Way)/Acrobat/Love Is Blindness PERSONNEL Bono (v), The Edge (g, k), Adam Clayton (b), Larry Mullen Jnr (d)

Achtung Baby marks Bono's welcome lyrical shift from the political to the personal and the band's assimilation of many recent stylistic developments. It is the first of U2's 'modern' pop records, recorded in the same studio in Berlin where producer Brian Eno

and David Bowie worked on their late Seventies experimental trilogy (**Low**, **Heroes** and **Lodger**). The result is a U2 album with an experimental edge, a U2 album you can dance to, with nods to techno, industrial, grunge and hip-hop.

With **Achtung Baby**, *U2 is once again trying to broaden its musical palette, but this time its ambitions are realised…. Few bands can marshal such sublime power….* **Elysa Gardner, Rolling Stone, January 1992**

Actually

ARTIST Pet Shop Boys RELEASE DATE September 1987 (UK)/October 1987 (US) LABEL Parlophone (UK)/EMI America (US) PRODUCER Pet Shop Boys, Stephen Hague UK CHART peak/weeks 2/59 US CHART peak/weeks 25/45 TRACK LISTING One More Chance/What Have I Done To Deserve This?/Shopping/Rent/Hit Music/It Couldn't Happen Here/It's A Sin/I Want To Wake Up/Heart/King's Cross PERSONNEL Neil Tennant (v), Chris Lowe (sy, k)

Having tested the water with a first album, **Please** and a dance remix version **Disco**, the Pet Shop Boys tackled their second album proper with aplomb. It would stay over a year in the charts and go gold in the States within three months. The US version was made available in Britain the following May, including the deliberately omitted chart-topping Presley cover *Always On My Mind* to go with the equally successful (and self-penned) *It's A Sin*.

European pop will come no cleaner, crisper or more impressive than the Pet Shop Boys. The genre demands a kind of quivery coldness imbued with a desire for memorability that has little time for hanging around outside the front door, but the Pet Shop Boys manage to do more than mere rote approximation. **Paul Mathur, Melody Maker, September 1987**

Affection

ARTIST Lisa Stansfield RELEASE DATE December 1989 (UK)/March 1990 (US) LABEL Arista (UK & US) PRODUCER Ian Devaney, Andy Morris, ColdCut UK CHART peak/weeks 2/31 US CHART peak/weeks 9/39 TRACK LISTING This Is The Right Time/Mighty Love/Sincerity/The Love In Me/All Around The World/What Did I Do To You?/Live Together/You Can't Deny It/Poison/When Are You Coming Back? PERSONNEL Lisa Stansfield (v), session musicians

Rochdale-born Stansfield had already enjoyed some success as lead singer of *People Hold On* by UK house act, Coldcut, but she entered the mega-league with *All Around The World*, a lushly produced, Seventies disco-style number from 1989. **Affection**, Stansfield's debut album, included  that global smash. Indeed, it was full of orchestral dance-pop whose debt to such masters of sensual Seventies grooves as Thom Bell and Barry White was obvious.

Affection *is a picture-perfect marriage between house beats and the torchy growl of late-night silky soul… the album is an ideal blend of club-land energy and the passion of soul music. A dance record you can listen to.* **Amy Linden, Rolling Stone, May 1990**

After The Gold Rush

ARTIST Neil Young RELEASE DATE October 1970 (UK)/September 1970 (US) LABEL Reprise (UK & US) PRODUCER Neil Young, David Briggs, Kendall Pacios UK CHART peak/weeks 7/68 US CHART peak/weeks 8/66 TRACK LISTING Tell Me Why/After The Goldrush/Only Love Can Break Your Heart/Southern Man/Till The Morning Comes/Oh Lonesome Me/Don't Let It Bring You Down/Birds/When You Dance I Can Really Love/I Believe In You/Crippled Creek Ferry PERSONNEL Billy Talbot (b), Greg Reeves (b), Nils Lofgren (p, v), Ralph Molina (d, v), Neil Young (h, g, v), Danny Whitten (g, v), Steve Stills (v)

Neil Young's first masterpiece contained some of his best folk-tinged ballads: *Tell Me Why*, a Top 40 hit *Only Love Can Break Your Heart*, the haunting, horn-flecked title track and finest rockers: *Southern Man* (which would later prompt Lynyrd Skynyrd's answer record, *Sweet Home Alabama*), *When You Dance You Can Really Love*. **After The Goldrush** reflected the sense of disillusion and burn-out felt by many in the early Seventies, providing succour and hope for acid casualties and hippy optimists let down by the late Sixties dream. It also established Young as rock's premier spokesman after Bob Dylan.

Despite the fact that the album contains some potentially first rate material, none of the songs here rise above the uniformly dull surface… most of this music was simply not ready to be recorded. **Langdon Winner, Rolling Stone, October 1970**

Aftermath

ARTIST The Rolling Stones RELEASE DATE April 1966 (UK)/July 1966 (US) LABEL Decca (UK)/London (US) PRODUCER Andrew Oldham UK CHART peak/weeks 1/28 US CHART peak/weeks 2/50 TRACK LISTING Mother's Little Helper/Stupid Girl//Lady Jane/Under My Thumb/Doncha Bother Me/Goin' Home/Flight 505/High And Dry/Out Of Time/It's Not Easy/I Am Waiting/Take It Or Leave It/Think/What To Do/Paint It Black PERSONNEL Mick Jagger (v, h), Keith Richards (rg), Brian Jones (lg), Charlie Watts (d), Bill Wyman (b), Ian Stewart (p)

The problem with **Aftermath**, the first Stones album composed completely of Jagger-Richards songs, is that it was released in a great year for rock. **Pet Sounds**, **Revolver** and **Blonde On Blonde** all got better reviews, leading to the following year's **Their Satanic Majesties Request** which saw the Stones follow trends for the first time. The last seven minutes of the lengthy *Going Home* was a studio jam, but elsewhere they kept it tight on an album whose original title was 'Could You Walk On The Water'.

Spanking new fourteen-track Rolling Stone LP. Undoubtedly this is the best they have made and should be their biggest British seller to date. The emphasis on the record is big beat… **Melody Maker, April 1966**

The Age Of Aquarius

ARTIST The 5th Dimension RELEASE DATE July 1969 (UK)/May 1969 (US) LABEL Soul City (US) PRODUCER Bones Howe UK CHART peak/weeks 0/0 US CHART peak/weeks 2/72 TRACK LISTING Aquarius/Let The Sunshine In/Blowing Away/Dontcha Hear Me Callin' To Ya/The Hideaway/Let It Be Me/Skinny Man/Sunshine Of Your Love/Those Were The Days/Wedding Bell Blues/Winds Of Heaven/Workin' On A Groovy Thing PERSONNEL Marilyn McCoo (v), Florence La Rue (v), Lamonte McLemore (v), Billy Davis Jr (v), Ron Townson (v)

Album sales had dipped after their US Top 10 debut **Up Up And Away**, but soul harmony quartet the Fifth Dimension hitched themselves to a fast-rising phenomenon by borrowing two songs from the hippy hit musical *Hair* for this album's chart-topping near-title track. The Laura Nyro-penned *Wedding Bell Blues* would give them a second US Number 1 in a year when group members McCoo and Davis, and LaRue and manager Marc Gordon, matched actions to words and got married!

A fabulous album from probably the world's top singing group. Tremendous excitement, bustling, yet tight arrangements socked out by skilled musicians, and the singing is out of this world. **Melody Maker, June 1969**

Aja

ARTIST Steely Dan RELEASE DATE October 1977 (UK & US) LABEL ABC (UK & US) PRODUCER Gary Katz UK CHART peak/weeks 5/10 US CHART peak/weeks 3/60 TRACK LISTING Black Cow/Aja/Deacon Blues/Peg/Home At Last/I Got The News/Josie PERSONNEL Donald Fagen (k, v), Walter Becker (b, v), session musicians

With its gatefold black sleeve and detailed liner notes, **Aja** had the sophisticated air of an obscure early Sixties cool jazz album. It was as if, after the international success of 1976's **The Royal Scam** LP, Steely Dan were turning their back on a pop scene that was always too juvenile for their fiercely intelligent brand of contemporary fusion. For all their efforts to reject the mainstream, **Aja** became their biggest seller yet, and on tracks like *Deacon Blues* (the inspiration for the mid-Eighties British group, Deacon Blue), *Peg* (the basis for hip hoppers De La Soul's *Eye Know*) and *Home At Last* they exuded an exquisite world-weary ennui.

Steely Dan have made a pronounced change of direction with a strong shift of emphasis away from songs and towards playing and arrangements…. Strangely enough, considering the number of musicians employed, they sound like a band again. **Steve Clarke, NME, September 1977**

Aladdin Sane

ARTIST David Bowie **RELEASE DATE** May 1973 (UK)/April 1973 (US) **LABEL** RCA Victor (UK & US) **PRODUCER** David Bowie, Ken Scott **UK CHART** peak/weeks 1/47 **US CHART** peak/weeks 17/22 **TRACK LISTING** Watch That Man/Aladdin Sane (1913-1938-197?)/Drive-In Saturday/Panic In Detroit/Cracked Actor/Time/The Prettiest Star/Let's Spend The Night Together/The Jean Genie/Lady Grinning Soul **PERSONNEL** David Bowie (v, g), Mick Ronson (g), T. J. Bolder (b), Woody Woodmansey (d), Mike Gason (p), Ken Fordham (s, f), Juanita Franklin (bv), Linda Lewis (bv), Mac Cormac (bv)

Another album, another face. Loving the smell of the greasepaint and the adulation of the crowd, this Aladdin showed fleeting glimpses of a touchy neuroticism, which gave an edge to Mike Garson's warped cabaret piano and the Stones-tinted rock of *Watch That Man* and *Panic In Detroit*. *Time* was monumental, allowing the cracked actor a stage for self-examination. *Drive-In Saturday* remains strangely prophetic despite its loopy sci-fi excesses, while *Lady Grinning Soul* was nothing if not flushed with deathless romance. Bowie was on one of the greatest rolls in rock history.

The Album

ARTIST Abba **RELEASE DATE** January 1978 (UK)/March 1978 (US) **LABEL** Epic/Atlanta **PRODUCER** Benny Anderson, Björn Ulvaeus **UK CHART** peak/weeks 1/61 **US CHART** peak/weeks 14/41 **TRACK LISTING** Eagle/Take A Chance On Me/One Man, One Woman/The Name Of The Game/Move On/Hole In Your Soul/The Girl With The Golden Hair/Thank You For The Music/I Wonder/I'm A Marionette **PERSONNEL** Benny Anderson (k, sy, v), Björn Ulvaeus (g, v), Agnetha Fältskog (v), Frida Lyngstad (v) with Rutger Gunnarsson (b), Ola Brunkert (d), Lasse Wellander (g), Malando Gassama (pc)

Abba's formula of brooding verses followed by huge barn-storming choruses was honed to an almost Zen perfection – the dodgy English lyrics and cute pronunciation adding to their charm, or irritation. The two overtly glamorous, ostentatiously in-love couples appealed to a bewildering cross-section of nationalities and age groups. The biggest chart-topper of the year (so much for punk rock), the album was eventually toppled, bizarrely enough, by a Buddy Holly compilation. Classic singles were Abba's life blood: this had its share.

The Album represents an interesting departure from past formulas and will undoubtedly receive a mixed response… side two is a real attempt to do something different, and, if not everything on it works, the effort is still laudable. **John Rockwell, Rolling Stone, March 1978**

Alf

ARTIST Alison Moyet **RELEASE DATE** November 1984 (UK)/April 1985 (US) **LABEL** CBS (UK)/Columbia (US) **PRODUCER** Tony Swain, Steve Jolley **UK CHART** peak/weeks 1/84 **US CHART** peak/weeks 45/25 **TRACK LISTING** Love Resurrection/Honey For The Bees/For You Only/Invisible/Steal Me Blind/All Cried Out/Money Mile/Twisting The Knife/Where Hides Sleep **PERSONNEL** Alison Moyet (v), session musicians

Former Southend punkette Alison 'Alf' Moyet only achieved so much job satisfaction singing Vince Clarke's songs as the female half of Yazoo. The bovver-booted tomboy used that as a step up, revamped herself as more of a *femme fatale*, and with the help of the production and songwriting team of Tony Swain and Steve Jolley, created an album that won her the 1983 Brit as Best Female Artist. *Invisible*, third of the hit singles that pushed the album to pole position, was custom-written by an admiring Lamont Dozier, one of the legendary Motown songwriters of the Sixties.

Of the current female singers, Alison was the only one with the strength of character to sound convincing. Here it sounds like too many record company questions and marketing suggestions have shaken her idea of herself… She's not sure – and it shows. **Don Watson, NME, November 1984**

Alice's Restaurant

ARTIST Arlo Guthrie **RELEASE DATE** December 1967 (UK)/November 1967 (US) **LABEL** Reprise (UK)/United Artists (US) **PRODUCER** Garry Sherman **UK CHART** peak/weeks 44/1 **US CHART** peak/weeks 17/99 **TRACK LISTING** Travelling Music/Alice's Restaurant Massacre Part 1/The Let Down/Songs To Ageing Children/Amazing Grace/Trip To The City/Alice's Restaurant Massacre Part 2/Crash Pad Improvs/You're A Fink/Harps And Marriage **PERSONNEL** Original Music by Arlo Guthrie, additional music composed and arranged by Garry Sherman, with Joni Mitchell, Trigger Outlaw (v), Al Schackman (v)

Eldest child of legendary troubadour Woody Guthrie, Arlo was singing his father's songs at age 13. Playing at Carnegie Hall in Radio WNYC's annual folk festival in 1967, he filled his 25-minute slot with *Alice's Restaurant Massacre*, an account of being arrested for dropping litter in Stockbridge, Massachussetts on Thanksgiving Day two years earlier, an 'offence' that excused him from the Vietnam draft. Though he rarely played it in concert, Guthrie re-recorded his hippy anthem in the Nineties but was critically panned.

Sadly, this film score is likely to be of little interest to anyone who hasn't seen the film. Arlo performs his two-part monologue **Alice's Restaurant Massacre** *to a simple ragtime accompaniment.* **Melody Maker, February 1970**

Alive!

ARTIST Kiss **RELEASE DATE** June 1976 (UK)/October 1975 (US) **LABEL** Casablanca (UK & US) **PRODUCER** Eddie Kramer **UK CHART** peak/weeks 49/2 **US CHART** peak/weeks 9/110 **TRACK LISTING** Deuce/Stutter/Got To Choose/Hotter Than Hell/Firehouse/Nothin' To Lose/C'mon And Love Me/Parasite/She/Watchin' You/100,000 Years/Black Diamond/Rock Bottom/Cold Gin/Rock And Roll All Nite/Let Me Go Rock N' Roll **PERSONNEL** Gene Simmons (v, b), Paul Stanley (g, v), Ace Frehley (lg, v), Peter Criss (d, v)

'Probably the greatest live album of all time' was how HM bible *Kerrang!* described this double recorded in Detroit's Cobo Hall. The spin-off single *Rock 'N' Roll All Nite* confirmed the breakthrough by hitting the US Top 20 (the studio version had stiffed at 68), while the invitation followed to put their footprints in the pavement outside Grauman's Chinese Theatre. A short British tour followed as **Alive!** went worldwide – though the band's insistence on wearing make-up off-stage coloured press reaction. A classic nonetheless.

It is a great recording, capturing the band exactly as they are on stage – brash, flash, loud, proud… and musically incompetent… the highs on **Alive!** *are few, and although Kiss play* **Rock Bottom** *only once, they manage to reach it frequently.* **M. O., Melody Maker, June 1976**

All Mod Cons

ARTIST The Jam **RELEASE DATE** November 1978 **LABEL** Polydor **PRODUCER** Vic Coppersmith-Heaven **UK CHART** peak/weeks 6/17 **US CHART** peak/weeks

- **TRACK LISTING** All Mod Cons/To Be Someone (Didn't We Have A Nice Time)/Mr Clean/David Watts/In The Crowd/Billy Hunt/It's Too Bad/Fly/The Place I Love/'A' Bomb In Wardour Street/Down In The Tube Station At Midnight **PERSONNEL** Paul Weller (v, g, ag, p, h, hp), Bruce Foxton (v, b), Rick Buckler (d, pc)

The third album from Paul Weller's talented trio in not much over a year found him hitting his stylistic stride. Ballads like *Fly* and *English Rose* (which would give The Stone Roses half of their name) added a new dimension to his art, while the whole tone of the album expressed a disillusionment with fame – a reaction perhaps to a mismatched US tour with Blue Oyster Cult – while underlining the band's Mod roots.

… not only several light years ahead of anything they've done before, but also the album that's going to catapult The Jam right into the front rank of international rock and roll… **Charles Shaar Murray, NME, October 1978**

All Things Must Pass

ARTIST George Harrison **RELEASE DATE** December 1970 (UK & US) **LABEL** Apple (UK & US) **PRODUCER** George Harrison, Phil Spector **UK CHART** peak/weeks 4/24 **US CHART** peak/weeks 1/38 **TRACK LISTING** I'd Have You Anytime/My Sweet Lord/Wah-Wah/Isn't It A Pity/What Is Life/If Not For You/Behind That Locked Door/Let It Down/Run Of The Mill/Beware Of Darkness/Apple Scruffs/Ballad Of Frankie Crisp (Let It Roll)/Awaiting On You All/All Things Must Pass/I Dug Love/Art Of Dying/Isn't It A Pity/Hear Me Lord/Out of The Blue/It's Johnny's Birthday/Plug Me In/I Remember Jeep/Thanks For The Pepperoni **PERSONNEL** George Harrison (v, g, var), session musicians

While Lennon and McCartney had enjoyed an outlet for their songs in The Beatles, guitarist George Harrison was lucky to squeeze a couple on to any one release. The result, when he finally went solo, was a triple solo album, though one disc was a jam session. Even though George's muse was clearly in overdrive, his million-selling hit from the album, **My Sweet Lord**, was ruled to have infringed the copyright of the Chiffons' girl-group classic **He's So Fine**.

Amazing Grace (Live)

ARTIST Aretha Franklin **RELEASE DATE** July 1972 (UK)/June 1972 (US) **LABEL** Atlantic (UK & US) **PRODUCER** Jerry Wexler, Arif Mardin, Aretha Franklin **UK CHART** peak/weeks 0/0 **US CHART** peak/weeks 7/23 **TRACK LISTING** Mary Don't You Weep/Precious Lord, Take My Hand/You've Got A Friend/Old Landmark/Give Yourself to Jesus/How I Got Over/What A Friend We Have In Jesus/Amazing Grace/Precious Memories/Climbing Higher Mountains/God Will Take Care You/Wholy Holy/You'll Never Walk Alone/Never Grow Old **PERSONNEL** Aretha Franklin (v, p, ce), Rev. James Cleveland (p), Cornell Dupree (g), Ken Lupper (o), Chuck Rainey (b), Bernard Purdie (d), Pancho Morales (pc), The Southern California Community Choir

While Aretha Franklin is rightly regarded as the Queen of Soul, we would do well to remember her roots: her ability to turn even the most mundane of material into something inspired within a studio was learnt within the church. After a hesitant start to her recording career, by 1972 she was one of the most popular R&B artists around. This, a timely return to gospel, recorded with the Southern California Community Choir, gave her the perfect opportunity to show her full vocal talents. If some later recordings were predictable, this set revealed Aretha at the peak of her powers.

An album that will not only go down in the annals of Aretha's history as an artist, but that will go down in the annals of the entire history of black music in the contemporary field… it is a fine album, full of power and belief… **P. V., Sounds, August 1972**

America

ARTIST America **RELEASE DATE** January 1972 (UK & US) **LABEL** Warner Bros. (UK & US) **PRODUCER** Ian Samwell, Jeff Dexter **UK CHART** peak/weeks 14/13 **US CHART** peak/weeks 1/40 **TRACK LISTING** Riverside/Sandman/Three Roses/Children/I Need You/Rainy Day/Never Found The Time/Clarice/Donkey Jaw/Pigeon Song **PERSONNEL** Dan Peek (v, g), Gerry Beckley (v, g), Dewey Bunnel (v, g)

An early Seventies reading of the Crosby Stills Nash and Young legacy, Dewey Bunnel, Dan Peek and Gerry Beckley were a California-based outfit who drew considerable flak for their sappy earnestness. Nevertheless, *Horse With No Name* made them all but a household name, and this album topped the charts Stateside. The soft sincerity and close harmonies it displayed were their trademark until George Martin later fleshed out their sound. The trio first met in Britain where their families were stationed in US military bases. By the decade's end they had out sold all country-rock competition save The Eagles.

I find: their vocal harmonies engagingly pretty, if samey, their individual lead singing manneredly sensitive/vulnerable and a little noxious, their tunes occasionally mildly pleasant… although mawkish sentiments and banal, pimply hyperboles abound therein. **John Mendelsohn, Rolling Stone, April 1972**

American Beauty

ARTIST The Grateful Dead **RELEASE DATE** December 1970 (UK & US) **LABEL** Warner Bros. (UK & US) **PRODUCER** Grateful Dead, Steve Barncard **UK CHART** peak/weeks 0/0 **US CHART** peak/weeks 30/19 **TRACK LISTING** Box Of Rain/Friend Of The Devil/Sugar Magnolia/Operator/Candyman/Ripple/Brokedown Palace/Till The Morning Comes/Attics Of My Life/Truckin **PERSONNEL** Jerry Garcia (g, ps, p, v), Phil Lesh (b, g, p, v), Bob Weir (g, v), Pig Pen (Ron McKernan) (h, v), Mickey Hart (pc), Bill Kreutzmann (d), Robert Hunter (w)

Second of the Dead's matching pair of acoustic-harmony albums to be issued in 1970, the gold, eventually platinum, success of **Workingman's Dead** and **American Beauty** would have persuaded less pig-headed musicians to follow that path – somewhere between the then mega Crosby Stills Nash & Young and Jerry Garcia's spin-off outfit New Riders of the Purple Sage (whose personnel guest here). The Dead's response was to release only extended live albums and solo projects for the next three years!

American Fool

ARTIST John Cougar Mellencamp **RELEASE DATE** November 1982 (UK)/May 1982 (US) **LABEL** Riva (UK & US) **PRODUCER** John Cougar Mellencamp, Don Gehman **UK CHART** peak/weeks 37/6 **US CHART** peak/weeks 1/120 **TRACK LISTING** Hurt's So Good/Jack And Diane/Hand To Hold On To/Danger List/Can You Take It/Thundering Hearts/China Girl/Close Enough/Weakest Moments **PERSONNEL** John Cougar Mellencamp (v, g), Larry Crane (g), Tom Wince (k), David Parman (b, g, vl, pc) Terence Salsa (d, pc), Wayne Hall (s, fl, pc)

Having survived six flop albums and discovering that his stage name had been changed to Johnny Cougar without his being consulted, Mellencamp defied the odds and perhaps shocked even himself by, as John Cougar, selling five million copies of this album. Its success was down to *Jack And Diane*, a massive worldwide single which welded snappily fatalistic lyrics with classic and instantly familiar rock structuring. The cornier *Hurt's So Good* was also a monster, at least Stateside, where his suspect 'rebel' image and 'honest man' social concerns were embraced throughout the heartland.

American Pie

ARTIST Don McLean **RELEASE DATE** March 1972 (UK)/November 1971 (US) **LABEL** United Artists (UK & US) **PRODUCER** Ed Freeman **UK CHART** peak/weeks 3/54 **US CHART** peak/weeks 1/48 **TRACK LISTING** American Pie/ Till Tomorrow / Vincent / Crossroads / Winterwood / Empty Chairs / Everybody Loves Me, Baby/Sister Fatima/The Grave/Babylon **PERSONNEL** Don McLean (v, g), session musicians

Cut in half to fit on both sides of a single, the full eight minutes of McLean's Buddy Holly-inspired *American Pie* inevitably overshadows the rest of this, his first album. But there was much else to enjoy from the former Hudson River troubadour who hitched lifts on sailboats and whose debut album **Tapestry** had been rejected by no fewer than 34 labels. They must have been kicking themselves as this collection spent a year in the UK charts, topped the pile at home and spun off his first UK Number 1 in the Van Gogh paean *Vincent*. But fame would sit uneasily on this bedsit bard's shoulders.

… sad, introspective almost sentimental. Occasionally, it is explicit… Don McLean's words are so often about the past. Their interpretation is relevant to today. **A. M., Melody Maker, March 1972**

And The Hits Just Keep On Comin'

ARTIST Mike Nesmith RELEASE DATE 1977 LABEL RCA PRODUCER Mike Nesmith UK CHART peak/weeks – US CHART peak/weeks - TRACK LISTING Tomorrow And Me/Upside Of Good-Bye/Lady Love/Listening/Two Different Roads/Candidate/Different Drum/Harmony Constant/Keep On/Roll With The Flow PERSONNEL Michael Nesmith (v, g, arr), Red Rhodes (g), O.J. Rhodes (stg)

They said the Monkees had no discernible musical talent – a fact guitarist Mike Nesmith (he of the woolly hat and sideburns) vehemently denied. This sarcastically titled solo album, the fourth since quitting the pre-fab four in 1970, continued in country-rock vein and proved satisfying enough for him to mix a reunion when the Monkees regrouped in 1975. Two decades later he would eat his pride to record and tour with them again, but this thoughtful yet unspectacular music (including the much covered *Different Drum*) remains worlds away from *Daydream Believer*.

… from ironic title with self-mocking sleeve picture, its bare lightbulb self-analysis skirting dangerously close to what the Sundays would call a 'suite' of scrupulously tailored songs that stand or fall as slivers of narrative. **David Hepworth, NME, January 1977**

The Angry Young Them

ARTIST Them RELEASE DATE June 1965 (UK & US) LABEL Decca (UK)/Parrot (US) PRODUCER Tommy Scott, Bert Berns UK CHART peak/weeks 0/0 US CHART peak/weeks - TRACK LISTING Here Comes The Night (US Only)/Mystic Eyes/If You And I Could Be As Two/Little Girl/Just A Little Bit/I Gave My Love A Diamond (UK Only)/Go On Home Baby/Gloria/You Just Can't Win/Don't Look Back/I Like It Like That/Bright Lights Big City/My Little Baby (UK Only)/Route 66 PERSONNEL Van Morrison (v, h), Billy Harrison (g), Eric Wrixen (p, k), Ronnie Mellings (d), Alan Henderson (b), Pete Bardens (k), Jimmy Page (g)

Formed by poet ruffian Van Morrison when he was 18, Them were Belfast's answer to The Animals and the Stones: their very own rough 'n' ready exponents of crude R&B, soul and blues. **The Angry Young Them**, their debut, featured a mixture of original songs and original material, including John Lee Hooker's *Don't Look Back* and such future Morrison classics as *Here Comes The Night* and the much covered *Gloria*.

The insidious and blatant sexuality of the music, and Van's tone of voice, never lets up. Played super-loud it's a revelation… **Geoffrey Cannon, Melody Maker, March 1971**

Animalisms

ARTIST The Animals RELEASE DATE May 1966 (UK)/December 1966 (US) LABEL Decca (UK)/M.G.M (US) PRODUCER Tom Wilson UK CHART peak/weeks 4/17 US CHART peak/weeks 20/30 TRACK LISTING One Monkey Don't Stop The Show/Maudie/Outcast/Sweet Little Sixteen/You're On My Mind/Clapping/ Gin House Blues/Squeeze Her - Tease Her/What Am I Living For/I Put A Spell On You/That's All I Am To You/She'll Return It PERSONNEL Eric Burdon (v), Dave Rowberry (k), Hilton Valentine (g), Chas Chandler (b), Barry Jenkins (d)

Were it not for internal squabbling and strife, The Animals could have duelled with the Stones as England's prime Sixties purveyors of R&B to the States. Eric Burdon sang with true Geordie working-class grit, but his ego clashed with that of original band leader Alan Price. Several hits in this album saw them brooding magnificently. Goffin/King's **Don't Bring Me Down** was elevated by Hilton Valentine's savage guitar, while **Gin House Blues** gave Burdon a chance to sing from a booze-soaked bluesy heart. Price left soon afterwards, and the first Animals line-up fell to LSD within months. There were several attempted comebacks.

The Animals are one of the few groups around still playing blues as it is written. On their new one, Eric sings with more restraint than he has shown on recent club appearances… **Melody Maker, May 1966**

Animals

ARTIST Pink Floyd RELEASE DATE February 1977 (UK & US) LABEL Harvest (UK)/Columbia (US) PRODUCER Pink Floyd UK CHART peak/weeks 2/33 US CHART peak/weeks 3/28 TRACK LISTING Pigs On The Wing (Part 1)/Dogs/Pigs (Three Different Ones)/Sheep/Pigs On The Wing (Part 2) PERSONNEL David Gilmour (g, v), Roger Waters (b, v, pc), Richard Wright (k), Nick Mason (d, pc)

After the critically savaged **Wish You Were Here**, the Floyd found renewed favour with a **Dark Side Of The Moon**-like concept album. The track titles are single-word animal names and the cover features an inflatable pig flying over Battersea Power Station. The pig, featuring as part of the stage show, would gain testicles as Roger Waters, ever the lyrical architect, sought to prevent the re-formed Floyd continuing to use the name and props of the earlier incarnation. So this is an album with bollocks — official!

Another Green World

ARTIST Brian Eno RELEASE DATE September 1975 (UK & US) LABEL Island (UK & US) PRODUCER Brian Eno, Rhett Davies UK CHART peak/weeks 0/0 US CHART peak/weeks 0/0 TRACK LISTING Sky Saw/Over Fire Island/St. Elmo's Fire/In Dark Trees/The Big Ship/I'll Come Running/Another Green World/Sombre Reptiles/Little Fishes/Becalmed/Zawinul/Lava Everthing Merges With The Night/Spirits Drifting PERSONNEL Phil Collins (d, pc), Percy Jones (b), Paul Rudolph (b, g), John Cale (va), Brian Eno (g, p, sy, pc), Robert Fripp (lg), Road Melvin (p), Brian Turrington (b, p)

1975 proved a busy year for Eno: as well as producing John Cale's **Slow Dazzle** LP, he released **Discreet Music**, the first of his now famous ambient recordings, **Evening Star**, his second collaboration with Robert Fripp, and this, his third solo LP. **Another Green World** combined elements from all areas of his earlier work. Characteristically wistful songs like *I'll Come Running* and *St Elmo's Fire* sat alongside dreamy instrumentals, all imbued with the distinctive sound which would make Eno such a highly regarded producer in subsequent years.

Another Green World sees the casting away of his egotistical gay blade role in favour of a new, quietly industrious Eno who is beginning – paradoxically – to lose his fear of being caught out as a secret cornball fanatic. **Pete Erskine, NME, November 1975**

Another Music In A Different Kitchen

ARTIST Buzzcocks RELEASE DATE March 1978 (UK & US) LABEL United Artists (UK)/I.R.S. (US) PRODUCER Martin Rushent UK CHART peak/weeks 15/11 US CHART peak/weeks 0/0 TRACK LISTING Fast Cars/No Reply/You Tear Me Up/Get On Our Own/Love Battery/16/I Don't Mind/Fiction Romance/Autonomy/I Need/Moving Away From The Pulsebeat PERSONNEL Steve Garvey (b), Pete Shelley (g, lv), Steve Diggle (g, v), John Maher (d)

Upon the timely departure of Howard Devoto to form Magazine, Pete Shelley was compelled to write, sing, and play ingeniously timid guitar solos for the punk band who brought preoccupation with love and sex to a movement previously dominated by so-called social concerns. Their fiery, short sharp power-pop and acerbic, often funny lyrics, attracted floating voters who otherwise might not have found a way into punk. While they were in their element as a singles band, the Buzzcocks' debut roared, with the surging *Fast Cars* a stand-out, and *Moving Away From The*

Pulsebeat promising imminent advances.

Pete Shelley irreverently opens his heart to self-doubting love-angst in that fabby, semi-androgynous, irony-tinged way which you can't help loving. Shelley doesn't need to shout, politick or sloganeer, 'cos he is punk's Neil Tennant (without the middle-class affection). **Carl Loben, Melody Maker, April 1994**

Appetite For Destruction

ARTIST Guns 'N' Roses RELEASE DATE August 1987 (UK & US) LABEL Geffen (UK & US) PRODUCER Mike Clink UK CHART peak/weeks 5/131 US CHART peak/weeks 1/147 TRACK LISTING Welcome To The Jungle/It's So Easy/Nightrain/Out To Get Me/Mr Brownstone/Paradise City/My Michelle/Think About You/Sweet Child O'Mine/You're Crazy/Anything Goes/ Rocket Queen PERSONNEL Steven Adler (d), Slash (lg, rg, ag), Duff 'Rose' McKagan (b, v), Izzy Stradlin (rg, lg, v, pc), Axel Rose (v, sy, pc)

By making a play for The Rolling Stones' title of most dangerous rock 'n' roll band in the world, Guns 'N' Roses succeeded in having as much written about their off-stage escapades (urinating on planes, etc.) as their music. But this, their official debut album after a privately- pressed six-track EP, justified the hype – even though it took two weeks short of a year to reach the US chart summit. Hit singles *Welcome To The Jungle*, *Paradise City* and the Number 1 *Sweet Child O'Mine* ensured a five-week stay and over a year's chart residency for a slow-burning, hard-biting album.

Basically this album consists of playing all the instruments very loud and very carefully along the kick-ass school of things, nodding towards sentimentality but never so much that people might think they're soft. **Paul Mathur, Melody Maker, July 1987**

Aqualung

ARTIST Jethro Tull RELEASE DATE March 1971 (UK)/May 1971 (US) LABEL Chrysalis (UK)/Reprise (US) PRODUCER Ian Anderson, Terry Ellis UK CHART peak/weeks 4/21 US CHART peak/weeks 7/76 TRACK LISTING Aqualung/Cross Eyed Mary/Cheap Day Return/Mother Goose/Wond'ring Aloud/Up To Me/My God, Hymn 43/ Slipstream/Locomotive Breath/Wind Up PERSONNEL Ian Anderson (v, fl), Mick Abrahams (g), Glenn Cornick (b), Clive Bunker (d)

It may not have been planned, but by early 1971 flute-playing Tull patriarch Ian Anderson had all but replaced the original members of the band and turned it into a vehicle solely for his own ambitions. **Aqualung** was the first Tull concept album, reflecting Anderson's religious obsessions and the wheezing-tramp character of the title. The striking sleeve painting, featuring a down-and-out with a touch of Fagin about him, bore more than a passing image to the band's celebrated leader. No surprise then that Anderson identified with such a figure – given the lean, often squalid years he had endured in Luton before success arrived.

… there is something depressingly anticlimatic about it all. There is a lot of misplaced emotion on this album. Thus, despite the fine musicianship and often brilliant structural organisaion of songs, this album is not elevated but undermined by its seriousness. **Ben Gerson, Rolling Stone, July 1971**

Arc Of A Diver

ARTIST Steve Winwood **RELEASE DATE** January 1981 (UK & US) **LABEL** Island (UK &US) **PRODUCER** Steve Winwood **UK CHART** peak/weeks 13/20 **US CHART** peak/weeks 3/43 **TRACK LISTING** While You Can See A Chance/Arc Of A Diver/Second-Hand Woman/Slowdown Sundown/Spanish Dancer/Night Train/Dust **PERSONNEL** Steve Winwood (v, var)

Steve Winwood was the boy wonder of British blues and R&B who enjoyed tremendous success in his late teens, first with The Spencer Davis Group, and then with Traffic. **Arc Of A Diver** was his third solo album and, although it came almost five years after his eponymous debut, it could not have sounded more fresh and contemporary. Playing all the instruments himself, and with lyrical assistance from, of all people, ex-Bonzo Dog Band member Viv Stanshall, it was a superbly crafted collection of mature rock and pop.

Are You Experienced

ARTIST Jimi Hendrix **RELEASE DATE** May 1967 (UK)/August 1967 (US) **LABEL** Track (UK)/Reprise (US) **PRODUCER** Kit Lambert **UK CHART** peak/weeks 2/33 **US CHART** peak/weeks 5/106 **TRACK LISTING** Foxy Lady/Manic Depression/ Red House/Can You See Me/Love Or Confusion/I Don't Live Today/May This Be Love/Fire/3rd Stone From The Sun/Remember/Are You Experienced **PERSONNEL** Jimi Hendrix (v, lg), Noel Redding (b), Mitch Mitchell (d)

When ex-Animal Chas Chandler brought Seattle-born Hendrix to the UK in the autumn of 1966, not even he could have imagined the lasting effect Jimi would have on rock 'n' roll. Seasoned on the southern 'chitlin' circuit, backing the likes of Little Richard, Hendrix let his imagination run riot. The album boasted snappy riff-orientated numbers like **Fire** which would shape the direction of rock over the next few years, while songs like **3rd Stone From The Sun** suggested the experimental way forward that became tagged as 'psychedelia'. With its sexual undercurrents and provocative lyrics, the album became the cornerstone of a legend.

Aretha: Lady Soul

ARTIST Aretha Franklin **RELEASE DATE** March 1968 (UK)/February 1968 (US) **LABEL** Atlantic (UK & US) **PRODUCER** Jerry Wexler **UK CHART** peak/weeks 25/18 **US CHART** peak/weeks 2/52 **TRACK LISTING** Chain Of Fools/Money Won't Change You/People Get Ready/Niki Hoeky/(You Make Me Feel Like) A Natural Woman/Since You've Been Gone (Sweet Sweet Baby)/Good To Me As I Am To You/Come Back Baby/Groovin'/Ain't No Way **PERSONNEL** Aretha Franklin (v, p), Joe South (g), Bobby Womack (g), King Curtis (ts), Joe Newman (t), Ralph Burns (con), Ellie Greenwich (bv), The Sweet Inspirations (bv), Gene Chrisman (d), Cissy Houston (v), Eric Clapton (g, gst), Frank Wess (fl, ts, ww), session musicians

It would have been easy for Aretha to have rested on the laurels of **I Never Loved A Man…** (which reached Number 2 in the US album charts) or to turn out more of the same, but Aretha has always been made of sterner stuff. It is not enough just to sing a song: she has to live it, feel it and make sure the listener ends up with the same emotion. **Lady Soul** is a logical progression and one of the finest moments in soul music. If there is a better delivered song than **You Make Me Feel Like A Natural Woman**, or a more impassioned version of **People Get Ready**, they have yet to be recorded.

On this record, Aretha is heard in command of absolutely everything. She's proved herself capable of encompassing a variety of moods, tempos, lyrics and styles and yet she remains on top of them all. **Jon Landau, Rolling Stone, July 1968**

Argus

ARTIST Wishbone Ash **RELEASE DATE** May 1972 (UK)/June 1972 (US) **LABEL** MCA (UK)/Decca (US) **PRODUCER** Derek Lawrence **UK CHART** peak/weeks 3/20 **US CHART** peak/weeks 169/13 **TRACK LISTING** Time Was/Sometime World/Blowin' Free/The King Will Come/Leaf And Stream/Warrior/Throw Down The Sword/No Easy Road **PERSONNEL** Steve Upton (d, pc), Martin Turner (b), Andy Powell (lg, ag, rg, hv), Ted Turner (lg, ag, rg, hv)

Prime exponents of British boogie, Wishbone Ash took advantage of progressive rock's emphasis of technical expertise over attitude or image: they were startlingly uncharismatic. **Argus** was by far their best album, and even the medieval imagery and swords-and-sorcery titles redolent of Merry Englande – **The King Will Come**, **Throw Down The Sword**, **Warrior** – did not get in the way of the band's powerful combination of folk influences and hard rock.

We've tried to get a looser sound, … we're known for our tight, arranged numbers, but this time we decided to loosen up in the studio. There is less guitar dominance, and more subtle playing with a better balance between instrumentals and vocals. **Chris Welch interviewing Andy Powell of Wishbone Ash, Melody Maker, May 1972**

Armed Forces

ARTIST Elvis Costello And The Attractions RELEASE DATE January 1979 (UK & US) LABEL Radar (UK)/Columbia (US) PRODUCER Nick Lowe UK CHART peak/weeks 2/28 US CHART peak/weeks 10/25 TRACK LISTING Senior Sevice/Oliver's Army/Big Boys/Green Shirt/Party Girl/Goon Squad/Busy Bodies/Sunday's Best/Moods For Moderns/Chemistry Class/Two Little Hitlers/Accidents Will Happen/Watching The Detectives/Alison PERSONNEL Elvis Costello (v, g), Steve Nieve (k), Bruce Thomas (b, v), Pete Thomas (d)

Sonically only slightly sweeter than **This Year's Model**, this was given added venom by Costello's most politically resonant lyrics yet. *Accidents Will Happen* and, predominantly, *Oliver's Army* (with its Abba-esque piano motif) burned up the charts. In the same year Costello produced the debut album by 2-Tone hopefuls The Specials.

Philosophically, he's still the jabbling, jangled Costello of the first two albums, but his big beat makes room for slightly slyer arrangements.... Costello remains the mad poet of modern, throttled, love... and his taut, grinding rock 'n' roll is the swiftest kick in the ass a party could ask for. **Fred Schruers, Rolling Stone, December 1979**

Arrival

ARTIST Abba RELEASE DATE November 1976 (UK)/February 1977 (US) LABEL Epic (UK)/Atlantic (US) PRODUCER Benny Anderson, Björn Ulvaeus UK CHART peak/weeks 1/92 US CHART peak/weeks 20/50 TRACK LISTING When I Kissed The Teacher/Dancing Queen/My Love, My Life/Dum, Dum, Diddle/Knowing Me, Knowing You/Money, Money, Money/That's Me/Why Did It Have To Be Me/Tiger/Arrival PERSONNEL Benny Anderson (k, sy, v), Björn Ulvaeus (g, v), Agnetha Fältskog (v), Frida Lyngstad (v)

Many thought that Abba, a seemingly naive but quite experienced Swedish pop combo consisting of Björn, Benny, Agnetha and Frida, would quickly fade in the manner of most grinning Eurostars after their effervescent, blue-sequinned triumph in the 1974 Eurovision Song Contest with *Waterloo*. Yet by the time of the deceptively titled **Arrival** (it was their fifth album, the fourth having already been a Greatest Hits compilation, the first of a franchise) they were usurping the British glam rock greats and heading for world domination. Only America remained lukewarm to their irresistibly obvious melodies and berserk sense of style. **Arrival** was jammed with perky hit singles.

Asia

ARTIST Asia RELEASE DATE April 1982 (UK & US) LABEL Geffen (UK & US) PRODUCER Mike Stone UK CHART peak/weeks 11/38 US CHART peak/weeks 1/64 TRACK LISTING Heat Of The Moment/Only Time Will Tell/Sole Survivor/One Step Closer/Time Again/Wildest Dreams/Without You/Cutting It Fine/Here Comes The Feeling PERSONNEL Geoffrey Downes (k, bv), Steve Howe (g, bv), Carl Palmet (d, pc), John Wetton (v, b)

In the early Eighties a supergroup seemed a distinctly dubious proposition: members of Yes (Steve Howe), King Crimson (John Wetton) and E.L.P. (Carl Palmer) could scarcely be thought to be in vogue. What saved them from immediate universal guffawing was, perhaps, the pop consciousness of one-time Buggle, Geoff Downes. They were not, of course, averse to long-winded instrumental noodling, but the hit *Heat Of The Moment* proved an acceptable red herring. For some reason, Asia were massive in Russia.

The dour magnitude of Wetton's bass grumble and chiselled, sure voice has made him the Charlton Heston of British Rock – dependable, enduring and uninspired.... It's not tragic, not even a little sad, only inevitable. Lie down and accept it. **Chris Bohn, NME, May 1982**

Astral Weeks

ARTIST Van Morrison RELEASE DATE September 1969 (UK)/November 1968 (US) LABEL Warner Bros. (UK & US) PRODUCER Lewis Merenstein UK CHART peak/weeks – US CHART peak/weeks 0/0 TRACK LISTING In The Beginning: Astral Weeks/Beside You/Sweet Thing/Cyprus Avenue/Afterwards: Young Lovers Do/Madame George/Ballerina/Slim Slow Slider PERSONNEL Van Morrison (v, g), Jay Berliner (g), Richard Davis (b), Connie Kay (d), John Payne (fl, ss), Warren Smith, Jr. (pc)

Many a camper van hitting the hippy trail to Nepal resounded to this stream-of-consciousness classic, improbably created in 48 hours of studio time with musicians Morrison had never met before. The seven-minute title track, considered the crux of the work, was cut as an afterthought without chord charts and in a first take: flautist John Payne, from Morrison's road trio, sat in as the regular player had gone home! Van has denied the influence of drugs in the making of this, which renders it even more amazing.

At Fillmore East

ARTIST The Allman Brothers **RELEASE DATE** July 1971 (UK & US) **LABEL** Capricorn (UK & US) **PRODUCER** Tom Dowd **UK CHART** peak/weeks 0/0 **US CHART** peak/weeks 13/47 **TRACK LISTING** Statesboro Blues/Done Somebody Wrong/Stormy Monday/You Don't Love Me/Hot 'Lanta/In Memory Of Elizabeth Redd/Whipping Post **PERSONNEL** Duane Allman (g), Gregg Allman (k, v, g), Dicky Betts (g, v), Berry Oakley (b), Butch Trucks (d), Jaimoe Johanson (d)

Forsaking heavy psychedelia, the Allmans took their cue from blues, soul and jazz, using their twin guitars (and drummers) to kick back and explore in their own sweet time. Their live shows were lazy and extended: the dishonoured art of jamming peaked somewhere on this double album. Duane's guitar (as featured on Derek And The Dominoes' **Layla**) and Gregg's voice deliver songs from the first two albums, and a batch of blues standards, with force and feeling over this double. The side-long **Whipping Post** builds to a peak before a euphoric foggy fade. Just months afterwards Duane Allman died in a motorcycle accident – he was 24 years old.

Turn the volume up all the way and sit through the concert; by the time it's over you almost imagine the Allman Band getting high and heading back to Macon. **George Kimball, Rolling Stone, August 1971**

Atlantic Crossing

ARTIST Rod Stewart **RELEASE DATE** August 1975 (UK)/September 1975 (US) **LABEL** Warner Bros. (UK & US) **PRODUCER** Tom Dowd **UK CHART** peak/weeks 1/88 **US CHART** peak/weeks 9/29 **TRACK LISTING** Three Times A Loser/All Right For An Hour/All In The Name Of Rock 'N' Roll/Drift Away/Stone Cold Sober/I Don't Want To Talk About It/It's Not The Spotlight/This Old Heart Of Mine/Still Love You/Sailing **PERSONNEL** Rod Stewart (v)

Produced by veteran knob-twiddler Tom Dowd, and with the assistance of the Muscle Shoals rhythm section, the title of **Atlantic Crossing** neatly pinpointed Rod Stewart's transformation from boozy British geezer-rocker to jet-setting tax exile complete with *de rigueur* blonde actress girlfriend, Britt Eckland. It was apparently Eckland's suggestion that the album be divided between a 'slow half' and a 'fast half'. Of the former, *I Don't Want To Talk About It* is a standout.

Rod has really made a personal statement that might fling off for ever the wrap of the old faces. He's treading out with this album for that elusive solo acceptance as an artist who is more than a beer-can swilling jester. **Chris Welch, Melody Maker, August 1975**

Atom Heart Mother

ARTIST Pink Floyd **RELEASE DATE** October 1970 (UK)/November 1970 (US) **LABEL** Harvest (UK & US) **PRODUCER** Pink Floyd **UK CHART** peak/weeks 1/23 **US CHART** peak/weeks 55/13 **TRACK LISTING** Atom Heart Mother a)Father's Shout b)Breast Milky c)Mother Fore d)Funky Dung e)Mind Your Throats Please f)Reeemergence/If Summer '68/Fat Old Sun/Alan's Psychedlic Breakfast/Rise And Shine/Sunny Side Up/Morning Glory **PERSONNEL** David Gilmour (g, v, b, k), Nick Mason (d, pc), Richard Wright (k, v), Jon Carin (k), Guy Pratt (b), Gary Wallis (pc), Tim Renwick (g), Dick Parry (ts), Bob Erzin (k, pc), Sam Brown (bv), Durga McBroom (bv), Carol Kenyon (bv), Jackie Sheridan (bv), Rebecca Leigh-White (bv)

In the aftermath of Syd Barrett quitting the band the Floyd were slow to find their future direction. And while side two saw each member writing and presenting a solo piece, as on its predecessor **Umma Gumma**, side one was given over to one long suite: the title cut which featured rock band, sound effects, plus radical orchestral and vocal arrangements by some-time alumnus Ron Geesin. The band would refine this style over the next few years to produce **Dark Side Of The Moon**. With its wonderfully surreal

sleeve of Friesian cows, **Atom Heart Mother** caught the Floyd at the crossroads, breaking with their underground ties and looking for more commercial appeal.

Possibly the most mature and finished piece of music the group has yet produced….The composition is credited to all four members, but it doesn't say who was responsible for the superb, majestic scoring for brass, strings and choir, which combines with the rock instruments in the most satisfying way. **R. W., Melody Maker, October 1970**

Attack Of The Killer B's

ARTIST Anthrax **RELEASE DATE** June 1991 (UK & US) **LABEL** Island (UK & US) **PRODUCER** Eddie Kramer **UK CHART** peak/weeks 13/5 **US CHART** peak/weeks 27/25 **TRACK LISTING** Milk (Ode To Billy)/Bring The Noise/Keep It In The Family (Live)/Startin' Up A Posse/Protest And Survive/Chromatic Death/I'm The Man '91/Parasite/Pipeline/Sects/Belly Of The Beast **PERSONNEL** Joey Belladonna (v), Dan Spitz (lg), Scott 'Not' Ian (rg), Frank Bello (b), Charlie Bonante (d)

The New York thrash band were well established but already gingerly probing new directions (they had recently covered Joe Jackson's *Got The Time*) when they hit on this unexpectedly palatable rap experiment. They rocketted out a version of **Bring The Noise**, teaming up with Public Enemy's Chuck D and Flavor Flav, gaining several credibility points and music press covers in the process. The bitching about categorization over *Startin' Up A Posse* expressed a desire to grow. Much of the album was odds 'n' sods and b-sides, but the response its best moments drew compelled the band to reassess their priorities. They sacked their vocalist and toured with Public Enemy.

Killer B's, *compiled by the band themselves, works both as one great album and as an explanation of how Anthrax came to be. Basically via a series of covers, reworkings of their own stuff and their self-penned sleeve notes.* **The Stud Brothers, Melody Maker, June, 1991**

Autobahn

ARTIST Kraftwerk **RELEASE DATE** November 1974 (UK)/February 1975 (US) **LABEL** Vertigo (UK & US) **PRODUCER** Ralf Hütter, Florian Schneider **UK CHART** peak/weeks 4/18 **US CHART** peak/weeks 5/22 **TRACK LISTING** I Autobahn/II

Kometenmelodie 1/Kometenmelodie 2/Mitternacht/Morgenspaziergang
PERSONNEL Ralf Hütter (v, e), Florian Schneider (v, e), Klaus Roeder (vl, g),
Wolfgang Flür (pc)

The German band, led by Ralf Hutter and Florian Schneider, were instrumental in inspiring the late Seventies synthesizer boom, and this hit album, especially the title track (edited down from 22 minutes and 30 seconds) which took synths into the singles charts in early 1975, was a crucial turning point. A transatlantic Top 5 placing opened the doors to others, while a compilation of early material, **Exceller 8** (a pun on accelerate), ended the band's first, most experimental period in 1976.

Automatic For The People

ARTIST R.E.M. RELEASE DATE October 1992 (UK & US) LABEL Warner Bros. (UK & US) PRODUCER Scott Litt, REM. UK CHART peak/weeks 1/64 (till end 1993) US CHART peak/weeks 2/75 TRACK LISTING Drive/Try Not To Breathe/The Sidewinder Sleeps Tonite/Everybody Hurts/New Orleans Instrumental No. 1/Sweetness Follows/Monty Got A Raw Deal/Ignoreland/Star Me Kitten/Man On The Moon/Nightswimming/Find The River PERSONNEL Michael Stipe (v), Peter Buck (g), Mike Mills (b), Bill Berry (d) and Bertis Downs, Jefferson Holt

Having scaled the commerical heights with **Out Of Time**, R.E.M. decided they didn't like the view and returned to the studio to cut their darkest album to date. The low-key collection was out of step with the grunge wave, living up to Stipe's claim that it was 'a punk record – just a very quiet one'. Led Zeppelin's Jon Paul Jones contributed string arrangements to four tracks, including the standout *Everybody Hurts*, completing an album that took shape in four different American cities but had a worldwide resonance.

Automatic For The People *turns out to be both aptly unfathomable and just the job. The contradictory elements of the band's rock 'n' roll cravings and the singer's ruminative tendencies sit together like completely different things in a pod…. R.E.M. can give a person quite a going over.* **Phil Sutcliffe, Q, November 1992**

Avalon

ARTIST Roxy Music RELEASE DATE May 1982 (UK)/June 1982 (US) LABEL Polydor (UK)/Atco (US) PRODUCER Rhett Davies UK CHART peak/weeks 1/57 US CHART peak/weeks 53/27 TRACK LISTING More Than This/The Space Between/India/While My Heart Is Still Beating/Main Thing/Take A Chance With Me/Avalon/To Turn You On/True To Life/Tara PERSONNEL Bryan Ferry (v, p), Phil Manzanera (g), MacKay (s, ob), Paul Thompson (d), Paul Carrack (k) Studio, David Skinner (k) Tours, Gary Tibbs (b)

In a year that saw David Sylvian of Japan, Martin Fry of ABC and Billy Mackenzie of The Associates all offer variations on Bryan Ferry's besuited aristocrat crooner, Ferry himself upped the ante and produced his slickest collection yet of polished funk and varnished soul. *More Than This*, *Avalon* and *Take A Chance With Me* were big hits, before Roxy disbanded once more in 1983, bequeathing for future generations their prototype Yuppie soundtrack muzak.

Avalon feels like a very unified album, in a way which is satisfying rather than monotonous. Overall its approach is soft, a little mournful, consistently mellow without blandness… a record which conveys emotion, intelligently, and it's nice to listen to. **Paul du Noyer, NME, May 1982**

Avalon Sunset

ARTIST Van Morrison RELEASE DATE May 1989 (UK)/July 1989 (US) LABEL Polydor (UK)/Mercury (US) PRODUCER Van Morrison UK CHART peak/weeks 13/14 US CHART peak/weeks 91/39 TRACK LISTING Whenever God Shines His Light/Contacting My Angel/I'd Love To Write Another Song/Have I Told You Lately/Coney Island/I'm Tired Joey Boy/When Will I Ever Learn To Live in God/Orangefield/Daring Night/These Are The Days PERSONNEL Van Morrison (lv, g), Neil Drinkwater (p, sy, ad), Arty McGlynn (g), Clive Culberson (b), Roy Jones (pc, d), Dave Early (pc, d), Henry Lowther (t), Cliff Hardie (tr), Stan Sultzman (as), Alan Barnes (bs), Steve Pearce (b), Georgie Fame (k)

Just as **Astral Weeks** and **Into The Music** had left succeeding decades with a landmark album, so Morrison closed the Eighties with a stunning summary of his art. Collaborators included organist Georgie Fame, who would become an integral part of Morrison's band and, less predictably, Cliff Richard, whose duet on *Whenever God Shines His Light* necessitated an uncomfortable-looking *Top Of The Pops* appearance. Named after the mystic isle, **Avalon Sunset** continued Morrison's spiritual quest, while throwing up a standard in the much covered *Have I Told You Lately That I Love You*.

When he gets it so right, it's rather like finding yourself transfixed by a particularly lovely sunset. You might turn away remembering the chores that need doing and the bills that must be paid, but the memory of the beauty will never leave you. **Dave Jennings, Melody Maker, June 1989**

Average White Band

ARTIST Average White Band **RELEASE DATE** July 1974 (UK & US) **LABEL** Atlantic (UK & US) **PRODUCER** Arif Mardin **UK CHART** peak/weeks 6/14 **US CHART** peak/weeks 1/43 **TRACK LISTING** You Got It/Got The Love/Pick Up The Pieces/Person To Person/Work To Do/Nothing You Can Do/Just Wanna Love You Tonight/Keepin' It To Myself/I Just Can't Give You Up/There's Always Someone Waiting **PERSONNEL** Alan Gorrie (lv, bv, b, g), Hamish Stuart (lv, bv, lg, b), Roger Ball (k, s), Onnnie McIntyre (bv, g), Malcolm (Molly) Duncan (ts), Robbie McIntosh (d, pc), with additional musicians: Randy Brecker, Marvin Stamm, Mel Davis, Glenn Ferris, Michael Brecker, Ken Bichel, Ralph McDonald

Emerging from a thriving soul and funk scene in Glasgow, The A.W.B. were given their name as a joke by Bonnie Bramlett. Emulating the tight arrangements of their heroes, they hit paydirt with the American Number 1 *Pick Up The Pieces*: to this day a radio and dance-floor staple. Their third album also included the much respected *Keepin' It To Myself*. They overcame the subsequent heroin-related death of drummer McIntosh to enjoy further hits and, as in-demand musicians, worked with everyone from Paul McCartney to Chuck Berry to Chaka Khan.

… sifting through what are generally regarded as last year's best black records I didn't find a single one as consistently moving as **Average White Band**. *Play it back-to-back with The Isleys'* **Live It Up** *and you'll see what I mean.* **Steve Clarke, NME, January 1975**

Axis: Bold As Love

ARTIST The Jimi Hendrix Experience **RELEASE DATE** December 1967 (UK)/February 1968 (US) **LABEL** Track (UK)/Reprise (US) **PRODUCER** Chas Chandler **UK CHART** peak/weeks 5/16 **US CHART** peak/weeks 3/53 **TRACK LISTING** Exp/Up From The Skies/Spanish Castle Magic/Wait Until Tomorrow/Ain't No Telling/Little Wing/If Six Was Nine/You've Got Me Floating/Castles Made Of Sand/She's So Fine/One Rainy Wish/Little Miss Lover/Bold As Love **PERSONNEL** Jimi Hendrix (v, lg), Noel Redding (b), Mitch Mitchell (d), Graham Nash (b), Roy Wood (v), Trevor Burton (v)

Having lived and played together for a year, manager Chas Chandler and the trio ably and concisely transferred the iconoclastic on-stage magic on to vinyl. A steady diet of hallucogenics had helped crystallize Jimi's songwriting capabilities and he was at the peak of his powers, creating a work that captured even better than The Beatles the heady atmosphere of 1967. While fans had become dependent on the band's classic riffs, **Axis** preferred to create its own sense of space, time and style.

The B52's

ARTIST The B52's **RELEASE DATE** July 1979 (UK & US) **LABEL** Island (UK)/Warner (US) **PRODUCER** Chris Blackwell **UK CHART** peak/weeks 22/12 **US CHART** peak/weeks 59/74 **TRACK LISTING** Planet Claire/52 Girls/Dance This Mess Around/Rock Lobster/Lava/There's A Moon In The Sky (Called The Moon)/Hero Worship/6060-842/Downtown **PERSONNEL** Cindy Wilson (g, v), Kate Pierson (o, v), Ricky Wilson (g), Fred Schneider (k, v), Keith Strickland (d)

Hailing from Athens, Georgia, the 'wacky', 'zany' B52's were among the first wave of post-punk combos to use irony as a sword. Wallowing in self-conscious hip and a love of all things trashy, their beehive hairdos and jerky dance steps endeared them to a seriousness-saturated era. Their awkward, insistent grooves were never better demonstrated than on the wigged-out workouts of *Rock Lobster*, *Planet Claire* and *Dance This Mess Around*. Eventually the shrieking 'schtick' grew tiresome, but here they were shocking pink.

While their long-awaited debut album doesn't come close to capturing the visual exuberance and rocking intensity that makes The B52's, above all, a great dance band… it promises great things. Right now, **The B52's** *is probably a livelier party than you've been invited to for quite a while.* **Tom Carson, Rolling Stone, September 1979**

Babes In The Wood

ARTIST Mary Black **RELEASE DATE** September 1991 (UK)/July 1991 (US) **LABEL** Grapevine **PRODUCER** Declan Sinnot **UK CHART** peak/weeks 0/0 **US CHART** peak/weeks 0/0 **TRACK LISTING** Still Believing/Bright Blue Rose/Golden Mile/Babes In The Wood/The Thorn Upon The Rose/Brand New Star/Prayer For Love/Adam At The Window/The Dimming Of The Day/Might As Well Be A Slave/Just Around The Corner/The Urge For Going **PERSONNEL** Mary Black (v), Declan Sinnott (g, db, md, 9bv), Pat Crowley (ad, p, bv), Garvan Gallagher (dbb), Noel Bridgeman (pc), Marie Bhreatnach (f, sy), Carl Geraghty (s)

In her native Ireland, Mary, who began singing with her sister and three brothers in The Black Family, is a superstar; this record entered the charts there at Number 1. Her pure, clear voice has tackled folk, old sea shanties and even some token 'contemporary' numbers with equal aplomb. The pensive songs in this collection were flavoured by mandolins, fiddles and saxophones, and drew in a wide audience – a subsequent Royal Albert Hall appearance was greeted with reverence.

Black's music – a savoury mix of folk with contemporary pop undertones – has potential for broad appeal, and the singer is not about to let herself get pigeon-holed as an earnest folkie….'There should be no walls,' Black says. 'Why can't I just do all sorts of stuff?' **Eliza Wing, Rolling Stone, January 1991**

Baby The Stars Shine Bright

ARTIST Everything But The Girl **RELEASE DATE** August 1986 (UK & US) **LABEL** Blanco Y Negro (UK)/Sire (US) **PRODUCER** Mike Hedges, Everything But The Girl **UK CHART** peak/weeks 22/9 **US CHART** peak/weeks 0/0 **TRACK LISTING** Come On Home/Don't Leave Me Behind/A Country Mile/Cross My Heart/Don't Let The Teardrops Rust Your Shining Heart/Careless/Sugar Finney/Come Hell Or High Water/Fighting Talk/Little Hitler **PERSONNEL** Tracey Thorn (v), Ben Watt (g), Mickey Harris (b), Robert Peters (d), Cara Tivey (p, o)

The third album from former college sweethearts Tracy Thorn and Ben Watt added lush orchestration to the earlier mix of voice and acoustic guitar. Yet when the opening *Come On Home* failed to chart despite being Radio 1's most played record for a fortnight, they decided to cut back to basics and were rewarded by greater success. Radio 1 acceptance would come later with the cover of Crazy Horse's *I Don't Want To Talk About It*, but **Baby The Stars Shine Bright** still repays repeated listening.

I've been examining this record with a stethoscope, trying to find some pulse, some surge of life or honest intention, but I'm not sure I've succeeded…. We haven't got a corpse on our hands… but… I think it's heartless. **Alan Jackson, NME, August 1986**

Back Home

ARTIST Chuck Berry **RELEASE DATE** January 1971 (UK), 1970 (US) **LABEL** Chess (UK & US) **PRODUCER** – **UK CHART** peak/weeks 0/0 **US CHART** peak/weeks 0/0 **TRACK LISTING** Tulane/Have Mercy Judge/Instrumental/Christmas/Gun/I'm A Rocker/Flyin' Home/Fish And Chips/Some People

PERSONNEL Chuck Berry (v, g), Johnnie Johnson (p), Jasper Thomas (d), Willie Dixon (b)

Returning to the Chess label after four unfulfilling years with Mercury – apart of course from the unfathomable **My Ding-A-Ling** smash – **Concerto In B Goode** is generally considered the low point of his career – Berry clawed back to something like his best, most incisive rock 'n' roll form. *Tulane*, which later became a one-off hit for The Steve Gibbons Band, and **Have Mercy Judge** told concise drug-bust anecdotes. During this period his live shows sizzled once more. In the view of many he has not made a decent record since, yet his influence on rock was immense, and endures.

Back Home *is the usual Berry mix: three or four dynamite tracks, two or three good ones, two or three bombs… this is rough, raw music, and it's all totally accessible, up front where you can grab it.* **Michael Goodwin, Rolling Stone, September 1970**

Back Home Again

ARTIST John Denver **RELEASE DATE** September 1974 (UK)/June 1974 (US) **LABEL** RCA Victor (UK & US) **PRODUCER** Milton Okun, Don Wardell, Susan Ruskin **UK CHART** peak/weeks 3/29 **US CHART** peak/weeks 1/96 **TRACK LISTING** Back Home Again/On the Road/Grandma's Feather Bed/Matthew/Thank God I'm A Country Boy/Music Is You/Annie's Song/It's Up To You/Cool And Green And Shady/Eclipse/Sweet Surrender/This Old Guitar **PERSONNEL** John Denver (g, v), Buddy Collette (cl), Eric Weissberg (stg, bj), James Gordon (d), Hal Blaine (d), Jim Connor (bj, h, v), Julie Connor (bv), Glen D. Hardin (p), Lee Holdridge (arr, con), David Jackson (b), Richard Kniss (b), John Sommers (bj, g, md, bv)

The loss of John Denver in an October 1997 air accident caused much reassessment of a man who had once epitomized the American apple-pie lifestyle but was not as wholesome as he seemed. This notwithstanding, his second US chart-topping album was defiantly unplugged before unplugged was fashionable, while *Back Home Again* was written from the viewpoint of an 'Air Force brat' and **This Old Guitar** was a three-minute autobiography in song. Surprisingly, *Thank God I'm A Country Boy*, another song much associated with him, was penned by a friend, John Martin Sommers. A live version later topped the singles chart.

Back In Black

ARTIST AC/DC **RELEASE DATE** July 1980 (UK & US) **LABEL** Atlantic (UK & US) **PRODUCER** Robert John 'Mutt' Lange **UK CHART** peak/weeks 1/40 **US CHART** peak/weeks 4/131 **TRACK LISTING** Back In Black/Hells Bells/Shoot To Thrill/Giving The Dog A Bone/What Do You Do For Money Honey/Rock 'N' Roll Ain't Noise Pollution/Let Me Put My Love Into You/You Shook Me All Night Long/Shake A Leg/Have A Drink On Me **PERSONNEL** Angus Young (g), Malcolm Young (g), Brian Johnson (v), Phil Rudd (d), Cliff Williams (b)

Brian Johnson, formerly with British teen-rock band Geordie, was a surprise choice to replace the deceased Bon Scott, but won the devoted headbanging fans loyalty with the supremely tasteless tribute *Have A Drink On Me*. His sandpaper vocals dovetailed well with the group's increasing, over-the-top noise pollution: **Back In Black** sold 10 million copies in the States alone, and led to massive stadium shows. *You Shook Me All Night Long* rang out as definitive. Speed metal, thrash and grunge were all, for better or worse, inspired by AC/DC's halcyon riffs. As wakes go, this album was positively celebratory.

… the sound is the usual grotesque perversion of vintage Led Zeppelin, all busy, squabbling guitars interspersed with the shrill squeak of new singer Brian Johnson's grating Plant parody. To a woman, the lyrics are at best an affront, at worst an infuriating affront. **Lynn Hanna, NME, August 1980**

Back In The USA

ARTIST MC5 RELEASE DATE November 1970 (UK)/Februar 1970 (US) **LABEL** Atlantic Records (UK &US) **PRODUCER** Jon Landau **UK CHART** peak/weeks 0/0 **US CHART** peak/weeks 13/7 **TRACK LISTING** Tutti Fruiti/Tonight/Teenage List/Looking At You/Let Me Try/High School/Call Me An Animal/The American Ruse/Shakin' Street/The Human Being Lawnmower/Back In The USA **PERSONNEL** Rob Tyner (v), Fred 'Sonic' Smith (g), Wayne Kramer (g), Michael Davies (b), Dennis Thompson (d)

Having kicked out the jams with a confrontational debut seething with White Panther Party political rage and the free-form spirit of Sun Ra and fellow jazz experimentalists, **Back In The USA** was something of a shock. Stripped down to essentials, the band unashamedly celebrated its garage roots, delivering a batch of lean originals that matched the intent of the album's opening and closing tunes by Little Richard and Chuck Berry. Producer Jon Landau failed to capture the MC5's sense of adventure, but instead helped to formulate a blueprint which would be adopted by hundreds of punk bands five years later.

… the band's newly re-issued 1970 follow-up, **Back In The USA***, constituted a far more radical call to arms. Trimming the feedback and baring their rock & roll roots on that album, the MC5 helped define the stripped-down beefed-up sound of the coming decade.* **Mark Coleman, Rolling Stone, December 1992**

Back Stabbers

ARTIST The O'Jays **RELEASE DATE** October 1972 (UK)/September 1972 (US) **LABEL** Philadelphia International Records **PRODUCER** Kenny Gamble, Leon Huff, Bunny Sigler, Thom Bell **UK CHART** peak/weeks 14/- **US CHART** peak/weeks 10/44 **TRACK LISTING** When The World's At Peace/Back Stabbers/Who Am I/Mr Lucky/Time To Get Down/992 Arguments/Listen to the Clock/Shiftless, Shady, Jealous/Sunshine/Love Train **PERSONNEL** Bunny Sigler (k), Ronald Baker (b), Thom Bell (st), Roland Chambers (g), Jon Renaldo (st, hn), Bobby 'Electronic' Eli (g), Dennis Harris (g), Norman Harris (g), Leon Huff (k), Eddie Lavert (v), Vince Montana (pc), Lenny Pakula (k), William 'Doc' Powell (v), Larry Washington (pc), Walter Williams (v), Earl Young (d)

When Leon Huff and Kenny Gamble formed Philadelphia International, their model was clearly Motown: that being the case, the O'Jays were a three-man Temptations, railing against injustice on the one hand and lauding the delights of romance the next. Their UK breakthrough single, *Backstabbers*, was followed by the US chart-topping *Love Train*, while the RIAA's gold certification in May 1973 was the first for both group and label. Its success was to send a collection of earlier Neptune label recordings, the cheekily titled **The O'Jays In Philadelphia**, into the lower US chart reaches.

… the O'Jays have a consistently grooving beat and more of a rock-singing format. **Back Stabbers** *is certainly one of the better R&B albums this year, despite its weak points, and the single is required listening.* **Daniel Goldberg, NME, October 1972**

Back To Basics

ARTIST Billy Bragg **RELEASE DATE** June 1987 **LABEL** Go! Discs **PRODUCER** Edward De Bono **UK CHART** peak/weeks 37/4 **US CHART** peak/weeks · **TRACK LISTING** Billy Bragg Back To Basics/The Milkman Of Human Kindness/To Have And To Have Not/Richard/Lovers Town Revisited/A New England/The Man In The Iron Mask/The Busy Girl Buys Beauty/It Says Here/Love Gets Dangerous/From A Vauxhall Velox/The Myth Of Trust/The Saturday Boy/Island Of No Return/This Guitar Says Sorry/Like Soldiers Do/St Swithin's Day/Strange Things Happen/A Lover Sings/Between The Wars/The World Turned Upside Down/Which Side Are You On **PERSONNEL** Billy Bragg (v, g), Kenny Craddock (o), Dave Woodhead (t)

Essex man Bragg's socialist preaching and rasping voice was not to everyone's taste, but the occasional heartfelt love song revealed a likeable soft underbelly. A collection of EPs and mini-albums – *Life's A Riot With Spy Vs Spy, Brewing Up With Billy Bragg,* and *Between The Wars* – all flaunted his typically frank and uncompromising lyrics, as did the near-classic *A New England,* which later became a hit single for Kirsty MacColl. His abrasive tones and Falkland references never translated Stateside.

Back To Front

ARTIST Gilbert O'Sullivan **RELEASE DATE** November 1973 (UK)/January 1973 (US) **LABEL** MAM (UK)/Columbia (US) **PRODUCER** Gordon Mills **UK CHART** peak/weeks 1/64 **US CHART** peak/weeks 48/19 **TRACK LISTING** Intro/I Hope You'll Stay/In My Hole/Clair/That's Love/Can I Go With You/But I'm Not/Outro/I'm In Love With You/Who Was It/What Could Be Nicer (Mum The Kettles Boiling)/Out Of The Question/The Golden Rule/I'm Leaving/Outro **PERSONNEL** Gilbert O'Sullivan (v, k)

Imagine Elton John in a cloth cap and with an Irish lilt – that's Gilbert O'Sullivan, who unlike Elt (Reg Dwight) changed just half of his name to find fame. The songs were nursery rhyme-style ditties about everyday dilemmas, the strings being pulled by former Tom Jones Svengali Gordon Mills. O'Sullivan would later successfully sue Mills regarding royalties and copyrights, giving Elton John the inspiration to do likewise to his own mentor Dick James, the only time the inspiration passed in that direction.

The melodies here are tedious to the point where I find it difficult to play the album all the way through… on the evidence of this he's on the downward curve to bland schmaltz. **M. W., Melody Maker, October 1972**

Bad

ARTIST Michael Jackson **RELEASE DATE** September 1987 (UK & US) **LABEL** Epic (UK & US) **PRODUCER** Quincy Jones **UK CHART** peak/weeks 1/115 **US CHART** peak/weeks 1/87 **TRACK LISTING** Bad/The Way You Make Me Feel/Speed Demon/Liberian Girl/Just Good Friends/Another Part Of Me/Man In The Mirror/I Just Can't Stop Loving You/Dirty Diana/Smooth Criminal **PERSONNEL** Michael Jackson (v), session musicians

To say this album was eagerly awaited is something of an understatement, with **Thriller** having notched up sales of over 40 million copies worldwide. After a five-year wait and countless delays the first single, *I Just Can't Stop Loving You*, was infinitely better than the first single from **Thriller**, and prospects looked good. **Bad** did not disappoint. Both artist and producer showed themselves aware that music had moved on, so the danceable cuts were heavier and more effective, and the ballads slightly more intense without being cloying. Even the accompanying videos, when released, showed Jackson had more than one move on the dance floor too.

Bad *beats up nearly anything else in the neighbourhood. Its lyrics might swerve from gung-ho simplicity to nebulous sentimentality, disclosing next-to-nothing about their creator, but singer-songwriter is not the tradition that Jackson works in…. The earth won't move, but the floors will shake.* **Paul Du Noyer, Q, October 1987**

Bad Company

ARTIST Bad Company **RELEASE DATE** June 1974 (UK & US) **LABEL** Island (UK)/Swan Song (US) **PRODUCER** Bad Company **UK CHART** peak/weeks 3/25 **US CHART** peak/weeks 1/64 **TRACK LISTING** Can't Get Enough/Rock Steady/Ready For Love/Don't Let Me Down/Bad Company/The Way I Choose/Movin' On/Seagull **PERSONNEL** Paul Rodgers (v, p), Mick Ralphs (g, k), Boz Burrell (b), Simon Kirke (d) with Mel Collins (s), Sue and Sunny (bv),

Perhaps responsible for the crime against humanity known as stadium rock, Bad Company were at first a genuine supergroup,

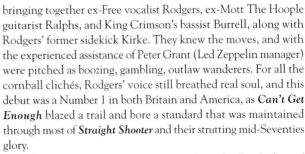

bringing together ex-Free vocalist Rodgers, ex-Mott The Hoople guitarist Ralphs, and King Crimson's bassist Burrell, along with Rodgers' former sidekick Kirke. They knew the moves, and with the experienced assistance of Peter Grant (Led Zeppelin manager) were pitched as boozing, gambling, outlaw wanderers. For all the cornball clichés, Rodgers' voice still breathed real soul, and this debut was a Number 1 in both Britain and America, as **Can't Get Enough** blazed a trail and bore a standard that was maintained through most of **Straight Shooter** and their strutting mid-Seventies glory.

The band has a past and it's a great one. That said, I'll go further and say Free never made an album as good as this one since **Tons of Sobs***… destined to be One Of The Great British Rock Bands Of This Year.* **G. B., Melody Maker, June 1974**

Bad Girls

ARTIST Donna Summer **RELEASE DATE** June 1979 (UK) / May 1979 (US) **LABEL** Casablanca (UK & US) **PRODUCER** Giorgio Moroder, Pete Bellote **UK CHART** peak/weeks 23/23 **US CHART** peak/weeks 1/49 **TRACK LISTING** Hot Stuff/Bad Girls/ Love Will Always Find You/ Walk Away/ Dim All The Lights/Journey To The Centre Of Your Heart/One Night In A Lifetime/Can't Get To Sleep At Night/On My Honor/There Will Always Be A You/All Through The Night/My Baby Understands/Our Love/ Lucky/ Sunset People **PERSONNEL** Donna Summer (v), session musicians

Her third double album in two years pushed Donna Summer ever further in her role as the first female crossover dance-pop star, well before the likes of Madonna and Paula Abdul. Another concept, this one starring Summer as hooker-with-a-heart, **Bad Girls** achieved maximum rotation on both black and white radio due to the equal emphasis on guitar lines and drum patterns on hits like **Hot Stuff** and the title track. The former arguably paved the way for the ultimate rock-funk fusion of Michael Jackson's **Thriller**.

The Band

ARTIST The Band **RELEASE DATE** January 1970 (UK)/September 1969 (US) **LABEL** Capitol (UK & US) **PRODUCER** John Simon **UK CHART** peak/weeks 25/11 **US CHART** peak/weeks 9/49 **TRACK LISTING** Across The Great Divide/Big Mam Rag/The Night They Drove Old Dixie Down/When You Awake/Up On Cripple Creek/Whispering Pines/Jemima Surrender/Rockin' Chair/Look Out Cleveland/Jawbone/The Unfaithful Servant/King Harvest (Has Surely Come) **PERSONNEL** Garth Hudson (o, cíte, p, ad, s, t), Richard Manuel (v, p, d, s, mh), Levon Helm (v, d, md, g), Rick Danco (v, b, vl, tb), Jaime Robbie Robertson (g), John Simon (ta, p, h)

Including perhaps their best-known songs, *Up On Cripple Creek* (a US hit) and *The Night They Drove Old Dixie Down* (later a hit for Joan Baez), The Band explored history and heritage with a novelist's eye for pertinent detail and memorable characters. They revelled in antiquated production standards, which served to bring out the best in their almost telepathic musical understanding. 'Their music,' said Greil Marcus, 'gave us a sense that the country was richer than we guessed.'

Band On The Run

ARTIST Paul McCartney And Wings RELEASE DATE December 1973 (UK & US) LABEL Apple (UK & US) PRODUCER George Martin UK CHART peak/weeks 1/124 US CHART peak/weeks 1/116 TRACK LISTING Band On The Run/Jet/ Bluebird/ Mrs Vanderbelt/Let Me Roll It/Mamunia/ No Words/ Picasso's Last Words (Drink To Me)/ Nineteen Hundred And Eighty Five PERSONNEL Paul McCartney (v, g, b), Linda McCartney (k, bv, p), Denny Laine (g, v)

With the exception of **John Lennon/The Plastic Ono Band**, this is probably the best of all the post-Beatles work, a Paul McCartney solo album in all but name. As if it needed proving, **Band On The Run** was an exemplary showcase for the Fab Four's ace melodicist, a hook-laden delight from beginning to end: from the dramatic two-part title track, to the horn-driven **Jet** and its echo-laden vocals, to the lilting, acoustic **Bluebird**, most of this music was as structurally ambitious as anything on **Abbey Road**.

McCartney may not sing with the clarity of voice he displayed in the heyday of The Beatles. But he sings more freely… his distinctive British sensibility now touches on things without belabouring them… **Jon Landau, Rolling Stone, June 1974**

Bandwagonesque

ARTIST Teenage Fanclub RELEASE DATE November 1991 (UK)/March 1992 (US) LABEL Creation (UK)/Geffen (US) PRODUCER Teenage Fan Club UK CHART peak/weeks 14/3 US CHART peak/weeks 137/4 TRACK LISTING The Concept/Satan/December/What You Do To Me/I Don't Know/Star Sign/ Metal Baby/Pet Rock/Sidewinder/Alcoholiday/Guiding Star/Is This Music? PERSONNEL Norman Blake (v, g), Raymond McGinley (b, v), Brendan O'Hare (b), Gerard Love (b, v), Dave Buchanon (pc, hc), Paul Chisholm (bv, g), Don Fleming (g, v, bv), Joseph McAlinden (hn, st, brs)

Voted Album Of The Year by America's prestigious *Spin* magazine, Bandwagonesque, the second LP from Teenage Fanclub, showed how thoroughly this Glaswegian band had assimilated their US influences, from the harmonies of the Beach Boys to the exquisitely melancholy jangle of cult favourites Big Star. Featuring an array of superb guitar-pop tunes – and Top 40 singles, from **The Concept** to **What You Do To Me** – **Bandwagonesque** remains the best example of Teenage Fanclub's ramshackle melodic approach.

Bandwagonesque *has not a single musical surprise in store… each song lopes along at a slowish mid tempo, made more endless by high thin vocals and moments of decorative guitar feedback. And it's all repetitive repetitive repetitive.* **Arion Berger, Rolling Stone, February 1992**

The Basement Tapes

ARTIST Bob Dylan RELEASE DATE July 1975 (UK & US) LABEL CBS (UK)/Columbia (US) PRODUCER Bob Dylan & The Band UK CHART peak/weeks 8/10 US CHART peak/weeks 7/14 TRACK LISTING Odds And Ends/Orange Juice Blues (Blues For Breakfast)/Million Dollar Bash/Yazoo Street Scandal/Goin' To Acapulco/Katie's Been Gone/Lo And Behold!/Bessie Smith/Clothes Line Saga/Apple Sucking Tree/Please, Mrs Henry/Tears Of Rage/Too Much Of Nothing/Yea! Heavy And A Bottle Of Bread/Ain't No More Cane/Crash On The Levee (Down In The Flood)/Ruben Remus/Tiny Montgomery/You Ain't Goin' Nowhere/Don't Ya Tell Henry/Nothing Was Delivered/Open The Door, Homer/Long Distance Operator/This Wheel's On Fire PERSONNEL Bob Dylan (ag, p, v), Robbie Robertson (ag, g, d, v), Richard Manuel (p, d, bv, v), Richard Danko (b, md, v), Gareth Hudson (o, ctte, ad, ts, p), Levon Helm (d, md, b, v)

Seeing the light in 1975 as a double album compiled and remixed by Robbie Robertson, these recordings had circulated since 1967, frequently on the 'Great White Wonder' series of bootlegs, and been covered by artists as diverse as Julie Driscoll, Manfred Mann and Peter Paul and Mary. They resulted from the 18 months following Dylan's motorcycle accident, which he spent writing and recording with Robertson.

The songs on **The Basement Tapes** *are the hardest, toughest, sweetest, saddest, funniest, wisest songs I know… they're about survival with honour and without bitterness. If there are tests, they've all been passed…* **Paul Nelson, Rolling Stone, September 1975**

Basket Of Light

ARTIST Pentangle RELEASE DATE October 1969 (UK)/January 1970 (US) LABEL Transatlantic (UK)/Reprise (US) PRODUCER Shel Talmy UK CHART peak/weeks 5/28 US CHART peak/weeks 200/2 TRACK LISTING Light Flight/Once I Had A Sweetheart/Springtime Promises/Lyke-Wake Dirge/Train Song/Hunting Song/Sally Go Round The Cuckoo/House Carpenter PERSONNEL Terry Cox (d, v, pc), Bert Jansch (g, v), Jacqui McShee (v), John Renbourn (g, v, si), Danny Thompson (b)

The mixture of jazz, blues and folk influences Pentangle offered was unique, and in John Renbourn and Bert Jansch they had two of the leading folk guitarists of the era. Picking up Blues Incorporated's rhythm section and the untried McShee, they found greatest success with this, their third album whose **Light Flight**, showcasing McShee's scat-singing abilities, was used as theme for a successful TV series, *Take Three Girls*. Re-formations after their early Seventies split have failed to recapture the magic here.

This Pentangle album disturbs me because it sounds as if the group has run out of things to do. Repetition, in style and material, dominates nearly every cut of this album. **Gary Von Tersch, Rolling Stone, Febuary 1970**

Bat Out Of Hell

ARTIST Meat Loaf RELEASE DATE January 1978 (UK)/October 1977 (US) LABEL Epic (UK)/Cleveland Epic (US) PRODUCER Todd Rundgren UK CHART peak/weeks 9/471 - US CHART peak/weeks 14/82 TRACK LISTING Bat Out Of Hell/You Took The Words Right Out Of My Mouth (Hot Summer Night)/Heaven Can Wait/All Revved Up With No Place To Go/Two Out Of Three Ain't Bad/Paradise By The Dashboard Light/For Crying Out Loud PERSONNEL Meatloaf (v), Jim Steinman (k, pc), Todd Rundgren (var), Roy Bittan (k, p), Max Weinberg (d), Kasim Sultan (b), Roger Powell (sy), Ellen Foley (bv), Rory Dodd (bv)

An overblown concept album written for Loaf (aka Marvin Lee Aday) by madcap composer Jim Steinman. It was constructed by producer/arranger/guitarist Todd Rundgren and, with the benefit

of a trio of early promo videos, shown on British TV, sold five million UK and 12 million worldwide. After a lengthy separation from Svengali Steinman, the 1993 follow-up **Bat Out Of Hell II**, proved Loaf's next best-seller, even if the protagonists admitted it shared little but the title and the singer with the first surprise hit. Movie shows, teen romances, motorbikes – all American life is here.

… there is a saving grace in this pretentious rubbish – the title track, an aggressive song about a motorcycle crash (into which Steinman injects every urban nightmare cliché in the book) which goes so far over the top one can only marvel. **Michael Oldfield, Melody Maker, February 1978**

Be Here Now

ARTIST Oasis RELEASE DATE August 1997 LABEL Creation Records PRODUCER Owen Morris & Noel Gallagher UK CHART peak/weeks 1/25 US CHART peak/weeks - TRACK LISTING D'You Know What I Mean?/My Big Mouth/Magic Pie/Stand By Me/I Hope, I Think,I Know/The Girl In The Dirty Shirt/Fade In-Out/Don't Go Away/Be Here Now/All Around The World/It's Gettin' Better (Man!)/All Around The World (reprise) PERSONNEL Liam Gallagher (v), Noel Gallagher (g, bv), Bonehead (g), Guigsy (b), Whitey (d, pc)

Few albums had inspired such expectation as Oasis's third, although the result revealed nothing we didn't already know. Eight minutes in album-track form, it set the tone for 11 long-winded creations, with the usual Beatles allusions (the title **It's Getting Better, Man!** and the piccolo trumpets of **All Around The World**), muscular rhythms and a Noel Gallagher vocal spot (**Magic Pie**). In late 1997 Noel proclaimed this 'our last album of the 1990s' – what next?

Noel Gallagher may be the master of the cliché, but that's way better than being its slave. He once again proves the ancient adage that mediocre artists borrow while great artists

steal: all his sources have the original tags still hanging off them…
Charles Shaar Murray, Mojo, September 1997

Be Yourself Tonight

ARTIST Eurythmics RELEASE DATE May 1985 (UK & US) LABEL RCA (UK & US) PRODUCER David A. Stewart UK CHART peak/weeks 3/80 US CHART peak/weeks 9/45 TRACK LISTING Would I Lie To You?/There Must Be An Angel (Playing With Heart)/I Love You Like A Ball And Chain/Sisters Are Doin' It For Themselves/Conditioned Soul/Adrian/It's (Baby Coming Back)/Here Comes That Sinking Feeling/Better To Have Lost In Love (Than Never To Have Loved At All) PERSONNEL Elvis Costello (v), Aretha Franklin (v), Michael Kamen (st), Mike Campbell (g), Annie Lennox (v, k, kp, fl), Angel Cross (bv), Martin Dobson (s), Nathan East (b), Dean Garcia (b), Stan Lynch (d), Dave Plews (t), Olle Romo (d), David A. Stewart (b, g, ag, d, v, dp), Benmont Tench (k), Charles Williams (bv), Stevie Wonder (h)

An all-star extravaganza that made a mockery of Lennox and Stewart's original stark duo image, this grab-bag nevertheless brought the pair their first UK Number 1 single thanks to Stevie Wonder's mellifluous harmonica lick underlying *There Must Be An Angel*. They had the ideal showcase to push the album up there too, but Lennox's throat problems caused a no-show at *Live Aid*. Consolation would come in 1986 with two Brits, Stewart winning Best Producer for the album and Lennox Best British Female.

*While derivativeness keeps this album from being an outright sparkler, they set up such a surprisingly raucous commotion on **Would I Lie To You?** that you're tempted to ask for an encore of this roof-raising stuff before their restless inventiveness moves them on to something quieter.*
The Year In Records 1985, Rolling Stone, December 1985

The Beach Boys Today

ARTIST The Beach Boys RELEASE DATE April 1966 (UK), May 1965 (US) LABEL Capitol (UK & US) PRODUCER Brian Wilson UK CHART peak/weeks 6/25 US CHART peak/weeks 4/50 TRACK LISTING Do You Wanna Dance?/Good To My Baby/Don't Hurt My Little Sister/When I Grow Up/Help Me, Rhonda/Dance, Dance, Dance/Please Let Me Wonder/I'm So Young/Kiss Me, Baby/She Knows Me Too Well/In The Back Of My Mind/Bull Session With The Big Daddy PERSONNEL Brian Wilson (b, k, v), Mike Love (v), Carl Wilson (g, v), Al Jardine (g, v), Dennis Wilson (d, v)

Even by this stage the Beach Boys' schizophrenia was evident: rousing peppy singles shimmied next to Brian Wilson's introspective studies of dream-like romances. The harmonies throughout were awe-inspiringly lovely. Wilson was influenced by Phil Spector, and was in thrall, perhaps too much, to The Beatles and The Byrds. Having almost lost his hearing in one ear the year previously, he cut out further touring and became a studio perfectionist.

Wilson's dream lovers were suddenly no longer simple happy souls harmonising their sun kissed innocence and undying devotion over a muted halcyon backdrop of surf and sand. They were vulnerable, insecure, at times almost neurotic. **Nick Kent, NME, June 1975**

A Beard Of Stars

ARTIST Tyrannosaurus Rex RELEASE DATE March 1970 (UK & US) LABEL Regal Zonophone (UK)/Blue Thumb (US) PRODUCER Tony Visconti UK CHART peak/weeks 21/6 US CHART peak/weeks 0/0 TRACK LISTING Prelude/A Day Late/The Woodland Bop/First Heart Mighty Dawn Dart/Pavillions Of Sun/Organ Blues/By The Light Of The Magical Moon/Wind Cheetah/A Beard Of Stars/Great Horse/Dragon's Ear/Lofty Skies/Dove/Elemental Child PERSONNEL Marc Bolan (v, g), Mickey Finn (bo, v)

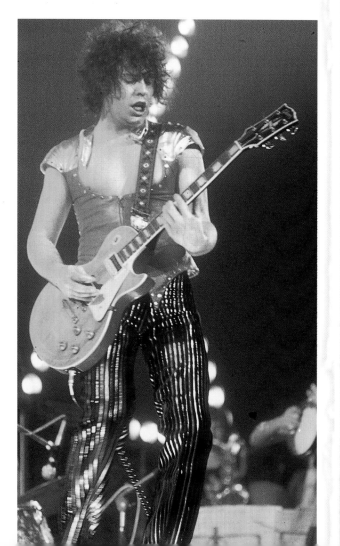

The replacement of Steve Took with an equally pretty sidekick, the bongo-playing Mickey Finn (he and Bolan had met in a health food restaurant), was less significant than Marc Bolan's decision to ditch his acoustic guitar for **A Beard Of Stars**: the first tentative step towards the glamification, and electrification, of folk-hippy outfit Tyrannosaurus Rex. Although Bolan's acid-tinged, visionary poesy were still present and correct (his collection of poems, *The Warlock Of Love*, made the British best-sellers lists), by **A Beard Of Stars** the whimsical imagery was offset by a rather more earthy sound. T.Rexstacy beckoned.

It is selfconcious as hell, largely uninteresting, and even grating to the ears…. Perhaps Bolan's mistakes lie in attempting more of a rock style – but you can't get rock from a bad fuzzy guitar and a bongo . **Ken Simmons, Rolling Stone, July 1970**

The Beast Inside

ARTIST Inspiral Carpets RELEASE DATE April 1991 (UK & US) LABEL Cow-Mute (UK)/Sire (US) PRODUCER Chris Nagle UK CHART peak/weeks 5/6 US CHART peak/weeks 0/0 TRACK LISTING Caravan/Please Be Cruel/Born Yesterday/Sleep Well Tonight/Brip/Beast Inside/Niagara/Mermaid/Further Away/Dreams Are All We Have PERSONNEL Graham Lambert (g), Tom Hingley (v), Martin Walsh (b), Craig Gill (d), Clint Boon (o, v)

Following the Number 2 album **Life** and a selection of critically lauded EPs, this continued the organ-dominated sound and inward-looking lyrics that had marked the Oldham-based Carpets out as a *nouveau* Doors. But there was a difference: brooding, dark and packed with ballads, it was not what had been expected from the single **Caravan**, and fell short of its predecessor in commercial terms. It would all fall apart for the Carpets, however, and in retrospect a carbon copy of **Life** might have kept them on track behind the Roses and Mondays as 'Madchester' giants.

… they never did seem to quite fit. Now they sound merely confused as to who or what exactly they want to be. A shame because it all starts off rather well with **Caravan***…. Long on attempted atmosphere but short on anything to hold on to.* **Peter Kane, Q, May 1991**

Beatles For Sale

ARTIST The Beatles RELEASE DATE December 1964 LABEL Parlophone PRODUCER George Martin UK CHART peak/weeks 1/46 US CHART peak/weeks 0/0 TRACK LISTING No Reply/I'm A Loser/Baby's In Black/Rock And Roll Music/I'll Follow The Sun/Mr Moonlight/Kansas City/Eight Days A Week/Words Of Love/Honey Don't/Every Little Thing/I Don't Want To Spoil The Party/What You're Doing/Everybody's Trying To Be My Baby PERSONNEL John Lennon (v, rg), Paul McCartney (v, b), George Harrison (v, lg), Ringo Starr (d)

Pretty love songs were on the wane: The Beatles were beginning to kick with venom and righteous, yet never pompous, protest. Lennon's *I'm A Loser* displayed a darker, more bitter twist to their tunefulness. While the six cover versions betrayed their over-commitment to work, with signs of understandable fatigue, the high point of Beatlemania was still imminent, even though the band held the top five places in the American chart simultaneously.

The Beatles (White Album)

ARTIST The Beatles **RELEASE DATE** November 1968 (UK & US) **LABEL** Apple (UK & US) **PRODUCER** George Martin **UK CHART** peak/weeks 1/21 **US CHART** peak/weeks 1/144 **TRACK LISTING** Back In The USSR/Dear Prudence/Glass Onion/Ob-la-di-ob-la-da/Wild Honey Pie/The Continuing Story Of Bungalo Bill/While My Guitar Gently Weeps/Happiness Is A Warm Gun/Martha My Dear/I'm So Tired/Blackbird/Piggies/Rocky Racoon/Don't Pass Me By/Why Don't We Do It In The Road/I Will/Julia/Birthday/Yer Blues/Mother Nature's Son/Everybody's Got Something To Hide Except Me And My Monkey/Sexy Sadie/Long Long Long/Revolution 1/Honey Pie/Savoy Truffle/Cry Baby Cry/Revolution 9/Good Night **PERSONNEL** George Harrison (o, g, vl, b, v), John Lennon (v, o, b, hn, s), Paul McCartney (v, fl, pc, d, p, b, o), Ringo Starr (pc, p, d, bo, v), Chris Thomas (hd, mln), Derek Watkins (t), Nicky Hopkins (p), Don Lang (tr), Yoko Ono (bv), George Martin (p, hn), session musicians

The Lennon-McCartney partnership and *simpatico* began to drift: individual obsessions, relationships and resentments were pulling the four friends in diverse directions. There was a notable absence of cohesive atmosphere or continuity to this patchy epic. The sessions exhausted the group and led them closer to the eventual split. Still, *Back In The USSR* and *Birthday* exhibited a defiantly rocking energy, which Lennon's regressive *Yer Blues* perhaps took too far. *Why Don't We Do It In The Road* was written by McCartney after watching two monkeys do just that (he was meditating at the time). Harrison's plaintive *While My Guitar Gently Weeps* was the album's, and his, best-ever song.

… there is at times a sadness that perhaps reflects their turbulent year… the album illustrates that the four members can each have their own direction under the artistic umbrella of the Beatles; pulling in different directions but never catapulting into anarchy… **Alan Walsh, Melody Maker, November 1968**

Beauty And The Beat

ARTIST Go-Go's **RELEASE DATE** August 1981 (UK)/July 1981 (US) **LABEL** I.R.S. (UK & US) **PRODUCER** Richard Gottehrer, Rob Freeman **UK CHART** peak/weeks 0/0 **US CHART** peak/weeks 1/72 **TRACK LISTING** Our Lips Are Sealed/How Much More/Tonite/Lust To Love/This Town/We Got The Beat/Fading Fast/Automatic/You Can't Walk In Your Sleep/Skidmarks On My Heart/Can't Stop The World **PERSONNEL** Belinda Carlisile (v), Charlotte Caffey (lg, v), Jane Wiedlen (rg, v), Margot Olaverra (b), Gina Shock (d)

When Los Angeles girl punks the Go-Go's put together a band, expectations varied. Singer Belinda Carlisle would have been happy with six-figure sales, while guitarist Jane Wiedlin would only be happy with platinum. Jane got her wish – but ironically it was Carlisle who professed herself 'horrified' by the way their rough edges had been smoothed in the studio and who would go on to be a million-selling solo artist with a sound so airbrushed that it made the Go-Go's sound like… punks!

Beck-Ola

ARTIST Jeff Beck **RELEASE DATE** September 1969 (UK)/July 1969 (US) **LABEL** Columbia (UK)/Epic (US) **PRODUCER** Mickie Most **UK CHART** peak/weeks 39/1 **US CHART** peak/weeks 15/21 **TRACK LISTING** All Shook Up/Spanish Boots/Girl From Mill Valley/Jailhouse Rock/Plynth (Water Down The Drain)/The Hangman's Knee/Rice Pudding **PERSONNEL** Rod Stewart (v), Ron Wood (b), Nicky Hopkins (p), Tony Newman (d), Jeff Beck (g)

Always acclaimed as 'the guitarist's guitarist' (other name axemen defer to his genius without hesitation), Beck has never capitalized commercially, though this album seems to many to have been the muse for Led Zeppelin's entire career. Subsequent Faces Rod Stewart and Ronnie Wood on bass – well, Beck was no slouch on the guitar – gelled well with the ex-Yardbird, who brought unexpected vitality to readings of *Jailhouse Rock* and *All Shook Up*. Mickie Most's production was criticized, but the personnel's

chemistry blazed. *Hi Ho Silver Lining* it ain't.

It's a shame Jeff's groups don't stay together longer. They tend to produce fine rock, especially with such talented sidemen as Nicky Hopkins and Rod Stewart on hand. Hopkin's piano feature on Girl From Mill Valley is particularly outstanding. **Melody Maker, September 1969**

Bedtime Stories

ARTIST Madonna **RELEASE DATE** October 1994 (UK & US) **LABEL** Maverick-Sire (UK & US) **PRODUCER** Madonna, Nellee Hooper, Babyface, Dallas Austin, Dave 'Jam' Hall **UK CHART** peak/weeks 3/- **US CHART** peak/weeks 3/48 **TRACK LISTING** Survival/I'd Rather Be Your Lover/Don't Stop/Inside Of Me/Human Nature/Forbidden Love/Love Tried To Welcome Me/Sanctuary/Bedtime Story/Take A Bow **PERSONNEL** Madonna (v), Tommy Martin (g), Me'Shell Ndege Ocello (b), Colin Wolfe (b), Dallas Austin (d, k), Babyface (sy, bv), Niki Harris (bv), Donna Delory (bv)

After setting out to shock with her book *Sex*, her album **Erotica** and her movie *Body Of Evidence*, Madonna returned to the innocence of her **True Blue** era for **Bedtime Stories**. Clean production, clean lyrics and her best collection of songs for some time made this a world-wide winner. Collaborations with Nellee Hooper and Björk produced some interesting results, but there is nothing controversial here, just an almost faultless collection of smooth ballads and laid-back grooves from a woman obviously more at ease with herself than ever before.

Princess Ciccone always resonates better when emoting from the other side of the American tracks. **Bedtime Stories** *uses modern black pop-swing beat et al as a bedrock for musings behind Hollywood shutters and is excellent in its evocations of loneliness, love and longing.* **NME, December 1984**

Before And After Science

ARTIST Brian Eno RELEASE DATE December 1977 (UK)/May 1978 (US) LABEL Polydor (UK)/Island (US) PRODUCER Brian Eno UK CHART peak/weeks – US CHART peak/weeks 171/5 TRACK LISTING No One Receiving/Backwater/Kurt's Rejoiner/Energy Fools The Magician/King's Lead Hat/Here He Comes/Julie With.../By This River/Through Hollow Lands/Spider And I PERSONNEL Brian Eno (sy)

Eno's final song-based album for over a decade was a masterpiece. If **Another Green World** had been a major step forward, **Before And After Science** was a giant leap, providing final proof of Eno's stature as a creator of atmospheric, intelligent music beyond easy categorization. It partly looked back to Eno's roots in Sixties pop, but influenced throughout by his love of musical experimentation and exploration. *Backwater* and *No One Receiving* are outstanding, but the standard never drops.

Brian Eno's records are much like his character: while the impression is of a forbidding intensity, the reality is much warmer and endearing....The long-term correctness of his original conception has been amply proved this past year. **Richard Williams, Melody Maker, December 1977**

Beggar's Banquet

ARTIST The Rolling Stones RELEASE DATE December 1968 (UK & US) LABEL Decca (UK)/London (US) PRODUCER Jimmy Miller UK CHART peak/weeks 3/12 US CHART peak/weeks 5/32 TRACK LISTING Sympathy For The Devil/No Expectations/Dear Doctor/Parachute Woman/Jigsaw Puzzle/Street Fighting Man/Prodigal Son/Stray Cat Blues/Factory Girl/Salt Of The Earth PERSONNEL Mick Jagger (v, h), Keith Richards (rg), Brian Jones (lg), Charlie Watts (d), Bill Wyman (b), Ian Stewart (p)

After the psychedelic *faux pas* of **Satanic Majesties** and various run-ins with the law, the Stones took their time to get back on track. The single *Jumping Jack Flash* was a statement of intent, while the album that followed was effectively a blueprint for the Stones' work to date. It was also the last album to feature Brian Jones who, edged out by the Jagger-Richards writing partnership, quit in 1969 and was found drowned a month later. The end of an era and the beginning of another...

The Belle Album

ARTIST Al Green RELEASE DATE September 1979 (UK)/December 1977 (US) LABEL Cream Label (UK)/Hi (US) PRODUCER Al Green, Fred Jordan, Reuben Fairfax Jr. UK CHART peak/weeks – US CHART peak/weeks 103/12 TRACK LISTING Belle/Loving You/Feels Like Summer/Georgia Boy/I Feel Good/All N' All/Chariots Of Fire/Dream PERSONNEL Al Green (g, v), Reuben Fairfax, Jr. (b), James Bass (g), Margaret Foxworth (v), Linda Jones & Harvey Jones (bv), Leon Thomas (cl), Johnny Brown (p), Fred Jordan (p), John Toney (d, pc), Rob Payne (epc) Ardis Hardin (d), Buddy Jarrett (as), Darryl Neely (t, hn), Ron Echols (s), Frd Jordan (t, hn)

Like Little Richard, who cast his jewellery off an Australian bridge, Al Green fought an inner battle between the sacred and the secular. **The Belle Album** was when it all came to a head, and saw Green, freed from the benevolent rule of producer Willie Mitchell who had overseen his career since 1969, following his own muse. Bassist Fairfax and trumpeter Jordan lent a compositional hand and Green's performance of the title track won the seventh Tokyo Music Festival, but a fall from stage (and grace?) the following year saw a return to full-time church music. **Belle** was his peak.

The Bends

ARTIST Radiohead RELEASE DATE March 1995 (UK)/May 1995 (US) LABEL Parlophone (UK)/Capitol (US) PRODUCER John Leckie UK CHART peak/weeks 6/- US CHART peak/weeks 88/24 TRACK LISTING Planet Telex/The

Bends/High and Dry/Fake Plastic Trees/Bones/Nice Dream/Just/My Iron Lung/Bullet Proof... I Wish I Was/Black Star/Sulk/Street Spirit (Fade Out) PERSONNEL Fender Gibson Musicman (g), Plank (g), Caroline Levelle (c), John Matthias (va, vl), Thom Yorke (st, v, g), Ed O'Brien (g, v), Jon Greenwood (g), Colin Greenwood (b), Phil Selway (d)

A change of direction from Sixties-inspired popsters proved fortuitous for Oxford's Radiohead. Their layered soundscapes struck a sombre chord amid the more buoyant sounds of the time, and York's anguished lyrics, delivered in tones of deepest despair, indicated that here was a band doing it 'for real'. While a number of genres were plundered in search of the ultimate statement, Radiohead nonetheless contrived a sound which was unique, while a low media profile merely added to their cult appeal.

Well, the **Creep** *single did threaten greatness, and Radiohead's second album seems to live up to that promise. The emotional range is not great, but their sulking grunge guitars have an epic stature and tunes like* **Black Star** *are mesmeric.* **Mojo, May 1995**

Berlin

ARTIST Lou Reed RELEASE DATE October 1973 (UK & US) LABEL RCA Victor (UK & US) PRODUCER Bob Ezrin UK CHART peak/weeks 7/5 US CHART peak/weeks 98/11 TRACK LISTING Berlin/Lady Day/Men Of Good Fortune/Caroline Says I/How Do You Think It Feels/Oh Jim/Caroline Says II/The Kids/The Bed/Sad Song PERSONNEL Lou Reed (v, g), Dick Wagner (g), Steve Hunter (g), Steve Winwood (k), Jack Bruce (b), Aynsley Dunbar (d)

Having left the Velvet Underground and taken the first step towards commercial success with the David Bowie-produced **Transformer**, Lou Reed, left to his own devices, created a truly downbeat concept album about a doomed, drugged affair in the German city of the title. It has been reassessed over the years and acclaimed as a *noir* classic, but at the time even the likes of Jack Bruce and Steve Winwood couldn't win **Berlin** fans, although it charted remarkably highly.

I't's not enough that all that 'decadent' bullshit is trotted out again, especially when it's given the cabaret-styled heading of **Berlin**. *Then again, maybe he does have to spell himself out once more for his new audience. But oh!, for that old terse style.* **M. W., Melody Maker, October 1973**

Between The Buttons

ARTIST The Rolling Stones RELEASE DATE January 1967 (UK)/February 1967 (US) LABEL Decca (UK)/London (US) PRODUCER Andrew Oldham UK CHART peak/weeks 3/22 US CHART peak/weeks 2/47 TRACK LISTING Yesterday's Papers/My Obsession / Back Street Girl / Connection / She Smiled Sweetly/ Cool, Calm And Collected/ All Sold Out/ Please Go Home/ Who's Been Sleeping Here?/ Complicated/Miss Amanda Jones/ Something Happened To Me Yesterday PERSONNEL Mick Jagger (v, h), Keith Richards (rg), Brian Jones (lg), Charlie Watts (d), Bill Wyman (b), Ian Stewart (p)

Situated between the underrated rock of **Aftermath** and the Sgt. Pepper carbon-copy of **Satanic Majesties**, **Between The Buttons** almost cast the Stones as classic British pop-rockers somewhere next to The Kinks and The Who. It was also the last album the Stones made coming straight off the tour-album-tour treadmill: henceforth they would take a more considered stance. **Connection** is Keith's first solo vocal on record, with Mick helping out on the choruses. Its drug theme was soon to be front page news.

Fun, excitement, great ballads and the full unveiling of Mick Jagger's voice… the Rolling Stones latest milestone. The group have achieved their best recording sound, far less complicated, much clearer, warmer, penetrating and communicating. **Melody Maker, January 1967**

Between Today And Yesterday

ARTIST Alan Price RELEASE DATE June 1974 (UK & US) LABEL Warner Bros. (UK & US) PRODUCER Alan Price UK CHART peak/weeks 9/10 US CHART peak/weeks 0/0 TRACK LISTING Left over People/Away, Away/Between Today And Yesterday/In Times Like These/Under the Sun/Jarrow Song/City Lights/Look at My Face/Angel Eyes/You're Telling Me/Dream of

Delight/Between Today And Yesterday PERSONNEL Alan Price (o, p, v), Dave Markee (b), Colin Green (g, b), Clive Thacker (d)

Having left The Animals because of a fear of flying, Newcastle's Alan Price's career became worthy but earthbound despite a series of American-inspired hit singles. This concept album – his first Top 10 solo LP – reunited him with his roots and included a surprise hit in **Jarrow Song**, celebrating the march on London by his fellow north-easterners. He was influenced by film-maker Lindsay Anderson, whose *O Lucky Man!* he had written the score of, and would continue addressing social themes with 1978's **England My England**.

Words like 'honesty', 'integrity' and 'gritty realism' come readily to mind when the subject of Alan Price comes up…. **Between Today And Yesterday…** *turns out to be something of a* tour de force. **M. W., Melody Maker, June 1974**

Big Science

ARTIST Laurie Anderson RELEASE DATE April 1982 (UK & US) LABEL Warner Bros. (UK & US) PRODUCER – UK CHART peak/weeks 29/6 US CHART peak/weeks 124/12 TRACK LISTING From The Air/Big Science/Sweaters/ Walking And Falling/ Born, Never Asked/O Superman (For Massnet)/Example PERSONNEL Laurie Anderson (v, vl, sy) with session David Van Tieghem (pc, d), Roma Peter Gordon (cl, s)

Distilled from her gargantuan performance-art concept *United States*, this mixture of sonic tomfoolery, musical experimentation (vocoders and violins) and spoken word thrilled critics. Intelligent discussion of technology's increasing dominance was then a relatively fresh topic, although Anderson was the first to point out that she was only doing 'what the avant-garde has been doing for 50 years'. Still, the inexplicable global success of the **O Superman** single made her a *cause célèbre*, and she was able to continue her search for post-modern meaning throughout the decade. It's ironic that she stepped out with the deity of old-school rock 'n' roll, Lou Reed.

Anderson's invention is astonishing – she's way ahead of technology's ability to record or reproduce her art in a way that will do it justice. So I guess until technology catches up with her, **Big Science** *will have to do.* **Chris Bohn, NME, April 1982**

Big 16

ARTIST The Impressions **RELEASE DATE** December 1965 (UK & US) **LABEL** H.M.V. **PRODUCER** – **UK CHART** peak/weeks – **US CHART** peak/weeks 0/0 **TRACK LISTING** Gypsy Woman/Talking About My Baby/I'm So Proud/Keep On Pushing/Ever Let Go/It's All Right/People Get Ready/Woman's Got Soul/You Must Believe Me/Sad, Sad Girl And Boy/I'm The One Who Loves You/Minstrel And Queen/Grow Closer Together/Amen/Meeting Over Yonder/I Need **PERSONNEL** Curtis Mayfield (lv, g), Fred Cash (v), Arthur Brooks (v), Richard Brooks (v), Sam Gooden (v)

The soul-gospel pioneers led by Curtis Mayfield were never really an album act, so this summation of their first five years was timely. It has since been superseded by 1989's CD-based **Definitive Impressions**, but the songs on here are legendary enough in their own right. Strangely, the first hit, *For Your Precious Love*, which featured early vocalist Jerry Butler rather than Mayfield, is not included. These songs were not just inspirational to US black musicians but also Jamaican – Bob Marley would cover *People Get Ready*.

One of The Impressions' strong points is that they do original material, and all of it comes from Curtis. Michael Alexander, **Rolling Stone, January 1969**

Billion Dollar Babies

ARTIST Alice Cooper **RELEASE DATE** March 1973 (UK & US) **LABEL** Warner Bros. (UK & US) **PRODUCER** Bob Ezrin **UK CHART** peak/weeks 1/23 **US CHART** peak/weeks 1/50 **TRACK LISTING** Hello Hooray/Raped And Freezin/Elected/Billion Dollar Babies/Unfinished Sweet/No More Mister Nice Guy/Generation Landslide/Sick Things/Mary-Ann/I Love The Dead **PERSONNEL** Alice Cooper (v), Glen Buxton (g), Michael Bruce (g, k), Dennis Dunaway (b), Neal Smith (d)

Alice's best, with snakeskin sleeve and a fine marriage of filthy rock and crossover choruses, plus some gratuitous sick bad taste thrown up for excess measure. Highly influential on the punks, the Godfather of shock-rock, Cooper displayed tremendous gall (*I Wanna Be Elected*), acted out bitter revenge fantasies (*No More Mr Nice Guy*), and had a penchant for ripping the heads off plastic dolls while allowing a lengthy snake to slither around his upper body. 'They say I hate babies,' quipped Alice, 'but it's not true – I just hate dolls.' He split the band, went solo, flew, crashed, and rose

again.

Billion Dollar Babies seems an abortion…. As it is now, with each member totally willing to submerge his musical development within the group personality, we'll continue to see a dependence on cheap tricks and illusions of decadence instead of rock 'n' roll. **Gordon Fletcher, Rolling Stone, May 1973**

Black Sabbath

ARTIST Black Sabbath **RELEASE DATE** February 1970 (UK)/July 1970 (US) **LABEL** Vertigo (UK)/Warner (US) **PRODUCER** Roger Bain **UK CHART** peak/weeks 8/42 **US CHART** peak/weeks 23/65 **TRACK LISTING** Black Sabbath/The Wizard/Behind The Wall Of Sleep/N.I.B./Evil Woman Don't Play Your Games With Me/Sleeping Village/Warning **PERSONNEL** Ozzy Ozborne (v), Tony Iommi (g), 'Geezer' Butler (b), Bill Ward (d)

Birmingham metal giants Sabbath's debut was doomy and definitive or dull and disastrous, depending on which critics you read. Plodding obsessively through muddy, murky riffs like a dinosaur in quicksand revealed that Tony Iommi didn't start life as a gifted guitarist and that wild frontman Ozzy Osbourne wasn't from the subtle-restraint school of singing. An overnight success, however, it launched the Sabs into the big rock league and was hailed as an influence a quarter century later by such bands as Nirvana.

The album is an accurate reflection of their music – hard driving and blues based with lyrics that have been influenced by Black Magic…. Their environment, they believe, is reflected in their music. **Royston Eldridge, Melody Maker, March 1970**

Black Sunday

ARTIST Cypress Hill **RELEASE DATE** July 1993 (UK & US) **LABEL** Columbia (UK)/Ruffhouse (US) **PRODUCER** Muggs **UK CHART** peak/weeks 13/21 **US CHART** peak/weeks 1/56 **TRACK LISTING** I Wanna Get High/I Ain't Goin' Out Like That/Insane In The Brain/When The Shit Goes Down/Lick A Shot/Cock The Hammer/Interlude/Lil' Putos/Legalize It/Hits From The Bong/What Goes Around Come Around/A To The K/Hand On The Clock/Break 'Em Off Some **PERSONNEL** B-Real (rap), Sen Dog (), DJ Muggs (dj)

Determinedly lazy production gave this L.A.-based rap trio a distinctive, menacing sound that many copied but failed to match. **Black Sunday**, following on a platinum-selling debut, was downright scary in parts, with its fabric of dope-hazed lyrics and near paranoid samples proving compulsive even to audiences who had not previously connected with hip-hop. Cuban-Americans, they soon moved from declaring themselves 'the biggest Latino crew of all time' to 'the biggest crew of all time', and topped the American charts again. *I Wanna Get High* became their manifesto. To keep in with more aggressive types they advocated guns almost as much as they did drugs.

Cypress's music blurs the borderline between the psychedelic and psychotic. The songs sound deceptively jaunty (the samples are all upful slices of Sixties soul, Meters-style proto-funk, jump-blues doo-wop), but the lowest-of-the-low-end bass exudes a baleful viscious menace. **Simon Reynolds, Melody Maker, July 1993**

Blackheart Man

ARTIST Bunny Wailer **RELEASE DATE** 1976 (US) **LABEL** Mango (US) **PRODUCER** Bunny Wailer **UK CHART** peak/weeks **US CHART** peak/weeks **TRACK LISTING** Blackheart Man / Fighting Against Conviction / Oppressed Song / The Fig Tree/ Dream Land / Rastaman / ReincarnatedSouls / Armageddon (Armagedon)/Bide Up/This Train **PERSONNEL** Aston Barrett (g), Carlton (Carlie) Barrett (d), Harold Butler (k), Dirty Harry (hn), Tyrone Downie (k), Bobby Ellis (hn), Fratter (g), Bunny Wailer (ag, b, g, pc, arr, d, v, bv, d),

Herman Marquis (hn), Tommy McCook (fl, s), Peter Tosh (g, bv), Willy Pep (bo), Robbie Shakespeare (b), Earl 'China' Smith (g), W. Wright (k), Neville Garrick (pc)

Bunny Wailer was, along with Bob Marley and Peter Tosh, one of the original Wailers. Possessed of a sweet, tender voice that has seen him described as reggae's own Marvin Gaye or Smokey Robinson, Wailer left his band-mates behind in 1973 to concentrate on a solo career that, while less widely celebrated than Tosh's and Marley's, rivals them for melodic pleasures and sheer spiritual intensity. **Blackheart Man**, his debut, is a beautiful collection that ranks alongside Marley's **Rastaman Vibrations** as Reggae Album of 1976.

It's a red eyed epic: the gospel according to Jah…. Had the album stuck to the personal, it would have been much more successful. The level of musicianship is very high… **Dan Oppenheimer, Rolling Stone, December 1976**

Blank Generation

ARTIST Richard Hell And The Void-Oids RELEASE DATE September 1977 (UK & US) LABEL Sire (UK & US) PRODUCER Richard Hell, Richard Gottehrer UK CHART peak/weeks 0/0 US CHART peak/weeks 0/0 TRACK LISTING Love Comes In Spurts/Liars Between/New Pleasure/Betrayal Takes Two/Down At The Rock And Roll Club/Who Says/Blank Generation/Walking On The Water/The Plan/Another World PERSONNEL Richard Hell (v, b), Robert Quine (g, v), Ivan Julian (g, v), Marc Bell (d)

Without Hell (born Richard Myers) and his groups Television and the Heartbreakers, both of which he left pre-fame, punk rock might never have been. Stiff Records picked up on him solo and this album's title track also titled an influential 1976 EP before being re-recorded. From a radical reworking of Creedence's **Walk Upon The Water** to the epic **Another World**, **Blank Generation** proved impossible to follow up, especially without Bell, who joined the Ramones, and Quine, who joined Lou Reed, both important contributors to a seminal work.

… his first album is going to provide him with an equally extreme congregate of aficionados and vicious back-stabbing critics. **Blank Generation** *is an extremely brave album, as ferociously successful as often as it fails in fulfilling its vision.* **Nick Kent, NME, October 1977**

Blind Faith

ARTIST Blind Faith RELEASE DATE August 1969 (UK)/July 1969 (US) LABEL Polydor (UK)/Atlantic (US) PRODUCER Jimmy Miller UK CHART peak/weeks 1/10 US CHART peak/weeks 1/37 TRACK LISTING Had To Cry/Can't Find My Way Home/Well All Right/Presence Of The Lord/Sea Of Joy/Do What You Like PERSONNEL Eric Clapton (v, g), Steve Winwood (v, k), Rick Grech (b), Ginger Baker (d)

Like most so-called supergroups, Blind Faith were short-lived, this being their only album. The teaming of Clapton and Baker from the recently split Cream, Winwood from Traffic and Grech from Family didn't quite flare up as might have been anticipated, and they indulged in some pretty pointless extended jamming. Redemption came in the shape of the gripping **Can't Find My Way Home** and the floating calm of **Presence Of The Lord**. After an impressive debut at Madison Square Garden their individual temperaments succumbed to the pressures of the industry's hype.

A beautiful set to put an end to doubts as to whether **Blind Faith** *was such a good idea after all. The four musicians work well together in a way that is quite different from Cream…* **Melody Maker, August 1969**

Blonde On Blonde

ARTIST Bob Dylan RELEASE DATE August 1966 (UK)/May 1966 (US) LABEL CBS (UK)/Columbia (US) PRODUCER Bob Johnston UK CHART peak/weeks 3/15 US CHART peak/weeks 9/34 TRACK LISTING Rainy Day Women #12 & 35/Pledging My Time/Visions Of Johanna/One Of Us Must Know/I Want You/Stuck Inside of Mobile With Thee/Leopard-Skin Pill-Box Hat/Just Like A Woman/Most Likely You Go Your Way And I'll Go Mine/Temporary Like Achilles/Absolutely Sweet Marie/4th Time Around/Obviously Five Believers/Sad Eyed Lady Of The Lowlands PERSONNEL Bob Dylan (bv, lg), Charlie McCoy, (bv) with Musicians: Wayne Moss, Kenneth Buttrey, Hargus Robbins, Jerry Kennedy, Joe South, Al Kooper, Bill Aikins, Henry Strzelecki, Jaime Robertson

The year of 1966 was an eventful one for Dylan: cat-called on his first electrified UK tour in May, he crashed his motorbike in July before releasing this critically-adored double album in August. Charting higher in Britain than at home, its centrepiece is the ambitious, side-long, **Sad Eyed Lady Of The Lowlands**, but it was overshadowed by the shorter tracks, notably the hit single **Rainy Day Women**, which attracted flak from supposedly being a 'drug song'.

Bob's back with a super gloss gatefold double album fifty shilling's worth of all that's best on the America rock scene. **Melody Maker, August 1966**

Blood And Chocolate

ARTIST Elvis Costello **RELEASE DATE** September 1986 (UK)/October 1986 (US) **LABEL** ImpDemon (UK)/Columbia (US) **PRODUCER** Nick Lowe, Colin Fairley **UK CHART** peak/weeks 16/5 **US CHART** peak/weeks 84/11 **TRACK LISTING** Uncomplicated/I Hope You're Happy Now/Tokyo Storm Warning/Home Is Anywhere You Hang Your Head/I Want You/Honey Are You Straight Or Are You Blind?/Blue Chair/Battered Old Bird/Crimes Of Paris/ Poor Napoleon/Next Time Round **PERSONNEL** Pete Thomas (d), Bruce Thomas (b), Steve Nieve (k), Napoleon Dynamite, Elvis Costello (v, g)

I Want You, fliply borrowing a Dylan title and outwriting the supposed master, remains one of the most emotional and affecting songs in the entire Costello canon. *I Hope You're Happy Now* and *Next Time Round* further illuminated his insight into every mood, every shade of optimism and pessimism, forgiveness and regret. The Attractions, with Nick Lowe as producer, had regrouped for this opus: it didn't flow easily – harder rockers sat uneasily next to tortured torch songs. Costello afterwards took a break from the band to explore artier avenues. Thom Yorke of Radiohead cited the album as a crucial influence.

*If **Blood And Chocolate** represents a return of sorts to the grit and bile that marked Costello's early albums, it is a welcome resurrection of a tough streak that has been underplayed since the turn of the decade.* Adrian Thrills, NME, September 1986

Blood On The Tracks

ARTIST Bob Dylan **RELEASE DATE** February 1975 (UK & US) **LABEL** CBS (UK)/Columbia (US) **PRODUCER** Bob Dylan **UK CHART** peak/weeks 4/16 **US CHART** peak/weeks 1/24 **TRACK LISTING** Tangled Up In Blue/Simple Twist Of Fate/You're A Big Girl Now/Idiot Wind/You're Gonna Make Me Lonesome When You Go/Meet Me In The Morning/Lily, Rosemary And The Jack Of Hearts/If You See Her, Say Hello/Shelter From The Storm/Buckets Of Rain **PERSONNEL** Bob Dylan (g, h, (v), Billy Preston (b), Eric Weissberg (g, bj), Tony Brown (b), Charlie Brown (g), Bill Berg (d), Charles Brown III (g), Buddy Cage (stg), Barry Cornfield (g, d), Richard Crooks (g, d), Paul Griffin (o, k), Gregg Inhofer (k), Barry Kornfield (g), Tom McFaul (k), Ken Odeguard (g), Bill Peterson (b), Chris Weber (g), Kevin Odegard (g)

After a couple of less than happy years with David Geffen's Asylum label, Dylan returned to his former home to deliver, arguably, his masterpiece. It was a return to the acoustic sound of the early Sixties, enhanced by the sparse backing of Eric Weissburg & Deliverance. Their skeletal input only served to enhance the bitter, often philosophical observations – impressionistic snapshots of the emotional turmoil Dylan was going through. *Idiot Wind* especially re-inforced the misogynistic temper of classics like *Positively 4th Street* in an uplifting, cathartic exercise that heralded Dylan's return to form and the throne as America's greatest songwriter.

*Bob Dylan… has produced in **Blood on the Tracks,** the most strikingly intelligent album of the Seventies… the work of a man who has lost not one iota of his devotion to, nor expertise with, a wide range of American music.* Michael Gray, Let It Rock, April 1975

Blood Sugar Sex Magik

ARTIST Red Hot Chilli Peppers **RELEASE DATE** September 1991 (UK)/October 1991 (US) **LABEL** Warner Bros. (UK & US) **PRODUCER** Rick Rubin **UK CHART** peak/weeks 25/34 **US CHART** peak/weeks 3/97 **TRACK LISTING** The Power Of Equality/If You Have To Ask/Breaking The Girl/Funky Monks/Suck My Kiss/I Could Have Lied/Mellowship Clinky In B Major/The Righteous & The Wicked/Give it Away/Blood Sugar Sex Magik/Under The Bridge/Naked In The Rain/Apache Rose Peacock/The Greeting Song/My Lovely Man/Sir Psycho Sexy/They're Red Hot **PERSONNEL** Anthony Keidis (v), John Frusciante (g), Chad Smith (d), Micheal 'Flea' Balzary (b)

Anyone entranced by the single *Under The Bridge* might have been horrified to find it referred to smack addict and pusher meeting, rather than two lovers, and equally shocked to find it

totally atypical of the album it came from. This was the swan song of guitarist John Frusciante – the guitarist who had replaced heroin victim Hillel Slovak – and the debut, Peppers-wise, of hard-rock producer Rick Rubin, the man best able to date to get their unique funk-meets-rock sound on to recording tape.

*On **BloodSugar**, their first album in many moons, the Chilli Peppers overdo it by at least a third, and even the good stuff, like, **Give It Away**, and **The Power Of Equality**, seems to pale among the so-so entries…* **The Year In Records 1991, Rolling Stone, December 1991**

Blood Sweat & Tears

ARTIST Blood Sweat & Tears **RELEASE DATE** March 1969 (UK)/January 1969 (US) **LABEL** CBS (UK)/Columbia (US) **PRODUCER** James William Guercio **UK CHART** peak/weeks 15/8 **US CHART** peak/weeks 1/109 **TRACK LISTING** Variations On A Theme (1st and 2nd Movements)/Smiling Phases/Sometimes In Winter/More And More/And When I Die/God Bless The Child/Spinning Wheel/You've Made Me So Very Happy/Blues Part II/Variations On A Theme By Eric Satie **PERSONNEL** Fred Lipsius (as, p), Chuck Winfield (t, h), Lew Soloff (t, h), Jerry Hyman (tb, rc), David Clayton-Thomas (v), Dick Halligan (o, p, fl, tb, v), Steve Katz (g, bv, v), Bobby Colomby (d)pc, v), Jim Fielder (b)

This million-selling Grammy winner overcame the band's loss of founder and Dylan sidekick Al Kooper and initial resistance to the showy vocal flourishes of new boy David Clayton-Thomas. One of the first groups to aspire to a fusion of rock and jazz, they laid the horns on thick and fast but still managed to attract the groovier end of the easy-listening market. The singles Brenda Holloway's *You've Made Me So Very Happy*, Laura Nyro's *And When I Die*, and Clayton-Thomas' *Spinning Wheel* each sold a million. The singer's melodramatic posturing became a robust part of the late Sixties tapestry.

… a brilliantly conceived consummation of sixty years of development, it draws from all categories, and defies categorisation… As a symbol, it shows the future has arrived today. **Melody Maker, March 1969**

Blue

ARTIST Joni Mitchell **RELEASE DATE** July 1971 (UK & US) **LABEL** Reprise (UK & US) **PRODUCER** David Crosby **UK CHART** peak/weeks 3/18 **US CHART** peak/weeks 15/28 **TRACK LISTING** All I Want/My Old Man/Little Green/Carey/Blue/California/This Flight Tonight/River/A Case Of You/The Last Time I Saw Richard **PERSONNEL** Joni Mitchell (v), Stephen Stills (b, g), James Taylor (g), Sneeky Pete (ps), Russ Kunkel (d)

While her previous three albums had partly consisted of stockpiled material, every song on **Blue**, bar the four-year-old *Little Green*, was newly written, hence its engagingly confessional stance. Stripped of extraneous instrumentation, Mitchell spoke from the bottom of her heart and both public and critics reacted favourably: *Rolling Stone* gave her a lengthy review, while the album would become her second million seller in time, despite a lack of a big hit single.

Each song seems not to have been worked out but to have been born whole and perfect and complete with shining guitar and velvety piano.... It is perhaps as a singer of exquisite, richly-contoured, beautifully singable songs, rather than anything more profound, that she now has her greatest strength. **A. L., Melody Maker, July 1970**

Blue Hawaii

ARTIST Elvis Presley **RELEASE DATE** December 1961 (UK)/October 1961 (US) **LABEL** RCA (UK & US) **PRODUCER** Don Wardell **UK CHART** peak/weeks 1/65 **US CHART** peak/weeks 1/79 **TRACK LISTING** Blue Hawaii/Almost Always True/Moonlight Swim/No More/Can't Help Falling In Love/Rock A Hula Baby/Island Of Love/Hawaiian Sunset/Hawaiian Wedding Song/Alohaoe/Beach Boy Blues/Slicin' Sands/Ku Ui Po/Ito Eats **PERSONNEL** Elvis Presley (v, g), with session musicians: Floyd Cramer (p), Scotty Moore (g)

Released in October, the **Blue Hawaii** soundtrack had been certified gold by 21 December – a suitable Xmas present for the King! But with 14 songs on board, more than any previous Elvis movie record, the customers were undoubtedly satisfied too. After taking eight weeks to hit the top, its 20-week stay would not be surpassed until Fleetwood Mac's **Rumours** in 1977, ironically the year of Presley's death.

Blue Hawaii affords full opportunity for the singer to demonstrate both his ballad and beat styles, so these 14 tracks fully cater for his admirer's tastes... this would make an ideal gift for any Elvis devotee. **Melody Maker, December 1961**

Blue Lines

ARTIST Massive Attack **RELEASE DATE** April 1991 (UK & US) **LABEL** Wild Bunch Circa (UK)/Virgin (US) **PRODUCER** Massive Attack, Johnny Dollar, Cameron McVey **UK CHART** peak/weeks 13/16 **US CHART** peak/weeks 0/0 **TRACK LISTING** Safe From Harm/One Love/Blue Lines/Be Thankful For What You've Got/Five Man Army/Unfinished Sympathy/Day Dreaming/Lately/Hymn Of The Big Wheel **PERSONNEL** Massive Attack: 3D (v), Mushroom (k), Daddy G (k); Guests: Shara Nelson (v), Horace Andy (v), Tony Bryan (v), Neneh Cherry (bv), Paul Johnson (b)

To receive a Brit nomination for your first album is an achievement for any group, particularly if like Bristol's Massive Attack they operate outside the musical mainstream. Its success attracted U2 to ask for their remix services, while the near hit single *Unfinished Sympathy* would prove enormously influential, notably on The Verve, whose *Bitter Sweet Symphony* 1997 hit even aped its video. Of the vocalists featured, Shara Nelson would go solo and Tricky would divide his time between his own work and the group's.

Bluejean Bop

ARTIST Gene Vincent **RELEASE DATE** November 1956 (UK)/September 1956 (US) **LABEL** Capitol (UK & US) **PRODUCER** – **UK CHART** peak/weeks 0/0 **US CHART** peak/weeks 16/29 **TRACK LISTING** Blue Jean Bop/Jezebel/Who Slapped John/Ain't She Sweet/I Flipped/Waltz Of The Wind/Jump Back, Honey Jump Back/The Old Gang Of Mine/Jumps, Giggles And Shouts/Up A Lazy River/Bop Street/Peg O' My Heart **PERSONNEL** Gene Vincent (v, g), Cliff Gallup (lg), Willie Williams (arr), Jack Neal (b), Dickie harris (d)

One of the most notable of the post-Presley rockers, Gene Vincent was an immediate international success with his first single, co-written with 'Sheriff' Tex Davis, *Be-Bop-A-Lula*, a million-selling burst of pure rock 'n' roll adrenaline with a powerful sexual undertow that charted on both sides of the Atlantic. **Bluejean Bop!** communicates much of the excitement of this libidinous, leather-clad young rocker. Unfortunately, Vincent was also one of the original tragic rockers: he had to wear a leg brace after a motorcycle accident and was critically injured in the car crash that killed Eddie Cochran, before succumbing to alcoholism and rupturing a stomach ulcer, aged 36.

Admirers of the Presley school may take this seriously, but unless they have keen ears or an exceptionally good hearing aid it is doubtful they will be able to decipher the words on either side. **Melody Maker, September 1956**

Bluesbreakers

ARTIST John Mayall **RELEASE DATE** July 1966 (UK & US) **LABEL** Decca (UK)/London (US) **PRODUCER** Mike Vernon UK CHART peak/weeks 6/17 US CHART peak/weeks 136/14 **TRACK LISTING** All Your Love/Hideaway/Little Girl/Another Man/Double Crossing Time/What'd I Say/Key To Love/Parchman Farm/Have You Heard/Ramblin' On My Mind/Steppin' Out/It Ain't Right **PERSONNEL** John Mayall (v, p, o, h), Eric Clapton (v, g), John McVie (b), Hughie Flint (d), Alan Skidmore (ts), John Almond (bs), Dennis Healey (t)

Probably the most influential recording in the history of British rock guitar, the 'Beano album' – so-called due to Eric Clapton's choice of reading matter on the front cover picture – encouraged a clutch of Seventies guitar stars in waiting to pick up an axe, Gary Moore prominent among them. Live recordings of this line-up are much sparkier and Clapton was the only one who dared turn up to stage volume in the studio. This remains a prime cut of British blues and a landmark for both band and guitarist, who was *en route* for Cream by the time of release.

It's been said to me many times that white men – particularly English white men – cannot really play the blues. But this is nonsense. Anyone can experience the blues. Anyone can play the blues. It's not restricted purely and simply to American Negroes. **John Mayall in interview with Alan Walsh, Melody Maker, October 1967**

The Book Of Invasions – A Celtic Symphony

ARTIST Horslips **RELEASE DATE** December 1976 (UK & US) **LABEL** DJM (UK & US) **PRODUCER** Alan O'Duffy, Horslips UK CHART peak/weeks 39/3 US CHART peak/weeks 0/0 **TRACK LISTING** 1st Movement – Geantrai/Daybreak/March Into Trouble/Trouble (With A Capitol T)/The Power And The Glory/The Rocks Remain/Dusk/Sword Of light/Dark/2nd Movement – Goltrai/Warm Sweet Breath Of Love/Fantasia (My Lagan Love)/King Of Morning, Queen Of Day/3rd Movement – Suantrai/Sideways To The Sun/Drive The Cold Winter Away **PERSONNEL** Charles O'Connor (f, md, cc, v), Jim Lockhart (k, fl, w), Barry Devlin (b, v), John Fean (g, v), Eamon Carr (d, pc)

Irish folk-rockers Horslips registered their only UK hit album in 1976 with their second concept album. Subtitled '**A Celtic Symphony**', it followed their 1973 offering **The Tain** by using myth and legend as its plot, twisting traditional melodies to fit rock rhythms in a tale of how pre-Christian Ireland was colonized and the Tuatha De Danann banished from the land. The result was a classic album, and it was no surprise when they returned to the concept format with **The Man Who Built America**, the last major success they had before their 1980 split.

There is a parallel… between the blues and Irish traditional music. They're both the music of an oppressed people… I find Irish traditional music very strange, it's almost cerebral. If you're high and you listen to some of those old guys, I'll tell you it almost takes the top of your head right off. **From an interview by Mark Plummer, Melody Maker, November 1972**

Bookends

ARTIST Simon And Garfunkel **RELEASE DATE** July 1968 (UK)/May 1968 (US) **LABEL** CBS (UK)/Columbia (US) **PRODUCER** Paul Simon, Arthur Garfunkel, Roy Halee UK CHART peak/weeks 1/77 US CHART peak/weeks 1/66 **TRACK LISTING** Bookends Theme (Instrumental)/Save The Life Of My Child/America/Overs/Voices Of Old People/Old Friends/Bookends Theme/Fakin It/Punky's Dilemma/Mrs Robinson/A Hazy Shade Of Winter/At The Zoo **PERSONNEL** Paul Simon (v, ag), Art Garfunkel (v, ag), session musicians

The second side of Simon And Garfunkel's fourth LP proper was given over to B-sides (Simon was never a prolific writer: seven studio solo albums in 25 years?), but there was one new track,

Mrs Robinson, as featured in *The Graduate*, that catapulted the pair, who began life as a high school duo called Tom And Jerry ten years previously, to international stardom. A concept album concerning friendship and ageing, **Bookends**, suggested Art Garfunkel's choir-boy vocals, and Paul Simon's deeply thoughtful songs were to be a major part of the post-*Woodstock* landscape.

Born Again

ARTIST Randy Newman **RELEASE DATE** September 1979 (UK)/August 1979 (US) **LABEL** Warner (UK & US) **PRODUCER** Randy Newman UK CHART peak/weeks 0/0 US CHART peak/weeks 41/11 **TRACK LISTING** It's Money That I Love/The Story of A Rock And Roll Band/Mr Sheep/Pretty Boy/They Just Got Married/Ghosts/Spies/The Girls In My Life (Part 1)/Half A Man/William Brown Pants **PERSONNEL** Randy Newman (v, p), Stephen Bishop (v, gst), session musicians

Having broken into the charts big time with the previous year's **Little Criminals** and its obvious hit **Short People**, Newman tried to strike a better balance between critical acclaim and commercial riches with this, its follow-up. It ONLY took him two years, being his fastest album to date, and led off with a **Short People**-style song in **It's Money That I Love**, promoted by a Kiss-style make-up job. But success and Newman were not to be as closely acquainted again.

The central joke of these songs… is that the sheer tedium of people's lives is funny in itself. It must have seemed to Newman an interesting exercise, but songs written about boredom are always likely to result in the state of mind that is being satirised. **Michael Watts, Melody Maker, August 1979**

Born In The USA

ARTIST Bruce Springsteen **RELEASE DATE** June 1984 (UK & US) **LABEL** CBS (UK)/Columbia (US) **PRODUCER** Bruce Springsteen, Jon Landau, Chuck Plotkin, Steve Van Zandt UK CHART peak/weeks 1/128 US CHART peak/weeks 1/139 **TRACK LISTING** Born In The USA/Cover Me/Darlington County/Working On The Highway/Downbound Train/I'm On Fire/No Surrender/Booby Jean/I'm Goin' Down/Glory Days/Dancing In The Dark/My Hometown **PERSONNEL** Bruce Springsteen (v, g), Nils Lofgren (lg), Danny Federici (k), Garry Tallent (b), Max Weinberg (d), Roy Bittan (p), Clarence Clemens (s), Patti Scialfa (bv)

BORN IN THE U.S.A./BRUCE SPRINGSTEEN

Selling over ten million copies and containing no less than seven hit singles (*Dancing In The Dark*, featuring a young Courteney Cox from *Friends* in the video; *Cover Me, I'm On Fire, Glory Days, I'm Goin' Down, My Hometown*, and the title track), **Born In The USA** catapulted Bruce Springsteen towards the pop firmament previously reserved for such deities as Prince, Madonna and Michael Jackson. Ironically, although the title track seemed to some, among them, President Reagan, to be a celebration of America, the excuse for a lot of jingoistic fist-punching and foot-stomping in the enormodomes Springsteen was now filling, **Born In The USA** was actually no less hard-hitting a critique of US society than his earlier work.

Throughout the album, his band – newly streamlined and rich with synthesizers – plays at peak power… And Springsteen himself sings with a force-of-nature power that's both raw and subtly, intuitively nuanced… Even an Englishman could get ino this one. **Rolling Stone, 1984**

Born To Run

ARTIST Bruce Springsteen **RELEASE DATE** October 1975 (UK)/September 1975 (US) **LABEL** CBS (UK)/Columbia (US) **PRODUCER** Bruce Springsteen, John Landau, Mike Appel **UK CHART** peak/weeks 17/50 **US CHART** peak/weeks 3/110 **TRACK LISTING** Thunder Road/Tenth Avenue Freeze Out/Night/Backstreets/Born To Run/She's The One/Meeting Across The River/Jungleland **PERSONNEL** Bruce Springsteen (g, v, h), Garry Tallent (b), Max Weinberg (d), Roy Bittan (gl, bv, p, hd), Clarence Clemens (s, ts), Mike Appel (bv), Steve Van Zandt (bv), Randy Brecker (t, fh), Michael Brecker (ts), Dave Sanborn (bs), Wayne Andre (tr), Ernst 'Boom' Carter (d), Danny Federici (o), Richard Davis (b)

With its over-the-top, Phil Spector-esque production and melodramatic ambience, **Born To Run** was like the promise of Fifties and Sixties rock 'n' roll fulfilled: unashamedly romantic, lyrical and intense. On songs like *Backstreets, She's The One* and *Jungleland*, Springsteen's sensitive tough-guy persona was married to vivid narratives and big pop hooks. The title track alone made him a national hero, landing him on the cover, simultaneously, of *Time* and *Newsweek*.

… it reached a point where it was a nightmare, we were not getting

close… Then John (Landau) came in and he was able to say 'Well you're not doing it because of this, and this… Me, you know, I just want to hear it, I don't want to know. **Bruce Springsteen interviewed by Lisa Robinson, NME, March 1977**

Born Under A Bad Sign

ARTIST Albert King **RELEASE DATE** February 1967 (UK & US) **LABEL** Atlantic (UK)/Sire (US) **PRODUCER** Albert King **UK CHART** peak/weeks 0/0 **US CHART** peak/weeks 0/0 **TRACK LISTING** Laundromat Blues/Oh, Pretty Woman/Crosscut Saw/Down Don't Bother Me/Born Under A Bad Sign/Personal Manager/Kansas City/The Very Thought Of You/The Hunter/Almost Lost My Mind/As The Years Go Passing By **PERSONNEL** Steve Cropper (g), The Memphis Horns (hn), Joe Arnold (hn), Donald 'Duck' Dunn (b), Isaac Hayes (p), Wayne Jackson (hn), Booker T. Jones (p), Albert King (g, v), Andrew Love (hn), Al Jackson Jr. (d)

The combination of southpaw blues guitar legend Albert King with crack-soul studio band Booker T and the MGs in 1966 proved a particularly creative one, and this album, released the following year, exposed him to a rock audience for the first time. His influence on Clapton, Knopfler, Stevie Ray Vaughan and others is immense, while it is said Hendrix knew his solos note for note. The title track alone has been covered by more than a score of top acts from Cream through Peter Green to Pat Travers.

Almost all of the material in **Born Under A Bad Sign** *originally appeared as singles, none of which ever really made it… King's guitar style is like no other. I asked him who he had learned from and he answered, 'Noboby. Everything I do is wrong.* **From an interview with Jon Landau, Rolling Stone, October 1968**

Boss Drum

ARTIST The Shamen **RELEASE DATE** October 1992 (UK & US) **LABEL** One Little Indian (UK)/Epic (US) **PRODUCER** The Shamen **UK CHART** peak/weeks 3/32 **US CHART** peak/weeks 0/0 **TRACK LISTING** Boss Drum/L.S.I: Love Sex Intelligence/Space Time/Librae Soldi Denari/Ebeneezer Goode Beat masters Mix/Comin' On/Phorever People/Fatman/Scientas/Re: Evolution/Boss Dub/ Phorever Dub **PERSONNEL** Colin Angus (v, g), Mr C. (v, rg), Jhelisa Anderson (v), Bob Breeks (k), Gavin Knight (d), Steve Hillage (g, gst)

Along with New Order and Happy Mondays, The Shamen built a bridge between the indie scene of the Eighties and the dance scene of the Nineties, their music a dazzling hybrid of rock guitars and technologically enhanced rhythms. Its predecessor, 1990's **En-Tact**, provided the blueprint, but **Boss Drum** was the commercial breakthrough, with *Ebeneezer Goode* reaching pole position amid controversy due to its chorus, which sounded suspiciously like 'E's are good! E's are good!' Original member Will Sinnot may have died in tragic circumstances in May 1991, but with the super-intelligent Colin Angus at the fore, together with zany cockney sidekick Mr C., The Shamen went supernova with this million-selling album.

… although it is easy to be cynical about some of The Shamen's ideas, their genuine concern for the environment is highly commendable, as is their overriding sense of optimism…. There are too many yawns between the thrills. **Push, Melody Maker, September 1992**

Bossanova

ARTIST The Pixies **RELEASE DATE** August 1990 (UK & US) **LABEL** 4.a.d. (UK)/Elektra (US) **PRODUCER** Gil Norton **UK CHART** peak/weeks 3/8 **US CHART** peak/weeks 70/12 **TRACK LISTING** Cecilia Ann/Rock Music/Velouria/Alison/Is She Weird/Ana/All Over The World/Dig For Fire/Down To The Wall/The Happening/Blown Away/Hang Fire/Stormy Weather/Havalina **PERSONNEL** Black Francis (v, g), Jerry Santiago (lg), Kim Deal (b, v), Dave Lovering (d)

References to aliens, flying saucers and journeys to the stars abound within the 14 songs that make up this album. It could almost have been the inspiration for the glut of the extra-terrestrial fantasies of the Nineties, but in reality it simply confirmed Boston's finest as the prime purveyors of apocalyptic guitar music. Taking the best elements of their two preceding albums, **Bossanova** remains Pixies' most listenable collection, without sacrificing any of the power.

… the Pixies are masters of the calculated incongruity… a song like **Havalina** *… which boasts a lead guitar of which Rubber Soul-era George Harrison would have been proud and a chorus so ethereally sweet it could score the next diet cola commercial.* **Mat Snow, Q, September 1990**

Boz Scaggs

ARTIST Boz Scaggs **RELEASE DATE** August 1969 (UK & US) **LABEL** Atlantic Records (UK & US) **PRODUCER** Jann Wenner, Boz Scaggs, Marlin Greene **UK CHART** peak/weeks 0/0 **US CHART** peak/weeks 0/0 **TRACK LISTING** I'm Easy/I'll Be Long Gone/Another Day (Another Letter)/Now You're Gone/Finding Her/Look What I Got/Waiting For A Train/Loan Me A Dime/Sweet Release **PERSONNEL** Boz Scaggs (g, v), Tracy Nelson (bv), Duane Allman (g, sg, db), Joe Arnold (s, ts), Barry Beckett (k), Ben Cauley (t), Charles Chalmers (ts), Joyce Dunn (bv), Jeannie Green (bv), Roger Hawkins (d), Eddie Hinton (g), Mary Holliday (v), David Hood (b), Jimmy Johnson (g), Al Lester (vl, f), Gene Miller (t, tr), James Mitchell (bs), Floyd Newman (bs), Irma Routen (bv), Donna Thatcher (bv)

A former rhythm guitarist with The Steve Miller Band, Scaggs recorded his second album (his debut, 1965's **Boz**, was issued only in Europe by Polydor) at the renowned *Muscle Shoals* with local sessioneers, assisted by Duane Allman and produced by Rolling Stone editor (and now publisher) Jann S. Wenner. **Boz Scaggs** was a critical hit but a commercial failure, although Allman's

memorable guitar solo on **Loan Me A Dime** helped it achieve some fame, paving the way for the enormous success of Scaggs' five-million selling LP from 1976, **Silk Degrees**, one of the high watermarks of Seventies blues-pop-soul.

Most of the transient residents at 3614 Jackson Highway, for example, site of the much favoured Muscle Shoals Sound Recorders, have no business recording there… what counts is what a musician brings into town with him. Fortunately Boz Scaggs travels with talent to spare. **Ed Leimbacker, Rolling Stone, November 1969**

Break Like The Wind

ARTIST Spinal Tap **RELEASE DATE** April 1992 (UK & US) **LABEL** MCA (UK & US) **PRODUCER** Spinal Tap **UK CHART** peak/weeks 51/2 **US CHART** peak/weeks 61/6 **TRACK LISTING** Bitch School/Majesty of Rock/Just Begin Again/Cash On Delivery/Sun Never Sweat/Rainy Day Sun/Break Like The Wind/Stinkin' Up The Great Outdoors/Springtime/Clam Caravan/Christmas With The Devil/All The Way Home **PERSONNEL** Jeff Beck (g), Joe Satriani (g), Dweezil Zappa (g), Nicky Hopkins (k), Luis Conte (pc), Tommy Funderburk (bv), Steve Lukather (g, p, arr, orc), David Mansfield (st), Timothy B. Schmit (bv), Ric Shrimpton (d), Slash (g), Derek Smalls (b, v), David St. Hubbins (g, v), Nigel Tufnel (g, v, sit), Caucasian Jeffrey Vanston (arr, k, orc), Waddy Wachtel (sg), Jimmie Wood (h), Eric 'Stumpy Joe' Childs (d)

Featuring complete versions of songs that featured in the now legendary movie satire of the rock business, *This Is Spinal Tap*, such as **Sex Farm**, **Big Bottom** and **Tonight I'm Gonna Rock You Tonight**, **Break Like The Wind** is a gloriously OTT parody of the hard rock/heavy metal genres. While the album is in hock to the likes of Black Sabbath, Deep Purple and Led Zeppelin up to its elbows, today it is regarded by *aficionados* almost as fondly as the music of the pioneers themselves.

Sure, this is a joke, but Spinal Tap is a joke that everyone is in on unlike most metal, which some people think isn't funny…. Clever criticism disguised as bathroom humour, **Break Like The Wind** *amplifies the absurdity of pop music in general.* **Christian Wright, Rolling Stone, April 1992**

Breakfast In America

ARTIST Supertramp **RELEASE DATE** March 1979 (UK & US) **LABEL** A&M (UK & US) **PRODUCER** Supertramp, Peter Henderson **UK CHART** peak/weeks 3/53 **US CHART** peak/weeks 1/88 **TRACK LISTING** Gone Hollywood/The Logical Song/Goodbye Stranger/Breakfast In America/Oh Darling/

Take The Long Way Home/Lord Is It Mine/Just Another Nervous Wreck/Casual Conversations/Child Of Vision PERSONNEL Richard Davies (v, k), Roger Hodgson (b, k, v), Dougie Thompson (b), Bob Benberg (d), John Anthony Helliwell (s, cl, v)

As befitting their most commercial record to date, **Breakfast In America** remains the band's biggest success, having sold upwards of 18 million copies worldwide. On their sixth LP, Supertramp went from one extreme – ponderous bombast – to another, delivering a collection of songs that were simple, verging on trite. The likes of **The Logical Song**, with its nursery rhyme line, 'Take a look at my girlfriend/She's the only one I've got', were never off the radio in summer 1979.

This is state of the art AOR, a last gasp for studio perfectionalism before New Wave makes the idea obsolete…. While the music is thoroughly, comfortingly seductive, Supertramp comes across as surprisingly asexual. Perfect music for the tape deck in a Mercedes Limo. **Jon Pareles, Rolling Stone, December 1979**

Bricks Are Heavy

ARTIST L7 RELEASE DATE April 1992 (UK)/August 1992 (US) LABEL Slash (UK)/London (US) PRODUCER Butch Vig UK CHART peak/weeks 24/6 US CHART peak/weeks 160/7 TRACK LISTING Wargasm/Scrap/Pretend We're Dead/Diet Pill/Everglade/Slide/One More Thing/Mr. Integrity/Monster/Shit List/This Ain't Pleasure PERSONNEL Donita Sparks (v, g), Suzi Gardner (g, v), Jennifer Finch (b, v), Dee Plakas (d)

Having taken their name from the American slang for 'square', L7, an all-girl band with gigantic attitude were on a mission to prove they could rock out as well as boys. **Bricks Are Heavy** made the point: monster guitar riffs, lyrics designed to cause offence, and hard-rocking songs which recalled the heavy/punk style of Motorhead and Metallica. A number of high-profile and confrontational media stunts after the album's release added to the band's notoriety, though not necessarily its credibility.

L7 are leather and denim rockers who have the sass of Girlschool plus the contemporary zip of Nirvana. **Bricks Are Heavy** *isn't a classic but in tracks like* **Wargasm** *and* **Diet Pill**, *L7 prove that they have their fist on the throttle.* **Dave Henderson, Q, April 1992**

Bridge Of Sighs

ARTIST Robin Trower RELEASE DATE April 1974 LABEL Chrysalis (UK & US) PRODUCER – UK CHART peak/weeks 0/0 US CHART peak/weeks 7/31 TRACK LISTING Day Of The Eagle/Bridge Of Sighs/In This Place/The Fool And Me/Too Rolling Stoned/About To Begin/Lady Love/A Little Bit Of Sympathy PERSONNEL Robin Torwer (g), Jim Dewar (b, v), Reg Isadore (d)

A founder member of Procul Harum, Robin Trower was, as a solo artist, the ultimate Hendrix acolyte. But he didn't just mimic his mentor's pyrotechnical ability: he learned to balance power with a subtlety and grace of which Jimi himself would have approved. Trower pulled together a Jimi Hendrix Experience/Cream-style power trio for **Bridge Of Sighs**, with Reg Isadore on drums and ex-Stone The Crowes bassist Jim Dewar on gritty vocals, affording Trower the freedom simultaneously to play hard rock riffs and blues solos with the fluidity of two men.

Bridge Over Troubled Water

ARTIST Simon And Garfunkel RELEASE DATE February 1970 (UK & US) LABEL CBS (UK)/Columbia (US) PRODUCER Paul Simon, Art Garfunkel, Roy Halee UK CHART peak/weeks 1/303 US CHART peak/weeks 1/85 TRACK LISTING Bridge Over Troubled Water/El Condor Pasa/Cecilia/Keep The Customer Satisfied/So Long Frank Lloyd Wright/The Boxer/Baby Driver/The Only Living Boy In New York/Why Don't You Write Me/Bye Bye Love/Song For The Asking PERSONNEL Paul Simon (v, g), Art Garfunkel (v), Fred Carter Jr (g), Hal Blaine (d), Joe Osborne (b), Larry Knechtel (k), Jimmy Haskell (st), Ernie Freeman (st)

Paul Simon's absorption of folk influences and appropriation of the new techniques of the singer-songwriter reached its apogee on this multi-platinum release, one of the biggest selling albums of all time. These haunting melodies spoke directly to the millions feeling shell-shocked after the death of the hippy dream at *Altamont*. Less overtly political than Bob Dylan or Neil Young, Paul Simon still managed to sum up the disillusionment of a generation.

Maybe Paul Simon has gotten fat and lazy. Maybe Arthur Garfunkel is devoting his time to acting or teaching. Whatever the cause, their music has gotten stale… everything they play someone else has played before, and everything they say they've said before. **Gregg Mitchell, Rolling Stone, May 1970**

Bring The Family

ARTIST John Hiatt RELEASE DATE May 1987 (UK & US) LABEL Demon Records (UK)/A&M (US) PRODUCER John Chelew UK CHART peak/weeks 0/0 US CHART peak/weeks 107/17 TRACK LISTING Memphis In The Meantime/Alone In The Dark/Thing Called Love/Lipstick Sunset/Have A Little Faith In Me/Thank You Girl/Tip Of My Tongue/Your Dad Did/Stood Up/Learning How To Love You PERSONNEL John Hiatt (ag, v, p), Ry Cooder (g, v), Jim Keltner (d), Nick Lowe (b, v)

Singer-songwriter Hiatt found his ideal musical setting in the company of messrs Keltner, Lowe and Cooder, who repaid his faith by enhancing his songs. But when the aggregation regrouped as Little Village for the eponymous 1992 recording, the magic had evaporated, allegedly because each member re-recorded his part in the search for perfection. Lesson: democracy does not work! This combination of superb songs and great musicianship was clearly a one-off. Joe Cocker later titled an album after **Have A Little Faith**.

Hiatt looked into selling the publishing for his songs: 'I took my lambs to the marketplace,' he says, 'I was 34 and I had just been married a month or so, and I wanted to buy a house.'… an often joyful, always soulful celebration of faith, survival and adult love. **From an interview by David Wilch, Rolling Stone, January 1989**

Bringing It All Back Home

ARTIST Bob Dylan RELEASE DATE May 1965 (UK & US) LABEL CBS (UK)/Columbia (US) PRODUCER Tom Wilson UK CHART peak/weeks 1/29 US CHART peak/weeks 6/43 TRACK LISTING Subterranean Homesick Blues/She Belongs To Me/Maggie's Farm/Love Minus Zero/No Limit/Outlaw Blues/On The Road Again/Bob Dylan's 115th Dream/Mr Tambourine Man/Gates Of Eden/It's Alright, Ma (I'm Only Bleeding)/It's All Over Now, Baby Blue PERSONNEL Bob Dylan (bv, lg), Charlie McCoy (bv), with Musicians: Wayne Moss, Kenneth Buttrey, Hargus Robbins, Jerry Kennedy, Joe South, Al Kooper, Bill Aikins, Henry Strzelecki, Jaime Robertson

When Dylan took his music to Britain in 1965, D. A. Pennebaker made a documentary of the tour called *Don't Look Back*. It was symbolic that this album replaced **Freewheelin'** at the top of the UK chart in May, its half-electric, half-acoustic format presaging things to come and containing landmarks in *Subterranean Homesick Blues, Maggie's Farm*' (electric) and **Mr Tambourine Man** (acoustic). Five albums in the UK Top 20 made this the peak of Dylan-mania.

It was Dylan's concept all the way, but he was able to draw out of the other musicians their ideas, their musical feel, using them to give his music a substance… The album erupted on the scene like an earthquake. Antony Scaduto, Rolling Stone, March 1972

Broken English

ARTIST Marianne Faithfull RELEASE DATE October 1979 (UK)/February 1980 (US) LABEL Island (UK & US) PRODUCER Mike Miller Mundy UK CHART peak/weeks 57/3 US CHART peak/weeks 12/31 TRACK LISTING Broken English/Witches' Song/Brain/Drain/Guilt/The Ballard Of Lucy Jordan/What's The Hurry/Working Class Hero/Why D'Ya Do It PERSONNEL Marianne Faithfull (v), with musicians: Diane Birch, Frankie Collins, Jim Cuomo, Guy Humphries, Joe Mavety, Maurice Pert, Barry Reynalds, Terry Stannard, Darryl Way, Steve Winwood, Steve York, Isabella Dulaney

With her celebrated relationship with Mick Jagger over and her health affected by heroin addiction, it looked as if Faithfull's singing career was over and it was astonishing that she should stand on the brink of a new decade with a new work of such magnitude. **Broken English** saw Faithfull re-inventing her bad-girl Sixties image as a weathered campaigner tramping the dark side of life. Her ravaged vocals lent an icy edge of honesty to a collection of self-composed songs about degradation and pain, all given a new-wave complexion by the use of synths and other keyboards, influencing a new generation of singers like Courtney Love, with whom she has since worked.

Broken English is the most fascinating and original LP to emerge from a British female singer this year… though it's not a comfortable album to deal with, it's still… an extraordinary piece of work. **Mark Williams, Melody Maker, November 1979**

Brothers And Sisters

ARTIST Allman Brothers Band RELEASE DATE September 1973 (UK)/August 1973 LABEL Capricorn (UK & US) PRODUCER Phil Walden UK CHART peak/weeks 42/3 US CHART peak/weeks 1/56 TRACK LISTING Wasted Words/Ramblin' Man/Come And Go Blues/Jelly Jelly/Southbound/Jessica/Pony Boy PERSONNEL Duane Allman (g), Gregg Allman (k, v, g), Dicky Betts (g, v), Lamar Williams (b), Butch Trucks (d), Jaimoe Johanson (pc)

Recuperating from gratuitous visits by the Grim Reaper, singer Greg's continuation of the seemingly cursed Allman Brothers Band proved worthwhile by this the album, which coined the term 'southern rock'. Pianist Chuck Leavell was a new recruit. It was wise not to attempt to replace the late Duane with another guitar hero. While this is generally considered their last great effort, it reached for the stars with the subtler-than-you-think *Ramblin' Man* and the freewheeling *Jessica*.

Brothers and Sisters is no masterpiece, but the new band has shown that it can carry on the work of the old, and add the appropriate new twists when necessary. **Bud Scoppa, Rolling Stone, September 1973**

Brothers In Arms

ARTIST Dire Straits RELEASE DATE May 1985 (UK)/June 1985 (US) LABEL Vertigo (UK)/Warner (US) PRODUCER Mark Knopfler, Neil Dorfsman UK CHART peak/weeks 1/196 US CHART peak/weeks 1/97 TRACK LISTING So Far Away/Money For Nothing/Walk Of Life/Your Latest Trick/Why Worry/Ride Across The River/The Man's Too Strong/One World/Brothers In Arms PERSONNEL Mark Knopfler (g, v), John Illsley (b), Terry Williams (d), Alan Clark (k), Sting (bv)

The first megaband of the CD age, Dire Straits had bought time with an EP and a double live album before releasing a finely honed collection of singer-guitarist Mark Knopfler's songs that positively begged to be heard in pristine digital form. The chart-topping *Money For Nothing* single helped it become their first US Number 1 album and their second in Britain, quoting MTV

in its lyric and boasting a computerized graphic video – but that was by some way the rockiest track on an album so laid-back it was positively horizontal. CD buffs lying on the living-room carpet using it to test out their system appreciated the result.

*Just when the working man thought it was safe to come out of his neighborhood, here comes a monumentally catchy, Led-Zep-for-yuppies song called, **Money For Nothing**. With its factory floor guitar and empyrean rhythm, it's quite irresistible.* **The Year In Records 1985, Rolling Stone, December 1985**

Bryter Layter

ARTIST Nick Drake **RELEASE DATE** November 1970 **LABEL** Island Records **PRODUCER** Joe Boyd **UK CHART** peak/weeks 0/0 **US CHART** peak/weeks - **TRACK LISTING** Introduction/Hazey Jane II/At The Chime Of A City Clock/One Of These Things First/Hazy Jane I **PERSONNEL** Nick Drake (v, g), Dave Pegg (b), Dave Mattacks (d), Richard Thompson (lg), Ray Warleigh (as), Mike Kowalski (d), Paul Harris (p), Ed Carter (b), Lyn Dobson (f), John Cale (va, hd, ce, o, p), Chris McGregor (p), Pat Arnold/Dorris Troy (bv), All bass and string arrangements by Robert Kirby

Having quit his Cambridge degree course with a year to go, Nick Drake had moved to Hampstead, north London, and his new urban surroundings were reflected in the music which is considerably more optimistic than the subdued but charming **Five Leaves Left**. A cast of talented session men contributed to an end product producer Joe Boyd and engineer John Eood then considered the only perfect album they made for the former's Witchseason production company. Only one more, **Pink Moon**, would result before Drake's untimely death.

Drake's guitar playing revolved around several complex open-tunings, principally certain mutations of the open-ended D and G chords. The instrumentals on **Bryter Layter** *give one potent example of the personal technique that was to reach full fruition on* **Pink Moon**. **Nick Kent, NME, February 1975**

Buddy Holly

ARTIST Buddy Holly **RELEASE DATE** July 1958 (UK)/March 1968 (US) **LABEL** Coral (UK & US) **PRODUCER** Milton De Lugg **UK CHART** peak/weeks 0/0 **US CHART** peak/weeks 0/0 **TRACK LISTING** I'm Gonna Love You Too/Peggy Sue/Look At Me/Listen To Me/Valley Of Tears/Ready Teddy/Everyday/Mailman Bring Me No More Blues/Words Of Love/Baby I Don't Care/Rave On/Little Baby **PERSONNEL** Buddy Holly (v, lg, ag, g), Niki Sullivan (rg), Joe Maudlin (b), Jerry Allison (d), Vi Petty (p), C.W. Kendall Jr. (p), Norman Petty (o)

The second and last album (after **The Chirping Crickets**) to be released during Buddy Holly's lifetime ironically came out on the Coral label that had rejected him not too long before. Though billed as Holly solo, the Crickets were still very much in evidence on all tracks, and Buddy had forgotten his trademark glasses for the cover pic (vanity?). One song, *Rave On*, was recorded in New York away from Norman Petty's Clovis studio, and that less than a month before release to complete a classic LP.

Buffalo Springfield Again

ARTIST Buffalo Springfield **RELEASE DATE** January 1967 (UK)/October 1966 (US) **LABEL** Atlantic (UK)/Atco (US) **PRODUCER** Stephen Stills, Neil Young, Jack Nitzsche, Richie Furay **UK CHART** peak/weeks – **US CHART** peak/weeks 44/14 **TRACK LISTING** Don't Scold Me/Go And Say Goodbye/Sit Down I Think I Love You/Nowadays Clancy Can't Even Sing/Everybody's Wrong/Hot Dusty Roads/Flying On The Ground/Burned/Do I Have To Come Right Out And Say It?/Leave/Pay The Price/Out Of My Mind **PERSONNEL** Stephen Stills (o, g, p, rg, k, v), Neil Young (g, h, v), Don Randi (p), James Burton (g, db), Dewey Martin (d), Jack Nitzsche (k, p), Bruce Palmer (b), Richie Furay (g, rg, v), Charlie Chin (bj), Jim Fielder (b), Bob West (b)

A virtual *who's who* of West Coast rock, Buffalo Springfield boasted, at various points in their brief yet stormy history, players as illustrious as Neil Young, Stephen Stills, Richie Furay, Dewey Martin and Jim Messina. While their eponymous debut LP marked them out as the leading folk-rock band apart from The Byrds, their second, **Buffalo Springfield Again**, expanded their commission to include country textures, psychedelic trickiness, hard rock and lavishly orchestrated balladry – of the latter, the heavily overdubbed and strings-drenched *Expecting To Fly* remains one of the most beautiful songs ever written by Neil Young.

Heartbeats, jazz piano, and rock 'n' roll beats are mixed into a programme that demands intensive listening to gain maximum understanding and musical rewards…. Most of the tracks are straightforward enough ballads or rockers… **Chris Welch, Melody Maker, February 1968**

Building The Perfect Beast

ARTIST Don Henley **RELEASE DATE** February 1985 (UK)/December 1984 (US) **LABEL** Geffen (UK & US) **PRODUCER** Don Henley, Danny Kortchmar, Greg Ladanyi **UK CHART** peak/weeks 14/11 **US CHART** peak/weeks 13/63 **TRACK LISTING** The Boys Of Summer/You Can't Make Love/Man With A Mission/You're Not Drinking Enough/Not Enough Love In The World/Building The Perfect Beast/All She Wants To Do Is Dance/Sunset Grill/Drivin' With Your Eyes Closed/Land Of the Living **PERSONNEL** Don Henley (v), Lindsey Buckingham (gst), Randy Newman (gst)

The Eagles singer and drummer had started his solo career hesitantly with 1982's **I Can't Stand Still**, but all the pieces fitted into place two years later when he jumped ship from his former group's long-time label to Geffen. A Grammy for *The Boys Of Summer*, which also had an award-winning black and white video, set him up to become unquestionably the most successful solo Eagle with the US Number 8 **End Of The Innocence**.

Sweet talk, tough talk and just about any form of pop discourse you could ask for are well within Don Henley's grasp on this impressive second solo outing. **Rolling Stone, December 1985**

Burnin'

ARTIST Bob Marley & The Wailers **RELEASE DATE** November 1973 (UK)/October 1975 (US) **LABEL** Island (UK & US) **PRODUCER** Chris Blackwell, The Wailers **UK CHART** peak/weeks 0/0 **US CHART** peak/weeks 151/6 **TRACK LISTING** Get Up, Stand Up/Hallelujah Time/I Shot The Sheriff/Burnin' And Lootin'/Put It On/Small Axe/Pass It On/Duppy Conquerer/One Foundation/Rasta Man Chant **PERSONNEL** Aston 'Family Man' Barrett (b), Bob Marley (v, ag), Carlton (Carlie) Barrett (d), Peter Mackintosh (p, o, g, v), Bunny Livingstone (cg, pc, v)

Marley's second Island album was considerably rootsier than its studio-sweetened predecessor, **Catch A Fire**. And though most of it had been laid down at Harry J's studios before the Wailers left for their first proper British tour, it would be promoted by a depleted band: Bunny Livingston had quit as a touring member, while Marley and Peter Tosh fell out in mid-tour, leaving Bob the undisputed leader. Yet his trilogy of *Burnin' And Lootin'*, *Get Up, Stand Up* and the much covered *I Shot The Sheriff* had already given him the whip hand.

Burnin' is a heavily committed album, both politically and religiously, reflecting… that Marley is an angry young man with a mission, and that mission is to spread the creed of Rastafari to a Western world that to him seems obsessed with triviality. **S.L., Melody Maker, October 1973**

Buscando America

ARTIST Ruben Blades **RELEASE DATE** 1984 **LABEL** Elektra **PRODUCER** Ruben Blades **UK CHART** peak/weeks – **US CHART** peak/weeks 0/0 **TRACK LISTING** – **PERSONNEL** Ruben Blades (ag, g, v), Oscar Hernandez (p, k), Ralph Irizarry (pc, tb), Ricardo Marrero (sy, pc, vp), Eddy Montalvo (pc, tr), Louis Rivera (pc, b), Michael Vinas (ag, bj, g)

Panama-born Blades's socially aware salsa was starting to reach a wider cross-section of the population when he signed to Elektra in 1984. Ten years earlier he had enjoyed the biggest selling salsa album ever, **Siembra Buscando America** (In Search Of America) pushed him further into the limelight. Soon he was collaborating with such names as Linda Ronstadt, Lou Reed and Elvis Costello, starring in films, and proving the catalyst behind the Sun City project. In 1994 he was a losing candidate in Panama's presidential election.

Buscando America is an album one feels obligated to like…. Unfortunately, though, Blades' talent just doesn't translate… he's not a terribly prepossessing singer… his playing never catches fire…. **Don Shewey, Rolling Stone, June 1984**

Business As Usual

ARTIST Men At Work **RELEASE DATE** June 1982 (UK)/July 1982 (US) **LABEL** Epic (UK)/Columbia (US) **PRODUCER** Peter Mcian **UK CHART** peak/weeks 1/44 **US CHART** peak/weeks 1/90 **TRACK LISTING** Who Can It Be Now/I Can See It In Your Eyes/Down Under/Underground/Helpless Automation/People Just Love To Play With Words/Be Good Johnny/Touching The Untouchables/Catch A Star/Down By The Sea **PERSONNEL** Colin James Hay (v, rg), Ron Strykert (g), Greg Ham (s, k, fl), John Rees (b, v), Jerry Speiser (d)

When CBS Records signed Australian bar band Men At Work, it was thanks not to an A&R man (Artist and Repertoire, biz-speak for a talent scout) but a member of the accounts department in their Melbourne office who dropped by a local bar to see them each Wednesday. Hopefully he got a bonus when they rose to world chart-topping status, aided by a support tour to Fleetwood Mac, the patronage of MTV for the single **Who Can It Be Now?** and the UK Number 1 **Down Under**, an anthem for all expatriate Aussies.

It didn't jar them people in the sense that I guess we use traditional, conventional methods of songwriting,' Colin replied, 'in the sense that there is a melodic content and 4/4 timing with words, things like that y'know… we don't have a formula…. **Adam Sweeting, Melody Maker, July 1983**

But Seriously

ARTIST Phil Collins **RELEASE DATE** November 1989 (UK)/December 1989 (US) **LABEL** Virgin (UK)/Atlantic (US) **PRODUCER** Phil Collins, Hugh Padgham **UK CHART** peak/weeks 1/69 **US CHART** peak/weeks 1/90 **TRACK LISTING** Hang In Long Enough/That's Just The Way It Is/Find A Way To My Heart/ Colours/ Father To Son/Another Day In Paradise/All Of My Life/Something Happened On The Way To Heaven/Do You Remember?/I Wish It Would Rain Down **PERSONNEL** Phil Collins (p, v), Stephen Bishop (gst), Eric Clapton (g, gst), David Crosby (gst), Don Myrick (gst), Steve Winwood (gst), Sting (bv, gst)

In which, as the title suggests, Collins wanted to leaven his MOR rock with some serious messages. Tracks with sociological undercurrents included *I Wish It Would Rain Down* (featuring Eric Clapton on guitar), *Do You Remember* and *Something Happened On The Way To Heaven*. Fans weren't turned off by Collins' bid for street credibility; this was as popular as any of his albums.

Butthole Surfers (Brown Reasons To Live)

ARTIST Butthole Surfers **RELEASE DATE** April 1984 (UK)/1983 (US) **LABEL** Alt.Tent (UK & US) **PRODUCER** Butthole Surfers **UK CHART** peak/weeks 0/0 **US CHART** peak/weeks 0/0 **TRACK LISTING** The Shah Sleeps In Lee Harvey's Grave/Hey/Something/Bar-B-Que/Pope/Wichita Cathedral/Suicide/The Legend Of Anus Presley **PERSONNEL** Gibby (v), Paul 'Pablo' Leary Warthall (g), King Koffee (d), Alan (b)

Guitarist Paul Leary claimed he had no regrets about his choice of name for this Texan band. Vocalist Gibby Haynes and drummer King Koffee moved to California with him where they forged their highly idiosyncratic and deeply deranged anti-style, influenced by anything unconventional, from Public Image to Captain Beefheart.

Pioneers of indie-rock underground who have been pushing the boundaries of good taste since 1981… **Jancee Dunn, Rolling Stone, May 1996**

Call Me

ARTIST Al Green **RELEASE DATE** November 1973 (UK)/May 1973 (US) **LABEL** London (UK)/Hi (US) **PRODUCER** Willie Mitchell, Al Green **UK CHART** peak/weeks 0/0 **US CHART** peak/weeks 10/41 **TRACK LISTING** Call Me (Come Back Home)/Have You Been Making Out O.K./Stand Up/I'm So Lonesome I Could Cry/Your Love Is Like The Morning Son/Here I Am (Come And Take Me)/Funny How Time Slips Away/You Ought To Be With Me/Jesus Is Waiting **PERSONNEL** Al Green (v), Donna Rhodes (v), Sandra Rhodes (v), Charles Chalmers (v), Wayne Jackson (t), Andrew Lone (v), Ed Logan (v), James Mitchell (bs), Jack Hale (tb), Howard Grimes (d), Al Jackson (d), Leroy Hodges (b), Charles Hodges (o, p), Tennie Hodges (g), Archie Turner (p), The Memphis Strings

This landmark album effectively brought to a close phase one in Green's career, most of which had shown an upward swing through to 1973. The following year's events, where an ex-girlfriend poured boiling grits over his back while he was taking a shower before shooting herself dead, had a profound effect on the singer, who later turned to the church and recorded gospel music. The transition was not immediate, for although there was some surprising material on the album (*Funny How Time Slips Away* and *I'm So Lonesome I Could Cry*) there was still the traditional material with which Green had made his reputation, including the title track and *Here I Am (Come And Take Me)*.

He is onto something, keeps on pushing and takes the listener with him. **Call Me** *is not an exceptional Al Green album, but it is solid as a rock at its centre. And that is what keeps me coming back for more.* **Jon Landau, Rolling Stone, July 1973**

Calypso

ARTIST Harry Belafonte **RELEASE DATE** – **LABEL** RCA Victor LPM-1248 **PRODUCER** – **UK CHART** peak/weeks – **US CHART** peak/weeks 172/2 **TRACK LISTING** Day O/I Do Adore Her/Jamaica Farewell/Will His Love Be Like His Rum?/Dolly Dawn/Star O/The Jack-Ass Song/Hosanna/Come Back Liza/ Brown Skin Girl/Man Smart (Woman Smarter) **PERSONNEL** Harry Belafonte with Tony Scott (orc), Millard Thomas (g)

More recently a reinvented social activist actor, Belafonte's lengthy career took off in the Fifties with his third album, which was Number 1 for an, even then, staggering 31 weeks. His catalogue embraced an abundance of international styles, but it was this record which established him in America's hearts as the king of the calypso movement. Joyful and spirited, it featured the much-mimicked *Banana Boat Song*, with its famous 'day-o, dee day-ay-o, daylight come and I wanna go home' refrain. A craze ensued.

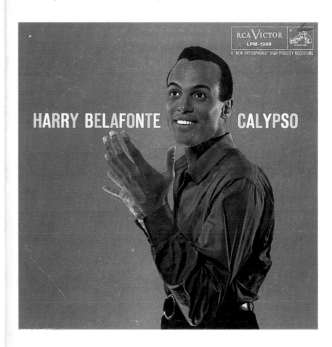

Can't Buy A Thrill

ARTIST Steely Dan **RELEASE DATE** December 1972 (UK)/November 1972 (US) **LABEL** Probe (UK)/ABC ABCL 5024 (US) **PRODUCER** Gary Katz **UK CHART** peak/weeks 0/0 **US CHART** peak/weeks 17/59 **TRACK LISTING** Do It Again/Dirty Work/Kings/Midnite Cruiser/Only A Fool Would Say That/Reelin' In The Years/Fire In The Hole/Brooklyn/Change Of The Guard/Turn That Heartbeat Over Again **PERSONNEL** Donald Fagen (p, ep, o, v), Walter Becker (b, b, v), Denny Dias (g, est), Jeff 'Skunk' Baxter (g, ps, ag), Jim Hodder (d, pc, v), David Palmer (v), Elliot Randall (g), Victor Feldman (pc), Jerome Richardson (ts), Snooky Young (fh), Clydie King (bv), Shirley Matthews (bv), Venetta Fields (bv)

Named after a dildo in William Burroughs' *Naked Lunch*, Steely Dan were more a studio concept than a full-fledged rock band, based around the cryptic lyrics and complex musicality of Donald Fagen and Walter Becker. **Can't Buy A Thrill**, the debut album, had a Top 10 single at the start of each side, the Latin shuffle of *Do It Again* and the harder *Reelin' In The Years*, but what surprised most was that such jazzily intricate songs and witty, literate word play could be so popular.

The first Steely Dan album was recorded in June 1972, after six fruitless months on the song squad. Both the Dan's hit singles are here, as well as a few songs that could've been hits if the band were greedy. **Wayne Robbins, NME, February 1974**

Can't Slow Down

ARTIST Lionel Richie **RELEASE DATE** October 1983 (UK)/November 1983 (US) **LABEL** Motown (UK & US) **PRODUCER** Lionel Richie, James Anthony Carmichael, David Foster **UK CHART** peak/weeks 1/154 **US CHART** peak/weeks 1/116 **TRACK LISTING** Can't Slow Down/All Night Long (All Night)/Penny Lover/Stuck on You/Love Will Find a Way/Running with the Night/Hello **PERSONNEL** Lionel Richie (v, k, d), David Foster (b, k), Louie Shelton (g), Joe Chemay (b), Michael Boddicker (sy), Sonny Burke (k), Diane Burt (v), Melinda Chatman (v), Dave Cochran (sy, g, s, v), Paulinho Da Costa (pc), Nathan East (b), John Hobbs (p), Mitch Holder (g), Steve Lukather (g), Richard Marx (v), Jeff Porcaro (d), session musicians

While there were no doubts about former Commodore Lionel Richie's ability to write compelling ballads, the standard of his up-tempo material was something altogether different. This is why **Can't Slow Down** represents the zenith of Lionel's solo career: the ballads are top notch, *Hello* and *Penny Lover* in particular, and the danceable tracks exceptional, with *All Night Long (All Night)* the standout – indeed, its success has tended to overshadow the ballads.

Richie rounds out the LP with two of the bland love ballads with which he's more commonly associated. They are, as usual, useless. The key flaw in all of Richie's music is its lack of personal assertion, its rampant tastefulness. **The year in music and entertainment 1984, Rolling Stone, 1984**

The Captain And Me

ARTIST The Doobie Brothers **RELEASE DATE** March 1973 (UK & US) **LABEL** Warner Bros. (UK & US) **PRODUCER** Ted Templeman **UK CHART** peak/weeks 0/0 **US CHART** peak/weeks 7/102 **TRACK LISTING** Natural Thing/Long Train Runnin'/China Grove/Dark Eyes Cajun Woman/Clear As The Driven Snow/Without You/South City Midnight Lady/Evil Woman/Ukiah/The Captain And Me **PERSONNEL** Tom Johnston (lg, bv, v), Pat Simmons (g, v), John Hartman (d, pc, v), Tiran Porter (b, v), Keith Knudson (d, v), Cornelius Bumpus (s)

Many UK fans would have assumed that the Doobies' hit single *Listen To The Music* would be on this album, but they were wrong. That re-activated song was from its predecessor, **Toulouse Street**, but the Doobies' arrival on UK soil in the autumn of 1973 proved the potency of this amped-up, Creedence-style rock album, powered by a twin-guitar, twin-drum combination. *Long Train Running*, a US Top 10 single, provided more riffery from Tom Johnston's pen, while *South City Midnight Lady* showcased Pat Simmons's more delicate balladry.

The band credits Templeman's production for their well-crafted second album. 'He translated all our musical ideas into the right electronics,' said Johnston. 'We also matured musically. We became more adventurous when we finally realised that the studio is always going to be different from a live performance.' **Tom Johnston from an interview by Steve Ditlea, Rolling Stone, January 1973**

Captain Fantastic And The Brown Dirt Cowboy

ARTIST Elton John **RELEASE DATE** June 1975 (UK & US) **LABEL** DJM (UK)/MCA (US) **PRODUCER** Gus Dudgeon **UK CHART** peak/weeks 2/24 **US CHART** peak/weeks 1/43 **TRACK LISTING** Captain Fantastic And The Brown Dirt Cowboy/Tower Of Babel/Bitter Fingers/Tell Me When The Whistle Blows/Someone Saved My Life Tonight/(Gotta Get A) Meal Ticket/Better Off Dead/Writing/We All Fall In Love Sometimes/Curtains **PERSONNEL** Elton John (v, p), Dee Murray (b), Davey Johnstone (g), Ray Cooper, Nigel Olsson (d)

An autobiographical effort, this included a mock-up teen mag featuring the stranger-than-fiction tale of Captain Fantastic (Elton) and the Brown Dirt Cowboy (rurally raised lyricist Bernie Taupin) who met via a music-paper small ad. Butterfly Ball artist Alan Aldridge designed the elaborate sleeve illustration. It would become a stage musical in 1998, 23 years after release, while the most controversy at the time came with *Someone Saved My Life Tonight*, the story of a suicide attempt that turned out to be true.

…while the stirring Elton John trademark is often strong enough to pull the songs through, the album remains a little wet… **R. C., Melody Maker, May 1975**

Catch A Fire

ARTIST Bob Marley & The Wailers **RELEASE DATE** April 1973 (UK & US) **LABEL** Island (UK & US) **PRODUCER** Bob Marley, Chris Blackwell **UK CHART** peak/weeks 0/0 **US CHART** peak/weeks 171/5 **TRACK LISTING** Concrete Jungle/Slave Driver/400 Years/Stop That Train/Stir It Up/Kinky Reggae/No More Trouble/Midnight Ravers **PERSONNEL** Aston 'Family Man' Barrett (b), Bob Marley (v, ag), Carlton (Carlie) Barrett (d), Peter Mackintosh (p, o, g, v), Bunny Livingstone (cg, pc, v)

With 'roots' such a buzzword in reggae circles it may be injudicious to point out that the success of Marley's first Island Records album was due as much to label boss Chris Blackwell's remixing and overdubbing as the core material. American guitarist Wayne Perkins embellished three tracks, countryman John 'Rabbit' Bundrick (of Free fame) appeared on most, and white Jamaican Blackwell's take on the undoubted talents of the Wailers, plus an elaborate Zippo-style album cover, piqued enough people's curiosity to make a mark.

Catch A Fire *is beautiful, reassuringly mellow, full-sounding music. Try it. Try listening to a track like* **Stop That Train** *or* **Stir It Up** *and try to forget about the damn song, try to get it out of your mind. It just won't leave you in peace.* **Phonograph Record Magazine, 1973**

Centerfield

ARTIST John Fogerty **RELEASE DATE** February 1985 (UK)/January 1985 (US) **LABEL** Warner Bros. (UK & US) **PRODUCER** John Fogerty **UK CHART** peak/weeks 48/11 **US CHART** peak/weeks 1/51 **TRACK LISTING** The Old Man Down The Road/Rock And Roll Girls/Big Train (From Memphis)/I Saw It On TV/Mr Greed/Searchlight/Centerfield/I Can't Help Myself/Vanz Kant Danz **PERSONNEL** John Fogerty (v, g), session musicians

Ex-Creedence Clearwater Revival frontman Fogerty had scores to settle on his second official solo effort, a US Number 1. Having fallen out with Creedence's old label boss, Saul Zaentz, he closed **Centerfield** with the vitriolic **Zanz Kant Dance**. The song was retitled **Vanz…** after the first pressing, but this didn't stop Zaentz (later the Hollywood film mogul behind *The English Patient*) claiming **The Old Man Down The Road** was a rip-off of Creedence's **Run Through The Jungle**, whose copyright he held! *Here, Fogerty comes back with all the elan of a born slugger, playing everything himself in the jaunty high style epitomised by the corkscrewing guitar that opens,* **The Old Man Down The Road**. **The Year In Records 1985, Rolling Stone, December 1985**

The Chase

ARTIST Garth Brooks **RELEASE DATE** September 1992 (UK & US) **LABEL** Capitol Records (UK)/Liberty (US) **PRODUCER** Allen Reynolds **UK CHART** peak/weeks - **US CHART** peak/weeks 1/64 **TRACK LISTING** We Shall Be Free/Somewhere Other Than The Night/Mr Right/Every Now and Then/Walkin' After Midnight/Dixie Chicken/Learning To Live Again/That Summer/Night Rider's Lament **PERSONNEL** Garth Brooks (g, v, bv), Donna McElroy (bv), Howard Smith (bv), Gary Chapman (bv), Bobby Wood (k), Robert Mason (st), Bruce Bouton (stg), Mark Casstevens (ag), John Catchings (st), Johnny Cobb (bv), Charles Cochran (arr), David Davidson (st), Connie Ellisor (st), Rob Hajacos (f), Vicki Hampton (bv), Yvonne Hodges (bv), Lee Larrison (st), Chris Leuzinger (g), Milton Sledge (pc, d), Mike Chapman (b), Debbie Nims (bv)

Though he meant little or nothing in Britain, Garth Brooks was a phenomenon Stateside: the biggest crossover country star ever. Questions of authenticity and credibility seemed to roll over and die in his slipstream. The Oklahoma-born singer/guitarist was allegedly selling a quarter of a million records A WEEK in the early Nineties. **The Chase** came at the front end of the roll, and proved he was not as bland as some maintained: *Face To Face* dealt with the controversial topic of date rape, and his takes on Patsy Cline's **Walkin' After Midnight** and Little Feat's **Dixie Chicken** had teeth.

Country just isn't the word for it: this is pure Garth music. His peaceful easy blend of under appreciated influences – twangy redneck rock, folksy balladry, shiny happy pop and honky tonk heartbreak – really has no precedent… this album contains his best recorded work. **The Year In Records 1992, Rolling Stone, December 1991**

Cheap Thrills

ARTIST Big Brother And The Holding Company **RELEASE DATE** September 1968 (UK)/August 1968 (US) **LABEL** CBS (UK)/Columbia (US) **PRODUCER** John Simon **UK CHART** peak/weeks 0/0 **US CHART** peak/weeks 1/66 **TRACK LISTING** Combination Of The Two/I Need A Man To Love/Summertime/Piece Of My Heart/Turtle Blues/Oh, Sweet Mary/Ball And Chain **PERSONNEL** Janis Joplin (v), Sam Andrew (g, v), Pete Albin (b, v), James Gurley (g), David Getz (d), Ed Bogus (vl)

The zenith – or nadir, depending on your view – of acid rock, overflowing with interminable wigged-out guitar solos, trippy-hippy Robert Crumb artwork and even a druggy reference within the band name. It has survived because of Janis Joplin's ferocious, elemental vocals. She attacks Erma Franklin's **Piece Of My Heart**, **Big Mama** and Thornton's **Ball And Chain** like a woman possessed, or at least fuelled by certain hush-hush substances and gargling whisky. The musicians are ragged, but then Joplin's take on Gershwin's **Summertime** is a rough diamond. No wonder she went solo thereafter.

Cherish

ARTIST David Cassidy **RELEASE DATE** May 1977 (UK & US) **LABEL** Bell (UK & US) **PRODUCER** Wes Farrell **UK CHART** peak/weeks 2/43 **US CHART** peak/weeks 15/23 **TRACK LISTING** Being Together/Blind Hope/Could It Be Forever/I Am A Clown/I Just Wanna Make You Happy/I Lost My Chance/My First Night Alone With You/Ricky's Tune/We Could Never Be Friends (Cause We've Been Lovers Too Long)/Where Is The Morning **PERSONNEL** David Cassidy (v, g, pc, k), session musicians

Graduating from the TV series *The Partridge Family*, in connection with which he had already sung on a handful of huge hits, Cassidy became one of the early Seventies most swoonsome teen pin-ups, displaying more of a rapport with puppy love than even Donny Osmond. His choice of hits showed a real affection for melancholy melody, as **Could It Be Forever** and **How Can I Be Sure** proved in romantic gushes. **Cherish** itself was a remarkably grandiose lyric, rising with near Yeatsean poeticism to a tear-jerking crescendo.

This first sold offering shows that he's much deeper than his image. He's an exceptionally good singer, with a strong, powerful voice… when Cassidy shakes off his teeny bop image he'll achieve more individually. **Pamela Holden, NME, June 1971**

Chicago V

ARTIST Chicago RELEASE DATE September 1972 (UK and US) LABEL Columbia (UK)/CBS (US) PRODUCER – UK CHART peak/weeks 24/2 US CHART peak/weeks 1/51 TRACK LISTING Saturday In The Park/A Hit By Varese/All Is Well/Now That You've Gone/Dialogue (Parts 1&2)/While The City Sleeps/State Of The Union/Alma Mater/Goodbye PERSONNEL Robert Lamm (v, k), Terry Kaths (v, g), Peter Cetera (v, b), Dan Seraphine (d), Lee Loughnane (t, v), James Pankow (tr), Waltzer Parazaider (r)

Revving up as pioneering avant-garde rockers with a huge horn section and Beach Boys-esque harmonies, Chicago lacked a truly charismatic front person but became one of America's most consistently big-selling and prolific album acts of the Seventies. They degenerated into flaccid middle-aged whimsy, as 1983's mega-hit *If You Leave Me Now* exemplified. Around the time of this album, however, they were relatively brave and ballsy: *A Hit By Varese* was an ambitious, complex opener, and *Saturday In The Park* was a loved gem. *Dialogue* also charted.

Instrumentally, then, no complaints. But, on record, there still seems to be no truly strong lead vocalist…. No new ground for Chicago, but when you're the best band around at what you're doing why worry? **G. B., Melody Maker, August 1972**

Chicken Skin Music

ARTIST Ry Cooder RELEASE DATE October 1976 (UK & US) LABEL Reprise (UK & US) PRODUCER Ry Cooder, Russ Titelman UK CHART peak/weeks 0/0 US CHART peak/weeks 177/5 TRACK LISTING The Bourgeois Blues/I Got Mine/Always Lift Him Up/He'll Have To Go/Smack Dab In The Middle/Stand By Me/Yellow Roses/Chloe/Goodnight Irene PERSONNEL Flaco Jimenez (ad), Ry Cooder (bj, g, ad, v, md), Bobby King (bv), Fred Jackson (s, ts), Jim Keltner (d), Russ Titelman (bj, v, b), session musicians

A melting pot of gospel, blues, soul and Hawaiian trad, with Cooder coaxing exceptional performances from his guest players. Flaco Jimenez and Gabby Pahinui were introduced to American music and flourished fearlessly, the former lighting up Ben E. King's *Stand By Me* with accordion magic. This Tex-Mex line was developed by Cooder on his live album of the following year,

Showtime. He then moved on through jazz, to rock 'n' roll, and then to his highly successful film scores.

Irene closes the album with one of Cooder's magnificent cross breedings: a mariachi feel filtered through a classic American folk song…. His ability to intergrate such diverse musical traditions should keep quite a few… towns singing. **Davis Leishman, Rolling Stone, September 1976**

The Chirping Crickets

ARTIST The Crickets RELEASE DATE February 1958 (UK)/Nvember 1957 (US) LABEL Vogue Coral (UK)/Brunswick (US) PRODUCER Norman Petty UK CHART peak/weeks 0/0 US CHART peak/weeks 0/0 TRACK LISTING Oh Boy/Not Fade Away/You've Got To Love/Maybe Baby/It's Too Late/Tell Me How/That'll Be The Day/I'm Looking For Someone To Love/An Empty Cup (And A Broken Date)/Send Me Some Lovin'/Last Night/Rock Me Baby PERSONNEL Buddy Holly (v, g), Niki Sullivan (rg), Joe B. Maudlin (b), Jerry J.I. Allison (d), session musicians

Originally Buddy Holly's backing band, The Crickets left the bespectacled one less than a year before his untimely death to pursue their own niche in the hall of pop fame. It wasn't to be, despite some small acclaim as a Sixties beat combo and a Seventies country-rock outfit. Drummer Jerry Allison, their leader, had recorded (as 'Ivan') the chestnut *Real Wild Child.* They were always bigger in Britain and Europe than America. Among their hits was *More Than I Can Say*, soon to do the business for Bobby Vee (with whom they recorded an album of Holly songs) and Leo Sayer. Generally, though, they found it tough to throw off the influence of *Peggy Sue*.

Jerry asserts that, unlike some of their contemporaries, they have no objection to being 'revived'. 'We need it! We really don't mind doing the old songs over again. It would be ridiculous for us to say we're current, when in fact we're old rock 'n' rollers from the Fifties.' **Jerry Allison From an interview by Richard Williams, Melody Maker, December 1972**

Choke

ARTIST The Beautiful South RELEASE DATE October 1990 (UK & US) LABEL Go! Discs (UK)/Elektra (US) PRODUCER Mike Hedges UK CHART peak/weeks 2/22 US CHART peak/weeks 0/0 TRACK LISTING Tonight I Fancy Myself/My Book/Let Love Speak Up Itself/Should've Kept My Eyes Shut/I've Come For My Award/Lips/I Think The Answer's Yes/A Little Time/Mother's Pride/I Hate You (But You're Interesting)/The Rising Of Grafton Street PERSONNEL Paul Heaton (v, g), Dave Hemingway (v), David Rotherray (g), Briana Corrigan (v), Sean Welch (b), David Stead (d)

Though seeming cynical to an extreme, the Hull-based band, formed from the ashes of The Housemartins, had the knack of appearing to enjoy huge pop success while despising all it entailed. Their second album featured the surprise Number 1 single *A Little Time*, an affecting and insightful kitchen-sink love duet sung by Dave Hemingway and Brianna Corrigan, who soon afterwards left to pursue a solo career. Throughout, Paul Heaton's jaundiced lyrics observed ailing relationships, ghastly children and human nature's worst side in general.

A year on from the band's debut, the quill of the boy Heaton is sharper in its observations and attitude to our everyday anxieties about relationships – not least with ourselves – and politics… Sweetening these bitter pills, the music seldom biffs you around the brow, cleverly preferring the softly-softly approach. **Q, January 1991**

The Christians

ARTIST The Christians **RELEASE DATE** October 1987 (UK & US) **LABEL** Island (UK & US) **PRODUCER** Laurie Latham **UK CHART** peak/weeks 2/68 **US CHART** peak/weeks 158/8 **TRACK LISTING** Forgotten Town/When The Fingers Point/Born Again/Ideal World/Save A Soul In Every Town/… And That's Why/Hooverville/One In A Million/Sad Songs **PERSONNEL** Garry A. Christian (lv), Russell Christian (s, v), Henry Priestman (k, g, v), Mike Bulger (g), Tony Jones (b), Paul Barlow (d)

With a deeper resonance and a greater proximity to 'real' soul than the white British soul acts that emerged through the mid Eighties, Liverpool's Christians – three brothers plus songwriter Priestman, formerly with The Yachts and It's Immaterial – laced their warm soft-shuffle ballads with political subtexts. *Ideal World* fizzed with barely concealed rage at social injustice, while *Living Blues* reckoned the welfare syndrome sucked. Roger Christian had left, but bald giant Garry gave the group a memorable image. *Forgotten Town* and *When The Fingers Point* were also hits.

What the album means to different people: 'To the abandoned lover it is solace and solitude. To the first year social awareness student it is resistance and heroism in the face of futility. To the bored housewife it is suffering and romance. To the advertising executive it is money and nostalgia, the perfect equation for improving market shares.' **Ted Mico, Melody Maker, October 1987**

A Christmas Gift For You

ARTIST Phil Spector **RELEASE DATE** 1963 **LABEL** Philies (US) **PRODUCER** Phil Spector **UK CHART** peak/weeks 0/0 **US CHART** peak/weeks 0/0 **TRACK LISTING** White Christmas/Frosty the Snowman/Bells of St. Mary's/Santa Claus is Coming to Town/Sleigh Ride/Marshmallow World/I Saw Mommy Kissing Santa Claus/Rudolph the Red-Nosed Reindeer/Winter Wonderland/Parade of the Wooden Soldiers/Christmas (Baby Please Come Home)/Here Comes Santa Claus/Silent Night **PERSONNEL** Leon Russell (p), Frank Capp (pc), Barney Kessel (g), Don Randi (p), Lou Blackburn (hn), Jack Nitzsche (pc), Darlene Love (v), Bob B. Soxx & the Blue Jeans (v), Nino Tempo (g), Hal Blaine (d), Sonny Bono (pc), Roy Caton (hn), Johnny Vidor Strings (s), session musicians

Generally considered the greatest Christmas album of all time, **A Christmas Gift For You** is a marvellous showcase for Phil Spector's legendary Wall Of Sound and his miniature pop symphonies. Featuring such Yuletide standbys as *Baby Please Come Home* and *Santa Claus Is Coming To Town* by acts from Spector's roster (Darlene Love, The Crystals), the success of the lavishly produced **A Christmas Gift…** was unfortunately scuppered by the fact that it was scheduled for release on November 22 1963 – the day John Kennedy was assassinated. Few felt inclined to buy it.

…never before has rock 'n' roll gripped so beautifully the spirit of a traditional event. The music is joyful, and if you like pop in its truest interpretation, produced by a man who has never given us trash you cannot really get through Christmas without this album. **R. C, Melody Maker, December 1973**

The Chronic

ARTIST Dr Dre **RELEASE DATE** February 1993 (UK & US) **LABEL** Interscope (UK)/Death Row Records (US) **PRODUCER** Dr Dre **UK CHART** peak/weeks 0/0 **US CHART** peak/weeks - **TRACK LISTING** The Chronic/Fuck Wit Dre Day (And Everybody's Celebrating)/Let Me Ride/The Day The Niggaz Took Over/Nuthin' But A 'G' Thang/Drreeez Nuuuts/Bitches Ain't Shit/Lil' Ghetto Boy/A Nigga Witta Gun/Rat-Tat-Tat-Tat/The $20 Sack Pyramid/The Roach (The Chronic Gum) **PERSONNEL** Dr Dre (v, var), Snoop Doggy Dogg (rap)

Though it received comparatively little of the critical acclaim of Snoop Doggy Dogg's debut, Dr Dre's slice of gangsta rap, which included contributions from Dogg, was arguably superior. Relying on samples from the Parliament/Funkadelic back catalogue (as with the Grammy-winning *Let Me Ride*), it would sell three million in the US alone in its first year on sale. The former NWA member could afford to smile as *Nothin' But A 'G' Thang*, based on a 1970's Leon Hayward hit, shot to Number 2.

… a sometimes frightening amalgam of inner-city street games that includes misogynist sexual politics and violent revenge scenarios. Throughout, **The Chronic** *drags raw realism and pays tribute to hip-hop virtuosity.* **Havelock Nelson, Rolling Stone, March 1993**

The Clash

ARTIST The Clash **RELEASE DATE** April 1977 (UK)/July 1979 (US) **LABEL** CBS (UK)/Epic (US) **PRODUCER** Mickey Foote **UK CHART** peak/weeks 12/16 **US CHART** peak/weeks 126/6 **TRACK LISTING** Janie Jones/Remote Control/I'm So Bored With The U.S.A./White Riot/Hate & War/What's My Name/ Deny/London's Burning/Career Opportunities/Cheat/Protex Blue/Police & Thieves/48 Hours/Garageland **PERSONNEL** Mick Jones (g, v), Joe Strummer (v, g), Paul Simonon (b), Tory Crimes (d)

One of punk rock's defining adrenaline rushes, sloganeering and breathless, placing energy over content and intent over order. The Clash were rivals to the less analytical Sex Pistols, and had equally fiery egos. Their debut was recorded in three weekends: appallingly produced and devoid of bottom end in the sound, it still captured the spirit of the simultaneously idealistic and exploitative 1977. Mick Jones's guitar lines gave it a semblance of melody, while Joe Strummer spat out manifestos and muddled rage on the classic spurt of **White Riot** and the shouldn't-work-but-does cod reggae of Junior Murvin's *Police And Thieves*.

Better than any other punk-rock album, **The Clash** *convincingly vents its outrage and frustration… and backs them with simple, careful, driving rock.* **Charley Walters, Rolling Stone, 1977**

Clear Spot

ARTIST Captain Beefheart & His Magic Band RELEASE DATE November 1972 (UK & US) LABEL Reprise (UK & US) PRODUCER Captain Beefheart UK CHART peak/weeks 0/0 US CHART peak/weeks 191/7 TRACK LISTING Low Yo Yo Stuff/Nowadays A Woman's Gotta Hit A Man/Too Much Time/Circumstances/My Head Is My Only House Unless It Rains/Sun Zoom Sparks/Clear Spot/Crazy little Thing/Long Neck Bottles/Her Eyes Are A Blue Million Miles/Big Eyed Beans From Venus/Golden Birdies PERSONNEL Captain Beefheart (v, h, g), John French 'Drumbo' (d), Jeff Cotton (g), Roy 'Orejon' Estrada (b), Rockette Norton (g, b, bv), Ed Marimba (cl), Russ Titelman (g)

Beefheart was making a conscious effort to rein in his ideas and attain a modicum of commercial success. This and its predecessor **The Spotlight Kid** were respectively over-jaunty and under-projecting hashes of pop-rock: yet as Beefheart goes, they're accessible. You can tell from the titles: *Big-Eyed Beans From Venus* and the bluesy *Nowadays A Woman's Gotta Hit A Man* show how hard he was trying to usher the mainstream in. Don't they?

Clear Spot *is sizzling heavy metal flash. It is without a doubt Beefheart's most commercial album… the weaker songs hit home with unexpected twists in the arrangements and committed, powerful playing from the band.* **Bob Palmer, Rolling Stone, December 1972**

Cliff Sings

ARTIST Cliff Richard RELEASE DATE November 1959 LABEL Columbia PRODUCER – UK CHART peak/weeks 2/36 US CHART peak/weeks - TRACK LISTING – PERSONNEL Cliff Richard (v)

Recorded in the earliest days of stereo sound, **Cliff Sings** was simultaneously mixed in two different control rooms, one working in mono the other in stereo. The album was 50-50 in content between ballads, backed by the Norrie Paramor Strings, and upbeat numbers with backing from The Shadows (who had just been renamed from the Drifters to avoid confusion with the US R&B vocalists). Two tracks, *I Gotta Know* and *The Snake And The Bookworm*, were re-cut in stereo after producer Paramor was

unhappy with the results, though the stereo issue was still considered of lesser importance.

… forgetting the fanatics, this is an LP which should be in the charts on it's own merits. It is literally streets ahead of so many of his contemporaries – both here and in America. **Melody Maker, November 1959**

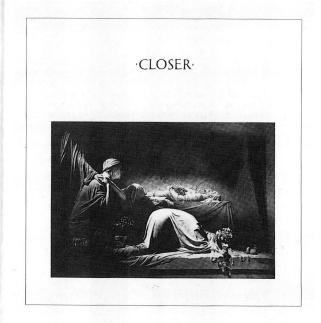

Closer

ARTIST Joy Division RELEASE DATE July 1980 LABEL Factory PRODUCER Martin 'Zero' Hannett UK CHART peak/weeks 6/8 US CHART peak/weeks - TRACK LISTING Heart And Soul/24 Hours/The Eternal/Decades/Atrocity/ Exhibition/Isolation/Passover/Colony/Means To An End PERSONNEL Ian Curtis (v), Bernard Albrecht (g), Peter Hook (b), Stephen Morris (d)

Coming as it did mere weeks after singer Ian Curtis's suicide, **Closer** was a minimalist masterpiece whose pessimistic lyrics were inevitably interpreted with even more doom and gloom than they deserved. Considerably more distant than its upfront predecessor, this put the instrumental emphasis on synthesizers and as such a pointer towards the band's work as New Order when keyboardist Gillian Gilbert was recruited and guitarist Bernard Albrecht/Sumner took on the vocal role. Only the non-inclusion of the single *Love Will Tear Us Apart* could be criticized.

Closer *is as magnificent a memorial as any post-Presley popular musician could have. In the most strict and literal sense of the term, it's a matter of life and death. Aren't you glad to live in the kind of times that make people produce music like this?* **Charles Shaar Murray, NME, July 1980**

Cloud Cuckoo Land

ARTIST The Lightning Seeds RELEASE DATE 10th February 1990 (UK)/May 1990 (US) LABEL Ghetto Ghet 3 (UK)/MCA (US) PRODUCER Ian Broudie UK CHART peak/weeks 50/2 US CHART peak/weeks 46/27 TRACK LISTING All I Want/Bound In A Nutshell/Pure/Sweet Dream/The Nearly Man/Joy/Love Explosion/Don't Let Go/Control The Flame/The Price/Fools/Frenzy/God Help Them PERSONNEL Ian Broudie (v, g, k), Peter Coyle, Paul Simpson

Liverpudlian Ian Broudie had been at the centre of Merseyside music for a decade, firstly as guitarist and songwriter with Big In Japan and later producer of Echo and the Bunnymen before this, his first 'solo' album albeit under a group name. It emerged on the Ghetto label before being picked up by Virgin and was released by MCA in the States.

*Broudie's voice drifts angelically through the LP counterpointed by a collection of neat and massively humable songs… the finest cut is the beautiful and quietly despairing ballad **Bound In A Nutshell**, which mourns the disenfranchised and put-upon city of Liverpool…* **Paul Davies, Q, February 1990**

Club Classics Volume One

ARTIST Soul II Soul RELEASE DATE April 1989 (UK & US) LABEL 10 Records (Virgin) (UK & US) PRODUCER Jazzie B, Nellee Hooper UK CHART peak/weeks 1/60 US CHART peak/weeks 14/51 TRACK LISTING Keep On Movin'/Fairplay/Holdin' On Bambelela/Feeling Free/African Dance/Dance/Feel Free/Happiness/Back To Life/Jazzie's Groove PERSONNEL Jazzie B (rap), Nellee Hooper (arr), Caron Wheeler (v), Rose Windross (v)

The luscious, slow-motion, 98bpm *Keep On Movin'* was not only the sound of summer 1989, it was also the most persuasive argument yet that Britain could match America in the smooth soul stakes. The title of **Club Classics Vol. One** was more than wishful thinking on the part of London's Soul II Soul. Apart from *Keep On Movin'*, this polyrhythmic, eclectic feast contained the Number 1 smash, **Back To Life**, and a variety of other mellifluous grooves, masterminded by DJ and occasional rapper Jazzie B, arranged by future Bjork producer Nellee Hooper and sung by Caron Wheeler.

*Soul II Soul is, of course, not so much a group as a collective. Centred around the system-reared funky entrepreneur Jazzie B…. It's not surprising then that the sheekily named **Classics** is a thoroughly unified record… it still goes boldly where no Brit soul merchant has gone before.* **Roger Morton, NME, April 1989**

Code

ARTIST Caberet Voltaire RELEASE DATE October 1987 (UK & US) LABEL Parlophone (UK)/Capitol (US) PRODUCER – UK CHART peak/weeks 0/0 US CHART peak/weeks 0/0 TRACK LISTING Don't Argue/Sex, Money, Freaks/Thank You Amercia/Here To Go/Trouble (Won't Stop)/White Car/No One Here/Life Slips By/Code/Here To Go (Little Dub) PERSONNEL Stephen Mallinder (v, b, oc, t, p) Richard H. Kirk (g, sy, bo, p), Alan Fish (d, pc), Dave Ball (k)

The Cabs, Stephen Mallinder and Richard H. Kirk, took their name from a group of Dada mavericks, and at their outset were considered similarly radical. Their daring fusion of electronic instrumentation and trance-like repetition was to prove highly influential, as was the use of tapes and random voices: a precursor of sampling. From Sheffield, the duo never reaped the commercial benefits as did, later, The Human League and Depeche Mode. **Code** arrived eight years into

their career, and was their first album for a major. It was both accessible and chillingly foreboding: a recipe they intermittently pulled together.

… there was a time when the Cabs' dislocations and swampy massiveness were really unsettling… Now that they've embraced this heavy-duty post-modernist groove thang, it's hard to know what they're doing. **Johnathon Romney, NME, October 1987**

Colour By Numbers

ARTIST Culture Club RELEASE DATE October 1983 (UK)/November 1983 (US) LABEL Virgin (UK)/Epic (US) PRODUCER Steve Levine UK CHART peak/weeks 1/56 US CHART peak/weeks 2/59 TRACK LISTING Karma Chameleon/It's A Miracle/Black Money/Changing Every Day/That's The Way (I'm Only Trying To Help You) PERSONNEL Boy George (v), Jon Moss (d, pc), Mike Craig (b), Roy Hay (g, k), Helen Terry (v), Phil Pickett (k), Steve Grainger (s), Terry Bailey (t)

Surprisingly Culture Club's only Number 1 album, this exemplified a group whose simple breezy pop was given charm and a brief magic by 'outrageous gender-bender' Boy George's soul-inflected, warm, honest voice. It bred a huge era-defining chart-topping single in **Karma Chameleon**, and a near miss Number 2 in the Motown steal **Church Of The Poison Mind**. George's sweet croon was given able back-up throughout by Helen Terry. Sadly, when these peacocks tried to infuse their work with some so-called seriousness, the resulting album, **Waking Up With The House On Fire**, marked the start of their decline. We already KNEW war was stupid…

Throughout, Culture Club never sound clumsy or forced but light-footed and sure as they create their modern pop, a delightful synthesis of the old and new, with masterly ease. **Paolo Hewitt, NME, October 1983**

Come Dance With Me

ARTIST Frank Sinatra RELEASE DATE May 1959 (UK)/February 1959 (US) LABEL Capital (UK) PRODUCER Dave Cavanaugh UK CHART peak/weeks 2/30 US CHART peak/weeks 2/141 TRACK LISTING Come Dance With Me/Something's Gotta Give/Just In Time/Dancing In The Dark/Too Close For Comfort/I Could Have Danced All Night/Saturday Night/Day In, Day Out/Cheek To Cheek/Baubles, Bangles And Beads/The Song Is You/The Last Dance PERSONNEL Frank Sinatra (v)

With Billy May, Sinatra revived the Big Band Sound of the swingin' Forties, although here the exuberance was tinged with the wisdom of experience. Casual and cool, cocky yet prone to moments of reflection, Sinatra's breathily intimate singing on Irving Berlin's *Cheek To Cheek* and Johnny Mercer's *Something's Gotta Give* are object lessons in how to approximate his less-is-more technique.

I believe Frank Sinatra adulation has something to do with hypnosis… It is as if the personality mesmerises and holds the crowd in unthinking subjection. I would be the first to allow that Sinatra has talent – but greatness is another quality altogether. **Tony Brown, Melody Maker, August 1959**

Come Fly With Me

ARTIST Frank Sinatra **RELEASE DATE** March 1958 (UK & US) **LABEL** Capitol (UK & US) **PRODUCER** Nelson Riddle **UK CHART** peak/weeks 2/18 **US CHART** peak/weeks 1/71 **TRACK LISTING** Come Fly With Me/Around The World/Brazil/Isle Of Capri/Let's Get Away From It All/April In Paris/Blue Hawaii/London By Night/It's Nice To Go Travelling/Moonlight In Vermont/On The Road To Mandalay **PERSONNEL** Frank Sinatra (v)

The Beatles' **Sgt. Pepper** or **Freak Out!** by The Mothers Of Invention are generally regarded as the first concept albums, but Frank Sinatra's eighth album for Capitol predated both by almost a decade, being a suite of songs that takes the listener around the world – from the Isle Of Capri to Vermont to New York to Paris to London to Brazil to Hawaii – in 40-odd minutes. **Come Fly With Me** was also notable for being Sinatra's first LP arranged and conducted by masterful orchestrator Billy May.

Come On Come On

ARTIST Mary Chapin Carpenter **RELEASE DATE** October 1992 (US) **LABEL** Columbia (US) **PRODUCER** John Jennings, Mary Chapin Carpenter **UK CHART** peak/weeks - **US CHART** peak/weeks 31/104 **TRACK LISTING** Hard Way/He Thinks He'll Keep Her/Rhythm Of The Blues/I Feel Lucky/Bug/Not Too Much To Ask/Passionate Kisses/Only A Dream/I Am A Town/Walking Through Fire/I Take My Chances/Come On Come On **PERSONNEL** Mary Chapin Carpenter (ag, g, v, bv), Jerry Douglas (db), Rosanne Cash (bv), Joe Diffie (v), Edgar Meyer (dbb, b), Shawn Colvin (bv), Indigo Girls (bv), John Jorgenson (g), Matt Rollings (p), Johnny Carroll (sy), J.T. Brown (b, bv), John Jennings (b, g, pc, bv), Benmont Tench (o), session musicians

A country-rocker with the suss to write about the relationship traumas of grown-ups, Carpenter's lyrics were seen to come on in leaps and bounds. After the over-angsty **Shooting Straight In The Dark**, she found room for fun here, covering songs by Lucinda Williams and Dire Straits and duetting with Dwight Yoakam and Lyle Lovett on **I Feel Lucky**, wherein she wins the lottery. This may have been a metaphor: the album sold over two million and in **He Thinks He'll Keep Her** she grabbed a Number 1 single among six hits.

Mary Chapin Carpenter hitches up her classiest songwriting instincts and a posse of quality musicians on **Come On Come On** *and emerges with an exquisitely tailored, finely modulated piece of work. Unfortunately, it's not much fun…* **Arion Berger, Rolling Stone, September 1992**

Come The Day

ARTIST The Seekers **RELEASE DATE** November 1966 **LABEL** Columbia **PRODUCER** Tom Springfield **UK CHART** peak/weeks 3/67 **US CHART** peak/weeks - **TRACK LISTING** Come The Day/Island Of Dreams/The Last Thing On My Mind/All Over The World/Red Rubber Ball/Well, Well, Well/Georgy Girl/Yesterday/I Wish You Could Be Here/Turn, Turn, Turn/Louisiana Man/California Dreamin' **PERSONNEL** Keith Potger, Bruce Woodley, Judith Durham

A quartet from Australia, The Seekers found success in the Sixties (and, later, with a completely different line-up in the Seventies, as The New Seekers) despite being regarded by some critics as anodyne exponents of folk muzak, **Come The Day** (titled 'Georgy Girl' in the US, after the theme for the celebrated Lynn Redgrave movie) was the best showcase for their rich, folk-tinged harmonies and the crystalline alto of Judith Durham. It also featured an excellent rendition of folk *politico* Tom Paxton's **The Last Thing On My Mind**.

This shows why the Seekers are so far ahead of their rivals. No other group has a lead singer to compare with Judith Durham and few can match the songwriting abilities of Tom Springfield and Seeker Bruce Woodley. **Melody Maker, January 1966**

The Confessions Of Dr Dream And Other Stories

ARTIST Kevin Ayers **RELEASE DATE** May 1974 **LABEL** Island **PRODUCER** Kevin Ayers, Rupert Hines **UK CHART** peak/weeks 0/0 **US CHART** peak/weeks 0/0 **TRACK LISTING** Day By Day/See You Later/Didn't It Feel Lonely Till I Thought Of You/Everybody's Sometimes And Some People's All The Time Blues/It Begins With A Blessing, But It Ends With A Curse/Once I Was Heard/Ball Bearing Blues/The Confessions Of Dr Dream a) Irreversible Neural Damage b) Invitation c) The One Chance Dance d) Doctor Dream Theme e) Two Into 4 Goes **PERSONNEL** Nico (v), Mike Oldfield (b, g, v), Lol Coxhill (s), Kevin Ayers (g, v), Rupert Hine (k, p), Sam Mitchell (g), John G. Perry (b), Doris Troy (v), Ray Cooper (pc), Henry Crallan (p), Trevor Jones (b), Michael Giles (d), Hulloo Choir (v), Mike Moran (p), session musicians

Signing up with Elton John's manager John Reid in 1974, this was supposed to be the album that would propel Kent hippie Kevin Ayers to the stardom his voice merited. The former Soft Machine vocalist had long been considered a kind of Bryan Ferry maverick poet on acid, but successive releases failed to cross over. This was one of the most accessible, despite the presence of guests Nico, Ollie Halsall and The Soporifics. **Why Are We Sleeping** was a homage to Ayers' lofty idol Gurdjieff. The voice brought fans to their knees and inspired the concert album **June 1st 1974** with Brian Eno, Nico, John Cale and Mike Oldfield.

Dr Dream *finds rock's most eloquent philosopher/observer more preoccupied than ever with 'sleeping'… and the need to awaken society to alternative realities… Ayer's messages to the world are contained within plenty of strong songs, good playing and good humour.* **J. W., Melody Maker, June 1974**

Connected

ARTIST The Stereo MCs **RELEASE DATE** 17th October 1992 (UK)/March 1993 (US) **LABEL** 4th & B'Way (UK & US) **PRODUCER** Stereo MCs **UK CHART** peak/weeks 2/45 **US CHART** peak/weeks 92/29 **TRACK LISTING** Connected/Ground Level/Everything/Sketch/Fade Away/All Night Long/Step It Up/Playing With Fire/Pressure/Chicken Shake/Creation/The End **PERSONNEL** Rob Birch (v), The Head (dj), Owen If (d), Cath Coffey (bv), Veronica (bv), Andrea (bv)

Connected was such an immediate success, most people believed it to be Stereo MCs' debut: it was actually their third, mainmen Rob Birch and Nick 'The Head' Hallam having been in bands together since the early Eighties, and having spent the early Nineties remixing virtually everyone on the dance scene. **Connected** was a supremely funky concoction of stoned rapping, live instrumentation and electronically triggered samples. Not surprisingly, it helped the band win that year's Brit Awards for Best Group and Best Album.

… a smooth, typically British approach to rap… Lyrically, they indulge themselves in the rather tired rapping obsessions with urban decay (**Playing With Fire**) *and the hoary old concept of 'one love'* (**Creation**). *Nevertheless, a valiant, if underachieving effort.* **Tom Doyle, Q, November 1992**

Cooley High Harmony

ARTIST Boyz II Men RELEASE DATE August 1991 (UK)/October 1992 (US) LABEL Biv Entertainment licensed to Motown (UK & US) PRODUCER Mark Nauseef, Dallas Austin, Walter Quintus, Kurt Renker UK CHART peak/weeks 7/18 US CHART peak/weeks 1/99 TRACK LISTING Please Don't Go/Lonely Heart/This Is My Heart/Uhh Ahh/It's So Hard To Say Goodbye To Yesterday/Motownphilly/Under Pressure/Sympin/Little Things/Your Love PERSONNEL Jack Bruce (b, v), Trilok Gurtu (v), Mark Nauseef (v, var), The Blackeyed Susans (g), Dallas Austin (pc, p, arr, d), Michael Bivins (v, arr), Rick Criniti (g), Nakia Keith (bv), Michael McCary (v), Nathan Morris (v, arr), Wanya Morris (v), Walter Quintus (vl), Rick Sheppard (kp), Shawn Stockman (v, arr), Troy Taylor (b, p, pc, d, k, arr), session musicians

Hitting on the formula of adapting doo-wop-based vocalizing to tame hip-hop grooves, the young Philadelphia outfit, under the guidance of Bell Biv Devoe singer Michael Bivins, cannot have anticipated the runaway success of this debut album. It sold over five million copies and encouraged a slight return to tender harmonies in an era when aggressive rap was all powerful. **Motownphilly** gave them a dance hit which appealed to two generations, but the ballad **It's So Hard To Say Goodbye** was more indicative of the path they would follow. Soon afterwards **The End Of The Road** topped the charts for longer than any other single before.

With their classic label affiliation and their clean-livin' ways, winsome lyrics that invite warm PG-13 romance and street corner sweetness of their singing, Boyz II Men echo the R&B of a time so innocent that it seems light years away… **The Year In Records 1991, Rolling Stone, December 1994**

Copperhead Road

ARTIST Steve Earle And The Dukes RELEASE DATE November 1988 (UK & US) LABEL MCA (UK & US) PRODUCER Steve Earle, Tony Browne UK CHART peak/weeks 44/8 US CHART peak/weeks 56/28 TRACK LISTING Copperhead Road/Snake Oil/Back To The Wall/The Devil's Right Hand/Johnny Come Lately/Even When I'm Blue/You Belong To Me/Waiting On You/Once You Love/Nothing But A Child PERSONNEL Steve Earle (v, g, h, dbb, md), Donny Roberts (g, dbb), Bill Lloyd (ag, g), Bucky Baxter (ps, ls, db), Ken Moore (sy, o), John Jarvis (p), Kelly Looney (b), Custer (d), Neil MacColl (md), John Cowan

(bv), Maria McKee (bv), Radney Foster (bv), The Pogues (gst), Telluride (gst)

Renegade country-star Earle's highway to glory started in 1986 with **Guitar Town**, but by now he had veered to the rock side of the road and acquired some undesirable rock-star habits. This, a Gram Parsons' take on country two decades on, gave him greater acceptance, especially in the UK, but little was heard after a live reprise until the cleaned-up Earle, fresh out of prison, resurfaced in 1995. Standout is **Johnny Come Lately**, a collaboration with the similarly hard-living Pogues.

Musically, it's his most diverse LP to date, although the themes are familiar…. I can't hear any reason why Steve Earle couldn't clean up a fair part of the Springsteen, Mellencamp or even Michael Hutchence market. His only obstacle on the road to stardom is his beer gut… and nothing to do with this man's fine music. **Andy Kershaw, Q, November 1988**

The Correct Use Of Soap

ARTIST Magazine RELEASE DATE May 1980 (UK & US) LABEL Virgin (UK)/IRS (US) PRODUCER Martin Hannett UK CHART peak/weeks 28/4 US CHART peak/weeks 0/0 TRACK LISTING Because You're Frightened/Model Worker/I'm A Party/You Never Knew Me/Philadelphia/I Want To Burn Again/Thank You (Falettinme Be Mice Elf Agin)/Sweetheart Contract/Stuck/A Song From Under The Floorboards PERSONNEL Howard Devoto (v), Barry Adamson (b, bv), John Doyle (d, pc), Dave Formula (k), John McGeoch (g, bv), Martin Jackson (d), Laura Teresa (bv)

The third album from Buzzcocks spin-off group Magazine was effectively their swansong, with guitarist John McGeoch – main man Howard Devoto's long-time lieutenant – quitting to join Siouxsie and the Banshees. Devoto himself, believing the band had already lost its cutting edge, quit after one more album and produced little of note since. In retrospect, this was the ideal compromise between commerciality and the experimental direction Devoto had left the 'Cocks to pursue.

… whether its name is intended to be irritating, ironic or a droll disguise, the album is an attempt to breath a less-rarefied air and break out of the precious atmosphere that had almost stifled them… Magazine's masterpiece. **Lynn Hanna, NME, June 1980**

Cosmo's Factory

ARTIST Creedence Clearwater Revival RELEASE DATE September 1970 (UK)/July 1970 (US) LABEL Liberty (UK & US) PRODUCER John Fogerty UK CHART peak/weeks 1/15 US CHART peak/weeks 1/69 TRACK LISTING Ramble Tamble/Before You Accuse Me/Travelin' Band/Ooby Dooby/Lookin' Out My Back Door/Run Through The Jungle/Up Around The Bend/My Baby Left Me/Who'll Stop The Rain/I Heard It Through The Grapevine/Long As I Can See The Light PERSONNEL Doug Clifford (d), Stu Cook (b), John Dogerty (lg, v), Tom Fogerty (rg)

Full of hit singles – three million sellers – despite a growing tendency to overrun the exemplary three-minute mark, **Cosmo's Factory** revealed a knack for worthwhile reinterpretation, proffering not just the famed cover of Marvin Gaye's *I Heard It Through The Grapevine*, but also Roy Orbison's *Oooby Dooby* and Elvis's *My Baby Left Me*. The range was further extended by John Fogerty's worthwhile dabbling on saxophone. *Long As I Can See The Light*, *Ramble Tamble* and *Lookin' Out My Back Door* were also to prove timeless, while *Run Through The Jungle* acknowledged the existence of a darker world outside the perimeters of a conventional Creedence ditty.

… another damn good album by a group which is going to be around a long time. **John Grissim, Rolling Stone, September 1970**

Countdown To Ecstasy

ARTIST Steely Dan RELEASE DATE July 1973 LABEL Probe (UK)/ABC (US) PRODUCER Gary Katz UK CHART peak/weeks 0/0 US CHART peak/weeks 35/34 TRACK LISTING Bodhisattva/Razor Boy/The Bouton Rag/Your Gold Teeth/Show Biz Kids/My Old School/Pearl Of The Quarter/King Of The World PERSONNEL Donald Fagen (k, v), Walter Becker (b), Jeff 'Skink' Baxter (g), Denny Dias (g), Jim Hodder (d)

Less commercially successful than its predecessor, nevertheless **Countdown To Ecstasy** represented a considerable progression. On the blackly humorous *Razor Boy* and scathing *Show Biz Kid*, Becker and Fagen offered cruel critiques of the self-obsessed 'Me' decade. Meanwhile their blend of cool jazz and bebop, Brill Building song craft and rock was unparalleled at the time (only Britain's 10cc were creating such intelligent pop in the early Seventies). By drafting in the cream of America's session men, their second album contained even more subtle pleasures and instrumental finesse than…**Thrill**.

Countdown To Ecstasy is far from an ambitious statement of a progressive musical philosophy; in fact, one could perhaps agree that the Steelies have found a formula and are exploiting it. **David Logan, Rolling Stone, August 1973**

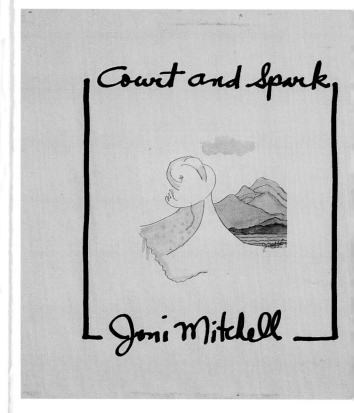

Court And Spark

ARTIST Joni Mitchell RELEASE DATE March 1974 (UK)/February 1974 (US) LABEL Asylum (UK & US) PRODUCER Joni Mitchell UK CHART peak/weeks 14/11 US CHART peak/weeks 2/64 TRACK LISTING Court And Spark/Help Me/Free Man In Paris/People's Parties/The Same Situation/Car On A Hill/Down To You/Just Like This Train/Raised On Robbery/Trouble Child/Twisted PERSONNEL Joni Mitchell (v, p, ctte, bv), John Guerin (d, pc), Max Bennett (b), Jim Hughart (b), Wilton Felder (b), Milt Holland (ch), Tom Scott (ww), Chuck Findley (t), Joe Sample (ep), David Cosby (bv), Graham Nash (bv), Susan Webb (bv), Cheech & Chong (bv), Wayne Perkins (g), Dennis Budimir (g), Robbie Robertson (g), Jose Feliciano (g), Larry Carlton (g)

Having found the West Coast coterie of musicans too straight-ahead to cope with her 'little eccentricities', Joni Mitchell employed jazz group LA Express to back her on **Court And Spark** – and the result was hugely successful both critically and commercially. The album went gold within a month of release and spawned hits in *Help Me* and *Free Man In Paris*, while *Raised On Robbery* that preceded it made up the hat-trick. Four Grammy nominations saw her win Best Arrangement for *Down To You*.

Cracked Rear View

ARTIST Hootie & The Blowfish RELEASE DATE March 1995 (UK)/July 1994 (US) LABEL Atlantic Records (UK & US) PRODUCER Don Gehman UK CHART peak/weeks 12/ US CHART peak/weeks 1/114 TRACK LISTING Hannah Jane/Hold My Hand/Let Her Cry/Only Wanna Be With You/Running From An Angel/I'm Goin' Home/Drowning/Time/Look Away/Not Even The Trees/Goodbye PERSONNEL Darius Rucker (v, ag, pc), Mark Bryan (g, ag, vpc, md, md), Dean Felber (b, cl, v, p), Jim 'Soni' Sonefield (d, v, p, pc)

The surprise US Number 1 album of 1995 owed much to others: label-mate David Crosby (backing vocals), admired singer-songwriter John Hiatt (whose lyric titled the record) and TV host David Letterman, who asked the unknown South Carolina band on his show three times. The unpretentious effort had racked up 12 million sales by January 1996, 18 months after release, ranking it with Whitney Houston's eponymous effort and Meat Loaf's **Bat Out Of Hell** as third best-selling debut album – but no-one's sure why!

Hearts-on-sleeves, widescreen rock anthems from the South Carolina band who have seduced the same trad-values market that welcomed Counting Crows and the Crash Test Dummies. Not unpleasant at all, but a touch too obvious, perhaps? **Mojo, May 1995**

Crime Of The Century

ARTIST Supertramp RELEASE DATE November 1974 (UK)/December 1974 (US) LABEL A&M (UK & US) PRODUCER Ken Scott, Supertramp UK CHART peak/weeks 4/22 US CHART peak/weeks 38/76 TRACK LISTING School/Bloody Well Right/Hide In Your Shell/Asylum/Dreamer/Rudy/If Everyone Was Listening/Crime Of The Century PERSONNEL Richard Davies (v, k), Roger Hodgson (b, k, v), Dougie Thompson (b), Bob Benberg (d), John Anthony Helliwell (s, cl, v)

An artful compromise between the instrumental excesses of the progressive rockers and the melodic brevity of pop, Supertramp's third album cut back on the meandering interludes of its predecessors, added some hooks, and reached Number 1. In fact, with such irresistible moments as *Dreamer*, a hit single in the UK, and *Bloody Well Right*, Supertramp proved they could have their cake and eat it: retain the credibility of album bands like Yes, ELP and Co., yet be able to propel individual songs into the Top 40.

…the more I play **Crime Of The Century…** *the more I appreciate the strength of Supertramp's writing and playing abilities… Seventies rock that stems from many sources but funnels down to an almost orchestral sound that's impressive, though not pretentious.* **Fred Dellar, NME, October 1974**

Crocodiles

ARTIST Echo And The Bunnymen RELEASE DATE July 1980 (UK & US) LABEL Korova (UK)/Sire (US) PRODUCER The Chameleons, Ian Broudie UK CHART peak/weeks 17/6 US CHART peak/weeks 0/0 TRACK LISTING Going Up/Stars Are Stars/Pride/Monkeys/Crocodiles/Rescue/Villiers Terrace/Pictures On

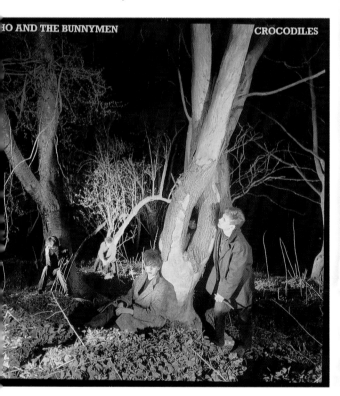

My Wall/All That Jazz/Happy Death Men **PERSONNEL Ian McCulloch (v), Will Sergeant (g), Les Pattinson (b), Pete de Freitas (d)**

Having debuted on the local Zoo label alongside rivals the Teardrop Explodes (whose singer Julian Cope had been with Ian McCulloch in the Crucial Three), Echo went national on Warners 'indie' subsidiary Korova with the Doors-influenced *Crocodiles*, re-cutting the Zoo single *Pictures On My Wall* but this time with a human drummer instead of the drum machine that gave them the first part of their name. It was a promising debut, though 1983's *Porcupine* saw them at their commercial if not creative peak.

… this crocodile is no imitation skin, and the whole is far greater than the sum of the various inputs. McCulloch's lyrical landscape is scattered with themes of sorrow, horror and despair, themes that are reinforced by stormy, animal, sexual imagery. **Adrian Thrills, NME, July 1980**

Crosby Stills And Nash

ARTIST Crosby, Stills And Nash RELEASE DATE August 1969 (UK)/June 1969 (US) LABEL Atlantic (UK & US) PRODUCER Crosby, Stills, Nash UK CHART peak/weeks 25/5 US CHART peak/weeks 6/107 TRACK LISTING Suite: Judy Blue Eyes/Marrakesh Express/Guinnevere/You Don't have To Cry/Pre-Road Downs/Wooden Ships/Lady Of The Island/Helplessly Hoping/Long Time Gone/49 Bye Byes PERSONNEL David Crosby (v, g), Stephen Stills (v, g, b, k), Graham Nash (v, g) with Dallas Taylor (d)

They brought baggage from previous unions but concocted something pertinent and new, catching the spirit of their time. Crosby had been in The Byrds, Stills in Buffalo Springfield, and Nash in The Hollies. Their harmonies gelled, their rock flickered from wispy-soft to grinding-hard. *Suite: Judy Blue Eyes*, written by Stills, was dedicated to Judy Collins, and was a groundbreaking hit, as was Nash's hippy devotional *Marrakesh Express*. Their second ever live show came at *Woodstock*, where Stills told the throng: 'We're scared shitless.'

'Our music is going in every direction that I've been able to figure out. One song comes out like Motown, one comes out like South African, one comes out like folk and one comes out like a Bulgarian harmony. There's no way I can tell in what direction we're going in… **Dave Crosby in an interview by Royston Eldridge, Melody Maker, August 1969**

The Crossing

ARTIST Big Country RELEASE DATE June 1983 (UK)/July 1983 (US) LABEL Mercury (UK & US) PRODUCER Steve Lillywhite UK CHART peak/weeks 3/80 US CHART peak/weeks 18/42 TRACK LISTING In A Big Country/Inwards/Chance/1000 Stars/The Storm/Harvest Home/Lost Patrol/Close Action/Fields Of Fire/Porrohman PERSONNEL Stuart Adamson (g, sy, v), Bruce Watson (g), Tony Butler (b), Mark Brzezicki (d)

After the demise of The Skids, few expected Scotsman Stuart Adamson's guitar-driven band to take off, for this was the era of *nouveau* synthesizer bands. Yet the single *Fields Of Fire* sounded so big and pure that Big Country were able to base a decent career on similar riffs and motifs, coloured by epic choruses and a naïve romanticization of all things Celtic – even the guitars sounded, to most, like bagpipes. They were soon outgunned by Simple Minds and U2, but the anthemic *In A Big Country* and live favourites such as *Harvest Home* successfully disguised Adamson's reedy vocals and thrilled loyal fans.

Though **The Crossing** *is far too well behaved and pretentious to steal my heart, there are sufficient adrenaline surges and inspiring thermals to keep my blood pulsing for most of its duration.* **Mat Snow, NME, July 1983**

Crown Of Creation

ARTIST Jefferson Airplane RELEASE DATE December 1968 (UK)/September 1968 (US) LABEL RCA Victor (UK & US) PRODUCER Al Schmitt UK CHART peak/weeks 0/0 US CHART peak/weeks 6/25 TRACK LISTING Lather/In Time/Triad/Star Track/Share A Little Joke/Chushingura/If You Feel/Crown Of Creation/Ice Cream Phoenix/Greasy Heart/The House At Pooneil Corners PERSONNEL Grace Slick (v), Marty Balin (v), Paul Kantner (g), Jorma Kaukonen (g), Jack Casady (b), Spencer Dryden (d)

After Bathing At Baxters had been a wild, experimental third album recorded while the band pursued all manner of hedonism in a $5000-a-month pink mansion in Hollywood – the kind of record only a group riding high could afford to release. This time there was a return to the song structures of a year previous. Most intriguing of all was the tribute *House At…* to renegade East Coast folkie Fred Neil – whose *Other Side Of This Life* was a live staple – and their rendition of *Triad*, the celebration of troilism which allegedly led to The Byrds sacking its writer, David Crosby.

Cut

ARTIST Slits RELEASE DATE September 1979 (UK & US) LABEL Island (UK)/Antilles (US) PRODUCER Dennis Bovell UK CHART peak/weeks 30/5 US CHART peak/weeks 0/0 TRACK LISTING Instant Hit/So Tough/Spend Spend Spend/Shoplifting/FM/Newtown/Ping Pong Affair/Love And Romance/Typical Girls/Adventures Close To Home PERSONNEL Ari Up (v), Vivien Albertine (g), Tessa Pollitt (b), Budgie (d, pc)

Produced by reggae-whiz Dennis Bovell and guest starring Budgie of the Banshees on drums, **Cut** was the main contribution to post punk rock by this all-girl bunch of Patti Smith devotees. From its cover (featuring the band, semi-naked and covered in mud) inwards, it exerted a tremendous influence on subsequent generations of would-be Riot Girls. **Cut** was essentially a white reggae album, Bovell bringing all manner of dub effects to bear on the trad-rock line-up. It coincided with the emergence of numerous avant-funk outfits – from Bristol's The Pop Group to Manchester's A Certain Ratio – and, with the teenage Ari Upp upfront, proved a significant step on the road to Girl Power.

They look and sound like the middle-class savages they surely were. The intricate mesh of their vocals falls somewhere between Nico, Althea, Donna and Zappa's GTO's; sometimes it shrieks, sometimes it's delicate and polite. **Q, June 1990**

Damaged

ARTIST Black Flag RELEASE DATE November 1981 (UK & US) LABEL S.S.T (UK & US) PRODUCER Black Flag UK CHART peak/weeks 0/0 US CHART peak/weeks 0/0 TRACK LISTING Rise Above/Spray Paint/Six Pack/What I See/TV Party/Thirsty And Miserable/Police Story/Gimmie Gimmie Gimmie/Depression/Room 13/Damaged II/No More/Padded Cell/Life Of Pain/Damaged I PERSONNEL Greg Ginn (g), Dez Cadena (v, g), Henry Rollins (v), Robo (d)

As hardcore as it gets, and twice as loud. Henry Rollins was both poet and pugilist, even though he had previously managed an ice-cream store. This was his debut. Over the next five years they released 23 records. Yet dumb as they tried to sound, Rollins' inquisitive intelligence kept coming to the fore. There were jokes, intentional and otherwise, rage and, of course, much much volume. Many cite the couplet 'My girlfriend asked which I liked better/I hope the answer don't upset her', from *Six Pack*, as an all-time gem.

Black Flag were at the centre of US Hardcore's initial assault on American rock and its suburban dreams. **Damaged** *was Hardcore's first great record and, in 1985, its psychotic brilliance is undiminished…*

it remains a definitive soundtrack for manic-depressive slam dancing. **Donald McRae, NME, November 1985**

Damn The Torpedoes

ARTIST Tom Petty & The Heartbreakers RELEASE DATE November 1979 (UK & US) LABEL MCA (UK)/Backstreet (US) PRODUCER Tom Petty, Jimmy Iovine UK CHART peak/weeks 57/4 US CHART peak/weeks 2/66 TRACK LISTING Refugee/Here Comes My Girl/Even The Losers/Shadow Of A Doubt (A Complex Kid)/Century City/Don't Do Me Like That/You Tell Me/What Are You Doin' In My Life?/Louisiana Rain PERSONNEL Tom Petty (lv, bv, g), Benmont Tench (p, o, hmm, v), Mike Campbell (g), Stan Lynch (d, v), Ron Blair (b)

Tom Petty's third album should have been the culmination of its two promising predecessors, shooting him into rock's first division alongside Springsteen, but ABC, parent company of Shelter, were bought by MCA: Petty objected and was sued, eventually filing for bankruptcy in a bizarre attempt to resolve matters. A compromise led to signing with MCA subsidiary Backstreet, dedicated solely to him and his group. Though this sold well, Petty would withhold his next album until MCA agreed to market it without a planned $1 price rise to $9.98: his fans, if not his label, appreciated the thought.

… what makes **Damn The Torpedos** *their best album yet isn't so much its sound… but its assurance. Mechanical rhythms are hip, but something more fluid makes better time with the flowing organ and guitar surges Petty uses so well.* **Ariel Swartley, Rolling Stone, December 1979**

Damned Damned Damned

ARTIST The Damned **RELEASE DATE** February 1977 **LABEL** Stiff **PRODUCER** Nick Lowe **UK CHART** peak/weeks 34/10 **US CHART** peak/weeks 0/0 **TRACK LISTING** Neat Neat Neat/Fan Club/I Fall/Born To Kill/Stab Yor Back/Feel The Pain/New Rose/Fish/See Her Tonite/1 Of The 2/So Messed Up/I Feel Alright **PERSONNEL** Dave Vanian (v), Brian James (g, v), Captain Sensible (b, v), Rat Scabies (d, v)

Recognized by most as the first punk album: there was no fourth chord but bags of adrenaline and scatter-gun aggression. 'Singer' Dave Vanian had been recruited on the grounds of his 'looking distinctive'; the others were regulars of the nascent punk scene, some of whom had played alongside Tony James, Mick Jones and journalist Nick Kent. Unfortunately for them The Damned were to gain a reputation as a fun, cartoon punk band. 'New Rose', on the new Stiff label, was the John The Baptist of punk rock. The album, produced with an extremely lo-fi attitude by Nick Lowe and fuelled by pills and drink as much as (ahem) political statement, was basically several versions of **New Rose**, but defined an era.

The Damned's music is as provocative as the cover that depicts them smeared with cream, jam, baked beans and other nameless gunge all over their faces. You are forced into either taking them to your heart or turning away repulsed. **Tony Parsons, NME, February 1977**

Dangerous

ARTIST Michael Jackson **RELEASE DATE** November 1991 (UK & US) **LABEL** Epic (UK & US) **PRODUCER** Michael Jackson, Bill Bottrell, Teddy Riley, Bruce Swedien **UK CHART** peak/weeks 1/96 **US CHART** peak/weeks 1/117 **TRACK LISTING** Jam/Why You Wanna Trip On Me/In The Closet/She Drives Me Wild/Remember The Time/Can't Let Her Get Away/Heal The World/Black Or White/Who Is It/Give In To Me/Will You Be There/Keep The Faith/Gone Too Soon/Dangerous **PERSONNEL** Michael Jackson (v), Slash (g, gst), Heavy D (gst), Rene Moore (gst), Jeff Porcaro (gst), David Paich (gst), session musicians

Having done much to define black music's past, Jackson showed himself with **Dangerous** intent on shaping its future. The easy option here would have been to recruit, once again, producer Quincy Jones and his entourage, and come up with an album that was effectively **Thriller** and **Bad** revisited, but Jackson knew how to spring a surprise – hence the appearance of Teddy Riley, the high priest of New Jack Swing, in the producer and writer's chair for six cuts. These tracks alone ensured the album was worthy of attention.

Dangerous *encompasses the entire range of what has come to be expected from Michael Jackson: aggression and schmaltz, paranoia and rose-tinted optimism, Godliness and megalomania, innovation and caution, the sublime and the ridiculous… Will he ever find true love and inner peace?* **Mat Snow, Q, January 1992**

Dare

ARTIST Human League **RELEASE DATE** October 1981 (UK & US) **LABEL** Virgin (UK)/A&M (US) **PRODUCER** Human League, Martin Rushent **UK CHART** peak/weeks 1/71 **US CHART** peak/weeks 3/38 **TRACK LISTING** The Things That Dreams Are Made Of/Open Your Heart/The Sound Of The Crowd/Darkness/Do Or Die/Get Carter/I Am The Law/Seconds/Love Action (I Believe In Love)/Don't You Want Me **PERSONNEL** Philip Oakley (v, sy), Ian Burden (b, Sy), Joanne Catherall (v), Susanne Sulley (v), Jo Callis (sy)

The album no-one could have expected – barely 12 months earlier Ian Craig Marsh and Martyn Ware had quit the Human League, leaving singer Phil Oakey and 'visual director' Adrian Wright with little more than the band name. Anyone else would have given up there and then, but Oakey and Wright picked themselves up, recruited two 17-year-old girls at a Sheffield disco, brought in bassist  Ian Burden and guitarist Jo Callis, and calmly went about crafting the perfect pop album of the early Eighties (which included electro-pop classics **Don't You Want Me** and **Love Action**). A worldwide Number 1 and not a duff track in sight – the perfect last laugh.

Dare *is a superb LP, blending politics and pop, glamour and statement. This is machine music that has a simple lyrical liveliness creating an LP of technology and emotion, but most of all the excitement of invention.* **Tony Stewart, NME, June 1982**

Daring Adventures

ARTIST Richard Thompson **RELEASE DATE** October 1986 (UK & US) **LABEL** Polydor (UK & US) **PRODUCER** Mitchell Froom **UK CHART** peak/weeks 1/92 **US CHART** peak/weeks 142/6 **TRACK LISTING** A Bone Through Her Nose/Valerie/Missiee How You Let Me Down/Dead Man's Handle/Long Dead Love/Lover's Lane/Nearly In Love/Jeenie/Baby Talk/Cash Down/Never Never/How Will I Ever Be Simple Again/Al Bowly's In Heaven **PERSONNEL** Richard Thompson (v, g), Mitchell Froom (o), Jerry Scheff (b), Mickey Curry (d), Jim Keltner (d), John Kirkpatrick (ad), Alex Acuna (pc)

Daring Adventures was Richard Thompson's second album for Polydor Records after a lengthy stint on Hannibal. Like its predecessor, 1983's **Across A Crowded Room**, it was a no less bitter examination of romance than his collaboration with his ex-wife, **Shoot Out The Lights**. Despite the easy tunefulness of songs like **How Will I Ever Be Simple Again?** or the simply affecting **Al Bowly's In Heaven**, Thompson had clearly lost none of his bile or bite.

No less than half the tunes are lugubrious in the extreme and shot through with the ache of his fretboard twine… One day Thomson will work out how to play fast tunes without sounding tense and bitchy. **Nick Coleman, NME, October 1986**

The Dark Side Of The Moon

ARTIST Pink Floyd RELEASE DATE March 1973 (UK&US) LABEL Harvest (UK & US) PRODUCER Pink Floyd UK CHART peak/weeks 2/310 US CHART peak/weeks 1/741 TRACK LISTING Speak To Me/Breathe/On The Run/Time/The Great Gig In The Sky/Money/Us And Them/Any Colour You Like/Brain Damage/Eclipse PERSONNEL David Gilmour (g, v), Roger Waters (b, v, pc), Richard Wright (k), Nick Mason (d, pc)

The test record of choice for hi-fi buffs in the Seventies, this was more than a lushly recorded album with ear-catching sound effects like the cash register in the intro to **Money**: it was also a Roger Waters treatise on mental illness, the things that drive people mad. The resulting concept album, previewed to the press at London's Planetarium in March 1973, was both shocking and compelling. It would re-emerge in live form, though *sans* Waters, as half of 1995's live double **Pulse** set.

The Dark Side Of The Moon *is a fine album with a textured and conceptual richness that not only invites but demands involvement. There is a certain grandeur here that exceeds mere musical melodramatics…* **Lester Bangs, Rolling Stone, May 1973**

Darklands

ARTIST Jesus And Mary Chain RELEASE DATE September 1987 (UK)/October 1987 (US) LABEL Blanco y Negro (UK)/Reprise (US) PRODUCER William Ried, Bill Price, John Loder UK CHART peak/weeks 5/7 US CHART peak/weeks 161/4 TRACK LISTING Darklands/Deep One Perfect Morning/Happy When It Rains/Down On Me/Nine Million Rainy Days/April Skies/Fall/Cherry Came Too/On The Wall/About You PERSONNEL Jim Reid (v, g), William Reid (g, v), John Moore (g), Douglas Hart (b), James Pinker (d)

The acceptance by radio and even *Top Of The Pops* of **April Skies** and **Happy When It Rains** helped the Chain's second album hit the Top 5 and prove they had overcome both the loss of percussionist Bobby Gillespie (who had returned to his job of vocalist with Primal Scream) and the split with manager Alan McGee (of Creation/Oasis fame). John Moore filled the former vacancy, but it would be three years before another proper album, and the Reids would be on their own by then.

Darklands *is a far more introverted affair than* **Psychocandy**… *with a brooding reverence that is by turns claustrophobic and exhilarating… The result is another complete mood piece that replaces the unrepeatable 'teenage' urgency of the old Mary Chain with something more staid and perhaps, more enduring.* **Mark Cooper, Q, October 1987**

Darkness On The Edge Of Town

ARTIST Bruce Springsteen RELEASE DATE June 1978 (UK & US) LABEL CBS (UK)/Columbia (US) PRODUCER Bruce Springsteen, Jon Landau UK CHART peak/weeks 16/40 US CHART peak/weeks 5/97 TRACK LISTING Badlands/Adam Raised A Cain/Something In The Night/Candy's Room/Racing In The Street/The Promised Land/Factory/Streets Of Fire/Prove It All Night/Darkness On The Edge Of Town PERSONNEL Bruce Springsteen (g, v, h), Garry Tallent (b), Max Weinberg (d), Roy Bittan (gl, bv, p, hd), Clarence Clemens (s, ts), Mike Appel (bv), Steve Van Zandt (bv), Randy Brecker (t, fh), Michael Brecker (ts), Dave Sanborn (bs), Wayne Andre (tr), Ernst 'Boom' Carter (d), Danny Federici (o), Richard Davis (b)

The flipside to **Born To Run** and its romantic perception of the American Dream, **Darkness On The Edge Of Town** dealt with the hopes and struggles of the blue-collar working classes in far bleaker terms than its predecessor. Despite the starkness and lyrical bite, there were glimpses of beauty on **Something In The Night** and **Racing In The Street**, only here they were tinged with a sadness that probably reflected the real-life difficulties Springsteen had with his management at the time.

Darkness On The Edge Of Town *walks a fine line between the outrageous claims made on Springstein's behalf and his tendency towards the grandiose, epic feel that encouraged those claims in the first place… the conquer-the-world romantic of before sounds oddly disillusioned, frustrated even.* **Paul Rambali, NME, 1978**

A Date With The Everly Brothers

ARTIST The Everly Brothers RELEASE DATE March 1961 (UK)/December 1960 (US) LABEL Warner Bros. (UK & US) PRODUCER The Everly Brothers UK CHART peak/weeks 3/14 US CHART peak/weeks 9/124 TRACK LISTING Cathy's Clown/That's Just Too Much/Stick With Me Baby/So How Come/Always It's You/Made To Love/Lucille/Love Hurts/Donna, Donna/A Change Of Heart/Baby What You Want Me To Do/Sigh, Cry, Almost Die PERSONNEL Don Everly (v, g), Phil Everly (v, g)

Second time round with Warner Brothers and the Everlys could have been rueing the fact that songwriters Felice and Boudleaux Bryant, a regular source of material in the Cadence days, were now lost to them. If so, they didn't show it, and the album equalled its predecessor's US chart position, falling one place short in Britain. But the month of release saw them up sticks, move from Nashville

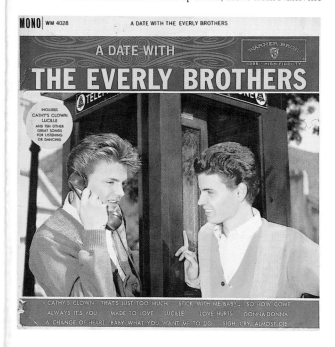

to Hollywood and – gulp! – start acting lessons. It would never get this good again.

Don and Phil Everly come on to a scene over-populated with vocal groups of all kinds, and stayed to achieve an undeniable pre-eminence. A Date With The Everly Brothers includes four numbers written by the boys… Everly fans can buy this with confidence. **Laurie Hernshaw, Melody Maker, February 1961**

Daydream Nation

ARTIST Sonic Youth RELEASE DATE October 1988 (UK & US) LABEL Blast First (UK)/Iridescene (US) PRODUCER Sonic Youth UK CHART peak/weeks 99/1 US CHART peak/weeks 0/0 TRACK LISTING Teenage Riot/Silver Rocket/ The Sprawl/'Cross The Breeze/Eric's Trip/Total Trash/Hey Joni/Providence/ Candle? / Rain King / Kissability / Trilogy: The Wonder-Hyperstation-Eliminator Jr PERSONNEL Thurston Moore (g), Kim Gordon (b, v), Lee Randaldo (g), Mike Watt (b), Steve Shelley (d)

Before Nirvana, there were Husker Du, R.E.M. and Sonic Youth at the vanguard of American rock. Guitar pioneers from the New York underground, Sonic Youth had been releasing innovative records of semi-accessible art-noise for half a decade before unleashing their masterpiece, the double LP, **Daydream Nation**. Although it had its fair share of atonal thrash-outs, there were also moments like *Teenage Riot* where the band reined in their avant-garde tendencies to create something approaching pop.

You don't have to notice the inclusion of a closing three-parter called Trilogy to realise that Sonic Youth are today's real progressive rock giants, lost in the bliss of their own creating. The avant garde has crashed into the side of punk… **Martin Aston, Q, November 1988**

Days Of Future Passed

ARTIST Moody Blues With The London Festival Orchestra Conducted By Peter Knight RELEASE DATE January 1968 (UK)/April 1968 (US) LABEL Deram (UK & US) PRODUCER Tony Clarke UK CHART peak/weeks 27/16 US CHART peak/weeks 3/106 TRACK LISTING The Day Begins/Dawn: Dawn Is A Feeling/The Morning: Another Morning/Lunch Break: Peak Hour/The Afternoon: Forever Afternoon (Tuesday)/Time To Get Away/Evening/The Sun Set: Twilight Time/The Night: Nights In White Satin PERSONNEL Denny Lane (v, g), Mike Pinder (k, v), Ray Thomas (fl, v, bv), Clint Warwick (b, v), Graham Edge (d)

This album should have been a rock version of Dvorak's 'New World Symphony'. Commissioned to show off the possibilities of then still new stereo sound, producer/arranger Peter Knight persuaded the record label to let the Moodies have their head with the orchestra: the result was a breakthrough album that turned them from R&B also-rans to symphonic-rock pioneers, selling over 150,000 copies in the US in a year and spawning the perennial hit *Nights In White Satin*. Even Dvorak might have approved…

Days Of Wine And Roses

ARTIST Andy Williams RELEASE DATE April 1963 (UK & US) LABEL CBS (UK)/Columbia (US) PRODUCER – UK CHART peak/weeks – US CHART peak/weeks 1/107 TRACK LISTING Falling In Love With Love/I Left My Heart In San Francisco/You Are My Sunshine/What Kind of Fool Am I?/When You're Smiling/Days Of Wine And Roses/It's A Most Unusual Day/My Coloring Book/Can't Get Used To Losing You/I Really Don't Want To Know/Exactly Like You/May Each Day PERSONNEL Andy Williams (v), session musicians

Andy Williams is the man in the cardigan with the golden tenor. He began as a small-time cabaret crooner in the Forties and achieved some success during the rock 'n' roll era before turning his back completely on youth-oriented pop and cashing in his chips with the chicken-in-a-basket set. A younger Perry Como, Williams' casually sung early Sixties hits such as *Can't Get Used*

To Losing You and *Moon River* remain easy-listening classics, while his choice of material has always been immaculate.

This man seems to churn out albums as often as you and I cross the road. They are all good, pure, wholesome… he's very nice, but 99 per cent of the time, he's totally predictable… **Melody Maker, July 1972**

Debut

ARTIST Björk RELEASE DATE July 1993 (UK & US) LABEL One Little Indian (UK)/Elektra (US) PRODUCER Nellee Hooper, Björk, David Arnold, Danny Cannon UK CHART peak/weeks 3/24 US CHART peak/weeks 61/31 TRACK LISTING Human Behaviour/Crying/Venus As A Boy/There's More To Life Than This/Like Someone In Love/Big Time Sensuality/One Day/Aeroplane/Come To Me/Violently Happy/The Anchor Song/Play Dead PERSONNEL Björk (v, k), Marius De Vries (k), Paul Waller (k), Marin Virgo (k), Garry Hughes (k, o), Luis Jardim (d, pc, b), Bruce Smith (d, pc), Nellee Hooper (d, pc), Jhelisa Anderson (bv), Corky Hale (hp), Jon Mallison (g), Talvin Singh (tl)

As Icelandic pop mavericks The Sugarcubes found their career stalling at the indie-favourites stage, many were of the opinion that Björk Gudmundsdottir, with her amazing rangey voice and pixie-like demeanour, should strike out on a solo career. Thankfully she did this with style and imagination. Teaming up with dance producer Nellee Hooper she succeeded in wrapping her idiosyncratic vocals around a winning blend of cutting edge techno, gregarious house, and simpler, sweeter acoustic songs. Shifting almost three million copies world-wide, Björk had, with disarming ease, become something of a user-friendly Sade for the Nineties. And this despite recording one song in a night-club toilet.

… in the relatively sparse setting of this solo album she reclaims all her old wit and jouissance. The combination of Björk's wonderfully untramelled vocals with former Soul II Soul producer Nellie Hooper's understated yet haunting grooves was surely made in heaven. **Mark Cooper, Q, July 1993**

Dedicated To You

ARTIST Five Royals **RELEASE DATE** 1957 **LABEL** – **PRODUCER** – **UK CHART peak/weeks** – **US CHART peak/weeks** - **TRACK LISTING** – **PERSONNEL** Obediah Carter, Clarence Pauling, Johnny Tanner, Johnny Moore, Lowman Pauling (v, bv)

Despite a raunchy image, the Five Royals started life as the Royal Sons Gospel Group in Winston-Salem, North Carolina, in the Forties. Moving to New York, they adopted their other name for the secular market to hide their dabbling in the Devil's Music. The album title comes from their most influential pop crossover, *Dedicated To The One I Love*, released in 1957 and reactivated four years later and would also hit for the Shirelles (1961) and the Mamas and the Papas (1967).

Deep Purple In Rock

ARTIST Deep Purple **RELEASE DATE** June 1970 (UK)/September 1970 (US) **LABEL** Harvest (UK)/Warner (US) **PRODUCER** Deep Purple **UK CHART peak/weeks** 4/68 **US CHART peak/weeks** 143/21 **TRACK LISTING** Speed King/Bloodsucker/Child In Time/Flight Of The Rat/Into The Fire/Living Wreck/Hard Lovin' Man **PERSONNEL** Ritchie Blackmore (g), Ian Gillan (v), Roger Glover (b), Jon Lord (k), Ian Paice (d)

Any band hitting the US Top 5 with their first single could be considered to be doing well – but not until Deep Purple replaced singer and bass player did they hit the creative as well as commerical heights. And after a false start with **Concerto For Group And Orchetsra**, the Ian Gillan-fronted Deep Purple Mark II laid down a hard-rock blueprint for the Seventies with this landmark album. *Speed King* and *Child In Time* added two classics to the repertoire while the simultaneous, non-album single *Black Night* hit Number 2 to confirm that orchestras were not wanted on this voyage.

… plodding along and hanging in there album after album in spite of being such quiet nonentities that they're not even good copy… if the 'Rock' in the title is meant to invoke the last 20 years' heritage, somebodies got their wires badly crossed. **Lester Bangs, Rolling Stone, December 1970**

Definitely Maybe

ARTIST Oasis **RELEASE DATE** August 1994 (UK)/February 1995 (US) **LABEL** Creation Records (UK & US) **PRODUCER** Oasis, Mark Coyle **UK CHART peak/weeks** 1/- **US CHART peak/weeks** 58/20 **TRACK LISTING** Rock 'N' Roll Star/Shaker Maker/Live Forever/Up In The Sky/Columbia/Supersonic/Bring It Down/Cigarettes And Alcohol/Digsy's Dinner/Slide Away/Married With Children/Sad Song **PERSONNEL** Liam Gallagher (v), Noel Gallagher (g, bv), Bonehead (g), Guigsy (b), Whitey (d, pc)

Recorded in no fewer than seven studios and preceded by three singles (all featured thereupon), the eagerly anticipated debut album from this Manchester quintet would become the fastest selling debut album in independent label history. It was all their own work, right down to the cover room which had been decorated by the versatile guitarist Paul 'Bonehead' Arthurs. But the stars of the show were the Gallaghers, songwriter Noel and vocalist Liam: names that would become ever more familiar in the coming months.

They're manna from heaven in a slow newspaper week: boorish, Northern, easily patronised, fluent in the quotable obscenity. Don't be put off: **Definitely Maybe** *is an outrageously exciting rock/pop album… such vigour and insouciance. A riot.* **Stuart Maconie, Q, October 1994**

Deja Vu

ARTIST Crosby, Stills, Nash & Young **RELEASE DATE** May 1970 (UK)/April 1970 (US) **LABEL** Atlantic (UK & US) **PRODUCER** David Crosby, Stephen Stills, Graham Nash, Neil Young **UK CHART peak/weeks** 25/5 **US CHART peak/weeks** 1/97 **TRACK LISTING** Carry On/Teach Your Children/Almost Cut My Hair/Helpless/Woodstock/Deja Vu/Our House/4+20/Country Girl/Everybody I Love You **PERSONNEL** David Crosby (v, g), Stephen Stills (v, g), Graham Nash (v, g), Neil Young (v, g), Dallas Taylor (pc), Gregory Reeves (b)

With Neil Young recruited to assist the overworked Stills on the musical side, CSN&Y took a heavier slant on their guitar tunes for their second album. It enjoyed advance sales of two million, with the group being perceived as America's replacement Beatles and angels of post-*Woodstock* optimism. Joni Mitchell's **Woodstock** song gave them another hit, and Crosby's enigmatic **Almost Cut My Hair** was both intimate and anthemic. 'Rejoice, rejoice, we have no choice,' opined the joyful **Carry On**. Anti-establishment and idealistic, the four could still be sentimental and cosy, as Nash's **Our House** and **Teach Your Children** betrayed. Only Young, who wrote **Helpless** and **Country Girl**, was to find a way forward from this landmark.

They've clearly been through some changes and the music here lacks some of the calm and limpid beauty of the first LP. It's heavier, tougher and funkier… And of course there's the brooding, inescapable presence of Neil Young. **A. L., Melody Maker, May 1970**

The Delfonics

ARTIST The Delfonics **RELEASE DATE** August 1970 (UK & US) **LABEL** Bell (UK & US) **PRODUCER** – **UK CHART peak/weeks** 0/0 **US CHART peak/weeks** 61/18 **TRACK LISTING** Baby I Love You/Delfonics Theme (How Could You)/Didn't I (Blow Your Mind This Time)/Dawn Is Up/Up 'N' Down/Funny Feeling I Gave To You/Over And Over/Think About Me/Trying To Make A Fool Of Me/When You Get Right Down **PERSONNEL** William Hart, Wilbert Mart, Ritchie Daniels, Randy Cain

Before there were Philadelphia International and the Stylistics, there were The Delfonics. William Hart's impassioned tenor voice was brought to the fore by Thom Bell's production skills and, aided by some lush orchestration, provided something of a blueprint that many other artists were to follow. Indeed, it was the success Bell

enjoyed with The Delfonics and, to a lesser extent, New York City, that enabled him to turn the Stylistics and Detroit Spinners into such consistent hit-makers. If Kenny Gamble and Leon Huff are regarded as having put Philadelphia on the musical map, then they owe a large debt to the groundbreaking work done by Stan Watson's Philly Groove label and The Delfonics.

old friends the Rolling Thunder Revue. **Desire** perfectly caught the tour mood and featured some of Dylan's strongest narratives: *Hurricane* explored his fascination with pugilism and was a plea to release 'wrongly convicted' boxer Ruben 'Hurricane' Carter, while *Sara* recalled life with his ex-wife as vividly as a Polaroid snapshot. Unfairly rubbished on release as a pale imitation of its predecessor **Blood On The Tracks**, **Desire** showed Dylan still capable of experimenting.

I have a feeling that this is going to be one of the difficult Dylan albums, one of those that initially get dismissed as aberrant rubbish, and then slowly draw people back to discover whole other levels beneath the crass surface of the tracks. **Mick Farren, NME, January 1976**

Delilah

ARTIST Tom Jones **RELEASE DATE** July 1968 (UK) **LABEL** Decca (UK) **PRODUCER** – **UK CHART** peak/weeks 1/29 **US CHART** peak/weeks - **TRACK LISTING** Delilah/I'm Coming Home/Things I Wanna Do/And I Tell The Sea/Key To My Heart/To Wait For Love/Where Do You Belong/The Lonely One/Smile/I've Got A Heart/Love Is A Burning Thing (Ring Of Fire)/The Rose/I Need Your Loving/I Still Love You (If You Need Me) **PERSONNEL** Tom Jones (v)

Never really an album artist, Welsh hip-swiveller Jones was nevertheless a regular in the Top 10 between 1967 and 1971, most efforts being live showcases or (as 1967's *Smash Hits*), a mish-mash of covers. This effort – still his only Number 1, barring a 1975 hits collection – deposed The Small Faces from the UK chart summit for a single week in September 1968, beating the Les Reed-penned title track by a single place.

Desire

ARTIST Bob Dylan **RELEASE DATE** January 1976 (UK & US) **LABEL** CBS (UK)/Columbia (US) **PRODUCER** Don Devito **UK CHART** peak/weeks 3/35 **US CHART** peak/weeks 1/35 **TRACK LISTING** Hurricane/Isis/Mozambique/One More Cup Of Coffee/Oh, Sister/Joey/Romance In Durango/Black Diamond Bay/Sara **PERSONNEL** Bob Dylan (v, rg, h, p), Emmylou Harris (bv), Ron Stoner (b, bv), Scarlet Rivera (vl), Howard Wyeth (d), Vincent Bell (bz), Dom Cortese (ad), Ronee Blakley (bv), Luther (cg)

Finally over his divorce, Dylan decided to have some fun with his

Desperado

ARTIST The Eagles **RELEASE DATE** April 1973 (UK)/May 1973 (US) **LABEL** Asylum (UK & US) **PRODUCER** Glyn Johns **UK CHART** peak/weeks 39/9 **US CHART** peak/weeks 41/70 **TRACK LISTING** Doolin-Dalton/Twenty One/Out Of Control/Tequilla Sunrise/Desperado/Certain Kind Of Fool/Outlaw Man/Saturday Night/Bitter Creek/Doolin-Dalton (reprise)/Desperado (reprise) **PERSONNEL** Glenn Frey (g, v), Bernie Leadon (g, v), Randy Meisner (b, v), Don Henley (d, v)

Concept albums and country-rock don't belong in the same sentence – or didn't until the Eagles hit on a cowboy setting for their second album. Recorded in London, with producer Glyn Johns, they evoked the spirit of frontier America, aided by songwriting accomplice John David Souther. The title track, though never an Eagles' single, is their most covered song, attracting everyone from Jess Roden to Linda Ronstadt, but its stately piano is far from typical of the guitar-driven sounds of *Outlaw Man* or the strum-along single *Tequila Sunrise*.

The whole country-rock movement,… was even connected to environmentalism, because it was a music that had grown in the past out of country music. It was very much connected to the earth, and everybody was wearing earthy clothes and celebrating the outdoors. **Don Henley in interview with Anthony DeCurtis, Rolling Stone, September 1990**

One of the definitive soundtracks of the Thatcher era, Sade's slick Eighties take on American blues and R&B predated the smooth soul of Simply Red and Wet Wet Wet. Formed from the ashes of the London-based Pride, Sade the group was a vehicle for Helen Folasade Adu. On the back of hits like *Your Love Is King* and *Smooth Operator*, as well as a cover of Timmy Thomas's *Why Can't We Live Together?*, **Diamond Life** earned international sales of over six million, making it the best-selling debut ever by a British female artist.

There's also a tangible rhythmic pulse on the other tracks here, and Sade's deft warm phrasing lets her glide through tasteful conga taps and sax hooks with a now chiming, now velvety style that's endlessly sure of itself. **The Year In Records 1985, Rolling Stone, December 1985**

Diamonds And Pearls

ARTIST Prince And The New Power Generation **RELEASE DATE** September 1991 (UK)/October 1991 (US) **LABEL** Paisley Park (UK & US) **PRODUCER** Prince **UK CHART** peak/weeks 2/51 **US CHART** peak/weeks 3/45 **TRACK LISTING** Thunder/Daddy Pop/Diamonds And Pearls/Cream/Strollin'/Willing And Able/Gett Off/Walk Don't Walk/Jughead/Money Don't Matter 2 Night/Push/Insatiable/Live 4 Love **PERSONNEL** Prince (v, sy) with Levi Seacer Jr. (g, v), Tommy Barbarella (k, sy), Sonny T (b, v), Rosie Gaines (v, o, sy), Michael B (d), Tony M (rap), Kirky Johnson (pc, v), Damon Dickson (pc, v)

After a brief blip (by his own high standards) with **Graffiti Bridge** it was a fine welcome back to top drawer material for **Diamonds And Pearls**. The album was preceded by the heaviest funk workout Prince could muster, **Gett Off**, and if subsequent singles were not of quite the same standard then it was merely because of the excellence of the first hit.

Diamonds and Pearls… *proves to be a modest, disappointing drizzle of commercial pop-funk songcraft. For all his commercial misfires in recent years, Prince has never stooped to sounding ordinary - until now.* **The Year In Records 1991, Rolling Stone, December 1991**

Diamond Dogs

ARTIST David Bowie **RELEASE DATE** May 1974 (UK & US) **LABEL** RCA Victor (UK & US) **PRODUCER** David Bowie **UK CHART** peak/weeks 1/17 **US CHART** peak/weeks 5/25 **TRACK LISTING** Future Legend/Diamond Dogs/Sweet Thing/Candidate/Sweet Thing (reprise)/Rebel Rebel/Rock 'n Roll With Me/We Are The Dead/1984/Big Brother/Chant Of The Ever Circling Skeletal Family **PERSONNEL** David Bowie (g, s, mln), Tony Newman (d), Aynsley Dunbar (d), Herbie Flowers (b), Mike Garson (k)

Often underrated, even by Bowie die-hards, this mixed futurism and a speed-reading of George Orwell to give birth to a dauntingly dramatic *magnum opus*. While the title song and the catchy **Rebel Rebel** relied on generic riffs and some unforgettable word play, it was on the spooky, huge ballads that Bowie sang like a god and moved mountains. The triptych of *Sweet Thing* (Parts 1 & 2) and *Candidate* was daringly structured, building to an impossibly theatrical climax. Visions of dictatorships gone bad were poetically evoked, and Bowie sang *Rock 'n' Roll With Me* with a sob in his heart. **Diamond Dogs** might have beens self-indulgent, but Bowie's talent pulled it off.

Diamond Dogs *was a strange album of transition, morbidly obsessed with encroaching decay, fascism etc…* **Dogs** *sounds rushed and scrappy, more like working notes than the fully fledged concept album it has claimed to be.* **Adam Sweeting, Melody Maker, January 1981**

Diamond Life

ARTIST Sade **RELEASE DATE** July 1984 (UK)/February 1975 (US) **LABEL** Epic (UK & US) **PRODUCER** Robin Millar **UK CHART** peak/weeks 2/98 **US CHART** peak/weeks 5/81 **TRACK LISTING** Smooth Operator/Your Love Is King/Hang On To Your Love/Frankie's First Affair/When Am I Going To Make A Living/Cherry Pie/Sally/I Will be Your Friend/Why Can't We Live Together? **PERSONNEL** Sade Adu (v) with Stuart Matthewman (g, s), Paul Denham (b), Andrew Hale (k), Paul Cook (d)

Diana

ARTIST Diana Ross **RELEASE DATE** October 1971 (UK)/April 1971 (US) **LABEL** Tamla Motown (UK & US) **PRODUCER** Bernard Edwards, Nile Rogers **UK CHART** peak/weeks 43/1 **US CHART** peak/weeks 46/15 **TRACK LISTING** Ain't No Mountain High Enough/Don't Rain On My Parade/I Love You (Call Me)/Love Story/Love You Save (Medley)/Remember Me/(They Long To Be) Close To You **PERSONNEL** Diana Ross (v), Bernard Edwards (b), Nile Rodgers (g), Alfa Anderson Barfield (bv), Michelle Cobbs (bv), Eddie Daniels (s), Raymond Jones (k), Luci Martin (bv), Bob Millikan (t), Meco Monardo (tr), Andy Schwartz (k), Tony Thompson (d), Fonzi Thornton (bv)

This highly underrated album, one of the singer's very finest in a 30-year-plus career, saw La Ross collaborate with Bernard Edwards and Nile Rodgers of Chic, the duo with the Midas touch whose uniquely elegant approach to dance had proved so chartworthy in the last few years of the Seventies. **Diana** features Edwards' fabulous basslines and Rodgers' trademark choppy guitar style on hits such as *Upside Down* (Number 1 in the US), *I'm Coming Out* and *My Old Piano*. The rhythmically divine *Tenderness*, aching *Friend*

To Friend and beautifully sparse *Now That You're Gone* make this as consistent a disco-era LP as anything by the Donna Summer/Giorgio Moroder team.

The latest LP from the former Supreme is oddly lacking lustre and impersonal for the erstwhile soul lady… Really it's slick, showy stuff aimed at the middle market, though a rocking spirit rears up through the gush now and then. **Melody Maker, April 1976**

Diesel And Dust

ARTIST Midnight Oil **RELEASE DATE** February 1988 **LABEL** CBS (UK)/Columbia (US) **PRODUCER** – **UK CHART** peak/weeks 19/16 **US CHART** peak/weeks 21/55 **TRACK LISTING** Beds Are Burning/Put Down That Weapon/ Dreamworld/Whoah/arctic World/Wara Kuma/The Dead Heart/ Bullroarer/ Sell My Soul/Sometimes **PERSONNEL** Peter Garrett (v), Martin Rotsey (g, v), Jim Moginie (g, k, v), Rob Hirst (d, v), Peter Gifford (b)

Despite competition from the likes of INXS and AC/DC, Midnight Oil broke all records with this 1987 release which went platinum in three days and shipped out more copies than any album in Australian record history. Singer Peter Garrett's lyrical obsession with domestic issues made them an unlikely international act, but the single *Beds Are Burning* was catchy enough to give them a hit in both UK and US markets. Success thereafter was sporadic, though they remained a huge domestic draw.

… a tuneful collection of chants blasted out with a rock 'n' roll fervour that is both likeable and oddly dated… the concerns remain abidingly contemporary and Midnight Oil's manner of expressing them as heartfelt as it is trapped in outmoded rock mannerisms. **Mark Cooper, Q, June 1988**

Different Class

ARTIST Pulp **RELEASE DATE** October 1995 **LABEL** Island Records **PRODUCER** Chris Thomas **UK CHART** peak/weeks 1/- **US CHART** peak/weeks - **TRACK LISTING** Mis-Shapes/Pencil Skirt/Common People/I Spy/ Disco 2000/Live Bed Show/Something Changed/Sorted For E's & Whizz/ F.E.E.L.I.N.G.C.A.L.L.E.D.L.O.V.E./ Underwear/ Monday Morning/Bar Italia **PERSONNEL** Jarvis Cocker (v, g, g, ag, mln), Russell Senior (g, vl), Candida Doyle (o, p), Steve MacKey (b), Mark Webber (g, ag, p), Nick Banks (d, pc)

In the wake of their critically acclaimed 1995 Glastonbury appearance, Pulp's **Different Class** always looked likely to succeed. This was no overnight success: the climax to a 13-year slog, **Different Class** takes a jaundiced look at a world full of losers, selecting its targets with pinpoint accuracy and going straight for the jugular. Jarvis Cocker assumes the mantle of voyeur, adulterer and social commentator to paint sordid pictures of social decay, delivering venomous judgement against a backdrop of perfectly crafted pop.

In its own twisted way, **Different Class** is one of the decade's most subversive albums.

If you've tagged Jarvis as a pervy poet and saucy sex maniac, you'll find plenty of titillating ditties on **Different Class**. *But the album title alone announces that Cocker's broadened his scope, has another axe to grind: social antagonism.* **Simon Reynolds, Melody Maker, October 1995**

Dire Straits

ARTIST Dire Straits **RELEASE DATE** June 1978 (UK)/October 1978 (US) **LABEL** Vertigo (UK)/Warner (US) **PRODUCER** Muff Winwood **UK CHART** peak/weeks 5/130 **US CHART** peak/weeks 2/41 **TRACK LISTING** Down To The Waterline/Water Of Love/Setting Me Up/Six Blade Knife/Southbound Again/Sultans Of Swing/In The Gallery/Wild West End/Lions **PERSONNEL** Mark Knopfler (g, v), John Illsley (b), Pick Withers (d), David Knopfler (g)

Local radio DJ and rock historian Charlie Gillett gave the Straits their break by playing a demo of *Sultans Of Swing* on his Sunday morning show. Record company execs were swiftly on the phone. The band committed their stage set to vinyl at the cost of £12,500, and though the original UK chart position of Number 38 was disappointing it paid back handsomely Stateside with a 41-week chart residency. Knopfler's template had been modelled on J. J. Cale, who once said 'I hope someday he covers one of my songs instead of sounding like them.'

Disintegration

ARTIST The Cure **RELEASE DATE** May 1989 (UK & US) **LABEL** Fiction-Polydor (UK)/Elektra (US) **PRODUCER** Robert Smith, Dave Allen **UK CHART** peak/weeks 3/26 **US CHART** peak/weeks 12/55 **TRACK LISTING** Plainsong/Pictures Of You/Closedown/Love Song/ Lullaby/Fascination Street/Prayers For Rain/The Same Deep Water As You/ Disintegration/Untitled **PERSONNEL** Robert Smith (v, g), Roger O'Donnell (k), Simon Galup (b), Porl Thompson (g), Borris Williams (d)

They had built and built on their sound and their incredibly loyal and large following, and this, their tenth album over 11 years, was a monument to their arch angst, ending in the divertingly spare yet tuneful *Untitled*. They had whet the palate with the incongruously sunny *Love Song* and, thanks to such occasional moments of light relief, were, perversely, beginning to make headway in America, where the previous and quite similar album **Kiss Me Kiss Me Kiss Me** had blazed a trail of sorts. *The Same Deep Water* became a fan favourite, typifying their more morbid, dreary yet compelling side.

While **Disintegration** *doesn't break new ground for the band, it successfully refines what the Cure does best. Even if his work no longer packs the shock value it once did, Smith has finally gotten things unequivocally, utterly and completely right.* **Michael Axerrad, Rolling Stone, July 1989**

Disraeli Gears

ARTIST Cream RELEASE DATE November 1967 (UK)/December 1967 (US) LABEL Reaction (UK)/Atco (US) PRODUCER Felix Pappalardi UK CHART peak/weeks 5/42 US CHART peak/weeks 4/77 TRACK LISTING Stange Brew/Sunshine Of Your Love/World Of Pain/Dance The Night Away/Blue Condition/Tales Of Brave Ulysses/SWLBRA/We're Going Wrong/Outside Woman Blues/Take It Back/Mother's Lament PERSONNEL Eric Clapton (v, g), Jack Bruce (v, b), Ginger Baker (d)

Eric Clapton had bragged, and this trio of late Sixties blues giants had worked and admired each other prior to forming this combo. Equal status was granted Bruce's singing and bass frills, Clapton's inevitable soloing, and Baker's rumbling drumming. Soon, the blues wasn't enough, and, influenced by Jimi Hendrix (to the point where Clapton unfortunately aped his hairdo), they turned psychedelic for **Disraeli Gears**. Cartoonist Martin Sharpe, of *Oz* magazine, wrote the lyrics to *Tales Of Brave Ulysses* as well as scratching together the record's sleeve. Recorded in New York, it yielded further breakout radio hits in *Strange Brew* and the now-ubiquitous *Sunshine Of Your Love.*

Diva

ARTIST Annie Lennox RELEASE DATE April 1992 (UK)/May 1992 (US) LABEL RCA (UK)/Arista (US) PRODUCER Stephen Lipson UK CHART peak/weeks 1/71 US CHART peak/weeks 23/72 TRACK LISTING Why/Walking On Broken Glass/Precious/Legend In My Living Room/Cold/Money Can't Buy It/Little Bird/Primitive/Stay By Me/The Gift/Keep Young And Beautiful PERSONNEL Annie Lennox (v, k), Stephen Lipson (g, k), Peter-John Vettese (k), Marius de Vries (k), additionally: Louis Jardim (pc), Ed Shearmur (p), Keith Leblanc (d), Doug Wimbish (b), Kenji Jammeer (g), Steve Jansen, Paul Moore (k), Dave Defries (t), Gavin Wright (vl)

It was well-nigh inevitable the former face and voice of the Eurythmics would continue to find success after going solo, and Lennox did not let anybody down by delivering a chart-topper. Nor, however, did she extend what we already knew: that she could deliver a tune with an expressionless yet pitch-perfect style. Her music was used in the soundtrack to the Demi Moore film *Striptease*, in which Mrs Bruce Willis revealed as little of herself as Lennox appeared willing to. And five years on, only one more album (of cover versions, also a Number 1) had added to the sum of human knowledge.

Lennox's first solo venture offers few radical departures from Eurythmics… **Diva***'s imagery may not be original – dark pools, melted snows, kicking down doors – but Lennox's trump card is the drama she injects, steering her usual graceful course between strength and pain.* **Ian Cranna, Q, May 1992**

The Divine Miss M

ARTIST Bette Midler RELEASE DATE March 1973 (UK)/December 1972 (US) LABEL Atlantic (UK & US) PRODUCER Joel Dorn UK CHART peak/weeks – US CHART peak/weeks 9/76 TRACK LISTING Do You Want to Dance?/Chapel of Love/Superstar/Daytime Hustler/Am I Blue/Friends/Hello In There/Leader of the Pack/Delta Dawn/Boogie Woogie Bugle Boy/Friends PERSONNEL Bette Midler (v), Melissa Manchester (bv), Barry Manilow (p), Ron Carter (b), Dick Hyman (p), Ralph MacDonald (pc), Don Arnone (g), Cissy Houston (bv), Kevin Ellman (d), William S. Fischer (arr), session musicians

The Divine Miss M *is a flawed piece of work but an exciting one… the identity surrounding her is just an extension of her burgeoning but very real art. She's a little over excited and manic on record, but she is alive and burning and hot to trot.* **Jon Landau, Rolling Stone, December 1972**

The Division Bell

ARTIST Pink Floyd RELEASE DATE April 1994 (UK & US) LABEL EMI (UK)/Columbia (US) PRODUCER Bob Ezrin & David Gilmour UK CHART peak/weeks 1/48 US CHART peak/weeks 1/51 TRACK LISTING Cluster One/What Do You Want From Me/Poles Apart/Marooned/A Great Day For Freedom/Wearing The Inside Out/Take It Back/Coming Back To Life/Keep Talking/Lost For Words/High Hopes PERSONNEL David Gilmour (g, v, b, k), Nick Mason (d, pc), Richard Wright (k, v), Jon Carin (k), Guy Pratt (b), Gary Wallis (pc), Tim Renwick (g), Dick Parry (ts), Bob Erzin (k, pc), Sam Brown (bv), Durga McBroom (bv), Carol Kenyon (bv), Jackie Sheridan (bv), Rebecca Leigh-White (bv)

The Division Bell *is a quieter, more atmospheric and contemplative Pink Floyd, with lyrics so opaque and inert one cannot hope to plumb their meaning… The album also gives off an uncomfortable whiff of old age and fraying sensibilities.* **Tom Graves, Rolling Stone, June 1994**

Dixie Chicken

ARTIST Little Feat RELEASE DATE February 1973 (UK & US) LABEL Warner Bros. (UK & US) PRODUCER Lowell George UK CHART peak/weeks 0/0 US CHART peak/weeks 0/0 TRACK LISTING Dixie Chicken/Two Trains/Roll Um Easy/On Your Way Down/Kiss It Off/Fool Yourself/Walkin All Night/Fat Man In The Bathtub/Juliette/Lafayette Railroad PERSONNEL Paul Barrere (g, v), Sam Clayton (cg), Lowell George (g, v, pc), Kenny Gradney (b), Richard Hayward (d, v), Bill Payne (k, v, sy) with additional musicians Bonnie Bramlett, Debbie Lindsey, Treet Fure, Gloria Jones, Stephanie Spurville, Bonnie Raitt

After their second album, the Feats's future looked distinctly short-term as bassist Roy Lestrada defected to Captain Beefheart & His Magic Band, and their leader fell prey to drugs. There was a mixture of songwriting contributions, even a cover of Allen Toussaint's **On Your Way Down**, but it was Lowell George's contributions as ever which were the standouts, notably the passionate *cri de coeur*, **Fat Man In The Bathtub**, an autobiographical account of his heroin problems.

I think that **Roll Um Easy** *is the tune that is most fully realised on* **Dixie Chicken**. *Dave Hutton,… had just come back from a tour and he was leaving that night for Japan. He was totally wasted, which was the perfect condition for that song.* **Lowell George in conversation with Steve Moore, Rolling Stone, August 1973**

Doc At The Radar Station

ARTIST Captain Beefheart And His Magic Band RELEASE DATE August 1980 (UK & US) LABEL Virgin (UK & US) PRODUCER Don Van Vliet UK CHART peak/weeks 0/0 US CHART peak/weeks 0/0 TRACK LISTING Hot Head/Ashtray Heart/A Carrot Is As Close As A Rabbit Gets To A Diamond/Run Paint Run Run/Sue Egypt/Brickbats/Dirty Blue Gene/Best Batch Yet/Telephone/Flavour Bud Living/Sheriff Of Hong Kong/Making Love To A Vampire With A Monkey On My Knee PERSONNEL Gary Lewis & the Playboys (g), Bruce Fowler (tr), Gary Lucas (g, fh), Captain Beefheart (g, h, v), Eric Drew Feldman (sy, b, k, ep), John French (d), Robert Pete Williams (d), John (Drumbo) French (b, g, mba, sg), session musicians

Don Van Vliet here gave up on his abortive attempts to make a commercial record and the result was his best work in a decade (some of it had been written years earlier): a kind of **Trout Mask Replica** with sane production values. Marimbas and Chinese gongs were purposefully rather than randomly thrown into the Magic Band's formula, and the wonderfully titled *Making Love To A Vampire With A Monkey On My Knee* grinded dirtily. Beefheart was soon to retire to the Mojave Desert and an extraordinarily successful career as a painter.

… country blues-derived slide guitar, bass and drum parts where the beat gets turned around in the first four bars and stays turned around… the sense of surprise and delight never wanes, since nobody else makes that sound… **Charles Shaar Murray, NME, September 1980**

Dock Of The Bay

ARTIST Otis Redding RELEASE DATE May 1968 (UK)/March 1968 (US) LABEL Stax (UK)/Volt (US) PRODUCER Steve Cropper UK CHART peak/weeks 1/15 US CHART peak/weeks 4/42 TRACK LISTING The Dock Of The Bay/Home In Your Heart/I Want To Thank You/Your One And Only Man/Nothing Can Change This Love/It's Too Late/For Your Precious Love/Keep Your Arms Around Me/Come To Me/A Woman, A Lover, A Friend/Chained And Bound/That's How Strong My Love Is PERSONNEL Steve Cropper (g), Otis Redding (v), Carla Thomas (v), Joe Arnold (ts), Sammie Coleman (t), Donald 'Duck' Dunn (b), Isaac Hayes (k), Booker T. Jones (k), Al Jackson, Jr.(d)

Otis Redding established himself as the premier soul performer of the age, releasing a series of highly acclaimed albums that had gone beyond the boundaries of traditional music to a sizeable white audience. Though we will never know the true extent of his potential, Otis remains one of the finest singers of any era, and this album encapsulates his artistry. The title track is the perfect example, mixing a variety of musical styles to produce a single of such beauty as to be timeless.

As the note says – 'Otis Redding was the best one-man campaign soul music ever had.' Here's proof… Eight of the tracks have never been on an album before so listen in at your friendly neighbourhood record store. You'll be hooked within four bars. **Melody Maker, June 1969**

Document

ARTIST R.E.M. RELEASE DATE September 1987 (UK & US) LABEL IRS (UK & US) PRODUCER Scott Litt UK CHART peak/weeks 28/3 US CHART peak/weeks 10/33 TRACK LISTING Finest Worksong/Welcome To The Occupation/Exhuming McCarthy/Disturbance At Heron House/Strange/It's The End Of The World As We Know It (And I Feel Fine)/The One I Love/Fireplace/Lightnin' Hopkins/King Of the Birds/Oddfellows Local PERSONNEL Michael Stipe (v), Peter Buck (g), Mike Mills (b), Bill Berry (d)

For a band with an unchanging line-up R.E.M. had produced four distinctively different albums before coming up with **Document**. Recorded in a new location (Nashville) with a new producer (Scott Litt), the album's tougher edge was represented by the single *It's The End Of The World As We Know It (And I Feel Fine)*; they threw the usual curve ball by covering UK avant-garde punks Wire's **Strange**. The hitherto organic growth of their following went exponential, with the album shipping 500,000 – equal to the total sales of its predecessor, **Life's Rich Pageant** – and setting them up for a major label deal.

Dog Man Star

ARTIST Suede **RELEASE DATE** October 1994 (UK & US) **LABEL** Nude-Sony (UK)/Sony (US) **PRODUCER** Ed Buller **UK CHART** peak/weeks 3/ **US CHART** peak/weeks 0/0 **TRACK LISTING** Introducing The Band/We Are The Pigs/Heroine/The Wild Ones/Daddy's Speeding/The Power/New Generation/This Hollywood Life/The 2 Of Us/Black Or Blue/The Asphalt World/Still Life **PERSONNEL** Brett Anderson (v), Bernard Butler (g, p), Matt Osman (b), Simon Gilbert (d)

The relationship between ostentatious frontman Brett Anderson and acclaimed guitarist Bernard Butler deteriorated during the recording of this, their second album, yet you could hardly tell from this seamless collection of cinematic, widescreen, symphonic rock. Suffused with a ruined romanticism, **Dog Man Star** is a concept album whose subtitle might well have been: Modern Life Is Sleazy. From *Introducing The Band* to the closing *Still Life*, Suede, boosted by strings and ambitious song structures, presented themselves as a sort of latterday Queen for bedsit miserabilists.

A lavish precious record, equal parts The Beatles, Prince and Andrew Lloyd Webber. Brett's imagination and ambition run riot, so much so that the whole fragrant confection sounds like an aesthete's riposte to the lad-rock of Blur and Co. **Writers top 50 LPs, NME, December 1984**

Doggystyle

ARTIST Snoop Doggy Dogg **RELEASE DATE** December 1993 (UK & US) **LABEL** Death Row East West (UK)/Death Row Interscope (US) **PRODUCER** Dr Dre **UK CHART** peak/weeks 38/3 **US CHART** peak/weeks 1/72 **TRACK LISTING** Bathtub/G Funk Intro/Gin And Juice/W Balls/Tha Shiznit/Domino Intro/Lodi Dodi/Murder Was The Case/Serial Killa/Who Am I (What's My Name)?/For All My Niggaz & Bitches/Ain't No Fun (If The Homies Can't Have None)/Chronic Relief Intro/Doggy Dogg World/Class Room Intro/GZ And Hustlas/Checkin'/GZ Up Hes Down/Pump Pump **PERSONNEL** Snoop Doggy Dogg (v, rap)

The first rap album ever to enter the US charts at Number 1, **Doggystyle**, the debut LP from Snoop Doggy Dogg was released amid controversy: not only did it coincide with Snoop's alleged involvement in a gangland killing, its lyrics were mired in a flippant attitude towards women that verged on misogyny. That said, **Doggystyle** was fantastically inventive: a cartoon concept produced by NWA's Dr Dre that drew on the Philly soul and Seventies funk records of Snoop's youth. G-Funk, they called it, built around slow, loping beats and menacing atmospherics worthy of a film soundtrack, over which the Doggman's louche vocals rhymed about life in the ghetto.

Dre's production can't hide Snoop's lurking paranoia. Most of Dre's hooks and nearly all his beats refuse to linger, as if the songs themselves are nervous, fearful of exposure, restless to get offscreen. **Toure, Rolling Stone, January 1994**

Don't Get Weird On Me, Babe

ARTIST Lloyd Cole **RELEASE DATE** September 1991 (UK & US) **LABEL** Polydor (UK)/Capitol (US) **PRODUCER** Lloyd Cole, Paul Hardiman, Fred Maher **UK CHART** peak/weeks 21/3 **US CHART** peak/weeks 0/0 **TRACK LISTING** Butterfly/Theme For Her/Margo's Waltz/Half Of Everything/Man Enough/What He Doesn't Know/Tell Your Sister/Weeping Wine/To The Lions/Pay For It/The One You Never Had/She's A Girl And I'm A Man **PERSONNEL** Lloyd Cole (o, b, h, p), Robert Quine (g), Matthew Sweet (b, v), Jack Johnson (g), Bashiri Johnson (pc), Paul Buckmaster (arr, con), Blair Cowan (g, p, ad, o), Fred Maher (g, pc, d), Carlos Vega (d), Leland Sklar (b), session musicians

Going solo after The Commotions' demise, Cole seemed to make all the right moves – heading to New York, working with cronies of Lou Reed and Television – but earned only the scorn of the British music press. His second album contained some beautifully polished old school songs and lyrical conceits, and tempered the showing-off with shafts of sincerity. *She's A Girl And I'm A Man* was a relatively jaunty pop gambit, but Cole couldn't convert the cynical critics.

… Lloyd Cole once again walks the fine line between self-indulgence and glossy cool… if Cole had stuck closer to home he might have had an album that, whatever the integrity of the songwriting, could have cleaned up instead of being too clean for its own good. **Jeremy Clarke, Q, October 1991**

Don't Shoot Me I'm Only The Piano Player

ARTIST Elton John **RELEASE DATE** February 1973 (UK & US) **LABEL** DJM (UK)/MCA (US) **PRODUCER** Gus Dudgeon **UK CHART** peak/weeks 1/42 **US CHART** peak/weeks 1/89 **TRACK LISTING** Daniel/Teacher I Need You/Elderberry Wine/Blues For My Baby And Me/Midnight Creeper/Have Mercy On The Criminal/I'm Going To Be A Teenage Idol/Texan Love Song/Crocodile Rock/High-Flying Bird **PERSONNEL** Elton John (p, v, k, cp), Davey Johnstone (sy, g, bv), Dee Murray (b), Nigel Olsson (d), Bernie Taupin (wor)

Having topped the US chart with **Honky Chateau,** Elton elected to stay on the album-tour treadmill to cut another album just eight months later. Fighting glandular fever, he returned to his favourite French studio to find he had only one complete song – so persuaded lyricist Bernie Taupin to send him more lyrics from the States! The first 45, **Crocodile Rock**, his first Stateside Number 1 single, paid homage to an early influence, Neil Sedaka, who, in a fascinating piece of symmetry, would be signed by Elton's Rocket records to record his own US chart-topper a few years hence.

Doolittle

ARTIST The Pixies **RELEASE DATE** April 1989 (UK)/May 1989 (US) **LABEL** 4AD (UK)/Elektra (US) **PRODUCER** Gil Norton **UK CHART** peak/weeks 8/9 **US CHART** peak/weeks 98/27 **TRACK LISTING** Debaser/Tame/Wave Of Mutilation/I Bleed/There Goes My Gun/Here Comes Your Man/Dead/Monkey Gone To Heaven/La La Love/Mr Grieves/Crakity Jones/3 Baby/Silver/Hey/Gouge Away **PERSONNEL** Black Franics (v, g), Jerry Santiago (lg), Kim Deal (b, v), Dave Lovering (d)

Picking up where they left off the previous year, Pixies' **Doolittle** is another storming set which has the ability to make the hair on the back of your neck stand on end. *Gouge Away* and *Debaser* boast memorable hooks, while the magnificent *Monkey Gone To Heaven* might have lyrics that no-one could fathom, but remained a captivating slice of vintage Pixies malevolence nonetheless. All this and *Tame*, undoubtedly the world's least appropriately titled song. Another masterpiece of psychopathic menace.

On **Doolittle**, *producer Gil Norton showcases the Pixies at their most diverse – distilling the band's sound and relying on the strong rhythm section... the emphasis on more textured production has in no way taken away from the band's intensity.* **Chris Mundy, Rolling Stone, July 1989**

The Doors

ARTIST The Doors **RELEASE DATE** March 1967 (UK)/January 1967 (US) **LABEL** Elektra (UK & US) **PRODUCER** Paul A. Rothchild **UK CHART** peak/weeks 43/12 **US CHART** peak/weeks 8/20 **TRACK LISTING** Break On Through/Soul Kitchen/The Crystal Ship/Twentieth Century Fox/Alabama Song (Whisky Song)/Light My Fire/Back Door Man/I Looked At You/End Of The Night/Take It As It Comes/The End **PERSONNEL** Jim Morrison (v), Ray Manzarek (o, p, b), Robby Krieger (g), John Densmore (d)

On a debut album chock-full of classic material were two of the Doors' greatest numbers: *Light My Fire* and *The End*. With its spiralling organ riff and pop hook, *Light My Fire* was destined to be a huge commercial single hit for them and others but, unlike most of their songs which revolved around Jim Morrison's word plays, was written mainly by the other three members. The centrepiece, the controversial 11-minute *The End*, was an ever-changing improvisational piece that has become the very foundation for the Doors' legend, full of Morrison's Oedipal poetic obsessions.

... widely thought to be the Doors' definitive album. In many ways it's also the definitive album of the era which still malingers on. Jim Morrison, the rebel in the pauper's grave with no cross or headstone or cold marble angels, epitomized the nervous malaise of America. **Julie Burchill, NME, February 1977**

Double Fantasy

ARTIST John Lennon **RELEASE DATE** November 1980 (UK)/December 1980 (US) **LABEL** Geffen (UK & US) **PRODUCER** Jack Douglas **UK CHART** peak/weeks 1/36 **US CHART** peak/weeks 1/74 **TRACK L'STING** (Just Like) Starting Over/EveryMan Has A Woman Who Loves Him/Cleanup Time/Give Me Something/I'm Losing You/I'm Moving On/Beautiful Boy (Darling Boy)/Watching The Wheels/I'm Your Angel/Dear Yoko/Beautiful Boys/Kiss Kiss Kiss/Woman/Hard Times Are Over **PERSONNEL** John Lennon (v, g), Yoko Ono (v)

As a writer of intensely personal songs, it was inevitable that Lennon's return to recording would reflect domestic bliss. Cynics said he had gone soft, but this was a celebration of his love for Yoko and Sean, which takes on a terrible poignancy in the light of his death just weeks after its release. For the first time John and Yoko recorded together, alternating contributions, further illustrating their closeness. The acerbic, militant, embittered Lennon of the past had gone for good.

Down By The Jetty

ARTIST Dr Feelgood **RELEASE DATE** December 1974 **LABEL** United Artists **PRODUCER** Vic Male **UK CHART** peak/weeks 0/0 **US CHART** peak/weeks 0/0 **TRACK LISTING** She Does It Right/Boom, Boom/The More I Give/Roxette/One Weekend/That Ain't The Way To Behave/I Don't Mind/Twenty Yards Behind/Keep It Out Of Sight/All Through The City/Cheque Book/Oyeh!/Bonie Moronie/Tequila **PERSONNEL** Wilko Johnson (lg, v), John B. Sparks (b), The Big Figure (d, v), Lee Brilleaux (lv, hp)

Some admirers of their impressive stage show have probably been disappointed by the lack of fireworks... but **Down By The Jetty** *approaches rhythm and blues at its rightest and best, and if they cut out the slack next time round, nothing will be so R&B as Doctor Feelgood.* **Phil McNeill, Let It Rock, April 1975**

The Dreamer

ARTIST Bobby Bland RELEASE DATE August 1974 (US) LABEL ABC Dunhill (US) PRODUCER Steve Barri UK CHART peak/weeks – US CHART peak/weeks 172/7 TRACK LISTING Ain't No Love In The Heart Of The City/I Wouldn't Treat A Dog (The Way You Treated Me)/Lovin' On Borrowed Time/When You Come To The End Of Your Road/I Ain't Gonna Be The First To Cry/Dreamer/Yolanda/Twenty-Four Hour Blues/Cold Day In Hell/Who's Foolin' Who PERSONNEL Bobby 'Blue' Bland (v), Larry Carlton (g), Ginger Blake (bv), B.B. King (g, v), Michael Omartian (o, p, con, arr, k, ctte), Sid Sharp (st), session musicians

Bland's career revived in the early Seventies with a new band leader in Mel Jackson and producer in Steve Barri. He followed the exquisite **California Album** – which included *It's Not The Spotlight* and *If Loving You Is Wrong* – with this sophisticated, soft-rock influenced set. Absurdly enough, Brit heavy-belters Whitesnake were to later interpret his *Ain't No Love In The Heart Of The City* with surprising sensitivity. A lack of commercial success saw his label teaming him up with his hero B.B. King for some minor works, but Bland, despite his name, had authoritative gravitas and a soulful delivery.

… the real star of **Dreamer** *is the voice of Robert Calvin Bland…. He has the ability to involve himself totally, and the gift to sound involved - share it with him.* **Bob Fisher, NME, November 1974**

A Drop Of The Hard Stuff

ARTIST The Dubliners RELEASE DATE May 1967 LABEL Major Minor PRODUCER – UK CHART peak/weeks 5/41 US CHART peak/weeks 0/0 TRACK LISTING – PERSONNEL Ronnie Drew, Barry MacKenna, Luke Kelly, John Sheahan, Ciaran Bourke

With the exception of the ever smiling Bachelors, the Dubliners (founded in 1963 by singer Ronnie Drew) single-handedly flew the flag for Irish music in the UK charts in the Sixties. They enjoyed three hit singles between May and October of 1967, most notable of which is *Seven Drunken Nights*, and this album, released on the independent Major Minor label, was their long-playing counterpart. The patronage of the Pogues, with whom they would enjoy chart success in the Eighties, was well deserved, for the Dubliners offered a different, rootsy perspective in an era when pop and rock was peace and love.

More than anything, the Dubliners sounded dangerous. They sang about whoring, guns, liquor and fist-fights – a rabid endorsement of Brendan Behan's rebel howl… [they] re-discovered the fierce qualities of urban (seaport) balladry, performing with a stout-swigging gut bucket zest that's defined them ever since. **Stuart Bailie, NME, June 1990**

Drums And Wires

ARTIST XTC RELEASE DATE August 1979 (UK)/January 1980 (US) LABEL Virgin (UK & US) PRODUCER Steve Lillywhite UK CHART peak/weeks 34/7 US CHART peak/weeks 176/8 TRACK LISTING Making Plans For Nigel/Helicopter/Life Begins At The Hop/When You're Near Me I Have Difficulty/Ten Feet Tall/Roads Girdle The Globe/Reel By Reel/Millions/That Is The Way/Outside World/Scissor Man/Complicated Game PERSONNEL Andy Partridge (v, g), Dave Gregory (sy, g), Colin Moulding (b, v), Terry Chambers (d)

Britain's own Talking Heads, XTC (formerly the Helium Kidz, Swindon's answer to the glam-trash rock of The New York Dolls) were the brainy kids at the front of the New Wave class, producing album after album of herky-jerky rhythms and lyrics that recoiled with a blend of sardonic detachment and horror from the modern whirl. **Drums And Wires**, XTC's third album, actually saw the band calm down the frenetic pace, achieving a sort of manic

control on the hit single *Making Plans For Nigel*.

Stealthily, XTC have plotted and laboured and produced an album that has an almost uncontrollably smug grin of confidence in its own resounding power and confounding cleverness …. With a mix of complexity, contrast, fluency and humour … XTC have broken cover, and broken ground. **John Orme, Melody Maker, August 1979**

Dry

ARTIST P. J. Harvey RELEASE DATE March 1992 LABEL Too Pure PRODUCER Head, Harvey, Ellis, Vernon UK CHART peak/weeks 11/5 US CHART peak/weeks - TRACK LISTING Oh My Lover/O Stella/Dress/Victory/Happy And Bleeding/Sheela-Na-Gig/Hair/Joe/Plants And Rags/Fountain/Water PERSONNEL P J Harvey (v, g, vl), StephenVaughan (b), Robert Ellis (d, v, h)

Dorset-born Polly Jean Harvey exploded on to the scene in 1992 on the Too Pure label, hitherto more famous for Stereolab, with this album by the band that bore her name. Initial copies included a limited edition album of demos, **Demonstration**, which like its parent showcased an uncompromising singer-songwriter whose extreme vocals, blunt lyrics and violent guitar style inspired love or hate in equal measure. Island Records picked her up and she was soon supporting U2 and playing the Brits with the equally wacky Björk, but this remains one of the era's most extreme albums.

There's an undeniable electricity to **Dry**, *the band's debut. These musical primitives make exciting use of dynamics and twisted arrangements. As a front woman, Harvey commands attention: she cunningly mixes sensuality and feminist awareness in conversational hooks.* **Mark Coleman, Rolling Stone, December 1992**

Dry And Heavy

ARTIST Burning Spear RELEASE DATE 1977 LABEL Mango PRODUCER Winston Rodney, Don Taylor UK CHART peak/weeks – US CHART peak/weeks – TRACK LISTING Any River/Sun, The/It's A Long Way Around/I W.I.N./Throw Down Your Arms/Dry & Heavy/Wailing/Black Disciples/Shout It Out PERSONNEL Richard Hall (s), Marquis (as), Aston Barrett (b, pc), Bobby Ellis (t), Angus Gaye (d), Vin Gordon (tr), Bernard Touter Harvey (k), Roots Kinsley (g), Earl Lindo (k), Willie Lindo (k),Winston Rodney (pc, v, arr), Earl 'Chinna' Smith (g)

Winston Rodney spins what was once called his 'mantra-like vocal web' over some of the tightest reggae known to man. On tracks such as *Any River* and the irresistible *Throw Down Your Arms* he is a force of nature. His musicians are on peak form, as you would expect from Robbie Shakespeare, and as you would at least hope for from men with nicknames like Chinna, Wire, Family Man, Dirty Harry and – this is my favourite – Horsemouth (the drummer, Leroy Wallace). There's message in their madness, and limitless allure to their grooves.

Burning Spear's music was born less in the grisly slums of Kingston

than in the dazzling panoramas of rural Jamaica. Likewise his songs are concerned less with any passing street youth fads than with the timeless quandaries of the soul. **Neil Spencer, NME, August 1977**

Dub Housing

ARTIST Pere Ubu **RELEASE DATE** November 1978 (UK & US) **LABEL** Chrysalis (UK & US) **PRODUCER** Pere Ubu, Kenneth Hamann **UK CHART** peak/weeks 0/0 **US CHART** peak/weeks 0/0 **TRACK LISTING** Codex/Blow Daddyo/Dub Housing/Cagliari's Mirror/Navvy/Spodyody/Pa/Ubu Dance Party/On The Surface/Thriller/I Will Wait/Goodbye **PERSONNEL** David Thomas (v), Tom Herman (g, b), R.Scott Krauss (d), Tony Maimone (b, p), Allen Ravenstine (sy), Thomas Laughner (g)

Recorded and released the same year as the band's astonishing debut, **Dub Housing** caught them on a roll both at home and in Europe where they toured with the Human League and Red Krayola singer, David Thomas now rechristened Crocus Behemoth! Packaged in anti-artwork (photos of the band were banned, for example, because they 'had no business being in close proximity to art'), the group took its name from the 'echo-like terraced housing of the streets of Baltimore'. Dark, fractured and almost impenetrable, this proved to be the last true creative gasp of the original band: subsequent albums were paler imitations and they split for the first time in 1983.

Dub Housing doesn't articulate. That's left to your listening, and what you're listening to is mostly an approximation of the moment's activity between apprehension and articulation… considered with the first album, **The Modern Dance**, *Dub Housing is more baffling, instrumental, banal and intimate, but less coherent.* **Ian Pennman, NME, November 1978**

Duke

ARTIST Genesis **RELEASE DATE** April 1980 (UK & US) **LABEL** Charisma (UK)Atlantic (US) **PRODUCER** Davis Hentschel, Genesis, assisted by Dave Bascombe **UK CHART** peak/weeks 1/30 **US CHART** peak/weeks 11/31 **TRACK LISTING** Behind The Lines/Duchess/Guide Vocal/Man Of Our Times/Misunderstanding/Heathaze/Turn It On Again/Alone Tonight/Cul-De-Sac/Please Don't Ask/Duke's Travels/Duke's End **PERSONNEL** Tony Banks (k, bv, g), Mike Rutherford (b, g, bv), Phil Collins (d, dm, v)

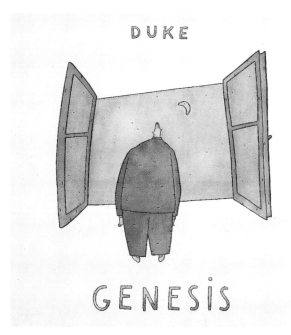

With extra-curricular recording projects, part-time bands, marriage problems and a two-year gap between albums, few would have guessed that **Duke** would be Genesis's first UK chart-topping album, let alone their second US gold record. Recorded at Abba's Polar Studio, it mirrored the Eurovision hit-makers by including a clutch of possible singles: Britain preferred the throbbing *Turn It On Again*, America the smoother *Misunderstanding*. By the following year they had the formula off pat and, with Collins's parallel solo career well-advanced, the Transatlantic charts began to look alike.

Foolishly they don't play to their strengths, choosing instead to showcase a set of appallingly trite songs, attributed to individual trio members…. Vocalist Phil Collins is hard put to instill some passion. **Chris Bohn, Melody Maker, March 1980**

Dummy

ARTIST Portishead **RELEASE DATE** August 1994 (UK)/January 1995 (US) **LABEL** Go Beat (UK)/Chrysalis (US) **PRODUCER** Portishead **UK CHART** peak/weeks 3/70 **US CHART** peak/weeks 79/17 **TRACK LISTING** Mysterons/Sour Times/Strangers/It Could Be Sweet/Wandering Star/Numb/Roads/Pedestal/Biscuit/Glory Box **PERSONNEL** Beth Gibbons (v), Geoff Barlow (sy), Adrian Utley (g), Clive Deamer (d), Dave McDonald (fl), Richard Newell (d), Neil Solman (sy, o), Andy Hague (t)

The debut album of the Nineties this groundbreaking record put trip-hop on the map in a big way, and the 1995 Mercury Music Prize was the icing on the cake. Singer Gibbons and mainman Barrow, whose home town near Bristol named the band, combined vocal emotion with musical elements like sampling, scratching, Hammond organ and reverb guitar that evoked Sixties film soundtracks. Back to the future might have been the motto… and it would take them three years to produce a follow-up.

The singer's frail, wounded sparrow vocals and Barrow's mastery of jazz-sensitive soul – hip-hop grooves and the almost forgotten art of scratching are an enthralling combination, and if Portishead tend to dwell within some groove, it's easy to forgive them. **Martin Aston, Q, October 1994**

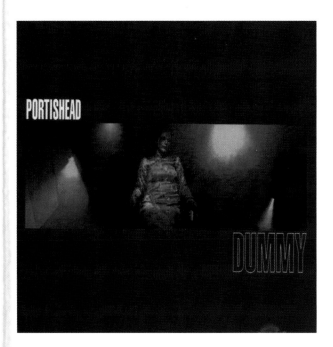

Dusty In Memphis

ARTIST Dusty Springfield **RELEASE DATE** April 1969 (UK)/March 1969 (US) **LABEL** Atlantic (UK & US) **PRODUCER** Jerry Wexler, Tom Dowd, Arif Mardin **UK CHART** peak/weeks 0/0 **US CHART** peak/weeks 99/14 **TRACK LISTING** Just A Little Lovin'/So Much Love/Son Of A Preacher Man/I Don't Want To Hear It Anymore/Don't Forget About Me/Breakfast In Bed/Just One Smile/The Windmills Of Your Mind/In The Land Of Make Believe/No Easy Way Down/I Can't Make It Alone **PERSONNEL** Dusty Springfield (v), Gene Chrisman (d), Reggie Young (g, st), Tommy Cogbill (b), Bobby Emmons (o, ep), Bobby Wood (p), The Sweet Inspirations (bv)

A white-soul landmark, **Dusty In Memphis** was recorded at the legendary Stax studios with the holy triumvirate of gritty R&B producers Tom Dowd, Arif Mardin and Jerry Wexler. The album does not just showcase Dusty Springfield's flexible, soulful voice, it also evinces her immaculate taste in songwriters. With tunes courtesy of the celebrated Goffin-King, Mann-Weill and Bacharach-David partnerships, as well as by Randy Newman, **Dusty In Memphis** is varied yet coheres superbly as an album of mature, melancholy pop.

Most of the songs … have a great deal of depth while presenting extremely direct and simple statements…. Dusty sings around her material, creating music that's evocative rather than overwhelming. Listening to this album will not change our life, but it'll add to it. **Greil Marcus, Rolling Stone, November 1969**

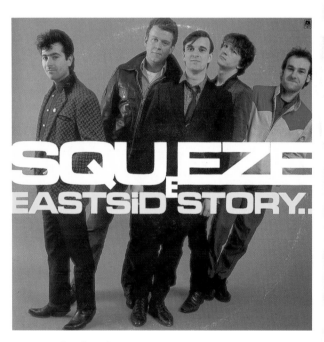

East Side Story

ARTIST Squeeze **RELEASE DATE** May 1981 (UK & US) **LABEL** A&M (UK & US) **PRODUCER** Roger Bechirian, Elvis Costello, Dave Edmunds **UK CHART** peak/weeks 19/26 **US CHART** peak/weeks 44/25 **TRACK LISTING** In Quintessence/Someone Else's Heart/Tempted/Piccadilly/There's No Tomorrow/Heaven/Woman's World/Is That Love/F-Hole/Labelled With Love/Someone Else's Bell/Mumbo Jumbo/Vanity Fair/Messed Around **PERSONNEL** Chris Difford (g, v), Glenn Tilbrook (g, v), Gilson Lavis (d), John Bentley (b, bv), Paul Carrack (k, v)

The album that marked out Glenn Tilbrook and Chris Difford as the Lennon & McCartney of New Wave British rock, **East Side Story** – co-produced by Elvis Costello, that other master of kitchen-sink vignettes – was the album that proved Squeeze were more than mere peddlers of the quirky novelty pop of their early hits, *Cool For Cats* and *Up The Junction*. From the country-tinged

Labelled With Love to *Tempted* – penned and sung by Paul Carrack of Ace, whose *How Long* was a blueprint for this kind of blue-eyed soul – Squeeze were now exhibiting a maturity of sound and vision that placed them well ahead of the competition.

Eat A Peach

ARTIST The Allman Brothers Band **RELEASE DATE** February 1972 (UK & US) **LABEL** Capricorn (UK & US) **PRODUCER** Tom Dowd **UK CHART** peak/weeks 0/0 **US CHART** peak/weeks 4/48 **TRACK LISTING** Ain't Wastin' Time No More/Les Brers In A Minor/Melissa/Mountain Jam/One Way Out/Trouble No More/Stand Back/Blue Sky/Little Martha/Mountain Jam Cont'd. **PERSONNEL** Duane Allman (g), Gregg Allman (k, v, g), Dicky Betts (g, v), Berry Oakley (b), Butch Trucks (d), Jaimoe Johanson (d)

By now wallowing in drugs and groupies and struggling to get over the deaths of Duane Allman and bassist Berry Oakley, Greg Allman managed to compile this stop gap of new and live (from Fillmore) tracks featuring Duane's gone-forever guitar. His tribute to Donovan, **Mountain Jam**, was of epic, possibly indulgent, length (45 minutes). Sonny Boy Williamson's **One Way Out** was covered with due respect. Given the rock-casualty lore surrounding the band name at this time, it's a miracle they produced any record, let alone one that's entered the canon.

The Allman Brothers are still the best goddamned band in the land… how many groups can you think of who really make you believe they're playing for the joy of it? **Tony Glover, Rolling Stone, April 1972**

Eat To The Beat

ARTIST Blondie **RELEASE DATE** October 1979 (UK & US) **LABEL** Chrysalis (UK & US) **PRODUCER** Mike Chapman **UK CHART** peak/weeks 1/38 **US CHART** peak/weeks 17/51 **TRACK LISTING** Dreaming/The Hardest Part/Union City Blue/Shayla/Eat To The Beat/Accidents Never Happen/Die Young Stay Pretty/Slow Motion/Atomic/Sound-A-Sleep/Victor/Living In The Real World **PERSONNEL** Jimmy Destri (k), Frank Infante (g), Chris Stein (g), Nigel Harrison (b), Clem Burke (d), Deborah Harry (v), Lorna Luft (v), Donna Destri (v)

Arguably even more vibrant than **Parallel Lines**, this arrived with a pioneering multi-video accompaniment that saw Debbie Harry both exploiting and subverting her niche as the world's most desirable woman. She was already dabbling in film acting. Yet *Atomic*, with sparkling bassline, all but outdid *Heart Of Glass*,

while *Dreaming* roared, with Burke at his hyperactive best, and *Union City Blue* felt like a warm wave crashing over your head. Pretensions to high art and health problems were soon to scupper the Blondie phenomenon, but right here they were gorged on pop and thoroughly gorgeous.

The components are similar – an ever increasing facility with pop forms, a couple of harder rock songs, and a very minor element of experimentation – but this is, at the very least, Blondie's most consistent album. **Chris Brazier, Melody Maker, September 1979**

Elastica

ARTIST Elastica **RELEASE DATE** March 1995 (UK)/April 1995 (US) **LABEL** Deceptive Records (UK)/Geffen (US) **PRODUCER** Marc Waterman, Elastica **UK CHART** peak/weeks 1/- **US CHART** peak/weeks 66/27 **TRACK LISTING** Line Up/Annie/Connection/Car Song/Smile/Hold Me Now/S.O.F.T./Indian Song/Blue/All-Nighter/Waking Up/2:1/Vaseline/Never Here/Stutter **PERSONNEL** Justine Frischmann (v, g), Donna Matthews (v, g), Annie Holland (b), Justin Welch (d)

Recruiting her band via the *Melody Maker* wanted ads, Justine Frischmann fused them into a streamlined outfit which pinched the best bits of classic punk and turned them into a cool, brash sardonic take on the Nineties. Guilty at times of plagiarism, and often accused of employing sound bites in favour of proper songs, **Elastica** nonetheless proved enormously popular, and well-publicized royalty payments to bands like Wire and The Stranglers did the band's reputation absolutely no harm.

'We're not writing songs for Women or things women might feel,' says Frischmann, glancing at Matthews and grimacing. 'We try not to marginalize ourselves. You have a different set of problems if you're a woman with an instrument, but they're not necessarily greater – just different.' **From an interview with Kara Manning, Rolling Stone, May 1995**

Electric Ladyland

ARTIST The Jimi Hendrix Experience **RELEASE DATE** November 1968 (UK)/October 1968 (US) **LABEL** Track (UK)/Reprise (US) **PRODUCER** Jimi Hendrix **UK CHART** peak/weeks 6/12 **US CHART** peak/weeks 1/37 **TRACK LISTING** And The Gods Made Love/Electric Ladyland/Crosstown Traffic/Voodoo Chile/Little Miss Strange/Long Hot Summer Night/Come On/Gipsy Eyes/Burning Of The Midnight Lamp/Rainy Day, Dream Away/1983 (A Merman I Should Turn To Be)/Moon, Turn The Tides...Gently Gently Away/Still Raining Still Dreaming/House Burning Down/All Along The Watchtower/Voodoo Chile (Slight Return) **PERSONNEL** Jimi Hendrix (v, lg), Noel Redding (b), Mitch Mitchell (d)

The Experience's last album together marked the end of Hendrix's golden period. The limitations of working as a trio were beginning to restrict him severely and as a result **Electric Ladyland** featured collaborations with most of Traffic and the Airplane's Jack Cassidy to name but two, as well as with Mitch Mitchell and Noel Redding. His most experimental work, it also showcased his interpretative skills, as *All Along The Watchtower* proved – a song that became wholly Jimi's rather than Bob Dylan's. With the Experience at an end, Jimi never again achieved the focused charge of the early days.

Electric Music For Mind And Body

ARTIST Country Joe McDonald (And The Fish) **RELEASE DATE** October 1967 (UK)/April 1967 (US) **LABEL** Fontana (UK)/Vanguard (US) **PRODUCER** Samuel B. Charters **UK CHART** peak/weeks 0/0 **US CHART** peak/weeks 39/38 **TRACK LISTING** Flying High/Not So Sweet Martha Lorraine/Death Sound Blues/Porpoise Mouth/Section 43/Superbird/Sad And Lonely Times/Love/Bass Strings/The Masked Marauder/Grace **PERSONNEL** Country Joe McDonald (v, g), Barry 'The Fish' Melton (g, v), Carl Shrager (wa), Bill Steel (b), Mike Beardside (hp, v), Bruce Barthol (b, h), Gary Hirsh (d), Dave Cohen (o, k, g)

Far from being just haze of a marijuana-smoke agit-prop, Country Joe & The Fish's debut album conveyed the rainbow-hued, incense-soaked atmosphere of the Bay Area LSD scene better than any. It pretty much defined the concept of acid rock, moving from dreamy, spooky psychedelic instrumentals to surreal ballads and back via erotic love songs to blues, and even boasted a paean to the Airplane's Grace Slick. As a result the band took *Woodstock* by storm. They couldn't maintain the high standards of this debut, but it still lives up to its title.

*Joe has a weird voice: strained but distinctive. And Mr. McDonald also wrote all the songs here except **Love**, a group composition. It's blues based, but it can also be very pretty, gentle and psychedelic. 'Acid Rock' is the general description.* **Melody Maker, December 1967**

Electric Warrior

ARTIST T. Rex **RELEASE DATE** September 1971 **LABEL** Fly-Emi **PRODUCER** - **UK CHART** peak/weeks 1/44 **US CHART** peak/weeks 32/ **TRACK LISTING** Mambo Sun/Cosmic Dancer/Jeepster/Monolith/Lean Woman Blues/Get It On/Planet Queen/Girl/The Motivator/Life's A Gas/Rip Off **PERSONNEL** Marc Bolan (g, v), Mickey Finn (pc, v), Steve Curry (b), Bill Legend (d)

In one of the most radical metamorphoses in pop history Marc Bolan transformed from trippy-dippy folk hippy to glam-rock guru of raunch 'n' roll within a couple of years. **Electric Warrior**, the second T. Rex album after the switch from the cosmic mumbo jumbo of Tyrannosaurus Rex, saw Bolan at the height of his powers, ushering in the glitter era with hit singles like *Jeepster* and *Get It On*, crude bursts of three-minute R&B perfection.

Marc Bolan and friends seem to be causing a great deal of confusion and upset lately. 'Boo, rubbish', is the cry, which is a shame because Marc's music is getting better all the time…. It's not exactly rock and roll, but New York juvenile delinquency, hub-cap stealing rumble music. **Melody Maker, September 1971**

Element Of Light

ARTIST Robyn Hitchcock And The Egyptians **RELEASE DATE** September 1986 (UK & US) **LABEL** Glass Fish Records (UK & US) **PRODUCER** Robyn Hitchcock, Andy Metcalfe **UK CHART** peak/weeks – **US CHART** peak/weeks 0/0 **TRACK LISTING** If You Were A Priest/Winchester/Somewhere Apart/Ted, Woody And Junior/The President/Raymond Chandler Evening/Bass/Airscape/Never Stop Bleeding/Lady Waters & The Hooded One **PERSONNEL** Robyn Hitchcock (b, g, p, v), Andy Metcalfe (b, pc, p, d, bv), Morris Windsor (g, pc, d, bv), Chris Cox (b, pc, t), James Fletcher (s), Roger Jackson (o, ep, bv, h)

Until R.E.M. took an interest, it seemed doubtful that former Soft Boy Robyn Hitchcock would make any kind of breakthrough. The band from Athens, Georgia, sang his praises on their first tour of Europe, and sure enough he soon became a hit on US college radio, many believing him to be the reincarnation of the late John Lennon. Backed mainly by ex-Soft Boys Andy Metcalfe and Morris Windsor, this proved to be Robyn's strongest collection of tunes: from the *noir* sensibility of **Raymond Chandler Evening** to the traditional folk pastiche of **Lady Waters** and on to the celebration of his old-school town, **Winchester**. He has since enjoyed major label if not major chart appeal.

Eli And The Thirteenth Confession

ARTIST Laura Nyro **RELEASE DATE** August 1968 (UK & US) **LABEL** C.B.S (UK)/Columbia (US) **PRODUCER** Charlie Calello, Laura Nyro **UK CHART** peak/weeks 0/0 **US CHART** peak/weeks 181/7 **TRACK LISTING** Luckie/Lu/Sweet Blindness/Poverty Train/Lonely Women/Eli's Comin'/Timer/Stoned Soul Picnic/Emmie/Woman's Blues/Once It Was Alright Now (Farmer Joe)/December's Boudoir/The Confession **PERSONNEL** Laura Nyro (v, p)

After debuting on Verve in 1966 while still a teenage prodigy with **More Than A New Discovery**, Laura Nyro's Columbia Records debut two years later was hailed by *Rolling Stone* as 'the work of an original and brilliant young talent'. Originally intended for Verve release as 'Soul Picnic' but held over, it included songs covered by Three Dog Night (**Eli's Comin'**), the Fifth Dimension (**Stoned Soul Picnic**), and more. What was even more impressive, she co-produced the whole thing.

A good first album from Laura Nyro, who not only sings well but writes all of her own material, mainly in the soul idiom. A young lady with great potential. **Melody Maker, September 1968**

Eliminator

ARTIST ZZ Top **RELEASE DATE** June 1983 (UK)/April 1983 (US) **LABEL** Warner Bros. (UK & US) **PRODUCER** Bill Ham **UK CHART** peak/weeks 3/135 **US CHART** peak/weeks 9/183 **TRACK LISTING** Gimmie All Your Lovin'/Got Me Under Pressure/Sharp Dressed Man/I Need You Tonight/I Got The Six/Legs/Thug/TV Dinners/Dirty Dog/If I Could Only Flag Her Down/Bad Girl **PERSONNEL** Billy Gibbons (g, v), Dusty Hill (b, v), Frank Beard (d)

A blues-rock trio from Texas, ZZ Top emerged in the early Seventies as bearded, semi-jokey exponents of swamp boogie. By the Eighties, they could so easily have become irrelevant. And yet with their ninth album, **Eliminator**, Billy Gibbons (guitar), Dusty Hill (bass) and Frank Beard (drums) did the unthinkable for a southern-bar band: drafted in some synthesizers. And so it was that, with gigantic hits such as **Legs**, **Sharp Dressed Man** and **Gimme All Your Lovin'** aided and abetted by some state-of-the-sexist-art videos, heavily rotated by the then new MTV, ZZ Top reinvented themselves as America's premier synth-boogie outfit.

The monumentally unfashionable Texas trio released its ninth album in March 1983 but continued pulling hits off it all through 1984… ZZ's ascendancy is a triumph of style over fashion, but this LP stands on its own as one of the great crunch-rock records of recent years. **The year in music and entertainment 1984, Rolling Stone, 1984**

Elite Hotel

ARTIST Emmylou Harris **RELEASE DATE** February 1976 (UK)/January 1976 (US) **LABEL** Reprise (UK & US) **PRODUCER** Brian Ahern **UK CHART** peak/weeks 17/11 **US CHART** peak/weeks 25/23 **TRACK LISTING** Amarillo/Together Again/Feelin' Single-Seeing Double/Sin City/One Of These Days/Till I Gain Control Again/Here There And Everywhere/Ooh Las Vegas/Sweet Dreams/Jambalaya/Satan's Jewel Crown/Wheels **PERSONNEL** Emmylou Harris (v) with James Burton (g), John Ware (d), Emory Gordy (b, v), Brian Ahern (g), Glen D Hardin (p), Hank deVito (ps), Micky Raphael (h), Herb Pederson (bj, v), Ron Tutt (d), Amos Garrett (g), Byron Berline (fd) Ben Keith (ps), Mike Auldridge (db), Rodney Crowel (g, v), Bill Payne (p), additional vocals - Linda Ronstadt, Dianne Brooks, Fayssoux Starling, Bernie Leadon, John Starling, Jonathon Edwards

Having opened her solo account respectably with **Pieces Of The Sky**, Harris cast off the shadow of singing partner the late Gram

Parsons with her second effort (actually her third: a debut on Jubilee in 1969, **Gliding Bird**, having been forgotten) which proved her US Top 30 debut. It also gave her an invite to *The Last Waltz*, representing The Band's country roots, while a cover of the familiar Beatles classic *Here There And Everywhere* helped her into the UK charts. With cameos on Dylan's **Desire** and Linda Ronstadt's **Prisoner In Disguise**, 1976 was a good year.

Emmylou's second solo album, is conclusive proof of her maturity and sophistication. It is also a masterpiece of contemporary country music. The album has been meticulously conceived, produced and arranged, and is performed with honesty and conviction. **A.J., Melody Maker, January 1976**

Elton John

ARTIST Elton John RELEASE DATE April 1970 (UK)/September 1970 (US) LABEL DJM (UK)/Uni - MCA (US) PRODUCER Gus Dudgeon UK CHART peak/weeks 11/14 US CHART peak/weeks 4/51 TRACK LISTING Your Song/I Need You To Turn To/Take Me To The Pilot/No Shoestrings On Louise/First Episode At Hienton/Sixty Years On/Border Song/The Greatest Discovery/The Cage/The King Must Die PERSONNEL Elton John (v, p, hd), Madeline Bell (bv), Leslie Duncan (bv), Kay Garner (bv), Tony Burrows (bv), Tony Hazzard (bv), Roger Cook (bv), Barry Morgan (d), Dave Richmond (b), Frank Clark (ag), Colin Green (g), Clive Hicks (g), Roland Barker (g), Skaila Kanga (hp), Alan Weighll (b), Caleb Quaye (lg), Alan Parker (rg), Dennis Lopez (pc), Diana Lewis (sy), Brian Dee (o), Colin Green (g),Terry Cox (d), Paul Buckmaster (c), Tex Navarra (pc), Les Hurdie (b)

Eponymous albums are often a statement of intent and Elton's second effort certainly confirmed him as a Stateside star. It sold a quarter of a million in its first six months on sale, while a Los Angeles showcase included Graham Nash, the Beach Boys and Leon Russell in the audience. Ace in the hole was **Your Song**, one of his favourite compositions.

The major problem with **Elton John** *is that one has to wade through so damn much fluff to get to Elton John… choirs and moogs and strings threaten to obscure Elton's voice and piano… he'll delight you senseless despite it all.* **John Mendelsohn, Rolling Stone, November 1970**

Elvis' Christmas Album

ARTIST Elvis Presley RELEASE DATE November 1957 (UK & US) LABEL RCA (UK & US) PRODUCER – UK CHART peak/weeks - (when re-issued in 1971, hit UK No 7) US CHART peak/weeks 1/7 TRACK LISTING Santa Claus Is Coming To Town/White Christmas/Precious Lord It Is No Secret (What God Can Do)/Blue Christmas/Santa Bring My Baby Back To Me/I'll Be Home For Christmas/Here Comes Santa Claus (Right Down Santa Claus Lane)/O Little Town Of Bethlehem/Silent Night/Take My Hand/I Believe/(There'll Be) Peace In The Valley (For Me) PERSONNEL Elvis Presley (v, g), Scotty Moore (g), Bill Black (b), D.J. Fontana (d), Floyd Cramer (p), Chet Atkins (g), Hank Garland (g), 'Boots' Randolph (s)

Combining eight specially recorded songs with the four spirituals already issued on the *Peace In the Valley* EP, **Elvis' Christmas Album** was the record to be seen with in the Yuletide season of 1957. It opened to reveal 10 photos of the King, while the original plastic bag outer had a 'From_____To_____' sticker on it. Deposed by Bing Crosby, the album regained the US top spot in January 1958 before yielding to Presley wannabe Ricky Nelson's debut long-player. A perennial favourite, it re-charted Stateside when converted to CD.

I made over a million dollars this year….I'm no musician at all. I can't play the guitar and I never wrote a song in my life….I learnt my singing style listening to coloured spiritual quartets down south…. **Interview by Howard Lucraft, Melody Maker, November 1957**

Elvis Is Back

ARTIST Elvis Presley RELEASE DATE June 1960 (UK)/May 1960 (US) LABEL RCA (UK & US) PRODUCER Steve Sholes, Chet Atkins UK CHART peak/weeks 1/27 US CHART peak/weeks 2/56 TRACK LISTING Make Me Know It/The Girl Of My Best Friend/Dirty Dirty/I Will Be Home Again/The Thrill Of Your Love/Feeling/Soldier Boy/Such A Night/It Feels So Right/Like A Baby/Fever/Reconsider Baby/The Girl Next Door PERSONNEL Elvis Presley (g, v), Floyd Cramer (p), Hank Garland (g), Scotty Moore (g), D.J. Fontana (d), Hoyt Hawkins (v), Bob Moore (b), Gordon Stoker (bv), Ray C. Walker (bv), Neal Jr. Matthews (bv)

Back from the army, of course – some copies of this album had a civvy Elvis on the front and a soldier Elvis at the rear, but all had bonus photos of the man a million fans had missed. Rumour has it some of the demos were produced by Phil Spector, but it is certain that this was the first Presley album to be released in true stereo.

Elvis is Back is what the disc's called and he proves it conclusively with a few tracks of this value-for-money LP… best tracks are **Fever**, *Make me know it*, *Such a night* *and* *Like a Baby*. **Melody Maker, July 1960**

Elvis Presley

ARTIST Elvis Presley RELEASE DATE March 1956 (US only) LABEL RCA PRODUCER – UK CHART peak/weeks Not Released Till Later (Rock 'N' Roll No.1) US CHART peak/weeks 1/48 TRACK LISTING Blue Suede Shoes/I'm Counting On You/Money Honey/I Got A Sweetie (I Got A Woman)/One Sided Love Affair/I'm Gonna Sit Right Down And Cry Over You/Tryin'To Get To You/I Love You Because/Just Because/Blue Moon/I'll Never Let You Go/Tutti Frutti PERSONNEL Elvis Presley (v, g), Scotty Moore (g), Bill Black (b), Floyd Cramer (p), Chet Atkins (g), Hank Garland (g), 'Boots' Randolph (s), Backing Vocals: The Jordanaires

The first album in history to sell one million copies, **Elvis Presley** consisted of five songs cut back in the Memphis studios of his first label Sun and seven at RCA studios in New York and Nashville. These were somehow filleted to provide five EPs! The very first copies had light pink lettering on the front, not dark, but if you missed out, don't worry: The Clash stole the design for 1979's **London Calling**, which is not a bad substitute!

An EP of our songs from **Love Me Tender** *is sure to cause a stampede amongst Elvis Presley fans… The three up-tempo titles reveal that Presley has the American's innate feeling for rhythm more than any singer I could mention in Britain.* **Laurie Henshaw, Melody Maker, December 1956**

Emergency On Planet Earth

ARTIST Jamiroquai **RELEASE DATE** June 1993 (UK & US) **LABEL** Sony (UK)/Epic (US) **PRODUCER** Jay Kay, J. K. Lewis, Mike Nielsen, Toby Smith **UK CHART** peak/weeks 1/21 **US CHART** peak/weeks 0/0 **TRACK LISTING** When You Gonna Learn (Digeridoo)/Too Young To Die/Hooked Up/If I Like It, I Do It/Music Of The Mind/Emergency On Planet Earth/Whatever It Is, I Just Can't Stop/Blow Your Mind/Revolution 1993/Diddn' Out **PERSONNEL** Jay Kay (v), Toby Smith (k), Nick Van Gelder (d), Stuart Zender (b), Kofi Karkikari (pc), Maurizio Ravalio (pc), Glenn Nightingale (g), Simon Bartholomew (g), D-Zire (dj), Gary Barnacle (s, fl), John Thirkell (t, fh), Richard Edwards (tr)

Ever since the Fifties white acts have made a killing through their take on black music, so while Jamiroquai singer Jay Kay was a vocal singer for Stevie Wonder, he defended his music as 'derivative but not appropriated'. His mother, singer Karen Kay, had been more of an influence than even Wonder had been, and in this jazz-funk fusion Kay found the sound of 1993, assiduously publicized by a high-powered PR campaign. An eight-album deal offered on the strength of one single, **When You Gonna Learn**, began to pay off with 300,000 plus sales – and the critics could eat dirt.

It all chugs along steadily with absolutely everything sounding like something you've heard before… Only less so, as although Jamiroquai can faithfully reproduce those 20-year-old sounds, they don't seem to understand what went into them sufficiently to be able to do anything other than copy. Thus while it's pleasant enough not to do anything wrong, it doesn't do that much right. **Lloyd Bradley, Q, August 1993**

The End Of Innocence

ARTIST Don Henley **RELEASE DATE** July 1989 (UK & US) **LABEL** Geffen (UK & US) **PRODUCER** Danny Kortchmar **UK CHART** peak/weeks 17/16 **US CHART** peak/weeks 8/148 **TRACK LISTING** The End Of Innocence/How Bad Do You Want It?/I Will Not Go Quietly/The Last Worthless Evening/New York Minute/Shangri-La/Little Tin God/Gimme What You Got/If Dirt Were Dollars/The Heart Of The Matter **PERSONNEL** Don Henley (v)

Five years between albums enabled former Eagle Henley to iron out his personal life and stockpile some great songs. Fortunately his public had not forgotten him, and both the album and its hit title track achieved identical US chart positions. It also gave backing singer Sheryl Crow the impetus to seek her own solo flight, since Henley sought her out and told her she was too good to be in anyone's shadow. She then went to join Michael Jackson's touring band.

…the former Eagle explores what happens to individuals and the society they live in when 'happily ever after fails' and seemingly intractable realities of the world set in. Probing and ambitious, the record raises provocative questions of the sort not typically encountered on pop albums. **Anthony De Curtis, Rolling Stone, August 1989**

Endless Flight

ARTIST Leo Sayer **RELEASE DATE** November 1976 (UK & US) **LABEL** Chrysalis (UK & US) **PRODUCER** Richard Perry **UK CHART** peak/weeks 4/66 **US CHART** peak/weeks 10/51 **TRACK LISTING** Hold On To My Love/You Make Me Feel Like Dancing/Reflections/When I Need You/No Business Like Love Business/I Hear The Laughter/Magdalena/How Much Love/I Think We Fell In Love Too Fast/Endless Flight **PERSONNEL** Leo Sayer (v), Chris Staunton (k), Grahame Jarvis (d), session musicians

Leo Sayer had endured four years on the fringes of the British music scene – busking on the London underground, singing with the Terraplane Blues Band, heading a group called Patches and co-writing an LP for Roger Daltrey – before reaching Number 2 in the UK in 1973 with **The Show Must Go On. Endless Flight**, Sayer's fourth album, saw him ditch the novelty Pierrot image and yielded three hit singles, ranging from up-tempo pop to schmaltzy balladry: **You Make Me Feel Like Dancing**, **When I Need You** (both US Number 1s) and **How Much Love**.

Enter The Wu-Tang

ARTIST Wu-Tang Clan **RELEASE DATE** May 1994 (UK)/November 1993 (US) **LABEL** Loud-R.C.A. (UK) **PRODUCER** Ol' Dirty Bastard, Method Man, Dennis Coles, Robert Diggs **UK CHART** peak/weeks 0/0 **US CHART** peak/weeks 41/42 **TRACK LISTING** Bring Da Ruckus/Shame On A Nigga/Clan In Da Front/7th Chamber (Wu-Tang)/Can It All Be So Simple/Da Mystery Of Chess Boxin'/Wu-Tang Clan Ain't Nuthing Ta Taf Wit/C.R.E.A.M./Method Man/Project Ya Neck/Tearz/7th Chamber (part 2) (Wu-Tang) **PERSONNEL** Method Man, Genius, Gza, Ol' Dirty Bastard, Chief Raekwon, Ghostface Killer, U-God, Prince Rakee, Rebel INS

Wu-Tang Clan were a crew of nine Staten Island MCs: production whiz Prince Rakeem aka The RZA, Method Man, Ol' Dirty Bastard, Genius, GZA, Chief Raekwon Ghostface Killa, U-God, Inspecta Deck and Masta Killa, five of whom would later record solo albums. **Enter The Wu-Tang** dropped a bomb on the complacent early Nineties hip-hop scene. A furious collage of insane ghetto rhymes, kung fu flick samples, dope beats and eerie B-movie interludes, it offered a disturbing East Coast alternative to the mellifluous skank of West Coast G-Funk.

Exuberantly mix-matching beats of prowling menace with snared funk licks... gleefully mixing in movie samples, slipped disc CD segments and shocking black humour, the Wu-Tangs present themselves as The Resevoir Dogs *of rap.* **Gavin Martin, NME, April 1994**

Entertainment

ARTIST Gang Of Four RELEASE DATE September 1979 (UK & US) LABEL EMI (UK)/Infinite Zero (US) PRODUCER Andrew Gill, Jon King, Rob Warr UK CHART peak/weeks 45/3 US CHART peak/weeks 0/0 TRACK LISTING Ether/Natural's Not In It/Not Great Men/Damaged Goods/Return The Gift/Guns Before Butter/I Found That Essence Rare/Glass/Contract/At Home He's A Tourist/5-45/Anthrax PERSONNEL Gang of Four (arr), David Allen (b), Hugo Burnham (d), Andrew Gill (g, d, v), Johnny King (v)

Spiky, uncompromising, thought-provoking agit-pop from the Gang Of Four, asking awkward questions and prompting a re-assessment of attitudes towards war, greed, social injustice and politics. The sound is sparse, repetitive and unsettling, the lyrics minimalist, but the strength of feeling is undeniable, and the end result curiously addictive. Ironically, given its attack on the media for their failings, this is a collection of somewhat unpalatable truths disguised as entertainment. Hear it, and you may never regard relationships, conflict, or the early evening news in the same way again...

... an important, intelligent and adventurous group who are doing their bit to raise our awareness of how things stand as we tumble Torily into the Eighties. **Chris Brazier, Melody Maker, November 1979**

Escape

ARTIST Journey RELEASE DATE August 1981 (UK & US) LABEL CBS (UK)/Columbia (US) PRODUCER Mike Stone, Kevin Elson UK CHART peak/weeks 32/16 US CHART peak/weeks 1/146 TRACK LISTING Don't Stop Believin'/Stone In Love/Who's Crying Now/Keep On Runnin'/Still They Ride/Escape/Lay It Down/Dead Or Alive/Mother, Father/Open Arms PERSONNEL Steve Perry (v), Neal Schon (g), Ross Valory (b), Jonathan Cain (k), Steve Smith (d)

With seven albums under their belt, the last four platinum, US AOR giants Journey were well overdue a Number 1. The catalyst was former Baby's keyboardist Jon Cain, whose replacement of long-time member Gregg Rolie brought a new freshness to the songwriting department: his ***Don't Stop Believin'*** was a highlight, along with trademark ballads like ***Who's Crying Now*** and ***Open Arms*** which quickly became radio staples. Like REO Speedwagon and the latter-day Chicago, Journey were safe and predictable – but oh so popular.

Even In The Quietest Moments

ARTIST Supertramp RELEASE DATE April 1977 (UK & US) LABEL A&M (UK & US) PRODUCER Supertramp UK CHART peak/weeks 12/22 US CHART peak/weeks 16/49 TRACK LISTING Give A Little Bit/Lover Boy/Even In The Quietest Moments/Downstream/Babaji/From Now On/Fool's Overture PERSONNEL Richard Davies (v, k), Roger Hodgson (b, k, v), Dougie Thompson (b), Bob Benberg (d), John Anthony Helliwell (s, cl, v)

Their first album to make inroads in America and featuring the typically catchy ***Give A Little Bit***, **Even In The Quietest Moments** was produced by erstwhile Beatles engineer, Geoff Emerick, who maintained a balance between the overwrought and the concise. Released at the height of punk, **Even In The Quietest Moments**, like the post-Gabriel Genesis, were virtually alone among their peers in withstanding the onslaught of the safety-pinned hordes.

'I think we're mellowing out in terms of songs and the sound we're creating,' John Helliwell said, *'I've introduced more sax as we've gone along, and of course most groups don't have a sax player at all...'* **From an interview by David Boothroyd, Melody Maker, October 1977**

Everybody Else Is Doing It, So Why Can't We?

ARTIST The Cranberries RELEASE DATE March 1993 (UK)/July 1993 (US) LABEL Island (UK & US) PRODUCER Stephen Street UK CHART peak/weeks 1/64 US CHART peak/weeks 18/130 TRACK LISTING I Still Do/Dreams/Sunday/ Pretty/Waltzing Black/Not Sorry/Linger/Wanted/Still Can't.../I Will Always/How/Put Me Down PERSONNEL Dolores O'Riordan (v, ag), Noel Hogan (g), Mike Hogan (b), Fergal Lawler (d)

America lapped up the agonized tones of Dolores O'Riordan before the UK did, though the Limerick band were already beloved in Ireland. The hit ballad ***Linger*** sent their gauche blend of folky guitars, sweeping strings and occasional lumpen rockisms into a gap left between The Smiths and U2. Despite the loathing of British critics, the album became only the fifth in history to top the charts here more than a year after its release. It has sold over 10 million worldwide, despite O'Riordan's stroppiness and occasionally iffy lyrics. A definitive case of gruelling touring schedules paid off.

'Why did the runts of our indie litter become the top-dogs?.... The answer, it seems, lies in the metamorphosis of the Cranberries from shy, retiring types to cool rock monsters.... In the way the Cranberries' music straddles the gulf between the traditional and the new.' **From an interview by Dele Fadele, NME, January 1994**

Every Good Boy Deserves Favour

ARTIST The Moody Blues RELEASE DATE July 1971 (UK)/August 1971 (US) LABEL Threshold (UK & US) PRODUCER Tony Clarke UK CHART peak/weeks 1/21 US CHART peak/weeks 2/43 TRACK LISTING Procession/The Story In Your Eyes/Our Guessing Game/Emily's Song/After You Came/One More Time To Live/Nice To Be Here/You Can Never Go Home/My Song PERSONNEL Denny Lane (v, g), Mike Pinder (k, v), Ray Thomas (fl, v, bv), Clint Warwick (b, v), Graham Edge (d)

The Moodies' third album on their own Threshold label – named after the notes on the lines of a treble stave (E-G-B-D-F) – saw them well set on their symphonic rock course that made them so successful in the States and chart-toppers back home without the aid of a single. Given the choice of presenter when the band was awarded their sixth US gold disc, the band chose Tonto (actor Jay Silverheels) from TV's *Lone Ranger*. One thing they did not need arranging was a loan….

It is obvious on this new album that the Moody Blues have not been motivated by the same degree of imagination that has peppered their creative past. **A.M., Melody Maker, July 1971**

Every Picture Tells A Story

ARTIST Rod Stewart RELEASE DATE June 1971 (UK & US) LABEL Mercury (UK & US) PRODUCER Rod Stewart UK CHART peak/weeks 1/52 US CHART peak/weeks 1/81 US CHART peak/weeks 1/52 TRACK LISTING Every Picture Tells A Story/Seems Like A Long Time/That's All Right/Tomorrow Is A Long Time/Maggie May/Mandolin Wind/(I Know) I'm Losing You/Reason To Believe PERSONNEL Rod Stewart (v, ag), Mick Waller (d), Peter Sears (p), Ron Wood (g, b, ps), Martell Brandy Martin Quittenton (ag), Ian McLagen (o), Danny Thompson (b), Andy Pyle (b), Dick Powell (v), Madeline Bell & Friends (v), Lindisfarne (md)

The first album to simultaneously reach pole position on both sides of the Atlantic, **Every Picture Tells A Story** is regarded by true Rod Stewart *aficionados* as his finest hour. The second record to do the same was another Stewart release, the single **Maggie May**.

Originally the B-side of Rod's cover of Tim Hardin's **Reason To Believe**, **Maggie May** became a monstrous success after DJs picked up on it; it remains one of the most memorable song-stories – about a young boy's adventures with a hooker – ever to top the charts, and is the highlight of this excellent set.

Sad to say, though, no amount of excellent, even occasionally breathtaking playing by his band behind quite satisfactory singing by Stewart himself can transform such massively inconsequential, nay, downright trivial, fare as **Seems Like A Long Time** *into anything memorable.* **John Mendelsohn, Rolling Stone, July 1971**

Everybody Knows This Is Nowhere

ARTIST Neil Young And Crazy Horse RELEASE DATE July 1969 (UK)/May 1969 (US) LABEL Reprise (UK & US) PRODUCER Jack Nitzsche UK CHART peak/weeks 0/0 US CHART peak/weeks 34/98 TRACK LISTING Cinnamon Girl/Everybody Knows This Is Nowhere/Round & Round (It Won't Be Long)/Down By The River/The Losing End (When You're On)/Running Dry (Requiem For The Rockets)/Cowgirl In The Sand PERSONNEL Neil Young (g), Danny Whitten (g), Ralph Molina (d), Billy Talbot (b), Bobby Notkoff (vl)

Neil Young's second album was his first gold-seller and the first to feature his three-piece backup band, Crazy Horse. It also contained three of Young's most memorable guitar workouts, **Cinnamon Girl**, **Down By The River** and **Cowgirl In The Sand**, which showcased his unique fretboard stylings: neither bluesy and rootsy nor acid-tinged, but as fluid and free-form as jazz.

Neil Young recorded these albums between leaving Buffalo Springfield and joining the Crosby, Stills Nash outfit. He has a strong, distinctive, rather plaintive voice, and is able to inject more than a touch of drama into his self-penned songs. **Melody Maker, September 1969**

Everything Must Go

ARTIST The Manic Street Preachers RELEASE DATE 1996 LABEL Sony Music Entertainment (UK) Ltd PRODUCER Mike Hedges, Dave Eringa, Ian Grimble UK CHART peak/weeks – US CHART peak/weeks – TRACK LISTING Elvis Impersonator: Blackpool Pier/A Design For Life/Kevin Carter/Enola/Alone/Everything Must Go/Small Black Flowers That Grow In The Sky/The Girl Who Wanted To Be God/Removables/Australia/Interiors (Song For William De Kooning)/Further Away/No Surface All Feeling PERSONNEL James Dean Bradfield (v, g, ag, p, bv), Sean Moore (d, pc, t, bv), Nicky Wire (b, bv), additional musicians: John Green, Martin Ditchum, Julie Aliss, Sally Herbert, Anne Stephenson, Chris Pitsillides, Claire Orsler, Martin Greene

The Welsh group's first album as a trio because of the disappearance of guitarist Richey Edwards; however, Richey's presence looms large due to a number of his lyrics used in the songs, and the almost palpable feeling of loss, suffering and despair which permeates every track. The Manics' most successful album up to this time, possibly due to the 'guilt factor' associated with Richey, but it is also a powerful, considered record in its own right, and one which sees the group throwing off the trappings of Americana and finding a voice distinctively its own.

Richey's influence remains strong – five songs were either written or co-written by him – and the music tingles the spine on a regular basis…. This is a bold and frequently remarkable album. **Richard Newson, Mojo, June 1996**

Exile In Guyville

ARTIST Liz Phair RELEASE DATE June 1993 (UK)/February 1994 (US) LABEL Matador Records (UK & US) PRODUCER Brad Wood, Liz Phair UK CHART peak/weeks 0/0 US CHART peak/weeks 196/1 TRACK LISTING 6'1"/Help Me Mary/Glory/Dance Of The Seven Veils/Never Said/Fuck And Run/Girls!Girls!Girls!/Divorce Song/Shatter/Flower/Soap Star Joe/Explain It To Me/Canary/Mesmerizing/Johnny Sunshine/Gunshy/Stratford On Guy/Strange Loop PERSONNEL Liz Phair (v, g), Brad Wood (d, pc), Casey Rice (g), Leroy Bach (b)

From Chicago, Liz Phair's debut album packs both a musical punch and reveals an artist in total control of her material and songwriting. A track-by-track feminist riposte to the Stones' **Exile On Main Street**, it shows a singer who both longs to be one of the boys and simultaneously implies that if men knew what it was like to be a woman, life might be a lot easier. The album's lyrics caused controversy from the outset but won an immediate audience through the way they so honestly, and without apology, articulated her emotions and desires.

Throbbing with ironic vows of vengeance upon the perfidious male of the species and delighting in a sexual candour that would leave Prince positively blushing… Phair dispenses wit and wisdom with a matter of factness that proves you don't have to scream to be heard. **Peter Kane, Q, August 1993**

Exile On Main Street

ARTIST The Rolling Stones RELEASE DATE June 1972 (UK & US) LABEL Rolling Stones (UK & US) PRODUCER The Rolling Stones UK CHART peak/weeks 1/15 US CHART peak/weeks 1/43 TRACK LISTING Rocks Off/Rip This Joint/Shake Your Hips/Casino Boogie/Tumbling Dice/Sweet Virginia/Torn And Frayed/Sweet Black Angel/Loving Cup/Happy/Turd On The Run/Ventilator Blues/I Just Want To See His Face/Let It Loose/All Down The Line/Stop Breaking Down/Shine A Light/Soul Survivor PERSONNEL Mick Jagger (v, h), Keith Richards (rg), Brian Jones (lg), Charlie Watts (d), Bill Wyman (b), Ian Stewart (p)

Listening to this landmark double is always a gentle surprise: can an album so half-heartedly produced, so murkily played and so depressingly downbeat really be a rock classic of white-hot motivational power? That it can is due to Richards' and Taylor's effortlessly effective guitar interplay and Jagger's discovery that, despite his best intentions, he does possess emotion and dimension. While *Happy*, *Rocks Off* and *Rip This Joint* describe themselves adequately, it is *Tumbling Dice* that best captures this curious blend of rootsiness and reverie. Recorded in tax exile in the basement of Richards' French villa, it granted the Stones several years more as a subject of debate and fascination.

Basically, **Exile On Main Street** *was an idea to try and get back to good old rock 'n' roll. Looking back over the recent albums, we felt there was a need to re-establish the rock thing.* **Jimmy Miller (producer) in interview with Ritchie Yorke, NME, June 1971**

Exit Planet Dust

ARTIST The Chemical Brothers RELEASE DATE June 1995 LABEL Freestyle Dust PRODUCER Tom Rolands, Ed Simons UK CHART peak/weeks 9/98 US CHART peak/weeks 0/0 TRACK LISTING Leave Home/In Dust We Trust/Song To The Siren/Three Little Birdies Down Beats/Fuck Up Beats/Chemical Beats/Life Is Sweet/Playground For A Wedgeless Firm/Chico's Groove/One Too Many Mornings PERSONNEL Tom Rowlands, Ed Simons, Tim Burgess (v), Beth Orton (v)

Originally named The Dust Brothers as a 'homage' to the American hip-hop producers of that name, this Mancunian DJ-ing pair found the tribute backfiring, and had to adopt their current moniker in 1995 after the threat of legal action. Paying their dues as remixers, they began surfing the *zeitgeist* as recording artists, pushing samples and beats beyond their assumed limitations. Featuring guest vocals from Tim Burgess of The Charlatans and Beth Orton, their debut yielded a hit in **Life Is Sweet**. A soundtrack for a new generation, The Chemical Brothers' powerful pulsating 'fucked-up beats' were just gathering momentum….

To call the Chemical Brothers formulaic is, of course, an understatement. But what a formula it is – 20 storey high beats fuse with techno pulses, acid squelches and rock 'n' roll poses to create a full-on, brat pack groove. **Martin James, Melody Maker, June 1995**

Exodus

ARTIST Bob Marley & The Wailers RELEASE DATE June 1977 (UK & US) LABEL Island (UK & US) PRODUCER Bob Marley & The Wailers UK CHART peak/weeks 8/56 US CHART peak/weeks 20/24 TRACK LISTING Natural Mystic/So Much Things To Say/Guiltiness/The Heather/Exodus/Jamming/Waiting In Vain/Turn Your Lights Down Low/Three Little Birds/One Love (People Get Ready) PERSONNEL Aston 'Family Man' Barrett (b), Bob Marley (v, ag), Carlton (Carlie) Barrett (d), Alvin 'Sheco' Patterson (pc), Bunny Livingstone (cg, pc, v), Tyrone Downie (k), Julian 'Junior' Murvin (g), Judy Mowat (bv), Marcia Griffiths (bv), Rita Marley (bv)

Marley spent the first half of 1977 in London after escaping an assassination attempt, but this did not harm his creative muse: sessions at Island's Basing Street studios produced enough songs for this, his first UK Top 10 album, plus its follow-up **Kaya**. *Guiltiness* and *So Much Things To Say* were inspired by the events of late 1976, while a Wailers staple, *One Love*, was re-recorded and made a medley with Curtis Mayfield's *People Get Ready*. But it was the title track and *Jammin'* that would really ignite the British audience, the former becoming his first Top 20 single here.

Exodus *arrives with felicitous timing: it's the first great summer album of 1977.* **Exodus** *seems like a reward for making it through winter.* **Charles Shaar Murray, NME, 1977**

Exotica

ARTIST Martin Denny RELEASE DATE May 1959 (UK & US) LABEL Liberty (US) PRODUCER Martin Denny UK CHART peak/weeks 0/0 US CHART peak/weeks 1/63 TRACK LISTING Ah Me Fun/Busy Port/China Nights (Shina No You)/Hong Kong Blues/Jungle Flower/Lotus Land/Love Dance/Quiet Village/Return To Paradise/Similau/Stone God/Waipio PERSONNEL Martin Denny (v, p, cp, arr), Julius Wechter (vbc), session musicians

New York-born pianist Denny came up with 1959's surprise hit album after migrating to Hawaii and playing at a beach-side bar. His quartet were spotted by Liberty Records and cut their first album locally at a reputed cost of $850. The single **Quiet Village** became a surprise hit, tugging the album in its wake and **Exotica** duly toppled the previously invincible **Peter Gunn** soundtrack in June, its sunny feel capturing the vibe for the US nation even though it had still to adopt its fiftieth state.

The Fabulous Little Richard

ARTIST Little Richard RELEASE DATE May 1959 (UK & US) LABEL London (UK)/Speciality (US) PRODUCER – UK CHART peak/weeks 0/0 US CHART peak/weeks 0/0 TRACK LISTING Shake A Hand/Chicken Little Baby/All Night Long/Most I Can Offer/Lonesome And Blue/Wonderin'/Whole Lotta Shakin' Goin' On/She Knows How To Rock/Kansas City/Directly From Your Heart/Maybe I'm Right/Early One Morning/I'm Just A Lonely Girl PERSONNEL Little Richard (v, p), Red Tyler (s), Lee Allen (s), Frank Fields (b), Ernest McLean (g), Justin Adams (g), Earl Palmer (d), session musicians

This third album from the Georgia Peach wouldn't spawn a whole clutch of hit singles like its predecessors, but then he had renounced secular music in favour of the religious life and this was the sound of Specialty scraping the barrel. Not bad pickings, though! *Kansas City*, a bigger hit here than in the States, where Wilbert Harrison's version topped the chart, would be picked up by Richard fans, The Beatles and, in a medley with his earlier *Hey Hey Hey Hey*, included on their **Beatles For Sale** album.

I used to play piano for the Church. The music is real, you know. In most places they just sing: 'Give me that old time religion,' but I didn't do it. I sang: "Give me that old time religion, boom boom boom, talking 'bout religion." I put that little thing in there. **From an interview by Chuck Pulin, Melody Maker, 28 March 1970**

Face To Face

ARTIST The Kinks RELEASE DATE October 1966 (UK)/February 1967 (US) LABEL Pye (UK)/Reprise (US) PRODUCER The Kinks UK CHART peak/weeks 12/11 US CHART peak/weeks 135/3 TRACK LISTING Party Line/Rosy Won't You Please Come Home/Dandy/Too Much On My Mind/Rainy Day In June/House In The Country/Holiday In Waikiki/Most Exclusive Residence For Sale/Fancy/Little Miss Queen Of Darkness/You're Looking Fine/Sunny Afternoon/I'll Remember PERSONNEL Ray Davies (v, g), Dave Davies (g, v), Peter Quaife (b)

Acerbic, cynical, incisive social comment from one of the greatest songwriters of the age, totally at odds with the prevailing atmosphere of optimism, patriotism and hedonism. Despite the fashionable sleeve illustration and the inclusion of songs with titles like *Dandy* and *You're Lookin' Fine*, this was a subtle collection of finely written attacks on the self-congratulation and decadence of 'Swinging London', undeniably English in its outlook, but carefully distancing itself from the pack. Ray Davies reached a creative peak in the mid Sixties and this is as fine an example of his craft as any.

By the time **Face to Face** *arrived, Ray Davies had attained some level of control over his muse: the flights of casual, diffident brilliance had become the rule rather than the exception.* **Charles Shaar Murray, NME, July 1980**

Face Value

ARTIST Phil Collins RELEASE DATE February 1981 (UK)/March 1981 (US) LABEL Virgin (UK)/Atlantic (US) PRODUCER Phil Collins assisted by Hugh Padgham UK CHART peak/weeks 1/274 US CHART peak/weeks 7/164 TRACK LISTING In The Air Tonight/This Must Be Love/Behind The Lines/The Roof Is Leaking/Droned/Hand In Hand/I Missed Again/You Know What I Mean/Thunder And Lightning/I'm Not Moving/I Leaving Me Is Easy/Tomorrow Never Knows PERSONNEL Phil Collins (p, d, v), John Giblin (b), Daryl Steurmer (g), Shorokav (vl), Alphonso (b), Don Myrick (ts), Louis (tb), Rahmlee Michael Davis (t), Michael Harris (t), Stephen Bishop (bv), Joe Partridge (sg), Ronnie Scott (gst), Martin Ford (st)

Lampooned as the ultimate soft mainstream ageing pop star, it's generally forgotten that as Genesis drummer-turned-singer and an all-round musician of some quality, Collins was once much revered. His first solo album pushed the cheeky chappie image to the irritation of many but the amusement of more. The songs showed real class, and his voice was just ravaged enough to express a soul beneath the charade. *In The Air Tonight* was a monster that managed to show off both that voice and a gargantuan drum sound. *I Missed Again* was an early dabble with light funk, while *If Leaving Me Is Easy*, surprisingly one of the lesser hits, dripped with genuine pathos.

Faith

ARTIST George Michael RELEASE DATE November 1987 (UK & US) LABEL Epic (UK)/Columbia (US) PRODUCER George Michael UK CHART peak/weeks 1/72 US CHART peak/weeks 1/87 TRACK LISTING Faith/Father Figure/I Want Your Sex/One More Try/Hard Day/Hand To Mouth/Look At Your Hands/Monkey/Kissing A Fool PERSONNEL George Michael (v, var), Deon Estus (b)

In **Wham!**, George Michael had left the guitar work to partner Andrew Ridgeley – though his lack of obvious ability led critics to suggest the axe was unplugged. But George grabbed the guitar for himself when it came to the cover of his first solo album, while an acoustic strummed Bo Diddley-style was the core of the title track and the first of four US Number 1 singles to be taken from a multi-platinum success.

Why is **Faith** *harder than the rest? Why has George stayed so long with leather? Because it's all part and packaging of the same con. He's an accountant in rebel's clothing and his songs are designer aggression.* **Steve Sutherland, Melody Maker, November 1987**

Faithful

ARTIST Todd Rundgren RELEASE DATE April 1976 (UK & US) LABEL Bearsville (UK & US) PRODUCER Todd Rundgren UK CHART peak/weeks 0/0 US CHART peak/weeks 54/15 TRACK LISTING Happenings Ten Years Time Ago/Good Vibrations/Rain/Most Likely You Go Your Way And I'll Go Mine/If Six Was Nine/Strawberry Fields Forever/Black And White/Love Of The Common Man/When I Pray/Cliche/The Verb 'To Love'/Boogies (Hamburger Hell) PERSONNEL Todd Rundgren (lg, v), Mark Klingman (k), Ralph Shuckett (b), John Siegler (b, c)

Side one featured note-perfect studio recreations of such epiphanal mid-Sixties moments as the Beach Boys' *Good Vibrations*, The Yardbirds' *Happenings Ten Years Time Ago*, Bob Dylan's *Most Likely You'll Go Your Way And I'll Go Mine*, The Beatles' *Rain* and *Strawberry Fields Forever* – as if Todd Rundgren was pitting himself against the all-time greats. Meanwhile, the flipside contained six new Rundgren compositions, at least three of which, *Love Of The Common Man*, *Cliche* and *The Verb 'To Love'*, were as beautiful as anything he had ever written.

The problem here isn't Rundgren's lack of vocal and instrumental chops of his influences…. Would even Rundgren listen to his versions in lieu of the originals? **John Milward, Rolling Stone, July 1976**

Falling Into You

ARTIST Celine Dion RELEASE DATE March 1996 (UK & US) LABEL Epic (UK & US) PRODUCER Vito Luprano, John Doelp (Exec prods) UK CHART peak/weeks 1/- US CHART peak/weeks 2/27 TRACK LISTING It's All Coming Back To Me Now/Because You Loved Me (Theme From Up Close And Personal)/Falling Into You/Make You Happy/Seduces Me/All By Myself/Declaration Of Love/(You Make Me Feel Like A) Natural Woman/Dreamin' Of You/I Love You/If That's What It Takes/I Don't Know/River Deep, Mountain High/Your Light/Call The Man PERSONNEL Celine Dion (v, bv), session musicians

Falling Into You had a hard act to follow, French-Canadian *chanteuse* Dion having broken through internationally with the mega-platinum **The Colour Of My Love**. The usual mixture of songwriters and producers made for a varied album, with Jim Steinman's three typically over-the-top efforts – including the Spector-esque *All Coming Back To Me Now*, with a *Bat Out Of Hell*-styled video – the pick of the bunch. That said, it was the Diane Warren-penned, David Foster-produced *Because You Loved Me* that gave her a US Number 1.

Falling Into You *is a pile of toss held together by Celine's hysterical screech and utterly preposterous lyrics. Celine doesn't write her own lyrics, but that doesn't excuse her.* **Kristy Baker, Melody Maker, April 1996**

Family Entertainment

ARTIST Family RELEASE DATE March 1969 (UK & US) LABEL Reprise (UK & US) PRODUCER John Gilbert, Glyn Lones UK CHART peak/weeks 6/3 US CHART peak/weeks 0/0 TRACK LISTING The Weaver's Answer/Observations From A Hill/Hung Up Down/Summer 67/How-Hi-The-Li/Second Generation Woman/From Past Archives/Dim/Processions/Face In The Cloud/Emotions PERSONNEL Jim King (ts, ss, bv, p), Rob Townsend (d, pc), John Witney (g,p,o), Roger Chapman (v, pc), Ric Grech (b, vl, v)

A less experimental album than its predecessor, **Family Entertainment** nevertheless delivers, including many of the band's live favourites of the time. *The Weaver's Answer*, *Hung Up Down* and *Observations From A Hill* alone make this essential, but there are further delights in a collection that deservedly reached the Top 10 of the UK charts. The production leaves something to be desired in places, but Chapman's magnificent vocals and some fine songwriting, distinguished by Ric Grech's deft bass and violin playing, more than compensate.

Unless you are irritated by one of the singers who has a vibrato like a ewe in lambing season, this should delight everyone who likes intelligent underground pop. It's all well played, the lyrics are both meaningful and witty and the material is all original. **Melody Maker, March 1969**

Fanny Hill

ARTIST Fanny Hill **RELEASE DATE** April 1972 (US) **LABEL** Reprise (UK & US) **PRODUCER** Richard Perry **UK CHART** peak/weeks – **US CHART** peak/weeks 135/6 **TRACK LISTING** Ain't That Peculiar/Knock On My Door/Blind Alley/You've Got A Home/Wonderful Feeling/Borrowed Time/Hey Bulldog/Think About The Children/Rock Bottom Blues/Sound And The Fury/The First Time **PERSONNEL** June Millington (g, v, ctte, pc), Nickey Barclay (p, k, v, o), Jean Millington (b, v), Alice de Buhr (d, pc), Jim Price (t,tb), Bobby Keys (ts)

Back in the early Seventies, the idea of an all-female band was something of a hoot. Beatle George Harrison was said to have come up with the cringe-worthy name (rechristened from Wild Honey), but Philippine-born sisters June and Jean Millington got on with the job of rocking out regardless. This their debut album coincided with a stint as Barbra Streisand's studio band for the **Stoney End** album, which was the more successful of the pair. The title track of the following LP was a hit single, but Jean quit one more album in and the impetus was lost.

Fanny have finally made it: their album is full of the best mainstream rock 'n' roll I've heard this year…. **Fanny Hill** *simply exudes with the confidence one finds in a young, energetic group who have finally put everything together.* **Mike Saunders, Rolling Stone, April 1972**

The Fat Of The Land

ARTIST The Prodigy **RELEASE DATE** July 1997 (UK & US) **LABEL** Warner Bros. (UK & US) **PRODUCER** L. Howlett **UK CHART** peak/weeks – **US CHART** peak/weeks 0/0 **TRACK LISTING** Smack My Bitch Up/Breathe/Diesel Power/Funky Shit/Serial Thrilla/Mindfields/Narayan/ firestarter/Climbatize/Fuel My Fire **PERSONNEL** Kool Keith Flint (v), Saffron (v), Jim Davies (g), Crispian Mills (v)

Three years on from the populist techno of **Music For The Jilted Generation**, The Prodigy were back with another winner. More rock and hip-hop influenced than its predecessor, **Fat Of The Land** sets the pulse racing, fusing monster beats with a raving-loony attitude. A punk-metal thrash cover of L7's *Fuel My Fire* sits easily alongside the almost straightforward hip-hop of *Diesel Power*, while *Funky Shit* is the nearest in spirit to the **Music For The Jilted Generation** material. An essential primer for those curious about dance music in the late Nineties, **Fat Of The Land** includes the Number 1 singles *Firestarter* and *Breathe*.

Prodigy finally swallow alive rock, dance, pop and all other contents of Planet Earth in incandescent post-everything beats-and-noise frenzy. **Q, December 1997**

Fear Of A Black Planet

ARTIST Public Enemy **RELEASE DATE** April 1990 (UK & US) **LABEL** Def Jam (UK & US) **PRODUCER** Public Enemy **UK CHART** peak/weeks 4/10 **US CHART** peak/weeks 10/27 **TRACK LISTING** Contract On The World Love Jam/Brothers Gonna Work It Out/911 Is A Joke/Incident At 66.6 FM/Welcome To the Terrordome/Meet The G That Killed Me/Pollywanacracka/Anti-Nigger Machine/Burn Hollywood Burn/Power To The People/Who Stole The Soul/Fear Of A Black Planet/Revolutionary Generation/Can't Do Nuttin' For Ya Man/Reggae Jax/Leave This Off Your Fuckin' Charts/B Side Wins Again/War At 33 1/3/Final Count Of The Collision Between Us And The Dammed **PERSONNEL** Chuck D (v), Flavor Flav (p), Terminator X (dj)

The growing popularity of Public Enemy was bound to bring about a backlash from middle America: it was revealed the group had appeared in an FBI report concerning rap music's effects on national security. Most groups would thereafter settle for a peaceful life, but it says much that the venom in their message shows little sign of being blunted. The standout track was *911 Is A Joke*, a reference to the response time by ambulances in the ghettos, but

such is the intense way the raps are delivered it is difficult to ignore any of the tracks.

The reason they're still with us… is the growth they've displayed with each new album. **Fear of a Black Planet** *follows this curve and is a living nightmare, delivered in a rage so focused, so purposeful, that even empathisers will be knocked back.* **Lloyd Bradley, Q, May 1990**

Fear Of Music

ARTIST Talking Heads **RELEASE DATE** September 1979 (UK & US) **LABEL** Sire (UK & US) **PRODUCER** Brian Eno, Talking Heads **UK CHART** peak/weeks 33/5 **US CHART** peak/weeks 21/30 **TRACK LISTING** Air/Animals/Cities/Drugs/Electric Guitar/Heaven/I Zimbra/Life During Wartime/Memories Can't Wait/Mind/Paper/Pyscho Killer/New Feeling **PERSONNEL** David Byrne (v, g), Tina Weymouth (b, v), Chris Frantz (d), Jerry Harrison (g, k)

Voted Album Of The Year by both British music weeklies, *NME* and *Melody Maker*, **Fear Of Music** saw Talking Heads' four-strong line-up augmented by numerous dance musicians, who helped to create this feast of Afrocentric polyrhythms and multi-textured atmospherics. David Byrne's neurotic-paranoic persona reached new heights (depths?) on *Life During Wartime*, while on *Air*, *Cities*, *Paper*, *Animals* and *Drugs* he declared his phobia of the modern world in general, and of, well, air, cities, paper, animals and drugs in particular. As for Talking Heads, they never funked so good.

…in their transfiguration from side-show to main event, Talking Heads had no visible need to expand and explore to the extent which **Fear Of Music** *shows them to have done. The result is their finest album yet: a development born of rock-as-reflex, as opposed to premeditated method.* **James Truman, Melody Maker, August 1979**

Feats Don't Fail Me Now

ARTIST Little Feat **RELEASE DATE** September 1974 (UK & US) **LABEL** Warner Bros. (UK & US) **PRODUCER** Lowell George **UK CHART** peak/weeks 0/0 **US CHART** peak/weeks 36/16 **TRACK LISTING** Rock 'N' Roll Doctor/Cold Cold Cold/Tripe Face Boogie/The Fan/Oh Atlanta/Skin It Back/Down The Road/Feats Don't Fail Me Now **PERSONNEL** Lowell George (v, g), Roy Estrada (b, v), Bill Payne (k, v), Richie Hayward (d), Bonnie Raitt (v, gst), Emmylou Harris (v, gst), Van Dyke Parks (gst), session musicians

Fate brought the band back together in early 1974 and this fourth album consolidated the promise shown by their early records. They continued to wallow in its love of funk, R&B and southern blues. Aside from the pointless revamping of two old tunes *Cold Cold Cold* and *Tripe-Face Boogie* as the closing medley, the album contained some of their most celebrated songs. *Rock 'N' Roll Doctor*, which opened proceedings, was to become a live perennial, while the rumbustious *Oh Atlanta* celebrated Lowell George's favourite southern city.

Contrary to popular belief, it never was just Lowell's entire baby. That's where the confusion was with the group before one person ran it. What one person did was to present a direction that everybody else tried to circumvent. **Bill Payne interviewed by Andy Gill, Q, February 1989**

Fifth Album

ARTIST Judy Collins **RELEASE DATE** October 1965 (UK)/September 1965 (US) **LABEL** London (UK)/Elektra (US) **PRODUCER** Joshua Rifkin **UK CHART** peak/weeks 0/0 **US CHART** peak/weeks 69/13 **TRACK LISTING** Pack Up Your Sorrows/The Coming Of The Roads/So Early, Early In The Spring/Tomorrow Is A Long Time/Daddy You've Been On My Mind/Thirsty Boots/Mr. Tambourine Man/Lord Gregory/In The Heat Of The Summer/Early Morning Rain/Carry It On/It Isn't Nice **PERSONNEL** Judy Collins (v), Eric Weissberg (g, v), Richard Fariña (du), Bill Takas (b), Bill Lee (b), Danny Kalb (g), John Sebastian (mh), Bob Sylvester (c), Jerry Dodgion, Chuck Israels (b)

One of the Sixties' prime purveyors of interpretative folk (along with Joan Baez and Joni Mitchell), Collins is better known in Britain for a career-resurrecting *Amazing Grace*. Yet she played a big part in bringing the songs of Mitchell, Dylan and Cohen to a resistant audience. By her fifth album, she was to try some less traditional angles. There were three Dylan numbers, Eric Andersen's *Thirsty Boots*, plus an interestingly minimal trad ballad in *Lord Gregory*. Her next two works, **In My Life** and **Wildflowers** were to grasp the nettle, tackling Lennon & McCartney, Donovan and Jacques Brel, and pushing the voice beyond reservation.

She radiates understanding and transports her lovely alto voice into new areas of passion and intelligence in folk song and interpretation. **The New York Times, 1965**

Fifth Dimension

ARTIST The Byrds **RELEASE DATE** September 1966 (UK)/August 1966 (US) **LABEL** CBS (UK)/Columbia (US) **PRODUCER** Allen Stanton **UK CHART** peak/weeks 27/2 **US CHART** peak/weeks 24/28 **TRACK LISTING** 5D (Fifth Dimension)/Wild Mountain Thyme/Mr Spaceman/I See You/What's Happening?!?!/I Come And Stand At Every Door/Eight Miles High/Hey Joe/John Riley/Captain Soul/2-4-2 Foxtrot (The Lear Jet Song) **PERSONNEL** Jim McGuinn (g, v), David Crosby (g, v), Chris Hillman (b, v), Michael Clarke (d)

If their second album **Turn! Turn! Turn!** relied too much on further Dylan cover versions, this, their third, proved their own song writing strength, despite Gene Clark leaving halfway through the recording. He had contributed the lyrics to *Eight Miles High*, an awesome slice of prescient psychedelia. It was banned by radio stations, thought to be a drugs song, but made Number 1 anyway. David Crosby and Roger (then called Jim) McGuinn came to the fore, drawing on diverse sources from jazz to Indian music. From the orchestrated *Wild Mountain Thyme* to the jovial hit *Mr. Spaceman*, this had multiple dimensions.

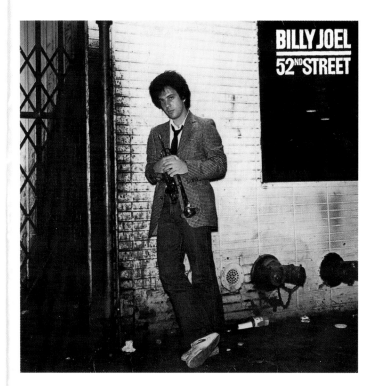

52nd Street

ARTIST Billy Joel **RELEASE DATE** November 1978 (UK)/October 1978 (US) **LABEL** CBS (UK)/Columbia (US) **PRODUCER** Phil Ramone **UK CHART** peak/weeks 10/43 **US CHART** peak/weeks 1/76 **TRACK LISTING** Big Shot/Honesty/My Life/Zanzibar/Stiletto/Rosalinda's Eyes/Half A Mile Away/Until The Night/52nd Street **PERSONNEL** Billy Joel (p, v), session musicians

Though 1974's *Piano Man* brought him world renown, it was this album, his fifth, that made Billy Joel a Number 1 act in a homage to **Abbey Road**. It was named after the New York 52nd Street location of the A&R studio where he recorded it, which had a collection of similarly diverse songs. It also prevented John Travolta's **Grease** returning to the US top spot, sweet revenge for **Saturday Night Fever** similarly baulking 1977's **The Stranger**.

Fire & Water

ARTIST Free **RELEASE DATE** July 1970 (UK)/September 1970 (US) **LABEL** Island (UK)/A&M (US) **PRODUCER** Free, John Kelly **UK CHART** peak/weeks 2/18 **US CHART** peak/weeks 17/27 **TRACK LISTING** Fire and Water/Oh I Wept/Remember/Heavy Load/Mr. Big/Don't Say You Love Me/All Right Now (long version) **PERSONNEL** Paul Rogers (v), Paul Kossof (g), Andy Fraser (b), Simon Kirke (d)

When Free co-headlined the 1970 Isle of Wight Festival they were the biggest name there thanks to this album and its hit single, the anthemic *All Right Now*. The success of both proved impossible to sustain and the band eventually fell apart after one more studio effort. They were still barely out of their teens, and tracks like *Oh I Wept, Heavy Load* and *Mr Big* were packed with bluesy bravado. But from the arresting cover photo – four angry young men shouldering into the camera lens – onwards this was a pinnacle of British blues rock.

A real pounding set from Free in this, their third album. At long last they seem to be getting the recognition they deserve and this album will go a long way to enhancing their already high reputation. **Melody Maker, July 1970**

First Take

ARTIST Roberta Flack **RELEASE DATE** July 1972 (UK)/Jan 1970 (US) **LABEL** Atlantic (UK & US) **PRODUCER** Joel Dorn **UK CHART** peak/weeks 40/2 **US CHART** peak/weeks 1/54 **TRACK LISTING** Compared To What/Angelitos Negros/Our Ages Or Our Hearts/I Told Jesus/Hey, That's No Way To Say Goodbye/First Time Ever I Saw Your Face/Tryin' Time/Ballad of the Sad Young Men **PERSONNEL** Roberta Flack (v, p), Ron Carter (b), Joe Newman (t), Bucky Pizzarelli (g), Seldon Powell (bs), Alfred Brown (vl), Ray Lucas (d), Charles McCracken (c)

Former schoolteacher Roberta Flack learnt the lesson of patience when her debut album fell off the US chart from a 1969 peak of Number 195. It would take nearly three years to reach Number 1, and then solely due to the success of the track *The First Time Ever I Saw Your Face*, written by Ewan MacColl (father of Kirsty). Exposure in the Clint Eastwood movie *Play Misty For Me* was the key, and the rest fell into place, thanks to Flack's second and third efforts reaching Numbers 33 and 18 respectively. And yes, they were nearly all first takes!

The hallmark of Roberta Flack is an ability to make sure that nothing stands between you and the experience of the song… if you can stand the intensity and don't mind risking your life, listen. **Julius Lester, October 1970**

Fisherman's Blues

ARTIST The Waterboys **RELEASE DATE** October 1988 (UK)/December 1988 (US) **LABEL** Ensign (UK)/Chrysalis (US) **PRODUCER** Bob Johnston **UK CHART** peak/weeks 13/19 **US CHART** peak/weeks 76/26 **TRACK LISTING** Fisherman's Blues/We Will Not Be Lovers/Strange Boat/World Party/And A Bang On The Ear/Has Anybody Here Seen Hank?/When Will We Be Married?/When Ye Go Away/The Stolen Child **PERSONNEL** Mike Scott (v, g, p), Anthony Thistlewaite (s), Steve Wicham (v), Colin Blakey (fl), Sharon Shannon (ad), Noel Bridgeman (d)

Mike Scott was a visionary Scot intent on becoming the post-punk Van Morrison (or, at least, a Kevin Rowland for the late Eighties and early Nineties). His marrying of folk influences and electric rock, Celtic poetry and spiritual mysticism earned the title 'big music' for its majesty and emotional resonance in a cynical, post-modern world. **Fisherman's Blues** featured a version of Morrison's *Sweet Thing* from **Astral Weeks** as well as a Yeats poem set to music. Only the hard-hearted could fail to be moved.

In common with other seekers of Celtic truth, Mike Scott walks a thin line between Mystic and Mental case – for much of the time here he sounds like a well intentioned outsider's view of what 'Irishness' is all about. **Sean O'Hagan, NME, December 1988**

Five Leaves Left

ARTIST Nick Drake **RELEASE DATE** September 1969 (UK)/1976 (US) **LABEL** Island (UK)/Antilles (US) **PRODUCER** Joe Boyd, Witchseason Productions Ltd **UK CHART** peak/weeks 0/0 **US CHART** peak/weeks 0/0 **TRACK LISTING** Time Has Told Me/River Man/Three Hours/Day Is Done/Way To Blue/Cello Song/The Thoughts Of Mary Jane/Man In A Shed/Fruit Tree/Saturday Sun **PERSONNEL** Nick Drake (v, ag, p), Paul Harris (p), Richard Thompson (g), Danny Thompson (b), Rocki Dzidzornu (cg), Clare Lowther (c), Tristam Fry (d, vp)

Cut while still a student at Cambridge University, Drake's debut album (named after a leaf in a Rizla packet) retains its beguiling freshness. His stubborn nature led to its original string arranger being replaced by fellow student Robert Kirby, though Harry Robinson did the honours on the excellent **River Man**. Sadly, disappointing sales plus Nick's inability to perform live (the two may well have been related) ensured only cult status.

… one of those albums that seem tied to exhorting and then playing on a particular mood in the listener – like **Astral Weeks** *and* **Forever Changes** *– certainly and arguably stationed on that particular echelon of creativity…* **Nick Kent, NME, February 1975**

5150

ARTIST Van Halen **RELEASE DATE** April 1986 (UK & US) **LABEL** Warner Bros. (UK & US) **PRODUCER** Van Halen, Mick Jones, Donn Landee **UK CHART** peak/weeks 16/18 **US CHART** peak/weeks 1/64 **TRACK LISTING** Good Enough/Why Can't This Be Love/Get Up/Dreams/Summer Nights/Best Of Both Worlds/Love Walks In/5150/Inside **PERSONNEL** Sammy Hagar (v, g), Eddie Van Halen (g), Michael Anthony (b), Alex Van Halen (d)

Following the departure of vocalist David Lee Roth, Sammy Hagar joined the band, his presence as both singer and guitarist allowing Eddie Van Halen the freedom to expand his technical repertoire and to experiment with keyboard sounds. **5150** – police code for 'escaped lunatic' – the seventh Van Halen album but the first not to feature Lee Roth, evinced a considerable musical advance and included the Number 3 US hit, **Why Can't This Be Love?**

They're not as oddball as before but still maintain that quirkiness that sets them apart and makes you smile. **Love Walks In** *sounds like REO Speedwagon mauling the famous final score theme.* **The Legendry Stud Brothers, Melody Maker, April 1986**

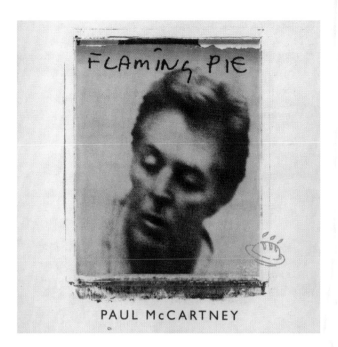

Flaming Pie

ARTIST Paul McCartney **RELEASE DATE** May 1997 (UK & US) **LABEL** Mpl/Parlophone (UK)/Mpl Capitol (US) **PRODUCER** Jeff Lynne, George Martin, Paul McCartney **UK CHART** peak/weeks 2/- **US CHART** peak/weeks – **TRACK LISTING** The Song We Were Singing/The World Tonight/If You Wanna/Somedays/Young Boy/Calico Skies/Flaming Pie/Heaven on A Sunday/Used To Be Bad/Souvenir/Little Willow/Really Love You/Beautiful Night/Great Day **PERSONNEL** Paul McCartney (lv, hv, g, ag, b, dbb, h, d, pc, p, hd), Jeff Lynne (bv, hd, g, ag, k), Steve Miller (hv, lv, g, ag, o), James McCartney (g), Linda McCartney (bv), Michael Thompson (frh), Richard Bissill (frh), Richard Watkins (frh), John Pigneguy (frh), Kevin Robinson (t), Chris 'Snake' Davis (s), Dave Bishop (bs), Ringo Starr (d, pc), session musicians

As the chief surviving Beatle turned 50, he marked the milestone with one of his most effective albums since the Seventies. US blues guitarist Steve Miller was selected as an appropriate vocal/instrumental foil (repaying a debt: Paul guested on his **My Dark Hour** as Paul Ramon), while Beatle flashbacks included the title, borrowed from a Lennon article in *Merseybeat* magazine, and a reunion with Ringo Starr. The single **Young Boy** could have come from George Harrison's Wilburys period, and was none the worse for that.

I'm another dinosaur… I will never stop competing with every other artist in this business. **Pet Sounds** *kicked me to make Pepper. It was direct competition with the Beach Boys. So what? That's what everyone's doing.* **Interviewed by David Fricke, Rolling Stone, February 1990**

Fleetwood Mac

ARTIST Fleetwood Mac **RELEASE DATE** August 1975 (UK & US) **LABEL** Reprise (UK & US) **PRODUCER** Fleetwood Mac, Keith Olsen **UK CHART** peak/weeks 23/20 **US CHART** peak/weeks 1/134 **TRACK LISTING** Monday Morning/Warm Ways/Blue Letter/Rhiannon/Over My Head/Crystal/Say You Love Me/Landslide/World Turning/Sugar Daddy/I'm So Afraid **PERSONNEL** Mick Fleetwood (d, pc), John McVie (k, sy, v), Lindsey Buckingham (g, v), Stevie Nicks (v)

When drummer Mick Fleetwood was looking for a studio to record his band's next album, he was checking out Sound City in Van Nuys, California, when engineer Keith Olsen played him tapes of a recently cut album by duo (Lindsey) Buckingham and (Stevie) Nicks. Both studio and musicians impressed him, so the new album

combined the talents of Fleetwood Mac, Buckingham, Nicks and Olsen, as well as featuring a re-recording of *Crystal* from the duo's eponymous release.

Flesh And Blood

ARTIST Roxy Music **RELEASE DATE** May 1980 (UK & US) **LABEL** Polydor (UK)/Atco (US) **PRODUCER** Talking Heads, Rhet Davies **UK CHART** peak/weeks 1/60 **US CHART** peak/weeks 35/19 **TRACK LISTING** In The Midnight Hour/Oh Yeah (On The Radio)/Same Old Scene/Flesh And Blood/My Only Love/Over You/Eight Miles High/Rain Rain Rain/No Strange Delight/Running Wild **PERSONNEL** Bryan Ferry (v, p), Manzanera (g), MacKay (s, ob), Thompson (d), Paul Carrack (k: Studio), Davud Skinner (k: Tour), Gary Tibbs (b)

The second album from the reformed Roxy Music, **Flesh And Blood** saw all the early Roxy dissonance polished away in favour of a sleek, elegant mid-Atlantic sound. The covers of Wilson Pickett's **Midnight Hour** and The Byrds' **Eight Miles High** were suitably airbrushed, while Bryan Ferry's anguished sighs bordered on the bored.

… the music was more clearly defined and controlled as opposed to the earlier stuff which was slightly more complex and not so easy on the ear. And I don't think it's necessarily a bad thing to make a record people can like and hear instantly. **Bryan Ferry interviewed by Kristine McKenna, NME, June 1982**

Flowers In The Dirt

ARTIST Paul McCartney **RELEASE DATE** June 1989 (UK & US) **LABEL** Parlophone (UK)/Capitol (US) **PRODUCER** Trevor Horn, Neil Dorfsman, Chris Hughes, David Foster **UK CHART** peak/weeks 1/20 **US CHART** peak/weeks 21/49 **TRACK LISTING** My Brave Face/Rough Ride/You Want Her Too/Distractions/We Got Married/Put It There/Figure Of Eight/This One/Don't Be Careless Love/That Day Is Done/How Many People/Motor Of Love/Ou Est Le Soleil **PERSONNEL** Paul McCartney (v, g), Linda McCartney (bv, k), Chris Whitten (d), Robbie McIntosh (g), Hamish Stuart (g, b)

The year 1989 was a landmark one even by Paul McCartney's standards. He received an Ivor for Outstanding Contribution to British Music, unveiled Elvis Costello as his new writing partner and celebrated his first Number 1 album in Britain for five years. *Rolling Stone* put him on their cover as a result, but more important was his decision to put a band (his recording line-up) on the road for the first time in years. Wings' lieutenant Denny Laine, though not involved, praised the album 'because it was a band again'.

Flowers In The Dirt *is the sound of Paul McCartney leaving the cosiness of his fame cocoon and actually competing again.* **Terry Staunton, NME, June 1989**

Fly Like An Eagle

ARTIST The Steve Miller Band **RELEASE DATE** June 1976 (UK)/May 1976 (US) **LABEL** Mercury (UK)/Capitol (US) **PRODUCER** Steve Miller **UK CHART** peak/weeks 11/17 **US CHART** peak/weeks 3/97 **TRACK LISTING** Fly Like An Eagle/Space Odyssey/Wild Mountain Honey/Serenade/Dance, Dance, Dance/Memory Blues/Take The Money & Run/Rock'n'Me/You Send Me/Blue Odyssey/Sweet Maree/The Window **PERSONNEL** Steve Miller (v, g, st), Gary Mallaber (d, pc), Lonnie Turner (b). Special Guests - James Cotton (h), Kenny Johnson (d), Charles Calamise (b), Curley Cooke (rg), Les Dudak (sg), John McFee (db), Joachim Young (o)

A veteran of the hippie era, Steve Miller had been releasing experimental pop albums for almost a decade before he hit international paydirt with **Fly Like An Eagle**, a considerable consolidation of the success he had already achieved in 1973 with **The Joker** album and single. Bolstered by the hits, *Rock'n'Me*, *Take The Money And Run* and the title track, **Fly Like An Eagle** became not just a multi-million seller, but also a well-crafted, mid Seventies adult radio staple on both sides of the Atlantic, as representative of the period as the Eagles and Fleetwood Mac.

The Flying Teapot

ARTIST Gong **RELEASE DATE** May 1973 **LABEL** Virgin **PRODUCER** Giorgio Gomelski **UK CHART** peak/weeks 0/0 **US CHART** peak/weeks 0/0 **TRACK LISTING** Radio Gnome Invisible/Flying Teapot/The Pot Head Pixies/The Octave Doctors & The Crystal Machine/Zero The Hero and The Witch's Spell/Witch's Song I am Your Pussy **PERSONNEL** Daevid Allen (g, v), Gilli Smyth (v), Didier Malherbe (s, fl), Rachid Houari (d, tb), Dieter Gewissler (ctb), Steve Hillage (g), Tim Blake (sy)

Australian guitarist Daevid Allen quit Soft Machine after the band had released its debut single, returned to Paris and set about forming Gong. Signed by Richard Branson to his new Virgin label, they recorded a loose trilogy of albums based on strong astrological, socio-political tenets. **Flying Teapot** was the first, introducing Zero The Hero, the Octave Doctors and other irrepressible Allen figures, and even if you could not actively engage in his philosophies the anarchic sound was totally riveting – ambient techno music years ahead of its time.

Once they stop chanting about Radio Gnome *and cups of tea it's really excellent; flowing rock themes, punctuated by weird effects… It's a great pity that much of the music is hidden behind the silly lyrics.* **M. O., Melody Maker, June 1973**

Focus III

ARTIST Focus **RELEASE DATE** December 1972 (UK)/April 1973 (US) **LABEL** Polydor (UK)/Sire (US) **PRODUCER** Mike Vernon **UK CHART** peak/weeks 6/15 **US CHART** peak/weeks 35/22 **TRACK LISTING** Round Goes The Gossip…/Love Remembered/Sylvia/Carnival Fugue/Focus III/Answers? Questions! Questions?/Anonymus II/Elspeth Of Nottingham/House Of The King **PERSONNEL** Thijs van Leer (v, o, p, pc, hd), Jan Akkerman (ag), Bert Ruiter (b), Pierre van der Linden (d)

Instrumental groups are usually classed as novelty outfits or singles sellers at best. But Dutch four-piece Focus rewrote the rule book and became favourites of BBC TV's *Old Grey Whistle Test* audience with some cultured early Seventies albums, featuring the keyboard/flute skills of Thijs Van Leer and the soaring guitar of Jan Akkerman. **Focus III**, a double, contained the hit single *Sylvia* and broke the band worldwide after the foundations had been laid by the previous year's **Moving Waves**.

'We certainly talked about what the band would be like though. We could either earn money or play progressive music. We did the last thing and it turned out to be commercial as well. Not in the first year when we didn't have anything to eat.' **From an interview by Chris Welch, Melody Maker, August 1972**

Fog On The Tyne

ARTIST Lindisfarne **RELEASE DATE** October 1971 (UK & US) **LABEL** Charisma (UK)/Elektra (US) **PRODUCER** Bob Johnston **UK CHART** peak/weeks 1/56 **US CHART** peak/weeks 0/0 **TRACK LISTING** Meet Me on The Corner/Alright On The Night/Uncle Sam/Together Forever/January Song/Peter Brophy Don't Care/City Song/Passing Ghosts/Train In G Major/Fog On The Tyne **PERSONNEL** Si Cowe (g, md, v), Ray Jackson (bv, md, v), Ray Laidlaw (d), Alan Hull (g, k, v), Rod Clements (g, vl)

The surprise chart-topper of the early Seventies, **Fog On The Tyne** must have been bought by everyone who had turned up to the band's cut-price 'three and six' tour – support acts Van Der Graaf Generator and Genesis – which played every hall in Christendom. As well as the title track becoming an anthem for exiled Geordies, the album's success focused attention on its ignored predecessor **Nicely Out Of Tune** which then climbed the chart in its wake, spawning the single *Lady Eleanor* en route. The good times quickly faded, but **Fog…**, despite a gruesome 1991 re-interpretation with soccer star Paul Gascoigne, remains evocative.

There are enough mature, flawlessly done songs here – **Meet Me On The Corner, January Song, Fog On The Tyne,** *and my favourite* **Train In G Major** *– to make it obvious that Lindisfarne is getting close to wherever it's headed.* **Bud Scoppa, Rolling Stone, June 1972**

For Those About To Rock We Salute You

ARTIST AC/DC **RELEASE DATE** November 1981 (UK & US) **LABEL** Atlantic (UK & US) **PRODUCER** Robert John 'Mutt' Lange **UK CHART** peak/weeks 3/29 **US CHART** peak/weeks 1/30 **TRACK LISTING** For Those About To Rock (We Salute You)/Evil Walks/C.O.D./Spellbound/Put The Finger On You/Let's Get It Up/Inject The Venom/Breaking The Rules/Snowballed/Night Of The Long Knives **PERSONNEL** Angus Young (g), Malcolm Young (g), Bon Scott (v), Phil Rudd (d), Cliff Williams (b), Brian Johnson (v)

The title 'song' became their theme tune (and that of an entire subculture) and, live, was just about audible above the firework display. Capitalizing on their resurrection, and relative new-boy Brian Johnson's determination to cut it, AC/DC pummelled away at deafening a new generation of HM fans. Only when the hooks matched the volume did they transcend the turgid limitations of their genre and, to non-converts, small doses are advisable. The lewd toilet humour of *Let's Get It Up* was typical of their childish sexual innuendo. They slumped in the Eighties.

… they're playing 'em hard, fast and furious on an album that confirms their reputation as the most fearsome metal machine imaginable. **Carol Clerk, Melody Maker, December 1981**

For Your Pleasure

ARTIST Roxy Music RELEASE DATE April 1973 (UK)/July 1973 (US) LABEL Island (UK)/Reprise (US) PRODUCER Brian Eno UK CHART peak/weeks 4/27 US CHART peak/weeks 193/2 TRACK LISTING Do The Strand/Beauty Queen/Strictly Confidential/Editions Of You/In Every Dream Home A Heartache/The Bogus Man/Grey Lagoons/For Your Pleasure PERSONNEL Bryan Ferry (v, p), Manzanera (g), Andy MacKay (s, ob), Graham Simpson (b, v), Thompson (d), Gary Tibbs (b), Brian Eno (sy)

Roxy Music's dual facility for succinct glam-rockers and extended prog-tronics was evinced on their second release, Bryan Ferry's personal favourite Roxy album. Featuring the celebrated *Do The Strand* (but not the band's recent hit, *Pyjamarama*) and the love letter to a blow-up doll, *In Every Dream Home A Heartache*, **For Your Pleasure** achieved in music what the cover art did with its glamorous depiction of Amanda Lear-plus-panther and Ferry-as-chauffeur against a neon futurescape: painting a picture of the modern world as beautiful yet melancholy, lonely and desperate.

Ferry's odd vocal styling and the group's sudden endings are all worth hearing, but mainly because they are interesting, not entertaining… the bulk of **For Your Pleasure** *is either above us, beneath us or on another plane altogether.* **Paul Gambaccini, Rolling Stone, July 1973**

Forces Of Victory

ARTIST Linton Kwesi Johnson RELEASE DATE April 1979 (UK & US) LABEL Island (UK & US) PRODUCER Linton Kwesi Johnson UK CHART peak/weeks 66/- US CHART peak/weeks 0/0 TRACK LISTING Want Fi Goh Rave/It Noh Funny/Sonny's Lettah (Anti-sus Poem)/Independant Intavenshan/Fite Dem Back/Reality Poem/Forces Of Vicktry/Time Come PERSONNEL Linton Kwesi Johnson: all words and music (v), Vivian Weathers (b, bv), Floyd Lawson (b), Jah Bunny (d, pc), Winston Crab Curniffe (d, pc), John Kaipye (g), Dennis Bovell (p, bv), Webster Johnson (p, o), The Invisible One (o), Fari (pc), Winston Bennett (bv), Rico (tb), Dick Cuthell (fh), Julio Finn (bv)

British reggae came of age in the late Seventies as the scene flourished in tandem with punk. Aswad, Merger, Black Slate, Steel Pulse and Misty were among those who took advantage, while dub poet Linton Kwesi Johnson, having debuted as Poet and the Roots, produced a classic under his own name. Tracks like *Sonny's Lettah* hit hard at oppression, while support slots with groups like the Beat saw him reach a wider audience. While his Nineties successors seemed rooted in straight poetry, L.K.J.'s mark was still recognized.

Forever Changes

ARTIST Love RELEASE DATE September 1966 (UK)/May 1966 (US) LABEL Elektra (UK & US) PRODUCER Arthur Lee, Bruce Botnick UK CHART peak/weeks 24/6 US CHART peak/weeks 57/18 TRACK LISTING Alone Again Or/A House Is Not A Motel/Andmoreagain/The Daily Planet/Old Man/The Red Telephone/Maybe The People Would Be The Times Or Between Clark And Hilldale/Live And Let Live/The Good Humor Man He Sees Everything Like This/Bummer In The Summer/You Set The Scene PERSONNEL Arthur Lee (v, g), John Echols (g), Bryan Maclean (g, v), Ken Forest (b)

Recording their third album, Love left behind their garage and folk roots to experiment with strings, woodwinds, strummed Spanish guitars and trumpets. Lyrically it both caught the dreamy acid mood of the times and remained in reality. Love were bad boys – Peter of Big Brother had once commented, 'their name's love but they're hate' – and leader Arthur Lee could be vindictive in his songwriting, whilst guitarist Johnny Echols added searing lead lines. Featuring the exquisitely orchestrated *Alone Again Or*, written by Bryan MacLean but a Lee vocal tour de force, this line-up released one subsequent single before passing into the realms of legend.

Some of the songs meander and lack real melodic substance. Leader Arthur Lee composed nine of the 11 cuts in his quest for originality… **The Red Telephone** *is an example of this. It contains both excellent and mediocre portions.* **Jim Bickhart, Rolling Stone, February 1968**

Forever Your Girl

ARTIST Paula Abdul **RELEASE DATE** October 1988 (UK)/July 1988 (US) **LABEL** Siren (UK)/Virgin (US) **PRODUCER** Glen Ballard, L.A. Reid **UK CHART peak/weeks** 3/39 **US CHART peak/weeks** 1/175 **TRACK LISTING** The Way That You Love Me/Knocked Out/Opposites Attract/State Of Attraction/I Need You/Forever Your Girl/Straight Up/Next To You/Cold Hearted/One Or The Other **PERSONNEL** Paula Abdul (v, bv), Babyface (k, bv), Jeff Lorber (k), St. Paul (b), Kayo (sy), Glen Ballard (d), Dave Cochran (g, bv), L.A. Reid (d), session musicians

Choreographer and Laker Girl Abdul timed her Madonna-lite debut album to perfection, and it became, almost implausibly, one of the most successful in history. Having previously put everyone from Janet Jackson to ZZ Top through their dance steps, as well as working on Oliver Stone's *The Doors* movie, Abdul at last appeared in her own very marketable videos, more memorable for her gyrations than the musical accompaniment. These videos included the mega-hits **Straight Up** and **Cold-Hearted**. A backing singer later sued, claiming she sang the lead vocal lines: the case was dismissed after two years. Abdul released further albums, and the exquisite **Rush Rush**, but the *zeitgeist* had moved on.

'*I'm no Aretha Franklin,*' *she says* – Abdul has managed, with the help of a vocal coach and savvy producers, to knock out a series of memorable Number 1 hits. And though it took more than a year… **Forever Your Girl** has also reached the top. **From an Interview by David Wild, Rolling Stone, November 1989**

4

ARTIST Foreigner **RELEASE DATE** July 1981 (UK & US) **LABEL** Atlantic (UK & US) **PRODUCER** Robert John 'Mutt' Lange, Mick Jones **UK CHART peak/weeks** 5/62 **US CHART peak/weeks** 1/81 **TRACK LISTING** Night Life/Juke Box Hero/Break It Up/Waiting For A Girl Like You/Luanne/Urgent/I'm Gonna Win/Woman In Black/Girl On The Moon/Don't Let Go **PERSONNEL** Mick Jones (lg, k, bv), Lou Gramm (lv, pc), Dennis Elliot (d, bv), Rick Wills (b, bv) with Tom Dolby, Mark Rivera, Hugh McCracken, Junior Walker, Larry Fast, Michael Fonfara, Bob Mayo, Ian Lloyd, 'Mutt' Lange

US AOR Giants Foreigner celebrated their fourth album by shedding two members to slim to a quartet. Yet less meant more and they binned Bad Company comparison with their first and only US chart-topper, thanks to two very contrasting hit singles. The Motown groove of *Urgent* was enhanced by a sax cameo by Junior Walker, whom they tracked down in the *Village Voice* gig guide and invited to the studio, while the synth-laced *Waiting For A Girl Like You* set the standard for future rock ballads.

461 Ocean Boulevard

ARTIST Eric Clapton **RELEASE DATE** August 1974 (UK)/July 1974 (US) **LABEL** RSO (UK & US) **PRODUCER** Tom Dowd **UK CHART peak/weeks** 3/19 **US CHART peak/weeks** 1/25 **TRACK LISTING** Motherless Children/Give Me Strength/Willie And The Hand Jive/Get Ready/I Shot The Sheriff/I Can't Hold Out/Please Be With Me/Let It Grow/Steady Rollin' Man/Mainline Florida **PERSONNEL** Eric Clapton (v, g, db), George Terry (g), Albhy Galuten (o), Dick Sims (o), Carl Radle (b), Al Jackson (d), Jamie Oldajer (d), Yvonne Elliman (v), Tom Bernfeld (bv), Jim Fox (d)

Clapton's solo career took off with this easy, laid-back set, highlighting his

comfortable voice as much as his renowned guitar technique. Choosing the accessibility and pull of his cover versions with some cunning, he brought Bob Marley (via *I Shot The Sheriff* – an American Number 1) to a wider audience, and was well suited to deliver Johnny Otis' *Willie And The Hand Jive* and Robert Johnson's *Steady Rollin' Man*, the title of which fairly summed up Clapton's niche and appeal after his late Sixties/early Seventies heroin excesses. Produced in Florida by Tom Dowd, *Motherless Children* was another stand-out.

Clapton has gone soft. A cosy little album this, with only a dash of the old spontaneity and flair, and oddly enough it seems over in a trice. **J. W., Melody Maker, July 1974**

Frampton Comes Alive!

ARTIST Peter Frampton RELEASE DATE May 1976 (UK)/January 1976 (US) LABEL A&M (UK & US) PRODUCER Peter Frampton UK CHART peak/weeks 6/39 US CHART peak/weeks 1/97 TRACK LISTING Introduction/Something's Happening/Doobie Wah/Show Me The Way/It's A Plain Shame/All I Want To Be (Is By Your Side)/Wind Of Change/Baby, I Love Your Way/I Wanna Go To The Sun/Penny For Your Thoughts/(I'll Give You) Money/Shine On/Jumping Jack Flash/Lines On My Face/Do You Feel Like We Do PERSONNEL Peter Frampton (g, v), John Siomos (d), Bob Mayo (g, v, p, o), Stanley Sheldon (b, v)

Four studio albums down and still no commercial breakthrough… Peter Frampton, dubbed the Face of '68 when lead guitarist with the Herd, took eight years to crack it, by dint of constant US touring. The 'talk-box' guitar gimmick quickly palled, but the songs themselves had an endearing charm, like the man himself. And after his career fell away (how do you top a six-million seller?) he had another crack at it in 1995 with **Frampton Comes Alive 2** – less hair but more know-how.

This is the best set of live performances heard for some time, and it marks the evolution of Peter Frampton into a major rock figure, armed with years of experience. **Chris Welch, Melody Maker, March 1976**

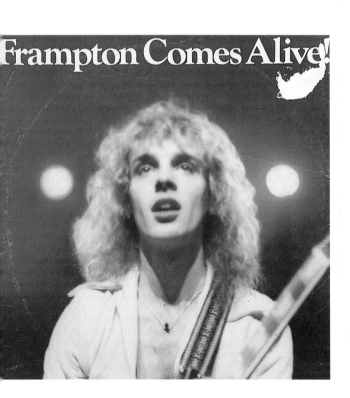

Frank Sinatra Sings For Only The Lonely

ARTIST Frank Sinatra RELEASE DATE December 1958 (UK)/September 1958 (US) LABEL Capitol (UK & US) PRODUCER Voyle Gilmore UK CHART peak/weeks 5/13 US CHART peak/weeks 1/120 TRACK LISTING Only For The Lonely/Angel Eyes/What's New/Willow Weep For Me/Good-Bye/Blues In The Night/Guess I'll Hang My Tears Out To Dry/Ebb Tide/Gone With The Wind/One For My Baby PERSONNEL Frank Sinatra (v), Nelson Riddle (arr, con), session musicians

The cover art, which won a Grammy, sets the tone, featuring Frank Sinatra as a sad clown with a tear falling down his cheek. For many, including Elvis Costello, this is Sinatra's masterpiece: the mood of unrestrained misery sustained beautifully over these 14 (on the CD) tracks. Again, Nelson Riddle manages to create lush soundscapes that never infringe on Sinatra's anguished, conversational croon.

Freak Out

ARTIST Mothers Of Invention RELEASE DATE March 1967 (UK)/February 1967 (US) LABEL Verve (UK)/Verve MGM (US) PRODUCER Tom Wilson UK CHART peak/weeks 0/0 US CHART peak/weeks 130/23 TRACK LISTING Hungry Freaks, Daddy/I Ain't Got No Heart/Who Are The Brain Police?/Go Cry On Somebody Else's Shoulder/Motherly Love/How Could I Be Such A Fool/Wowie Zowie/You Didn't Try To Call Me/Any Way The Wind Blows/I'm Not Satisfied/You're Probably Wondering Why I'm Here/Trouble Every Day/Help, I'm A Rock/The Return Of The Son Of Monster Magnet PERSONNEL Frank Zappa (g, v), Ray Collins (v), Elliott Ingber (g), Roy Estrada (b)

In the mid Sixties pop scene no-one had released a double album as a debut, and concept albums were as rare as hen's teeth. Having been discovered by Dylan-producer Tom Wilson and signed to MGM/Verve for a $2,500 advance, Frank Zappa and his Mothers broke the mould. This highly unconventional result featuring improvisations, conversation and all manner of fragments more or less single-handedly invented psychedelic rock. The group's name was extended for the label at Verve's insistence.

Throwing off their social chains, freeing themselves from their national social slavery and realising whatever potential they possess for free expression the Mothers of Invention toss the moral code aside like spare sugar lumps. That is they're sending up American society… **Melody Maker, March 1967**

Free Live

ARTIST Free RELEASE DATE June 1971 (UK)/September 1971 (US) LABEL Island (UK)/A&M (US) PRODUCER Free, Andy Johns UK CHART peak/weeks 4/12 US CHART peak/weeks 89/8 TRACK LISTING All Right Now/I'm A Mover/Be My Friend/Fire And Water/Ride On Pony/Mr Big/The Hunter/Get Where I Belong PERSONNEL Paul Rogers (v), Paul Kossoff (g), Andy Fraser (b), Simon Kirke (d)

It took the first of several break-ups to force the stop-gap release of **Free Live** – but maybe it was listening to it that made the band members realise what they were giving up. Intuitive, instinctive and powerful, the set catches the four-man blues rockers at their best: Fraser's thick, pumping bass sound is the ideal counterpoint to Kossoff's Les Paul wail, while Rodgers is as ever the consummate blues shouter. The final track, a studio effort *Get Where I Belong*, suggests they were too spent to do another encore – but who could fail to be satisfied with what had gone before?

Essentially a live group, it seems surprising that they have waited until they are no more before releasing a live album… It's a must for Free fans… for it could easily have been titled 'The Best Of Free'. **C. C., Melody Maker, June 1971**

Free Peace Sweet

ARTIST Dodgy **RELEASE DATE** June 1996 **LABEL** A&M (UK & US) **PRODUCER** Hugh Jones **UK CHART** peak/weeks – **US CHART** peak/weeks – **TRACK LISTING** Intor/In A Room/Trust In Time/You've Gotta Look Up/If You're Thinking Of Me/Good Enough/Ain't No Longer Asking/Found You/One Of Those Rivers/Prey For Drinking/Jack The Lad/Long Life/U.K.R.I.P./Homegrown **PERSONNEL** Nigel Clark (v, g, ag, b), Matthew Priest (d, pc, v), Andy Miller (g, v), Richard Payne (k)

Mixing the Stone Roses' blissed-out messages with the Who's muscular trad (dad?)-rock and a smattering of West Coast harmonies, Birmingham Brit-popsters Dodgy hit paydirt with their third album – two years on from **Homegrown**, which might have done the trick in 1994 but for the delayed release of the single *Staying Out For The Summer*. At festival time, *Good Enough* – one of four hits here – proved an infectious anthem, while horns, strings, vibes and Richard Payne's guest keyboards broadened the palette effectively.

If **Free Peace Sweet** *was the work of one of the genre's less imaginative ensembles… it would sound fine indeed. But from Dodgy it sounds like a group treading water… a fine pop album then. But not a great Dodgy album.* **Paul Moody, NME, June 1996**

Free Your Mind And Your Ass Will Follow

ARTIST Funkadelic **RELEASE DATE** 1971 (UK)/October 1970 (US) **LABEL** Pye Int (UK)/Westbound (US) **PRODUCER** George Clinton **UK CHART** peak/weeks 0/0 **US CHART** peak/weeks 92/11 **TRACK LISTING** Free Your Mind And Your Ass Will Follow/Friday Night, August 14th/Funky Dollar Bill/I Wanna Know If It's Good To You/Some More/Eulogy And Light **PERSONNEL** George Clinton (v), Charles Butch Davis (v), Calvin Simon (v), Robert Lambert (v), Grady Thomas (v), Bernie Worrell (k)

With contractual wrangles having temporarily curtailed the Parliaments, George Clinton regrouped his troops, gave them a change of direction and unleashed Funkadelic (the name being reflective of the group's music – hard and heavy funk laced with psychedelia) upon an unsuspecting public. Coming at a time when Sly, Hendrix and Whitfield were pushing black music's boundaries ever outwards to the rock market, Funkadelic are equally worthy of interest. Westbound are also worthy of mention: to have allowed the Ohio Players free reign over their sleeves and Clinton the final say on album titles spoke volumes!

Sheer boredom – but FUNKY boredom, you dig? Almost 50 minutes of endlessly repeated guitar and organ riffs freaked up with that funkadelic to psyche-soul sound… **A. L., Melody Maker, September 1970**

The Freewheelin' Bob Dylan

ARTIST Bob Dylan **RELEASE DATE** November 1963 (UK)/September 1963 (US) **LABEL** CBS (UK)/Columbia (US) **PRODUCER** John Hammond **UK CHART** peak/weeks 1/49 **US CHART** peak/weeks 22/33 **TRACK LISTING** Blowin' In The Wind/Girl From The North Country/Masters Of War/Down The Highway/Bob Dyaln's Blues/A Hard Rain's A-Gonna Fall/Don't Think Twice It's Alright/Bob Dylan's Dream/Oxford Town/Talking World War III Blues/Corrina, Corrina/Honey, Just Allow Me One More Chance/I Shall Be Free **PERSONNEL** Bob Dylan (v), session musicians

Having released an influential first album the previous year, Dylan hit his stride – much to the delight of Peter Paul and Mary, who took *Blowin' In The Wind* and *Don't Think Twice It's Alright* to the chart. Bizarrely it would be April 1965 before **Freewheelin** would top the UK listings, by which time Dylan had released two more albums and been mentioned in dispatches by the clearly besotted Beatles. The cover, incidentally, features his then

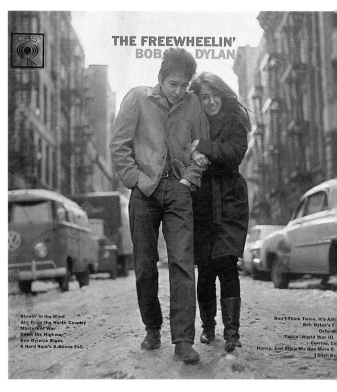

girlfriend Suze Rotolo.

His repertoire is stuffed with original material which gives a really individual slant on the way we are living and, as he puts it, not living… he lashes out hard in such songs as **Masters of War** *and* **With God on our Side**. **Melody Maker, May 1964**

French Record

ARTIST Kate & Anna McGarrigle **RELEASE DATE** 1980 **LABEL** /Hannibal (US) **PRODUCER** Joe Boyd, Anna McGarrigle, Ken McKenzie, David Nichtern **UK CHART** peak/weeks – **US CHART** peak/weeks – **TRACK LISTING** Entre Lajeunesse Et La Sagesse/Complainte Pour Ste Catherine/Mais Quand Tu Danses/Cheminant a La Ville/Excursion a Venise/In Filant Ma Quenouille/La Belle S'est Etourdie/Naufragee Du Tendre/Avant La Guerre/A Boire/Prends Ton Manteau **PERSONNEL** Janie McGarrigle (o, v), Anna McGarrigle (v, bv, p, k, bv), Kate McGarrigle (o, g, ad, k, v, bv), session musicians

Having been plucked from the musical backroom after writing hits for Linda Ronstadt (**Heart Like a Wheel**), Maria Muldaur (**The Work Song**), etc., and cast back again after their own commercial potential proved limited, the Canadian sisters celebrated both their freedom and their French language heritage with this album, cut for Kebec Disc and titled **Entre La Jeunese et La Sagesse** (between youth and experience). Signing to Polydor, they found this rarity had become much sought after by fans, so it appeared on Hannibal for the rest of the world under a somewhat simpler title.

From Elvis In Memphis

ARTIST Elvis Presley **RELEASE DATE** August 1969 (UK)/June 1969 (US) **LABEL** RCA (UK & US) **PRODUCER** Felton Jarvis, Chips Moman **UK CHART** peak/weeks 8/13 **US CHART** peak/weeks 13/34 **TRACK LISTING** Wearin That Loved-In Look/Only The Strong Survive/I'll Hold You In My Heart/Long Black Limousine/It Keeps Right On A-Turnin'/I'm Moving On/Power Of My Love/Gentle On My Mind/After Loving You/True Love Travels On A Gravel Road/Any Day Now/In The Ghetto **PERSONNEL** Elvis Presley (g, p, v), Ronnie Milsap, Bobby Wood (p), The Memphis Horns (brs), Gene Chrisman (d), Mike Leech(gst), Tommy Cogbill (b), Bobby Emmons (o), Ed Hollis (h), John Hughey (stg), Reggie Young (g), session musicians

As Elvis mounted his comeback, fans in Britain, where this topped the chart, were considerably more receptive than at home, where he was now filed firmly under 'country'. To remind everyone of the previous year's TV special that had proved the springboard, an 8 ft by 10 ft photo was included as a bonus. **In The Ghetto** was the gem, proving that the King had successfully re-invented himself.

… the King is still producing commercial music – and has moved into the second half of the twentieth century. Given superb modern backing on a selection of good songs he more than lives up to the legend that began back in 1958. **Melody Maker, August 1969**

Fruit At The Bottom

ARTIST Wendy & Lisa RELEASE DATE March 1989 (UK)/April 1989 (US) LABEL Virgin (UK & US) PRODUCER – UK CHART peak/weeks 45/2 US CHART peak/weeks 88/13 TRACK LISTING Lolly Jolly/Are You My Baby/Satisfaction/Always In My Dreams/Everyday/From Now On (We're One)/Tears Of Joy/Someday I/I think It Was December/Fruit At The Bottom PERSONNEL Wendy Melvoin (g, v), Lisa Coleman (k, b)

Wendy Melvoin and Lisa Coleman grew up together in L.A.: the former a student of jazz, the other of classical piano. In 1979 Coleman began working with Prince, while by 1984 the pair were playing in his band, The Revolution, providing arrangements and even appearing in his film *Purple Rain*. Wendy and Lisa went out on their own in the mid Eighties, to work on their own Prince-ly fusion of pop and funk. **Fruit At The Bottom**, their second album, saw the multi-instrumentalists cook up an eclectic dance-rock stew that, sadly, pleased the critics far more than it did the fans.

Wendy & Lisa produced the album and played just about everything on it, but this time they took a slightly different songwriting approach, emphasising grooves over hooks, danceability over hummability. Alternately feisty and cute. **Michael Azewad, Rolling Stone, June 1989**

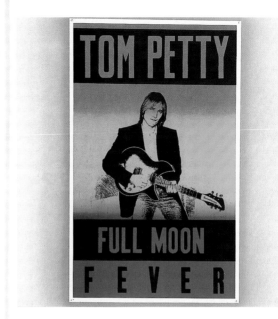

Full Moon Fever

ARTIST Tom Petty RELEASE DATE June 1989 (UK)/May 1989 (US) LABEL MCA (UK & US) PRODUCER Jeff Lynne, Tom Petty, Mike Campbell UK CHART peak/weeks 8/16 US CHART peak/weeks 3/71 TRACK LISTING Free Fallin'/I Won't Back Down/Love Is A Long Road/A Face In The Crowd/Runnin' Down A Dream/Feel A Whole Lot Better/Yer So Bad/Depending On You/The Apartment Song/Alright For Now/A Mind With A Heart Of Its Own/Zombie Zoo PERSONNEL Tom Petty (v, g), Jeff Lynne (g, b, k, v), Mike Campbell (g, b, md, k), Phil Jones (d, pc), Guests

Having served 15 years as frontman of the Heartbreakers, Tom Petty had no qualms about going solo. Besides, he had the not inconsiderable assistance of producer Jeff Lynne, a band-mate in the Travelin' Wilburys, as well as long-time Heartbreakers guitarist Mike Campbell. One or other contributed to most songs, while a cover of The Byrds' *Feel A Whole Lot Better* was a nod to the group who had been so influential on his breakthrough **American Girl**. Going forward while looking back.

…even if **Full Moon Fever** *isn't Petty's best record, it sure sounds like it was the most fun to make.* **Jimmy Guterman, Rolling Stone, May 1989**

Fun House

ARTIST The Stooges RELEASE DATE 1970 LABEL /Elektra (US) PRODUCER Don Gallucci, Brian Ross Myring UK CHART peak/weeks – US CHART peak/weeks – TRACK LISTING Down on the Street/Loose (Stooges)/T.V. Eye/Dirt/1970/Fun House/L.A.Blues PERSONNEL Iggy Pop (v), Dave Alexander (b), Ron Asheton (g), Scott Asheton (d), Steven MacKay (ts), The Stooges (arr)

Iggy Pop's snotty attitude (**T.V. Eye**) and self-loathing (**Dirt**) are present and correct on The Stooges' second album, only this time his players (Dave Alexander on bass, Ron Asheton on guitar and brother Scott on pummelling drums) prove they can do more than emit a cacophonous din. Despite the primal screams, atonal freak-outs and honking free jazz saxophones (courtesy of extra member, Steven Mackay), this band could swing, which makes sense when you remember their home base was the Motor City: Motown.

Do you long to have your mind blown open so wide it'll take weeks for you to pick up the little bitty pieces?…. Then by all means, you must come visit us at the Stooges' **Funhouse**. **Charlie Burton, Rolling Stone, October 1970**

Funky Divas

ARTIST En Vogue RELEASE DATE May 1992 (UK)/April 1992 (US) LABEL East West (UK)/Atlantic (US) PRODUCER Thomas McElroy, Denzil Foster UK CHART peak/weeks 4/29 US CHART peak/weeks 8/86 TRACK LISTING This Is Your Life/My Lovin' (Your'e Never Gonna Get It)/Hip Hop Lover/Free Your Mind/Desire/Giving Him Something He Can Feel/It Ain't Over Till The Fat The Lady Sings/Give It Up/Turn It Loose/Yesterday/Hooked On Your Love/Love Don't Give You/What Is Love/Thanks, Prayer PERSONNEL Terry Ellis (v), Cindy Herron (v), Maxine Jones (v), Dawn Robinson (v)

San Franciscan soul vocal quartet En Vogue were formed by producers Denzil Foster and Thomas McElroy, but soon showed a feisty quality that suggested they were no-one's puppets. 1990's album **Born To Sing** yielded the US Top 3 single *Born To Sing* but it was **Funky Divas** that put them on the map with an incendiary hat-trick of hits in *My Lovin*, *Giving Him Something He Can Feel* and *Free Your Mind*. All were US Top 10 hits, the last covered unwisely by old-timers The Band. They lost a solo-bound Dawn Robinson in 1997 just before *EV3*, her vocal parts unceremoniously deleted. These girls took no shit!

Playful and passionate, smart and sexy, they strut their stuff without selling the songs short.... **Funky Divas** *is the kind of musically adventurous pop album that rockers might find intriguing.* **The Year In Records 1992, Rolling Stone, December 1992**

Funky Kingston

ARTIST Toots And The Maytals RELEASE DATE November 1975 (US) LABEL Trojan PRODUCER Warwick Lyn, Chris Blackwell, Dave Bloxham UK CHART peak/weeks - US CHART peak/weeks 164/13 TRACK LISTING Sit Right Down/Pomp And Pride/Loiue Loiue/I Can't Believe/Redemption Song/Daddy/Funky Kingston/It Was Written Down PERSONNEL Brass by Sons of the Jungle

The title of Toots And The Maytals' third album spoke volumes about their dual commitment to the gentle lilt of Jamaican reggae and the rhythmic force of funk. In mainman Toots Hibbert's delivery, too, there was evidence of his love of the great soul vocalists, from Otis Redding to Solomon Burke. Although **Funky Kingston** earned The Maytals a support slot on one of The Who's early Seventies US tours, they never had the crossover impact of Bob Marley's Wailers. Nevertheless, cover versions of *Louie Louie*, and the inclusion of *Pressure Drop*, which also appeared on the landmark reggae soundtrack, **The Harder They Come**, demonstrate the breadth of Hibbert's vision.

This is perhaps the best lurching album of all time. Listening to it, you can't help but sway from side to side in a way which closely approximates the state of drunkeness... Every track here is a gas. **R. W., Melody Maker, June 1973**

Future Days

ARTIST Can RELEASE DATE June 1973 (UK & US) LABEL United Artists (UK & US) PRODUCER Can UK CHART peak/weeks 0/0 US CHART peak/weeks 0/0 TRACK LISTING Future Days/Spray/Moonshake/Bel Air PERSONNEL Irmin Schmidt (k), Holger Czukay (b), David Johnson (fl), Michael Karoli (g, vl), Jaki Liebezeit (d), Malcolm Mooney (v)

The Krautrock kings inspired every shade of hyperbole, with Julian Cope describing them as heroes, wizards and stars. They saw themselves as anarchists rather than rockers. Five years into their career, **Future Days** moved them from sonic groovemeisters to melancholy texture-teasers. Atypically embracing jazzier indulgences, it boosted their cult following massively; on subsequently signing to Virgin though, they seemed perversely intent on burying their own legend under a series of unpalatable experiments.

Lots of repetition, ponderous bass riffs, tiny guitar and organ motifs, like miniature splinters of electronic sound, and the battering, unrelenting drumming Jaki Liebezeit. This time, Can have eased up slightly on their overpowering heaviness, and whilst this one is just as insistent its not so out-and-out loud. **S. L., Melody Maker, January 1974**

Fuzzy

ARTIST Grant Lee Buffalo RELEASE DATE July 1994 (UK)/June 1993 LABEL Slash (UK & US) PRODUCER Paul Kimble UK CHART peak/weeks – US CHART peak/weeks 0/0 TRACK LISTING The Shining Hour/Jupiter And Teardrop/Fuzzy/Wish You Well/The Hook/Soft Wolf Tread/Stars 'N' Stripes/Dixie Drug Store/America Snoring/Grace/You Just Have To Be Crazy PERSONNEL Grant Lee Phillips (v, ag, g.), Paul Kimble (b, p, v), Joey Peters (d, pc)

A beautifully understated, lovingly textured debut that demonstrates how a simple three-piece band can seem like the most important thing on this planet. **Fuzzy** is uniquely American, combining all the best parts of Neil Young, Woody Guthrie and Tom Waits. Evocatively sparse soundscapes, cinematic vision, emotional rollercoastering and a storyteller's ability to draw the listener into the song's visual heartland are a few of the reasons why this is the soundtrack to the best road movie never made.

…a debut album suffused with a swaggering air of precocious authority that prompts all those cliches about 'trainee stadium rock'. Therein, of course, lies GLB's appeal… there is a bold sense of drama that makes **Fuzzy** *a heartstopping tour de force.* **NME, December 1994**

Fuzzy Logic

ARTIST Super Furry Animals RELEASE DATE 1996 LABEL Creation Records (UK & US) PRODUCER Gorwell Owen & SFA UK CHART peak/weeks – US CHART peak/weeks – TRACK LISTING God! Show Me Magic/Fuzzy Birds/Something For The Weekend/Frisbee/Hometown Unicorn/Gathering Moss/If You Don't Want Me To Destroy You/Bad Behaviour/Mario Man/Hangin' With Howard Marks/Long Gone/For Now And Ever PERSONNEL Gruff Rhys (v, g), Dafydd Ieuan (d, pc, v, p), Cian Ciaran (k, v), Guto Pryce (b, o), Huw Bunford (g, v, c)

Originally a techno outfit, Super Furry Animals emerged from Wales in the early Nineties with an equal fondness for new technology and classic pop structures. Unlike most of the Brit-pop pack, who were content to draw on the obvious Beatles, Stones and Kinks, on their debut album, **Fuzzy Logic**, SFA harked back to the pomp and circumstance of prog-rock (spot the balalaika!) as well as to such masters of synth-driven glam-pop as Roxy Music.

Super Furry Animals peel back the decades for inspiration. Crucially, however, the Furries ignore the pious bleatings of the saucy Sixties sycophants, because in Super Furry Town, the year is always 1974. Think Wombles! Think bubble gum fumblings! Think vast glam chords, mad pianos and the odd perky flute! **Simon Williams, NME, May 1996**

G.I. Blues

ARTIST Elvis Presley RELEASE DATE December 1960 (UK)/October 1960 (US) LABEL RCA (UK & US) PRODUCER Don Wardell UK CHART peak/weeks 1/55 US CHART peak/weeks 1/111 TRACK LISTING Tonight Is So Right For Love/What's She Really Like/Big Boots/Frankfurt Special/Wooden Heart/Shoppin' Around/Pocketful Of Rainbows/G.I.Blues/Doin The Best I Can/Didja Ever/Blue Suede Shoes PERSONNEL Elvis Presley (v, g), Scotty Moore (g), Floyd Cramer (p)

When **G.I. Blues** entered *Billboard*'s album chart at Number 6 in October 1960, it was the highest debut for any of Presley's albums: the 110-week stay was also a record. All 11 movie songs were included, though curiously **Wooden Heart**, such a success in Britain, was overlooked as a US single release. Joe Dowell cleaned up with a million-selling cover version! Another case of confusion came with Presley's character, Tulsa McLean (originally Tulsa McCauley), and even the film itself (original title *Café Europa*).

Elvis runs the gauntlet of his individualistic vocals on this original soundtrack release and his fans have already delivered their favourable verdict on it by giving the disc best-seller status. It's a must for those who love Elvis. **Pop Vocal Discs, Melody Maker, January 1961**

Garbage

ARTIST Garbage RELEASE DATE October 1995 LABEL Mushroom (UK)/Geffen (US) PRODUCER – UK CHART peak/weeks – US CHART peak/weeks 20/49 TRACK LISTING Supervixen/Queer/Only Happy When It Rains/As Heaven Is Wide/Not My Idea/A Stroke Of Luck/Vow/Stupid Girl/Dog New Tricks/My Lover's Box/Fix Me Now/Milk PERSONNEL Shirley Manson (v, g), Steve Marks (g, b), Dave Erikson (g, k, b), Butch Vig (d)

After a couple of low-key single releases, the Garbage bandwagon got rolling in earnest with their eponymous debut album. A kaleidoscope of contemporary sounds and rhythms, their unique blend of grunge and groove, with multi-layered guitars and punchy beats (from Nirvana producer Butch Vig) gave the whole an atmosphere of seductive menace. No less than five tracks were eventually lifted for singles release as Garbage carved a niche for themselves, purveying industrial pop-rock with a commercial edge. Dynamic, shimmering, and utterly worthy of the hype.

Garbage *is dazzlingly multi-layered, full of tape loop samples, double-tracked vocals, assorted percussive bangings and mysterious scratches and rumblings. It's audaciously of its time, queasily bright in its vicious darkness…* **Sharon O'Connell, Melody Maker, September 1995**

Gasoline Alley

ARTIST Rod Stewart **RELEASE DATE** September 1970 (UK)/June 1970 (US) **LABEL** Vertigo (US)/Mercury (US) **PRODUCER** Rod Stewart, Lou Reizner **UK CHART** peak/weeks 62/1 **US CHART** peak/weeks 27/57 **TRACK LISTING** Gasoline Alley/It's All Over Now/Only A Hobo/My Way Of Giving/County Comfort/Cut Across Shorty/Lady Day/Jo's Lament/I Don't Want To Discuss It **PERSONNEL** Rod Stewart (v), Ron Wood (g), Ronnie Lane (b), Kenneth Jones (d)

In the same year that the Faces released their debut album, the band's lead singer, Rod Stewart, put out his second LP, **Gasoline Alley**, which cemented his burgeoning reputation as a strong songwriter and even more remarkable singer. Featuring cover versions of Elton John (**Country Comfort**) and Bob Dylan (**Only A Hobo**) material alongside some original compositions, **Gasoline Alley** was also notable for the slide guitar of the Faces' (and future Rolling Stone) Ronnie Wood.

Stewart has a rare sensitivity for the delicate moments in a person's existence…. His music speaks with a gentleness and depth which seems to heal the wounds and ease the pain… a supremely fine artist. **Langdon Winner, Rolling Stone, September 1970**

Gaucho

ARTIST Steely Dan **RELEASE DATE** November 1980 (UK)/December 1980 (US) **LABEL** M.C.A. (UK & US) **PRODUCER** Gary Katz **UK CHART** peak/weeks 27/12 **US CHART** peak/weeks 9/36 **TRACK LISTING** Babylon Sisters/Hey Nineteen/Glamour Profession/Gaucho/Time Out Of Mind/My Rival/Third World Man **PERSONNEL** Donald Fagen (k, v), Walter Becker (b, v), Jeff 'Skunk' Baxter (lg), Denny Dias (rg), Jim Hodder (d), Rick Derringer (sg, gst), Mark Knopfler (g, gst)

The final album before Becker and Fagen went their separate ways, **Gaucho** won a Grammy, bequeathed a pair of surefire FM radio classics in **Babylon Sisters** and **Hey Nineteen** and became *de rigueur* as sonically immaculate soundtrack muzak for urban swingers in wine bars around the world. And this, despite the fact that Don and Walt had spent the previous decade lampooning the *faux* sophisticated manners of the upwardly mobile set.

Generation Terrorists

ARTIST The Manic Street Preachers **RELEASE DATE** February 1992 (UK & US) **LABEL** Columbia (UK & US) **PRODUCER** Steve Brown **UK CHART** peak/weeks 13/10 **US CHART** peak/weeks 0/0 **TRACK LISTING** Slash N' Burn/Nat West-Barclays-Midland-Lloyds/Born To End/Motorcycle Emptiness/You Love Us/Love's Sweet Exile/Little Baby Nothing/Repeat (Stars & Stripes)/Tennessee/Another Invented Disease/Stay Beautiful/So Dead/Repeat (UK)/Spectators Of Suicide/Damn Dog/Crucifix Kiss/Methadone Pretty/Condemned To Rock 'N' Roll **PERSONNEL** James Dean Bradfield (v, g, ag, p, bv), Sean Moore (d, pc, t, bv), Nicky Wire (b, bv), Richey Edwards (rg), additional musicians: May McKenna, Jackie Challenor, Lorenza Johnson, Dave Eringa, Traci Lords, Spike Edney, Richard Cottle

The Manics' provocative, arrogant and over-ambitious first album came amid a concentrated press backlash which seems incongruous today. In 1992 their image was that of mouthy, leopard skin-clad Welsh chancers, and **Generation Terrorists** reinforced it superbly. This double album should have been their swan song, but they did not split, as promised, after its release and it now forms an intriguing snapshot of their formative years where raw punk energy rubbed shoulders with intelligent, considered balladry indicative of their later development.

Unsurprisingly, the hype… has outweighed the music. What the many detractors of the Welsh outsiders seem to have ignored is their melodic aplomb, which aids a quest not to prolong their Clash-inspired, thrashy origins. Only a handful of the 17 songs are duff… **Martin Aston, Q, March 1992**

The Genius Of Ray Charles

ARTIST Ray Charles **RELEASE DATE** February 1960 (UK & US) **LABEL** London (UK)/Atlantic (US) **PRODUCER** – **UK CHART** peak/weeks 0/0 **US CHART** peak/weeks 17/82 **TRACK LISTING** Let The Good Times Roll/It Had To be You/Alexander's Ragtime Band/Two Years Of Torture/When Your Lover Has Gone/'Deed I Do/Just For A Thrill/You Won't Let Me Go/Tell Me You'll Wait For Me/Don't Let The Sun Catch You Crying/Am I Blue?/Come Rain Or Come Shine **PERSONNEL** Ray Charles (v, p), Milton Garrad (b), Gisady McGhee (g)

One of the most influential figures of black music, Charles had taken on various genres: blues, gospel, country, jazz, soul and pop, and triumphed with his voice supreme. Blind from the age of seven, he idolised Nat King Cole and Charles Brown. At 29, he recorded the seminal hit (and his first top tenner) *What'd I Say*, but was already demonstrating his versatility by cutting this album: predominantly string-led ballads but coloured with berserk covers such as **Alexander's Ragtime Band** and **Come Rain Or Come Shine**.

Genius + Soul = Jazz

ARTIST Ray Charles **RELEASE DATE** November 1961 (UK)/March 1961 (US) **LABEL** HMV (UK)/ABC Paramount (US) **PRODUCER** Creed Taylor **UK CHART** peak/weeks 0/0 **US CHART** peak/weeks 4/48 **TRACK LISTING** From The Heart/I've Got News For You/Moanin'/Let's Go/One Mint Julep/I'm Gonna Move To The Outskirts Of Town/Stomping Room Only/Mister C/Strike Up The Band/Birth Of The Blues **PERSONNEL** Ray Charles (o, p), Charles Terry, Phillip Guibeau, Joe Newman, Thad Jones, Eugene Young, Joe Wilder, John Frosk, Jimmy Nottingham (t), Frank Wess, Marshall Royal, George Dorsey, Earle Warren (as), Frank Foster, Billy Mitchell, Budd Johnson, Seldon Powell (ts), Charlie Fowlkes, Haywood Henry (s), Urbie Green (tb), Benny Powell, Jimmy Cleveland, Keg Johnson, George Matthews, Henry Cocker, Al Grey (tb), Freddy Greene (g), Eddy Jones, Sam Herman, Joe Benjamin (b), Sonny Payne, Roy Haynes (d)

The eclectic Charles' only big-band jazzy get-together of the early Sixties, this gave the great man an instrumental hit in **One Mint**

Julep. Arranged by Quincy Jones, it saw the versatile singer cool and confident enough to let the musicians do the talking, while he played organ throughout. Yet his mixing together of various styles was vastly influential, and his legacy to singers was what Chuck Berry's was to guitarists.

Singing came to me naturally as a small child. I've since come to consider blues the greatest expression of Negro America.… I will sing anything I like, for what I like is good for me and I hope that the way I sing it is good for those who listen. **Ray Charles interview with Henry Kahn, Melody Maker, October 1961**

Germ Free Adolescents

ARTIST X-Ray Spex RELEASE DATE November 1978 LABEL EMI International PRODUCER Falcon Stuart UK CHART peak/weeks 30/14 US CHART peak/weeks - TRACK LISTING Art-I-Ficial/Obsessed With You/Warrior In Woolworths/Let's Submerge/I Can't Do Anything/Identity/Genetic Engineering/I Live Off You/I Am A Poseur/Germ Free Adolescents/Plastic Bag/The Day The World Turned Day-glo, Oh Bondage Up-Yours PERSONNEL Poly Styrene (v), Jak 'Airport' Stafford (g), Lora Logic (s), Paul Dean (b), B. P. Hurding (d)

X-Ray Spex were the band formed by school friends Poly Styrene and Lora Logic, both of whom became essential role models for *femme* punks everywhere. Not that X-Ray Spex attacked conventional punk targets such as the government and the law. Instead, they aimed their fluorescent bile at the vapidity and sterility of the modern world, specifically the increasingly consumerist nature of society, in classic sax-drenched anthems such as *Oh Bondage, Up Yours* and *The Day The World Turned Day-Glo*.

… barriers mark the world which X-Ray-Spex inhabit and the world about which Poly Styrene writes with the sophisticated innocence that gives a tree and a supermarket equal value.… **Charles Shaar Murray, NME, November 1978**

Get Happy!

ARTIST Elvis Costello And The Attractions RELEASE DATE February 1980 (UK & US) LABEL F-Beat (UK)/Columbia (US) PRODUCER Nick Lowe UK CHART peak/weeks 2/14 US CHART peak/weeks 11/15 TRACK LISTING I Can't Stand Up For Falling Down/Black & White World/Five Gears In Reverse/B Movie/Motel Matches/Human Touch/Beaten To The Punch / Temptation / I Stand Accused/Riot Act/Love For Tender/Opportunity/The Imposter/ Secondary Modern / King Horse / Possession/ Man Called Uncle/ Clown Time Is Over/New Amsterdam/ High Fidelity PERSONNEL Elvis Costello (v, g), Steve Nieve (k), Bruce Thomas (b), Pete Thomas (d)

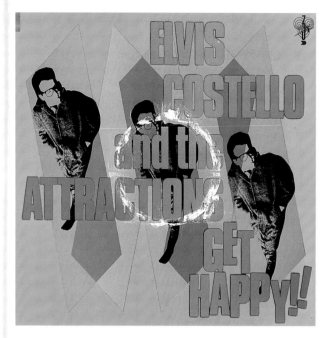

With manager Jake Riviera, Costello formed his own F-Beat label, and the ironically-named **Get Happy!** was its manifesto. It gave the singer a chance to cover some favourite soul numbers, including Sam And Dave's *I Can't Stand Up For Falling Down*, which relished the crack in his voice and gave him a Top 3 hit. While the album's 20 cuts could have benefited from quality control, it was perhaps the relentless ungiving nature of the collection which made it so feverishly exciting. Costello freely admitted to drawing hooks and propulsions from The Four Tops, Al Green, and other soul messiahs.

At 47 odd minutes the album is long, but not extraordinarily so, which means the 10 songs on each side have to rattle through like a fusillade… Twenty-track avalanches are difficult to absorb… but **Get Happy** *will do fine for the moment.* **Chris Brazier, Melody Maker, February 1980**

Get The Knack

ARTIST The Knack RELEASE DATE July 1979 (UK)/June 1979 (US) LABEL Capitol (UK & US) PRODUCER Mike Chapman UK CHART peak/weeks 65/2 US CHART peak/weeks 1/40 TRACK LISTING Let Me Out/Your Number Or Your Name/Oh Tara/(She's) So Selfish/Maybe Tonight/Good Girls Don't/My Sharona/Heartbeat/Siamese Twins (The Monkey And Me)/Lucinda/That's What Little Girls Do/Frustrated PERSONNEL Doug Fieger (v, rg), Berton Averre (lg), Bruce Gay (d), Prescott Niles (b)

Power pop was a US concept, taking the energy of punk but rendering it radio friendly. And The Knack took their cues from even further back: the back cover of this album being a parody of The Beatles' **A Hard Day's Night**. Fuelled by the chart-topping single **My Sharona**, it turned out to be a record-breaking debut, having been recorded in 11 days for $18,000; it went gold in 13 days, platinum in seven weeks and sold a reported five million! But the 1980's, 600,000-selling follow-up **But Little Girls Understand**, indicated that The Knack had clearly lost it.

Don't bother. Unless you've got a taste for cheerfully plundered pop perpetrated by a crew which has as much respect for its sources as the early Sweet had for theirs… Got The Knack? You've been done, too. Yuk. Yuk. **Chris Bohn, Melody Maker, July 1979**

Get Yer Ya-Ya's Out

ARTIST The Rolling Stones **RELEASE DATE** September 1970 (UK & US) **LABEL** London (UK)/Decca (US) **PRODUCER** – **UK CHART** peak/weeks 1/15 **US CHART** peak/weeks 6/23 **TRACK LISTING** Jumpin'Jack Flash/Carol/Stray Cat Blues/Love In Vain/Midnight Rambler/Sympathy For The Devil/Live With Me/Little Queenie/Honky Tonk Women **PERSONNEL** Mick Jagger (v, h), Keith Richards (rg), Brian Jones (lg), Charlie Watts (d), Bill Wyman (b), Ian Stewart (p)

A live album recorded at Madison Square Garden over two November nights in 1969, it begins with godly arrogance: 'Ladies and gentlemen, please welcome the greatest rock 'n' roll band in the world'. Mick Jagger was finding his niche, adding immensely to **Stray Cat Blues** and **Love In Vain**. There was a feral punkish energy to **Sympathy For The Devil**. Although this American tour was to end in tears at Altamont – the end of the Sixties, as many have said – The Stones were burning through the already inspired songs of the last two albums. They released this to spoil the racketeering of a then hot bootleg **Liver Than You'll Ever Be**.

The Seventies may not have started with bright prospects for the future of rock… The form may be in trouble… but The Rolling Stones are most assuredly not in trouble…. The Stones, alone among their generation of groups, are not about to fall by the wayside. **Lester Bangs, Rolling Stone, 12 November 1970**

Ghost In The Machine

ARTIST The Police **RELEASE DATE** October 1981 (UK & US) **LABEL** A&M (UK & US) **PRODUCER** The Police, Hugh Padgham **UK CHART** peak/weeks 1/27 **US CHART** peak/weeks 2/109 **TRACK LISTING** Spirits In The Material World/Every Little Thing She Does Is Magic/Invisible Sun/Hungry For You (J'Aurais Toujours Faim De Toi)/Demolition Man/Too Much Information/Rehumanize Yourself/One World (Not Three)/Omegaman/Secret Journey/Darkness **PERSONNEL** Andy Summers (g), Stewart Copeland (d), Sting (b, v), Jean Roussel (k)

By 1981 the Police were big business: the digital group representation on the cover was 'a service mark of Roxanne Music Overseas Limited', and a music machine they certainly were. **Invisible Sun**, the first single at home and inspired by the Irish Troubles, followed the Specials' **Ghost Town** as a dark soundtrack to a sombre year. Everywhere else it was the sunniest song, *Every*

Little Thing She Does Is Magic, ironically recorded in Canada, with Cat Stevens keyboardist Jean Roussel, rather than the sunshine isle of Montserrat.

The Ghost In The Machine *is amaaaaaaaaazingly dull… dull music with worthy sentiments attached is, ultimately, no more rewarding an aesthetic experience than dull music with foul sentiments attached.* **Charles Shaar Murray, NME, October 1981**

Giant Steps

ARTIST The Boo Radleys **RELEASE DATE** July 1993 (UK & US) **LABEL** Creation (UK)/Columbia (US) **PRODUCER** Boo! Productions **UK CHART** peak/weeks 17/4 **US CHART** peak/weeks 0/0 **TRACK LISTING** I Hang Suspended/Upon 9th and Fairchold/Wish I Was Skinny/Leaves And Sand/Butterfly McQueen/Thinking Of Ways/Barney/Spun Around/If You Want It, Take It/Best Lose The Fear/Take The Time Around/Lazarus/One Is For/Run My Way Runaway/I've Lost The Reason/The White Noise Revisted **PERSONNEL** Rob Cieka (d, pc), Time Brown (b, k), Martin Carr (g, k, fh), Lindsay Johnston (c), Jackie Roy (cl, bc), Meriel Barham (v), Chris Moore (t), Margaret Fiedler (c)

Joining the Brit-pop explosion as American grunge wilted, Liverpool's Boos came up with the marathon opus that was **Giant Steps**. A hodge-podge of Beatlesque Sixties melodies, dubby basslines, guitars, brass and bizarre samples, it wowed the critics and gave the band, led by twin song-smiths Carr and Rowbottom, a reinforced credibility, which they strengthened by drinking the said critics under the table. They also displayed a love of Beach Boys harmonies and shoe-gazing guitar blurs. Unsatisfied with the acclaim of mere reviewers, Carr soon whipped out the naff pop hit *Wake Up Boo*.

Giant Steps *is a fresh fruit salad of an LP. Sometimes it's even cosmic enough to live up to its title. As a role model for British guitar bands, you will hear none better this year.* **Robert Prieur, Melody Maker, August 1993**

The Gilded Palace Of Sin

ARTIST The Flying Burrito Brothers **RELEASE DATE** April 1969 (UK)/March 1969 (US) **LABEL** A&M (UK & US) **PRODUCER** The Flying Burrito Brothers **UK CHART** peak/weeks 0/0 **US CHART** peak/weeks 164/7 **TRACK LISTING** Christine's Tune/Sin City/Do Right Woman/Dark End Of The Street/My Uncle/Wheels/Juanita/Hot Burrito £1/Hot Burrito £2/Do You Know How It Feels/Hippie Boy **PERSONNEL** Gram Parsons (v, g), Chris Hillman (g, v), Sneaky Pete Kleinow (ps), Chris Etheridge (b), Jon Corneal (d)

The Burritos recorded one of the most influential albums of the late Sixties, even if commercially it did little. The partnership of ex-Byrds Chris Hillman and Gram Parsons produced a clutch of classic tunes, paving the way for lesser country-rock outfits like the Eagles, but this stunning debut was never bettered, right down to the sleeve photography with Parsons sporting a Nudie suit – a company renowned for its outfits for traditional country stars like Buck Owens – lavishly decorated with marijuana leaves!

Glass Houses

ARTIST Billy Joel **RELEASE DATE** March 1980 (UK & US) **LABEL** CBS (UK)/Columbia (US) **PRODUCER** Phil Ramone **UK CHART** peak/weeks 9/24 **US CHART** peak/weeks 1/73 **TRACK LISTING** You may Be Right/Sometimes A Fantasy/Don't Ask Me Why/It's Still Rock 'N' Roll To Me/All For Leyna/I Don't Want To Be Alone/Sleeping With The Television On/C'Etait Toi (You Were The One)/Close To Borderline/Through The Long Night **PERSONNEL** Billy Joel (v), David Brown (g), Ritchie Cannata (o), Liberty DeVito (d), Russell Javors (g), Doug Stegmeyer (b)

Billy Joel's second US Number 1 album saw him honing his material to come across in the larger venues he was now playing. He even on occasion abandoned his piano for a guitar in order to belt out bigger, brasher anthems. While the lead single, *You May Be Right*, reached the Top 10 it was the simple, direct, almost Presley-esque *It's Still Rock 'N' roll To Me* that suggested the 'Piano Man' had really been a rocker all along.

I listen to him stabbing out punch lines and punching out stab-lines and the band whacking into some finely sharpened arrangements… a rocker followed by a weepie followed by a smokie sax solo, etc… I'm not sure I can believe Joel on **Glass Houses**. **Colin Irwin, Melody Maker, March 1980**

Going To A Go-Go

ARTIST Smokey Robinson and The Miracles **RELEASE DATE** February 1966 (UK)/November 1965 (US) **LABEL** Tamla-Mowtown (UK)/Tamla (US) **PRODUCER** Smokey Robinson **UK CHART** peak/weeks 0/0 **US CHART** peak/weeks 8/40 **TRACK LISTING** The Tracks Of My Tears/Going To A Go-Go/Ooh Baby Baby/My Girl Has Gone/In Case You Need Love/Choosey Beggar/Since You Won My Heart/From Head To Toe/All That's Good/My Baby Changes Like The Weather/Let Me Have Some/A Fork In The Road **PERSONNEL** Smokey Robinson (lv), Ronnie White (v), Bobby Rodgers (v), Pete Moore (v), Marvin Tarplin (g)

Robinson's craft, honed by none other than Berry Gordy, is best revealed on the lead cut, *The Tracks Of My Tears*, one of Motown's finest-ever singles. If, like Lionel Richie, Robinson excelled on ballads, then there were still moments when he could raise the tempo and come up with the goods: the title track (later covered by The Rolling Stones!) is as important to Motown's dance heritage as *Dancing In The Street*.

Robinson moved quickly from writing period pieces that seemed influenced by Atlantic's R&B sound, to composing and singing a smooth, poetic brand of blues. **Rolling Stone, August 1972**

Gold Mother

ARTIST James **RELEASE DATE** June 1990 (UK & US) **LABEL** Fontana (UK)/Mercury (US) **PRODUCER** Booth, Gott, Glennie, Garside **UK CHART** peak/weeks 2/34 **US CHART** peak/weeks 0/0 **TRACK LISTING** Come Home/Lose Control/Government Walls/God Only Knows/You Can't Tell How Much Suffering (On A Face That's Always Smiling)/How Was It For You/Sit Down/Walking The Ghost/Gold Mother/Top Of The World **PERSONNEL** Tim Booth (v, w), Jim Glennie (b, bv), Larry Gott (g, bv), Saul Davies (vl, g, cb), Andy Diagram (t, bv), David Baynton-Power (d, pc), Mark Hunter (k, ad). (Backing Vocals on 'Gold Mother' by Inspiral Carpets. Saxophone on 'Gold Mother' by Vinny Corrigan.)

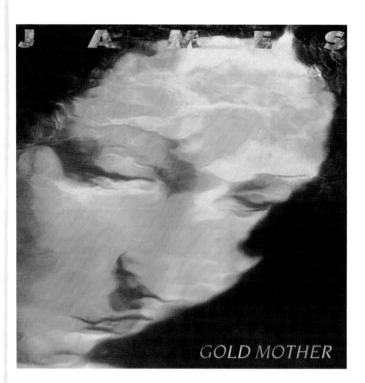

GOLD MOTHER

Having formed in 1983 and taken home £34 a week as an unconventional part of a government-funded Enterprise Scheme, indie-hopefuls James showed considerable enterprise in re-recording two long-time stage standards, *Sit Down* and *Come Home*, first released in 1989, after signing with Fontana. The former would hit Number 2 in April 1991 behind one-hit wonder Chesney Hawkes, while this album was hastily repackaged and repromoted to similarly successful effect.

… a bold, brazenly confident fulfillment of promises made… a multi-tiered extravaganza of organically upbeat intuition which challenges and chills with one hand and comforts with the other. James… are creating pop as disposable as a test tube of panda sperm. Enter and enjoy. **Simon Williams, NME, June 1990**

The Golden Age Of Lonnie Donegan

ARTIST Lonnie Donegan **RELEASE DATE** September 1962 **LABEL** Pye Golden Guinea **PRODUCER** Pye Records (Sales) Ltd **UK CHART** peak/weeks 3/23 **US CHART** peak/weeks 0/0 **TRACK LISTING** Have A Drink On Me/Lost John/Nobody Loves Like An Irishman/Cumberland Gap/Seven Daffodils/Puttin' On The Style/Battle Of New Orleans/Love Is Strange/Rock O' My Soul/Fort Worth Jail/Grand Coulee Dam/My Old Man's A Dustman **PERSONNEL** Lonnie Donegan (v)

The king of skiffle was never really an album artist, but in the year The Beatles had their first hit he not only recorded his last chart single, *Pick A Bale Of Cotton*, but also this, his first chart album. **Volume 2** would reach Number 15 the following year, but by 1964 he was in cabaret – his job as the midwife between music hall and Merseybeat completed. All the classics are here.

I draw my material from blues and spirituals. Admittedly, the songs have to be polished-up to suit the variety stage. But although there is a vast resevoir of material to draw from, very few songs are suitable. They have got to have a story – something different. **Lonnie Donegan interviewed by Jerry Dawson, Melody Maker, May 1959**

The Golden Age Of Wireless

ARTIST Thomas Dolby RELEASE DATE May 1982 (UK)/March 1983 (US) LABEL Venice In Peril (UK)/Capitol (US) PRODUCER Thomas Morgan Dolby Robertson, Tim Friese Green UK CHART peak/weeks 65/10 US CHART peak/weeks 13/28 TRACK LISTING She Blinded Me With Science/Radio Silence/Airwaves/Flying North/Weightless/Europa And The Pirate Twins/Windpower/Commercial Breakup/One Of Our Submarines/Cloudburst At Shingle Street PERSONNEL Thomas Dolby (v, k, s)

A criminally neglected gem from the era of synth-pop, **Golden Age** was an album that proved that synthesizers were not simply a way for the creatively challenged to make a living. Dolby took technology and gave it a soul, producing a richly varied showcase for his talents as musician and songwriter. *Europa And The Pirate Twins*, *Windpower* and *Airwaves* are outstanding examples of Dolby's craft, but beware the mid-Eighties reissue, on which the later *She Blinded Me With Science* and *One Of Our Submarines* replace some of the original.

Thomas Dolby sees the opportunity of making an LP as a kind of vehicle for a very faddish boffinism… he sings with an antiseptic punctiliousness, sets his synthesisers to tick towards doomsday. A grey way of pilfering – which is all this amounts to, I'm afraid. **Richard Cook, NME, May 1982**

Good Old Boys

ARTIST Randy Newman RELEASE DATE October 1974 (UK & US) LABEL Reprise Records (UK & US) PRODUCER Lenny Waronker, Russ Titelman UK CHART peak/weeks 0/0 US CHART peak/weeks 36/23 TRACK LISTING Rednecks/Birmingham/Guilty/Naked Man/Marie/Mr. President (Have Pity On The Working Man)/Louisiana 1927/Every Man A King/Kingfish/A Wedding In Cherokee County/Back On My Feet Again/Rollin' PERSONNEL Randy Newman (v, p), session musicians

After three critically acclaimed but low-selling albums, this collection of songs about the south, where he'd grown up, was an unlikely chart debut for singer-pianist Newman. While cover possibilities had been plentiful and obvious on its predecessors, little here stood out as hit material; however, biting compositions like *Rednecks*, on racial attitudes and *Louisiana 1927*, a reflection on the lot of the farmer, repaid repeated listening.

Good Old Boys is a momentary dream of a little song-cycle, pursued halfway then allowed to rust and stand in the weeds. Nevertheless, its failure, in Randy Newman's philosophical terms, is itself a kind of success. **Ian MacDonald, NME, October 1974**

Goodbye

ARTIST Cream RELEASE DATE March 1969 (UK)/February 1969 (US) LABEL Polydor (UK)/Atco (US) PRODUCER Felix Pappalardi by arrangement with Robert Stigwood UK CHART peak/weeks 1/28 US CHART peak/weeks 2/26 TRACK LISTING I'm So Glad/Politician/Sitting On Top Of The World/Badge/Doing That Scrapyard Thing/What A Bringdown PERSONNEL Eric Clapton (g, v), Jack Bruce (p, b, v, o), Ginger Baker (d) with Felix Pappalardi (b, mln, p), L'Angelo Misterioso (rg)

Cream had already split by the time this aptly named farewell album was released. Three left-over studio sessions (one from the pen of each member) were coupled with live renditions of *Politician*, *I'm So Glad*, and *I'm Sitting On Top Of The World*. Yet the best ever Cream moment was surely *Badge*, co-written by Clapton with George Harrison, who lent it melody, and credited as L'Angelo Misterioso. Jimi Hendrix paid homage to Cream's demise by warping into *Sunshine Of Your Love* on Lulu's exceptionally groovy television show.

So they were together for a while and now they are apart. But something else will happen. For many they represent five years of British music history and more. They also represent the future…. **Melody Maker, March 1969**

Goodbye And Hallo

ARTIST Tim Buckley RELEASE DATE December 1967 (UK)/October 1967 (US) LABEL Elektra (UK & US) PRODUCER Jerry Yester UK CHART peak/weeks 0/0 US CHART peak/weeks 171/5 TRACK LISTING No Man Can Find The Warm/Carnival Song/Pleasant Street/Hallucinations/I Never Asked To Be Your Mountain/Once I Was/Phantasmagoria In Two/ Knight Errant/Morning Glory/ Goodbye And Hello PERSONNEL Tim Buckley (v, g), Lee Underwood (g, k), Billy Mundi (d), Jim Fielder (b), Van Dyke Parks (p), Jack Nitzsche (st, arg)

With a voice that could move from falsetto to low rumble to something indescribable within seconds, Tim Buckley was only 28 when he died, which gives a fair indication of the demons son Jeff had to grapple with.

Joining Elektra's folk roster early on alongside Judy Collins and Phil Ochs, Buckley was, at the least, insanely prolific, sometimes tossing out albums with only weeks in between. This, his second, divides opinion. Verbose and leaning towards a shuffling rock beat, Buckley was at the time heavily influenced by now-neglected singer/songwriter Fred Neil, and covered his *Dolphins* with eyebrow-raising vocal agility.

It's a full-blown artistic failure, bedevilled by ambition and Beckett and Buckley's preoccupation with courtly love and second-hand moralising about the Vietnam war. As a product of its time the resulting artefact is fascinating, painfully sincere, bloated with overwrought metaphors and quaint images. **Max Bell, NME, December 1979**

Goodbye Jumbo

ARTIST World Party **RELEASE DATE** May 1990 (UK)/June 1990 (US) **LABEL** Ensign (UK & US) **PRODUCER** World Party **UK CHART** peak/weeks 36/10 **US CHART** peak/weeks 73/23 **TRACK LISTING** Is It Too Late?/Way Down Now/When The Rainbow Comes/Put The Message In The Box/Ain't Gonna Come Till I'm Ready/And I Fell Back Alone/Take It Up/God On My Side/Show Me To The Top/Love Street/Sweet Soul Dream/Thankyou World **PERSONNEL** Karl Wallinger (v, k, s), Guy Chambers (k, gst), Sinead O'Connor (v, gst), session musicians

Former Waterboy Karl Wallinger swapped the Celtic obsessions of his ex-boss, Mike Scott, for a healthy interest in all things Sixties: 'retrodelic' is what you could term Wallinger's marriage of Beatles chord structures and Prince-ish Nineties mix'n'match dance-pop. **Goodbye Jumbo** was Wallinger's State of the Disunited Nations address, featuring a series of grim, though entertaining warnings, from the eco-fear of *Take It Up* and *Put The Message In The Box* to the tale of communication breakdown between lovers' countries that was *And I Fell Back Alone*.

As it moves from fevered desperation to a romantic, almost dreamy utopianism, **Goodbye Jumbo** *displays an ambition as broad as the emotional range of its music.* **Don McLeese, Rolling Stone, May 1990**

Goodbye Yellow Brick Road

ARTIST Elton John **RELEASE DATE** October 1973 (UK & US) **LABEL** DJM (UK)/MCA (US) **PRODUCER** Gus Dudgeon **UK CHART** peak/weeks 1/84 **US CHART** peak/weeks 1/103 **TRACK LISTING** Funeral For A Friend/Love Lies Bleeding/Candle In The Wind/Bennie And The Jets/Goodbye Yellow Brick Road/This Song Has No Title/Grey Seal/Jamaica Jerk-Off/I've Seen That Movie Too/Sweet Painted Lady/The Ballad Of Danny Bailey (1909-34)/Dirty Little Girl/All The Girls Love Alice/Your Sister Can't Twist (But She Can Rock 'N' Roll)/Saturday Night's Alright For Fighting/Roy Rogers/Social Disease/Harmony **PERSONNEL** Elton John (v, p), Dee Murray (b), Davey Johnstone (g), David Hentschel (sy), Nigel Olsson (d), Del Newman (st arg)

With two songs left over from **Don't Shoot Me...** Elton followed The Rolling Stones' lead and headed for Jamaica, where he wrote 20 more in short order. Sadly, producer Gus Dudgeon's reconnaissance trip had been optimistic and recording facilities were not up to scratch, so all 22 songs were stowed in the hand luggage and taken back to the Château in France where the previous two albums had been recorded. Ironically, the album it knocked off the top of the US charts was the Stones' **Goat's Head Soup**.

Goodbye Yellow Brick Road is thoroughly enjoyable, the rockers moving out with more gusto than those of many bands who work exclusively in that genre, the ballads exploring his and lyricist Bernie Taupin's romanticism without apology. **Jon Landau, Rolling Stone, June 1974**

Grace

ARTIST Jeff Buckley **RELEASE DATE** 1994 **LABEL** Columbia **PRODUCER** Andy Walce 'The Fist', Jeff Buckley **UK CHART** peak/weeks – **US CHART** peak/weeks 149/7 **TRACK LISTING** Mojo Pin/Grace/Last Goodbye/Lilac Wine/So Real/Hallelujah/Lover, You Should've Come Over/Corpus Christi Carol/Eternal Life/Dream Brother **PERSONNEL** Jeff Buckley (v, g, h, o, du), Mick Grondahl (b), Matt Johnson (d, pc), Michael Tighe (g), Gary Lucas (g), Loris Holland (o), Misha Masud (tl)

The tragic death of Jeff Buckley in 1997, aged just 31, means that **Grace**, his only full album, will forever be treated with a religious reverence. In truth, it already was. Its release in 1995 was greeted by press reviews of unprecedented adulation, and laid to rest any suspicions that he was trading on his father Tim's reputation. His song structures were wildly diverse and often inspired, meshing brute force and fine-spun delicacy on numbers like *Lilac Wine* and *Lover, You Should've Come Over*. He raised hell and kissed the heavens with that breeze of a voice, which echoed artists from Piaf to Plant, but was ultimately unique.

.. ranging from delicate and dreamy to highly charged and nakedly emotional – swooping from choir boy to intense Led Zeppelin blues ballad. This is no pretty folk LP, it's a powerful album of unlocked emotions, poetry and drama… Grace is variously fascinating, uneasy listening and hard work, but you could never confuse it with anything else. **Ian Cranna, Q, September 1994**

Grace And Danger

ARTIST John Martyn **RELEASE DATE** October 1980 (UK & US) **LABEL** Island (UK)/Atlantic (US) **PRODUCER** Martin Levan **UK CHART** peak/weeks 54/2 **US CHART** peak/weeks 0/0 **TRACK LISTING** Some People Are Crazy/Grace And Danger/Lookin' On/Our Love/Johny Too Bad/Sweet Little Mystery/Hurt In Your Heart/Baby Please Come Home/Save Some For Me **PERSONNEL** John Martyn (v), Phil Collins (v, d)

Phil Collins would top the charts worldwide in 1981 with **Face Value**, an album charting the break-up of his marraige. Ironically, close friend John Martyn had done the same the previous year, with Collins contributing drums and vocals, though sadly for him to less than platinum effect. Scots popsters Wet Wet Wet would appropriate some of the lyrical concerns of **Sweet Little Mystery** later in the decade, but they couldn't hope to rival the emotional depth and frayed nerve ends of their grizzled fellow countryman.

PAUL·SIMON
GRACELAND

Graceland

ARTIST Paul Simon **RELEASE DATE** September 1986 (UK & US) **LABEL** Warner Bros. (UK & US) **PRODUCER** Paul Simon **UK CHART** peak/weeks 1/101 **US CHART** peak/weeks 3/97 **TRACK LISTING** The Boy in The Bubble/Graceland/I Know What I Know/Gumboots/Diamonds On The Soles Of Her Shoes/You Can Call Me Al/Under African Skies/Homeless/Crazy Love Vol II/That Was Your Mother/All Around The World or The Myth Of Fingerprints **PERSONNEL** Paul Simon (v), Tao Ea Matsekha, Baghiti Khumalo (b), Ray Phiri (g), Demola Adepoju (g), King Sonny Ade Band, Shangaan Group, Ladysmith Black Mambazo, Soweto Rhythm Section, Youssou N'Dour, Isaac Mtshali, Morris Goldberg (w), Stimela Good Rockin' Dopsie And The Twisters, Los Lobos

Simon's second Grammy Award winner was a wholly successful marriage of Western pop and South African sounds and rhythms. **Graceland** was recorded in Johannesburg and featured the vocals of local group Ladysmith Black Mambazo, as well as the Everly Brothers and Los Lobos. The presence of indigenous musicians led Simon, accused of transgressing anti-apartheid restrictions, to be blacklisted by the United Nations and the African National Congress. Today, however, **Graceland**, including the hits *You Can*

Call Me Al and *The Boy In The Bubble*, is regarded as a modern classic.

Simon has taken contemporary mbaqanga dance music of the South African townships and fused it with his own peculiarly New Yorkian preoccupations and incidentally regenerated his own muse in the process. **Penny Reel NME, September 1986**

Gratitude

ARTIST Earth, Wind & Fire **RELEASE DATE** December 1975 (UK)/November 1975 (US) **LABEL** CBS (UK)/Columbia (US) **PRODUCER** Earth, Wind & Fire **UK CHART** peak/weeks 0/0 **US CHART** peak/weeks 1/54 **TRACK LISTING** Sing A Song/Gratitude/Celebrate/You Can't Hide Love/Sunshine/Shining Star/Sun Goddess/Devotion/Africano/Poer Medley/Yearnin' Learnin' **PERSONNEL** Maurice White (v, d, p), Verdine White (b), Wade Flemons (k, v), Don Whitehead (p, v), Michael Beal (g), Chet Washington (ts), Alex Thomas (tr)

The Seventies was the decade for successful live albums: Earth, Wind & Fire set the standard for Wings, Peter Frampton and Donna Summer, among others. Side four of the double vinyl format consisted of new material, notably the title track and subsequent hit single *Sing A Song*. The only thing the package could not hope to include was the band's extravagant costumes and over-the-top stage sets– for that, perhaps, we should be grateful!

Proof at last that EWF deserve all the acclaim that's been heaped on them in the last couple of years… we get to hear them at their very best and it's suddenly apparent that they knock most other 'progressive' black groups into a cocked hat. **Cliff White, NME, February 1976**

The Great Escape

ARTIST Blur **RELEASE DATE** September 1995 (UK & US) **LABEL** Parlophone (UK)/Virgin (US) **PRODUCER** Stephen Street **UK CHART** peak/weeks – **US CHART** peak/weeks 150/1 **TRACK LISTING** Stereotypes/Country House/Best Days/Charmless Man/Fade Away/Top Man/The Universal/Mr. Robinsons' Quango/He Thought Of Cars/It Could Be You/Ernold Same/Globe Alone/Dan Abnormal/Entertain Me/Yuko And Hiro **PERSONNEL** Damon Albarn (v, p, o, sy), Graham Coxon (g, ag, bv, s), Alex James (b), Dave Rowntree (d)

Damon Albarn was now established as the country's prime lust object for teen girls, but attention just prior to this album's release was focused on the drummed-up 'war' between Blur, supposedly soft 'arty' southerners, and Oasis, emergent dead-hard 'working class' northerners. As Blur's *Country House* single, complete with video directed by Damien Hirst and a rhyme of 'Balzac' with 'prozac', which Ray Davies would have killed for, swept to Number 1 ahead of the Mancunians' *Roll With It*: it appeared Blur had 'won'. But they had won the battle, not the war. Nevertheless this deceptively dark album showed intelligence and verve behind a jaunty façade of wacky characters.

The Great Escape is ambitious and perhaps a tad longer than necessary for maximum listening pleasure, although you have to dig very deep to find any filler… this is a most gong-worthy sound, complete with head-slicing guitars, catchy tunes and very funny words. **Will Birch, Mojo, October 1995**

Green

ARTIST R.E.M. **RELEASE DATE** November 1988 (UK & US) **LABEL** Warner Bros. (UK & US) **PRODUCER** R.E.M., Scott Litt **UK CHART** peak/weeks 27/20 **US CHART** peak/weeks 12/40 **TRACK LISTING** Pop Song '89/Get Up/You Are Everything/World Leader Pretend/Stand/The Wrong Child/Orange Crush/Hairshirt/Turn Your Inside Out/I Remember California/Untitled Song **PERSONNEL** Michael Stipe (v), Peter Buck (g), Mike Mills (b), Bill Ferry (d)

A five-album, reported $10 million record deal can concentrate the mind: if long-time fans complained of a sellout, Warner

blur *The Great Escape*

Brothers' corporate clout ensured the move from theatre to arena status was accompanied by a leap in sales. Three months in the recording, a record by R.E.M.'s standards, yielded an album Pete Buck dubbed a 'big rock record' as opposed to the 'weird art-folk' of yesteryear.

Green reveals a much wider range than previous efforts, including a playfulness that wasn't there before… REM may be dangerously close to becoming a conventional rock 'n' roll band, but Green proves it's a damn good one. **Michael Azerrad, Rolling Stone, January 1989**

Green Mind

ARTIST Dinosaur Jr RELEASE DATE February 1991 (UK & US) LABEL Blanco Y Negro (UK)/Sire (US) PRODUCER J.Mascis UK CHART peak/weeks 36/2 US CHART peak/weeks 168/6 TRACK LISTING The Wagon/Puke & Cry/Blowing It - I Live For That Look/FLying Cloud/How'd You Pin That One On Me/Water/Muck/Thumb/Green Mind PERSONNEL Charlie Nakajima (v), Donna Biddell (g), Scott Helland (b), J. Mascis (v, d), Murph (d)

Coming to Blanco Y Negro with a reputation for producing high quality hardcore, Dinosaur Jr repaid the label's confidence in them with the excellent **Green Mind**. In effect a J. Mascis solo project – long-term cohort Murph made only a limited contribution – this was an album that had the usual quota of full-tilt metal mayhem, but also revealed an unexpected softer side to the Mascis character in the doleful *Flying Cloud*. Other highlights included the unsuccessful single, *The Wagon*, a more typical offering which deserved to do better.

… an LP which should consolidate their reputation as purveyors of quality hardcore… Effectively, J. Mascis has made an album which will spawn truckloads of inferior imitations, the major label cloak hangs around their shoulders comfortably, and they might even start to turn critical acclaim into hard sales. **Graeme Kay, Q, April 1991**

Green River

ARTIST Creedence Clearwater Revival RELEASE DATE December 1969 (UK)/September 1969 (US) LABEL Liberty (UK)/Fantasy (US) PRODUCER John Fogerty UK CHART peak/weeks 20/6 US CHART peak/weeks 1/68 TRACK LISTING Tombstone Shadow/Bad Moon Rising/Sinister Purpose/Lodi/Wrote A Song For Everyone/Night Time Is The Right Time/Cross-tie Walker/Green River/Commotion PERSONNEL John Fogerty (v, g), Tom Fogerty (rg), Stu Cook (b), Doug 'Cosmo' Clifford (b)

John Fogerty may have been a Californian but his songs cried out from the heart of the Louisiana swamplands with bluesy roots. *Proud Mary* (from **Bayou Country**) made Number 2 in America, then *Bad Moon Rising* hit Number 1 in Britain. Creedence continued this run of single successes while simultaneously being prolific with albums. Songs such as *Wrote A Song For Everyone* and *Tombstone Shadow* perfectly captured the simple skills of the band and met the acclaim of both rock brow furrowers and hit parade funsters. *Lodi* was adopted as a definitive 'travellin' man' anthem.

Creedence's deficiencies are readily apparent… But their distinctive driving sound, when fused with Fogerty's vocals, results in something so fine that it makes such criticisms seem irrelevant. **Green River**, *whatever its flaws, is a great album.* **Bruce Miroff, Rolling Stone, October 1969**

Grievous Angel

ARTIST Gram Parsons RELEASE DATE February 1974 (UK & US) LABEL Reprise (UK & US) PRODUCER Gram Parsons UK CHART peak/weeks 0/0 US CHART peak/weeks 195/3 TRACK LISTING Love Hurts/Las Vegas/In My Hour Of Darkness/Return Of Grievous Angel/Hearts On Fire/Can't Dance/Brass Buttons/1,000 Wedding/Medley: (a)Cash On Barrel (b)Hickory Wind PERSONNEL Gram Parsons (v, g), Emmylou Harris (v), James Burton (g), Glen D. Hardin (p), Rik Grech (b), Linda Ronstadt (bv)

Having kick-started country-rock as a Byrd and a Burrito, Gram Parsons would get only two shots at a solo career before his drug-induced late-1973 death. Those albums were released exactly a year apart, **Grievous Angel** posthumously: It was originally titled 'Sleepless Nights', but that song didn't make it to the final cut. The *Medley Live From Northern Quebec* was dubbed with fake applause when a live session fell through. Instrumental support came from various Elvis Presley sidemen, former Burrito Bernie Leadon and, most crucially, harmony vocalist Emmylou Harris, the Tammy to his George Jones, who would keep Parsons' flame burning.

Love in a plaid flannel shirt, brought to you by the same folks who'd sooner milk a pig than listen to some pretty boy crooning about Max Factor and tight assholes. **Chrissie Hynd, NME, February 1974**

Gris-Gris

ARTIST Dr John, The Night Tripper RELEASE DATE 1968 (UK & US) LABEL Atlantic (UK)/Atco (US) PRODUCER Harold Battiste UK CHART peak/weeks 0/0 US CHART peak/weeks 0/0 TRACK LISTING Gris-Gris Gumbo Ya Ya/Danse Kalinda Ba Doom/Mama Roux/Danse Fambeaux/Croker Courtbullion/Jump Sturdy/I Walk On Gilded Splinters PERSONNEL Dr John (p, v), session musicians

Hailed by *Rolling Stone* as 'one of the most bizarre LPs of the late Sixties', the first solo album from Mac Rebennack, alias Dr John, contained many of his theme tunes, not least *I Walk On Gilded Splinters*– covered by everyone from Marsha Hunt (Sixties) to Paul Weller (Nineties) – *Gris Gris Gumbo Ya Ya*'and *Croker Courtbouillion*. Heavy friends on the session included Jesse Hill and Harold Battiste, labouring under the *noms de disque* of Dr Poo Pah Doo and Dr Battiste of Scorpio, and the result is a Crescent City party in the studio that unfortunately overshadowed the good Doctor's later excellent, though not quite as wacky, work.

Grotesque (After The Gramme)

ARTIST Fall RELEASE DATE November 1980 LABEL Rough Trade PRODUCER – UK CHART peak/weeks 0/0 US CHART peak/weeks - TRACK LISTING Pay Your Rates/English Scheme/New Face In Hell/C 'N' C Smithering/The Container Drivers/Impressions Of J. Temperance/In The Park/W.M.C. Blob 59/Gramme Friday/The N.W.R.A. PERSONNEL Craig Scanlon (g), Steve Hanley (b), Paul Hanley (d), Mark Riley (b, g), Mark E. Smith (v)

Fall's third studio album proved that if ever a band was truly miscast in the post-punk generalization of the time, this was it. Mark E. Smith's perverse vision and vicious, surreal, often hilarious wordplay was proficiently underpinned by the band – 'five wacky English proletariat idiots'. Their hard, mesmeric grooves and proto-psychobilly stomps added intriguing, sub-pop elements to a record remarkable for its subliminal and disturbing power. *Grotesque* featured a brief stint by Marc Riley, now better known as Radio 1 DJ Mark Radcliffe's comedy sidekick Lard, on bass guitar.

Guilty

ARTIST Barbra Streisand RELEASE DATE October 1980 (UK & US) LABEL CBS (UK)/Columbia (US) PRODUCER Barry Gibb UK CHART peak/weeks 1/82 US CHART peak/weeks 1/49 TRACK LISTING Guilty/Woman In Love/Run Wild/Promises/Love Inside/What Kind Of Fool/Life Story/Never Give Up/Make It Like A Memory PERSONNEL Barbra Streisand (v), Barry Gibb (bv), session musicians

The cover said it all – the then-reigning king and queen of MOR mugging it up for the camera: La Streisand and Bee Gee Barry Gibb arm in arm. Although only Streisand's name was featured on the cover, Gibb had a songwriting credit on every song and duetted on two tracks, *What Kind Of Fool* and *Guilty*. The latter was a moderate chart single, but it was *Woman In Love* which hit Number 1 on both sides of the Atlantic, as did the album, certified quintuple platinum.

If you like disco, Barry Gibb or Barbra Streisand, you'll go a bundle on **Guilty**, *but really it's music which wallpapers your imagination, plugging every critical orifice with its bland professionalism.* **Patrick Humphries, Melody Maker, October 1980**

The Hangman's Beautiful Daughter

ARTIST The Incredible String Band RELEASE DATE April 1968 (UK)/July 1968 (US) LABEL Elektra (UK&US) PRODUCER Joe Boyd UK CHART peak/weeks 5/21 US CHART peak/weeks 161/9 TRACK LISTING Koeeoaddi There/The Minotaur's Song/Witches Hat/A Very Cellular Song/Mercy I Cry City/Waltz Of The New Moon/The Water Song/Three Is A Green Crown/Swift As The Wind/Nightfall PERSONNEL Robin Williamson (v, g), Clive Palmer (g, v), Mike Heron (v, rg), Licorice McKechnie (v, k), Rose Simpson (b, pc)

Formed in 1966 by Edinburgh-based beat folkniks Robin Williamson, Mike Heron and (briefly) Clive Palmer, the ISB were the first major British signings by hip US label Elektra. This early 1968 masterpiece consolidated their achievements in world music eclecticism, no more so than on Heron's 12-minute *A Very Cellular Song*. This combined a mind-bending array of different musical styles and instrumentation that ranged from Deep South gospel to calypso and featured xylophone, fiddle and guitar, ending in almost hymn-like solemnity. There were also surprising flashes of humour, as on *Kooeeaddi There*, that later albums lacked.

Heron and Williamson are superb musicians working within the folk idiom; on this album they apparently forgot it … and left folk music for something else. Unfortunately they didn't know where they were going. **James Pomeroy, Rolling Stone, September 1968**

Happy Trails

ARTIST QuickSilver Messenger Service RELEASE DATE March 1969 (UK & US) LABEL Capitol (UK & US) PRODUCER Quick Silver Messenger Service UK CHART peak/weeks 0/0 US CHART peak/weeks 27/30 TRACK LISTING Who Do You Love Suite;- Who Do You Love (pt.1) - Who Do You Love - Where Do You Love - How Do You Love - Which Do You Love - Who Do You Love (pt.2)/Maiden Of The Cancer Moon/Mona/Calvary/Happy Trails PERSONNEL John Cippollina (v, g), Gary Duncan (g, v), David Freiberg (b, v), Greg Elmore (d)

After dissatisfaction with their debut album San Francisco's Quicksilver decided to record the next in concert. Side one was spliced together from performances at the Fillmores' East and West, based on Bo Diddley's *Who Do You Love*, a tribal celebration that featured the almost telepathic interplay between all members of the band, especially guitarists Gary Duncan and John Cipollina. Even better was Duncan's *Calvary*, his last contribution before temporarily quitting the band. Inspired by Christ's final journey to the cross – 'we were really swacked when we conceived that one,' admitted Cipollina – its spiralling layers of Spanish electric guitar epitomized the free-blowing spirit of the Haight.

Hard Again

ARTIST Muddy Waters RELEASE DATE April 1977 (UK)/February 1977 (US) LABEL Blue Sky (UK & US) PRODUCER Johnny Winter UK CHART peak/weeks 0/0 US CHART peak/weeks 143/7 TRACK LISTING Mannish Boy/Bus Driver/I Want To Be Loved/Jealous Hearted Man/I Can't Be Satisfied/The Blues Had A Baby And They Named It Rock And Roll/Deep Down In Florida/Crosseyed Cat/Little Girl PERSONNEL Muddy Waters (g, v), Johnny Winter (g, bv), James Cotton (hp), 'Pine Top' Perkins (p), Bob Margolin (g), Charles Calmese (g), Willie 'Big Eyes' Smith (d)

Muddy Waters cut three of his best-selling albums when in his sixties, employing members of his old band from the Fifties, as well as hot, young(ish) producer and virtuoso blues guitarist, Johnny

Winter. **Hard Again**, like its successors, 1978's **I'm Ready** and 1981's **King Bee**, saw Waters rehabilitate ancient material and some of his own compositions, making them palatable for the rock generation while still remaining faithful to his gritty blues roots. The results were as consistently pleasing as anything he had ever produced.

A Hard Day's Night

ARTIST The Beatles RELEASE DATE July 1964 (UK & US) LABEL Parlophone (UK)/Capitol (US) PRODUCER George Martin UK CHART peak/weeks 1/38 US CHART peak/weeks 1/51 TRACK LISTING A Hard Day's Night/I Should Have Known Better/If I Fell/I'm Happy Just To Dance With You/And I Love Her/Tell Me Why/Can't Buy Me Love/Any Time At All/I'll Cry Instead/Things We Said Today/When I Get Home/You Can't Do That/I'll Be Back PERSONNEL John Lennon (v, rg), Paul McCartney (v, b), George Harrison (v, lg), Ringo Starr (d)

High on success, The Beatles wrote an entire album for the first time and Lennon revealed glimpses of a less breezy nature. The title track hinted at the trippy wordplay that was to become a Beatles trait. Despite limited time, the group produced unerring melodic pop songs which have enjoyed staggering longevity: *Can't Buy Me Love*, *If I Fell*, *&And I Love Her*. The film of the same name pre-empted the rock video style with its pacey editing and frenetic inventiveness.

The quintessential Beatles album, chocka with melody, optimism and invention. They wrote all 13 songs and none of them are rubbish… the title track features the most inventive use of a crashing chord in pop ever. **David Quantick, NME, October 1991**

The Harder They Come

ARTIST Jimmy Cliff RELEASE DATE March 1975 (UK & US) LABEL Island (UK)/A & M (US) PRODUCER Jimmy Cliff, Byron Lee, Leslie Kong, Derrick Harriot UK CHART peak/weeks 0/0 US CHART peak/weeks 140/8 TRACK LISTING Draw Your Brakes/Rivers Of Babylon/Many Rivers To Cross/Sweet And Dandy/Johnny Too Bad/Shanty Town/Pressure Drop/Sitting In Limbo/You Can Get It If You Really Want/The Harder They Come PERSONNEL Jimmy Cliff, Scotty, Melodians, Maytals, The Slickers, Desmond Dekker

At the age of 24, the most successful Jamaican singer/songwriter other than Marley starred in the Perry Henzell film *The Harder*

They Come as a rude boy-cum-local icon. His contributions to the soundtrack included the classic **Sitting In Limbo** and the infectious **Many Rivers To Cross** – a hit for UB40 11 years later. Cliff had a knack with sweet melodies which particularly endeared him to Britain. He embraced certain soul phrasings and techniques, as well as gospel. In the Eighties his credibility took a dive after a 1982 South African tour, but he continued to score hits.

I think reggae music is the freshest music going around in the world today… it's been keeping in the corner for some time, but everything that's good has to come out eventually and that's what's happening to reggae now. **From an interview by Bob Randall, Melody Maker, August 1972**

Hard Nose The Highway

ARTIST Van Morrison RELEASE DATE July 1973 (UK)/August 1973 (US) LABEL Warner Bros. (UK & US) PRODUCER Van Morrison UK CHART peak/weeks 22/3 US CHART peak/weeks 27/19 TRACK LISTING Snow In San Anselmo/Warm Love/Hard Nose The Highway/Wild Children/The Great Deception/Bein' Green/Autumn Song/Purple Heather PERSONNEL Jack Schroer (h), Jules Broussard (h), Joseph Ellis (h), William Atwood (h), Nathan Rubin, Zaven Melikian, Nancy Ellis, Theresa Adams, John Tenny, Michael Gerling (str), Jef Labes (p), John Platania (g), Van Morrison (g, v), David Haynes (b), Marty David (b), Gary Mallaber (d), Rick Schlosser (d), Jackie DeShannon (bv), with the Oakland Symphony Chamber Chorus on 'Snow In San Anselmo'

Unique in containing two non-original songs, *Bein' Green* from *The Muppet Show*, and the traditional *Wild Mountain Thyme* (retitled **Purple Heather**), this album started with a trio of Morrison-penned classics but faded out in uncertainty. Next, Morrison would turn to a live album to recharge his creative batteries before returning to Irish roots with **Veedon Fleece**. Yet it was not surprising that after such an outpouring of creativity since **Astral Weeks** he should turn in this flawed but entertaining effort.

Hard Nose the Highway *is psychologically complex, musically somewhat uneven and lyrically excellent… Van demonstrates his ability to fuse jazz, pop and rock ideas into a fluid format whose stylistic identity ends up being his and his alone.* **Stephen Holden, Rolling Stone, September 1973**

Harvest

ARTIST Neil Young **RELEASE DATE** March 1972 (UK & US) **LABEL** Reprise (UK & US) **PRODUCER** Elliot Mazar, Jack Nitzsche, Henry Lewy, Neil Young **UK CHART** peak/weeks 1/33 **US CHART** peak/weeks 1/41 **TRACK LISTING** Out On The Weekend/Harvest/A Man Needs A Maid/Heart Of Gold/Are You Ready For The Country/Old Man/There's A World/Alabama/The Needle And The Damage Done/Words (Between The Lines Of Age) **PERSONNEL** Neil Young (v, g), Ben Keith (g), Kenny Buttrey (d), Tim Drummond (b), Jack Nitzsche (p, sg), John Harris (p)

Harvest reached Number 1 and sold three million, but is considered by now a weak successor to **After The Gold Rush**, relying too much on formula, saccharine-emoting and overblown, string-drenched production. Nevertheless, Neil Young's fourth solo LP did contain some memorable songs, such as *The Needle And The Damage Done* (prompted by Crazy Horse guitarist Danny Whitten's fatal drug overdose), the huge-selling title track and *A Man Needs A Maid*, which was genuinely moving in spite of, or perhaps even because of, its chauvinist sentiment. Such is Young's genius.

It is the elusiveness, the mysteriousness, of many of Young's songs, which makes them so precious. Because they are not explicit, each listener can interpret them in a way which is meaningful to him or her. **A. L., Melody Maker, February 1972**

Hats

ARTIST The Blue Nile **RELEASE DATE** October 1989 (UK)/February 1990 (US) **LABEL** Linn-Virgin (UK)/A&M (US) **PRODUCER** The Blue Nile **UK CHART** peak/weeks 12/4 **US CHART** peak/weeks 108/14 **TRACK LISTING** Over The Hillside/The Downtown Lights/Let's Go Out Tonight/Headlights On The parade/From A Late Night-train/Seven AM/Saturday Night **PERSONNEL** Paul Buchanan (v, g, sy), Robert Bell (k, sy), Paul Joseph Moore (sy, b)

The anticipation surrounding The Blue Nile's second album was intense; its majesty transcended genre and had people describing them as music's answer to Venice. The most commonly used lyric was 'I love you', and it was hard not to swoon as Bell and Moore's washes of keyboard-led sound evoked travel, hope and despair. *The Downtown Lights* was later covered by both Annie Lennox and Rod Stewart, but neither matched Buchanan's easy urgency. The Blue Nile even conquered their fear of playing live, and the singer began an unlikely romance with actress Rosanna Arquette. It was to be six years before their next album, **Peace At Last**, but it was well worth the wait.

Hats has a peculiar power; unfortunately, its risky departure from pop conventions will cause many to overlook it. It is surely a fine second act from a trio that deserves encouragement. **David Thigpen/Rolling Stone, May 1990**

The Healer

ARTIST John Lee Hooker **RELEASE DATE** November 1989 (UK)/October 1989 (US) **LABEL** Silvertone (UK)/Chameleon (US) **PRODUCER** Roy Rogers, Co-produced by Carlos Santana, Jim Gaines **UK CHART** peak/weeks 63/8 **US CHART** peak/weeks 62/38 **TRACK LISTING** The Healer/I'm in The Mood/Baby Lee/Cuttin' Oil/Think Twice Before You Go/Sally Mae/That's Alright/Rockin' Chair/My Dream/No Substitute **PERSONNEL** John Lee Hooker (v, g), Carlos Santana (g), Chipito Areas (tb), Armando Peraza (cg), Nduga Chancler (d), Chester Thompson (k, sy), Bonnie Raitt (v, g), Roy Rogers (g), Scott Matthews (d), Robert Crat (g), Richard Cousins (b), Scott Matthews (d), Henry Destine (g), Larry Taylor (b), Filo De La Parra (d), Charlie Musselwhite (h), Cesar Rosas (g), David Hildago (g, ad), Louie Perex (d), Conrad Lozano (b), Steve Berlin (s), George Thorogood (g), Steve Ehrmann (b)

Aside from a cameo appearance in *The Blues Brothers*, the legendary John Lee Hooker could as well have been dead and buried to the music world at large until a group of those he had played with and influenced joined forces to re-cut some of his greatest songs. The result was **The Healer**, originally pressed in limited numbers but becoming a million seller. The Bonnie Raitt duet, *In The Mood*, took Grammy honours for Best Traditional Blues Song as Hooker finally claimed his due.

Take pure John Lee Hooker, add strong doses of Santana, Bonnie Rait, Robert Cray, Canned Heat, Los Lobos and George Thorogood (all of whom appear on **The Healer***), and what do you get? Brilliant, 100-proof blues, that's what.* **Janie Matthews, Rolling Stone, October 1989**

Heart

ARTIST Heart **RELEASE DATE** October 1985 (UK)/July 1985 (US) **LABEL** Capitol (UK & US) **PRODUCER** Ron Nevison **UK CHART** peak/weeks 19/43 **US CHART** peak/weeks 1/92 **TRACK LISTING** Tell It Like It Is/Barracuda/Straight On/Dog & Butterfly/Even It Up/Bebe Le Strange/Sweet Darlin'/I'm Down/Long Tall Sally/Unchained Melody/Rock and Roll **PERSONNEL** Ann Wilson (v), Nancy Wilson (g, v), Roger Fisher (g), Howard Leese (k, g), Steve Fossen (b), Michael Derosier (d)

Signing to a new label after a decade of mixed fortunes, Heart were persuaded to include outside material on this re-launch album. Sisters Ann and Nancy Wilson were less than enamoured, but were forced to eat their words when the album topped the US chart in late 1985, two Top 10 singles being followed by another pair in early 1986. **These Dreams**, by Bernie Taupin and Martin Page, topped the pile.

On Heart's latest comeback album, a desperate desire to make music that complies with current radio formats overwhelms what made the band interesting in the first place… pumped-up AOR-happy production. **Jimmy Guterman, Rolling Stone, October 1985**

Heart Like A Wheel

ARTIST Linda Ronstadt **RELEASE DATE** January 1975 (UK)/December 1974 (US) **LABEL** Asylum (UK & US) **PRODUCER** Peter Asher **UK CHART** peak/weeks 0/0 **US CHART** peak/weeks 1/51 **TRACK LISTING** You're No Good/It Doesn't Matter Anymore/Faithless Love/The Dark End Of The Street/Heart Like A Wheel/When Will I Be Loved/Willing/I Can't Help It (If I'm Still In Love With You)/Keep Me Blowing Away/You Can Close Your Eyes **PERSONNEL** Linda Ronstadt (v), session musicians

The half-Mexican, half-German Linda Ronstadt was one of the most popular female recording artists of the Seventies, making her name singing a mixture of astutely chosen old covers and contemporary songs. The two-million selling **Heart Like A Wheel** spawned the Number 1 hit, *You're No Good*; its flip side, Hank Williams' *I Can't Help It (If I'm Still In Love With You)* rocked the country & western charts and won that year's Grammy for Best Female Country Vocal. A version of the Eagles' *Desperado* rounded off what many consider the then nascent superstar's finest hour.

Heart Like A Wheel is far from being simply A Country Album, with the first side of the set having a distinctive contemporary air about it… the atmosphere is generally gloomy and at times miserably drab…
Tony Stewart, NME, January 1976

Heart Shaped World

ARTIST Chris Isaak RELEASE DATE July 1989 LABEL Warner Bros PRODUCER Erik Jacobsen UK CHART peak/weeks - US CHART peak/weeks 7/74 TRACK LISTING Heart Shaped World/I'm Not Waiting/Don't Make Me Dream About You/Kings Of The Highway/Wicked Game/Blue Spanish Sky/Wrong To Love You/Forever Young/Nothing's Changed/In The Heart Of The Jungle/Diddley Daddy PERSONNEL Chris Isaak (v, g), James Calvin Wilsey (lg), Rowland Sally (b, v), Kenny Dale Johnson (d, v)

Californian ex-boxer Isaak proved his label, Warner Brothers, wrong, with a little help from a friend, when they failed to promote this collection of Fifties-style retro love songs. They were out of tune with the synth ridden Eighties all right, but in tune completely with Hollywood director David Lynch, who had already used Isaak's music in *Blue Velvet* and did likewise in his new movie *Wild At Heart* starring Nicolas Cage. Atlanta radio station Power 99 aired **Wicked Game** thanks to its film connection and a nation followed. Isaak, having frolicked with Helena Christensen in the video, went on to film stardom.

His compositions, which have developed from teenage bedroom tapes into sleek, cinematic epics and tragic soul wrenchers… don't step outside the precincts of the love song… 'I'm not going to start writing about anything else, there's still a million angles to be written on the love story.'
From an interview by Gavin Martin, NME, October 1987

Heaven Or Las Vegas

ARTIST The Cocteau Twins RELEASE DATE September 1990 (UK & US) LABEL 4 a.d. (UK)/Capitol (US) PRODUCER Cocteau Twins UK CHART peak/weeks 7/12 US CHART peak/weeks 99/19 TRACK LISTING Cherry-Coloured Funk/Pitch The Baby/Iceblink Luck/Fifty-Fifty Clown/Heaven Or Las Vegas/I Wear Your Ring/Fotzepolitic/Wolf In The Breast/Road, River And Rail/Frou-Frou Foxes In Midsummer Fires PERSONNEL Elizabeth Fraser (v), Robin Guthrie (g, dp, k), Richard Thomas (b, s)

This saw the Cocteaus leaning slightly more towards conventional song structures, and even tasting a rare chart single with *Iceblink Luck*. They had just opened their own new studio in London but were keen to take the opulent fruits of their labours out on the road. This perhaps accounted for a greater 'rationale' to Liz Fraser's lyrics. Fans were divided as to whether this gravitation towards the centre of things was a joy or a loss: the band weren't and signed to a major label soon afterwards, where they continued to explore this vein.

Like classical composers who they can resemble with their lush, baroque atmosphere and sweeping cadences, the Cocteaus don't waste time on agendas but concentrate on distilling emotions…. One thing's for sure; this particular destination isn't Las Vegas, but Heaven. **Martin Aston, Q, October 1990**

Heavenly

ARTIST Johnny Mathis RELEASE DATE September 1959 (UK & US) LABEL CBS (UK)/Columbia (US) PRODUCER – UK CHART peak/weeks – US CHART peak/weeks 1/295 TRACK LISTING Heavenly/Hello, Young Lovers/Lovely Way To Spend An Evening/Ride On A Rainbow/More Than You Know/Something I Dreamed Last Night/Misty/Stranger In Paradise/Moonlight Becomes You/They Say It's Wonderful/I'll Be Easy to Find/That's All PERSONNEL Johnny Mathis (v)

Mathis's first collaboration with arranger Glenn Osser saw him tackle a mixture of contemporary ballads leavened with show tunes and standards. The songs were in many cases identified with Mathis's early influences: Nat King Cole, Sarah Vaughan and Errol Garner – a personal friend. Garner's **Misty** was nearly omitted but included at the singer's insistence, and would be hailed as the record's standout track. **Heavenly** made up three Mathis albums in the US Top 10 when it hit the top in late 1959, underlining his commercial status. Little wonder he was still on Columbia two decades later!

'They tell me you're the biggest selling record artist in the world now… and without doing a single rock 'n' roll song.' Johnny smiled as if he didn't realise he was that popular. **Gilbert King, Melody Maker, April 1960**

Hejira

ARTIST Joni Mitchell **RELEASE DATE** November 1976 (UK & US) **LABEL** Asylum (UK & US) **PRODUCER** – UK CHART peak/weeks 11/5 US CHART peak/weeks 13/18 **TRACK LISTING** Coyote/Amelia/Furry Sings The Blues/A Strange Boy/Hejira/Song For Sharon/Black Crow/Blue Motel Room/Refuge Of The Roads **PERSONNEL** Joni Mitchell (v, rg, g,), Jaco Pastorius (b), Larry Carlton (lg, ag), Bobbye Hall (pc), John Guerin (d), Max Bennett (b), Neil Young (h), Abe Most (cl), Chuck Domanico (b), Chuck Findley, Tom Scott (hn)

The man who shared the spotlight with Mitchell on this release was fretless bass player Jaco Pastorius. The songs were written while she was on a road trip across America; its release coincided with her appearance at The Band's **Last Waltz** concerts. Lyrically, it returned to self-examination, and lacked a hit single, but would still represent one of the last albums of Mitchell's commercially successful period. The advent of Linda Ronstadt, whose *Hasten Down The Wind* pipped her for Best Pop Vocal Grammy, showed she was slipping from vogue in favour of more sexy, straightforward fare.

Hello I Must Be Going

ARTIST Phil Collins **RELEASE DATE** November 1982 (UK & US) **LABEL** Virgin (UK)/Atlantic (US) **PRODUCER** Phil Collins UK CHART peak/weeks 2/164 US CHART peak/weeks 8/141 **TRACK LISTING** I Don't Care Anymore/I Cannot Believe It's True/Like China/Do You Know, Do You Care?/You Can't Hurry Love/It Don't Matter To Me/Thru These Walls/Don't Let Him Steal Your Heart Away/The West Side/Why Can't It Wait Till Morning **PERSONNEL** Phil Collins (v, d, k), session musicians

Collins adopted soul and funk mannerisms here without alienating the core Genesis audience. His stabs at authenticity were hit-and-miss affairs: the Motown retread *You Can't Hurry Love* was nothing special, and relied heavily on a gimmicky video to take it to the top of the charts. The ballads were not quite oozing as intended although two years later he carved one out with *Take A Look At Me Now* from the soundtrack to *Against All Odds*. Whereas **Face Value** had been written as his marriage broke up, this album seemed over-compromised and calculated. It failed to top the charts.

Help!

ARTIST The Beatles **RELEASE DATE** July 1965 (UK)/September 1965 (US) **LABEL** Parlophone (UK)/Capitol (US) **PRODUCER** George Martin UK CHART peak/weeks 1/37 US CHART peak/weeks 1/44 **TRACK LISTING** Help!/The Night Before/You've Got To Hide Your Love Away/I Need You/Another Girl/You're Going To Lose That Girl/Ticket To Ride/Act Naturally/It's Only Love/You Like Me Too Much/Tell Me What You See/I've Just Seen A Face/Yesterday/Dizzy Miss Lizzy **PERSONNEL** John Lennon (v, ep, g), Paul McCartney (v, b), George Harrison (lg, bv), Ringo Starr (d)

Their second 'movie soundtrack' (it's easy to forget how insanely prolific the group were), contained seven numbers from the film plus seven others. It was a comparatively gentle, reflective set: lyrics were more considered and centre stage and acoustic guitars were granted greater prominence, a good example being Lennon's *You've Got To Hide Your Love Away*. McCartney sang *Yesterday* over a string quartet and offered it as a single but Chris Farlowe turned it down for being 'too soft'. It has since become one of the most played and performed songs of all time.

Help!, the title of the Beatle's new LP, will be the cry of all British groups who will try to equal the standard of this brilliant album…. There's something of the medieval minstrels in the Beatles…. They communicate. **Chris Welch, Melody Maker, July 1965**

Here Come The Warm Jets

ARTIST Brian Eno **RELEASE DATE** March 1974 (UK)/August 1974 (US) **LABEL** Island (UK & US) **PRODUCER** Brian Eno UK CHART peak/weeks 26/2 US CHART peak/weeks 151/6 **TRACK LISTING** Baby's On Fire/Needles In The Camel's Eye/Blank Frank/Cindy Tells Me/Driving Me Backwards/Dead Finks Don't Talk/Some Of Them Are Old/The Paw-Paw Negro Blowtorch/On Some Faraway Beach/Here Come The Warm Jets **PERSONNEL** Brian Eno (s, var), Robert Fripp (g), Manzanera (g)

Fresh out of Roxy Music, Eno's first solo project came as a surprise. Rejecting the polished chic of his former band, he moved into altogether rougher terrain, producing a quirky collection of simple songs overlaid with a wide variety of textures and sounds. A springboard for what was to follow, it has an undeniable charm, and still sounds startling. Check out *Baby's On Fire*, *Blank Frank* and *On Some Faraway Beach* to get an idea of the album's sheer variety.

Bailey/San Miguel/E Inu Tatou E/A Rollin' Stone/Goober Peas/A Worried Man PERSONNEL Dave Guard (g, v), Nick Reynolds (g, v), Bob Shane (g, v)

In September 1959, the Kingston Trio released their fifth album, **Here We Go Again!**, which, like its predecessor, made top spot in the *Billboard* album charts. *A Worried Man* was the big single, the Trio's fourth Top 20 entry inside 15 months, and the last during Dave Guard's membership of the group. This album contained another 12 tracks of clean-cut popular folk music from the very clean-cut Californian-based Trio, who were the first to bridge the gap between the pop charts and the more politically inspired work of traditional folkies like Pete Seeger.

…underlines the reason why the Kingstons are currently riding high in the States…. Discerning admirers of folky offerings cannot afford to miss this outstanding release. **Melody Maker, August 1959**

Here's Little Richard

ARTIST Little Richard RELEASE DATE August 1957 (UK & US) LABEL London (UK)/Speciality (US) PRODUCER Robert 'Bumps' Blackwell UK CHART peak/weeks 0/0 US CHART peak/weeks 13/5 TRACK LISTING Tutti Fruiti/True Fine Mama/Ready Teddy/Baby/Slippin' And Slidin' (Peepin' And Hidin')/Long Tall Sally/Miss Ann/Oh Why/Rip It Up/Jenny, Jenny/She's Got It/Can't Believe You Want To Leave PERSONNEL Little Richard (v, p), Earl Palmer (d), Red Tyler (s), Lee Allen (s), Frank Fields (b), Ernect McClean (g), Juston Adams (g), Huey Smith (p), Edward Frank (p), Little Booker (p), Salvador Doucette (p)

Albums were definitely not what Little Richard was about, hence his absence from the UK listings and only one entry, with this album, in the US chart in his Fifties heyday. Not long after it started a five-week run, he renounced rock 'n' roll while on an Australian tour, cast his jewellery off a bridge into a river and began one of several splits with 'the Devil's Music': as good a last testament as one could have wanted.

The semi-hysterical blues shouting of Little Richard is OK in small doses but I find 12 tracks of his bleating, croaking and lisping too much at one sitting. But doubtless the dwindling Rock 'n' Roll element will welcome this release. **Laurie Hernshaw, Melody Maker, August 1957**

Heroes

ARTIST David Bowie RELEASE DATE October 1977 (UK & US) LABEL RCA Victor (UK & US) PRODUCER Bowie, Visconti UK CHART peak/weeks 3/18 US CHART peak/weeks 35/19 TRACK LISTING Beauty And The Beast/Joe The Lion/Heroes/Sons Of The Silent Age/Blackout/V-2 Schneider/Sense Of Doubt/Moss Garden/Neuköln/The Secret Life Of Arabia PERSONNEL David Bowie (v, k, g, s, bv), Carlos Alomar (rg), Dennis Davis (pc), George Murray (b), Brian Eno (sy, k, g), Robert Fripp (lg), Tony Visconti (bv), Antonia Maass (bv)

Perversely interweaving jauntily sung staccato reels and morbid instrumentals, Bowie was beginning to make the point he had begun formulating on **Low**. Robert Fripp joined the secret society and the soundscapes grew ever more chilling. *Joe The Lion* was a tribute to Bowie's son Zowie; *Sons Of The Silent Age* was a blissed-out revisitation of earlier sci-fi themes, but it was the title song which cut through the uncertainty. A romantic anthem of insuperable dignity, *Just For One Day*, has been since covered by many artists who wish they could do it justice. Bowie's first performance of this song on Marc Bolan's TV show, showed him looking lean and fit again.

… for all its pessimism **Heroes** *ultimately overcomes its own depression…. Bowie, virtually alone … is attempting to create truly modern popular music for a modern world … its courage can not be denied.* **Allan Jones, Melody Maker, October 1977**

Here, My Dear

ARTIST Marvin Gaye RELEASE DATE January 1979 (UK & US) LABEL Motown (UK & US) PRODUCER Marvin Gaye UK CHART peak/weeks 0/0 US CHART peak/weeks 26/21 TRACK LISTING Here, My Dear/I Met A Little Girl/When Did You Stop Loving Me, When Did I Stop Loving You/Anger/Is That Enough/Everybody Needs Love/Time To Get It Together/Sparrow/Anna's Song/When Did You Stop Loving Me, When Did I Stop Loving You (Instrumental)/A Funky Space Reincarnation/You Can Leave, But It's Going To Cost You/Falling In Love Again/When Did You Stop Loving Me, When Did I Stop Loving You (Reprise) PERSONNEL Marvin Gaye (v), Delta Ashby, Ed Townsend (w), with session musicians

Countless artists have used their wives, husbands, girlfriends or boyfriends as the inspiration for songs pledging undying love, and here Marvin Gaye used his divorce as inspiration for an album – and the royalties it generated were part of the divorce settlement! Largely ignored at the time of release, it has since gone on to be regarded as something of a masterpiece, not least for the honesty with which Marvin tackled the subject. Never has such famous dirty laundry been washed so publicly.

Here We Go Again!

ARTIST The Kingston Trio RELEASE DATE November 1959 LABEL Capitol PRODUCER Voyle Gilmore UK CHART peak/weeks – US CHART peak/weeks 1/126 TRACK LISTING Molly Dee/Across The Wide Missouri/Haul Away/The Wanderer/'Round About The Mountain/Oleanna/The Unfortunate Miss

Hi Infidelity

ARTIST REO Speedwagon **RELEASE DATE** April 1981 (UK)/December 1980 (US) **LABEL** Epic (UK & US) **PRODUCER** Gary Richrath, Kevin Cronin **UK CHART** peak/weeks 6/29 **US CHART** peak/weeks 1/101 **TRACK LISTING** Don't Let Him Do/Keep On Loving You/Follow My Heart/In Your Letter/Take It On The Run/Tough Guys/Out Of Season/Shakin' It Loose/Someone Tonight/I Wish You Were There **PERSONNEL** Gary Richrath (lg), Neal Doughty (k, o), Alan Gratzer (d), Kevin Cronin (v, g), Bruce Hall (b)

Named after a fire engine, Illinois' REO Speedwagon had worked a decade as a perennial support act before unseating John Lennon from the top of the US charts. Their radio-friendly rock defined AOR for the Eighties as Journey, Styx (the band who replaced them at Number 1) and others made ever increasing and often bland million sellers. Their previous peak had been 1978's Number 29 **You Can Tune A Piano But You Can't Tuna Fish** – a title that says it all. Naff but occasionally inspired…

The sound is hard and heavy, very polished and most of all, crystal clear. You've seen it all before, of course – the lead singer in tight leather pants… but only a select few can do it as well as REO. **Kevin Cronin, Melody Maker, May 1981**

High Land, Hard Rain

ARTIST Aztec Camera **RELEASE DATE** April 1983 (UK)/August 1983 (US) **LABEL** Rough Trade (UK)/Sire (US) **PRODUCER** Bernie Clarke, John Brand **UK CHART** peak/weeks 22/18 **US CHART** peak/weeks 129/10 **TRACK LISTING** Oblivious/The Boy Wonders/Walk Out To Winter/The Bugle Sounds Again/We Could Send Letters/Pillar To Post/Release/Lost Outside The Tunnel/Back On Board/Down The Dip **PERSONNEL** Roddy Frame (v, g), Dave Ruffy (d), Campbell Owens (b), Bernie Clarke (k)

After a few indie singles with the then crucial Postcard and Rough Trade, East Kilbride's Roddy Frame (who, to all intents and purposes, IS Aztec Camera) released this remarkably composed and mature debut album, which supported his witty semi-acoustic love songs with hints of gospel, jazz, even calypso. Intimate enough for bedsit musings but airy enough to enjoy *en masse*, Frame's vignettes cast him as a visionary innocent. His tidy guitar decorated the chart hits **Oblivious** and **Walk Out To Winter**.

If they played it a touch tougher Aztec Camera could draw blood. On this album they've found some feelings they had left behind, and

high land, hard rain

there's an indication they are coming to terms with the sweet pain they are capable of inflicting. **Don Watson, NME, April 1983**

Highway 61 Revisited

ARTIST Bob Dylan **RELEASE DATE** September 1965 (UK)/August 1965 (US) **LABEL** CBS (UK)/Columbia (US) **PRODUCER** Bob Johnston, Tom Wilson **UK CHART** peak/weeks 4/15 **US CHART** peak/weeks 3/47 **TRACK LISTING** Like A Rolling Stone/Tombstone Blues/It Takes A Lot To Laugh, It Takes A Train To Cry/From A Buick Six/Ballard Of A Thin Man/Queen Jane Approximately/Highway 61 Revisited/Just Like Tom Thumbs Blues/Desolation Row **PERSONNEL** Bob Dylan (g, h, k, v), Michael Bloomfield (g), Al Kooper (o, g, p, k), Sam Lay, Bobby Gregg (d), Harvey Brooks, Harvey Goldstein, Russ Savakus (b), Paul Griffin (o, p, k), Frank Owens (p), Charlie McCoy (g, h)

Aggressive, argumentative and addressed at his many critics, **Highway 61 Revisited** followed on from the half-acoustic **Bringing It All Back Home** and told the world that Bob Dylan was going his own, electrified way, no matter what. ***Ballad Of A Thin Man*** accused the traditionalists directly of not knowing what was going on, while the Al Kooper organ-fuelled ***Like A Rolling Stone*** was a showstopper and the 11-minute plus ***Desolation Row*** drew its fascinating cast of characters from myth and medicine shows. Folk-rock Dylan-style at its brilliant best.

Bob Dylan's sixth LP, like all others, is fairly incomprehensible but nevertheless an absolute knockout. On all nine tracks Dylan uses some form of accompaniment, ranging from guitar, organ, to a siren, and the accent is mainly on the swing. **Chris Hayes, Melody Maker, October 1965**

Highway To Hell

ARTIST AC/DC **RELEASE DATE** August 1979 (UK & US) **LABEL** Atlantic (UK & US) **PRODUCER** Robert John Lange **UK CHART** peak/weeks 8/32 **US CHART** peak/weeks 17/83 **TRACK LISTING** Highway To Hell/Girls Got Rythm/Walk All Over You/Touch Too Much/Beating Around The Bush/Shot Down In Flames/Get It Hot/If You Want Blood (You've Got It)/Love Hungry Man/Night Prowler **PERSONNEL** Angus Young (g), Malcolm Young (g), Bon Scott (v), Phil Rudd (d), Cliff Williams (b)

It was still credible to like this Heavy Metal group through much of the Seventies and Eighties. The comical Australian noiseniks had just broken into the American Top 20 with this album when their Scottish vocalist, Bon Scott, choked on his own vomit after an excessive boozing binge and died. The band, if only in myth, still retain a taste for boozing. Guitarist Angus Young, the grubby, mooning perennial schoolboy, was the focus on stage with his surreal source of daft antics and bludgeoning, monstrous riffs. You either laughed or leapt about. Scott's death, ironically, gave them a near heroic kudos.

AC/DC play powerhouse rock – raw, aggressive sounds that are so hard to capture in the confines of a recording studio. **Highway To Hell,** *however, shows that at last they seem to have retained a little of that on-stage magic.* **Steve Gett, Melody Maker, August 1979**

The Hissing Of Summer Lawns

ARTIST Joni Mitchell **RELEASE DATE** November 1975 (UK & US) **LABEL** Asylum (UK & US) **PRODUCER** Joni Mitchell **UK CHART** peak/weeks 14/10 **US CHART** peak/weeks 4/17 **TRACK LISTING** In France They Kiss On Mainstreet/The Jungle Line/Edith And The Kingpin/Don't Interupt The Sorrow/Shades Of Scarlett Conquering/The Hissing Of Summer Lawns/The Boho Dance/Harry's House-Centerpiece/Sweet Bird/Shadows And Light **PERSONNEL** Joni Mitchell (v, bv, ag, k), Robben Ford (g, db, g), Jeff Baxter (g), Victor Feldman (ep, cg), John Guerin (d), Max Bennett (b), Joe Sample (ep), Larry Carlton (g), Wilton Felder (b), Chuck Findley (h, fh, t), Bud Shank (s, fl), James Taylor (g), Max Bennett (b)

Patti Smith Horses

It took nearly two years for Joni Mitchell to follow up her enormously successful **Court And Spark**, and this, her eighth album, saw her return to an earlier observational approach as opposed to the first-person confessional that had brought such praise from **Blue** onwards. Despite a poor press it still reached the US Top 5 and Prince, no less, has confessed it a favourite. Musically it merged her West Coast friends (Nash, Crosby and Taylor) with the jazz-rockers used so successfully on **Spark**, though *The Jungle Line* featured the Warrior Drums of Burundi.

Joni has produced an album which successfully puts the finger on Western Society as she sees it, and in doing so reveals her talent to be awesome in the extreme. **Steve Clarkem, NME, November 1975**

Honky Chateau

ARTIST Elton John RELEASE DATE May 1972 (UK)/June 1972 (US) LABEL D.J.M. (UK)/Uni (US) PRODUCER Gus Dudgeon UK CHART peak/weeks 2/23 US CHART peak/weeks 1/61 TRACK LISTING Honky Cat/Mellow/I Think I'm Going To Kill Myself/Susie (Dramas)/Rocket Man (I Think It's Going To Be A Long, Long Time)/Salvation/Slave/Amy/Mona Lisas And Mad Hatters/Hercules PERSONNEL Elton John (v, p), Dee Murray (b), Davey Johnstone (g), Nigel Olsson (d)

Ex-Magna Carta guitarist Davey Johnstone brought the Elton John Band up to a four-piece as they headed for the Château d'Hierouville outside Paris to record his fifth studio album. It took just three weeks to record ('being in the middle of nowhere,' he explained, 'you couldn't yield to temptation') and contained *Rocket Man*, a song that would prove his most successful British single to date. The package, with an elaborate gatefold sleeve, was to prove his first US chart-topper.

This album may not be as 'clever' or as full of instantly memorable melodies as Elton's early albums. But it's a warm and satisfying set which improves with every listen… **A. L., Melody Maker, May 1972**

Horses

ARTIST Patti Smith RELEASE DATE December 1975 (UK & US) LABEL Arista (UK & US) PRODUCER John Cale UK CHART peak/weeks 0/0 US CHART peak/weeks 47/17 TRACK LISTING Gloria/Rodondo Beach/Birdland/Free Money/Kimberley/Break It Up/Land/Elegie PERSONNEL Patti Smith (v), Richard Sohl (p), Lenny Kaye (lg), Ivan Kral (g, b), Jay Dee Daugherty (d)

Horses arrived in 1975, generally regarded as rock's lowest ever point, just before punk's Year Zero, and it appears now to be the album that paved the way for punk's mimimalist techniques. The negative to Debbie Harry of Blondie's positive, Patti Smith drew on base elements from the past – the riffs of The Rolling Stones, the nihilism of The Velvet Underground, the poetry of the Doors – to provide rock with a new future.

… Patti's startling freewheeling poetry, too raw, uninhibited, and spontaneous to shine in print, in its proper context, nestling up against and screwing with the primal rhythms of rock 'n' roll. **Chris Brazier, Melody Maker, March 1978**

Hot Buttered Soul

ARTIST Isaac Hayes RELEASE DATE October 1969 (UK)/July 1969 (US) LABEL Stax (UK)/Enterprise (US) PRODUCER Alan Jones, Al Bell UK CHART peak/weeks 0/0 US CHART peak/weeks 8/81 TRACK LISTING Walk On By/Hyperbollesyllaciscesquelalymistc/One Woman/By The Time I Get To Phoenix PERSONNEL Isaac Hayes (v, k), session musicians

When Stax label linked with Paramount and Gulf & Western, it released no fewer than 27 albums to coincide. The second solo effort by Hayes, a former writer and session musician, was something of a makeweight alongside the likes of Johnnie Taylor, Eddie Floyd and Booker T, but comfortably outsold all competition. Rap-style monologues and just four songs on the album theoretically restricted airplay possibilities, but cover versions *Walk On By* and *By The Time I Get To Phoenix* charted in the US thanks to familiarity combined with innovation. Soul II Soul, Massive Attack and many others followed the blueprint.

A huge American success – the first solo album from Isaac Hayes, better known as one half of Stax's famous hit writing team of Hayes and Porter. Beautiful but not funky enough to be a soul best seller. **Melody Maker, January 1970**

Hot Licks, Cold Steel And Truckers Favorites

ARTIST Commander Cody And His Lost Planet Airmen RELEASE DATE September 1972 (UK & US) LABEL Paramount (UK & US) PRODUCER – UK CHART peak/weeks 0/0 US CHART peak/weeks 94/13 TRACK LISTING Cravin' Your Love/Diggy Liggy Lo/It Should've Been Me/Kentucky Hills Of Tennessee/Looking At The World Through A Windscreen/Momma Hated Diesels/Rip It Up/Semi-Truck/Truck Drivin' Man/Truck Stop Rock/Tutti Fruitti/Watch My 0.38 PERSONNEL Bill Kirchen (g, v), Bruce Barlow (b, v), Bobby Black (stg, v), Lance Dickerson (d, v), Billy C. Farlow (h, v), Andy Stein (vl, s), John Tichy (g)

These Texans were a fun mob, extolling the joys of country, rockabilly, and anything that encouraged wild live antics and copious intakes of beer. Refusing to follow the dreamy whimsy of such as The Byrds, they cranked it up and enjoyed a one-off smash with **Hot Rod Lincoln**. They ironically feigned nostalgia on **The Kentucky Hills Of Tennessee** and bashed through Little Richard's **Rip It Up**. They both sucked up to and blew raspberries at truck-drivin' men: **Diggy Liggy Lo** was a straight tribute, **Momma Hated Diesels** was a hysterical parody. The band's eventual 'Best Of' was called **Too Much Fun**. Appropriate.

There are three types of songs here: early Sun Records style of rockabilly, regular honky-tonk country & western, and several off-brand oddities…. Commander Cody and His Lost Planet Airmen will be remembered for being the first long-haired group to completely cross the country barrier. **Chet Flippo, Rolling Stone, September 1972**

Hot Rats

ARTIST Frank Zappa RELEASE DATE February 1970 (UK)/October 1969 (US) LABEL Reprise (UK)/Bizarre (US) PRODUCER Frank Zappa UK CHART peak/weeks 9/27 US CHART peak/weeks 0/0 TRACK LISTING Peaches In Regalia/Willie The Pimp/Son Of Mr Green Genes/Little Umbrella/The Gumbo Variations/It Must Be A Camel PERSONNEL Frank Zappa (g, b, pc), Ian Underwood (p, o, fl, cl, s)

One of Frank Zappa's more focused solo albums, **Hot Rats** showcased the talented virtuoso guitarist as he ran the gamut of modern guitar styles, particularly the sort of dexterous jazz-rock fusions that would dominate the early Seventies. As well as the memorable instrumental *Peaches In Regalia*, **Hot Rats** featured *Willie The Pimp*, containing the album's only vocal courtesy of old school chum, Don Van Vliet aka Captain Beefheart, whose **Trout Mask Replica** Zappa had produced the previous year. **Hot Rats** proved that, were he to stand still for a single moment, Zappa could have carved a successful career as a standout guitarist, ace melodicist, pop songsmith – anything he put his brilliant mind to. Fortunately, he resisted any such categorization.

*If **Hot Rats** is any indication of where Zappa is headed on his own, we are in for some fiendish rides indeed… this album suggests he may be off on a new and much more individual direction.* **Lester Bangs, Rolling Stone, March 1970**

Hotel California

ARTIST The Eagles RELEASE DATE December 1976 (UK & US) LABEL Asylum (UK & US) PRODUCER Bill Szymczyk UK CHART peak/weeks 2/63 US CHART peak/weeks 1/107 TRACK LISTING Hotel California/New Kid In Town/Life In The Fast Lane/Wasted Time/Wasted Time (reprise)/Victim Of Love/Pretty Maids All In A Row/Try And Love Again/The Last Resort PERSONNEL Glenn Frey (g, v), Bernie Leadon (g, v), Randy Meisner (b, v), Don Henley (d, v)

Having prepared the grounds with the US chart-topping **Greatest Hits**, the Eagles then topped even that with an album whose sales exceeded 10 million. The replacement of country-rock pioneer

and former Burrito Brother Bernie Leadon with Joe Walsh gave the band three out-and-out rock guitarists, while the band's depiction of the hedonistic West Coast culture would become required listening. Barney Hoskyns' *Waiting For The Sun* would call it 'a grandiose critique of the entertainment business which itself seemed to eptomise all that was bogus and overblown about the world'.

Hounds Of Love

ARTIST Kate Bush RELEASE DATE September 1985 (UK & US) LABEL EMI (UK)/EMI America (US) PRODUCER Kate Bush UK CHART peak/weeks 1/51 US CHART peak/weeks 30/27 TRACK LISTING Running Up That Hill (A Deal With God)/Hounds Of Love/The Big Sky/Mother Stands For Comfort/Cloudbusting/And Dream Of Sleep/Under Ice/Waking The Witch/Watching You Without Me/Jig Of Life/Hello Earth/The Morning Fog PERSONNEL Kate Bush (v, k), Paddy Bush (md, var), Del Palmer (b), John Williams (c, gst), session musicians, with orchestral arrangements by Michael Kamen

Bush's masterpiece, this was dramatic and sensual and saw her revelling in the fruits of her experimental labours on the only partially successful **The Dreaming**. Working in her home studio for the first time proper, she allowed her imagination free rein but retained her pop awareness. Thus **Running Up That Hill**, a favourite single of that year, became her first Top 3 hit for seven years, and her first sizeable success in America. **Cloudbusting**, **The Big Sky**, and the title track were also hits – again aided by big-thinking videos, while the album's James Joyce-inspired second side, **The Ninth Wave**, describing the thought processes of a drowning woman, brought credibility back to the notion of 'concept' rock. Howling genius.

*The biggest plus of the album is, in fact, her singing: she squawked and shrieked her way through **The Kick Inside** and **Lionheart** and even on **Never For Ever** (surely her greatest work) there were moments when hysteria got the better of her.* **Colin Irwin, Melody Maker, September 1985**

How Do You Like It

ARTIST Gerry & The Pacemakers **RELEASE DATE** October 1963 **LABEL** Columbia **PRODUCER** George Martin **UK CHART** peak/weeks 2/28 **US CHART** peak/weeks 0/0 **TRACK LISTING** A Shot Of Rhythm And Blues/ Jambalaya/ Where Have You Been/Here's Hoping/Pretend/ Maybellene/You'll Never Walk Alone/The Wrong Yo Yo/You're The Reason/Chills/You Can't Fool Me/Don't You Ever/Summertime/Slow Down **PERSONNEL** Gerry Marsden (v, lg), Les Chadwick (b), Freddie Marsden (d), Les Maguire (p, s)

When *Mersey Beat* published its first readers' poll in 1962, Gerry Marsden's group came second to The Beatles. And despite a trio of chart-topping singles with their first three releases, it was situation normal in October 1963 when **Please Please Me** ruled the chart, giving way two months later to **With The Beatles**. Gerry's album, his first, contained only his latest chart-topper, *You'll Never Walk Alone*, along with covers of US standards from Hank Williams, Chuck Berry and Carl Perkins.

Hunky Dory

ARTIST David Bowie **RELEASE DATE** December 1971 (UK & US) **LABEL** RCA Victor (UK & US) **PRODUCER** Ken Scott **UK CHART** peak/weeks 3/69 **US CHART** peak/weeks 93/16 **TRACK LISTING** Changes/Oh! You Pretty Things/Eight Line Poem/Life On Mars?/Kooks/Quicksand/Fill Your Heart/Andy Warhol/Song For Bob Dylan/Queen Bitch/The Bewlay Brothers **PERSONNEL** Michael Ronson (g), Woody Woodmansey (d), Trevor Bolder (b), Richard Wakeman (p), David Bowie (p, g, s, v)

A reasonably straightforward album of pretty ballads and strong piano-led craftsmanship which has stood the test of time. **Hunky Dory** demonstrated that even without the era-defining chameleon images, Bowie was a force and talent to be reckoned with. *Changes* was all but a theme song; the grandiose and ambitious *Life On Mars* was a hit much later. *Quicksand* is a performance favourite, while *Oh! You Pretty Things* survived even a Peter Noone cover version. *The Bewlay Brothers* and the sweetly romantic *Kooks* showcased Bowie's knack for colouring stream-of-consciousness

words with loaded meaning and resonance.

Possibly, just possibly, David Bowie could be the biggest thing to come out of Britain this year, and if this album is any indication, it won't be through hype either. **Hunky Dory** *is… the most inventive piece of songwriting to have appeared on record for a considerable time.* **M. W., Melody Maker, January 1972**

Hysteria

ARTIST Def Leppard **RELEASE DATE** August 1987 (UK & US) **LABEL** Vertigo (UK)/Mercury (US) **PRODUCER** Robert John 'Mutt' Lange **UK CHART** peak/weeks 1/95 **US CHART** peak/weeks 1/133 **TRACK LISTING** Women/Rocket/Animal/Love Bites/Pour Some Sugar On Me/Armageddon It/Gods Of War/Don't Shoot Shotgun/Run Riot/Hysteria/Excitable/Love And Affection **PERSONNEL** Joe Elliot (lv), Steve 'Steamin' Clark (g), Phil Collen (g), Rick Savage (b), Rick Allen (d), Pete Williams (g)

Topping **Pyromania**, the album only Jacko's **Thriller** kept from the peak of the US charts, would have been hard enough without drummer Rick Allen losing an arm in an auto smash. But Leppard topped their best despite it all, ditching Meat Loaf's Jim Steinman in favour of long-time producer Mutt Lange who contributed to the songs before he too was hospitalized after another, thankfully less serious, car accident. Overdubbed to the nth degree during its lengthy gestation, the result is sonic and songwriting perfection.

The hour of music on **Hysteria** *is laundered and wholesome, guaranteed not to offend. With the exception of* **Rocket**'s *big drums and* **Gods Of War**'s *political comment, there's little that makes a statement. Having said that, millions of people are going to love it.* **Emily Fraser, Q, October 1987**

I Do Not Want
What I Haven't Got

ARTIST Sinead O'Connor **RELEASE DATE** March 1990 (UK)/April 1990 (US) **LABEL** Ensign (UK & US) **PRODUCER** Sinead O'Connor, Nellee Hooper **UK CHART** peak/weeks 1/51 **US CHART** peak/weeks 1/52 **TRACK LISTING** Feel So Different/I Am Stretched On Your Grave/Three Babies/The Emperor's New Clothes/Black Boys On Mopeds/Nothing Compares 2 U/Jump In The River/You Cause As Much Sorrow/The Last Day Of Our Acquaintance/I Do Not Want What I Haven't Got **PERSONNEL** Sinead O'Connor (v), John Reynolds (gst), Andy Rourke (gst), Jah Wobble (gst), session musicians

Though her debut, **The Lion And The Cobra**, had shown how capable a songwriter Sinead O'Connor was, the success of her second album was attributable to a cover of Prince's **Nothing Compares 2 U**. But it was not as easy as picking a hit: her relationship with manager/boyfriend Fachtna O'Kelly (who suggested the song) ended just as she shot the video, leading to a tearfully real performance, while she later claimed Prince had 'threatened her' when they met…needless to say, he denied it.

With her high, yelping voice glowing like a torch in the sparse, frosty setting, O'Connor delivers a performance that becomes a beacon of dangerously uninhibited yet life-affirming lust on an album fraught with anger, heartache and fragile hope. **David Fricke, Rolling Stone, December 1990**

I Just Can't Stop It

ARTIST English Beat **RELEASE DATE** May 1980 (UK)/August 1980 (US) **LABEL** Go-Feet BEAT (UK)/Sire (US) **PRODUCER** Bob Sargeant **UK CHART** peak/weeks 3/32 **US CHART** peak/weeks 142/14 **TRACK LISTING** Mirror In The Bathroom/Hands Off...She's Mine/Two Swords/Twist & Crawl/Tears Of A Clown/Rough Rider/Click Click/Ranking Full Stop/Big Shot/Whine & Grine/Stand Down Margaret/Noise In This World/Can't Get Used To Losing You/Best Friend/Jackpot **PERSONNEL** Dave Wakeling, Bob Sargeant, Ranking Roger, Andy Cox, David Steele, Everett Moreton

Madness and the Beat (English Beat in the US) were the most successful bands to have used 2-Tone as a leg-up to pop fame. This album, plus a clutch of singles, represented the peak of their creativity; a third album did better in America but lost the plot slightly. Whether poking fun at sexism (**Hands Off She's Mine**), vanity of either gender (**Mirror In the Bathroom**) or dipping a tie in political waters (the anti-Thatcher **Stand Down Margaret**) their sureness of touch was enviable. And you could dance to it.

I Left My Heart In San Francisco

ARTIST Tony Bennett **RELEASE DATE** May 1965 (UK)/July 1962 (US) **LABEL** CBS (UK)/Columbia (US) **PRODUCER** Ernest Altschuler **UK CHART** peak/weeks 13/14 **US CHART** peak/weeks 5/149 **TRACK LISTING** I Left My Heart In San Francisco/Once Upon A Time/Tender Is The Night/Love For Sale/Taking A Chance On Love/Candy Kisses/Have I Told You Lately?/Rules Of The Road/Marry Young/I'm Always Chasing Rainbows/Best Is Yet To Come **PERSONNEL** Tony Bennett (v, p), Ralph Sharon (p, arr), session musicians

Seemingly forever untouched by shifting trends in music, Bennett enjoyed a revival of popularity as new generations, encouraged by such fans as kd lang and Elvis Costello, discovered the *tendresse* of the great man's voice. Sinatra's only serious rival as the ultimate crooner, Bennett sang for 40 years with a lazy laid-back charm, and swung effortlessly. Born in New York as Anthony Dominick Benedetto, he saw this album spend nearly two years in the charts, with the title track, written by Douglas Cross and George Cory, becoming something of a theme song. **Tender Is The Night** and **The Best Is Yet To Come** are not without their *aficionados*.

It's another marvelous album from one of the best singers around, who can handle a song with style, warmth and in-tune... Don't miss this one. **Melody Maker, January 1964**

I Never Loved A Man The Way I Love You

ARTIST Aretha Franklin **RELEASE DATE** July 1967 (UK)/April 1967 (US) **LABEL** Atlantic (UK & US) **PRODUCER** Jerry Wexler **UK CHART** peak/weeks 36/2 **US CHART** peak/weeks 2/79 **TRACK LISTING** Respect/Drown In My Own Tears/I Never Loved A Man (The Way I Love You)/Soul Serenade/Don't Let Me Lose This Dream/Baby, Baby, Baby/Dr. Feelgood/Good Times/Do Right Woman-Do Right Man/Save Me/A Change Is Gonna Come **PERSONNEL** Aretha Franklin (v), session musicians

Such had been the faltering way Aretha's career had begun (six years with Columbia that found both her and her label struggling to establish an identity for herself) that it was hard to believe this album was her tenth release. All the years of uncertainty were washed away with a triumphant release. More importantly, this album opened up many hitherto closed markets for Aretha; in hitting Number 2 on the US album charts, many white record buyers were exposed to the delights of Aretha singing her own unique brand of soul.

'At Columbia, I'd make a tape to give them an idea of what I wanted, and they would write the music around that... At Atlantic... they just let me come in and start playing; the musicians would work

around what I was doing and as soon as it seemed to fit, we went right ahead and made the record.' **Interview with Leanard Feather, Melody Maker, February 1968**

I Remember You

ARTIST Frank Ifield **RELEASE DATE** February 1963 **LABEL** Columbia **PRODUCER** – **UK CHART** peak/weeks 3/36 **US CHART** peak/weeks 0/0 **TRACK LISTING** Just One More Chance/I've Got That Sad And Lonely Feeling/The Glory Of Love/Gone/Lonely Teardrops/San Antonio Rose/Heart And Soul/I'm A Fool To Care/The Wisdom Of A Fool/(I Heard That) Lonesome Whistle/Any Time/Before This Day Ends/I Just Can't Lose The Blues/In A Mansion Stands My Love **PERSONNEL** Frank Ifield (v), Norrie Paramor and his Orchestra

The first British recording artist to score three UK chart-toppers in successive singles, Coventry-born Frank Ifield emigrated to Australia at age nine and, presaging the Bee Gees, returned to knock the mother country dead. While the brothers Gibb boasted a mean falsetto, Frank's gimmick was the yodel, which was all over this album named after the first chart-topper. But despite his singles success only the film theme tie-in **Born Free** later in the year would prove equally popular in the LP stakes, and cabaret beckoned.

I Should Coco

ARTIST Supergrass **RELEASE DATE** May 1995 **LABEL** Parlophone **PRODUCER** Sam Williams **UK CHART** peak/weeks 1/– **US CHART** peak/weeks - **TRACK LISTING** I'd Like To Know/Caught By The Fuzz/Mansize Rooster/Alright/Lose It/Lenny/Strange Ones/Sitting Up Straight/She's So Loose/We're Not Supposed To/Time/Sofa (Of My Lethargy)/Time To Go **PERSONNEL** Gaz Coombes (v, g), Nick Goffey (g), Danny Goffey (d)

Sounding like a 'Best Of The Sixties, Seventies and Eighties' compilation, the debut album by Oxford's Supergrass offered a superb, compact version of the last three decades of British pop. Ferociously energetic, maddeningly infectious, **I Should Coco** features numerous chart smashes: the bubblegum punk of **Caught By The Fuzz**, the Madness meets Kinks effervescence of **Mansize Rooster**, and one *bona fide* adolescent pop classic, **Alright**, which

almost reached Number 1 in the summer of Brit-pop, 1995.

Sex 'n' drugs 'n' rock 'n' roll are the stuff of **I should Coco**, *which celebrates them with a happy shrug. Debauchery is fun, and fun is good for you…* **David Bennun, Melody Maker, May 1995**

I Want To See The Bright Lights Tonight

ARTIST Richard & Linda Thompson **RELEASE DATE** April 1974 (UK & US) **LABEL** Island (UK)/Reprise (US) **PRODUCER** Richard Thompson **UK CHART** peak/weeks 0/0 **US CHART** peak/weeks 0/0 **TRACK LISTING** I Want To See The Bright Lights Tonight/When I Get To The Border/The Calvary Cross/Withered & Died/Down Where The Drunkards Roll/We Sing Hallelujah/Has He Got A Friend For Me?/The Little Beggar Girl/The End Of The Rainbow/The Great Valero **PERSONNEL** Richard Thompson (v, g), Linda Thompson (v), with Sour Grapes; Simon Nichol (du), Steve Borrell (b), William Murray (d)

An original member of British folk-rock pioneers, Fairport Convention, Richard Thompson's chosen *métier* was the delicate fusion of Celtic, folk and rock 'n' roll music as a means of exploring the darker side of the human condition. **I Want To See The Bright Lights Tonight** juxtaposed the fear and loathing of Richard's lyrics – and his deep baritone – with the warmer, softer alto of his then wife, Linda. On tracks such as **Calvary Cross**, the battle between the sexes never sounded so sad, sombre or sweet.

One of the most enjoyable albums of an admittedly, limpid year… Richard Thompson… is the least lauded yet most accomplished guitarist in this land… don't get the idea that this album is for the manic depressive only. It isn't. It leaves me feeling at peace. **G. B., Melody Maker, May 1974**

I Was Born A Man

ARTIST Babybird **RELEASE DATE** August 1995 (UK)/July 1995 (US) **LABEL** Babybird Recordings **PRODUCER** – **UK CHART** peak/weeks Limited Addition - 1000 copies only **US CHART** peak/weeks 0/0 **TRACK LISTING** Blow It To The Moon/Man's Tight Vest/Lemonade Baby/C.F.C./Corner Shop/Kiss Your Country/Hong Kong Blues/Dead Bird Sings/Baby Bird/Farmer/Invisible Tune/Alison/Love, Love, Love **PERSONNEL** Stephen Jones (v, var)

Stephen Jones emulated the Sheffield pop stars of a decade earlier by taking on the critical establishment at their own game: self-consciously arty and intellectual, he tore up the rule book by releasing five home-recorded albums in little over a year, whilst pushing an image of inverted glamour. He staged ugliness as cool, and wrote idiosyncratic love/hate songs arranged with wilful tackiness. Prior to his surprise runaway hit **You're Gorgeous**, this debut album was lo-fi and high concept – and paid for by an Arts Council grant!

I Was Born A Man *is the only record I've heard this year with lyrics worth remembering and music that's impossible to forget… I'd rather you listen to it than me talk about it.* **Mark Luffman, Melody Maker, August 1995**

I'm Nearly Famous

ARTIST Cliff Richard **RELEASE DATE** May 1976 (UK)/August 1976 (US) **LABEL** EMI (UK)/Rocket (US) **PRODUCER** Bruce Welch **UK CHART** peak/weeks 5/21 **US CHART** peak/weeks 76/15 **TRACK LISTING** I Can't Ask for Anymore Than You/It's No Use Pretending/I'm Nearly Famous/Lovers/Junior Cowboy/Miss You Nights/I Wish You'd Change Your Mind/Devil Woman/Such is the Mystery/You've Got to Give Me All Your Lovin'/If You Walked Away/It's Alright Now **PERSONNEL** Cliff Richard (v)

Having suffered the first hitless year of his career Cliff Richard got into new gear in 1976 with this album. Not only did it contain two hit singles in **Miss You Nights** and **Devil Woman** – the latter his first sizeable US hit – it became his first Top 5 album since 1964's **Wonderful Life**. His next three albums would be accompanied by stage shows featuring a permanent band, while a revitalized decade would close with **We Don't Talk Anymore**, his best-selling single ever written by one of the band, Alan Tarney.

… all the fast songs are very good, all the slow songs are not. Unfortunately, the fast ones are unremittingly alternated with the slow ones, so there's no avoiding the dross. The album simply lacks direction. **Ken Tucker, Rolling Stone, August 1976**

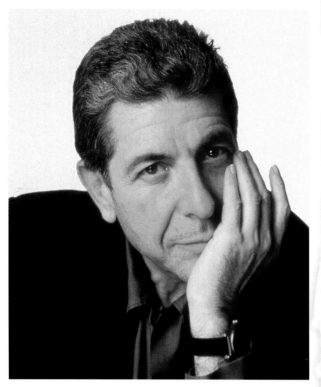

I'm Your Man

ARTIST Leonard Cohen RELEASE DATE February 1988 (UK & US) LABEL CBS (UK)/Passport (US) PRODUCER Leonard Cohen UK CHART peak/weeks 48/13 US CHART peak/weeks 0/0 TRACK LISTING First We Take Manhattan/Ain't No Cure For Love/Everybody Knows/I'm Your Man/Take This Waltz/Jazz Police/I Can't Forget/Tower Of Song PERSONNEL Leonard Cohen (v, g), Jennifer Warnes (gst), session musicians

Cohen's comeback success, which saw him allowing humour (eating a banana on the cover shot, for example) and examining both middle age and Middle Europe with wry wit. Perennial acolyte Jennifer Warnes guested, while Cohen bit into some of his most acerbic lyrics ever on love, lust, loss and loneliness. He was engaging a whole new audience: surprisingly enough riveting the post-punks who, as punks, had ridiculed his sombre side. *Tower Of Song* inspired a later tribute album which drew offerings from R.E.M., John Cale and Nick Cave. *Everybody Knows* and the title song were among the best studies of the male psyche in his entire canon.

Nowadays he tempers his world-weary innocence with a touch of cynicism… **I'm Your Man** *is Cohen's best LP since the mid-Seventies… there are no real departures here, just the usual gorgeous melodies and an ageing poet taking himself very seriously… until he twinkles.* **Mark Cooper, Q, March 1988**

The Idiot

ARTIST Iggy Pop RELEASE DATE April 1977 (UK&US) LABEL RCA Victor (UK & US) PRODUCER David Bowie UK CHART peak/weeks 30/3 US CHART peak/weeks 72/13 TRACK LISTING Sister Midnight/Nightclubbing/Funtime/Baby/China Girl/Dum Dum Boys/Tiny Girls/Mass Production PERSONNEL Iggy Pop (v), David Bowie (k), Ricky Gardiner (g), Tony Sales (b), Hunt Sales (d), Carlos Alomar (g)

The Idiot was James Osterberg's third crack at fame, having cut two Elektra LPs that failed to sell but are now regarded as precursors of punk rock and another pre-punk classic in 1973's **Raw Power**,

on whose release the band promptly folded! Its producer David Bowie resurrected Iggy once more in 1977 with this debut solo LP, which included the first appearance of **China Girl**, and which would prove a transatlantic Top 10 hit for co-writer Bowie in 1983.

The Idiot… *steeped in the so-called 'minimalist' ambience currently so fashionable amongst young bands who've spent too much time listening to Iggy and taking him seriously, is the most savage indictment of rock posturing ever recorded.* **The Idiot** *is a necrophiliac's delight.* **John Swanson, Rolling Stone, 1977**

If Only I Could Remember My Name

ARTIST David Crosby RELEASE DATE February 1971 (UK & US) LABEL Atlantic (UK & US) PRODUCER David Crosby UK CHART peak/weeks 12/7 US CHART peak/weeks 12/18 TRACK LISTING Music Is Love/Laughing/Tamalpais High (At About 3)/Cowboy Music/What Are Their Names/Traction In The Rain/Song With No Words (Tree With No Leaves)/Orleans/I'd Swear There Was Somebody Here PERSONNEL David Crosby (g, v), Graham Nash (gst), Neil Young (gst), Joni Mitchell (gst), Jerry Garcia (gst), Phil Lesh (gst), Michael Shrieve (gst), Grace Slick(gst)

After **Four Way Street**, the individual members of CSN&Y drifted apart and together with hippie uncertainty. Crosby's solo claim was assisted by half the working musicians in California: Neil Young, Joni Mitchell, Grace Slick and Jerry Garcia were among his willing collaborators. His impressive voice, however, domininated. Some pruning might have been welcome, and *I'd Swear There Was Somebody Here* and *Song With No Words (Tree With No Leaves)* veered towards self-indulgence. The attitude, like the title, now seems almost a comic parody of the stoners' turn-of-the-decade dream, but the feel is as authentic as they come.

Crosby's album is not likely to go down in history, but it is not a bad album. While it's true that it all sounds pretty much the same, we must also note that nothing really jars. **Lester Bangs, Rolling Stone, April 1971**

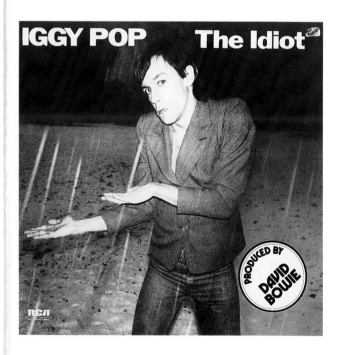

Imagine

ARTIST John Lennon **RELEASE DATE** October 1971 (UK)/September 1971 (US) **LABEL** Apple (UK & US) **PRODUCER** John Lennon, Yoko Ono, Phil Spector **UK CHART** peak/weeks 1/101 **US CHART** peak/weeks 1/45 **TRACK LISTING** Imagine/Crippled Inside/Jealous Guy/How Do You Sleep?/It's So Hard/I Don't Want To Be A Soldier/Oh My Love/Give Me Some Truth/How?/Oh Yoko! **PERSONNEL** John Lennon (v, g, var), Yoko Ono (v, ww), Klaus Voorman (b), Mike Pinder (b), Jim Keltner (d), Alan White (d), Nicky Hopkins (p)

Lennon's second solo album revealed a man still at odds with himself and the world at large. Personal problems surfaced once more on **Crippled Inside**, **Jealous Guy** and the thinly veiled attack on Paul McCartney that was **How Do You Sleep?**, and he raged against the corruption of Nixon's America on **Give Me Some Truth**. But Phil Spector's lush production and the inclusion of the title track plus simple love songs like **Oh Yoko** and **Oh My Love** showed the mellower side of an artist in transition.

Lennon's won, hands down. If this were a new name, it would be deemed the gutsy answer to the feeble state of rock. Instead a lot of people are going to be talking about it rather than playing it. **R. H., Melody Maker, September 1971**

Immigrés

ARTIST Youssou N'Dour Et Le Super Etoile De Dakar **RELEASE DATE** August 1988 (UK & US) **LABEL** Celluloid **PRODUCER** – **UK CHART** peak/weeks 0/0 **US CHART** peak/weeks 0/0 **TRACK LISTING** Immigrés - Britim Rew/Pitche Mi/Taaw/Badou **PERSONNEL** Youssou N'Dour (v), Pape Ohmar Ngomn (g), Jimmy Mbaya (g), Assane Thaim (pc), Babacar Faye (pc), session musicians

After leaving the Star Band of Dakar in 1979 and promoting his music by a series of no less than 13 cassettes, N'Dour visited Paris in 1982 and London in 1984. This set's appearance on the Celluloid label was his first British release and the first to attract Western attention. It was less frantic and more sophisticated than his earlier efforts which had brought *mbalax* (Senegalese popular music) to a wider audience. His experience with Virgin was a salutary one, failing to meet high commercial expectations, but he remained a superstar into the Nineties. **Immigrés** is where it started.

… the first record to demonstrate his smooth mastery of international communication… there's an explosive excitement to his growing sense of power over himself and his listeners… **Mark Sinker, NME, August 1988**

Imperial Bedroom

ARTIST Elvis Costello And The Attractions **RELEASE DATE** July 1982 (UK & US) **LABEL** Radar (UK)/Columbia (US) **PRODUCER** Geoff Emerick **UK CHART** peak/weeks 6/12 **US CHART** peak/weeks 30/24 **TRACK LISTING** Beyond Belief/Tears Before Bedtime/The Long Honeymoon/Shabby Doll/Man Out

In My Tribe

ARTIST 10,000 Maniacs **RELEASE DATE** August 1987 (UK)/September 1987 (US) **LABEL** Elektra (UK & US) **PRODUCER** Peter Asher **UK CHART** peak/weeks 0/0 **US CHART** peak/weeks 37/77 **TRACK LISTING** What's The Matter Here?/Hey Jack Kerouac/Like The Weather/Cherry Tree/The Painted Desert/Don't Talk/Peace Train/Gun Shy/My Sister Rose/A Campfire Song/City Of Angels/Verdi Cries **PERSONNEL** Natalie Merchant (v), Jerome Augustyniak (d), Dennis Drew (o), Robert Buck (g, sy), Steven Gustafson (b, g)

Formed in 1981 in Jamestown, New York, 10,000 Maniacs brought folk-rock to alternative college radio, like a Fairport Convention for the slacker generation. Produced by Peter Asher (formerly of Sixties duo Peter And Gordon and the man at the controls of James Taylor's first three albums), **In My Tribe** combined socially conscious lyrics with strong hooklines, the icing on the cake being Natalie Merchant's oddly beguiling warble and new waif persona. Hit single **What's The Matter Here?** was about child abuse, while the band won a moral victory when they stopped performing their version of Cat Stevens' **Peace Train** live after the born-again Moslem expressed his support for death threats against Salman Rushdie.

Where do you start with a record so full, so completely realised…. It's as though, when I start speaking, just a little of the magic will seep away. **John Wilde, Melody Maker, September 1987**

In Search Of Space

ARTIST Hawkwind **RELEASE DATE** October 1971 (UK & US) **LABEL** United Artists (UK & US) **PRODUCER** Hawkwind, George Chkiantz **UK CHART** peak/weeks 18/19 **US CHART** peak/weeks 0/0 **TRACK LISTING** Technicians Of Space/Ship Earth/This Is/Your Captain Speaking/Your Captain Is Dead **PERSONNEL** Nik Turner (as, ag, v), Dave Brock (v, g, ag), Dave Anderson (b, g), Del Dettmar (sy), Terry Ollis (d, pc), Dik Mik (ag), Stacia Dances (gst), Huw, Colin and Bill Strong Arms (gst), Electric Heads (gst)

Hawkwind have been space-rock pioneers since 1969 and this album, their second, was an early landmark. Festival appearances with poet Robert Calvert and dancer Stacia pushed this to the Top 20 and offered a launchpad for 1972's surprise hit **Silver Machine**, where new bassist Lemmy overdubbed Calvert.

… this album, friends, is Psychedelic from the cover to the fade-out of the last groove. The music itself mostly sounds pretty much the same: monotone jammings with hypnotic rhythms and solos unravelling off into… well space. **Lester Bangs, Rolling Stone, June 1972**

In The Court Of The Crimson King

ARTIST King Crimson **RELEASE DATE** October 1969 (UK)/December 1969 (US) **LABEL** Island (UK)/Atlantic (US) **PRODUCER** King Crimson **UK CHART** peak/weeks 5/18 **US CHART** peak/weeks 28/25 **TRACK LISTING** Epitaph incl. (a)March For No Reason, (b)Tomorrow And Tomorrow/The Court Of The Crimson King incl. (a)The Return Of The Fire Witch, (b)The Dance Of The Puppets/I Talk To The Wind/21st Century Schizoid Man/Moonchild (a)Mirrors, (b)Illusion **PERSONNEL** Robert Fripp (g), Greg Lake (v, b), Ian MacDonald (s), Mike Giles (d), Pete Sinfield (w)

Progressive certainly, but with very little in common with rock, King Crimson's opening salvo took its spirit and inspiration from free-form jazz, and its discipline and sense of scale from the world of the classics. There are, undeniably, moments of sheer self-indulgence, most notably the tedious improvisation that forms most of **Moonchild** – but Greg Lake's superb lead vocals and bass playing, and the inclusion of **21st Century Schizoid Man**, the achingly beautiful **Epitaph** and the mellotron-heavy title track, make this an outstanding collection. And then there's that cover…

There's usually a tendency to regard weirdness as an end in itself, and excesses often ruin good ideas. Happily King Crimson avoids these obstacles most of the time… they have combined aspects of many musical forms to create a surreal work of force and originality. **John Mortland, Rolling Stone, December 1969**

In The Wee Small Hours

ARTIST Frank Sinatra **RELEASE DATE** May 1955 **LABEL** Capitol **PRODUCER** Voyle Gilmore **UK CHART** peak/weeks – **US CHART** peak/weeks 2/44 **TRACK LISTING** In the Wee Small Hours of the Morning/Mood Indigo/Glad to Be Unhappy/I Get Along Without You Very Well/Deep in a Dream/I See Your Face Before Me/Can't We Be Friends?/When Your Lover Has Gone/What Is This Thing Called Love/Last Night When We Were Young/I Be Around/Ill Wind/It Never Entered My Mind/Dancing On The Ceiling/I'll Never Be the Same/This Love Of Mine **PERSONNEL** Frank Sinatra (v), Nelson Riddle (arr, con), session musicians

His third album for Capitol introduced a rather different Frank Sinatra. Compared to the swinging sessions he recorded with Tommy Dorsey for the bobby-soxers in the early Forties and the happy-go-lucky romanticism of his work at Columbia in the mid to late Forties, Sinatra in the Fifties evinced a greater depth, the passion and perception in his voice easily matched by Nelson Riddle's beautiful arrangements. Sinatra's thoughtful delivery of material by the likes of Rodgers and Hart's **Glad To Be Unhappy**, Van Heusen's **Deep In A Dream** and Cole Porter's **What Is This Thing Called Love?** revealed the vulnerability beneath the swagger.

In The Wind

ARTIST Peter, Paul And Mary **RELEASE DATE** March 1964 (UK)/October 1963 (US) **LABEL** Warner Bros (UK & US) **PRODUCER** Albert B. Grossman **UK CHART** peak/weeks 11/19 **US CHART** peak/weeks 1/80 **TRACK LISTING** Very Last Day/Hush-A-Bye/Long Chain On/Rocky Road/Tell It On The Mountain/Polly Von/Stewball/All My Trials/Don't Think Twice, It's All Right/Freight Train/Quit Your Lowdown Ways/Blowin' In The Wind **PERSONNEL** Peter Yarrow (g, v), Paul Stookey (g, v), Mary Travers (v), Eddie DeHaas (b), Bob Dylan (gst)

The folksy trio's third album and second US chart-topper contained three songs by the as-yet unheralded Bob Dylan. Two, the title track and *Don't Think Twice, It's All Right*, had already been released as singles before the album appeared, but the third *Quit Your Low Down Ways* would not be heard officially until the 1991 **Bootleg Series** box set. Not that the apple-pie-cute singers listened to bootlegs – the link was Albert Grossman, the man who managed them both.

What we try to do is to present the original meaning of the song. But to do it as it was done in the original is to be reporters. We're interpreters, and it's a case of being ourselves… Experience is the great teacher… **Paul interviewed by Max Jones, Melody Maker, April 1964**

In Through The Out Door

ARTIST Led Zeppelin **RELEASE DATE** September 1979 (UK & US) **LABEL** Swan Song (UK & US) **PRODUCER** Jimmy Page **UK CHART** peak/weeks 1/16 **US CHART** peak/weeks 1/41 **TRACK LISTING** Fool In The Rain/In The Evening/ South Bound Saurez/All My Love/I'm Gonna Crawl/ Carouselambra/ Hot Dog **PERSONNEL** Robert Plant (v), Jimmy Page (lg), John Paul Jones (b), John Bonham (d)

Cut at Abba's Polar Studios, this proved that Zeppelin were still a going concern after a series of problems, not least of which was the tragic death of Robert Plant's five-year-old son. Bassist John Paul Jones had also apparently quit, feeling the band were stagnating – and it's his influence, most notably on keyboards, that pervades this album, with Jimmy Page uncharacteristically low-key. *Carouselambra* continues the Eastern lead of *Kashmir*, while *All My Love* and *Fool In The Rain* would be highlights on any album.

The impressionable first play had everyone in the office rolling around laughing, splatting their heads against the wall in an effort to control mirth… It's that funny… Led Zeppelin are displaying the first intimations of mortality, and it's time they accepted their fate like men. **Chris Bohn, Melody Maker, August 1979**

In Utero

ARTIST Nirvana **RELEASE DATE** September 1993 (UK & US) **LABEL** D.G.C. (UK & US) **PRODUCER** Nirvana **UK CHART** peak/weeks 1/14 **US CHART** peak/weeks 1/87 **TRACK LISTING** Serve The Servants/Scentless Apprentice/Heart-shaped Box/Rape Me/Frances Farmer Will Have Her Revenge On Seattle/Dumb/Very Ape/Milk It/Penny Royal Tea/Radio Friendly Unit Shifted/Tourette's/All Apologies/Gallons Of Rubbing Alcohol Flow Through The Strip **PERSONNEL** Kurt Cobain (v, g), Chris Novoselic (b), Dave Grohl (d), Kera Shaley (c)

Just over six months after the release of this album Kurt Cobain was dead. This album was troubled, but not a suicide note, despite the originally suggested title 'I Hate Myself And Want To Die'. It couldn't hope to live up to the breakthrough **Nevermind**, and didn't try: Steve Albini's production values ensuring a much less polished product. It was a halfway house between **Nevermind** and the earlier, low-fi **Bleach** – not what Geffen wanted but it went straight into the UK and US charts at the very top.

It's the last thing most people would expect from Angst Central, and its an inspired sign-off that shows how Nirvana have been reborn in the face of suck-cess… brilliant, corrosive, enraged and thoughtful, most of them all at once. **David Fricke, Rolling Stone, September 1993**

Infected

ARTIST The The **RELEASE DATE** November 1986 (UK & US) **LABEL** Some Bizarre (UK)/Epic (US) **PRODUCER** Matt Johnson, Gary Langan, Warne Livesey **UK CHART** peak/weeks 14/30 **US CHART** peak/weeks 89/18 **TRACK LISTING** Infected/Out Of The Blue (Into The Fire)/Heartland/Angels Of Deception/ Sweet Bird Of Truth/Slow Train to Dawn/Twilight Of A Champion/ The Mercy Beat **PERSONNEL** Matt Johnson (v, g), session musicians

Less a band and more a solo project that allowed tormented whiz-kid Matt Johnson to vent his spleen, The The formed in London on the eve of the Eighties, and foreshadowed the experimental bedsit electro-melancholia of Soft Cell, Pet Shop Boys et al. **Infected**, The The's third album, dealt with Johnson's usual favourites, millenial psychosis, urban alienation, apocalypse paranoia, the gamut of post-punk obsessions, but the synthetic beats and crystalline melodies were sufficiently irresistible to make you put up with – enjoy, even – the grim subject matter.

Infected is at once a delicious pop sweetmeat for under the Christmas tree and at the same time the sort of thing that'll make the family pet howl in fear. Subtle snapshots of decay distributed to the sounds of angels losing their wings. **Paul Mathur, Melody Maker, November 1986**

Ingénue

ARTIST k.d. lang **RELEASE DATE** March 1992 (UK & US) **LABEL** Sire (UK & US) **PRODUCER** Greg Penny, Ben Mink, k.d. Lang **UK CHART** peak/weeks 3/34 **US CHART** peak/weeks 18/90 **TRACK LISTING** Save Me/The Mind Of Love/Miss Chatelaine/Wash Me Clean/So It Shall Be/Still Thrives This Love/Season Of Hollow Soul/Outside Myself/Tears Of Love's Recall/Constant Craving **PERSONNEL** k.d. lang (v, g), session musicians

Lang's first album after turning 30 years old won her a third Grammy, indicating that she had the country field at her feet. Its success encouraged her not only to move further towards the pop *milieu* but to declare her lesbianism publicly. The major hit **Constant Craving** would earn her a credit on the Rolling Stones' closely related **Has Anybody Seen My Baby**.

Although her lyrics are generally simple, clear and strong, the odd stumbling clumsiness does escape quality control… But the imperial elegance of her singing effortlessly rescues any stray syllable, **Ingenue** *is open, self-assured and sexy as a cobra.* **Phil Sutcliffe, Q, April 1992**

Innervisions

ARTIST Stevie Wonder **RELEASE DATE** August 1973 (UK & US) **LABEL** Tamala Motown (UK)/Tamla (US) **PRODUCER** Stevie Wonder **UK CHART** peak/weeks 8/55 **US CHART** peak/weeks 4/89 **TRACK LISTING** Too High/Visions/Living For The City/Golden Lady/Higher Ground/Jesus Children Of America/All In Love Is Fair/Don't You Worry 'Bout A Thing/He's Misstra Know-It-All **PERSONNEL** Stevie Wonder (v, p, h), Lani Groves (bv), Tasha Thomas (bv), Jim Gilstrap (bv), Malcolm Cecil (b), Dean Parks (ag), David 'T' Walker (g), Clarence Bell (o), Ralph Hammer (ag), Larry 'Nastyee' Latimer (cg), Scott Edwards (b), Yusuf Roahman (pc), Sheila Wilkerson (pc), Willie Weeks (b)

His second masterpiece, **Innervisions** featured massive hits: *Higher Ground*, *Living For The City*, *Don't You Worry 'Bout A Thing*, *Golden Lady* and the pop-perfect *He's Misstra Know-It-All*. *Living For The City* and *All In Love Is Fair* also showed Wonder was equally adept at scorching politicized funk and gorgeous balladry. It is no wonder **Innervisions** won four Grammy awards.

A master stylist and arranger, his music has a grace, a studied balance, that does more than just set off each cut in perfect harmony with its neighbours. Indeed, **Innervisions** *may be as close to a concept album as Stevie will ever produce.* **Lenny Kaye, Rolling Stone, September 1973**

Interiors

ARTIST Rosanne Cash **RELEASE DATE** November 1990 **LABEL** CBS (UK)/Columbia (US) **PRODUCER** Rosanne Cash **UK CHART** peak/weeks – **US CHART** peak/weeks 175/4 **TRACK LISTING** On The Inside/Dance With The Tiger/On The Surface/Real Woman/This World/What We Really Want/Mirror Image/Land Of Nightmares/I Want A Cure/Paralyzed **PERSONNEL** Rosanne Cash (v, bv, arr), Jerry Douglas (db), Edgar Meyer (b), Eddie Bayers (d), Richard Bennett (ag, md), John Jarvis (k, p), Mike Lawler (k), Vince Melamed (k, arr), Mark O'Connor (md, vl), Stuart Smith (g)

Daughter of Johnny, Cash had carved her own niche as a perceptive and daring country vocalist. **Interiors** forsook her previous safety valve of light wit and came in dark and heavy as a scathing assault on the illusory benefits of intimate relationships: 'We crawled night and day through the tears and debris,' it begins. With astutely supportive guitar from the highly rated Stuart Smith, Cash (who had pointedly sung **My Old Man** five years earlier) proved, with this work, that she was a visionary lyricist in her own right, with a heart duly dressed in black.

Interiors *flies in the face of the happy-ending fairy tales that pass for entertainment in this country. It is disturbing, and it offers no answers.* **Wayne King, Rolling Stone, November 1990**

Introspective

ARTIST Pet Shop Boys **RELEASE DATE** October 1988 (UK & US) **LABEL** Parlophone (UK)/EMI America (US) **PRODUCER** Pet Shop Boys, Trevor Horn, Stephen Lipson, Lewis A. Martinee, David Jacob, Julian Mendelsohn **UK CHART** peak/weeks 2/39 **US CHART** peak/weeks 34/22 **TRACK LISTING** Left To My Own Devices/I Want A Dog/Domino Dancing/I'm Not Scared/Always On My Mind/In My House/It's Alright **PERSONNEL** Neil Tennant (v), Chris Lowe (sy, k), Fro Sossa (k), Mike Bakst (k), Nestor Gomez (g), Tony Conception, Kenneth William Faulk, Dana Tebor, Ed Calle (brs), The Voice In Fashion (bv)

After two earlier albums, both also blessed with single-word titles, the Pet Shop Boys made a conscious decision to broaden their electro-pop horizons with this 1988 effort. It contained a remix of the Christmas chart-topping cover of Presley's **Always On My Mind**, originally cut for a 10th anniversary TV special, plus their own version of **I'm Not Scared**, a Top 10 hit earlier in the year for Patsy Kensit's Eighth Wonder, Frankie Knuckles' house mix of **I Want A Dog** and two new tracks recorded with Trevor Horn. A grab-bag then, but an entertaining one.

…it's a rather oddly conceived release but, as advertised, it dances. There are a couple of brilliant new songs and a running time of over 50 minutes in all formats is ample proof that there's no complacency or carelessness creeping in. **Phil Sutcliffe, Q, November 1988**

Irish Heartbeat

ARTIST Van Morrison & The Chieftains **RELEASE DATE** June 1988 (UK & US) **LABEL** Mercury (UK)/Warner (US) **PRODUCER** Van Morrison **UK CHART** peak/weeks 18/7 **US CHART** peak/weeks 102/13 **TRACK LISTING** Star At County Down/Irish Heartbeat/Ta Mo Chleamhnas Deanta/Ranglan Read/She Moved Through The Fair/I'll Tell Yer Mama/Carrickfergus/Celtic Ray/My Lagan Love/Marie's Wedding **PERSONNEL** Van Morrison (v, g, s), with The Chieftains; Paddy Maloney (up, w), Derek Bell (hp, hd, tp), Martin Fay (fd), Kevin Conneff (v), Matt Malloy (fl), Sean Keane (fd)

Tying up with the Chieftains and co-producing with their leader, Morrison chose a track first recorded for 1983's **Inarticulate Speech Of The Heart** as his title track, then bulked up with traditional classics like **Carrickfergus** and **My Lagan Love** that told us little new about him but resulted in an eminently entertaining meeting of minds. The ensemble toured together in 1988, their live shows every bit as joyous as the album that became his first since **Inarticulate…** to reach the UK Top 20. He was even seen to smile!

The inescapable feeling is of a man positively revelling in the chance to play great songs of old and of home in the company of one of the finest groups of musicians to be found in the world anywhere. **D. C., NME, December 1988**

It Takes A Nation Of Millions To Hold Us Back

ARTIST Public Enemy RELEASE DATE July 1988 (UK & US) LABEL Def Jam (UK & US) PRODUCER Rick Rubin UK CHART peak/weeks 8/9 US CHART peak/weeks 42/51 TRACK LISTING Countdown To Armageddon/Bring The Noise/Don't Believe The Hype/Flavor Flav Cold Bumpin'/Terminal To The Edge Of Panic/Mind Terrorist/Louder Than A Bomb/Caught/Can We Get A Witness/Show Em' Watcha Got/She Watch Channel Zero/Night Of The Living Baseheads/Black Steel In The Hour Of Chaos/Security Of The First World/Prophets Of Rage/Rebel Without A Pause/Party For Your Right To Fight PERSONNEL Chuck D (v), Flavor Flav (p), Terminator X (dj), Professor Griff (v)

Grandmaster Flash's crown as the most politically aware of rappers has passed on to Public Enemy. As such they have frequently tackled the establishment head on with a series of incisive and cutting raps designed to provoke a reaction. This album bursts with the sound of a dissatisfied black America: court procedure, prisons and stop and search being the frequent causes for complaint. What lifts this album above the paranoia is the the way such anger is expertly mixed with the music and sound effects and the tight production of Rick Rubin.

It's like baby-sitting dynamite, holding stolen goods or just waiting for the dam to burst. We are in full agreement that once again they've brought the noise, still filled the decks and written the most power-cutting crazy LPs of the year. **James Brown, NME, December 1988**

It's A Shame About Ray

ARTIST Lemonheads RELEASE DATE July 1992 (UK & US) LABEL Atlantic (UK & US) PRODUCER Robb Bros., Evan Dando UK CHART peak/weeks 33/12 US CHART peak/weeks 68/19 TRACK LISTING Rockin Stroll/Confetti/It's A Shame About Ray/Rudderless/Buddy/The Turnpike Down/Bit Part/Alison's Starting To Happen/Hannah & Gabi/Kitchen/Ceiling Fan In My Spoon/Frank Mills/Mrs Robinson PERSONNEL Evan Dando (g, v), David Ryan (d), Juliana

Hatfield (b, bv), Gunnar Nelson (gst), Barry Goldberg (gst), Jeff 'Skunk' Baxter (gst)

Just 29 minutes long, this album could be subtitled 'What Evan Dando Did On His Holidays'. Though cut in the USA, it was conceived in Australia, where Dando had fled after his group fell apart. Enlisting Tom Morgan from local group Sneeze as a writing partner, he came up with the title track and **Bit Part**, while **Frank Mills** was borrowed from the Sixties hippie musical *Hair* – though you'd not have known. Dando credited the 'nature and solitude' of Australia, not to mention its 'distance and Valium feel' for his creative rebirth.

Lemonheads prove themselves masters at the pop art of taking a simple musical idea and maximising it to thrilling, melodious effect. With Lemonheads' former Grunge excesses now streamlined… this album thrills at neighbourhood-waking volume. **David Roberts, Q, August 1992**

It's Everly Time

ARTIST The Everly Brothers RELEASE DATE June 1960 (UK)/May 1960 (US) LABEL Warner Bros. (UK & US) PRODUCER – UK CHART peak/weeks 2/23 US CHART peak/weeks 9/10 TRACK LISTING So Sad/Just In Case/Memories Are Made Of This/That's What You Do To Me/Sleepless Nights/What Kind Of Girl Are You/Oh, True Love/Carol Jane/Some Sweet Day/Nashville Blues/You Thrill Me/I Want You To Know PERSONNEL Don Everly (v, g), Phil Everly (v, g)

Having left the homespun Cadence label for the mighty Warner Brothers in a 10-year, $1 m contract, it wasn't just Everly time – it was payback time! Eight songs cut in the original sessions had not been seen to produce a potential hit, so they rushed home and came back with **Cathy's Clown**: the remainder of the tracks got an airing here and despite their 'lack of potential' nevertheless gave the Evs – the era's consummate singles artists, to be fair – their most successful album ever.

*Here's an album that warmly deserves its MM Top Pop spotlight. This is an album without established hits – not even **Cathy's Clown** – but it makes up for this with 12 good numbers performed in crisp Nashville fashion.* **Melody Maker, July 1960**

It's Great When You're Straight… Yeah!

ARTIST Black Grape **RELEASE DATE** August 1995 **LABEL** Radioactive Records (UK & US) **PRODUCER** Danny Saber, Stephen Lironi, Shaun Ryder, Gary Kurfirst **UK CHART** peak/weeks 0/0 **US CHART** peak/weeks 0/0 **TRACK LISTING** Reverend Black Grape/In The Name Of The Father/Tramazi Parti/Kelly's Heroes/Yeah Yeah Brother/A Big Day In The North/Shake Well Before Opening/Submarine/Shake Your Money/Little Bob **PERSONNEL** Shaun Ryder (v), Paul 'Kermit' Leveridge (v), Bez 'Bez' Bez (vp), Paul 'Wags' Wagstaff (g), Ged Lynch (d, pc)

When Manchester's baggy gods The Happy Mondays crashed and burned, most expected the apparently disorganized Shaun Ryder to disappear into drug-addled oblivion. Before you could say bellyache, however, he was back with another boisterous, boyishly scatological punk-funk outfit. All similarities to The Mondays were entirely undeniable, but with cohort Kermit helping him write songs and, reportedly, 'go straight', Ryder found energy not seen during the previous band's decline. Singles *Reverend Black Grape* and *In The Name Of The Father* preceded what, for all its open pilfering, became another cheeky triumph with press and populace.

With two fingers firmly aloft, Black Grape plunder soul and funk back catalogues to create crisply-cut, boisterous rhythms, then cover 'em up with guitar licks so rip-roaringly yobbish they could go out ram-raiding…. It's surprisingly compelling…. Here, at least, at last, is a British group that sound like they're genuinely enjoying themselves. **Lloyd Bradley, Mojo, October 1995**

It's Too Late To Stop Now (Live)

ARTIST Van Morrison **RELEASE DATE** February 1974 (UK & US) **LABEL** Warner Bros. (UK & US) **PRODUCER** Van Morrison, Ted Templeman **UK CHART** peak/weeks 0/0 **US CHART** peak/weeks 53/17 **TRACK LISTING** Ain't Nothing You Can Do/Warm Love/These Dreams Of You/Into The Mystic/I Believe My Soul/I've Been Working/Help Me/Wild Children/I Just Wanna Make Love To You/Domino/Bring It On Home To Me/Saint Dominic's Preview/Take Your Hand out Of My Pocket/Listen To The Lion/Gloria/Caravan/Here Comes The Night/Cypress Avenue **PERSONNEL** Van Morrision (v, g, s), with the Caledonian Soul Orchestra

Possibly one of the best realized live albums of all time, this (vinyl) double featured both horn and string sections – feasible in the pre-depression Seventies but rarely seen today – giving Morrison the opportunity to re-present his entire career from *Gloria* onwards without compromise. Absolutely no overdubs were attempted, *Moondance* being a notable absentee since no perfect version existed: covers of Sam Cooke, Ray Charles and Willie Dixon are ample compensation.

… highly atmospheric album, dominated by Morrison's intensely soulful vocals 100 per cent soul and nothing but the best. It may not convince you that he's a genius, but if you still don't believe that, then woe betide you, mama, it's too late to start now! **Graham Taylor, Let it Rock, June 1974**

Jackson Browne

ARTIST Jackson Browne **RELEASE DATE** April 1972 (UK)/March 1972 (US) **LABEL** Asylum (UK & US) **PRODUCER** Jackson Browne, Richard Sanford Orshoff **UK CHART** peak/weeks 0/0 **US CHART** peak/weeks 53/23 **TRACK LISTING** A Child In These Hills/Song for Adam/From Silver Lake/Doctor My Eyes/Jamaica Say You Will/I'm Looking Into You/Rock Me On The Water/My Opening Farewell/Something Fine/Under The Falling Sky **PERSONNEL** Jackson Browne (v), Russ Kunkel (d), Craig Doerge (k), David Crosby (bv), Albert Lee (g), Clarence White (g), Leland Sklar (b), session musicians

Browne addressed broad social concerns in his work before it was fashionable to make glib apologies, but introspection was ever his keynote. Committedly a West Coast writer, he had seen his songs interpreted by Nico, The Byrds (*Jamaica Say You Will*) and the Eagles (*Take It Easy*, co-written with Glenn Frey). His debut solo album gave him a hit with *Doctor My Eyes*, which was also bundled through by The Jackson Five. Suddenly he was everybody's friend – the follow-up album bore the title **For Everyman** – as the guests here, David Crosby and Albert Lee, confirmed.

For a debut album, Browne could not have wished to achieve a more profound impact. Broadly speaking his songs are romantic, heart-in-the mouth affairs, but structured with such subtlety, earnestness and intensity of feeling that their cumulative effect is rather like a return to innocence… **M. W., Melody Maker, March 1972**

Jagged Little Pill

ARTIST Alanis Morissette **RELEASE DATE** June 1995 **LABEL** Maverick (UK)/Reprise (US) **UK CHART** peak/weeks 1/- **US CHART** peak/weeks 1/- **TRACK LISTING** All I Really Want/You Oughta Know/Perfect/Hand In My Pocket/Right Through You/Forgiven/You Learn/Head Over Feet/Mary Jane/Ironic/Not The Doctor/Wake Up **PERSONNEL** Alanis Morissette (v, h), Glen Ballard (g, k), Gota Yashiki (ga), Dave Navarro (g), Flea (b), Benmont Tench (o), Matt Laug (d), Rob Ladd (d, pc), Lance Morisson (b), Michael Thompson (o), Basil Fung (g), Joel Shearer (g), Michael Landau (g)

Singer-songwriter Morissette was lauded for her outspoken, sexually explicit lyrics on this surprise worldwide best-seller, but few outside her native Canada realized she had a two-album career as a Tiffany-style teen star to live down. Madonna saw potential that had yet to be realized, signed her to her Maverick label and the result was an album that spawned innumerable hit singles and made history by making her, at 21, the first Canadian woman to top the US chart.

… with this album she has comprehensively ditched her past and relaunched herself as a Gen X darling. Even more amazingly, she's quite good… the air of connivance… means you can't quite swallow **Jagged Little Pill** *whole. But if this is illusion, Alanis Morissette is mighty good at using it.* **Mark Sutherland, NME, September 1995**

Jailbreak

ARTIST Thin Lizzy **RELEASE DATE** April 1976 (UK & US) **LABEL** Vertigo (UK & US) **PRODUCER** John Alcock **UK CHART** peak/weeks 10/50 **US CHART** peak/weeks 18/28 **TRACK LISTING** Jailbreak/Angel From The Coast/Running Back/Romeo And The Lonely Girl/Warriors/The Boys Are Back In Town/Fight Or Fall/Cowboy Song/Emerald **PERSONNEL** Phil Lynott (b, ag, v), Scott Gorham (lg, g), Brian Downey (d, pc), Brian Robertson (lg, g)

Jailbreak was the breakthrough album for this bunch of hard rockers, led by black Irish singer-songwriter, bassist and vocalist Phil Lynott. Thin Lizzy had been making records since 1970, although it wasn't until a rock rendition of Irish folk stand-by *Whisky In The Jar*, in 1973, that they enjoyed any Top 10 success. Jailbreak, Lizzy's sixth LP, propelled them into the UK and US mainstreams. The title track and their most famous song, *The Boys Are Back In Town*, best represented this archetypal bunch of wild rockers – guitarists Scott Gorham and Brian Robertson trading licks over some of Lynott's finest melodies.

The realisation of potential, especially when that potential has been obvious for years, is a joy to witness… With **Jailbreak***, Thin Lizzy finally establish themselves as an outstanding albums band. I'm bound to say that it's been worth the long wait.* **H. D., March 1976**

Janet

ARTIST Janet Jackson **RELEASE DATE** May 1993 (UK & US) **LABEL** Virgin (UK & US) **PRODUCER** Janet Jackson, Jimmy Jam, Terry Lewis, Jellybean Johnson **UK CHART** peak/weeks 1/24 **US CHART** peak/weeks 1/106 **TRACK LISTING** Morning/That's The Way Love Goes/You Know…/You Want This/Be A Good Boy/If/Back/This Time/Go on Miss Janet/ Throb/What'll I Do/Lounge/Funky Big Band/Racism/New Agenda/Love Pt. 2/Because Of Love/Wind/Again/Another Lover/Where Are You Now/Hold On Baby/Body That Loves You/Rain/Anytime, Anyplace/Are You Still Up/ Sweet Dreams **PERSONNEL** Janet Jackson (v), Steve Wright (t), Dave Barry (g), Lee Blaskey (orc), David Bullock, Carolyn Daws, Hanley Daws (vl), David Carr (fl), Chuck D. (rap), Bernie Edstrom (t, arr), Mark Haynes (b, dp), Stevie Wonder (h, gst), session musicians

While brother Michael peeled ever increasing numbers of singles off each album, sister Janet did even better with her 1993 debut for a new label, Virgin. She started paying off her $32 m 'transfer fee' with an album that debuted in the US Number 1 position and spun off no fewer than seven singles, each a US Top 10 entry.

Swingbeat and sex are **Janet's** *chosen themes, but instead of exploring subtleties or developing new aspects, it crossly labours the obvious… as a serious post-rap soul contender it pales next to today's techno-literate 19-year-olds. And as proof of maturity, this 75 minutes of risibly relentless rumpo will probably only fool her brother.* **Lloyd Bradley, Q, July 1993**

Joan Baez In Concert (Live)

ARTIST Joan Baez **RELEASE DATE** October 1962 (UK & US) **LABEL** Fontana (UK)/Vanguard (US) **PRODUCER** – **UK CHART** peak/weeks 0/0 **US CHART** peak/weeks 10/114 **TRACK LISTING** Babe, I'm Gona Leave You/ Geordie/Copper Kettle/Kumbaya/What Have They Done To The Rain/Black Is The Colour/Danger Waters/Gospel Ship/The House Carpenter/Pretty Boy Floyd/Lady Mary/Ate Amanha/Matty Groves **PERSONNEL** Joan Baez (v, ag)

A collection of Scottish and Irish traditional folk songs that typified what most either loved or hated about Joan Baez: her completely po-faced seriousness. Her reverence for the form was seen as either very touching or tediously academic. At this point she was yet to enter her phase of promoting radical new songwriters with a voice of protest such as Dylan, Ochs and Hardin. Her political activism and pensive humanitarianism were, however, already to the fore on and off stage. She lightened up later…two decades later.

'You have to be free floating in music or just get in a bind. I like to do it all, but most important is to try to find a way to have it all make sense… to get people to stop murdering each other.' **From an interview by John Grissim Jr., Rolling Stone, December 1968**

John Barleycorn Must Die

ARTIST Traffic **RELEASE DATE** July 1970 (UK & US) **LABEL** Island (UK)/United Artists (US) **PRODUCER** Chris Blackwell, Steve Winwood, Guy Stevens **UK CHART** peak/weeks 11/9 **US CHART** peak/weeks 5/38 **TRACK LISTING** Glad/Freedom Rider/Empty Pages/Stranger To Himself/John Barleycorn/Every Mother's Son **PERSONNEL** Steve Winwood (o, p, pc, ag, v, b, ep), Chris Wood (s, fl, es, pc), Jim Capaldi (d, pc)

A showcase for versatile multi-instrumentalist Steve Winwood, as well as for the band's eclectic merging of R&B, jazz, rock and pastoral folk influences, **John Barleycorn Must Die** was a masterpiece of proficient musicianship: the rendition of traditional ballad *John Barleycorn*, for example, with its distinctive keyboard sounds, evinced a highly adventurous outfit reaching a creative peak. Meanwhile, saxaphonist/flautist Chris Wood added texture while percussionst Jim Capaldi injected some funk into Traffic's complex grooves.

It's all so perfect, so exquisite and so dull…. Perhaps part of my problem is my high expectations of any Traffic album. This is a good album of rock 'n' roll music… maybe the next album will soar again. **Jon Carroll, Rolling Stone, September 1970**

John Lennon And The Plastic Ono Band

ARTIST John Lennon And The Plastic Ono Band RELEASE DATE December 1970 (UK & US) LABEL Apple (UK & US) PRODUCER Phil Spector, John Lennon, Yoko Ono UK CHART peak/weeks 11/11 US CHART peak/weeks 6/33 TRACK LISTING Mother/Hold On/I Found Out/Working Class Hero/Well Well Well/Look At Me/Isolation/Remember/God/My Mummy's Dead PERSONNEL John Lennon (v, g), Yoko Ono (v, ww), Klaus Voorman (b), Ringo Starr (d)

Powerful and uncompromising, John Lennon's first solo effort was as far removed from The Beatles as anything could be. Even after all these years, rock music has yet to produce a more intense articulation of personal pain and discontent than this. On *Mother*, Lennon relives the rejection he suffered in childhood, with *Working Class Hero* he sneeringly dismisses his status as a cultural icon and *God* sees him cast aside his past: 'I don't believe in Beatles,' he says, '…the dream is over…' No-one hearing this terrifyingly stark confessional could have been in any doubt.

John Prine

ARTIST John Prine RELEASE DATE March 1972 (UK)/February 1972 (US) LABEL Atlantic Records (UK & US) PRODUCER Arif Marden UK CHART peak/weeks – US CHART peak/weeks 154/3 TRACK LISTING Illegal Smile/Spanish Pipedream/Hello In There/Sam Stone/Paradise/Pretty Good/Your Flag Decal Won't Get You Into Heaven Anymore/Far From Me/Angel From Montgomery/Quiet Man/Donald And Lydia/Six O'Clock News/Flashback Blues PERSONNEL John Prine (ag, g, v), Bobby Wood (p, k), Gene Chrisman (d, tm), Johnny Christopher, Leo LeBlanc, Reggie Young (g), Bobby Emmons (o, k), Noel Gilbert, Dave Prine (fd), Bishop Heywood (pc, d), Mike Leach, Neal Rosengarden (b)

Discovered by Canadian crooner Paul Anka, John Prine was one of many to follow in the wake of Bob Dylan, and their vocal similarity did Prine no favours. He was still recording great albums in the Nineties on his own Oh Boy label, but this debut album remains the all-time classic of his canon. Bonnie Raitt's *Angel From Montgomery* is one of many covers, but no-one has bettered these songs, while *Sam Stone* has a special place in the many songs inspired by the horror of Vietnam. An all-round triumph.

There are 13 tracks here and though not melodically outstanding the lyrics are, without exception, excellent. Arrangements are purposefully simple, the guitar backing being laced sparingly with pedal guitar… fiddles… and organ… all of which concentrates on Prine's vocals, which occasionally betray a Dylanish twang. **G. B., Melody Maker, March 1972**

John Wesley Harding

ARTIST Bob Dylan RELEASE DATE February 1968 (UK & US) LABEL CBS (UK)/Columbia (US) PRODUCER Bob Johnston UK CHART peak/weeks 1/29 US CHART peak/weeks 2/52 TRACK LISTING John Wesley Harding/As I Went Out One Morning/I Dreamed I Saw St. Augustine/All Along The Watchtower/The Ballard Of Frankie Lee And Judas Priest/Drifter's Escape/Dear Landlord/I Am A Lonesome Hobo/I Pity The Poor Immigrant/The Wicked Messenger/Down Along The Cove/I'll Be Your Baby Tonight PERSONNEL Bob Dylan (v, g, bv, p), Charles McCoy (b), Kenny Buttrey (d), Pete Drake (g)

Having linked up with The Band, electrified folk to spine-tingling effect and crashed out of rock after a motorbike accident, Dylan wound the clock back with a gentle, country-tinged album that was noticeably simpler than its predecessors and swam against the year's musical tide. No single would be taken from the album named after a real-life outlaw but it topped the UK chart anyway, and *All Along The Watchtower* is perceived as a hit simply on the strength of Jimi Hendrix's interpretation – he also cut *Drifter's Escape*.

Johnny Cash At Folsom Prison

ARTIST Johnny Cash RELEASE DATE May 1968 (UK & US) LABEL CBS (UK)/Columbia (US) PRODUCER Bob Johnston UK CHART peak/weeks 8/53 US CHART peak/weeks 13/122 TRACK LISTING Folsom Prison Blues/Dark As The Dungeon/I Still Miss Someone/Cocaine Blues/25 Minutes To Go/Orange Blossom Special/The Long Black Veil/Send A Picture Of Mother/The Wall/Dirty Old Egg-Sucking Dog/Flushed From The Bathroom Of Your Heart/Jackson/Give My Love To Rose/I Got Stripes/Green, Green Grass Of Home/Greystone Chapel PERSONNEL Johnny Cash (v, g), session musicians

Country legend Cash – 'the man in black' – always appealed to rock fans, from his 1955 association with Carl Perkins to his alliance three decades on with U2 on **Zooropa**. Battling with drug addiction at this stage, having survived competition with Elvis Presley and collaborated with Bob Dylan, he toured prisons for some time when this first of two legendary 'prison albums' demonstrated his sublime hard-boiled rapport with the definitive captive audience. This sold in millions: he was embraced by the mainstream and given his own TV show.

Johnny Cash At San Quentin

ARTIST Johnny Cash RELEASE DATE August 1969 (UK)/June 1969 (US) LABEL CBS (UK)/Columbia (US) PRODUCER – UK CHART peak/weeks 2/114 US CHART peak/weeks 1/70 TRACK LISTING Wanted Man/Wreck Of The Old 97/I Walk The Line/Darling Companion/Starkville City Jail/San Quentin/A Boy Named Sue/Peace In The Valley/Folsom Prison Blues PERSONNEL Johnny Cash (v, g), session musicians

The second of Cash's near-mythical prison albums, this gave him a funny-sad crossover hit, his biggest ever, in Shel Silverstein's *A Boy Named Sue*, which used his stoical, manly voice to inspired effect. His cover of Bob Dylan's **Wanted Man** was lacerating. He was free of his drug habit and was to enjoy a sustained period of chart presence for several years after this watershed.

'The idea was to obtain a background picture of the climate of patriotism, violence and Mom's apple pie that is part of the American scene and which is, to some extent, captured in Counrty and Western music.' **Jo Durden-Smith in interview with Laurie Hernshaw, Melody Maker, August 1969**

Johnny Winter And… Live

ARTIST Johnny Winter RELEASE DATE May 1971 (UK)/March 1971 (US) LABEL CBS (UK)/Columbia (US) PRODUCER Johnny Winter UK CHART peak/weeks 20/6 US CHART peak/weeks 154/4 TRACK LISTING Good Morning/It's My Own Fault/Jumpin' Jack Flash/Rock 'n' Roll Medley: Great Balls Of Fire, Long Tall Sally, Whole Lotta Shakin' Goin' On, Mean Town Blues, Johnny B. Goode PERSONNEL Johnny Winter (v, g, md), Rick Derringer (g), Randy Jo Jobbs (b), Randy Zehringer (d), Edgar Winter (k, as)

One of the few credible white bluesmen, Johnny Winter was more than just a 'cross-eyed albino with long, fleecy hair', as an article in *Rolling Stone* put it in 1968 – he was also a demon guitarist with an impressive voice who learned his trade playing roots music in bars around the South. Assembling a band with former McCoy Rick Derringer, another guitar whiz, enabled Winter to move off in different directions, playing melodic psychedelia, hard rock and southern-fried boogie.

The material is surprisingly good…. Winter's compositions, though intense and moving tend to lack form… But what the hell. This is fine stuff, by far the best thing Johnny Winter has done. And that's saying something. **David Gancher, Rolling Stone, October 1970**

Jordan: The Comeback

ARTIST Prefab Sprout RELEASE DATE August 1990 (UK & US) LABEL Kitchenware (UK)/Epic (US) PRODUCER Thomas Dolby UK CHART peak/weeks 7/17 US CHART peak/weeks 0/0 TRACK LISTING Looking For Atlantis/Wild Horses/Machine Gun Ibiza/We Let The Stars Go/Carnival 2000/Jordan: The Comeback/Jesse James Symphony/Jesse James Bolero/Moon Dog/All The World Loves Lovers/All Boys Believe Anything/The Ice Maiden/Paris Smith/The Wedding March/One Of The Broken/Michael/Mercy/Scarlet Nights/Doo Wop In Harlem PERSONNEL Paddy McAloon (v, g), Wendy Smith (g, v), Martin McAloon (b), Neil Conti (d), Luis Jardim (pc, gst), Judd Lander (h, gst), Jenny Agutter (gst)

Having travelled from Langley Park to Memphis, the centrepiece of Prefab Sprout's fourth LP release was a four-song set about Elvis Presley. British rock's most noted Amerophile, Paddy McAloon, contributed 15 more compositions which, since the album failed to include a big single, sold badly. It would be seven years before the comeback, **Andromeda Heights**. McAloon busied himself as backroom songwriter for fellow country & western-fixated Geordie

Jimmy Nail in his *Crocodile Shoes* persona.

*Most impressive… is Jordan's comprehensiveness of arrangement: never losing sight of the original rhythms and melodies, it fills every nook and cranny with sounds, and can… transform a simple sketch like **Paris Smith** into a shimmering canvas of emotion… it's all shot through with the driest of humour.* **Lloyd Bradley, Q, September 1990**

Joshua Judges Ruth

ARTIST Lyle Lovett RELEASE DATE April 1992 (UK & US) LABEL MCA Records (UK & US) PRODUCER George Massenburg, Billy Williams, Lyle Lovett UK CHART peak/weeks 0/0 US CHART peak/weeks 57/34 TRACK LISTING I've Been To Memphis/Church/She's Already made Up Her Mind/North Dakota/You've Been So Good Up To Now/All My Love Is Gone/Since The Last Time/Baltimore/Family Reserve/She's Leaving Me Because She Really Wants To/Flyswatter/Ice Water Blues (Monty Trenckmann's Blues)/She Makes Me Feel Good PERSONNEL Lyle Lovett (v, ag), Leland Sklar (b), Russ Kunkel (d), Matt Rollings (p, o), Ray Herndon (g), Dean Parks (asg), Willis Alan Ramsey (hv), Arnold McCuller (hv), Emmylou Harris (gst), Sweet Pea Atkinson (gst), Rickie Lee Jones (gst), Leo Kottke (gst), Francine Reed (gst), Sir Harry Bowens (gst)

'The songs are all conversations with God about three topics: death, food and women.' That was Lyle Lovett's explanation to *Rolling Stone* of the album that transformed him from country cult to superstar singer-songwriter. Ironically it came as country was enjoying a resurgence and like its three predecessors, **Joshua…** contained new songs and ones from further back: *Since The Last Time*, the oldest, dated from 1979. And though a marriage to Julia Roberts was yet to come, this was an album from someone on the fast track to fame.

If Lovett is himself a misfit, he sings to the misfit that lives within every listener… for all the darkness permeating the songs, the sense lingers that our hero will somehow make his way from day to day, taking sustenance where he finds it. **Don McLeese, Rolling Stone, April 1992**

The Joshua Tree

ARTIST U2 RELEASE DATE March 1987 (UK & US) LABEL Island (UK & US) PRODUCER Daniel Lanois, Brian Eno UK CHART peak/weeks 1/129 US CHART peak/weeks 1/103 TRACK LISTING Where The Streets Have No Name/I Still Haven't Found What I'm Looking For/With Or Without You/Bullet The Blue Sky/Running To Stand Still/Red Hill Mining Town/In God's Country/Trip Through Your Wires/One Tree Hill/Exit/Mothers Of The Disappeared PERSONNEL Bono (v), The Edge (g, k), Adam Clayton (b), Larry Mullen Jnr (d)

This was the globe-straddling album that saw U2 ascend to the very highest level of success, placing them on the front cover of

America's prestigious *Time* magazine, an accolade previously only afforded The Beatles and The Who. **The Joshua Tree** was chock-full of anthems that although perfectly constructed for stadium celebration, explored Bono's personal search for meaning in this fast-moving, multi-media world. *I Still Haven't Found What I'm Looking For* and *With Or Without You* remain two of his most affecting works, while *Where The Streets Have No Name* is as poignant a song as rock has thrown up.

U2 are massive but minimal, majestic but free of pomp or flourish. There are no solos, power chords, curlicues – just a weave of closechording texture, an exhilarating shimmer. **Simon Reynolds, Melody Maker, March 1987**

The Journeyman

ARTIST Eric Clapton RELEASE DATE November 1989 (UK & US) LABEL Duck Warner (UK)/Duck (US) PRODUCER Russ Titelman UK CHART peak/weeks 2/32 US CHART peak/weeks 16/51 TRACK LISTING Pretending/Anything For Your Love/Bad Love/Running On Faith/Hard Times/Hound Dog/No Alibis/Run So Far/Old Love/Breaking Point/Lead Me On/Before You Accuse Me PERSONNEL Eric Clapton (v, g), Alan Clarke (k), Robert Cray (g, bv), George Harrison (g), Phil Collins (d, bv)

A relaxed, typically sleepy album, with Clapton in fine guitar form which distracted sufficiently from the wishy-washiness of some of the songs. The over-cooked modesty of the title was perhaps a smart reaction to recent revivals of the cause to canonize him. Nevertheless this year saw him play a season of concerts at the Royal Albert Hall: these were to become an annual event of some stature. Compilations aside, **Journeyman** was Clapton's biggest seller for some time.

If **Journeyman** *seems less than heroic, that's only because Clapton approaches each song on its own terms instead of dominating the material to flatter his vanity. That may not seem exciting, but don't worry: the result is Clapton's most consistent and satisfying album since* **461 Ocean Boulevard**. **J. D. Considine, Rolling Stone, November 1989**

Judy At Carnegie Hall

ARTIST Judy Garland RELEASE DATE March 1962 (UK)/July 1961 (US) LABEL Capitol (UK & US) PRODUCER Andy Wiswell UK CHART peak/weeks 13/3 US CHART peak/weeks 1/95 TRACK LISTING Overture: The Trolley Song/Over The Rainbow/The Man That Got Away/When You're Smiling/Medley: Almost Like Being In Love/This Can't Be Love/Do It Again/You Go To My Head/Alone Together/Who Cares? (As Long As You Care For Me)/Puttin' On The Ritz/How Long Has This Been Going On?/Just You, Just Me/San Francisco/I Can't Give You Anything But Love/That's Entertainment/Come Rain Or Come Shine/You're Nearer/A Foggy Day/If Love Were All/Zing! Went The Strings Of My Heart/Stormy Weather/Medley: You Made Me Love You/For Me And My Girl/The Trolly Song/Rock-A-Bye Baby With A Dixie Melody/Over The Rainbow/Swanee/After You've Gone PERSONNEL Judy Garland (v), Orchestra under the direction of Mort Lindsey

If the sleeve-note is to be believed, 3,165 'privileged people' packed out the Carnegie Hall to witness the concert immortalized by this 26-song album. It won four Grammies, including Album of the Year and Best Female Vocal Performance. The songs here, from a buoyant *When You're Smiling* to the climactic *I Can't Give You Anything But Love*, almost back up the sleeve-note writer in suggesting this was 'probably the greatest occasion in show business history'.

Nowadays Judy Garland has passed into that small class of vocalists who can pack concerts and sell records on sheer personality appeal... her performances are charged with some sort of emotional magic that transcends the projection of notes and words. **Melody Maker, March 1962**

Kick

ARTIST INXS RELEASE DATE November 1987 (UK & US) **LABEL** Mercury (UK)/Atlantic (US) **PRODUCER** Chris Thomas **UK CHART** peak/weeks 9/99 **US CHART** peak/weeks 3/81 **TRACK LISTING** Guns In The Sky/New Sensation/Devil Inside/Need You Tonight/Need You Tonight/Mediate/The Loved One/Wild Life/Never Tear Us Apart/Mystify/Kick/Calling All Nations/Tiny Daggers **PERSONNEL** Michael Hutchence (v), Tim Farriss (g), Kirk Pengilly (g, s, v), Andrew Farriss (k), Garry Beers (b, v), John Farriss (d, v)

Established in 1979, Australia's INXS, and in particular swaggering front man Michael Hutchence, established themselves in the States with the help of MTV as the new Rolling Stones, but Poms smelled a rat and kept them at arm's length until this all-round powerhouse rock album. It spent 99 weeks on the UK listings, and when the band sold out Wembley Arena in June 1988 it was apparent Britain had succumbed. *Need You Tonight* would hit Number 2 on reissue, and while America still loved them most the UK (and Paula Yates in particular) henceforth took them to their bosom. Michael Hutchence, alas, committed suicide in 1997.

The album consists of 'tunes that your Bryan Adamses could knock out before breakfast, sound worked at, planned with the aid of a T.Square and a Berlitz Oz-to-American phrase book.' **Caroline Sullivan, Melody Maker, November 1987**

The Kick Inside

ARTIST Kate Bush **RELEASE DATE** February 1978 (UK & US) **LABEL** EMI (UK)/EMI America (US) **PRODUCER** Andrew Powell **UK CHART** peak/weeks 3/70 **US CHART** peak/weeks 0/0 **TRACK LISTING** Moving/The Saxophone Song/Strange Phenomena/Kite/The Man With The Child In His Eyes/Wuthering Heights/James And The Cold Gun/Feel It/Oh To Be In Love/L'Amour Looks Something Like You/Them Heavy People/Room For The Life/The Kick Inside **PERSONNEL** Kate Bush (v, bv, p), various backing musicians, Orchestral contractor: David Katz

Plumstead girl Bush was only 20 when this debut, quite breathtaking in its ambition and range, planted her in the Brits' affections. The *Wuthering Heights* single had given her an instant Number 1. Its lyricism and emotional grandeur were representative of her music, which was then being encouraged by Pink Floyd's Dave Gilmour, her mentor. *The Man With The Child In His Eyes*, another hit, was reportedly written when she was just 12 years old. Kate's elaborate dance routines and early videos were eye-catching, but she moved away rapidly from live performance after an exhaustive initial tour.

… there are occasional pieces of brilliance that make me shudder when I think of her future. She is still only nineteen…. At the moment, Kate's lyrics are steeped in romanticism, although she occasionally touches eroticism, and if Feel It doesn't arouse something, you'd better see the doctor. **Harry Doherty, Melody Maker, March 1978**

Kiko

ARTIST Los Lobos **RELEASE DATE** May 1992 (UK & US) **LABEL** London-Slash (UK)/Slash (US) **PRODUCER** Los Lobos, Mitchell Froom **UK CHART** peak/weeks 0/0 **US CHART** peak/weeks 143/10 **TRACK LISTING** Dream In Blue/Wake Up Delores/Angels With Dirty Faces/The Train Don't Stop Here/Kiko And The Lavender Moon/Saint Behind The Grass/Reva's House/When The Circus Comes/Arizona Skies/Short Side Of Nothing/Two Janes/Wicked Rain/Whiskey Trail/Just A Man/Peace/Rio De Tenampa **PERSONNEL** David Hidalgo (v, g, ad), Cesar Rosas (g, v), Conrad Lozano (b), Steve Berlin (s), Luis Perez (d)

Many people thought Los Lobos had peaked with **La Bamba**, good-time cover-version theme to a Ritchie Valens bio-pic in 1987 – Tex-Mex party music, pure and simple. But **Kiko** was in many ways the album they had waited 18 years to make…a gamble, but one that paid off handsomely. From the New Orleans rhythms of *Dream In Blue* to the Zimbabwean beat of *Wake Up Delores*, this was world music that showed them capable of much more than their pigeon-hole.

'People have to remember that rock and roll came from a cross-pollination of a lot of different cultures,' says drummer and songwriter Luis Perez, 'The black, the hillbilly, the rural culture, that's what rock and roll is all about.' **From an interview by Michael Goldberg, Rolling Stone, April 1985**

Kilimanjaro

ARTIST Teardrop Explodes **RELEASE DATE** October 1980 (UK & US) **LABEL** Mercury (UK & US) **PRODUCER** Zoo Production Team **UK CHART** peak/weeks 24/35 **US CHART** peak/weeks 156/6 **TRACK LISTING** Ha,Ha, I'm Drowning/Second Head/Bouncing Babies/Treason/Thief Of Baghdad/Brave Boys Keep Their Promises/Went Crazy/Sleeping Gas/Poppies In The Field/When I Dream/Books **PERSONNEL** Julian Cope (v, b), Gary Dwyer (d), David Balfe (k), Alan Gill (g)

Of Liverpool's 'Crucial Three' – Pete Wylie of Wah!, Ian McCulloch of Echo & The Bunnymen and Julian Cope – the latter's Teardrop Explodes always seemed The Band Most Likely To, due to Cope's colourful madcap persona, pretty-boy good looks and pop sensibility. **Kilimanjaro**, the Teardrops' debut album, features three hit singles, *When I Dream*, *Treason (It's Just A Story)* and the Top 10 smash, *Reward*, and offers a marvellous compromise between Saint Julian's melodic nous and the sort of wayward musical and lyrical tendencies that one has now come to expect from this latter-day Syd Barrett.

Kill 'Em All

ARTIST Metallica **RELEASE DATE** July 1983 (UK & US) **LABEL** M.F.N. (UK)/Megaforce (US) **PRODUCER** Pail Curcio **UK CHART** peak/weeks 0/0 **US CHART** peak/weeks 155/10 **TRACK LISTING** Hit The Lights/Jump In The Fire/Motorbreath/Whiplash/Phantom Lord/Seek And Destroy/(Anaethesia) Pulling Teeth/Metal Militia/The Four Horsemen/No Remorse **PERSONNEL** James Hatfield (v, g), Kirk Hammett (g), Jason Newsted (b), Lars Ulrich (d)

The debut album from this Californian quartet bore the motto 'Bang the head that doesn't bang' – and proceeded to lay down the new rules for headbangers worldwide. Influenced by British bands Motorhead and Venom (the latter soon becoming touring partners), it was the guitar sound of James Hetfield and Kirk Hammett that would define thrash metal in the next decade, pushed ever onwards by band founder Lars Ulrich on drums. And though the sound has been refined, this, a five-star *Kerrang!* selection, was the breakthrough disc.

Kill 'Em All *is the original and archetypal thrash metal album… I write lyrics 'cos I've got to sing something. When it comes out it's like, wow, that's almost kinda good – what the fuck am I doing?!* **James Ketfield interviewed by Mat Snow, Q, September 1991**

Killing Joke

ARTIST Killing Joke RELEASE DATE October 1980 (UK)/ LABEL Polydor (UK)/EG (US) PRODUCER Killing Joke UK CHART peak/weeks 39/4 US CHART peak/weeks 0/0 TRACK LISTING Requiem/Tomorrow's World/S.O. 36/Complications/The Wait/Bloodsport/Wardance/Primitive PERSONNEL Jaz Coleman (v, k), Geordie (g, sy), Pig Youth (b, v), Paul Ferguson (d)

Uncompromising has to be the word where Jaz Coleman and his cohorts were concerned. How a self-taught band formed in a squat ended up on the same record label as progressive rock virtuosi King Crimson is unknown, but this debut album was a classic: all the way from its graffiti-strewn artwork to the apocalyptic mix of heavy metal, dub and anarchy that rendered them unmistakeable. *Wardance* and *Requiem* were peeled off as singles, but the full effect had to be savoured in this uncompromising slab.

There's doom aplenty here – post nuclear apocalyptic visions, chilling threats, a sense we're standing on the threshold of a new dark age…. The musical attacks here are a form of self-flagellation and if you need to know why it's so enjoyable then ask a psychologist. **Melody Maker, October 1980**

Kimono My House

ARTIST Sparks RELEASE DATE May 1974 (UK & US) LABEL Island (UK & US) PRODUCER Muff Winwood UK CHART peak/weeks 4/24 US CHART peak/weeks 101/14 TRACK LISTING This Town Ain't Big Enough For Both Of Us/Amateur Hour/Falling In Love With Myself Again/Here In Heaven/Thank God It's Not Christmas/Hasta Manana, Monsieur/Talent Is An Asset/Complaints/In My Family/Equator PERSONNEL Russell Mael (v, b), Ron Mael (k), Martin Gordon (b, v), Dinky Diamond (d), Adrian Fisher (g), Peter Oxendale (k)

Formerly Halfnelson, Sparks were, give or take the odd sessioneer, a two-piece comprising one straight man, the Hitler-moustached Ron Mael, and his gregarious, falsetto-voiced brother Russell – forerunners of such Eighties electro-duos as Orchestral Manoeuvres In The Dark, Soft Cell and Erasure. **Kimono My House** was Sparks' most consistent collection of quirkily intelligent pop, containing *Amateur Hour*, *Here In Heaven* and the UK Number 1, *This Town Ain't Big Enough For Both Of Us*.

Sparks branch out on their own and display an impressive and legitimate musical ability, as well as an image. This could well stand against them in the current climate of popular music which seems to have gone backwards about fifteen years… **C. W., Melody Maker, May 1974**

A Kind Of Magic

ARTIST Queen RELEASE DATE May 1986 (UK & US) LABEL EMI (UK)/Capitol (US) PRODUCER Queen, Mack Richards, David Richards UK CHART peak/weeks 1/63 US CHART peak/weeks 46/13 TRACK LISTING Princess Of The Universe/A Kind Of Magic/Gimme The Prize/One Year Of Love/Pain Is So Close To Pleasure/One Vision/Don't Lose Your Head/Who Wants To Live Forever/Friends Will Be Friends PERSONNEL Freddie Mercury (v, p), Roger Taylor (d, v), Brian May (g, v, k), John Deacon (b)

Having entered the Eighties in uncertain fashion, Queen found their second wind at Live Aid, the ultimate showcase for Mercury and Co. With their commercial fortunes revived, this was the album to kickstart their creativity: **One Vision** had been inspired by the Live Aid experience, while other songs owed their genesis to the *Highlander* film project starring Christopher Lambert. What was certain was that the circus was on the road again, and the touring that followed, including some huge gigs in Hungary, Knebworth and Wembley, would end up being their live swansong.

Drop the needle of the record at random… with two exceptions, each and every offering is distinguished by the heroic vocals, the guitardammerung that unmistakably spell **'Seven Seas of Rhye'.** *In their approach, they've never really progressed from those halycon days of '74, except to add the odd topical fillip.* **Caroline Sullivan, Melody Maker, June 1986**

King Creole

ARTIST Elvis Presley RELEASE DATE October 1958 (UK)/September 1958 (US) LABEL RCA (UK & US) PRODUCER Don Wardell UK CHART peak/weeks 4/14 US CHART peak/weeks 2/15 TRACK LISTING King Creole/As Long As I Have You/Crawfish/Lover Doll/Hard Headed Woman/Don't Ask Me Why/Trouble/New Orleans/Dixieland Rock/Steadfast, Loyal And True/Young Dreams PERSONNEL Elvis Presley (v, g), session musicians

It must have been a blow when Elvis failed to dislodge Mitch Miller's easy-listening **Sing Along With Mitch** from the top of the US album chart, but the bonus black and white picture of Presley in his army uniform suggested the reason why – he needed a 60-day draft deferment to finish the feature. Even in his absence, *King Creole,* his fourth film and the first to be shot on location, did well enough at the box office.

… after listening to the disc, I objectively report that it contains at least two numbers that could easily make the hit parade… I feel that Presley scores best with his beat specialities. I find his projection of the slower numbers over-affected. **Laurie Kernshaw, Melody Maker, September 1958**

King Tubby Meets Rockers Uptown

ARTIST Augustus Pablo RELEASE DATE 1976 LABEL Yard Music (UK)/ Shanachie (US) PRODUCER Augustus Pablo UK CHART peak/weeks 0/0 US CHART peak/weeks 0/0 TRACK LISTING Keep On Dubing/Stop Them Jah/Young Generation Dub/Each One Dub/555 Dub Street/Brace's Tower Dub/Brace's Tower Dub 2/King Tubby Meets Rockers Uptown/Corner Crew Dub/Shanking Dub/Frozen Dub/Satta Dub/ PERSONNEL Augustus Pablo (v, mo)

Horace Swaby took his name from The Upsetters' keyboardist who in 1971, upon leaving Kingston for America, bequeathed the Augustus Pablo 'concept' to the young admirer. This Pablo proceeded to shake the reggae genre by its boots. With sidekick producer King Tubby he is often hailed as 'the man who invented dub'. This was achieved with distorted bass and drum sounds and a liking for the haunting twang of cinematic instrumental pieces. Swaby formed his own Rockers label, and on this album engaged the assistance of Robbie Shakespeare and various members of the Bob Marley band.

Kings Of The Wild Frontier

ARTIST Adam Ant And The Ants RELEASE DATE November 1980 (UK & US) LABEL CBS (UK)/Epic (US) PRODUCER Chris 'Merrick' Hughes UK CHART peak/weeks 1/66 US CHART peak/weeks 44/35 TRACK LISTING Dog Eat Dog/'Antmusic'/Feed Me To The Lions/Los Rancheros/Ants Invasion/Killer In The Home/Kings Of The Wild Frontier/The Magnificent Five/Don't Be Square (Be There)/Joll Roger/Making History/The Human Beings PERSONNEL Stuart 'Adam Ant' Goddard (v, g), Marco Pirroni (g, v), Kevin Mooney (b, v), Chris 'Merrick' Hughes (d), Terry Lee Miall (d)

Just another punk but the Prince Charming of New Romanticism, Adam Ant was for a brief moment the biggest, loudest and most colourful thing in British pop. Burundi conga drums sat uneasily alongside Duane Eddy guitar snaps, and the image – peacock make-up veering from Red Indian to Renaissance fop – carried all before it on the crest of a wave, after the New Wave. Ant-music was more of a narcissistic, persuasive conviction than a fully thought-out sound, but this ANT-hemic collection hogged the charts for the whole year, making ridicule nothing to be scared of.

Kite

ARTIST Kirsty McColl RELEASE DATE April 1989 (UK) LABEL Virgin (UK)/Charisma (US) PRODUCER Steve Lillywhite UK CHART peak/weeks 34/12 US CHART peak/weeks 0/0 TRACK LISTING Innocence/Free World/Mother's Ruin/Days/No Victims/Fifteen Minutes/Don't Come The Cowboy With Me Sonny Jim!/Tread Lightly/What Do Pretty Girls Do?/Dancing In Limbo/The End Of A Perfect Day/You And Me Baby/You Just Haven't Earned It Yet Baby/La Foret De Moinosas/Complainte Pour Ste Catherine PERSONNEL Kirsty MacColl (pc, g, b, stg), Mark Berrow, Wilfred Gibson, Roy Gillard, Dave Woodcock, Ben Cruft, Dave Woodcock, Gavyn Wright (vl), Stuart Brooks, Guy Baker (t), Paul Crowder (tm), James Eller, Steve Lillywhite, Pino Palladino, Guy Pratt (b), Mel Gaynor, David Palmer (d), Pete Glenister, Colin Stuart (ag, g), Malcolm Griffiths (tr), Robbie McIntosh (ag), Johnny Marr(g), Yves N'Djock (g), Philip Todd (cl)

Daughter of folkie Ewan, Kirsty had punked up with the Adicts before a novelty pop hit (something about a chip shop and Elvis) left her in search of a third musical identity. She had the talent and **Kite** was the album where she took off, thanks to an alliance with ex-Smiths guitarist Johnny Marr, a hit cover of the Kinks' 1968 *Days* and some classic self-penned songs. It set up another successful effort in 1991's **Electric Landlady.**

The effect, at least lyrically, is a sort of distaff Elvis Costello: sharp-tongued, literate and in it's own distinctive way – charming. The charm is derived in no small part from MacColl's songwriting skill. **Rolling Stone, November 1990**

L.A. Woman

ARTIST The Doors RELEASE DATE June 1971 (UK)/May 1971 (US) LABEL Elektra (UK & US) PRODUCER Bruce Botnick, The Doors UK CHART peak/weeks 28/4 US CHART peak/weeks 9/34 TRACK LISTING The Changeling/Love Her Madly/Been Down So Long/Cars Hiss By My Window/L.A. Woman/L'America/Hyacinth House/Crawling King Snake/The WASP/Riders On The Storm PERSONNEL Jim Morrison (v), Robbie Krieger (g), Ray Manzarek (p, o), John Densmore (d), Jerry Scheff (b), Marc Benno (rg)

Recorded to fulfil their contract to Elektra, **L.A. Woman** became Jim Morrison's swansong with the Doors and one of their most critically acclaimed albums. It was very much back to that live-in-the-studio sound of the first album. Not even the ubiquitous drinking and extra-curricular activities could derail the sessions and Morrison completed his singing duties efficiently and quickly. Within three months of its release, however, Morrison was found dead of a heart attack in Paris, fulfilling his wish to burn out like a comet.

*… And I'll be a monkey's uncle if **The WASP**… doesn't showcase Morrison's finest command of spoken jive to date, far superior to **Horse Latitudes** and a demonstration of lyric supporting timing at least the equal of George Burns in his prime… this is the Doors' greatest album.* **R. Meltzer, Rolling Stone, May 1971**

The Lamb Lies Down On Broadway

ARTIST Genesis RELEASE DATE November 1974 (UK)/December 1974 (US) LABEL Charisma (UK)/Atco (US) PRODUCER John Burns, Genesis UK CHART peak/weeks 10/6 US CHART peak/weeks 41/16 TRACK LISTING The Lamb Lies Down On Broadway/Fly On A Windshield/Broadway Melody Of 1974/Cuckoo Cocoon/In The Cage/The Grand Parade Of Lifeless Packaging/ Back In New York City/Hairless Heart/Counting Out Time/Carpet Crawlers/ The Chamber Of 32 Doors/Lilywhite Lilith/The Waiting Room/ Anyway/Here Comes The Supernatural/Anaesthetist/The Lamia/ Silent Sorrow In Empty Boats/The Colony Of Slippermen/The Arrival-A Visit To The Doktor-Raven/Ravine/The Light Dies Down On Broadway/Riding The Scree/In The Rapids/It PERSONNEL Tony Banks (k, bv, g), Mike Rutherford (b, g, bv), Phil Collins (d, dm, v), Peter Gabriel (v)

It is impossible to make any meaningful summary of the epic tale of redemption that lies at the heart of **The Lamb Lies Down On Broadway**, but this was Genesis' finest hour (and a half), a superbly cinematic work that set Peter Gabriel's complex storyline against a rich variety of musical backdrops. From the storming **Back In New York City** to the haunting **Carpet Crawlers** and **Silent Sorrow In Empty Boats** this was a triumph, a creative peak that very few progressive rock bands could even hope to emulate.

To parody Peter Gabriel: I suppose listening to this is a bit like busting for a crap and having to wade across a ploughed field in wellies to reach the hedge on the other side. **Pete Erskine, NME, November 1974**

Land Of Dreams

ARTIST Randy Newman RELEASE DATE September 1988 (UK & US) LABEL Reprise Records (UK & US) PRODUCER Mark Knopfler, James Newton Howard, Tommy Lipuma, Jeff Lynne UK CHART peak/weeks 0/0 US CHART peak/weeks 80/19 TRACK LISTING Dixie Flyer/New Orleans Wins The War/Four Eyes/Falling In Love/Something Special/Bad News From Home/Roll With The Punches/Masterman And Baby J/Red Bandana/Follow The Flag/It's Money That Matters/I Just Want You To Hurt Like I Do PERSONNEL Randy Newman (v, p)

This was a departure for Newman: an album on which he sang about himself. It was also a return to form after five years concentrating on film soundtracks and scripting the film *Three Amigos*, but with his *amigo*, Dire Straits guitarist and co-producer Mark Knopfler, he returned to pop with aplomb. The key track,

I Just Want You To Hurt Like I Do, could be read as a comment on his recent divorce or, as he laughingly claimed, an answer to USA For Africa's *We Are The World* to whose sessions he had not been invited.

… the heart of the record is a series of songs that seem to speak directly and frankly about Randy Newman… a subdued palette of piano-based but near-orchestral hues, **Land of Dreams** *works in subtler, more unsettling ways.* **Steve Pond, Rolling Stone, October 1988**

The Land Of Rape And Honey

ARTIST Ministry RELEASE DATE January 1989 (UK)/November 1988 (US) LABEL Sire (UK & US) PRODUCER Hypo Luxa, Hermes Pan, Eddie Cho UK CHART peak/weeks 0/0 US CHART peak/weeks 164/4 TRACK LISTING Stigmata/The Missing/Deity/Golden Dawn/Destruction/The Land Of Rape And Honey/You Know What You Are/Flashback/Abortive. PERSONNEL Al Jourgensen (k, g, s, v), Chris Connelly (v), Barker (b), Rieflin (d)

Having been pushed in a more commercial direction by his former record company, Cuba-born Al Jourgensen regrouped with bassist Barker and drummer Rieflin plus sometime Finitribe vocalist Chris Connelly to evolve a heavy duty brand of industrial metal that reached its zenith on an album they considered their true debut. The ultra-powerful opening track, *Stigmata*, a deserved club hit, was just one highlight of this groundbreaking, sample-strewn fusion which established Ministry alongside the likes of Big Black as masters of the genre.

Land Of Rape And Honey *simulates, ambiguously, both the noise of torment and the anguish of the oppressed – ambiguous and formidable.* **David Stubbs, Melody Maker, February 1989**

Lark's Tongues In Aspic

ARTIST King Crimson RELEASE DATE March 1973 (UK & US) LABEL Island (UK)/Atlantic (US) PRODUCER – UK CHART peak/weeks 20/4 US CHART peak/weeks 61/14 TRACK LISTING Book Of Saturday/Lark's Tongues In Aspic (Pts. 1 & 2)/The Talking Drum/Exiles/Easy Money PERSONNEL Robert Fripp (g), John Wetton (v, b), Bill Bruford (d), David Cross (vl, fl), Jamie Muir (pc), Richard Palmer-James (w)

By 1973, Robert Fripp was the only remaining member of the original King Crimson line-up, but the ideals that had driven the band were unaltered. Unsettling, perverse and gut-wrenchingly powerful by turns, this was every bit as startling as their debut had been four years earlier. The brooding menace that lurks at every turn is largely due to the presence of Jamie Muir, whose unorthodox percussion work meshed perfectly with Bill Bruford's intense drumming and John Wetton's forceful bass to create an almost unparalleled *tour de force*.

Listening to certain parts can frequently produce nothing as crassly simple as severe brain damage but a rather more civilised basic aural pain… The psychic melodramas do, though, have the saving grace of being carried out with an appropriate sense of artistic folly. **Chris Salewicz, NME, October 1974**

The La's

ARTIST The La's RELEASE DATE October 1990 (UK & US) LABEL Go! Disks (UK)/London (US) PRODUCER Steve Lillywhite UK CHART peak/weeks 30/19 US CHART peak/weeks 0/0 TRACK LISTING Son Of A Gun/I Can't Sleep/Timeless Melody/Liberty Ship/There She Goes/Doledrum/ Feelin'/Way Out/I.O.U./Freedom Song/Failure/Looking Glass PERSONNEL Lee Mavers (v, g), Neil Mavers (d), James Joyce (b), John Byrne (g), Paul Hemmings (g), Cammy (g)

'La' is scouse slang for lad and Lee Mavers' gang were briefly the talk of Merseyside, thanks to a jangly, intensely catchy Sixties throwback called **There She Goes**. It charmed radio into making it a hit and **Timeless Melody** was a more than adequate follow-up, but Mavers' painstaking slowness in the studio caused dissension in the ranks and in the end bassist John Power would find more lasting fame as leader of Cast.

… one of the freshest and craftiest offerings of the year. The spirit of Merseybeat infuses some addictive melodies and the impatient energy of punk informs their delivery; but there is no retro cutesiness about it… The La's seem… to have finally landed. **Q, January 1991**

The Last Record Album

ARTIST Little Feat RELEASE DATE November 1975 (UK & US) LABEL Warner Bros. (UK & US) PRODUCER Lowell George UK CHART peak/weeks 36/3 US CHART peak/weeks 36/15 TRACK LISTING Down Below The Borderline/ Somebody's Leaving/All That You Dream/Mercenary Territory/One Love Stand/Romance Dance/Day Or Night/Long Distance Love PERSONNEL Lowell George (g, v), Bill Payne (k, p, g, v), Richard Hayward (d, v), Ken Gradney (b), San Clayton (cg), Paul Barrere (g, v), John Hall (g), Valerie Cater (bv)

After making their live European debut to critical acclaim, drummer Richie Hayward was almost killed in a road accident. When the next record surfaced (with Richie's medical bills festooning its back sleeve), keyboardist Bill Payne and guitarist Paul Barrere were prominent in the songwriting credits as rumours circulated of Lowell George's continued drug problems – but this fifth album contained his finest moment, **Long Distance Love**. Little Feat never got near it again and George inevitably left to pursue a tragically short solo career: he died of a heart attack aged 34 on 29 June 1979.

…they've managed to combine the stilted tangential feeling of their hitherto best, **Sailin' Shoes**, *with the more immediate (but again, stilted) and easily assimilated black funk feel of Feats.* **Pete Erskine, NME, November 1975**

The Last Waltz

ARTIST The Band RELEASE DATE April 1978 (UK & US) LABEL Capitol (UK & US) PRODUCER Robbie Robertson UK CHART peak/weeks 39/ US CHART peak/weeks 16/20 TRACK LISTING Theme From The Last Waltz/Up On Cripple Creek/Helpless/Who Do You Love/Stage Fright/Dry Your Eyes/Such A Night/Coyote/It Makes No Difference/Mystery Train/The Shape I'm In/The Night They Drove Old Dixie Down/Mannish Boy/Further On Up The Road/Down South In New Orleans/Baby Let Me Follow You Down (Reprise)/Life Is A Carnival/Out Of The Blue/Ophelia/Tura Lura Larai (That's An Irish Lullaby)/Caravan/Forever Young/I Shall Be Released/The Weight/I Don't Belong To You (She Acts Like We Never Met)/The Well/Evangeline/The Last Refrain (Reprise)/Theme From The Last Waltz (with orchestra) PERSONNEL Robbie Robertson (g, v), Richard Manuel (p, v), Garth Hudson (o), Rick Danko (b, v), Levon Helm (d, v), Bob Dylan (gst), Neil Young (gst), Joni Mitchell (gst), Eric Clapton (gst), Van Morrison (gst), Neil Diamond (gst), Muddy Waters (gst), Bobby Charles (gst), Dr John (gst), Ronnie Hawkins (gst), Stephen Stills (gst), Ronnie Wood (gst), Ringo Starr (gst), Paul Butterfield (gst), Emmylou Harris (gst)

At the climax of their final tour The Band elected to play a farewell show on Thanksgiving Day at San Francisco's Winterland Hall. Filmed with panache by Martin Scorsese for the film of the same name, it attracted guest appearances from Bob Dylan, Neil Young, Eric Clapton, Van Morrison, Joni Mitchell, Neil Diamond, The Staple Singers, Dr. John, and Muddy Waters. Somehow both emotional and stiff-upper-lipped it nevertheless made a legend of The Band. Robertson opted out of later reunion tours, but the link established with Scorsese led him into further film and soundtrack work.

… there is an overabundance of good music here – music that transcends the mere presence of the celebrities involved and actually delivers… this all adds up to a bunch of greats shooting their best shot. **Nick Kent, NME, April 1978**

Late For The Sky

ARTIST Jackson Browne RELEASE DATE December 1974 (UK)/October 1974 (US) LABEL Asylum (UK & US) PRODUCER Jackson Browne, Al Schmitt UK CHART peak/weeks 0/0 US CHART peak/weeks 14/29 TRACK LISTING Late For The Sky/Fountain Of Sorrow/Farther On/The Late Show/The Road And The Sky/For A Dancer/Walking Slow/Before The Deluge PERSONNEL David Lindley (g, fd), Doug Haywood (b, v), Larry Zack (d, pc), Jai Winding (p, o), Jackson Browne (p, ag), Don Henley (bv, gst), Dan Fogelberg (bv, gst)

Gaining in confidence as a performer of his own material, Browne was finding the perfect blend for the times: gentle political comment and reflective self-analysis: **Before The Deluge** demonstrated the former, while **Fountains Of Sorro'** was deeply personal, though Joan Baez later made it as good as her own. Violins weaved in and out; **The Late Show** made people cry. He needed to move on though: critics started to snipe at his material's 'saminess'.

Late For The Sky *is unlikely to win Jackson Browne any new admirers and while it doesn't exactly damage his reputation there isn't that much on the album which enhances it.* **Steve Clarke, NME, November 1974**

Late Night Grande Hotel

ARTIST Nanci Griffith **RELEASE DATE** September 1991 (UK & US) **LABEL** MCA (UK & US) **PRODUCER** Rod Argent, Peter Van Hooke **UK CHART** peak/weeks 40/5 **US CHART** peak/weeks 185/1 **TRACK LISTING** It's Just Another Morning Here/Late Night Grande Hotel/It's Too Late/Fields Of Summer/Heaven/The Power Lines/Hometown Streets/Down 'N' Outer/One Blade Shy Of A Sharp Edge/The Sun, Moon And Stars/San Diego Serenade **PERSONNEL** Nanci Grffith (v, ag), Tanita Tikaram (gst), session musicians

Having graduated to major label status via Rounder Records, Texan country-folk songstress Griffith had found greater success in Britain than her native country. But linking with UK musicians Rod Argent and Peter Van Hooke as producers resulted in an album which performed so badly back home that MCA promptly dropped her! A work like this proved she fitted no defining genre, with country, folk and rock influences that attracted UK audiences but confused Americans. Her next step on a new label would be that old standby, the classic covers album.

The end result lacks nothing in poise, with plenty of strong, easy-paced melodies…. It's simply too constrictive to get the best out of a voice that, lets face it, can kick like a mule and needs to be pushed harder than here. **Peter Kane, Q, October 1991**

Laughter And Tears

ARTIST Neil Sedaka **RELEASE DATE** July 1976 **LABEL** Polydor **PRODUCER** – **UK CHART** peak/weeks 2/25 **US CHART** peak/weeks 0/0 **TRACK LISTING** Standing On The Inside/Love Will Keep Us Together/Solitaire/The Other Side Of Me/A Little Lovin'/Lonely Night (Angel Face)/Brighton/(I'm A Song) Sing Me/Breaking Up Is Hard To Do/Laughter In The Rain/Cardboard California/Bad Blood/The Queen Of 1964/The Hungry Years/Betty Grable/Beautiful You/That's When The Music Takes Me/Our Last Song Together **PERSONNEL** Neil Sedaka (v)

The Number 1 US single from 1974, *Laughter In The Rain*, signalled a strong return to form from a songwriter and performer whose run of late Fifties/early Sixties hits – **Oh! Carol**, **Calendar Girl**, **Happy Birthday Sweet Sixteen** – were among the best of the pre-Beatles era. **Laughter And Tears** is a compilation that focuses on Sedaka's comeback phase, when he worked with Graham Gouldman of 10cc, signed to fan Elton John's Rocket label and gave away some of his best ever material: The Carpenters hit big

with *Solitaire* while The Captain And Tennille's *Love Will Keep Us Together* was America's best-selling single of 1975.

'Music today isn't as predictable. When you're writing or listening now, you don't want to know the whole of the song in the first eight bars. It should be a surprise.' **From an interview with Richard Williams, Melody Maker, December 1972**

Layla And Other Assorted Love Songs

ARTIST Derek And The Dominos **RELEASE DATE** December 1970 (UK)/November 1970 (US) **LABEL** Polydor (UK)/Atco (US) **PRODUCER** The Dominos, Tom Dowd **UK CHART** peak/weeks 0/0 **US CHART** peak/weeks 16/65 **TRACK LISTING** I Looked Away/Bell Bottom Blues/Keep On Growing/Nobody Knows You When You're Down And Out/I Am Yours/Anyday/Key To The Highway/Tell The Truth/Why Does Love Got To Be So Sad?/Have You Ever Loved A Woman/Little Wing/It's Too Late/Layla/Thorn Tree In The Garden **PERSONNEL** Eric Clapton (g, lv), Bobby Whitlock (o, p, v, ag), Jim Gordon (d, pc, p), Carl Radle (b, pc), Duane Allman (g, gst), Albee (p)

Eric Clapton's obsession with avoiding the spotlight after the excesses of Cream led to an invented frontman ('Derek') and a six-string guitar partner in Duane Allman, on loan from the Allman Brothers. The result was incendiary but spectacularly unsuccessful: not till the title track hit two years later did anyone take much notice of the double album. Now it is regarded as a landmark, though by its twenty-fifth anniversary Allman and Carl Radle were dead, and drummer Jim Gordon imprisoned for murder!

… forget any indulgences and filler – it's one hell of an album. Clapton's not God, but him and Skydog and the Dominos together do make for an hour or so of heaven. Maybe the critics, audience and musicians can agree, just this once. **Ed Leimbacher, Rolling Stone, December 1974**

Lazer Guided Melodies

ARTIST Spiritualized **RELEASE DATE** April 1982 **LABEL** Dedicated **PRODUCER** Barry Clempson, Jason Pierce **UK CHART** peak/weeks 27/2 **US CHART** peak/weeks - **TRACK LISTING** You Know It's True/If I Were With Her Now/

I Want You/Run/Smiles/Step Into The Breeze/Symphony Space/Take Your Time/Shine A Light/Angel Sigh/Angel Sigh/Sway/200 Bars **PERSONNEL** Jason Pierce (v, g), Willie B.Carruthers (b), Jon Matlock (d), Kate Radley (v, k, o), Mark Refroy (g, du)

Formed out of the ashes of British trance-rockers Spacemen 3, Spiritualized are a kind of latterday Pink Floyd. The brainchild of vocalist/guitarist Jason Pierce, their debut album, **Lazer Guided Melodies**, was a four-track affair, each song broken up into three or four sections. Alternating between droning guitar mantras and gossamer lullabies, with Pierce's soft, almost devotionally whispery vocals heightening the sacred ambience, **Lazer Guided Melodies** provided the perfect prescription at the height of grunge.

Infused with the essence of April, this album is the true blossoming of Pierce's genius. Bask in its beauty. **Simon Reynolds, Melody Maker, March 1992**

Leave Home

ARTIST The Ramones **RELEASE DATE** March 1977 (UK)/February 1977 (US) **LABEL** Sire (UK & US) **PRODUCER** Tony Bongiovi, Tommy Erdely **UK CHART** peak/weeks 45/1 **US CHART** peak/weeks 148/10 **TRACK LISTING** Glad To See You Go/Gimme Gimme Shock Treatment/Pinhead/Oh Oh I Love Her So/I Remember You/Suzy Is A Headbanger/Now I Want To Be A Good Boy/Swallow My Pride/You're Gonna Kill That Girl/You Should Never Have Opened That Door/California Sun/Babysitter **PERSONNEL** Joey Ramone (v), Jonny Ramone (g, v), Dee Dee Ramone (b, v), Tommy Ramone (d)

Many groups face a 'difficult' second album – the Ramones, however, solved the problem of coming up with a new effort by cloning the eponymous first one. The 'gabba gabba hey!' chorus of Pinheads, inspired by the Tod Browning film *Freaks*, would inspire fans' placards at gigs, while **Carbona Not Glue** was removed from some British pressings by 'the moral majority'. Chart success was minimal, but in the jubilee year of punk the Ramones were just glad to be there.

Led Zeppelin

ARTIST Led Zeppelin **RELEASE DATE** March 1969 (UK)/February 1969 (US) **LABEL** Atlantic (UK & US) **PRODUCER** Jimmy Page **UK CHART** peak/weeks 6/79 **US CHART** peak/weeks 10/95 **TRACK LISTING** Good Times Bad Times/Babe I'm Gonna Leave You/You Shook Me/Dazed And Confused/Your Time Is Gonna Come/Black Mountain Side/Communication Breakdown/I Can't Quit You Baby/How Many More Times **PERSONNEL** Robert Plant (v, bv), Jimmy Page (lg, g, bv), John Paul Jones (b, o, bv), John Bonham (d, bv, pc)

The first album by one of Britain's most legendary rock acts was cut at a cost of £1,782, the money being put up by manager Peter Grant, no recording contract having yet been signed. A facsimile of their live set, it took just 30 hours to record, compared with the reputed 100 hours Simon and Garfunkel were then spending on their single **The Boxer**. The master tapes landed Zep a reported £50,000 contract: at that time the largest amount paid for a new band.

Jimmy Page… has been a rather mystical figure to British fans… now, with his own group, the legend comes to life…. Their material does not rely on obvious blues riffs, although when they do play them, they avoid the emaciated feebleness of most so-called British blues bands. **Melody Maker, 1969**

Led Zeppelin II

ARTIST Led Zeppelin **RELEASE DATE** October 1969 (UK & US) **LABEL** Atlantic (UK & US) **PRODUCER** Jimmy Page **UK CHART** peak/weeks 1/138 **US CHART** peak/weeks 1/98 **TRACK LISTING** Whole Lotta Love/What Is And What Should Never Be/The Lemon Song/Thank You/Heart Breaker/Livin' Lovin' Maid (She's A Woman)/Ramble On/Moby Dick/Bring It On Home **PERSONNEL**

Robert Plant (v), Jimmy Page (lg), John Paul Jones (b), John Bonham (d)

While its predecessor had been a straightforward 'bang down the live set' effort, Zeppelin's second long-player made far more use of the studio – and while Robert Plant's songwriting activities had been curtailed on the first album due to contractual problems, five songs here would be Page-Plant and all the remainder (barring the instrumental **Moby Dick**) band-credited. Despite a frantic touring schedule, the result was a cohesive and stunningly powerful statement of intent, which also remains a quintessential Zep album.

OK, I'll concede that until you've listened to the album eight hundred times, as I have, it seems as if it's just one especially heavy song extended over the space of two whole sides. But, hey! You've got to admit that the Zeppelin have their distinctive and enchanting formula down stone-cold, man. **John Mendelsohn, Rolling Stone, 1969**

Led Zeppelin III

ARTIST Led Zeppelin **RELEASE DATE** October 1970 (UK & US) **LABEL** Atlantic (UK & US) **PRODUCER** Jimmy Page **UK CHART** peak/weeks 1/40 **US CHART** peak/weeks 1/42 **TRACK LISTING** Immigrant Song/Friends/Celebration Day/Since I've Been Loving You/Out On The Tiles/Gallows Pole/Tangerine/That's The Way/Bron-Y-Aur Stomp/Hats Off To (Roy) Harper **PERSONNEL** Robert Plant (v), Jimmy Page (lg), John Paul Jones (b), John Bonham (d)

Having shelved their first album's folk roots in creating a rock monster of a second album, Zep went unplugged for number three, retreating to the Welsh country hideaway of Bron-Y-Aur to get their heads and songs together. But there were rockers, too, the 'Viking' lyric of **Immigrant Song** inspired by a trip to Iceland. The critical flak they received, plus problems with the elaborate cover (designed to imitate a crop rotation chart), would lead to a return to more straightforward fare.

*The best way to dig **III** is to put on your headphones, close your eyes and light a cigarette. From the opening bars of **Immigrant Song** with its thumping, aggressive, 'out-of-my-way' riff we know they mean business.* **Chris Welch, Melody Maker, 1970**

Led Zeppelin IV (Four Symbols)

ARTIST Led Zeppelin RELEASE DATE November 1971 (UK & US) LABEL Atlantic (UK & US) PRODUCER Jimmy Page UK CHART peak/weeks 1/63 US CHART peak/weeks 2/259 TRACK LISTING Stairway to Heaven/Misty Mountain Hop/Rock And Roll/Goin' To California/The Battle Of Evermore/4 Sticks/Black Dog/When The Levee Breaks PERSONNEL Robert Plant (v), Jimmy Page (g), John Paul Jones (b), John Bonham (d)

Also known as the 'Four Symbols', or 'Runes' album, it was colossally presumptuous in not stating the band's name or an album title on the sleeve. The band experimented with new instruments, Page debuting on mandolin on *Battle Of Evermore* and Jones on recorder on the intro to *Stairway To Heaven*, perhaps the band's best known track of all time with its Tolkienesque lyrics and gradually building rock backing. Page would order a double-neck Gibson specifically to play the track live, adding to its mythical status.

The march of the dinosaurs that broke the ground for their first epic release has apparently vanished, taking with it the splattering electronics of their second effort and the leaden acoustic moves that seemed to weigh down their third. **Lenny Kaye, Rolling Stone, 1971**

Let It Be

ARTIST The Beatles RELEASE DATE May 1970 (UK & US) LABEL Apple (UK & US) PRODUCER Phil Spector UK CHART peak/weeks 1/59 US CHART peak/weeks 1/59 TRACK LISTING Two Of Us/I Dig A Pony/Across The Universe/I Me Mine/Dig It/Let It Be/Maggie Mae/I've Got A Feeling/One After 909/The Long And Winding Road/For You Blue/Get Back PERSONNEL John Lennon (v, rg), Paul McCartney (v, b), George Harrison (v, lg), Ringo Starr (d)

This unfocused collection was inexpertly edited and overdubbed by Phil Spector, and the largely Yoko-induced bad vibes, coupled with McCartney and Harrison seething at each other, put paid to any aspirations to genuine grandeur. Nevertheless it would be a stony heart that did not throb a little to the melancholy musings of the title cut and *The Long And Winding Road*. *Get Back* cannot be heard without the mind's eye seeing that legendary last performance up on the roof at Apple – ' hope we've passed the audition' – and *Two Of Us* features Paul and John harmonizing together for the final time.

Musically, boys, you passed the audition. In terms of having the judgement to avoid either over-producing yourselves or casting the fate of your 'Get-Back' statement to the most notorious of all over-producers, you didn't. Which somehow doesn't seem to matter much any more anyway. **John Mendelsohn, Rolling Stone, June 1970**

Let It Be

ARTIST The Replacements RELEASE DATE October 1984 (UK & US) LABEL Zippo (UK & US) PRODUCER The Replacements, Peter Jesperson, Steve Fjelstad UK CHART peak/weeks 0/0 US CHART peak/weeks 0/0 TRACK LISTING I Will Dare/Favourite Thing/We're Comin' Out/Tommy Gets His Tonsils Out/Androgynous/Black Diamond/Unsatisfied/Seen Your Video/Gary's Got A Boner/Sixteen Blue/Answering Machine PERSONNEL Paul Westerberg (v, g), Bob Stinson (g), Tommy Stinson (b), Chris Mars (d)

The third album from the Minneapolis four-piece was their last studio effort on the indie Twin/Tone label, and gained *kudos* by featuring guest guitarist Pete Buck from R.E.M.. But signing to Sire did not bring them the expected breakthrough, while a mismatched tour supporting Tom Petty closed the Eighties in confidence-sapping fashion. None of their albums in a 12-year history truly convinced, this bizarrely titled (well, who copies The Beatles?) effort combining the sensitive and the senseless to confusing effect.

This is a brilliant rock & roll album as loose as it is hard rocking and as pissed off at all the right things… as it is hilarious… in an age when most rock records are studied and wimpy, this rugged album feels truly fresh. **Debby Miller, Rolling Stone, February 1985**

Let It Bleed

ARTIST The Rolling Stones RELEASE DATE December 1969 (UK & US) LABEL Decca (UK)/London (US) PRODUCER Jimmy Miller UK CHART peak/weeks 1/129 US CHART peak/weeks 3/44 TRACK LISTING Gimme Shelter/Love In Vain/Country Honk/Live With Me/Let It Bleed/Midnight Rambler/You Got The Silver/Monkey Man/You Can't Always Get What You Want PERSONNEL Mick Jagger (v, h, k, hp), Keith Richards (rg, k, v), Brian Jones (lg, pc, hp), Charlie Watts (d), Bill Wyman (b), Ian Stewart (p), Ry Cooder (g, gst), Merry Clayton (gst), London Bach Choir (v, gst), session musicians

Brian Jones died a month after being replaced in the band by Mick Taylor. Thus Keith Richard was forced – or allowed – to push his guitar further forward, resulting in the flashy strutting of *Midnight Rambler* and *Monkey Man*. A twisted country & western leaning could be spotted on *Love In Vain* and *Country Honk*, and Keith even sang, in a sharp, nasal offhand way, on *You Got The Silver*. Jagger meanwhile was becoming increasingly self-regarding, but on the peaks, *You Can't Always Get What You Want* and the sublime *Gimme Shelter* (which wears perhaps the most visceral intro ever), this band was *in excelsis*.

Back to a simpler, more funky style for the Stones after their recent offerings. This is the sort of country rock that made the Stones one of the world's top pop names. **Melody Maker, January 1970**

Let's Dance

ARTIST David Bowie RELEASE DATE April 1983 (UK & US) LABEL EMI (UK & US) PRODUCER Nile Rodgers UK CHART peak/weeks 1/56 US CHART peak/weeks 4/68 TRACK LISTING Criminal World/Let's Dance/China Girl/Ricochet/Shake It/Without You/Modern Love/Cat People (Putting Out Fire) PERSONNEL David Bowie (v, var), Stevie Ray Vaughan (g), Bernard Edwards (b), Tony Thompson (d), session musicians

Bowie calculated that by playing it simple he could make a serious commercial comeback. His cheap-rate stuff was better than the family jewels of most. He rehashed **China Girl** – from an old Iggy Pop album – to sweeping effect, and in Nile Rodgers, ex-Chic dance floor guru, found the perfect *producer du jour*. The palatable title cut gave him the requisite chart-topper, but by his standards was rather anaemic. The image, too, was straight as an arrow. He was now in the Eighties: no longer the prince of alienation, he had become 'success'. Few deserved it as much. Yet he knew he could do better, and in subsequent years grew interested in other creative media.

Like most of Bowie's records, this one says absolutely nothing while recognising precisely the time, date and circumstance of its creation. It saddens me slightly that it took me so long to appreciate the full extent of Bowie's unerring, instinctive duplicity… **Adam Sweeting, Melody Maker, April 1983**

Let's Get It On

ARTIST Marvin Gaye RELEASE DATE September 1973 LABEL Tamla Motown (UK)/Tamla (US) PRODUCER Marvin Gaye, Ed Townsend UK CHART peak/weeks 39/1 US CHART peak/weeks 2/61 TRACK LISTING Let's Get It On/Please Don't Stay (Once You Go Away)/If I Should Die Tonight/Keep Gettin' It On/Come Get To This/Distant Lover/You Sure Love To Ball/Just To Keep You Satisfied PERSONNEL Marvin Gaye (v), session musicians

Having successfully explored spiritual matters with **What's Goin' On**, Marvin turned his attentions to more physical pursuits for **Let's Get It On**, perhaps one of the most sensuous albums ever released. The velvet voice was still in evidence, but the pleading for tolerance on **What's Goin' On**', was replaced by pleading of an altogether different sort. With this and its later companion **I Want You** you have the ideal seduction kit. While many other artists have since pursued similar themes (most notably Barry White and Isaac Hayes), few have done so with such panache.

Let's Get It On…. *ebbs and flows, occasionally threatening to spend itself on an insufficiency of ideas, but always retrieved, just in time, by Gaye's performance. From first note to last, he keeps pushing and shoving…* **Jon Landau, Rolling Stone, December 1973**

The Lexicon Of Love

ARTIST ABC RELEASE DATE July 1982 (UK)/September 1982 (US) LABEL Neutron (UK)/Mercury (US) PRODUCER Trevor Horn UK CHART peak/weeks 1/50 US CHART peak/weeks 19/27 TRACK LISTING Show Me/Poison Arrow/Many Happy Returns/Tears Are Not Enough/Valentine's Day/The Look Of Love (Part One)/Date Stamp/All Of My Heart/4 Ever 2 Gether/The Look Of Love (Part Two) PERSONNEL Martin Fry (v), Mark White (g), David Palmer (b), session musicians.

The Sheffield group's debut soared to success due to its ultra-savvy marriage of new wave attitude and mainstream pop production values. Gloriously caressed into life by a peak performance from Trevor Horn, it showcased Martin Fry's terrific romanticism and wit with hits like **The Look Of Love** and **Poison Arrow**. Other less heralded but equally perfectly formed odes to beauty, such as **Date Stamp** and **Many Happy Returns**, also featured on the album. The band, short-lived in this line-up, wore their hearts on their gold lamé sleeves – a new, sussed, smart-ass pop was born: Ferry without mercy, Dollar with currency.

… Listening to certain parts can frequently produce nothing as crassly simple as severe brain damage but a rather more civilised basic aural pain… The psychic melodramas do, though, have the saving grace of being carried out with an appropriate sense of artistic folly. **Chris Salewicz, NME, October 1974**

Liberty Belle And The Black Diamond Express

ARTIST The Go-Betweens RELEASE DATE March 1986 (UK & US) LABEL Beggars Banquet (UK & US) PRODUCER – UK CHART peak/weeks 0/0 US CHART peak/weeks 0/0 TRACK LISTING Spring Rain/Ghost And The Black Hat/Head Full Of Steam/Wrong Road/To Reach Me/Twin Layers Of Lightening/In The Core Of The Flames/Bow Down/Palm Sunday/Apology Accepted PERSONNEL Grant McLellan (v, lg), Rob Forster (g, v), Lindy Morrison (d), Robert Vickers (b), session musicians

Having established themselves as critical favourites, Australia's Go-Betweens all but foundered after a dalliance with Sire Records (home of major influences like Talking Heads) ended after just one album. Beggars Banquet provided a safe haven where, unpressured, they could come up with their fourth and best long-player to date. A move into string and woodwind instrumentation led to the expansion of the line-up to include multi-instrumentalist Amanda Brown: a commercial breakthrough of sorts would be the next step with 1987's **Tallulah**, but this remains their most rounded achievement.

For every song you have to make an emotional investment. The Go-Betweens aren't easy or obvious. Their world is full of despairing, melancholy people hanging about. The weather is in their moods and it always seems to be raining. **Eithne, Melody Maker, April 1996**

Licensed To Ill

ARTIST The Beastie Boys **RELEASE DATE** January 1987 (UK)/November 1986 (US) **LABEL** Def Jam (UK & US) **PRODUCER** Beastie Boys, Rick Rubin **UK CHART** peak/weeks 7/40 **US CHART** peak/weeks 1/68 **TRACK LISTING** Time To Get Ill/(You Gotta) Fight For Your Right (To Party)/Slow And Low/No Sleep 'Til Brooklyn/It's The New Style/Hold It Now Hit It/Posse In Effect/Paul Revere/Girls/Brass Monkey/She's Crafty/Slow Ride/Rhymin' And Stealin' **PERSONNEL** King Ad-Rock (Adam Horovitz) (v), MCA (Adam Yauch) (v), Mike D (Michael Diamond) (v), Rick Rubin (dj)

Bringing the rap spirit to the suburban mall and appropriating a black music genre in the time-honoured white tradition, Ad-Rock, MCA and Mike D hollered pumped-up rhymes with high-school horniness and self-deluding sass. They wanted so much to be bad but, basically, they were merely naughty. This was the appeal to America, who made the album a monster. Its samples from, and nods to, AC/DC, Aerosmith, Led Zeppelin and Mister Ed helped. In *Fight For Your Right (To Party)* the Beasties came clean with the joke, delivered a generation's 'rebel' anthem, and ensured baseball caps would be reversed for years to come…

Licensed To Ill hasn't got time for ballads… The album's a one-trick pony. But what a trick. Grindy-metal and nuclear backbeats smeared with bouncy amphetamine rapping. And lots of gesticulating. **Paul Mathur, Melody Maker, July 1995**

Liege And Lief

ARTIST Fairport Convention **RELEASE DATE** December 1969 (UK & US) **LABEL** Island (UK)/A&M (US) **PRODUCER** Joe Boyd **UK CHART** peak/weeks 17/15 **US CHART** peak/weeks 0/0 **TRACK LISTING** Come All Ye/Reynardine/Matty Groves/Farewell, Farewell/The Deserter/Medley (The Lark In The Morning)/Rakish Paddy/Fox Hunters' Jig/Toss The Feathers/Tam Lin/Crazy Man Michael **PERSONNEL** Sandy Denny (v), Ashley Hutchings (b), Dave Mattacks (d), Simon Nicol (g), Dave Swarbrick (v, va), Richard Thompson (g)

This album, Fairport's fourth, opened up new vistas for English folk by its application of rock instrumentation to traditional material like the song **Matty Groves**. That they should record this weeks after a motorway smash in which drummer Martin Lamble lost his life was truly astonishing, but his replacement, Dave Mattacks, would prove to be one of the longest-staying of the band's notoriously changing personnel. The writing partnership of Thompson and Swarbrick (**Crazy Man Michael**) was destined to be brief but fruitful: this being the first of two albums they both appeared on.

Where are the exhilarating many-voiced harmonies, the sense of fun and the feeling of harnessed electricity that made their first two albums

together such treats? Where, essentially, is something to excite those of us who find artiness worthy enough of quiet admiration but a little boring? **John Mendelsohn, Rolling Stone, June 1970**

Like A Prayer

ARTIST Madonna **RELEASE DATE** March 1989 (UK & US) **LABEL** Sire (UK & US) **PRODUCER** Madonna, Patrick Leonard, Stephen Bray, Prince **UK CHART** peak/weeks 1/65 **US CHART** peak/weeks 1/77 **TRACK LISTING** Like A Prayer/Express Yourself/Love Song/Till Death Do Us Part/Promise To Try/Cherish/Dear Jessie/Oh Father/Keep It Together/Spanish Eyes/Act Of Contrition **PERSONNEL** Madonna (v), session musicians

Far from being the rebel she had portrayed in earlier days, Madonna let her parents inspire her on her fourth (non-soundtrack) album. It was dedicated to her late mother, who 'taught me how to pray' (a reference to the opening *Like A Prayer*), while the track *Oh Father* dealt with her relationship with the surviving parent. The video for the title track attracted profanity allegations as she frolicked with a black priest and led to Pepsi dropping a sponsorship deal…. What would Mummy have thought?

Daring in its lyrics, ambitious in its sonics… you may see her navel on the inner sleeve, but what you hear once you get inside the package is as close to art as pop music gets. **J. D. Considine, Rolling Stone, April 1989**

Like A Virgin

ARTIST Madonna **RELEASE DATE** November 1984 (UK & US) **LABEL** Sire (UK & US) **PRODUCER** Nile Rogers, Madonna, Steve Bray **UK CHART** peak/weeks 1/152 **US CHART** peak/weeks 1/108 **TRACK LISTING** Material Girl/Angel/Like A Virgin/Over And Over/Love Don't Live Here Anymore/Into The Groove/Dress You Up/Shoo-Bee-Doo/Pretender/Stay **PERSONNEL** Madonna (v), session musicians

A culture clash informed the recording of this album, with early-rising Madonna at odds with the schedule of guitarist and producer Nile Rodgers. The Chic mainman rarely surfaced before midday, being a keen club-goer, leaving Madonna to take a swim and a

leisurely walk before work began on her second (and first chart-topping) effort. **Into The Groove** from the film *Desperately Seeking Susan* would be added to later pressings, helping this become an album that sold seven million plus in the US alone.

The droning male chorus and Mr Machine synth riff behind **Material Girl** *strike just the right note of snickering wit: that song and the whipped cream tastiness of the title cut, guarantee at least two hits and a very, very clever, er, repositioning of Madonna's image.* **The Year In Records 1985, Rolling Stone, December 1985**

Listen To Cliff

ARTIST Cliff Richard RELEASE DATE April 1961 LABEL Columbia (UK)/Paramount (US) PRODUCER – UK CHART peak/weeks 2/28 US CHART peak/weeks 0/0 TRACK LISTING What'd I Say/Blue Moon/True Love Will Come To You/Lover/Unchained Melody/Idle Gossip/First Lesson/Almost Like Being In Love/Beat Out That Rhythm On A Drum/Memories Linger On/Temptation/I Live For You/Sentimental Journey/I Want You To Know/We Kiss In A Shadow/It's You/It'll Be Me/So I've Been Told/How Long Is Forever?/I'm Walkin' The Blues/Turn Around/Blueberry Hill/Let's Make A Memory/When My Dreamboat Comes Home/I'm On My Way/Spanish Harlem/You Don't Know/Falling In Love With Love/Who Are We To PERSONNEL Cliff Richard (v)

As with its predecessor-but-one, **Cliff Sings**, this album contrasted the MOR ballads and rockier fare: its original title being **Stringy And Swingy**. The original Shadows line-up, including the rhythm section of Jet Harris and Tony Meehan, made their swansong on this release. With two Number 2 albums in the previous three, there were high hopes of a chart-topper this time, but any disappointment at falling just short paled against the death of Cliff's father, Rodger Webb, the following week.

This amounts to a musical adventure for Cliff and with the assistance of The Shadows, Norrie Paramor's orchestra and the swinging Bernard Ebbinghouse band, he tackles many songs outside the teen idiom. **Pop Vocal Discs, Melody Maker, May 1961**

Little Earthquakes

ARTIST Tori Amos RELEASE DATE January 1992 (UK)/December 1991 (US) LABEL East West (UK)/Atlantic (US) PRODUCER Eric Rosse, Davitt Sigerson, Ian Stanley UK CHART peak/weeks 14/16 US CHART peak/weeks 54/38 TRACK LISTING Crucify/Girl/Silent All These Years/Precious Things/Winter/Happy Phantom/China/Leather/Mother/Tear In Your Hand/Me And A Gun/Little Earthquakes PERSONNEL Tori Amos (v, p), Steve Farris (g), Matt Sorum (d), Steve Canton (g), Will McGregor (b), Eric Rosse (k), Jeff Scott (b, g), Paulinho DaCosta (pc)

Compared to Kate Bush and Joni Mitchell, Tori Amos wooed an enormous fan base with her deeply confessional, emotional and imaginative ballads. Unafraid to take risks lyrically, and making her piano sound like an orchestra or a kick-ass rock 'n' roll band, flame-haired Amos touched a nerve with sensitive females. Her writhing and wriggling on stage may have increased her percentage of male admirers. **Crucify, Silent All These Years** and the dramatic title track were wonderfully realized, and **Me And A Gun** courageously dealt with her own experience of rape. Born in North Carolina, and once in a band with Guns'N'Roses drummer Matt Sorrum, Amos saw this album go gold in Britain before breaking in America.

The omens do not look good for Tori Amos… It's as if she'd set herself that most difficult of tasks – to be even drabber than Michelle Shocked… Lyrically, she's something special… **Little Earthquakes** *is disturbing, funny and sexy by turns… Where on earth can she go from here?* **John Aizlewood, Q, February 1992**

Little Stevie Wonder/The Twelve Year Old Genius

ARTIST Stevie Wonder RELEASE DATE July 1963 (UK & US) LABEL Tamla Motown (UK & US) PRODUCER – UK CHART peak/weeks – US CHART peak/weeks 1/20 TRACK LISTING Don't You Know In My own Tears/Fingerib Part 2/Hallelujah I Love Her So/(I'm Afraid) The Masquerade Is Over/La La La La La/Soul Bongo PERSONNEL Stevie Wonder (k, v), session musicians

Little Stevie Wonder was the third album from a true soul prodigy, blind since infancy. Recorded live before the Michigan-born Steveland Judkins Morris had even entered his teens, **Little Stevie Wonder** featured his Number 1 hit, *Fingertips*, and introduced this energetic whiz-kid to a startled world. A junior version of Ray Charles, that other blind soulman to whom the whiz-kid was often compared (there are three Charles covers here), Wonder showed he could already play harmonica, drums, piano and organ, and sing with passion and conviction.

Live!

ARTIST Bob Marley & The Wailers RELEASE DATE December 1975 (UK & US) LABEL Island (UK & US) PRODUCER Bob Marley & The Wailers UK CHART peak/weeks 38/11 US CHART peak/weeks 90/9 TRACK LISTING Trenchtown Rock/Burnin' And Lootin'/Them Belly Full/Lively Up Yourself/No Woman, No Cry/I Shot The Sheriff/Get Up, Stand Up PERSONNEL Bob Marley (v, g), Aston Barrett (b), Al Anderson (g), Tyrone Downie (k), Alvin 'Sheco' Patterson (pc), Julian 'Junior' Murvin (g)

Following a breakthrough US tour, the Wailers hit Britain in July 1975 to play just four dates, two in London's Lyceum. The second of these was recorded by Island label boss Chris Blackwell for possible release – and his hunch was confirmed when **No Woman, No Cry**, released as a single in advance of the LP, reached Number 22 and pulled **Natty Dread** (where the studio cut had appeared) into the Top 50. **Live** would better its position by five places, suggesting that Marley, and reggae, had arrived.

… it's a toss-up whether this record or **Natty Dread** *is better. The audience response is electrifying and both the Wailers and the I-Threes vocalists are in top form. One of the best live albums ever.* **Ed Ward, Rolling Stone, 1976**

Live At Leeds

ARTIST The Who **RELEASE DATE** May 1970 (UK & US) **LABEL** Track (UK)/Decca (US) **PRODUCER** The Who, Jon Astley, Kit Lambert, Shel Talmy **UK CHART** peak/weeks 3/21 **US CHART** peak/weeks 4/44 **TRACK LISTING** Young Man Blues/Substitute/Summertime Blues/Shaking All Over/My Generation/Magic Bus **PERSONNEL** Roger Daltrey (v, h), Pete Townsend (g, v, k), John Entwistle (b, g, k, v), Keith Moon (d)

Featuring many of their best known hits as well as several nods to their mod/R&B roots in the cover versions, **Live At Leeds**, one of the few essential live albums, does more than prove The Who's mastery of the three-minute single; it also demonstrates what a powerful live attraction they were, and would be throughout the Seventies, a decade during which they would be widely hailed alongside The Rolling Stones and Led Zeppelin as The Greatest Rock 'n' Roll Band in the World.

… the formal commercial end of the first great stage of their great career… thanks to their vision and sound… Peter Townshend and his band will begin to translate the Seventies into rock 'n' roll. **Greil Marcus, Rolling Stone, July 1970**

Live At The Apollo

ARTIST James Brown **RELEASE DATE** December 1962 (UK & US) **LABEL** London (UK)/King (US) **PRODUCER** – **UK CHART** peak/weeks 0/0 **US CHART** peak/weeks 32/39 **TRACK LISTING** I'll Go Crazy/Try Me/Think/I Don't Mind/Lost Someone/Please, Please, Please/You've Got The Power/I Found Someone/Why Do You Do Me Like You Do/I Want You So Bad/I Love You Yes I Do/Why Does Everything Happen To Me/Bewildered/Please Don't Go/Night Train **PERSONNEL** James Brown (v, var), with The Famous Flames; Bobby Byrd (o), Johnny Terry (g), Sylvester Keels (g), Nafloyd Scott (g)

Even in 1963 James Brown, the Godfather of Soul, was better known for his live shows, or 'revues', than for his recorded output: his ideas and grooves were years ahead of their time. Bizarrely, his record company didn't see the point in releasing a live album, so Brown, never one to doubt his abilities, made **Live At The Apollo** using his own money. Revelling in the tight pizzazz of the band (The Flames) as they tore the roof off the New York theatre, the audience screamed with unabashed delight. James milked the rapport and the hits come thick and fast: *Night Train*, *Please*

Please Please, *Think*, *I'll Go Crazy*, *Try Me*, et al. Funk was rarely so funky.

Over the years, soul music has produced many fine albums and its share of true classics, but over and above even these stand a handful of recordings which stand as true landmarks in the music's development out of the Black American Ghettos and into its present major role on the wider pop scene around the world. **Roger St. Pierre, NME**

Live At The Regal

ARTIST B. B. King **RELEASE DATE** July 1965 (UK & US) **LABEL** HMV (UK)/ABC Paramount (US) **PRODUCER** – **UK CHART** peak/weeks 0/0 **US CHART** peak/weeks 0/0 **TRACK LISTING** Everyday (I Have The Blues)/Sweet Little Angel/It's My Own Fault/How Blue Can You Get/Please Love Me/You Upset Me Baby/Worry, Worry/Woke Up This Mornin'/You Done Lost You Good Thing/Help The Poor **PERSONNEL** B. B. King (v, g), session musicians

Riley B King, the Beale Street Blues Boy, made his name in the Fifties on the Kent label before moving into the mainstream with ABC in the next decade. The Chicago-recorded **Live At The Regal** let him reprise the glories of the past decade while breaking through to a new white audience which included the likes of Eric Clapton. U2 would recognise this live magic three decades later by co-opting him into their own act for the 'Rattle And Hum' tour, most notably on **When Love Comes To Town**. You can bet this is in Bono's record collection – Clapton's too.

B. B. King is captured at the height of his popularity performing for a very vocal black audience… it is made into something of an occasion by the very presence of that audience and by the performer's own response to its reaction. **Peter Guralnick, Rolling Stone, April 1971**

Live Bullets

ARTIST Bob Seger & The Silver Bullet Band **RELEASE DATE** August 1976 (UK)/April 1976 (US) **LABEL** Capitol (UK & US) **PRODUCER** Bob Seger, Punch **UK CHART** peak/weeks 0/0 **US CHART** peak/weeks 34/167 **TRACK LISTING** Nutbush City Limits/Travelin' Man/Beautiful Loser/Jody Girl/I've Been Working/Turn The Page/U.M.C./Bo Diddley/Ramblin' Gamblin' Man/Heavy Music/Katmandu/Lookin' Back/Get Out Of Denver/Let It Rock **PERSONNEL** Bob Seger (lv, g, p), Drew Abbott (lg, bv), Alto Reed (ts, as, bs), (pc, bv), Robin Robbins (k), Chris Campbell (b, bv), Charlie Allen Martin (d, bv, v)

Sometimes described as one of the greatest live albums ever made, **Live Bullets** was gruff rocker Bob Seger's eighth LP: a double, recorded at Detroit's Cobo Hall some 15 years after emerging from Michigan with a hometown three-piece, The Decibels. Featuring blistering versions of **Nutbush City Limits** and **Get Out Of**

Denver, **Live Bullet** stayed on the American charts for over three years and eventually went quadruple platinum.

… it would negate Seger's method of working to say that the live versions are superior to the studio ones. He's always kept a strict line between the two; in the studio he uses both his band of the moment and top session men to lay down the version, while on stage he substitutes energy for expertise. **M. O., Melody Maker, September 1976**

Live Dead (Live In The Studio)

ARTIST The Grateful Dead **RELEASE DATE** February 1970 (UK)/December 1969 (US) **LABEL** Warner (UK & US) **PRODUCER** The Grateful Dead **UK CHART** peak/weeks 0/0 **US CHART** peak/weeks 64/15 **TRACK LISTING** Dark Star/St Stephen/The Eleven/Turn On Your Lovelight/Death Don't Have No Mercy/Feedback/And We Bid You Goodnight **PERSONNEL** Jerry Garcia (v, lg), Bob Weir (rg), Ron 'Pigpen' McKernan (k, v, h), Phil Lesh (b), Bill Kreutzmann (d), Tom Constanten (k), Mickey Hart (pc), Robert Hunter (w)

The Dead had always found the studio a constraint. They were primarily a live band who had developed a wild and improvisatory sound out of their jug-band roots as the musical accompanists to Ken Kesey & His Merry Pranksters' public experiments with LSD. It was no surprise then that they should issue a live set that confirmed their underground reputation and, with its guitar feedback, still sounds wholly contemporary. This remains one of the pinnacle live-rock albums of all time and set a trend that was to see them regularly release live works throughout the subsequent 25 years of their existence.

I wasn't expecting too much from this, having been bored silly by the Dead on their previous three albums. But all the fuss is clarified on this double-album, recorded in person, which allows them to stretch out and take their time layin' the licks down. **R. W., Melody Maker, March 1970**

Live In Europe

ARTIST Rory Gallagher **RELEASE DATE** May 1972 (UK)/August 1972 **LABEL** Polydor (UK & US) **PRODUCER** Rory Gallagher **UK CHART** peak/weeks 9/15 **US CHART** peak/weeks 101/15 **TRACK LISTING** Messin' With The Kid/Laundromat/I Could've Had Religion/Pistol Slapper Blues/Going To My Home Town/In Your Town/Bullfrog Blues **PERSONNEL** Rory Gallager (v, g, md, bv), Wilgar Cambell (d), Gerry McAvoy (b)

Profoundly unhip yet strangely popular, work-shirted Irish guitarist Gallagher and his battered Strat had been staples on European stages ever since the days of Taste. Like that band, whose **Live At The Isle Of Wight** was a posthumous hit, Gallagher made the breakthrough after two solo albums with a Top 10 live set that remained a chart staple for 15 weeks and showcased his versatility and viruosity by mixing acoustic and electric with ease. 'Playing live is always instinctive for me, more primal,' he said – and this album is the proof.

'I don't consider all my material is blues. Let's say I'm a blend of blues, rock, jazz and folk music… it doesn't really worry me what I'm playing, it's just the emotional hold the blues has…' **From an interview by Mark Plummer, Melody Maker, July 1972**

Live MCMXCIII

ARTIST The Velvet Underground **RELEASE DATE** October 1993 (UK & US) **LABEL** Sire (UK)/Warner (US) **PRODUCER** Mike Rathke **UK CHART** peak/weeks 70/1 **US CHART** peak/weeks 180/1 **TRACK LISTING** We're Gonna Have A Good Time Together/Venus In Furs/Guess I'm Falling In Love/After Hours/All Tomorrow's Parties/Some Kinda Love/I'll Be Your Mirror/Beginning To See The Light/The Gift/I Heard Her Call My Name/Femme Fatale/Hey Mr Rain/Sweet Jane/Velvet Nursery Rhyme/White Light/White Heat/I'm Sticking With You/Black Angel's Death Song/Rock 'N' Roll/I Can't Stand It/I'm Waiting For The Man/Heroin/Pale Blue Eyes/Coyote **PERSONNEL** Lou Reed (v, g), Sterling Morrison (b, g), John Cale (b, k, v, va), Maureen Tucker (d)

With every claim to being the most influential cult band of all time, the Velvet Underground were arch-experimenters both in pharmaceutical as well as musical spheres. They re-formed to play dates in England then record the double CD set **Live MCMXCIII** in Paris in 1993. Original member Nico had died earlier in 1988 after falling off her bike on holiday in Ibiza. This live set features rousing renditions of songs familiar to every Velvets fans such as **Sweet Jane**, **White Light/White Heat** and **I'm Waiting For The Man**. The band would be named 'Comeback of the Year' in *Rolling Stone's* 1994 Music Awards Critics' Picks.

… it reafirms the V.U's place in history… for all of the music's spontaneous combustion, **MCMXCIII** *side-steps the key issue of where the Velvets go from here.* **Don McLeese, Melody Maker, November 1993**

Live Through This

ARTIST Hole **RELEASE DATE** April 1994 (UK & US) **LABEL** City Slang (UK)/D.G.C. (US) **PRODUCER** Paul Q Kolderie, Sean Slade **UK CHART** peak/weeks 13/ **US CHART** peak/weeks 52/68 **TRACK LISTING** Violet/Miss World/Plump/Asking For It/Jennifer's Body/Doll Parts/Credit In The Straight World/Softer, Softest/She Walks On Me/I Think That I Would Die/Gutless/Rock Star **PERSONNEL** Courtney Love (v, g), Eric Erlandson (g), Kristen Pfaff (b, p, bv), Patty Schemel (d)

A nasty twist of fate found this record released shortly after Courtney Love's husband, Kurt Kobain, committed suicide. It acts to some extent as a document of the couple's relationship, as well as being one of Hole's most accessible records. Kurt's influence can be felt throughout a strong collection of songs that benefit greatly from potent dynamics. The lyrical themes deal prominently with lack of self-esteem and confidence – not surprising given the stick Love received from the media.

Even if you have serious reservations about punk-rock brats living on major-label largesse or believe profanity is the last refuge of the inarticulate, the sheer force of Love's corrosive, lunatic wail… is impressive stuff, a scorched earth blast of righteous indignation. **David Fricke, Rolling Stone, April 1994**

Live (X Cert)

ARTIST The Stranglers **RELEASE DATE** March 1979 (UK & US) **LABEL** United Artists (UK)/IRS (US) **PRODUCER** The Stranglers **UK CHART** peak/weeks 7/10 **US CHART** peak/weeks 0/0 **TRACK LISTING** (Get A) Grip (On Yourself)/ Dagenham Dave/Burning Up Time/Dead Ringer/Hanging Around/I Feel Like A Wog/Straighten Out/Curfew/Do You Wanna?/Death And Night And Blood (Yukio)/5 Minutes/Go Buddy Go **PERSONNEL** Hugh Cornwall (v, g), Jean-Jaques Burnel (b, v), Dave Greenfield (k), Jet Black (d)

Recorded at a variety of gigs throughout 1977 and 1978, **Live (X Cert)** features The Stranglers at their most confrontational – some might say repulsive – as the band, particularly Cornwall, insult the audience between songs. For lovers of the Sex Pistols and The Clash, The Stranglers's anti-social 'schtick' was just too calculated. Musically, too, they went against the grain: this is dexterously played, technically proficient stuff. No wonder the punks hated them.

The band is musically excellent, their songs are structured interestingly, and the overall impression of the album is unquestionably powerful. Aggressive, atmospheric and mean. But this was all the stuff of 1977. **Susan Hill, Melody Maker, February 1979**

Living The Blues

ARTIST Canned Heat **RELEASE DATE** December 1968 (UK & US) **LABEL** Liberty (UK & US) **PRODUCER** – **UK CHART** peak/weeks 0/0 **US CHART** peak/weeks 18/17 **TRACK LISTING** Refried The Boogie (Live 45 Mins)/Bullfrog Blues/Going Down South/Going Up The Country/Time Was/Pony Blues/My Mistake/Five Owls/Sandy's Blues/Walking By Myself/Boogie Music/One Kind Of Flavour/Parthenogenesis/Nebulosity/Rollin' And Tumblin' **PERSONNEL** Bob 'The Bear' Hite (v, h), Al 'Blind Owl' Wilson (g, h, v), Henry Vestine (g), Larry Taylor (b), Fito De La Parra (d)

A double album of equally rationed live and studio material, this warmed Canned Heat up nicely for *Woodstock*, where their *Going Up The Country*, an ancient blues standard, was clasped to the collective bosom as a theme song: certainly the subsequent *Woodstock* movie conveyed that impression. Al Wilson's high-pitched vocal phrasings gave a distinctive lilt to the blues band, one of the few such white acts to enjoy chart success at the time. They are perhaps best remembered for the hits **On The Road**

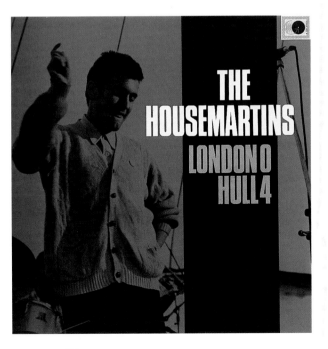

Again and **Let's Work Together** (later revamped by Bryan Ferry as **Let's Stick Together**). When Wilson died of a drug overdose in 1970, the band struggled to continue, although they still roamed the nostalgia circuit.

Loaded

ARTIST The Velvet Underground **RELEASE DATE** April 1971 (UK)/August 1970 (US) **LABEL** Atlantic (UK)/Cotillion (US) **PRODUCER** Geoffrey Haslam, Shel Kagan, The Velvet Underground **UK CHART** peak/weeks 0/0 **US CHART** peak/weeks 0/0 **TRACK LISTING** Who Loves The Sun/Sweet Jane/Rock & Roll/Cool It Down/New Age/Head Held High/Lonesome Cowboy Bill/I Found A Reason/Train Round The Bend/Oh! Sweet Nuthin' **PERSONNEL** Doug Yule (o, p, b, d, lg, ag, v), Sterling Morrison (lg, rg), Lou Reed (rg, p, v), Moe Tucker (d)

Recorded with Doug Yule (John Cale's replacement) during the band's summer-long residency at New York's now legendary Max's Kansas City, **Loaded** features at least two all-time primitive rock 'n' roll classics: **Sweet Jane** and **Rock 'n' roll**, both of which have cropped up on aspiring punk, grunge and Brit-pop bands' set-lists. Lou Reed left the Velvets during the mixing and editing of **Loaded**.

*The Velvet Underground on **Loaded** are more loose and straightforward than we've yet heard them… (it) shows off some of the incredible finesse that Lou Reed has… as a songwriter.* **Lenny Kaye, Rolling Stone, December 1970**

Lodger

ARTIST David Bowie **RELEASE DATE** May 1979 (UK & US) **LABEL** RCA (UK & US) **PRODUCER** Brian Eno **UK CHART** peak/weeks 4/17 **US CHART** peak/weeks 20/15 **TRACK LISTING** Fantastic Voyage/African Night Flight/Move On/Red Sails/D. J./Look Back In Anger/Boys Keep Swingin'/Repitition/Red Money **PERSONNEL** David Bowie (v), Mick Ronison (g), John Cambridge (d)

As if revving up to re-enter the mainstream, this combined the chilling fatalism of **Low** and **Heroes** with some almost manically enthused attempts to kick-start rock rhythms. **Look Back In Anger** and **Red Sails** tripped over themselves with eagerness, yet Eno's off-centre production made them sound as if they were dragging a metal bucket behind one leg. The good humour could not be denied: **D.J.** was an entertaining single, while **Boys Keep Swingin'** was a classic of sarcastic gender-bending. In the video for this single Bowie dragged it up with a vicious glee.

A strange jumble of travel diaries, character sketches and private riddles, **Lodger** *has the colourful illogic of an oracular dream… the tracks chortle and percolate with exotic cross rhythms and wildly tangent solos.* **Jon Pareles, Rolling Stone, December 1979**

London 0 Hull 4

ARTIST The Housemartins **RELEASE DATE** June 1986 (UK)/February 1987 (US) **LABEL** Go! Discs (UK)/Elektra (US) **PRODUCER** Jeffrey Wood **UK CHART** peak/weeks 3/41 **US CHART** peak/weeks 124/14 **TRACK LISTING** Flag Day/Happy Hour/Lean On Me/Think For A Minute/Freedom/Sitting On A Fence/Over There/Sheep/Caravan Of Love/Anxious/Get Up Off Your Knees/We're Not Deep/Reverends Revenge **PERSONNEL** Norman Cook (v), Paul Heaton (v, g), Stan Cullimore (b), Hugh Whitaker (d)

Its title cheekily celebrating the four-piece band's Humberside origins, this debut, the seventh album to be issued by the Go! Discs label, surprised all and sundry by scaling the UK chart heights in the summer of 1986. Its light, happy, yet sussed tone fitted the season, and two more Top 10 albums were to follow before the band imploded and frontman Heaton spun off to form the Beautiful South.

The Housemartins are like the callow youth who sits in the corner of the pub sipping half a mild, while the local boyos give the one-arm bandit an almighty hammering, for no reward. As they retire to the bar in search of more coins the youth in the corner nonchalantly ambles across to the machine munching his pork scratchings, shoves in the only 10p in his pocket… and hits the jackpot. **Colin Irwin, Melody Maker, June 1986**

London Calling

ARTIST The Clash RELEASE DATE December 1979 (UK)/January 1980 (US) LABEL C.B.S. (UK)/Epic (US) PRODUCER Guy Stevens UK CHART peak/weeks 9/20 US CHART peak/weeks 27/33 TRACK LISTING London Calling/Brand New Cadillac/Jimmy Jazz/Hateful/Rudie Can't Fail/Spanish Bombs/The Right Profile/Lost In The Supermarket/Clampdown/Guns Of Brixton/Wrong 'Em Boyo/Death Or Glory/Koka Kola/The Card Cheat/Lover's Rock/Four Horsemen/I'm Not Down/Revolution Rock/Train In Vain PERSONNEL Mick Jones (g, v), Joe Strummer (v, rg), Paul Simonon (b, v), Topper Headon (d, pc)

Allowing themselves to venture into a broader church of styles and sounds, The Clash here proved themselves prolific and prophetic. The title song still rings true, and was an anthemic hit, while *Guns Of Brixton* further explored their reggae leanings. A double album priced as a single one, this also shamelessly embraced rock 'n' roll in *Brand New Cadillac*, and even a *bona fide* American hit in *Train In Vain*. The band's ability to pinpoint perceptions of London life, with its overbearing American influences, was archly demonstrated on Jones' *Lost In The Supermarket*. For *Rolling Stone*, this was 'the album of the Eighties'.

The Clash love rock 'n' roll, which is why they play it, but they want it to live up to its promises, which is why they play it the way they do… **London Calling** *makes up for all the bad rock 'n' roll played over the last decade.* **Charles Shaar Murray, NME, 1979**

The Long Run

ARTIST The Eagles RELEASE DATE September 1979 (UK & US) LABEL Asylum (UK & US) PRODUCER Bill Szymczyk UK CHART peak/weeks 4/16 US CHART peak/weeks 1/57 TRACK LISTING The Long Run/I Can't Tell You Why/In The city/The Disco Strangler/King Of Hollywood/Heartache Tonight/Those Shoes/Teenage Jail/The Greeks Don't Want No Freaks/The Sad Café PERSONNEL Glenn Frey (g, v), Bernie Leadon (g, v), Randy Meisner (b, v), Don Henley (d, v), David Sanborn (s, gst), Jimmy Buffet (gst)

By the time the Eagles recorded their sixth album the pressures of superstardom had well and truly caught up with them. There came a two-year, $1 m gestation period. The result, though it became their fourth US chart-topper, was in truth not up to the standard of **Hotel California**, despite the pressure to top it. Asylum Records were banking on a golden goose and there was no prospect of a break to recharge the batteries. When the band split, drummer Don Henley said it would take till 'hell freezes over' before any reunion.

This is easily the worst Eagles album to date. Continuous playing over several days may establish a few songs in your mind, but there's nothing as tenacious as the earlier classics. **Mark Williams, Melody Maker, September 1979**

Look Sharp!

ARTIST Joe Jackson RELEASE DATE January 1979 (UK & US) LABEL A&M (UK & US) PRODUCER David Kershenbaum UK CHART peak/weeks 40/11 US CHART peak/weeks 20/39 TRACK LISTING One More Time/Sunday Papers/Is She Really Going Out With Him?/Happy Loving Couples/Throw It Away/Baby Stick Around/Look Sharp!/Fools In Love/(Do The) Instant Mash/Pretty Girls/Got The Time PERSONNEL Joe Jackson (v, p, h), Gary Sanford (g), Graham Maby (b), Dave Houghton (d)

Classically trained, pinstriped keyboardist Joe Jackson was championed by the (now defunct) *Sounds* music paper as heading a 'spiv rock' wave… and with everyone looking for the next big post-punk thing, the buzz was considerable. Jackson and his three-piece backing band did not disappoint, combining taut Police/Costello-style pop with lyrical rants against the tabloid press – **Sunday Paper**, marriage – **Happy Loving Couples**, and more. Twenty years on, Jackson was back playing classical music.

This is ready made New Wave, saved from the accusation of irrelevance by Joe's tough-but-tender singing, reggae influenced band sound that never gets crowded and the hand-wringing anomie that the songwriter's love life (or lack of it) has inspired in him. **Fred Schruers, Rolling Stone, December 1979**

Los Angeles

ARTIST X **RELEASE DATE** June 1980 **LABEL** Slash **PRODUCER** Ray Manzerek **UK CHART** peak/weeks - **US CHART** peak/weeks 0/0 **TRACK LISTING** Your Phone's Off The Hook, But You're Not/Johnny Hit And Run Pauline/Soul Kitchen/Nausea/Sugarlight/Los Angeles/Sex And Dying In High Society/The Unheard Music/The World's A Mess, It's In My Kiss **PERSONNEL** Exene Cervenka (v), Billy Zoom (g), John Doe (b, v), D. J. Bonebrake (d)

As the London and New York punk scenes were fading, Los Angeles threw up the critically lauded X, led by husband and wife team John Doe and Exene Cervenka. Debut album **Los Angeles**, produced by Ray Manzarek of the Doors, was more complex, musically, than basic punk, betraying the players' roots in rockabilly, rock 'n' roll and country, while the lyrics were more sophisticated than the bog-standard nihilism exhibited by most New Wave noiseniks.

Los Angeles is so committed to today that tomorrow it might be out of date. To be level with X they obviously don't worry about anything as mundane as tailoring their material to include entertainment value… loud, obnoxious, ordinarily arcane. **Max Bell, NME, July 1980**

Lotus

ARTIST Santana **RELEASE DATE** December 1974 **LABEL** CBS (UK)/Columbia (US) **PRODUCER** Santana **UK CHART** peak/weeks 0/0 **US CHART** peak/weeks 0/0 **TRACK LISTING** Meditation/Going Home/A-1 Funk/Every Step Of The Way/Black Magic Woman - Gypsy Queen/Oye Como Va/Yours Is The Light/Batuka/Xibaba (She-Ba-Ba)/Savor/Stone Flower/(Introduction)/Castillos De Arena (Part 1)/Waiting/Se A Cabo/Samba Pa Ti/Toussaint L'Overture/Incident At Neshabur **PERSONNEL** Carlos Santana (g), Gregg Rolie (k, v), David Brown (b), Mike Shrieve (d), Jose 'Cheoito' Areas (pc), Mike Carabello (cg) Tom Frazer (g)

A triple album featuring 22 tracks, this live set was released in Japan in 1974 but remained unavailable in America until 1991. Bearing the influence of Miles Davis' **Bitches Brew**, **Lotus** highlights the band's propensity for long, intense jams and aggressive musicianship, notably Carlos Santana's blazing guitar playing. As Eric Clapton once reputedly said, 'For pure spirituality and emotion, Carlos Santana is number one.'

Musically, the albums do present the best ever Santana band… Unless you feel that you can't live without **Lotus***, or that if you buy it you need never buy another Santana album, I'd settle for the next genuinely current recording…* **Max Bell, NME, September 1976**

Love

ARTIST The Cult **RELEASE DATE** December 1985 **LABEL** Beggar's Banquet (UK)/Sire (US) **PRODUCER** – **UK CHART** peak/weeks 4/22 **US CHART** peak/weeks 87/34 **TRACK LISTING** Nirvana/She Sells Sanctuary/Rain/Black Angel/Love/The Hollow Man/Revolution/Big Neon Glitter/The Phoenix/Brother Wolf, Sister Moon **PERSONNEL** Ian Astbury (v), Mark Brzezicki (d), Billy Duffy (g), Jamie Stewart (b)

Metamorphosing from Bradford Goth rockers Southern Death Cult, these eventual stadium heavies still carried an air of American Indian and Aboriginal mysticism as they hurled themselves into shameless power-riffing, dominated by the pile-driving guitars of ex-Theatre Of Hate man Billy Duffy. Singer Ian Astbury gave them a bleary charisma and a time-honoured full-blooded vocal whine-cum-roar. **She Sells Sanctuary**, with its memorable motifs, gave them their breakthrough hit, and the **Love** album neatly interweaved indie and psychedelia. The epic sprawling **Brother Wolf, Sister Moon** met with derision from critics: The Cult got their revenge by going even heavier, and America-friendly, on the logical extension of their next album, **Electric**.

The Cult have strayed too far into the realm of the ridiculous to irk or annoy. One false move and it's parody. As it is, it's just grotesque… No, you don't need **Love***.* **William Leith, NME, October 1985**

Love Bites

ARTIST Buzzcocks **RELEASE DATE** September 1978 (UK & US) **LABEL** United Artists (UK)/IRS (US) **PRODUCER** Pete Shelley, Howard Devoto **UK CHART** peak/weeks 13/9 **US CHART** peak/weeks 0/0 **TRACK LISTING** Real World/Ever Fallen In Love With Someone You Shouldn't/Operator's Manuel/Nostalgia/Just Lust/Sixteen Again/Walking Distance/Love Is Lies/Nothing Left/E.S.P./Late For The Train. **PERSONNEL** Howard Devoto (v), Pete Shelley (g, v), Steve Diggle (b, v), John Maher (d)

The Mancunians' second burst of in-a-hurry punk-pop encouraged input from all four members, and while it still boasted Shelley's mastery of three-minute failed romantics Bibles, it also tried on some longer, more instrumentally involved, muso workouts. With Steve Diggle's guitar almost as elementally visceral as Shelley's, this never resulted in prog-rock: rather, in stabs of concise sonic statement which perhaps the more highly praised Clash could have benefited from. The sardonic waggishness and sense of wonder at love of Shelley's lyrics added an extra smile-inducing, edge.

Love Bites is rammed with wingy-wangy guitar over perfect poppy-punk. **Carl Loben, Melody Maker, April 1994**

Love Is The Thing

ARTIST Nat 'King' Cole **RELEASE DATE** April 1957 (US) **LABEL** Capitol (US) **PRODUCER** Arranged by Gordon Jenkins **UK CHART** peak/weeks – **US CHART** peak/weeks 1/94 **TRACK LISTING** When I Fall In Love/Stardust/Stay As Sweet As You Are/Where Can I Go Without You/Maybe It's Because I Love You Too Much/Love Letters/Ain't Misbehavin'/I Thought About Marie/At Last/It's All In The Game/When Sunny Gets Blue/Love Is The Thing **PERSONNEL** Nat 'King' Cole (v), with the orchestra of Gordon Jenkins

Cole transcended genre boundaries as well as racial ones. It's easy to forget now that he initially came to prominence as a jazz pianist, influencing even Oscar Peterson, before gracing us with his silky-smooth baritone and relaxed, overtly content demeanour. Settling on a form of pop-jazz, which sold him millions of records and made many eternal easier-than-easy favourites, he had just enjoyed great acclaim and success with the **After Midnight** sessions when he released this, his initial foray into the court of the great American popular song. Truly unforgettable.

A change of pace would have livened things up. **Melody Maker, June 1957**

Love Over Gold

ARTIST Dire Straits **RELEASE DATE** September 1982 (UK & US) **LABEL** Vertigo (UK)/Warner Bros (US) **PRODUCER** Mark Knopfler **UK CHART** peak/weeks 1/198 **US CHART** peak/weeks 19/32 **TRACK LISTING** Telegraph Road/Private Investigations/Industrial Disease/Love Over Gold/It Never Rains/If I Had You/Twisting By The Pool/Two Young Lovers/Badges, Posters, Stickers, T-Shirts **PERSONNEL** Mark Knopfler (g, v), John Illsley (b), Pick Withers (d), Alan Clark (k)

The Straits' fourth album and their first UK chart-topper, was the last to feature original drummer Pick Withers, who would be replaced by ex-Man sticksman Terry Williams. It was boosted by the unusually long seven-minute single *Private Investigations*, which stalled at Number 2 behind *Eye Of The Tiger*, but included an even longer showcase for Mark Knopfler's guitar in the 14-minute *Telegraph Road*. Yet the song they could not fit on, 'Private Dancer', would prove a huge hit for Tina Turner three years later.

Although still secure in his own ability, and still possessed of a superlatively easy touch, Knopfler sounds like a man who knows great things are expected of him… the continuity has gone, and suddenly they're staggering under the weight of commercial expectations, trying to make Art. **Phil McNeill, NME, October 1982**

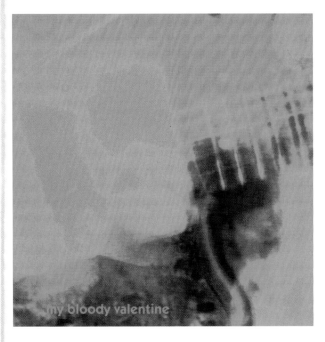

Love Songs

ARTIST Barbra Streisand **RELEASE DATE** January 1982 (UK & US) **LABEL** CBS (UK)/Columbia (US) **PRODUCER** – **UK CHART** peak/weeks 1/129 **US CHART** peak/weeks **TRACK LISTING** Memory/You Don't Bring Me Flowers/My Heart Belongs To Me/Wet/New York State Of Mind/A Man I Loved/No More Tears (Enough Is Enough)/Comin' In And Out Of Your Life/Evergreen (Love Theme From 'A Star Is Born')/I Don't Break Easily/Kiss Me In The Rain/Lost Inside Of You/The Love Inside/The Way We Were **PERSONNEL** Barbra Streisand (v), Neil Diamond (v, gst), Donna Summer (v, gst), session musicians

By 1981, the versatile Streisand had dabbled in pop-rock, covering the songs of Laura Nyro and Jimmy Webb; she had duetted with contemporary Lotharics Neil Diamond and Barry Gibb of the Bee Gees; and she had experimented with disco, on the collaboration with Donna Summer, *No More Tears (Enough Is Enough)*. The Summer and Diamond tunes feature on **Love Songs**, as do two of her signature ballads, both from Streisand movie vehicles, *The Way We Were* and *Evergreen* (The Love Theme from *A Star Is Born*), co-written by Streisand and Paul Williams.

Loveless

ARTIST My Bloody Valentine **RELEASE DATE** April 1991 (UK & US) **LABEL** Creation (UK & US) **PRODUCER** K. Shields, C. O'Ciosoig **UK CHART** peak/weeks 24/2 **US CHART** peak/weeks 0/0 **TRACK LISTING** Only Shallow/Loomer/Touched/To Here Knows When/When You Sleep/I Only Said/Come In Alone/Sometimes/Blown A Wish/What You Want/Soon **PERSONNEL** Colm O'Ciosoig (d), Bilinda Butcher (v, g), Debbie Googe (b), Kevin Shields (g, v)

When an album credits 18 different engineers, it's fair to suggest they have used rather more studios than the average indie band. But **Loveless**, which followed MBV's acclaimed debut by three years, was worth the wait: an amazing selection of samples and instrumentation transforming their music from their 'shoegazing' roots to a higher plane. But switching from Creation to Island saw them setting up their own studio, and an even longer period would ensue before anything else was heard.

What gives the band their undeniable edge is their murky, muggy sensuality – imagine that still-dreaming feeling when you first wake up – which seeps through to the vocals…. The rock-is-dead argument could very well stop here. **Martin Aston, Q, January 1992**

Loving You

ARTIST Elvis Presley RELEASE DATE October 1977 (UK & US) LABEL RCA (UK & US) PRODUCER Ernst Michael Jorgensen, Roger Semon UK CHART peak/weeks 24/3 US CHART peak/weeks 1/29 TRACK LISTING Kiss Me Quick/Just For Old Time Sake/Gonna Get Back Home Somehow/(Such An) Easy Question/Steppin' Out Of Line/I'm Yours/Something Blue/Suspicion/I Feel That I've Known You Forever/Night Rider/Fountain Of Love/That's Someone You Never Forget PERSONNEL Scotty Moore (g), Bill Black (b, d),Gordan Stroker (bv), Hoyt Hawkins (bv), Neal Matthews (bv), Hugh Garrett (bv)

With side one containing all seven songs from Elvis's second film, plus five early 1957 recordings on the flip, this album became the fastest-rising Presley album to date when it shot from Number 11 to Number 1 in the *Billboard* listings. The film went through several titles, including *The Lonesome Cowboy* and *Running Wild*, before coming up with *Loving You*. Presley's character, Deke Rivers, so entranced young Welsh teenager Roger Leonard that he appropriated his Christian name: the guitarist fronted Man 40 years on!

Elvis stares broodingly from the coloured sleeve and inside are packed eight numbers from his film Loving You. *Elvis scores best with the beat numbers* **Mean Woman Blues** *… but his admirers will find no faults with the rest.* **Laurie Hernshaw, Pop Discs, Melody Maker, August 1957**

Low

ARTIST David Bowie RELEASE DATE January 1977 (UK & US) LABEL RCA (UK & US) PRODUCER David Bowie, Tony Visconti. UK CHART peak/weeks 2/18 US CHART peak/weeks 11/9 TRACK LISTING Speed Of Life/Breaking Glass/What In The World/Sound And Vision/Always Crashing In The Same Car/Be My Wife/A New Career In A New Town/Warszawa/Art Decade/Weeping Wall/Subterraneans PERSONNEL David Bowie (v), Tony Visconti (b), Mick Ronson (g), John Cambridge (d)

The first of three studio albums made in Berlin with Brian Eno, where again Bowie dared his fans to take a leap of faith: this time into experimental minimalist ambience. Reportedly heavily into cocaine and all manner of very-Berlin decadence, he made an image of no image, and an album of beguiling and frosty mystery. The short sharp shocks of Side One – the ambiguous *Be My Wife* and forlorn *Always Crashing In The Same Car* – gave way to a second side of unprecedented atmospheric brooding. The album was incontestably influential and Bowie even squeezed a hit, *Sound And Vision*, from it.

Low serves as a moderately interesting conduit through which a wider audience will be exposed to Bowie's latest heroes, and in this sense is an interesting addition to his recorded catalog. **John Milward, Rolling Stone, April 1977**

Low Spark Of High Heeled Boys

ARTIST Traffic RELEASE DATE December 1971 (UK & US) LABEL Island Records (UK & US) PRODUCER Steve Winwood UK CHART peak/weeks 0/0 US CHART peak/weeks 7/30 TRACK LISTING Hidden Tresure/The Low Spark Of The High Heeled Boys/Rock And Roll Stew/Many A Mile To Freedom/Light Up Or Leave Me Alone/Rainmaker PERSONNEL Steve Winwood (v, k), Dave Mason (g, v), Jim Capaldi (d, v), Chris Wood (fl, s), James Gordon (d), Rebop Kwaku Baah (con)

Traffic's ability to stretch out and doodle on their instruments was best demonstrated on their fifth album, a triumph of improvisation and dexterous fretwork, one that earned a gold disc for sales in the States. The title cut of *The Low Spark Of High-Heeled Boys* addressed, over 12 minutes, the problems incurred by successful bands faced with armies of adoring fans, although, for some, Traffic's penchant for the extended 'jam' was getting too much.

In the past, when you heard a Traffic recording… you were bound to gain new perceptions about how well music can be played and put together. **The Low Spark of High-Heeled Boys** *is no exception.* **David Lubin, Rolling Stone, January 1972**

Lucky 13 Shades Of Val Doonican

ARTIST Val Doonican RELEASE DATE December 1964 LABEL Decca PRODUCER – UK CHART peak/weeks 2/27 US CHART peak/weeks 0/0 TRACK LISTING – PERSONNEL Val Doonican (v)

Making his way into the TV entertainment field via radio, Doonican and his unthreatening image – a smiling Irish singer, sweater-clad in a rocking chair – was tailor-made for the pre-rock generation. The MOR 'country and Irish' torch has been picked up today by the likes of Daniel O'Donnell, but Doonican's wry self-mocking humour evidenced on some of these tracks are closer to Terry Wogan – the radio connection?

Lust For Life

ARTIST Iggy Pop RELEASE DATE September 1977 (UK & US) LABEL RCA (UK & US) PRODUCER David Bowie UK CHART peak/weeks 28/5 US CHART peak/weeks 120/6 TRACK LISTING Lust For Life/Sixteen/Some Weird Sin/The Passenger/Tonight/Success/Turn Blue/Neighbourhood Threat/Fall In Love With Me PERSONNEL Iggy Pop (v), David Bowie (p), Carlos Alomar (g), Ricky Gardiner (g), Hunt Sales (d), Tony Sales (b)

Along with its Bowie-produced predecessor **The Idiot,** released the same year and 1978's live **TV Eye,** Iggy enjoyed no fewer than three splashes of stardust from Ziggy, and this, the title track of which entertained a new generation when extracted for use in

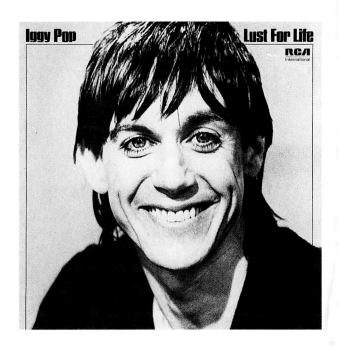

Trainspotting, was as worthy as any. Optimism only interrupted by the drug OD nightmare of **Turn Blue**, it set the blueprint for a series of Arista label releases that divided this and his next encounter with Bowie in 1986 for **Blah Blah Blah**.

Lust for Life was finished completely after a mere two-and-a-half-weeks in the studio. Iggy stayed on to work when everyone else had gone home because he wanted the record to be his not David Bowie's. **Tony Parsons, NME, September 1977**

Machine Head

ARTIST Deep Purple RELEASE DATE April 1972 (UK & US) LABEL Purple (UK)/Warner (US) PRODUCER Deep Purple UK CHART peak/weeks 1/24 US CHART peak/weeks 7/118 TRACK LISTING Highway Star/Maybe I'm A Leo/Pictures Of Home/Never Before/Smoke On The Water/Lazy/Space Truckin' PERSONNEL Ritchie Blackmore (g), Ian Gillan (v), Roger Glover (b), Jon Lord (k), Ian Paice (d)

Deep Purple's third studio album with their definitive line-up was to be recorded in Montreux, Switzerland, in a mobile studio. But the intended venue, the Casino, was burned down after an accident with a flare gun so recording took place in the Grand Hotel. The whole episode was recounted in **Smoke On The Water**, a hit US single and probably one of the most played tracks by would-be guitarists anywhere. A 1997 25th anniversary reissue included a bonus disc of remixes by bassist Roger Glover.

On first hearing, it might seem that Purple are indeed a machine-like band, who play rather obvious riffs without much soul. But probe a little deeper. The band actually play a lot looser and with more feel than many similar heavy rock outfits. **C. W., Melody Maker, April 1972**

Mad Not Bad

ARTIST Madness RELEASE DATE October 1985 (UK & US) LABEL Zarjazz (UK)/Virgin (US) PRODUCER Clive Langer, Alan Winstanley UK CHART peak/weeks 16/9 US CHART peak/weeks 0/0 TRACK LISTING I'll Compete/Yesterday's Men/Uncle Sam/White Heat/Mad Not Bad/Sweetest Girl/Burning The Boats/Tears You Can't Hide/Time/Coldest Day PERSONNEL Suggs (v), Mike Barson (k), 'Chrissie Boy' Foreman (g), 'Bedders' (b), Lee 'Kix' Thompson (s, v), 'Woody' Woodgate (d), Chas Smash (hn)

By the time Madness made this their first LP release on their own

label, Zarjazz, they had long since matured from the 'nutty' ska beginnings into a Kinks/Squeeze-style pop group of class and quality. All the more surprising that the single **Uncle Sam** should have attempted to wind back the musical clock. It became the first of 21 to miss the Top 20 completely. The preceding **Yesterday's Men** was more typical, while a cover of Scritti Politti's **Sweetest Girl** betrayed how much they missed keyboardist-songwriter Mike Barson, who moved to Holland in 1983. A split soon followed.

For a proper sense of the nation's increasing entropic state you'd do better to listen to a Madness song. No one else in popular music is presently reading Britain's physiognomy so accurately. **Biba Kopf, NME, October 1985**

The Madcap Laughs

ARTIST Syd Barrett RELEASE DATE January 1970 (UK & US) LABEL Harvest (UK & US) PRODUCER Roger Waters, Malcom Jones, David Gilmour UK CHART peak/weeks 40/1 US CHART peak/weeks 163/4 TRACK LISTING Terrapin/No Good Trying/Love Tou/No Man's Land/Dark Globe/Here I Go/Octopus/ Golden Hair/Long Gone/She Took A Long Cold Look/Feel/If It's In You/Late Night. PERSONNEL Syd Barret(v, g), Mike Ratledge (k), Hugh Hopper (b), Robert Wyatt (d), John Willie Watson & Jerry Shirley (r)

The idiosyncratic Pink Floyd founder refused to go quietly: his solo work was honest and exposed, revealing a troubled soul and a drug-induced paranoia. Complete with false openings and botched changes, this was tortured art to true believers and unlistenable to others. Yet David Gilmour's production reined the maverick in for some dotty songs which influenced an array of artists from Marc Bolan to Julian Cope. The crazy diamond's solo debut took a year to bring even to this state: the octopus was in his mind. He became a reclusive painter, but his legend was perpetuated by the jobbing Floyd.

Syd has been through some tough times since he formed Pink Floyd and disappeared. Now his old colleagues Dave Gilmour and Roger Waters have helped him produce a fine solo album… representing the Barrett mind unleashed. **Melody Maker, January 1970**

Made In Heaven

ARTIST Queen RELEASE DATE November 1995 (UK and US) LABEL Parlophone (UK)/Hollywood (US) PRODUCER Queen UK CHART peak/weeks 1/- US CHART peak/weeks 58/11 TRACK LISTING It's A Beautiful Day/Made In Heaven/Let Me Live/Mother Love/My Life Has Been Saved/I Was Born To Love You/ Heaven For Everyone/Too Much Love Will Kill You/You Don't Fool Me/ A Winter's Tale/It's A Beautiful Day (Reprise) PERSONNEL Freddie Mercury (v, p, k), John Deacon (b, k), Roger Taylor (d, pc, k, v), Brian May (g, k, v)

Queen had returned to their hard-rock roots, leavened with not a little humour, as the Nineties began. But it was clear from **The Show Must Go On** on 1991's **Innuendo** that singer Freddie Mercury was preparing to take his final curtain. He went on recording right up to his Aids-related death late that year, and the results were patched together for this swansong. Notable was the 17-minute final track, **A Winter's Tale**, while young film makers were commissioned to make videos for the single **Heaven For Everyone** – a retread from a Taylor solo album. Not a classic, but a fond farewell.

…consistent with the ongoing programme entitled Freddie: The Remake. He's now perceived as being warm, selfless and tragic – his physicality quite literally replaced on the cover by a bronze statue giving a straight-arm salute. Lovely… vulgar, creepy, sickly and in dubious taste. Freddie would have loved it. **Stuart Bailie, NME, November 1995**

Made In Japan

ARTIST Deep Purple **RELEASE DATE** December 1972 (UK)/April 1973 (US) **LABEL** Purple (UK)/Warner (US) **PRODUCER** Deep Purple **UK CHART** peak/weeks 16/14 **US CHART** peak/weeks 6/52 **TRACK LISTING** Highway Star Osaka - 6th August 1972/Child In Time Osaka-16th August 1972/Smoke On The Water Osaka - 15th August 1972/The Mule Tokyo - 17th August 1972/Strange Kind Of Woman Osaka - 16th August 1972/Lazy Tokyo - 17th August 1972/Space Truckin' Osaka - 16th August 1972 **PERSONNEL** Ritchie Blackmore (g), Ian Gillan (v), Roger Glover (b), Jon Lord (k), Ian Paice (d)

Live albums are rarely definitive, but Purple's 1972 concert double not only proved a landmark in hard rock but inspired a spate of similar *Unleashed in the East* efforts, few of which came close. Concerts in Tokyo and Osaka were welded together to produce a flawless riff-fest, originally intended for Japanese consumption, but import sales caused their next studio release to be pushed back the best part of a year! The entire concerts emerged in 1993 on a triple-CD set for those who had not headbanged enough over the two intervening decades.

Deep Purple is a tried-and-true Seventies group that has proven itself time and time again, a favourite of many a serious musician. **Jon Tiven, Rolling Stone, May 1973**

Magical Mystery Tour

ARTIST The Beatles **RELEASE DATE** December 1967 (UK & US) **LABEL** Parlophone (UK)/Capitol (US) **PRODUCER** George Martin **UK CHART** peak/weeks 31/2 **US CHART** peak/weeks 1/91 **TRACK LISTING** Magical Mystery Tour/The Fool On The Hill/Flying/Blue Jay Way/Your Mother Should Know/I Am The Walrus/Hello Goodbye/Strawberry Fields Forever/Penny Lane/Baby You're A Rich Man/All You Need Is Love **PERSONNEL** John Lennon (v, g), Paul McCartney (v, g), George Harrison (v, lg), Ringo Starr (d)

A kind of **Sgt. Pepper**: the out-takes grab-bag, this ride rescued *Penny Lane* and *Strawberry Fields Forever* from those sessions. Indeed the pair made an unorthodox double A-side (the group's first single since 1962 not to make Number 1: Engelbert Humperdinck's *Release Me* did the damage). *I Am The Walrus* further showed off Lennon's burgeoning 'visionary' lyrical preoccupation, while *Hello Goodbye*, *The Fool On The Hill* and the definitively anthemic *All You Need Is Love* weren't exactly throwaway fillers.

'Records can't be seen so it's good to have a film of some sort to go with the new music.' **John Lennon in article by Susan Lydon, Rolling Stone, December 1967**

Make It Big

ARTIST Wham! **RELEASE DATE** November 1984 (UK & US) **LABEL** Epic (UK)/Columbia (US) **PRODUCER** George Michael **UK CHART** peak/weeks 1/72 **US CHART** peak/weeks 1/80 **TRACK LISTING** Wake Me Up Before You Go-Go/Everything She Wants/Heartbeat/Like A Baby/Freedom/If You Were There/Credit Card Baby/Careless Whisper **PERSONNEL** George Michael (v, b), Andrew Ridgley (g, k), session musicians

Wham! were that rarity: a teeny-bop duo who combined commercial success and critical acclaim. The presence of George Michael helped. More than just some teen-dream himbo in tennis shorts, Michael had been reared on the piano-led song structures of Elton John and clearly knew a thing or two about how to contrive a perfect pop song. Like Duran Duran's **Rio** and Spandau Ballet's **True**, **Make It Big** featured so many infectious dance-pop delights, such as the ingenious Motown pastiches, *Wake Me Up Before You Go Go* and *Freedom*, that even hardened rockers found it difficult to resist. As for the ballads, *Careless Whisper* and *Everything She Wants*, they hinted quite strongly that Michael would be able to survive without hapless partner in rhyme Andrew Ridgeley.

How will we, in time, judge the pop music being made today?… And what, then, of Wham!, currently Britain's most popular group and the most reviled!… I doubt if the music will last. It's too synthetic and transparent. **Paolo Hewitt, NME, November 1984**

Make Way

ARTIST The Kingston Trio **RELEASE DATE** May 1959 **LABEL** Capitol **PRODUCER** – **UK CHART** peak/weeks 0/0 **US CHART** peak/weeks 1/39 **TRACK LISTING** – **PERSONNEL** –

Released in May 1959, this was the prolific Kingston Trio's fourth album inside 12 months. As before, it contained the usual eclectic mix of old and new material. Complementing such traditional songs as *Scarlet Ribbons* and *All My Sorrows* was the amusing original number 'MTA', which provided the Trio with their third US Top 20 single. This was late Fifties, pre-Dylan folk music, which owed as much to the close harmony singing of the Four Freshmen as it did the protest songs of Woody Guthrie. The formula worked, however, and earned the group their first Number 1 album.

Making Movies

ARTIST Dire Straits **RELEASE DATE** October 1980 (UK & US) **LABEL** Vertigo (UK)/Warner Bros (US) **PRODUCER** Jimmy Iovine **UK CHART** peak/weeks 4/249 **US CHART** peak/weeks 19/31 **TRACK LISTING** Tunnel Of Love/Romeo And Juliet/Skateaway/Expresso Love/Hand In Hand/Solid Rock/Less Boys **PERSONNEL** Mark Knopfler (g, v), John Illsley (b), Terry Williams (d), Alan Clark (k)

While the first two Straits albums featured guitar-sparring siblings Mark and David Knopfler, the younger man's departure for a low-key solo career left Mark in sole charge. And while American Hal Lindes was recruited to restore parity, it was the impact of the keyboards that broadened the Dire Straits sound – Springsteen sideman Roy Bittan among those contributing in that area. *Romeo And Juliet* was the key cut, a transatlantic hit that finally and successfully followed up *Sultans Of Swing*.

The nine months off the road haven't diminished the fire of Mark Knopfler's writing: the quality is as high as ever. The Straits' way of doing things may not be the usual way – but who's complaining. **Michael Oldfield, Melody Maker, October 1980**

Mama Said

ARTIST Lenny Kravitz **RELEASE DATE** April 1991 (UK & US) **LABEL** Virgin America (UK)/Virgin (US) **PRODUCER** Lenny Kravitz **UK CHART** peak/weeks 8/27 **US CHART** peak/weeks 39/40 **TRACK LISTING** Fields Of Joy/Always On The Run/Stand By My Woman/It Ain't Over 'Til It's Over/More Than Anything In This World/What Goes Around Comes Around/The Difference Is Why/Stop Draggin' Around/Flowers For Zoe/Fields Of Joy (Reprise)/All I Ever Wanted/When The Morning Turns To Night/What The . . . . Are We Saying?/Butterfly **PERSONNEL** Lenny Kravitz (v, g, p, b, d), with a few on session, Henry Hirsch (k), Karl Densen (S)

Permeated by the heartbreak of his split from actress wife Lisa Bonet, most notably the hit single *It Ain't Over Till It's Over*, New York-born Kravitz found huge home-country success with a second album that broadened the musical base of his Sixties-fixated debut **Let Love Rule** but lost none of the zeal. Its success would attract the likes of Madonna, Aerosmith and Jagger to beat a path to his door, but by his 1993 third album Kravitz had lost his sure touch and seemed happy to ape Hendrix.

… he's not soft, he's sussed right down to the socks he never wears and… full of 'positivity'. **Mama Said** *is a 14-track holiday – and even at give-away recession prices still cheaper than a week in Majorca.* **Phil Sutcliffe, Q, May 1991**

Mama Said Knock You Out

ARTIST L.L. Cool J **RELEASE DATE** October 1990 (UK)/August 1990 (US) **LABEL** Def Jam (UK)/Columbia (US) **PRODUCER** L.L. Cool J, Marley Marl **UK CHART** peak/weeks 49/2 **US CHART** peak/weeks 16/76 **TRACK LISTING** The Boomin' System/Around The Way Girl/Eat Em Up L Chill/Mr Good Bar/Mordergram (Live at Rapmania)/Cheesy Rat Blues/Farmers Blud (Our Anthem)/Mama Said Knock You Out/Milky Cereal/Jingling Baby (Remixed But Still Jingling)/To Da Break Of Dawn/6 Minutes of Pleasure/Illegal Search/The Power of God **PERSONNEL** L.L. Cool J (v, rap), Darren Lighty (k, bv), Flex (bv), Eric Williams (bv)

Five years on from **Radio** and L.L. Cool J was still a big star, aided by numerous acting appearances, a couple of anti-drugs performances and steadily selling albums. There were those within the rap community who resented his success, but L.L. always seemed to have the last word. With the success of **Mama Said** he got to have quite a few last words as well, one or two that revealed his views on the state of rap past, present and future. L.L. Cool J obviously saw himself having a say and a role in all three.

L.L. … obliges big time with producer Marley Marl's steely, stripped-back beats and his own verbal fisticuffs on the likes of **Eat Em Up L Chill** *… L.L. also cooks up quality New Jack for the ladies, with the sassy gab and slinky rhythm of* **Around The Way Girl**. … **The Year In Records 1991, Rolling Stone, December 1991**

The Man Machine

ARTIST Kraftwerk **RELEASE DATE** May 1978 (UK & US) **LABEL** Capitol (UK & US) **PRODUCER** Ralf Hütter **UK CHART** peak/weeks 9/13 **US CHART** peak/weeks 130/9 **TRACK LISTING** The Robots/Spacelab/Metropolis/The Model/Neon Lights/The Man-Machine **PERSONNEL** Ralf Hütter (v, e), Florien Schneider (v, e), Karl Bartos (ep), Wolfgang Flur (ep)

Having created an album that promoted the superiority of machines over their human makers, Düsseldorf's Kraftwerk scored a surprise UK chart-topper in *The Model* – but only three years after the album's release, by which time the world was catching up with them. Many electro-pop acts, from the Human League to Orchestral Manoeuvres in the Dark and Gary Numan owe much to this groundbreaking six-tracker, which sold over 100,000 copies in Britain alone and was entitled **Mensch Maschine** in the band's home country.

The Man Machine *stands as one of the pinnacles of Seventies rock music, and one which… I doubt Kraftwerk will ever surpass. You will buy it, or be deemed mentally unstable.* **Andy Gill, NME, April 1978**

The Man Who Sold The World

ARTIST David Bowie RELEASE DATE April 1971 (UK)/November 1970 (US) LABEL Mercury (UK & US) PRODUCER Tony Visconti UK CHART peak/weeks 26/22 US CHART peak/weeks 105/23 TRACK LISTING The Width Of A Circle/All The Madmen/Black Country Rock/After All/Running Gun Blues/Saviour Machine/She Shook Me Cold/The Man Who Sold The World/The Supermen PERSONNEL David Bowie (v, g), Tony Visconti (b, p, g), Mick Ronson (g), Mick Woodmansey (d), Ralph Mace (sy)

With *Space Oddity*, Bowie had begun to make his first of a multitude of subsequent transitions, from folky minstrel with Anthony Newley inflections to cosmic visionary. Now he strapped on some hard rock, with Tony Visconti's peculiar but compelling bass-heavy production bringing out the beast in the band. *The Width Of A Circle* was a sprawling theatrical epic; *After All* was a sad fairground requiem. Elsewhere though, Bowie kicked ass with an unselfconscious abandon not seen again till the ill-fated *Tin Machine* project. The title song was later adapted by, surreally, Lulu, then later on by Nirvana.

It's a heavy rock album par excellence: indeed, on most of the tracks… Bowie and his men beat Sabbath at their own game with the sheer density of the white-hot guitar, stomach-churning bass and pneumatic-drill drumming… **A. L., Melody Maker, November 1972**

Marcus Garvey

ARTIST Burning Spear RELEASE DATE November 1975 (UK & US) LABEL Island (UK)/Mango (US) PRODUCER Jack Ruby UK CHART peak/weeks 0/0 US CHART peak/weeks 0/0 TRACK LISTING Marcus Garvey/On Slavery Days/Invasion/Live Good/Give Me/Old Marcus Garvey/Tradition/Jordan River/Red, Gold And Green/Resting Place PERSONNEL Delroy Hines (v), Robbie Shakespeare, Aston Barrett (b), Tony Chin, Earl 'Chinna' Smith (g), Bernard Touter Harvey (k), Leroy 'Horsemouth' Wallace (d), Winston Rodney (v), session musicians

Bob Marley may have taken it to the masses, but Burning Spear looked deeper INTO reggae, and raised its level of consciousness. Winston Rodney's sub-sonic voice was mesmeric and vaguely threatening, but also mournful. *On Slavery Days*, the refrain of 'do you remember the days of slavery?' is hugely effective in its dry simplicity. Burning Spear insisted that the lessons of history should not be forgotten. Rodney had taken his name from Kenyan independence fighter Jomo Kenyatta, although he was often referred to as 'The Spear'. As for Marcus Garvey, he was to become a recurring symbol in later releases.

Rodney and Ruby have collaborated on producing the heaviest, most uncompromising roots music around – stuff that makes most of the current dub craze look the way it is: a little too light-headed. **Ian MacDonald, NME, November 1975**

Maria Muldaur

ARTIST Maria Muldaur RELEASE DATE September 1973 (UK & US) LABEL WEA (UK)/Reprise (US) PRODUCER Lenny Waronker, Joe Boyd UK CHART peak/weeks 0/0 US CHART peak/weeks 3/56 TRACK LISTING Any Old Time/Long Hard Climb/I Never Did Sing You A Love Song/Mad Mad Me/My Tennessee Mountain Home/The Work Song/Vaudeville Man/Walkin' One And Only/Midnight At The Oasis/Don't You Feel My Leg (Don't Get Me High)/Three Dollar Bill PERSONNEL Maria Muldaur (v), Amos Garrett (ag), Andrew Gold (ag), David Lynley (g), Jim Keltner (d), Dave Holland (b), Mac Rebennack (p), Jim Gordon (cl, o), session musicians

The Brand New Heavies' reworking of *Midnight At The Oasis*, this album's standout track, over two decades after its 1974 success, proved the former Jim Kweskin Jug band vocalist was ahead of her time. By the time it came round again, Muldaur (born Maria D'Amato) had turned to inspirational material…so songs like *Don't You Feel My Leg* were, presumably, not now part of the repertoire! Guitarist Amos Garrett based his subsequent career on his *Oasis* solo, while Muldar's next album fell 20 places short of this glorious effort– hardly an answer to prayer!

Maria Muldour's art is mature, sophisticated, sensual and wise. She moves among the genres of jazz, Dixieland, jug band, country, pop and rock… as if they were flowers in a garden each worthy of her tenderest loving care. **Jon Landau, Rolling Stone, September 1973**

Mariah Carey

ARTIST Mariah Carey RELEASE DATE September 1990 (UK)/June 1990 (US) LABEL CBS (UK)/Columbia (US) PRODUCER Narada Michael Walden, Rhett Lawrence, Ric Wake, Mariah Carey, Ben Margulies, Walter Afanasieff UK CHART peak/weeks 6/36 US CHART peak/weeks 1/113 TRACK LISTING Vision of Love/There's Got To Be A Way/I Don't Wanna Cry/Someday/Vanishing/All In Your Mind/Alone In Love/You Need Me/Sent From Up Above/Prisoner/Love Takes Time PERSONNEL Mariah Carey (v, bv), Nile Rogers (g), Omar Hakim (d), Jimmy Rip (g), Vernon Ice Black (g), Rich Tancredi (k), Billy T. Scott Ensemble (bv), Jamiliah Muhammed (bv), Narada Michael Walden (d), Chris Camozzi (ag, g), Bob Cadway (g), Richard Tee (p), David Williams (d), Michael Landau (g), Ben Margulies (d, dp), Ren Klyce (dp), Rhett Lawrence (k), Joe Franco (pc, dp), Louis Biancaniello (k, b, dp), Ric Wake (dp), Walter 'Babylove' Afanasieff (k, dp, syh, syb)

With the mega-smash and Grammy-winner *Vision Of Love*, overnight sensation Mariah Carey – coincidentally then married

Marquee Moon

ARTIST Television RELEASE DATE February 1977 (UK & US) LABEL Electra (UK & US) PRODUCER Andy Johns, Tom Verlaine UK CHART peak/weeks 28/13 US CHART peak/weeks 0/0 TRACK LISTING See No Evil/Venus/Friction/Marquee Moon/Elevation/Guiding Light/Prove It/Torn Curtain PERSONNEL Tom Verlaine (v, g), Richard Lloyd (g, v), Fred Smith (b, v), Billy Ficca (d)

Unarguably the most ambitious, innovative rock album to emerge from New York's CBGBs scene, **Marquee Moon** is the **Sgt. Pepper** of post-punk guitar-pop. At a time when brevity and simplicity were the watchwords, **Marquee Moon** featured long, complex instrumental interludes, notably from duelling twin lead guitarists Tom Verlaine and Richard Lloyd, and Verlaine's unfathomable poetic lyrics. Epic in scope they may be, nevertheless tracks like the near 10-minute title song never outstay their welcome.

Maxinquaye

ARTIST Tricky RELEASE DATE February 1995 (UK & US) LABEL 4th & Broad (UK & US) PRODUCER Tricky, Mark Saunders, Kevin Petre, Howie B UK CHART peak/weeks 3/ US CHART peak/weeks 0/0 TRACK LISTING Overcome/ Ponderosa/Black Steel/Hell Is Around The Corner/Pumpkin/ Aftermath (Hip Hop Blues)/Abba On Fat Tracks/Brand New You're Retro/Suffocated Love/You Don't/Strugglin'/Feed Me PERSONNEL Tricky (v), Howie B (v), C. Ridenhour (v), E. Sadler (v), H. Shocklee (v), Pete Briqutte (b), Mark Saunders (k), FTV (g, d), Tony Wrafter (fl), James Stevenson (g)

A former member of Bristol's pioneering Massive Attack, Tricky took their blueprint – deathly slow hip hop beats underpinning a series of dark, melancholy melodies with awkward chord structures – and turned it into a chart-topping, award-winning formula. **Maxinquaye**, Tricky's astonishing debut, was, along with Portishead's eponymous debut, the first trip-hop masterpiece, all lugubrious raps, deceptively sweet, ethereal female vocals (courtesy of one Martine), dope beats and sinister soundscapes, drenched in foreboding. With samples from sources as diverse as Public Enemy and Smashing Pumpkins, **Maxinquaye** shook mid-Nineties Brit-pop to its foundations.

… an abrasive mix of animated beauty and technological skank… a mercurial style of dance music that immediately finds its own fast feet. He's a scavenger with the formal acuity of a scientist. **James Hunter, Rolling Stone, June 1995**

McCartney

ARTIST Paul McCartney RELEASE DATE May 1970 (UK & US) LABEL Apple (UK & US) PRODUCER Paul McCartney UK CHART peak/weeks 2/32 US CHART peak/weeks 1/47 TRACK LISTING The Lovely Linda/That Would Something/ Valentine Day/Every Night/Hot As Sun/Glasses/Junk/Man We Was Lonely/ Momma Miss America/Teddy Boy/Singalong Junk/Maybe I'm Amazed/Kreen-Akrove PERSONNEL Paul McCartney (v, b, g, k, d), Linda McCartney (bv)

In contrast to the boundary-stretching **Sgt. Pepper** which took Sixties recording to its ultimate, ex-Beatle Paul McCartney chose to cut his first solo album in his living room: remarkably simply. The release, timed as it was a fortnight before The Beatles' **Let It Be** (which deposed it from the US Number 1 spot), effectively ended any lingering hopes of their continuation into a new decade, and as if to parallel the Lennons' musical collaborations, 'The Lovely Linda', his bride of less than a year, played her part by contributing vocals and cover photography.

For most of the trip it's just a man alone in a small recording studio fiddling around with a few half-written songs and a load of instruments. **Richard Williams, Melody Maker, April 1970**

---

to the head of Sony Records – showed off her unfeasible multi-octave voice and gave America and the world a white answer to Whitney Houston. Sales soon hit the stratospheric, with Narada Michael Walden producing with guile and skill. Carey sometimes oversung her vapid material, but then you got the impression it would be hard to find any song that would seriously tax her. Her mother was an opera singer.

Asked to evaluate what's right or wrong with her first album, Carey answers diplomatically. 'I wasn't used to working that way,' she says… But as she returns to her rehearsal, far from her label's supervision, Carey continues to rearrange her hit single the way she wants to hear it. **From an article by Rob Tannenbaum, Rolling Stone, August 1990**

Marjory Razor Blade

ARTIST Kevin Coyne RELEASE DATE 1973 LABEL Virgin (UK & US) PRODUCER David Clague UK CHART peak/weeks 0/0 US CHART peak/weeks 0/0 TRACK LISTING Marjory Razorblade/Marlene/Talking To No One/Eastbourne Ladies/ Old Soldiers/I Want My Crown/Nasty, Lonesome Valley/House On The Hill/ Cheat Me/Jackie And Edna/Everybody Says/Mummy/Heaven In My View/ Karate King/Dog Latin/This Is Spain/Chairman's Ball/Good Boy/Chicken Wing/Lovesick Fool/Sea Of Love PERSONNEL Kevin Coyne (v, g), David Clague (b, g)

Utilizing his experiences as a social worker, Kevin Coyne became one of left-field rock's most challenging and ambitious lyricists. His first album for Virgin was packed with literate and detailed character analyses, shifting confidently from the seemingly flippant *Eastbourne Ladies* and *Karate King* to the indisputably gruelling and provocative *Old Soldier* and *House On The Hill*. His distinctive voice won die-hard admirers but didn't prove commercial. Coyne moved to Germany and became a very successful prose writer, painter, and actor.

Kevin's got a very unusual voice to say the least – very high pitched and nasal…. It's very reminiscent of Captain Beefheart: they both have their roots in acoustic blues; and both have adapted the tradition into an individual style. **M. O., Melody Maker, September 1973**

Me And My Shadows

ARTIST Cliff Richard **RELEASE DATE** 15th October 1960 **LABEL** Columbia **PRODUCER** – **UK CHART** peak/weeks 2/33 **US CHART** peak/weeks - **TRACK LISTING** I'm Gonna Get You/You And I/I Cannot Find A True Love/Evergreen Tree/She's Gone/Left Out Again/You're Just The One To Do It/Lamp Of Love/Choppin' 'n' Changin'/We Have It Made/Tell Me/Gee Whiz It's You/I Love You So/I'm Willing To Learn/I Don't Know/Working After School **PERSONNEL** Cliff Richard (v), Jet Harris (b), Hank B. Marvin (lg), Bruce Welch (rg), Tony Meehan (d)

The album took its title from a series of weekly shows taped in London and sent out to the Grand Duchy of Luxembourg for broadcast. 'No home should be without this album by Cliff!' proclaimed music paper headlines, while two weeks later EMI's managing director revealed that the former Harry Webb had sold 5.5 million records in the two years since his career had begun.

Cliff sings with commendable control and a fine innate rhythmical feeling. And he is supported in stellar fashion by his four Shadows… who really know the score when it comes to laying down a firm rhythmical foundation for a solo artist. **Melody Maker, October 1960**

Me Myself I

ARTIST Joan Armatrading **RELEASE DATE** May 1980 (UK & US) **LABEL** A&M (UK & US) **PRODUCER** Richard Gottehrer **UK CHART** peak/weeks 5/23 **US CHART** peak/weeks 28/23 **TRACK LISTING** Me Myself I/Ma-Me-O-Beach/Friends/Is It Tomorrow Yet/Turn Out The Light/When You Kisses Me/All The Way From America/Feeling In My Heart (For You) Simon/I Need You **PERSONNEL** Will Lee, Marcus Miller (b), Anton Fig (d), Chris Spedding, Hiram Bullock, Ricky Hirsh, Joan Armatrading (lv) (g), Danny Federici (o), Paul Shaffer, Clifford Carter, Phillip St. John (p), Clarence Clemons (s), George Kerr, Sammy Turner (bv)

In the early Eighties the first black woman to gain acclaim as a pop writer turned to a more punchy, rockier sound, taking a break from both folk structures and regular producer Glyn Johns. Richard Gottehrer was brought in, as were several name musicians –from Chris Spedding to members of Springsteen's E Street Band to Sly and Robbie – and Armatrading adopted a more throwaway lyrical tone. Although popular in Britain, the album didn't make the sought-after American breakthrough.

*… Joan Armatrading said she'd like her music to get closer to rock 'n' roll… **Me Myself I** takes it further – and brilliantly. Only towards the end, with two ill-advised stabs at reggae, does she allow the pace and intensity to tail off.* **Graham Lock, NME, June 1983**

Meat Is Murder

ARTIST The Smiths **RELEASE DATE** February 1985 (UK & US) **LABEL** Rough Trade (UK)/Sire (US) **PRODUCER** – **UK CHART** peak/weeks 1/13 **US CHART** peak/weeks 110/32 **TRACK LISTING** The Headmaster Ritual/Barbarism Begins At Home/Rusholme Ruffians/I Want The One I Can't Have/What She Said/Nowhere Fast/That Joke Isn't Funny Anymore/Well I Wonder/Meat Is Murder **PERSONNEL** Stephen Patrick Morrissey (v), Johnny Marr (g, h, md, p), Andy Rouke (b), Mike Joyce (d)

Morrissey expanded his field of vision beyond the bedsit to address, among other things, vegeterianism and sadistic teachers on The Smiths' second LP. As ever, Johnny Marr was able to match the singer's mournful, ruminating note for a more plangent one, while the rhythm section of Mike Joyce and Andy Rourke provided varied backings for tracks as different as the frantic **Rusholme Ruffians** and the haunting **Well I Wonder**.

Lyrically, these nine new tracks display the Bard of Whalley Range at his most direct. Disciplined and succinct, each song relates an affecting tale or makes a point with killing precision. **Paul du Noyer, NME, 16 February 1985**

Meaty Beaty Big & Bouncy

ARTIST The Who **RELEASE DATE** December 1971 (UK)/November 1971 (US) **LABEL** Track (UK)/Decca (US) **PRODUCER** – **UK CHART** peak/weeks 9/8 **US CHART** peak/weeks 11/21 **TRACK LISTING** Compilation Album I Can't Explain/The Kids Are Alright/Happy Jack/I Can See For Miles/Pictures Of Lilly / My Generation / The Seeker / Anyway, Anyhow, Anywhere / Pinball Whizard/A Legal Matter/Boris The Spider/Magic Bus/Substitute/I'm A Boy **PERSONNEL** Roger Daltrey (v), Pete Townsend (g, v), John Entwistle (b, v), Keith Moon (d, v)

For a band with The Who's extensive catalogue, there are bound to be several retrospectives and compilations: **Meaty, Beaty, Big & Bouncy** was the first and remains one of the best. It includes many of their early teen anthems such as **My Generation** as well as hits like **I Can See For Miles**, tracing their development from London mods to world-class rock 'n' roll band.

*The definitive 'Who Greatest Hits' compilation. Version of **I'm A Boy** is totally different to the single cut.* **Roy Carr, Charles Shaar Murray, NME, November 1973**

Meet The Searchers

ARTIST The Searchers **RELEASE DATE** August 1963 (UK)/April 1964 (US) **LABEL** Pye (UK)/Mercury (US) **PRODUCER** – **UK CHART** peak/weeks 2/44 **US CHART** peak/weeks 22/21 **TRACK LISTING** Sweets For My Sweet/ Alright/ Love Potion No 9/Farmer John/Stand By Me/Money/Da Doo Ron Ron/Ain't Gonna Kiss Ya/Since You Broke My Heart/Tricky Dicky/Where Have All The Flowers Gone/Twist And Shout **PERSONNEL** Tony Jackson (v, b), Chris Curtis (v, d), Michael Pender (lg, v), Larry John McNally (rg, v)

One of the best of the bands to emerge from Liverpool in the wake of The Beatles, this Buddy Holly/Everly Brothers-infatuated four-piece anticipated the folk-rock sound of The Byrds *et al* with their exquisite harmonies and ringing 12-string guitar lines. **Meet The Searchers** contains their second UK Number 1, a cover of The Drifters' **Sweets For My Sweet**, as well as their biggest ever US hit, **Love Potion No9**. The versions of **Money**, **Stand By Me**, **Da Doo Ron Ron** and **Twist And Shout** were less groundbreaking.

Mellon Collie
And The Infinite Sadness

ARTIST The Smashing Pumpkins **RELEASE DATE** October 1995 (UK)/November 1995 (US) **LABEL** Hut Virgin (UK)/Virgin (US) **PRODUCER** Flood, Alan Moulder, Billy Corgan **UK CHART** peak/weeks 4/ **US CHART** peak/weeks 1/47 **TRACK LISTING** Mellon Collie And The Infinate Sadness/Tonight, Tonight/Jellybelly/ Zero/Here Is No Why/Bullet With Butterfly Wings/To Forgive/An Ode To No One/Love/Cupid De Locke/Galapagos/Muzzle/ Porcelina Of The Vast Oceans/Take Me Down/Where Boys Fear To Tread/ Bodies/Thirty-Three/In The Arms Of Sleep/1979/Tales Of A Scorched Earth/Thru The Eyes Of Ruby/ Stumbleine/X.Y.U./We Only Come Out At Night/Beautiful/Lily (My One And Only)/By Starlight/Farewell and Goodnight **PERSONNEL** Billy Corgan (v, g), James Iha (g), D'Arcy (b, v), Jimmy Chamberlain (d)

Never ones to under reach themselves, Chicago's Smashing Pumpkins followed the six-million selling **Siamese Dream** with these two hour-long CDs, subtitled **Dawn To Dusk** and **Twilight To Starlight**. **Mellon Collie…** was accused by many critics of being an opportunity for vocalist/frontman Billy Corgan to indulge his every whim; others, meanwhile, applauded its astonishing breadth of styles, its audacity and inventiveness as the Pumpkins took hard rock to a higher level.

Adore or despise Billy Corgan's unmistakable musical shitstorm of hubris and angst… it is refreshing to encounter a Yank who isn't shy about proclaiming his desire to have it all… the tracks are more intricately layered than ever. **Ben Edmonds, Mojo, December 1995**

Metallica

ARTIST Metallica **RELEASE DATE** August 1991 (UK & US) **LABEL** Vertigo (UK)/Elektra (US) **PRODUCER** – **UK CHART** peak/weeks 1/69 **US CHART** peak/weeks 1/266 **TRACK LISTING** Enter Sandman/Sad But True/Holier Than Thou/The Unforgiven/Wherever I May Roam/Don't Tread On Me/Through The Never/Nothing Else Matters/Of Wolf And Man/The God That Failed/My Friend Of Misery/The Struggle Within **PERSONNEL** James Hatfield (v, rg), Lars Ulrich (d), Lloyd Grand (g)

Every band gets to release an eponymous album – and that often means an attempt at a definitive musical statement. It was like that with Metallica, though it took five albums to try it. A blank, black cover gave nothing away, but the attempt to write songs as opposed to riffs, plus the input of co-producer Bob Rock turned them into US chart-toppers for the first time. Strings, on **Nothing Else Matters** were an innovation, while the fact the first single, **Enter Sandman**, had an optional five CD holder for follow-ups betrayed their ambition.

Refreshingly free of the airbrushed production and ham-fisted imagery that dominates so much of the genre, Metallica manage to rekindle the kind of intensity that fired the likes of Black Sabbath before metal fell in love with its own cliches. **Mark Cooper, Q, October 1991**

Mind Games

ARTIST John Lennon **RELEASE DATE** December 1973 (UK)/November 1973 (US) **LABEL** Apple (UK & US) **PRODUCER** John Lennon **UK CHART** peak/weeks 13/12 **US CHART** peak/weeks 9/31 **TRACK LISTING** Mind Games/Tight A\$/Aisumasen (I'm Sorry)/One Day (At A Time)/Bring On The Lucie (Freda Peeple)/Nutopian International Anthem/Intuition/Out The Blue/Only People/I Know (I Know)/You Are Here/Meat City **PERSONNEL** John Lennon (v, g), Yoko Ono (w, v)

Although Lennon's confidence undoubtedly took a dive after the critical backlash which followed 1972's heavily politicized **Some Time In New York City** album, the follow up was nevertheless inspired by social idealism of a kind. Gentler and more personal than its predecessor, **Mind Games** led to accusations that Lennon was abandoning social concerns for sentimentality, but in reality he had simply chosen a more commercial framework for his ideas. **Intuition**, **Out The Blue** and the title track stand out from a well-rounded collection.

… the complete pop star – wracked by domestic strife, impractical in his application of ideas into his music business, persistently experimental and clutching at every piece of modern gimmickry or musical technology that pops up… the sweet naiveté of it all is somehow charming. **R. C., Melody Maker, December 1973**

Mirage

ARTIST Fleetwood Mac **RELEASE DATE** July 1982 (UK & US) **LABEL** Warner Bros. (UK & US) **PRODUCER** Lindsey Buckingham **UK CHART** peak/weeks 5/39 **US CHART** peak/weeks 1/5 **TRACK LISTING** Love In Store/Can't Go Back/That's Allright/Book Of Love/Gypsy/Only Over You/Empire State/Straight Back/Hold Me/Oh Diana/Eyes Of The World/Wish You Were Here **PERSONNEL** Mick Fleetwood (d), John McVie (b), Christine McVie (k, v), Lindsey Buckingham (g, v), Stevie Nicks (v)

After the near unfollowable **Rumours** and the inevitable anticlimax of the album that had the misfortune to follow it, **Tusk**, there was perhaps a more even field for **Mirage** to play on. It could never be a global phenomenon on a par with **Rumours**, but was among the five best-sellers of the year – a Number 1 in America– and gave the group more hit singles. While *Gypsy* and *Love In Store* were the American tasters, *Oh Diane* was the surprise choice in Britain, where the album stalled at Number 5 but spent nearly a year deciding to drop out, by which time Nicks and Buckingham had returned to solo projects, foiling plans for a tour.

Miss America

ARTIST Mary Margaret O'Hara **RELEASE DATE** 1988 (US) **LABEL** Virgin (UK & US) **PRODUCER** Jody Colero, Mary Margaret O'Hara, Michael Brook. **UK CHART** peak/weeks 0/0 **US CHART** peak/weeks – **TRACK LISTING** To Cry About/The Year In Song/Body's In Trouble/Dear Darling/A New Day/When You Know Why You're Happy/My Friends Have/Help Me Lift You Up/Keeping You In Mind/Not Be Alright/You Will Be Loved Again **PERSONNEL** Mary Margaret O'Hara (v), Michael Brook, Rusty McCarty (g), David Piltch, Henrik Riik (b), Michael Sloski (d), session musicians

Canadian singer O'Hara has gained a coven of celebrity fans, from Michael Stipe to Morrissey, on the strength of this one album. And it would never have seen the light of day had not avant-garde composer Michael Brook witnessed a typically quirky concert performance and taken charge of an act record-label Virgin, having signed her in 1984, had all but given up on (original producer Andy Partridge of XTC quit after a day). Acting diverted her, but the unconventional nature of this album makes it either impossible to listen to or a classic, depending on your viewpoint.

'The reaction to the record was, um, overwhelming,' she remembers, *'Especially in Britain. There was so much genuine love. I still get letters from people who say they loved the record but their friends thought it was so depressing.'* **From an interview by Jon Wilde, NME, December 1991**

Moby Grape

ARTIST Moby Grape **RELEASE DATE** June 1967 (UK & US) **LABEL** CBS (UK)/Columbia (US) **PRODUCER** David Rubinson **UK CHART** peak/weeks – **US CHART** peak/weeks 24/27 **TRACK LISTING** Hey grandma/Mr. Blues/Fall On You/8:05/Come In The Morning/Omaha/Naked If Want To/Someday/Ain't No Use/Sitting By The Window/Changes/Lazy Me/Indifference. **PERSONNEL**

Alexander 'Skip' Spence (g, lv), Peter Lewis (g, v), Jerry Miller (g), Bob Mosley (b), Don Stevenson (d)

The Grape were an 'ornery' bunch who paid respect to NO-one. At the photo sessions for the cover the band got so pissed off that drummer Don Stevenson gave the finger; shocked corporate bosses had it airbrushed out after initial copies had offended the nation! Every song had hit potential, and a confused Columbia ended up simultaneously releasing the LP as five singles, which lessened the chances of any of the songs making the Top 10. But there wasn't a turkey among them, and they didn't need to improvise: the Grape could play the classic LSD-soaked celebrated San Francisco sound in the context of three-minute pop songs.

A set that grows on you from the smoothest of America's underground groups. A varied programme showing country influences as well as a touch of the Beach Boys here and there and moments of hard rock. **Melody Maker, March 1969**

The Modern Dance

ARTIST Pere Ubu **RELEASE DATE** January 1978 (US Only) **LABEL** Blank (US only) **PRODUCER** – **UK CHART** peak/weeks - **US CHART** peak/weeks 0/0 **TRACK LISTING** Non Alignment Pact/The Modern Dance/Laughing/Street Waves/Chinese Radiation/Life Stinks/Real World/Over My Head/Sentimental Journey/Humour Me **PERSONNEL** David Thomas (v), Peter Laughner (g), Tim Wright (b, g), Tom Herman (g, b), R. Scott Krause (d), Allen Ravenstine (s)

Wrought on the urban anvil of Cleveland, Ohio, Pere Ubu pushed rock into uncharted territories with their album debut, one of the most important 'rock' releases since Zappa and Beefheart. Tape loops, sound effects from synths to smashing crockery collided with pop-song structures, whilst frontman David Thomas, looking uncannily like David Lynch's *Eraserhead*, gibbered lyrics that seemed to owe a lot to the beat poetry of local artist D. A. Levy. In the face of the more orthodox three-minute pop songs of the New Wave on both sides of the Atlantic this was a total eye-opener, saluted by everyone from Joy Division to Julian Cope.

… some tracks are more accessible than others. No, the album isn't an egghead's fantasy come true. The singles plus **Non-Alignment Pact** *attack with spine-tingling vigour and chrome plated frenzy in the most time honoured gutsy manner.* **Ian Birch, Melody Maker, March 1978**

Modern Sounds In Country & Western Music

ARTIST Ray Charles **RELEASE DATE** July 1962 (UK) March 1962 (US) **LABEL** HMV (UK)/ABC Parlophone (US) **PRODUCER** Sid Feller **UK CHART** peak/weeks 6/16 **US CHART** peak/weeks 1/101 **TRACK LISTING** Bye Bye Love/You Don't Know Me/Half As Much/I Love You So Much It Hurts/Just A Little Lovin'/Born To Lose/Worried Mind/It Makes No Difference Now/You Win Again/Careless Love/I Can't Stop Loving You/Hey, Good Looking **PERSONNEL** Ray Charles (v, p), Gisady McGee (g), Milton Garrad (b)

The first of two such concept albums – the second featured the classic *Your Cheatin' Heart*, but also a version of *You Are My Sunshine* which still divides opinion as to whether it was spoof or sincerity – this was split between string arrangements and big-band razzmatazz. A hit was forged with Don Gibson's *I Can't Stop Loving You*, the chorus of which boasted a scorching, heart-tearing Charles vocal. More followed.

…the album is not played in a country & western thing, but the songs were known for their country & western ties…. What we tried to do was put a modern sound to them. **Ray Charles in an interview with Chris Roberts, Melody Maker, October 1962**

predecessor, the remainder of the ten songs being the most commercial of his offerings since the hit single **Brown Eyed Girl**. The influence of The Band, his neighbours in *Woodstock*, can be heard in **Brand New Day**, and the result is glorious optimism for a new decade.

Moondance *is an album of musical invention and lyrical confidence; the strong moods of* **Into the Mystic** *and the fine, epic brilliance of* **Caravan** *will carry it past many good records we'll forget in the next few years.* **Greil Marcus and Lester Bangs, Rolling Stone, March 1970**

More Of The Monkees

ARTIST The Monkees **RELEASE DATE** April 1967 (UK)/February 1967 (US) **LABEL** RCA (UK)/Colgems (US) **PRODUCER** Tommy Boyce, Bobby Hart, Neil Sedaka, Carole Bayer, Michael Nesmith, Jeff Barry, Jack Keller, Gerry Goffin, Carole King **UK CHART** peak/weeks 1/25 **US CHART** peak/weeks 1/70 **TRACK LISTING** She/When Love Comes Knockin' (At Your Door)/Mary, Mary/Hold On Girl/Your Auntie Grizelda/(I'm Not Your) Steppin' Stone/Look Out (Here Comes Tomorrow)/The Kind Of Girl I Could Love/Sometime In The Morning/Laugh/I'm A Believer **PERSONNEL** Davey Jones (v, g), Mike Nesmith (v, g), Peter Tork (v, k, b, g), Mickey Dolenz (v, d)

Riding high on the phenomenal success of their TV series, the Monkees were about to show that there was more to them than met the eye. Album number two continued the tradition of their debut and was mainly reliant on others' songwriting skills, as with **(I'm Not Your) Steppin' Stone**, one of two Boyce-Hart songs and a version of which would feature heavily in the Sex Pistols' repertoire. Mike Nesmith ensured that the band actually played on ensuing albums and increased their creative input. But **More of the Monkees** exuded a sense of fun that slowly dissipated with subsequent releases.

More Of The Monkees *is as much a brilliant production job as the TV series…. Nobody is trying too hard, either with the actual performance or content. All is lightweight, youthful, happy – pleasant. Nothing rude, nothing nasty or violent.* **Melody Maker, April 1967**

The Monkees

ARTIST The Monkees **RELEASE DATE** January 1967 (UK)/October 1967 (US) **LABEL** RCA Victor (UK)/Colegems (US) **PRODUCER** Tommy Boyce, Bobby Hart, Jack Keller, Michael Nesmith **UK CHART** peak/weeks 1/36 **US CHART** peak/weeks 1/78 **TRACK LISTING** (Theme From) The Monkees/Saturday's Child/I Wanna Be Free/Tomorrow's Gonna Be Another Day/Papa Jean's Blues/Take A Giant Step/Last Train To Clarksville/This Just Doesn't Seem To Be My Day/Let's Dance On/I'll Be True To You/Sweet Young Thing/Gonna Buy Me A Dog **PERSONNEL** Davey Jones (v, g), Mike Nesmith (v, g), Peter Tork (v, k, b, g), Mickey Dolenz (v, d)

Put together by movie director Bob Rafelson and Bert Schneider as America's answer to The Beatles, as portrayed in *A Hard Day's Night* and *Help!*, the Monkees might have boasted Charles Manson and Steve Stills – both turned down at the auditions! The TV series was a worldwide success and fuelled hits like **Last Train To Clarksville**. A heated debate ensued when it was discovered that the Monkees themselves did not actually play on the record, but nonetheless it remains a stunning introduction to a band that, despite its origins, was to dominate the latter half of the Sixties.

… however much they are upsetting people with their brand of instant success, the facts can't be argued. People are buying their records and watching their TV shows… Rumour spreaders say that the Monkees aren't actually playing on this very pleasant and entertaining album. **Melody Maker, January 1967**

Moondance

ARTIST Van Morrison **RELEASE DATE** March 1970 (UK & US) **LABEL** Warner Bros. (UK & US) **PRODUCER** Van Morrison **UK CHART** peak/weeks 32/2 **US CHART** peak/weeks 29/22 **TRACK LISTING** Stoned Me/Moondance/Crazy Love/Caravan/Into The Mystic/Come Running/These Dreams Of You/Brand New Day/Everyone/Glad Tidings **PERSONNEL** Van Morrison (lg, rg, tm), Jack Schrorer (as, ss), Collin Tillton (ts, fl), Jeff Labes (o, ctte, p), John Platania (lg, rg), John Klingberg (b), Garry Malabar (d, vp), Guy Masson (cg)

After the free-form streams of consciousness of **Astral Weeks**, this presented Morrison in a very much more radio-friendly form. Only **Into The Mystic** harked back to the album's impenetrable

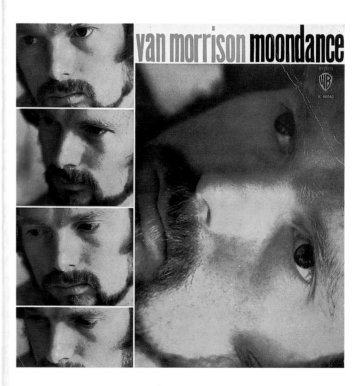

More Songs About Buildings And Food

ARTIST Talking Heads **RELEASE DATE** July 1978 (UK & US) **LABEL** Sire (UK & US) **PRODUCER** Brian Eno **UK CHART** peak/weeks 21/3 **US CHART** peak/weeks 29/42 **TRACK LISTING** Thank You For Sending Me An Angel/New Feeling/Tentative Decisions/Happy Day/Who Is It/No Compassion/The Book I Read/Don't Worry About The Goverment/First Week-Last Week...Care Free/Psyco Killer/Pulled Up. **PERSONNEL** David Byrne (v, g), Tina Weymouth (b, v), Chris Frantz (d) Jerry Harrison (k)

For their second album, Talking Heads began a collaboration with ex-Roxy Music electronics whiz, Brian Eno, which saw a toughening of their sound as David Byrne's anxiety-attack vocals spluttered a series of lyrics that possessed more rhythmic value than they did lyrical sense. One year ahead of Britain's white funk explosion (ABC, Heaven 17, Spandau Ballet), **More Songs About Buildings And Food** became the album to be seen with in 1978. The inclusion of a typically Heads-ified rendition of Al Green's *Take Me To The River* suggested all manner of possibilities for re-examining the past during pop's post-modern era.

These songs are Stooges. Music to muse uselessly by, music to make lists to. Make of it what you will... Talking heads seem like nicer people and better entertainers than television. **Julie Birchill, NME, July 1978**

Morrison Hotel

ARTIST The Doors **RELEASE DATE** 11th April 1970 (UK)/March 1970 (US) **LABEL** Elecktra (UK & US) **PRODUCER** – UK CHART peak/weeks 12/8 US CHART peak/weeks 4/127 **TRACK LISTING** Land Ho/The Spy/Queen Of The Highway/Indian Summer/Maggie McGill/Roadhouse Blues/Waiting For The Sun/You Make Me Real/Peace Frog/Blue Sunday/Ship Of Fools **PERSONNEL** Jim Morrison (v), Ray Manzarek (k), Robbie Krieger (g), John Densmore (d)

Following the critically mauled **The Soft Parade**, and with the very real possibility of a jail sentence looming for the self-pronounced Lizard King after his alleged indecent exposure in Miami, the Doors cut this fifth album which went some way to restoring their credibility. Aside from the ethereal raga-esque **Indian Summer**, the band had taken a harder, grittier, rootsier direction for the new decade. All the stress from the court cases, arrests and adverse

publicity, not to mention the drinking, had taken their toll, and through songs like **Maggie McGill** Morrison was pouring out his pain and grief.

They came perilously close to schmaltz on their last album, and it seems they've taken heed of the cries of 'sell-out!'... here the Doors have gone right back to the biting hard rock of their first two albums, and it's a knockout. **A.L., Melody Maker, March 1970**

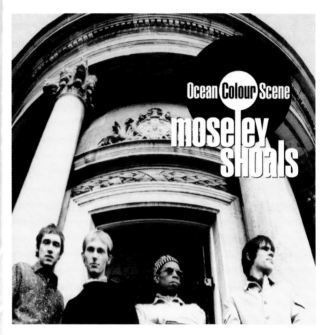

Moseley Shoals

ARTIST Ocean Colour Scene **RELEASE DATE** April 1996 (UK & US) **LABEL** MCA (UK & US) **PRODUCER** Brendan Lynch, Ocean Colour Scene **UK CHART** peak/weeks – **US CHART** peak/weeks – **TRACK LISTING** The Riverboat Song/The Day We Caught The Train/The Circle/Lining Your Pockets/Fleeting Mind/40 Past Midnight/One For The Road/It's My Shadow/Policemen And Pirates/The Downstream/You've Got It Bad/Get Away **PERSONNEL** Simon Fowler (v, ag, h), Steve Cradock (g, p, v), Oscar Harrison (d, p, v), Damon Minchella (b), Paul Weller (g, o, p, bv)

Having been forced into psychedelic territory by first record company Fontana, Ocean Colour Scene came again with this impressive effort, their cause helped by two members' part-time employment as Paul Weller's backing musicians. Tagged 'dad-rock' by a hostile press due to their retro influences (The Small Faces were particular favourites), they nevertheless prospered in the Brit-pop boom, with the 1997 follow-up **Marchin' Already** equalling the success of this album.

Ocean Colour Scene's retro... is mere duplication and reproduction, the self deluded belief that they actually WERE a successful group in the sixties, as though remembering what they sounded like, not imagining what it COULD have been like. **Daniel Booth, Melody Maker, April 1996**

The Mothership Connection

ARTIST Parliament **RELEASE DATE** June 1976 (UK)/February 1976 (US) **LABEL** Casablanca (UK & US) **PRODUCER** George Clinton **UK CHART** peak/weeks 0/0 **US CHART** peak/weeks 13/37 **TRACK LISTING** P.Funk (Wants To Get Funked Up)/Mothership Connection (Star Child)/Unfunky UFO/Supergroovalistic-Prosifunksication/Handcuffs/Give Up The Funk (Tear The Roof Off The Sucker)/Night Of The Thumpasorus Peoples **PERSONNEL** George Clinton (v), Bootsie Collins (v, b, g, pc), Bernie Worrell (k, sy), Fred Wesley (hn), Maceo

Parker (hn), Michael Brecker (hn), Randy Brecker (hn), Boom (hn), Joe Farrell (hn), Tiki Fulwood (pc, d), Jerome Brailey (pc, d), Gary Cooper (pc, d), Gary Shiler (g), Michael Hampton (g), Glen Goins (g), Cordell Mosson (b)

George Clinton pointed out that three quarters of funk was fun and this album encapsulates that *modus operandi* to a tee. With a cast of characters straight out of *Eagle* magazine and music reminiscent of James Brown at his very best, **Mothership Connection** became essential listening. One of those few albums that revealed something new with successive plays.

The mothership has arrived, the hand-picked team of funksters are abroad, watch out for the orbiting Psychotic-bumpschool to put a glide in your stride and a dip in your hip, improving your interplanetary funkshionship. They're chocolate coated, freaky, and habit forming. **Cliff White, NME, July 1976**

Mott

ARTIST Mott The Hoople **RELEASE DATE** July 1973 (UK)/August 1973 (US) **LABEL** CBS (UK)/Columbia (US) **PRODUCER** Production supervisor: Dan Loggins **UK CHART** peak/weeks 7/15 **US CHART** peak/weeks 35/ **TRACK LISTING** All The Way From Memphis/Whizz Kid/Hymn For The Dudes/Honaloochie Boogie/Violence/Drivin' Sister/Ballad Of Mott The Hoople/I'm A Cadillac/El Camino Dolo Roso/I Wish I Was You Mother **PERSONNEL** Ian Hunter (v, g), Mick Ralphs (g), Verden Allen (k), Overend Watts (b), Dale 'Buffin' Griffin (d)

A hard-working second division British rock outfit, Mott the Hoople had split up in Switzerland in March 1972 – an occurrence chronicled in this album's **Ballad Of Mott**. But help came in the shape of famous fan David Bowie, whose gift of **All The Young Dudes** revitalized Ian Hunter and his crew. This album was their first unaided step and proved the swansong of guitarist Mick Ralphs, who quit to form Bad Company. But the combination of Ralphs' craft and Hunter's *chutzpah* created something special here.

Mott *is an album of new music, and the group emerges as original, funky rock and rollers instead of tired musicians with a chip on their shoulders brought about by hard work and few rewards.* **C.C., Melody Maker, July 1973**

Mr Fantasy

ARTIST Traffic **RELEASE DATE** December 1967 (UK)/April 1968 (US) **LABEL** Island (UK)/United Artists (US) **PRODUCER** Jimmy Miller **UK CHART** peak/weeks 8/16 **US CHART** peak/weeks 88/22 **TRACK LISTING** Heaven Is In Your Mind/Berkshire Poppies/House For Everyone/No Name, No Number/Dear Mr. Fantasy/Dealer/Utterly Simple/Coloured Rain/Hope I Never Find Me There/Giving To You/Paper Sun/Hole In My Shoe **PERSONNEL** Steve Winwood (o, g, b, p, hd, pc, v), Jim Capaldi (d, pc, v), Chris Wood (fl, s, o, v), Dave Mason (g, st, tm, b, v)

Traffic were one of the few late Sixties acts who successfully bridged the gap between the highbrow pretensions of the art-rockers, the whimsical explorations of psychedelia and the complex musicianship of the progressive era. **Mr Fantasy** featured the soulful rasp of teen prodigy Steve Windwood – already famous for his work with The Spencer Davis Group – on a number of trippily ambitious tracks, including the vaudevillian **Berkshire Poppies** and the sitar-driven hit, **Paper Sun**, which appeared on the US version of the LP.

Mr Tambourine Man

ARTIST The Byrds **RELEASE DATE** August 1965 (UK)/June 1965 (US) **LABEL** CBS (UK)/Columbia (US) **PRODUCER** Terry Melcher **UK CHART** peak/weeks 7/12 **US CHART** peak/weeks 6/38 **TRACK LISTING** Mr Tambarine Man/I'll Feel A Whole Lot Better/Spanish Harlem Incident/You Won't Have To Cry/Here Without You/The Bells Of Rhymney/All I Really Want To Do/I Knew I'd Want

You/It's No Use/Don't Doubt Yourself, Babe/Chimes Of Freedom/We'll Meet Again. **PERSONNEL** Gene Clarke (v, t), Jim McGuinn (g, v), David Crosby (g, v), Chris Hillman (b, v), Michael Clarke (d)

Variously hailed as responsible for folk rock, country-rock, and even psychedelia, The Byrds' ever shifting line-up owed their flying start to impressive management: the hit cover of Dylan's **Mr Tambourine Man** showed off their jingle-jangle 12-strings and rich harmonies to beautiful effect. Gene Clark emerged as a mature songwriter too, with **I'll Feel A Whole Lot Better** lifting the spirits of teen fans and serious musos alike. **All I Really Want To Do** still features as a Sixties landmark.

All the tracks are tremendous singly, but the overall sound is too samey despite different tempos and composers. They are a very good group and we're going to hear a lot more of the Byrds. **Nick Jones, Melody Maker, August 1965**

Muddy Waters At Newport

ARTIST Muddy Waters **RELEASE DATE** September 1961 (UK & US) **LABEL** Pye Jazz (UK)/Chess (US) **PRODUCER** – **UK CHART** peak/weeks 0/0 **US CHART** peak/weeks 0/0 **TRACK LISTING** Tiger In Your Tank/I've Got My Mojo Working/I Got My Brand On You/Baby, Please Don't Go/Soon Forgotten/I Feel So Glad/Goodbye Newport Blues/ **PERSONNEL** Muddy Waters (v, g), Francis Clay (d), Andrew Stephenson (b), Pat Hare (g), Otis Spann (p), James Cotton (h)

Apart from bequeathing one of rock's most important bands their name, and inspiring the title of Bob Dylan's most famous song, Muddy Waters was one of the founding fathers of rock 'n' roll, dragging blues out of his native Delta and electrifying, amplifying and modernizing it. **Muddy Waters At Newport** had a profound impact on legions of young guitarists, among them future members of The Animals, The Yardbirds and the Stones, who became mesmerized by the gospel vocalizing and inspirational fretwork of the inventor of the rock riff.

Murmur

ARTIST R.E.M. **RELEASE DATE** August 1983 (UK)/May 1983 (US) **LABEL** I.R.S. (UK and US) **PRODUCER** Mitch Easter, Don Dixon **UK CHART** peak/weeks 0/0 **US CHART** peak/weeks 36/30 **TRACK LISTING** Radio Free Europe/ Pilgrimage/Laughing/Talk About The Passion/Moral Kiosk/Perfect Circle/ Catapult/Sitting bull/9-9/Shaking Through/We Walk/West Of The Fields **PERSONNEL** Michael Stipe (v), Peter Buck (g), Mike Bills (b), Bill Berry (d)

The first full-length album from the future American music legends is recognizable as the band that produced **Out Of Time** and **Automatic For The People**, but was considerably harder to fathom. *Talk About The Passion* and *Radio Free Europe*, the latter a re-recording of their first indie-label single, could well have hoped for radio play, but what exactly Stipe was banging on about remained obscure. You would have been hard pushed to choose R.E.M. above their many fine contemporaries as future chart-toppers.

R.E.M. are reticent and introspective, veiling their observations and remembrances in gauzy cloud… R.E.M. are the champions of soft-focus enigmatic pop. R.E.M. have a claim to being one of the most evocative pop practitioners around. **Richard Grabel, NME, September 1983**

Music Box

ARTIST Mariah Carey **RELEASE DATE** September 1993 (UK & US) **LABEL** CBS (UK)/Columbia (US) **PRODUCER** Robert Clivilles, David Cole, Walter Afanasieff, Dave Hall, Babyface, Daryl Simmons, Mariah Carey **UK CHART** peak/weeks 1/16 **US CHART** peak/weeks 1/128 **TRACK LISTING** Dreamlover/Hero/Anytime You Need A Friend/Music Box/Now That I Know/Never Forget You/Just To Hold You Once Again/I've Been Thinking About You/All I Ever Wanted/Everything Fades Away **PERSONNEL** Dave Hall (k), Walter Afanasieff (k, sy, o, b, ag), Michael Landau (g), Mark Rooney (bv), Cindy Mizelle (bv), Melanie Daniels (bv), Kelly Price (bv), Shanrae Price (bv), David Cole (k), Robert Clivilles (d, pc), Babyface (k, d, bv), Kayo (b), Mariah Carey (v)

If anything, Carey learnt restraint for this album. Though panned by sniping critics alarmed by its success, it features some divinely slinky funk and, despite her reputation, some genuinely moving ballads. Among the hit singles, her take on Badfinger's/Nilsson's *Without You* was remarkably tasteful, and *Dreamlover* was joyfully sexy. The collaboration with C&C Music Factory, *I've Been Thinking About You*, showed a good ear for funk partners. The album sold 20 million and then some.

Music Box *would be an exercise in bombast if Carey didn't infuse these greeting-card sentiments with a sustained passion that enhances the wedding-album feel.* **Stephen Holden, Rolling Stone, October 1993**

Music For The Jilted Generation

ARTIST The Prodigy **RELEASE DATE** July 1994 (UK)/March 1995 (US) **LABEL** X.L. (UK)/Mute (US) **PRODUCER** L.Howlett, Neil McLellan, K.Palmer **UK CHART** peak/weeks 1/ **US CHART** peak/weeks 0/0 **TRACK LISTING** Intro/Break And Enter/Their Law/Full Throttle/Voodoo People/Speedway/The Heat (The Energy)/Poison/No Good (Start The Dance)/One Love (Edit)-The Narcotic Suite/3 Kilos/Skylined/Claustrophobic Sting **PERSONNEL** Phil Bent (fl), Lance Riddler (g), Liam Howlett (k), Mc Maxim Reality (v)

A barnstorming call to arms to those under siege from the Criminal Justice Bill, **Music For The Jilted Generation** popularized techno almost at a stroke. A deserving winner of a Brit Award for Best Dance Act, the second Prodigy album took samples, voices, dialogues, juddering breakbeats and crazy electronic noises, wedded them to a wide range of musical settings, added a healthy dash of their own distinctive character, and then turned up the volume. Including the earlier single *No Good (Start The Dance)*: this is a frantic, uninhibited rollercoaster ride from beginning to end.

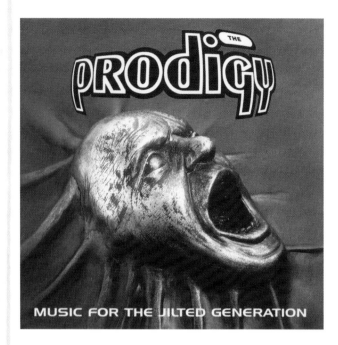

MUSIC FOR THE JILTED GENERATION

…an accessible, condensed double album; but where its predecessor was celebratory, it is dark and claustrophobic… a soundtrack for the times: a disturbing, intoxicating joyride through a land of police clamp downs, where hedonism is re-invented as a gesture of rebellion. **Sam Taylor, Q, September 1994**

Music From Big Pink

ARTIST The Band **RELEASE DATE** August 1968 (UK & US) **LABEL** Capitol (UK & US) **PRODUCER** John Simon **UK CHART** peak/weeks 0/0 **US CHART** peak/weeks 30/40 **TRACK LISTING** Tears Of Rage/To Kingdom Come/In A Station/Caledonia Mission/The Weight/We Can Talk/Long Black Veil/Chest Fever/Lonesome Susie/Wheels On Fire/I Shall Be Released **PERSONNEL** Jaime Robbie Robertson (g, v), Rick Danco (b, v), Richard Manuel (p, v), Garth Hudson (o), Levon Helm (d, v)

Acclaimed as the 'maturing' of rock, The Band had already backed Ronnie Hawkins and of course Bob Dylan for years when they got around to recording an album themselves. This featured no overdubs and the emotionally affecting vocal interplay of Danko, Helm and Manuel. *I Shall Be Released* and *The Weight* have become classics. Strikingly, this downbeat, almost stately record swam against the tide of heavy rock and trippy psychedelia. 'If everybody was going east,' Robertson later said, 'we were going west.' Into an America of lyrical, believable depth.

The chord changes are refreshing, the stories are told in a subtle yet taut way; country tales of real people you can relate to…. This album was recorded in approximately two weeks. There are people who will work their lives away in vain and not touch it. **Al Kooper, Rolling Stone, August 1968**

Music In The Doll's House

ARTIST Family **RELEASE DATE** August 1968 (UK & US) **LABEL** Reprise RLP 6312 (UK & US) **PRODUCER** John Gilbert, David Mason, Jimmy Miller **UK CHART** peak/weeks 35/3 **US CHART** peak/weeks **TRACK LISTING** The Chase/Mellowing Grey/Never Like This/Me My Friend/Variation On A Theme Of Hey Mr. Policeman/Winter/Old Songs New Songs/Variation On A Theme Of The Breeze/Hey Mr. Policeman/See Through Windows/Variation On A Theme Of Me And My Friend/Peace Of Mind/Voyage/The Breeze/3 x Time **PERSONNEL** Roger Chapman (lv, bv, ts), John Witney (lg, g), Jim King (s), Ric Grech (b, v, c, vl), Rob Townend (d, p)

An all-time classic debut, **Music In A Doll's House** was ambitious without being pretentious and has, unlike most albums of the period, aged remarkably well. Eleven self-penned songs, plus Dave Mason's *Never Like This*, some cross-faded, others linked by short variations on themes found elsewhere, and the standard set by *The Chase* is maintained throughout. Roger Chapman's distinctive vocals sit as easily astride the gentle balladry as they do the thunderous roar of, say, *Peace Of Mind*.

… it lacks spontaneity and excitement. It is studied, very serious, yet not heavy enough to bear much serious listening. Like a doll's house, it is a miniature replica of the real thing, intricate, but lifeless. **David Gancher, Rolling Stone, December 1968**

Music Of My Mind

ARTIST Stevie Wonder RELEASE DATE May 1972 (UK)/March 1972 (US) LABEL Tamla Motown PRODUCER Stevie Wonder, Robert Margouleff, Malcolm Cecil (Assoc. Prod) UK CHART peak/weeks - US CHART peak/weeks 21/- TRACK LISTING Love Having You Around/Superwoman/I Love Every Little Thing About You/Sweet Little Girl/Happier Than The Morning Sun/Girl Blue/Seems So Long/Keep On Running/Evil PERSONNEL Stevie Wonder (v, p), Buzzy Feiton (lg), Art Baron (tr)

Music Of My Mind was, astonishingly, the 21-year-old Stevie Wonder's twelfth studio album. Although he had already wrested control of his career from Motown (as had Marvin Gaye with **What's Going On**) with his first album as a mature artist, 1971's **Where I'm Coming From**, it was **Music Of My Mind** that really showed what Wonder was capable of. More than the usual Motown fare of a couple of hits plus filler, this was a serious album from a serious albums artist, a self-contained studio master who could produce, arrange and play virtually every note on his own breathtakingly inventive brand of synthesized funk-pop-soul.

A multi track one man band with Stevie on piano, drums, harmonica, organ, clavichord, clarinet plus the harp and moog synthesizers with their various attachments… sounds like an ego extravaganza… the effect is both satisfying and exciting. **Vince Alleti, Rolling Stone, April 1972**

My Aim Is True

ARTIST Elvis Costello RELEASE DATE August 1977 (UK)/March 1977 (US) LABEL Stiff (UK)/Columbia (US) PRODUCER Nick Lowe UK CHART peak/weeks 14/12 US CHART peak/weeks 30/17 TRACK LISTING Welcome To The/Working Week/Miracle Man/No Dancing/Blame It On Cain/Alison/Sneaky Feelings/(The Angels Wanna Wear My) Red Shoes/Less Than Zero/Mystery Dance/Pay It Back/I'm Not Angry/Waiting For The End Of The World PERSONNEL Elvis Costello (v, g), with backing band The Shamrocks, John McFee (g), Alex Call (g, v), Sean Hopper (k), John Ciambotti (b), Michael Shine (d)

Costello's debut shared punk's passion, but already he showed a broader, more probing vision. He had the ability to turn any genre to his advantage, and the lyrics to transcend genre. This was recorded on a nothing budget for new label Stiff, but gave more than a hint of his soon-to-come majesty, with remarkable mature song writing and fiery vocals evidenced by the (perhaps now over familiar) *Alison* and *Miracle Man*. *(The Angels Wanna Wear My) Red Shoes* gave him a first hit of sorts: was this the song that gave birth to 'new wave'? *Less Than Zero* gave birth to a Bret Easton Ellis novel.

My Aim Is True isn't just the title track of Mr Costello's auspicious album debut, but is indicative of a quirky line of vision which painfully – often to the point of total humiliation – examines the recurring traumas of love and other related adolescent dilemmas. **Roy Carr, NME, July 1977**

My Generation

ARTIST The Who RELEASE DATE December 1965 (UK & US) LABEL Brunswick (UK)/Decca (US) PRODUCER – UK CHART peak/weeks 5/11 US CHART peak/weeks – TRACK LISTING Out In The Street/I Don't Mind/The Good's Gone/La-La-La-Lies/Much Too Much/My Generation/The Kids Are Alright/Please Please Please/It's Not True/I'm A Man/A Legal Matter/The Ox PERSONNEL Pete Townsend (lg), Keith Moon (d), Roger Daltrey (v), John Entwistle (b)

The third most important British rock band of the Sixties (with the Kinks and The Small Faces at four and five), The Who burst on to the scene with a reputation for off-stage loutishness – singer Roger Daltrey was the prototype Lad, while drummer Keith Moon was as self-destructive as any rocker before or since – and on-stage melodramatics – Pete Townshend would regularly smash his guitars. **My Generation** unveiled the writing talents of Pete Townshend, an angry young man with a knack for focusing his fury into three-minute songbites. Nowhere was this more apparent than on **My Generation** (featuring the immortal line, 'hope I die before I get old') and *The Kids Are Alright*.

Long-awaited LP from the **My Generation** *hit-makers. Nine of the twelve varied tracks are from the pen of Pete Townshend…. Singer Roger Daltrey adapts his voice excellently to each track…. A very big seller.,* **Melody Maker, 4 December 1965**

My People Were Fair And Had Sky In Their Hair But Now They're Content To Wear Stars On Their Brows

ARTIST Tyrannosaurus Rex RELEASE DATE July 1968 (UK) LABEL Regal Zozophone (UK)/A&M (US) PRODUCER Toni Visconti UK CHART peak/weeks 15/9 US CHART peak/weeks – TRACK LISTING Red Hot Mama/Scenesof/ Child Star/Strange Orchestra/Chateau In Virgina Waters/Dwarfish Trumpet Blues/Mustang Ford/Arghan Woman/Knight/ Graceful Fat Shake/Weilder Of Woods/Frowning Alahuallpa PERSONNEL Marc Bolam (v)/Steve Peregrine (b, v)

After Marc Bolan's departure from John's Children, but before the shortening of his band's name and his subsequent tranformation into the first glam star, the erstwhile mod and former model was one half of Tyrannosaurus Rex: a folk duo co-starring that other corkscrew-curled figure straight out of a Botticelli painting, Steve Peregrine Took, on percussion. **My People Were Fair…**, with its blend of acoustic and exotic instrumentation, such as the Chinese gong, introduced Bolan's fantastical pseudo-mystical gobbledegook and ear for a catchy tune, making them darlings of the UK underground circuit at the height of Flower Power.

Marc and Steve seemed like strange, gentle creatures caught out of sequence, and their music seemed to come straight from a time when many things were simpler, and many other things had existed that were now lost to us. **Charles Shaar Murray, NME, April 1973**

My Son, The Folk Singer

ARTIST Allan Sherman RELEASE DATE November 1962 (US) LABEL Warner Bros (US) PRODUCER – UK CHART peak/weeks US CHART peak/weeks 1/51 TRACK LISTING The Ballad Of Harry Lewis/Shake Hands With Your Uncle Max/Sir Greenbaum's Madrigal/My Zelda/The Streets Of Miami/Sarah Jackman/Jump Down, Spin Around (Pick A Dress O' Cotton)/Oh Boy Shticks And Stones PERSONNEL Allan Sherman (v), Christine Nelson (v), Orchestra and Chorus under the Direction of Lou Busch

Sherman's parodies may seem quaint by Nineties standards, but his ability to address the social and political issues of the day using pop and folk styles was hard to beat. He had already had three Number 1 albums before he enjoyed his first hit single in August 1963 with *Hello Mudduh, Hello Fadduh*, the tale of a young boy's first experience at summer camp. Compassionate yet cutting, like a less vicious Lenny Bruce, it turned Sherman, albeit briefly, into a reluctant star.

The Mystery Of Love (Is Greater Than The Mystery Of Death)

ARTIST Jackie Leven RELEASE DATE June 1995 LABEL Cooking Vinyl PRODUCER – UK CHART peak/weeks 0/0 US CHART peak/weeks 0/0 TRACK LISTING Clay Jug/Shadow In My Eyes/Call Mother/A Lonely Field/The Crazy Song/Farm Buy/The Garden/Snow In Central/Looking For Love/Heartsick Land/Gylen Gylen/I Say A Little Prayer For You/Bars Of Dundee PERSONNEL Jackie Leven (v, ag, g), James Helawell (v, k, b), Glen Nightingale (g), Chuck Merchan (b), Steve 'Killer' Jackson (d), session musicians

This release confirmed the rebirth of singer-guitarist Jackie Leven whose previous band, Doll By Doll, had been perennial under-achievers. An attack in a London street threatened Leven's voice and he found himself with a serious heroin habit. Relocating to Argyll, in Scotland, his rehabilitation dictated the lyrical pace of the new material, which is almost traditional in its timbre. Leven's voice carries new conviction as he recounts loss and hurt in what is a mature and, against the odds, uplifting album.

Nashville Skyline

ARTIST Bob Dylan RELEASE DATE May 1969 (UK & US) LABEL CBS (UK)/Columbia (US) PRODUCER Bob Johnston UK CHART peak/weeks 1/42 US CHART peak/weeks 3/47 TRACK LISTING Girl From The North Country (With Johnny Cash)/Nashville Skyline Rag/To Be Alone With You/I Threw It All Away/Peggy Day/Lay Lady Lay/One More Night/Tell me That It Isn't True/Country Pie/Tonight I'll Be Staying/Here With You PERSONNEL Bob Dylan (v, g), Kenny Buttrey, Charles McCoy, Peter Drake, Norman Blake, Charlie Daniels, Bob Wilson, Johnny Cash

Continuing the country theme of its predecessor **John Wesley Harding**, **Nashville Skyline** saw Dylan co-opt veteran Johnny Cash who contributed liner notes and duetted on *Girl From The North Country*. It had already topped the chart here by the time Dylan flew across to play the 1969 *Isle of Wight Festival*, after which *Lay Lady Lay*, allegedly written as a commission for the *Midnight Cowboy* film but rejected by its makers, would give him a final UK hit single.

His lightest thing yet, with the new smooth, Dylan voice with a country flavour. No lengthy, poetical stanzas, no social protest, no mysticism. Plenty of variety including the addition of Johnny Cash on **Girl From The North Country**. **Melody Maker, June 1969**

Natty Dread

ARTIST Bob Marley & The Wailers RELEASE DATE May 1975 (UK and US) LABEL Island (UK and US) PRODUCER Lee 'Scratch' Perry UK CHART peak/weeks 43/5 US CHART peak/weeks 92/28 TRACK LISTING Lively Up Yourself/No Woman No Cry/Them Belly Full (But We Hungry)/Rebel Music (3 O'Clock Road Block)/So Ja Seh/Natty Dread/Bend Down Low/Talkin' Blues/Revolution PERSONNEL Bob Marley (v, k), Aston Barrett (k, b), Carlton Barrett (k, d), Earl Lindo (k), Bernard Harvey (k), Al Anderson (g)

This was the first album to give Bob Marley star billing following the retirement of Messrs Tosh and Livingston – not only that, but a portrait by Jamaican artist Neville Garrick filled the front sleeve. The I-Threes were drafted in to provide a vocal counterpoint to the main man and the album's US chart success was the Wailers' first outside their native land. White-rock radio stations (rather

compared to the technicolour extravaganza that was **Born To Run**, the stripped-down nature of **Nebraska** makes it sound today like a prototype for MTV's series of *Unplugged* sessions. Minus the E Street Band, Springsteen deployed acoustic guitar and harmonica to sing, in his trademark gravelly voice, songs about characters ripped straight from the edge of town.

No longer ground down by the need to prove his honesty by wearing his heart in his holler, he's now writing and singing in the testy troubadour tradition of entertaining with a kick. **Chris Bohn, NME, September 1982**

Never A Dull Moment

ARTIST Rod Stewart RELEASE DATE July 1972 (UK & US) LABEL Mercury (UK & US) PRODUCER Rod Stewart UK CHART peak/weeks 1/36 US CHART peak/weeks 2/36 TRACK LISTING True Blue/Lost Paraguayos/Mama You Been On My Mind/Italian Girls/Angel/Interludings/You Wear It Well/I'd Rather Go Blind/Twistin' The Night Away PERSONNEL Rod Stewart (lv), Brian (cp), Dick Powell (vl), Martin Quittenton (ag), Kenny Jones (d), Spike Heatley, Speedy (cg), Gordon Huntley (sg), Ian McLagan (o), Pete Sears (p, b), Ronnie Lane (b), Woody (g, ag, b)

Another fine example of Rod Stewart's skills as a compelling storyteller, **Never A Dull Moment** almost repeated the enormous success of **Every Picture Tells A Story**. The formula was replicated to near perfection on the mixture of covers (Sam Cooke's *Twistin' The Night Away*, wherein Stewart approximates Cooke's husky soulfulness) and originals, such as the timeless *You Wear It Well*.

Rod Stewart and his merrie men rock on, with the image of a happy-go-lucky tippler-musician managing to spread cheer, style and common sense through miserable times. **Never A Dull Moment** *– I guess the title is its own best review.* **Stephen Davis, Rolling Stone, September 1972**

than black R&B) were playing the album, hinting at the crossover to come.

Natty Dread *is exquisite. It does for reggae what Marvin Gaye's* **Let's Get It On** *did for soul – spreads it right out, lays it right back and turns it around and around on itself.* **Idris Walters, Let It Rock, 1975**

Nazz

ARTIST Nazz RELEASE DATE October 1968 (US&US) LABEL Screen Gem (US) PRODUCER – UK CHART peak/weeks 0/0 US CHART peak/weeks 188/26 TRACK LISTING Back Of Your Mind/Open My Eyes/When I Get My Plane/If That's The Way You Feel/Hello It's Me/Wildwod Blues/She's Going Down/The Lemming Song/etc. PERSONNEL Todd Rundgren (lg, v, cp), Robert Antoni (v, p), Carsten Van Osten (b, v), Thom Mooney (d), Stewkey (o, p, v)

Todd Rundgren has never been a conventional pop star, so it's no surprise that his first band, the Nazz, were far from textbook successes. Influences from the Move and Small Faces to The Beatles surfaced in this first album, which climbed no higher than Number 188, failing to become Philadelphia's answer to the New York and Bosstown (Boston) groups dominating the US scene. The first single *Hello It's Me* would be a greater success when later reworked by not only Rundgren but the Isley Brothers.

… the Nazz here prove their all-round competence in the field of contemporary rock. Nothing to get worked up about except that they're better than a lot of other mobs about… Nazz weigh in around the cruiser weight division… **Melody Maker, March 1969**

Nebraska

ARTIST Bruce Springsteen RELEASE DATE September 1982 (UK & US) LABEL CBS (UK)/Columbia (US) PRODUCER Bruce Springsteen, Mike Batlin UK CHART peak/weeks 3/19 US CHART peak/weeks 3/29 TRACK LISTING Nebraska/Atlantic City/Mansion On The Hill/Johnny 99/Highway Patrolman/State Trooper/Use Cars/Open All Night/My Father's House/Reason To Believe PERSONNEL Bruce Springsteen (v, g), Danny Federici (k), Garry Talent (b), Max Weinberg (d), Clarence Clemens (s), Steve van Zandt (lg)

Just as Springsteen was becoming a household name, he made his sparsest, bleakest album yet. A low-key, black-and-white affair

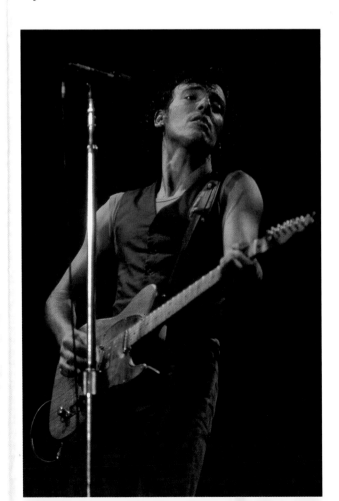

Never Mind The Bollocks, Here's The Sex Pistols

ARTIST The Sex Pistols **RELEASE DATE** November 1977 (UK)/December 1977 (US) **LABEL** Virgin (UK)/Warner (US) **PRODUCER** – **UK CHART** peak/weeks 1/48 **US CHART** peak/weeks 106/12 **TRACK LISTING** Holidays In The Sun/Bodies/No Feelings/Liar/God Save The Queen/Problems/Seventeen/Anarchy In The UK/Submission/Pretty Vacant/New York/E.M.I. **PERSONNEL** Johnny Rotten (v), Steve Jones (g), Sid Vicious (v, b), Paul Cook (d)

The **Sgt. Pepper** of punk, the debut album by the Sex Pistols altered the face of British rock as irrevocably as had The Beatles 10 years earlier. Virtually every one of these 11 tracks was notorious, from the venomous singles that almost brought a nation to its knees – *Anarchy In The UK*, *Pretty Vacant*, *God Save The Queen*, *Holidays In The Sun* – to the anthems of alienation and adolescent self-loathing – *Bodies*, *No Feelings*. The Clash may have had a more coherent political agenda, the Jam may have been better musicians, but the Pistols were the agents of cultural change.

Musically, **Never Mind The Bollocks, Here's The Sex Pistols** *is just about the most exciting Rock 'n' Roll record of the Seventies… Rotten's jabbing, gabbing vocals won't leave you alone.* **Paul Nelson, Rolling Stones, February 1978**

Nevermind

ARTIST Nirvana **RELEASE DATE** October 1991 (UK & US) **LABEL** DGC (UK & US) **PRODUCER** Butch Vig **UK CHART** peak/weeks 7/103 **US CHART** peak/weeks 1/250 **TRACK LISTING** Smells Like Teen Spirit/In Bloom/Come As You Are/Breed/Lithium/Polly/Territorial Pissings/Drain You/Lounge Act/Stay Away/On A Plain/Something In The Way **PERSONNEL** Kurt Cobain (v,g), Chris Novoselic (b), David Grohl (d, v)

Nirvana's second album pioneered a new musical genre: 'grunge'. Kurt Cobain's instinctive grasp of dynamics applied to this collection of songs proved, like the Pixies before, that melody and power need not be mutually exclusive. Cobain's vocal extremity, coupled with the band's psychotic energy, placed **Nevermind** in previously untrodden territory. While enough primal pop sentiment remained to ensure it crossed into the mainstream, the raw delivery and potent emotion struck a major chord with the youth of the western world. Seminal.

A dynamic mix of sizzling power chords, manic energy and sonic restraint, Nirvana erects sturdy melodic structures – sing-along hard rock as defined by groups like the Replacements, Pixies and Sonic Youth – but then attacks them with frenzied screaming and guitar havoc. **Ira Robbins, Rolling Stone, November 1991**

New Boots And Panties

ARTIST Ian Dury And The Blockheads **RELEASE DATE** September 1977 (UK)/May 1978 (US) **LABEL** Stiff (UK & US) **PRODUCER** Peter Jenner, Laurie Latham, Rick Walton **UK CHART** peak/weeks 5/90 **US CHART** peak/weeks 168/5 **TRACK LISTING** Wake Up And Make Love With Me/Sweet Gene Vincent/I'm Partial To Your Abracadabra/My Old Man/Billericay Dickie/Clevor Trevor/If I was With A Woman/Blockheads/Blackmail Man/There's Nothing With It !!! **PERSONNEL** Ian Dury (v), Charley Charles (d), Norman Watt Roy (b), Chaz Jankel (g, k) with Davey Payne (s), Edward Speight (g) and Geoff Castle

Having found little success with theatrical rock combo Kilburn & the High Roads, ex-art school graduate Ian Dury's fortunes changed on signing to Stiff in 1977. Lyrically he was as sharp as the razor blade he wore as an earring. His observations of working-class life in his beloved East End of London were both humorous and human, all delivered in cockney rhyming slang. Although Dury went on to write some outstanding singles, his ensuing albums failed to match this power-charged debut.

… typically versatile examples of the force, humour and ingenuity of Dury's imagination…Dury's songs are rooted in the streets and their populations: the lives and frustrations and aspirations of ordinary people… **Allan Jones, Melody Maker, October 1977**

New Forms

ARTIST Roni Size & Reprazent **RELEASE DATE** October 1997 (US) **LABEL** Mercury (UK)/Talkin' Loud (US) **PRODUCER** Various **UK CHART** peak/weeks **US CHART** peak/weeks 0/0 **TRACK LISTING** Railing/Brown Paper Bag/New Forms/Let's Get It on/Digital/Matter Of Fact/Mad Cat/Heroes/Share The Fall/Watching Windows/Beatbox/Morse Code/Destination **PERSONNEL** Roni Size, D J Krust, D J Die, D J Suv (Reprazent), Onallee (v), Bahamadia (v)

New Forms was arguably the first drum & bass, or jungle, album to infiltrate the mainstream. It rendered palatable the fast, jittery rhythms of jungle, and even allied those cutting-edge beats to a sharp melodic sense, with comprehensible singing over the top – as opposed to the gibberish rants of most jungle Djs. When **New Forms** beat all-comers, including Radiohead, The Prodigy, the Chemical Brothers and the Spice Girls, to win 1997's prestigious Mercury Prize, it sealed jungle's reputation as the most happening sound around.

The songs veer between joyous optimism and bleak resignation; moods which are combined in the album's peak moment, the impassioned **Share The Fall** *– simultaneously a love song and an elegy for the comedown from the rare dream. A landmark work.* **Matthew Collin, Mojo, August 1997**

New Gold Dream (81-82-83-84)

ARTIST Simple Minds **RELEASE DATE** September 1982 (UK)/Febuary 1983 (US) **LABEL** Virgin (UK)/A&M (US) **PRODUCER** Peter Walsh **UK CHART** peak/weeks 3/52 **US CHART** peak/weeks 69/19 **TRACK LISTING** Someone Somewhere In Summertime/Colours Fly And Catherine Wheel/Promised You A Miracle/Big Sleep/Somebody Up There Likes You/New Gold Dream (81-82-83-84)/Glittering Prize/Hunter And The Hunted/King Is White And In The Crowd **PERSONNEL** Charles Burchill (g), Derek Forbes (b), Michael McNeil (b), Jim Kerr (v), Mike Ogletree (d, pc), Mel Gaynor (d), Kenny Hyslop (d), Sharon Campbell (v)

Simple Minds' fifth studio album, **New Gold Dream (81-82-83-84)** was their commercial breakthrough, containing three hit singles in *Promised You A Miracle*, *Someone, Somewhere In Summertime* and *Glittering Prize*, and remaining in the UK charts for a year. It also represented this Scottish band's artistic peak, as the obvious influence of early Roxy Music and the David Bowie/Brian Eno LP trilogy waned in favour of a more original art-disco sound. Even though they would soon rival U2 for stadium appeal, they would never again match this work.

Suddenly the group sound acutely aware of space and emptiness, and their impact is a lot harder because of that (when I say harder, I am just as likely to mean 'softer' – it depends whether you're stood on your head or not). **Paul Morley, NME, September 1982**

New York

ARTIST Lou Reed RELEASE DATE January 1989 (UK & US) LABEL Sire (UK & US) PRODUCER Lou Reed, Fred Maher UK CHART peak/weeks 14/22 US CHART peak/weeks 40/22 TRACK LISTING Romeo Had Juliette/Halloween Parade/Dirty Blvd./Endless Cycle/There Is No Time/Last Great American Whale/Beginning Of A Great Adventure/Busload Of Faith/Sick Of You/Hold On/Good Evening Mr Waldheim/Xmas In February/Strawman/Dime Store Mystery PERSONNEL Lou Reed (v, g), Mike Rathke (g), Rob Wasserman (b), Fred Maher (fdg, d), Maureen 'Mo' Tucker (pc)

The year of 1989 saw Lou Reed lurching towards a Velvet Underground reunion, playing two live shows with John Cale in memory of Svengali Andy Warhol and inviting Mo Tucker to drum on two tracks of this first album for a new label, Sire. Its back-to-basics approach won him his best UK chart placing since 1973's **Berlin**, though US fans seemed less impressed, perhaps waiting for the main event – they reunited in November on a recording session for Mo Tucker's album.

… what makes **New York**, *the album, so compulsively entertaining is the edgy neurotic energy it shares with* New York, *the place, in the way it flaunts its extremes…. Lou reed has seldom paid tribute to his favourite place with such sensitivity and style.* **Robert Sandall, Q, February 1989**

New York Dolls

ARTIST New York Dolls RELEASE DATE August 1973 (UK)/September 1973 (US) LABEL Mercury (UK & US) PRODUCER Todd Rundgren UK CHART peak/weeks US CHART peak/weeks 116/12 TRACK LISTING Personality Crisis/Looking For A Kiss/Vietnamese Baby/Lonely Planet Boy/Frankenstein/Trash/Bad girl/Subway Train/Pills/Private World/Jet Boy PERSONNEL David Johansen (v), Johnny Thunders (g, v), Sylvain Sylvain (g, v), Arthur Kane (b)

Introduced by a witheringly scornful Bob Harris on TV's *Old Grey Whistle Test* as bearing the same relation to the Stones as the Monkees to The Beatles, the Dolls were nevertheless, along with the Stooges, the nearest thing to a punk blueprint. This Todd Rundgren-produced debut was recorded and mixed in a week but remained promising enough for Malcolm McLaren to show an interest. He could not stop them self-destructing, but took their essence and made his own version in the Sex Pistols, who

were to the Dolls as the Monkees…(etc.)

… singer David Johansen shamelessly apes Jagger's voice and mannerisms, while lead guitarist Johnny Thunders functions as a blend of Keith Richard and Ron Wood. This dual axis is the band's storm-centre, the focus of energy and attention, and they perform their roles to perfection. **R.W., Melody Maker, August 1973**

Nice 'N' Easy

ARTIST Frank Sinatra RELEASE DATE January 1961 (UK)/August 1960 (US) LABEL Capitol (UK & US) PRODUCER – UK CHART peak/weeks 4/27 US CHART peak/weeks 1/86 TRACK LISTING Nice 'N' Easy/That Old Feeling/How Deep Is The Ocean?/I've Got A Crush On You/You Go To My Head/Fools Rush In/Nevertheless/She's Funny That Way/Try A Little Tenderness/Embraceable You/Mam'selle/Dream PERSONNEL Frank Sinatra (v), Orchestra conducted by Nelson Riddle, Herbie Hancock, Graham Nash, David Crosby (gst)

His first album of the Sixties was the perfect compromise between sad-Sinatra and swingin'-Sinatra, and the fact that it charted high on both sides of the Atlantic was vindication for both of Ol' Blue Eyes' approaches. Again, the cover, with Frank laid back in his armchair, all comfy cardigan and wry grin, spoke volumes about the content. The title track was virtually self-descriptive, while *Fools Rush In* hinted at the heartache (failed marriages and a career that floundered until his first non-singing role in 1953's *From Here To Eternity*) behind the bravado.

Sinatra is in his most languid sensuous mood on this release. The 'master' is again in great form, projecting a selection of melodious evergreens against more of those immaculate Nelson Riddle accompaniments. **Pop Vocal Discs, Melody Maker, February 1961**

Nick Of Time

ARTIST Bonnie Raitt **RELEASE DATE** April 1989 (UK & US) **LABEL** Capitol (UK & US) **PRODUCER** Don Was **UK CHART** peak/weeks 51/5 **US CHART** peak/weeks 1/85 **TRACK LISTING** Nick Of Time/Thing Called Love/Love Letter/Cry On My Shoulder/Real Man/Nobody's Girl/Have A Heart/Too Soon To Tell/I Will Not Be Denied/I Ain't Gonna Let You Break My Heart Again/The Road's My Middle Name **PERSONNEL** Bonnie Raith (p, v), sessions musicians

Having progressively glossed up her blues-based sound and found diminishing commercial and critical returns, Bonnie Raitt decided her tenth album would go back to basics. And just five days in the studio yielded a three-time Grammy-winner, with a little help from producer Don Was and guests Herbie Hancock, Graham Nash and David Crosby. The title song, dealing with a woman wanting a baby, could as easily have referred to one looking for a Number 1 album – and the happy event came true!

Bonnie Raitts' tenth album is a strong if surprisingly conservative offering…. For almost any other pop singer, **Nick Of Time** *would be a solid victory. For Raitt, who is clearly capable of being great, it is another beautiful miss.* **Fred Goodman, Rolling Stone, April 1989**

A Night At The Opera

ARTIST Queen **RELEASE DATE** December 1975 (UK & US) **LABEL** EMI (UK)/Elektra (US) **PRODUCER** Roy Thomas Baker & Queen **UK CHART** peak/weeks 1/50 **US CHART** peak/weeks 4/56 **TRACK LISTING** Death On Two Legs (Dedicated To…)/Lazing On A Sunday Afternoon/I'm In Love With My Car/You're My Best Friend/'39/Sweet Lady/Seaside Rendezvous/The Prophet's Song/Love Of My Life/Good Company/Bohemian Rhapsody/God Save The Queen **PERSONNEL** Freddie Mercury (v), Brian May (g), John Deacon (b), Roger Taylor (d)

The most expensive record ever made at the time of release, this saw Queen extend their musical frontiers from guitar-based hard rock to include theatre and opera in their repertoire. Its centrepiece, *Bohemian Rhapsody*, was overdubbed so much the tape could be seen through, and producer Roy Thomas Baker was essentially co-opted as a fifth member to 'play the studio'. *Prophet's Song* was another elaborate creation, while *You're My Best Friend*

was pure pop and *Death On Two Legs* was dedicated to an unloved former manager. This band did it all.

Rhapsody with changing moods, operatic vocals and above all a logical progression to a beautiful climax, is the definitive track of the album… these attributes are common to most of the songs; and if it's the most expensive album ever made in a British studio, its also arguably the best. **Tony Stewart, NME, November 1975**

The Night I Fell In Love

ARTIST Luther Vandross **RELEASE DATE** April 1985 (UK & US) **LABEL** Epic (UK & US) **PRODUCER** Luther Vandross & Marcus Miller **UK CHART** peak/weeks 19/10 **US CHART** peak/weeks 19/56 **TRACK LISTING** 'Til My Baby Comes Home/The Night I Fell In Love/If Only For One Night/Creepin'/It's Over Now/Wait For Love/My Sensitivity (Gets In My Way)/Other Side Of The World **PERSONNEL** Luther Vandross (v), session musicians

He first came to the public's attention after working on David Bowie's **Young Americans**, but in the next decade he really came into his own. Basically, Luther Vandross was the Marvin Gaye of the Eighties and early Nineties, a black *auteur* – and loverman – who wrote and produced his own material. **The Night We Fell In Love** was one of Vandross's many platinum and double-platinum albums, a superb collection of polished romantic ballads and gentle up-tempo pop-funk tracks.

A Night On The Town

ARTIST Rod Stewart **RELEASE DATE** July 1976 (UK & US) **LABEL** Riva (UK)/Warner (US) **PRODUCER** – **UK CHART** peak/weeks 1/47 **US CHART** peak/weeks 2/57 **TRACK LISTING** Tonight's The Night (Gonna Be Alright)/The First Cut Is The Deepest/Fool For You/The Killing Of Georgie (part 1 & 2)/The Balltrap/Pretty Flamingo/Big Bayou/The Wild Side Of Life/Trade Winds I And II **PERSONNEL** Rod Stewart (v), session musicians

Rod's transition from rough Scots rocker to purveyor of smoothly soulful pop-rock continued apace on **A Night On The Town**, his first album to outsell **Every Picture Tells A Story**, which was largely due to the inclusion of *Tonight's The Night (Gonna Be Alright)*, the biggest selling single of 1976, topping the American charts for eight weeks. More impressive still were a cover of Cat Stevens' *The First Cut Is The Deepest*, and the LP's centrepiece, *The Killing Of Georgie (Part I and II)*, an epic tale about the murder of one of Stewart's gay friends.

This is Stewart's real strength: a working class eloquence, a belief in the simplest truths that won't let him get caught up in the canonization of mere punks and gangsters. **Dave Marsh, Rolling Stone, August 1976**

Nightflight To Venus

ARTIST Boney M **RELEASE DATE** July 1978 (UK & US) **LABEL** Atlantic (UK)/Hansa (US) **PRODUCER** A Frank Farian **UK CHART** peak/weeks 1/65 **US CHART** peak/weeks 134/10 **TRACK LISTING** Nightflight To Venus/Rasputin/Painter Man/He Was A Steppenwolf/King Of The Road/Rivers Of Babylon/Voodoonight/Brown Girl In The Ring/Never Change Lovers In The Middle Of The Night/Heart Of Gold **PERSONNEL** Bobby Farrell (v), Marcia Barrett (v), Liz Mitchell (v), Maisie Williams (v)

German producer Frank Farian had rifled out disco hits for Silver Convention, and caught the bug. It seemed so easy. He put out his own recordings under the name Boney M; when they started to sell he had to find some visual types to front the releases. Soon Boney M were covering traditionals to meet the demand for Christmas hits, and the camp dance steps of Bobby Farrell were being emulated, with tongue in cheek, across Europe. Not, however in

America, whose understandable apathy to the project wound down the 'group' with the dawning of the Eighties.

Instead of swamping the group's identity in a confusion of electronic nastiness… the group's producer might attempt to express the individual personalities and musical attributes of its members. **Penny Reel, NME, August 1978**

The Nightfly

ARTIST Donald Fagen RELEASE DATE 20th October 1982 (UK & US) LABEL Warner Bros. (UK & US) PRODUCER Gary Katz UK CHART peak/weeks 44/16 US CHART peak/weeks 11/27 TRACK LISTING I.G.Y. (What A Beautiful World)/Green Flower Street/Ruby Baby/Maxine/New Frontier/The Nightfly/The Goodbye Look/Walk Between Raindrops PERSONNEL Donald Fagen (sy, ep, o, v, p), session musicians

The Fagen-Becker axis that had survived innumerable personnel changes around them finally sundered in 1981. Steely Dan were no more and Fagen's solo career would remain just one album's length for another decade. But this, an account of one night at a fictional jazz radio station, WJAZ in the Kennedy era, was no bad way to start. Standout tracks were a languorous cover of the Drifters' **Ruby Baby** and the US hit single **IGY (What A Beautiful World)**.

A mandatory purchase for all old farts with a few Steely Dan albums stashed away at the back of the pile, and a fine introduction to Donald Fagan… Anybody who responds to genuine wit and craftsmanship and who is interested in a non-rocking look at the Kennedy era could do worse than investigate. **NME, October 1982**

Nils Lofgren

ARTIST Nils Lofgren RELEASE DATE April 1975 (UK & US) LABEL A&M Records (UK & US) PRODUCER Nils Lofgren, David Briggs UK CHART peak/weeks – US CHART peak/weeks 141/9 TRACK LISTING Be Good Tonight/Back It Up/One More Saturday Night/If I Say It, It's So/I Don't Want To Know/Keith Don't Go (Ode To The Glimmer Twin)/Can't Buy A Break/Duty/The Sun Hasn't Set On This Boy Yet/Rock And Roll Crook/Two By Two/Goin' Back PERSONNEL Nils Lofgren (v, g, o, p, bv), Wornell Jones (b), Aynsley Dunbar (d)

After making his name as a sideman on Neil Young's **After The Goldrush**, it was time Nils Lofgren made a name for himself. It would not happen until 1976's **Cry Tough** which made the UK pre-punk Top 10, but this first solo album contained many songs around which his stage act would revolve for the next two decades. Most notable was **Keith Don't Go (Ode To The Glimmer Twin)**, a plea to the errant Rolling Stone (which, a couple of years hence, would have a new lyric pertaining to his Canadian drug bust) and **The Sun Hasn't Set On This Boy Yet**, a plea that he not be written off.

… for a while it looked as though Nils would fall into a sad and premature reclusive studio career. **Nils Lofgren** *is forceful evidence that this isn't going to be so…* **G. B., Melody Maker, April 1975**

Nilsson Schmilsson

ARTIST Nilsson RELEASE DATE January 1972 (UK)/December 1972 (US) LABEL RCA Victor (UK & US) PRODUCER Richard Perry UK CHART peak/weeks 4/22 US CHART peak/weeks 3/46 TRACK LISTING Gotta Get Up/Driving Along/Early In The Morning/The Moonbeam Song/Down/Without You/ Coconut/Let The Good Times Roll/Jump Into The Fire/I'll Never Leave You PERSONNEL Harry Nilsson (v, p), Jim Gordon (d), Klaus Voorman (b), Chirs Spedding (g), Jim Price (t, tr),Herbie Flowers (b)

From writing songs for Three Dog Night and scoring the animated hit TV movie *The Point* to the US Top 3 was quite a jump for Harry Edward Nelson III. But it was one he negotiated in no little style, thanks in the main to the transatlantic chart-topper **Without You**. Another (US-only) hit **Coconut** gilded the lily, but after a carbon-copy album Nilsson fell in with John Lennon in his 'lost weekend' mode and the creative momentum was lost. Hard to pigeonhole but undoubtedly talented, Nilsson's masterpiece, albeit sometimes overblown, remains this Richard Perry production.

As a songwriting talent, Nilsson always seems to be several steps away from true originality and genius, but high enough up there to merit the plaudits that come…. Where he doesn't quite measure up in his songwriting is in a kind of inability to create an oeuvre, a distinct style for himself. **M. W., Melody Maker, January 1972**

1999

ARTIST Prince And The Revolution RELEASE DATE February 1983 (UK)/November 1982 (US) LABEL Warner Bros. (UK & US) PRODUCER Prince UK CHART peak/weeks 30/21 US CHART peak/weeks 9/153 TRACK LISTING 1999/Little Red Corvette/Delirious/Free/Let's Pretend We're Married/Something In The Water (Does Not Compute)/Lady Cab Driver PERSONNEL Prince (v, sy, var)

Alongside Michael Jackson, Prince is the most important black performer of the last two decades. But, whereas Jackson has confined his subject matter to everyday topics, Prince has shown time and again there are no taboos when it comes to music. While **1999** revealed Prince to be a unique artist, it also revealed an abundance of subconscious influences: mixing the best funk lines of Clinton and Sly with the rock licks of Hendrix and Ernie Isley – a potent cocktail.

You (Prince) use partying, like many of your nasty nationality, as a carwash for the brain – having fun to hide from fear, most graphically in the title track. The end of the world – don't worry your pretty little head about it, Prince, leave the social comment to Grandmaster Flash and revel in your role of pretty boy's pin-up! **Julie Burchill, NME, November 1982**

1977

ARTIST Ash **RELEASE DATE** May 1996 (UK)/May 1996 (US) **LABEL** Infectious Records (UK)/Reprise (US) **PRODUCER** Owen Morris, Ash **UK CHART** peak/weeks 10/4 **US CHART** peak/weeks 0/0 **TRACK LISTING** Lose Control/Goldfinger/Girl From Mars/I'd Give You Anything/Gone The Dream/Kung Fu/Oh Yeah/Let It Flow/Innocent Smile/Angel Interceptor/Lost In You/Darkside Lightside **PERSONNEL** Tim Wheeler (g, st), Mark Hamilton (b), Rick McMurray (d), Lisa Moorish (v), Nick Ingman (st), Owen Morris (st)

Young, lucky, and obsessed with comic books and tacky TV shows, Ash hit the UK indie-pop upsurge with all cylinders firing. The Northern Irish trio had already turned down tours with Pearl Jam and Soul Asylum (due to school commitments!) when their singles started to garner rave reviews and chart showings. **1977** buzz-sawed to number one, high on adrenaline, named after the year of punk rock, *Star Wars*, and the birth of Tim Wheeler, Mark Hamilton and Rick McMurray. *Oh Yeah* demonstrated an ear for poignant melody and dynamics which suggested Ash might not burn out as quickly as one might at first have expected.

… 1977 is sprightly if ineffectual, with more in the way of youthful ebullience than any real musical artistry. **N.D., Mojo, June 1996**

He goes and gets his audience with hard clipped rhythms and brash horns that epitomise white R&B bounce, and he holds them with unexpected melodies… it's still a homey familiarity that Collins creates. **The Year In Records 1985, Rolling Stone, December 1985**

No Secrets

ARTIST Carly Simon **RELEASE DATE** January 1973 (UK)/December 1972 (US) **LABEL** Elektra (UK & US) **PRODUCER** Richard Perry **UK CHART** peak/weeks 3/26 **US CHART** peak/weeks 1/171 **TRACK LISTING** The Right Thing To Do/The Carter Family/You're So Vain/His Friends Are More Than Fond Of Robin/We Have No Secrets/Embrace Me, You Child/Waited So Long/It Was So Easy/Night Owl/When You Close Your Eyes **PERSONNEL** Carly Simon (v, p, g, bv), Lowell George, Paul Keough (g), Jim Keltner, James Gordon (d), Bill Payne (o), Jim Ryan, Klaus Voorman (b), Mick Jagger (bv, gst), Paul & Linda McCartney (bv, gst)

If *You're So Vain* (reputedly a savagely sweet put-down of Warren Beatty, and featuring the vocals of fellow big lipper, Mick Jagger) put her on the map, it was **No Secrets** which presented Carly Simon as a considerable force: a sort of glossier Joni Mitchell or less homespun, more urban Carole King. Simon's marriage to fellow icon of early Seventies singer-songcraft, James Taylor, was celebrated on *The Right Thing To Do*, yet her lyrical obsession was the vapidity of mature relationships.

No Jacket Required

ARTIST Phil Collins **RELEASE DATE** Febuary 1985 (UK)/March 1985 (US) **LABEL** Virgin (UK)/Atlantic (US) **PRODUCER** Phil Collins, Hugh Padgham **UK CHART** peak/weeks 1/176 **US CHART** peak/weeks 1/123 **TRACK LISTING** Sussudio/Only You Know And I Know/Long Long Way To Go/I Don't Wanna Know/One More Night/Don't Lose My Number/Who Said I Would/Doesn't Anybody Stay Together Anymore/Inside Out/Take Me Home **PERSONNEL** Phil Collins and Musicians

Mastering the art of the middle ground – melodic, nothing too challenging – Collins had another mammoth money-spinner with this. *One More Night* was its anticipated ballad hit, but *Sussudio* was an extraordinarily misguided hash of Prince's *1999*. With the customary blend of white soul and saccharine rock-with-the-rock-taken-out, chummy Phil was sailing the mid-Eighties *zeitgeist*, even following this up with an album of dance remixes. And all the while still keeping up the Genesis day job…

No Sleep Til Hammersmith

ARTIST Motorhead **RELEASE DATE** June 1981 (UK & US) **LABEL** Bronze (UK)/Mercury (US) **PRODUCER** Vic Maile **UK CHART** peak/weeks 1/21 **US CHART** peak/weeks 0/0 **TRACK LISTING** Ace Of Spades/Stay Clean/Metropolis/The Hammer/Iron Horse/No Class/Overkill/(We Are) The Road Crew/Capricorn/Bomber/Motorhead **PERSONNEL** Lemmy (b,v), Eddie Clarke (g), Phil Taylor (d)

Recorded during the tour to promote the **Ace Of Spades** album, this is the definitive Motorhead album, a live greatest hits collection that captured much of the power of the band on stage. Eleven tracks lasting a touch over 40 minutes – Motorhead had no time for the self-indulgent posturing and posing which mars so many live albums – and the pace never let up for a single second. Rightly regarded as a classic of the *genre*, this album proved just why Motorhead had earned the respect they commanded.

Motorhead… are simple, straightforward rock 'n' rollers who put the most colossal physical effort into their performance… **No Sleep** *has set the standard for heavy metal in the Eighties.* **Brian Harrigans, Melody Maker, June 1981**

A Nod's As Good As A Wink… To A Blind Horse

ARTIST The Faces RELEASE DATE November 1971 (UK)/December 1971 (US) LABEL Warner Bros. (UK & US) PRODUCER Glyn Johns UK CHART peak/weeks 2/22 US CHART peak/weeks 6/24 TRACK LISTING Miss Judy's Farm/You're So Rude/Love Lives Here/Last Orders Please/Stay With Me/Debris/ Memphis/Too Bad/That's All I Need PERSONNEL Rod Stewart (v), Ron Wood (g), Ian McLaglan (k), Ronnie Lane (b, v), Kenney Jones (d)

The Faces' third album since dropping the 'Small' suffix and replacing Steve Marriott by Rod Stewart was unavoidably overshadowed by their lead singer's solo breakthrough. But by any other yardstick than that transatlantic chart-topper, this was a classic ramshackle rock album, with some fabulous Ronnie Lane songs, most notably *Debris*, alongside Stewart and Wood's misogynistic *Stay With Me*, inevitably the single. It never got better than this: Lane left, producer Glyn Johns went on to the Eagles and the cracks became chasms. Here, though, there were laughter lines showing.

… a basic track that is usually… undistinguished, unimaginatively arranged, and sounds as much of a bore to listen to as it must have been to record. **Jon Landau, Rolling Stone, January 1972**

Non-stop Erotic Cabaret

ARTIST Soft Cell RELEASE DATE December 1981 (UK)/August 1982 (US) LABEL Some Bizzare (UK)/Sire (US) PRODUCER Mike Thorne UK CHART peak/weeks 5/46 US CHART peak/weeks 22/41 TRACK LISTING Frustration/Tinted Love/ Seedy Films/Youth/Sex Dwarf/Entertain Me/Chips On My Shoulder/ Bedsitter/Secret Life/Say Hello, Wave Goodbye. PERSONNEL Marc Almond (v), Dave Ball (k, s, dp)

While Duran Duran explored the glamorous side of life, fellow early Eighties pop act Soft Cell exposed its sleazy underbelly. A duo formed in Leeds, comprising poker-faced keyboard whiz David Ball and camp vocal tragedian-cum-self-styled sex dwarf Marc Almond, Soft Cell found enormous international success with their second single, a synth-pop rendition of Northern Soul classic, *Tainted Love*, that reached Number 1 in the UK and stayed on the US charts for a year. **Non-Stop Erotic Cabaret** was exactly that: gorgeously seedy pop songs – *Bedsitter, Say Hello, Wave Goodbye* – rendered by low-budget electronics.

Jealousy, deceit, blackmail, and how the backdrop (the rest of the world) sucks – these are the savagely emotional mainlines. Miraculously, humour and camp and the love of a good tune not only survive but thrive in this festering environment. **Chris Roberts, Melody Maker, April 1992**

A Northern Soul

ARTIST The Verve RELEASE DATE July 1995 (UK & US) LABEL Hut (UK)/Vernon Yard (US) PRODUCER Owen Morris, The Verve UK CHART peak/weeks 13/7 US CHART peak/weeks 0/0 TRACK LISTING A New Decade/This Is Music/On Your Own/So It Goes/A Northern Soul/Brainstorm Interlude/Drive You Home/History/No Knock On My Door/Life's An Ocean/Stormy Clouds/ Reprise PERSONNEL Nick McCabe (g, p, ag, o), Richard Ashcroft (v, ag, pc, ep), Simon Jones (b, pc, k, ag), Peter Salisbury (d, pc), Owen Morris (o, sys)

The Verve entered the history books with 1997's **Urban Hymns**, regarded by many as the album of the year. Arriving on the scene in late 1991, Wigan's finest were immediately pigeonholed with the 'shoegazer' bands such as Slowdive, Ride and Moose – all feedback and artily obscure lyrics. By 1995, however, The Verve had learned to focus their drone-rock into powerful, four or five-minute chunks: *This Is Music*, *A New Decade* and, in particular, *History*, were anthemic clarion calls to Britain's Gen X-ers – rays of hope on the approach to a new century. As for 'mad' Richard Ashcroft, he was swiftly becoming the most charismatic frontman in the land, a sort of articulate, sensitive Liam Gallagher with poetic sensibilities.

With this scuzzy realism, you get an ace summer soundtrack, the sky-swallowing bass, the jazzy slither of the drums, the wild card guitars turning every pigeon that flies past into a cosmically choreographed omen. **Victoria Segal, Melody Maker, July 1995**

Nothing's Shocking

ARTIST Jane's Addiction RELEASE DATE September 1988 (US)/December 1988 (UK) LABEL Warner Bros. (UK & US) PRODUCER Dave Jerden UK CHART peak/weeks 0/0 US CHART peak/weeks 103/35 TRACK LISTING Up The Beach/Ocean Size/Pigs In Zen/1%/I Would For You/My Time/Jane Says/Rock 'N' roll/Sympathy/Chip Away/Idiot's Rule PERSONNEL Penny Farrell (v), Dave Navarro (g), Eric A's (b), Stephen Perkins (d)

From its challenging cover art of plaster Siamese twins with heads ablaze, Jane's Addiction's major label debut was designed to live up to its title: as Warners dithered early copies were sheathed in rubber sleeves. Flea, on loan from the Red Hot Chili Peppers, played brass on the funky *Idiots Rule*, presaging his involvement in the band's 1997 re-formation along with Dave Navarro who joined the Chilis after Jane's Addiction split. A very influential release thanks to the guitar and vocal interplay over hypnotic rhythms.

Nothing's Shocking *is constantly on the scam, pulling different faces and moods to suit the beguiling lyrics and flexible larynx of Penny Farrell. It's a record that's quite unafraid to take risks where other angels fear to tread… Jane's Addiction have innovation and intrigue on their side.* **Martin Aston, Q, November 1988**

The Notorious Byrd Brothers

ARTIST The Byrds **RELEASE DATE** April 1968 (UK)/January 1968 (US) **LABEL** CBS (UK)/Columbia (US) **PRODUCER** Gary Usher, Bob Irwin **UK CHART peak/weeks** 12/11 **US CHART peak/weeks** 47/19 **TRACK LISTING** Artificial Energy/Goin' Back/Natural Harmony/Draft Morning/Wasn't Born To Follow/Get To You/Change Is Now/Old John Robertson/Tribal Gathering/Dolphin's Smile/Space Odyssey **PERSONNEL** Gene Clark (v, tm), Roger McGuinn (g, v), David Crosby (g, v), Chris Hillman (b, v), Michael Clarke (d), Clarence White (g), Jim Gordon (d)

Midway through this recording, both David Crosby (who'd started hanging out with Buffalo Springfield and thus alienated the proud, quiet McGuinn) and drummer Michael Clarke left. McGuinn retaliated by portraying Crosby on the album sleeve as a horse. Still, with horn sections, pioneering vari-speeded vocals, sound effects and even Moog synthesizers meshing effectively, **T.N.B.B.** wed pop songs and hippy trippiness on this their last indisputably great album. The towering triumphs were **Wasn't Born To Follow** (a key moment in the *Easy Rider* movie) and the yearning pathos of Carole King's **Goin' Back**.

*… there is much on **Notorious Byrd Brothers** that positively reeks of the psychedelic. Seemingly out-of-context trumpet parts appear in songs and actually work… a Byrds album that is innovative and hints at things to come.* **Steve Clarke and John Tobler, NME, August 1976**

Now And Then

ARTIST The Carpenters **RELEASE DATE** July 1973 (UK & US) **LABEL** A&M (UK & US) **PRODUCER** Jack Dougerty **UK CHART peak/weeks** 2/65 **US CHART peak/weeks** 2/41 **TRACK LISTING** Sing/This Masquerade/Heather/Jambalaya/I Can't Make Music/Yesterday Once More/Fun, Fun, Fun/End Of The World/Da Doo Ron Ron/Dead Man's Curve/Johnny Angel/Night Has A Thousand Eyes/Our Day Will Come/One Fine Day **PERSONNEL** Karen Carpenter (v, d), Richard Carpenter (k, v)

Albums from Richard and Karen were generally less consistent than Greatest Hits compilations, but this boasted a second side of unabashed nostalgia: revisiting old rock 'n' roll standards with a heartily kitsch affection and practising what the brother and sister duo had preached on **Yesterday Once More**. As we now know The Carpenters were never quite the puritanical Waltons of mythology, and Karen's untimely death from anorexia in 1982 has given a tragic edge to their seemingly over-creamy songs of love and loss. The yearning in her voice is painfully evident here.

The Number Of The Beast

ARTIST Iron Maiden **RELEASE DATE** March 1982 (UK)/April 1982 (US) **LABEL** EMI (UK)/Harvest (US) **PRODUCER** Martin Birch **UK CHART peak/weeks** 1/31 **US CHART peak/weeks** 33/65 **TRACK LISTING** Invaders/Children Of The Damned/The Prisoner/22, Acacia Avenue/The Number Of The Beast/Run To The Hills/Gangland/Hallowed Be Thy Name **PERSONNEL** Bruce Dickinson (v), Dave Murray (g), Adrian Smith (lg), Steve Harris (b, v), Clive Burr (d)

With new recruit Bruce Dickinson fronting the band as if born to it and one-time Deep Purple producer Martin Birch adding studio muscle to live chops, Maiden made the breakthrough to world domination status with their third album. It borrowed its title from Satanist Aleister Crowley, also an influence on Led Zeppelin's Jimmy Page, but otherwise was all their own work. It well deserved its five-star *Kerrang!* review: 'Polished but exciting, a thunderous set of performances.'

The great strength of this album is the songwriting. Steve Harris, who's written five of the eight songs here and co-composed two of the others, has finally fulfilled the potential he's previously only suggested. **Brian Harrigan, Melody Maker, March 1982**

O. G. Original Gangster

ARTIST Ice-T **RELEASE DATE** May 1991 (UK)/June 1992 (US) **LABEL** Sire (UK & US) **PRODUCER** Aladdin, D.J. Bilial Bashir, Ice-T, Afrika Islam **UK CHART peak/weeks** 42/2 **US CHART peak/weeks** 15/33 **TRACK LISTING** Home Of The Bodybag/First Impressions/Ziplock/Mic Contract/Mind Over Matter/New Jack Hustler/Ed/Bitches 2/Straight Up Nigger/O. G. Original Gangster/The House/Evil E-What About Sex?/Fly By/Midnight Fried Chicken/M.V.P.'s/Lifestyles Of The Rich And Famous/Body Count/Prepared To Die/Escape From The Killing Fields/Street Killer/Pulse Of The Rhyme/The Tower/Ya Should Killed Me Last **PERSONNEL** Ice-T (v, w), Africa Islam (s)

After Ice-T's role in *New Jack City*, one of the year's most talked-about movies, he might have been expected to clean up his act a little to capitalize on the attention it brought him. Instead, he came on like the rap equivalent of Nine Inch Nails, rockhard and uncompromising, determined and oozing aggression. **O. G. – Original Gangster** was tight, musically adventurous and dynamic, and helped to redefine the *genre* at a time when rap was in danger of becoming stale.

… raps are as little life-enhancing as it's possible for music this dynamic to be…. The cynicism of this LP is inescapable, and the fact that the grooves are consistently rock hard only makes the bile harder to swallow. **Jonathan Romney, Q, July 1991**

Ocean Drive

ARTIST The Lighthouse Family **RELEASE DATE** February 1996 **LABEL** Polydor (UK)/Wildcard (US) **PRODUCER** Mike Peden **UK CHART peak/weeks** 3/99 **US CHART peak/weeks TRACK LISTING** Lifted/Heavenly/Loving Every Minute/The Way You Are/Keep Remembering/Sweetest Operator/What Could Be Better/Beautiful Night/Goodbye Heartbreak **PERSONNEL** Tunde (v), Paul Tucker (k), Pete Wingfield (p), Timm Kellett (t, fh)

Having secured a deal by dint of playing a demo of the title track down the phone, Newcastle University students Paul Tucker and Tunde Baiyewu went on to register Polydor's biggest selling debut album in recent history. Their seamless blend of soul and pop, reminiscent of a Nineties Hot Chocolate, brought four hit singles, including the aforementioned **Ocean Drive**, but they remained ordinary enough to continue travelling by bus.

*Quality R&B based music is the order of the day on The Lighthouse Family's debut album **Ocean Drive**. The unusual and attractive style they demonstrated on their hit single **Lifted** is to the fore, as is musicianship on a sturdy collection of songs…* **Alan Jones, Music Week, March 1996**

album of unusual eclecticism and vigour, blending sampling and song-writing skills to throw 30 odd years of rock and funk into an unholy melting pot and come up smiling. He may have had just 'two turntables and a microphone', but his knowing post-modern irony and stubborn (if veiled) talent made him a press darling and the hip guru of Nineties appropriation.

This… is the 'true' follow-up to Beck's **Mellow Gold***…. Arrangements are of the stew-pot variety, with ingredients thrown in almost randomly, their flavours combining and clashing in arresting manner… Intriguingly eclectic, and occasionally bordering on the sensible.* **Andy Gill, Mojo, July 1996**

Odessey & Oracle

ARTIST The Zombies **RELEASE DATE** February 1965 (UK & US) **LABEL** Parrot (US) **PRODUCER** – **UK CHART** peak/weeks 0/0 **US CHART** peak/weeks 39/17 **TRACK LISTING** Derelict/Devils Haircut/High 5 (Rock The Catskills)/ Hotwax/Jack-Ass/Lord Only Knows/Minus/ New Pollution/ Novocane/Ramshackle/Readymade/ Sissyneck/ Where It's At **PERSONNEL** Rod Argent (k), Colin Bilinstone (v), Paul Atkinson (g), Chris White (b), Hugh Grundy (p)

Apart from the much lauded Beatles, there was another, far less celebrated band intent on bringing intricate, lushly orchestrated pop to the masses: The Zombies, St Albans' leading pioneers of baroque 'n' roll. Although they achieved considerable success with the hits, **She's Not There** and **Tell Her No**, **Odessey & Oracle** remains The Zombies' most cohesive statement, and certainly their finest LP, an undervalued masterpiece of melancholy symphonia, featuring Colin Blunstone's breathily affecting vocals and the adventurous arrangements of Rod Argent (later of Argent) and Chris White.

On this album they have handled the problems of added orchestration and elaborate production quite well while generally improving on their original sound, a sound which established them as one of England's very best rock groups. **Paul Album, Rolling Stone, February 1969**

Off The Bone

ARTIST The Cramps **RELEASE DATE** June 1983 (UK) **LABEL** Illegal (UK)/IRS (US) **PRODUCER** Alex Chilton from 'Human Fly', The Cramps from 'Goo Goo Muck' **UK CHART** peak/weeks 44/4 **US CHART** peak/weeks – **TRACK LISTING** Human Fly / The Way I Walk / Domino / Surfin' Bird / Lonesome Town / Garbageman/Fever/Drug Train/Love Me/I Can't Hardly Stand It/Goo Goo Muck/She Said/The Crusher/Save It/New Kind Of Kick **PERSONNEL** Lux Interior (v), Poison Ivy Rorschach (g), Brian Gregory (g), Nick Knox (d)

Louche, leering and so politically incorrect you had to laugh along with them, The Cramps churned out a psychedelic rockabilly of ebullient twisted honesty. They loved rock 'n' roll, dodgy Fifties records and B-movies, and all things trashy – as their dress sense happily displayed. **Off The Bone** brought together their debut EP **Gravest Hits** and the swampy **Psychedelic Jungle**. Their voodoo venom emanated largely from Poison Ivy's guitar, which was so muddy no bass was usually required. Lux Interior was a lecherous, unstable frontman who writhed in ecstatic abandon at the tortuous tainted riffs of the *genre* classic **Human Fly** and **The Trashmen's Surfin' Bird**. Truly BAD rock 'n' roll indeed.

Ode To Billy Joe

ARTIST Bobbie Gentry **RELEASE DATE** September 1967 (UK & US) **LABEL** Capitol (UK & US) **PRODUCER** – **UK CHART PEAK/WEEKS** 0/0 **US CHART PEAK/ WEEKS** 1/30 **TRACK LISTING** – **PERSONNEL** Bobbie Gentry (v, g, p, bj, b), session musicians

Most people think of **Ode To Billy Joe** as Bobbie Gentry's chart-topping single of 1967. The album of the same name was a hastily conceived affair: veteran arranger Jimmie Haskell joked that the artwork took longer than the recording, which was completed in seven days, from the basic tracks to final mix, by producer Kelly Gordon. But the real reason **Ode To Billy Joe** is a significant album is, surely, that it ended **Sgt. Pepper**'s 15-week stay atop *Billboard*'s listings!

Bobbie manages to combine an earthy sexiness with an authentic Southern sound and yet remains a pop singer not a folk performer… the one snag on the album… is the sameness of her songs. **Melody Maker, December 1967**

Odelay

ARTIST Beck **RELEASE DATE** July 1996 (UK & US) **LABEL** DGC (US) **PRODUCER** Beck Hansen, The Dust Brothers **UK CHART** peak/weeks 0/0 **US CHART** peak/weeks 16/13 **TRACK LISTING** Devils Haircut/Hotwax/Lord Only Knows/ The New Pollution/Derelict/Novacane/Jack-Ass/Where It's At/Minus/ Sissyneck/Readymade/High 5 (Rock The Catskills)/Ramshackle/ Diskobox **PERSONNEL** Beck (v, ag), Rachel Haden (d, v), Anna Waronker (b, v), Petra Haden (vl, v), Mike Boito (o), David Harte (d), Rob Zabrecky (b)

Kansas-raised all-rounder Beck Hansen seemed destined to dwell forever in One Hit Wonderland when his **Loser** hit *I'm a loser baby, so why don't you kill me* became a slacker-nerd anthem. He then stunned everyone, including himself, by producing a second

Off The Wall

ARTIST Michael Jackson RELEASE DATE September 1979 (UK & US) LABEL Epic (UK & US) PRODUCER Quincy Jones UK CHART peak/weeks 5/176 US CHART peak/weeks 3/169 TRACK LISTING Don't Stop 'Til You Get Enough/Rock With You/Working Day And Night/Get On The Floor/Off The Wall/Girlfriend/She's Out Of My Life/I Can't Help It/It's The Falling In Love/Burn This Disco Out PERSONNEL Michael Jackson (v, bv, pc), Louis Johnson (b), John Robinson (d, pc), Greg Phillinganes (ep, sy, cite), David Williams (g), Marlo Henderson (g), Randy Jackson (pc), Richard Heath (pc), Paulinho Da Costa (pc), The Seawind Horns (hn), Jerry Hey (t, fl), Larry Williams (as, ts, f), Kim Hutchcroft (bs, ts, f), William Reichenbach (t), Bobby Watson (b), session musicians

This first solo album for Epic linked Michael Jackson with top producer Quincy Jones and the songwriting talents of Rod Temperton. While Temperton had previously proven himself adept at writing excellent soul/pop tunes for Heatwave, the cuts he penned for Jackson were altogether funkier and lent themselves perfectly to video. In among the up-tempo material – standout cuts being *Don't Stop Till You Get Enough*, *Rock With You* and the title track – were some equally excellent ballads, with *She's Out Of My Life* becoming a staple part of Jackson's live show. The delivery throughout never dips below excellent.

… an oddly mixed bag – Carole Bayer-Sager here, Earth, Wind and Fire there – yet it's possible to see both as culmination (in Gavin Martin's words 'the final summation of the great disco party') and as the inauguration of a new, softer funk for the Eighties. **Barney Hoskins, NME, September 1983**

Ogden's Nut Gone Flake

ARTIST The Small Faces RELEASE DATE June 1968 (UK)/September 1968 (US) LABEL Immediate (UK & US) PRODUCER Ian Samwell-Smith UK CHART peak/weeks 1/19 US CHART peak/weeks 159/9 TRACK LISTING Ogden's Nut Gone Flake/Afterglow (Of Your Love)/Long Agos And Worlds Apart/Rene/Son Of A Baker/Lazy Sunday/Happiness Stan/Rollin' Over/The Hungry Intruder/The Journey/Mad John/Happy Days/Toy Town PERSONNEL Steve Marriott (v, g), Jimmy Winston (o), Ronnie Lane (b, v), Kenney Jones (d)

The fourth Small Faces album and the last one before the departure of lead vocalist/guitarist Steve Marriott, **Ogden's Nut Gone Flake** is the band's most acclaimed work, and not just because of its original flattened, circular sleeve, designed to resemble a tin of pipe tobacco. Apart from the hit single, *Lazy Sunday* – one of their signature tunes – the LP was a kind of mod concept, with gimmicky between-track links courtesy of comedian Stanley Unwin. Side one featured some of their finest trad-mod rockers, while on side two the acid ethos permeated their consciousness for a trippy, post **Sgt. Pepper** fairytale.

It's all real nice and truthfully freaky, a refreshing change from a lot of the 'progressive' garbage we've been hearing recently. Everybody owes it to themselves to get this record and be refreshed. **James Pomeroy, Rolling Stone, October 1968**

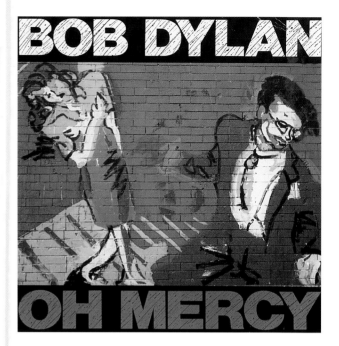

Oh Mercy

ARTIST Bob Dylan RELEASE DATE October 1989 (UK & US) LABEL CBS (UK)/Columbia (US) PRODUCER Daniel Lanois UK CHART peak/weeks 6/7 US CHART peak/weeks 30/123 TRACK LISTING Political World/Where Teardrops Fall/Everything Is Broken/Ring Them Bells/Man In The Long Blackcoat/Most Of The Time/What Good Am I?/Disease Of Conceit/What Was It You Wanted/Shooting Star PERSONNEL Bob Dylan (v, g, h)

The year from October 1988 was an unusually active and diverse one by Dylan's standards. Having banded with Harrison, Orbison, Petty and Lynne in the Travelin' Wilburys, he released a live album, **Dylan And The (Grateful) Dead,** which found precious few converts. Then he headed for New Orleans where, under Daniel Lanois' (U2, etc) supervision and with Crescent City house band the Neville Brothers in attendance, he whipped out an album in **Oh Mercy** that took him to his highest UK chart position since the beginning of the decade! Some year…

Oh Mercy can perhaps best be thought of as a collaboration between Dylan and producer Daniel Lanois. Lanois has… fashioned evocative, atmospheric soundscapes that elicit every nuance of meaning from Dylan's songs while never overwhelming them. **Anthony De Curtis, Rolling Stone, September 1989**

OK Computer

ARTIST Radiohead RELEASE DATE July 1997 (UK & US) LABEL Parlophone/EMI Records (UK)/Capitol (US) PRODUCER Radiohead UK CHART peak/weeks 1/30 US CHART peak/weeks 0/0 TRACK LISTING Airbag/Paranoid Android/Subterranean Homesick Alien/Exit Music (For A film)/Let Down/Karma Police/Fitter Happier/Electioneering/Climbing Up The Walls/No Surprises/Lucky/The Tourist PERSONNEL Thom Yorke (v, g), Colin Greenwood, Jonny Greenwood (g), Bill Selway (d), Ed O'Brien (g)

When *Paranoid Android* appeared as a single, it was obvious that something important had been happening in deepest Oxfordshire, but the reality of **OK Computer** still came as something of a shock. Thom Yorke had articulated his feelings of hopelessness and impotence and his eventual acceptance of a world he could not change with such unnerving force that it made for distinctly uncomfortable listening, a discomfort amplified by the alien soundscapes created by the rest of the band. Powerful, claustrophobic and disorienting, this is the sound of Radiohead singing as the walls close in.

… once you've been hooked it never stops growing on you. Better than The Bends? Probably. Record of the year? Conceivably… in 20 years time I'm betting **OK Computer** *will be seen as the key record of 1997.* **Nick Kent, Mojo, July 1997**

Older

ARTIST George Michael RELEASE DATE June 1996 (UK & US) LABEL Virgin (UK)/Dream Works (US) PRODUCER George Michael UK CHART peak/weeks 1/ US CHART peak/weeks 6/18 TRACK LISTING Jesus To A Child/Fast Love/Older/Spinning The Wheel/It Doesn't Really Matter/The Strangest Thing/To Be Forgiven/Move On/Star People/You Have Been Loved/Free PERSONNEL George Michael (v, k, b, d), Hugh Burns (ag), John Douglas (k), Dave Clews (k), Andy Hamilton (s), Steve Sidwell (t), Chris Cameron (st, k, p), John Thirkell (fh, t), Stuart Brooks (t, fh), Chris Davies (s), Phil Smith (s), Fayyaz Virji (tr), Alan Ross (g), Danny Jacobs (g)

After settling an acrimonious court case with former label Sony, with whom he had signed (as CBS) when part of teen duo Wham!, George Michael came back with a mature piece of work which reflected both a new-found fascination with South American rhythms and the loss of a close friend, Anselmo Feleppa. Singles (which were still being peeled from **Older** 18 months after release) included the post-Aids ode *Spinning The Wheel*, as world-weary as Wham! had been carefree.

Hip-swaying beat-box percussion pops around background strings and other sampled orchestral colourings… easy-going and low on excitement… George Michael is excellent… But he's still telling us about himself, giving us information where the immortals present us with a piece of their soul. **Phil Sutcliffe, Mojo, June 1996**

Ommadawn

ARTIST Mike Oldfield RELEASE DATE November 1975 (UK)/December 1975 (US) LABEL Virgin (UK & US) PRODUCER Mike Oldfield UK CHART peak/weeks 4/23 US CHART peak/weeks 146/7 TRACK LISTING Ommadawn (Side 1), Ommadawn (Side 2) PERSONNEL Mike Oldfield (g, b, evthg), Tom Newman (g), Jon Field (fl), Stan Broughton (d), Lindsay Cooper (wi)

Having knocked **Tubular Bells** off the top of the charts with its successor **Hergest Ridge**, multi-instrumentalist Oldfield, still just

OK COMPUTER
RADIOHEAD

22, had given himself a hard act to follow with his third solo work. He did so by co-opting the likes of the Chieftains' Paddy Moloney to vary the musical mix and add ethnic folk influences. The new wave would overtake him, however, and by 1978's **Incantations** he had reduced his ambient creations to the length of an album side, giving the other over to short songs.

Not only committed to massive, intense creative effort, but also prepared to stand up for naivety and innocence. Not to mention truth and beauty…. The hippie dream doesn't have to end in paranoia, sickness and decay, after all. **Bob Edmands, NME, November 1975**

On Tour With Eric Clapton

ARTIST Delaney & Bonnie & Friends RELEASE DATE June 1970 (UK)/April 1970 (US) LABEL Atlantic (UK)/Atco (US) PRODUCER Jimmy Miller & Delaney Bramlett UK CHART peak/weeks 39/3 US CHART peak/weeks 29/17 TRACK LISTING Things Get Better/Poor Elijah/Only You And I Know/I Don't Want To Discuss It/That's What My Man Is For/Where There's A Will There's A Way/Coming Home/Little Richard Medley: Long Tall Sally/Jenny Jenny/The Girl Can't Help It/Tutti-Frutti PERSONNEL Delaney Bramlett (rg, v), Bonnie Bramlett (v), Eric Clapton (lg), Dave Mason (g), Carl Raddle (b), Jim Gordon (d), B. Whitlock (o, v), Jim Price (t, tb), Bobby Keys (s), Tex Johnson (pc), Rita Coolidge (v)

The turbulent career of Cream, rock's first supergroup, proved so traumatic to Eric Clapton that he decided his next move would be to link with the Bramletts, Delaney and Bonnie, as a mere lead guitarist. They basked in his reflected glory for a short while in 1970 as this album charted due to his patronage, but euphoria evaporated somewhat as three backing musicians, Bobby Whitlock, Carl Radle and Jim Gordon departed to form Eric's Dominos.

Sure it made a difference in England to be able to say Eric Clapton was playing with us, because we were an unknown. If Eric hadn't gone over there and said 'this is the best band in the world'… they wouldn't have seen us for the longest time probably. **Bonnie in interview with Jacoba Atlas, Melody Maker, March 1970**

Once Upon A Star

ARTIST The Bay City Rollers RELEASE DATE May 1975 (UK)/September 1975 (US) LABEL Arista (UK & US) PRODUCER – UK CHART peak/weeks 1/37 US CHART peak/weeks 20/35 TRACK LISTING Bye Bye Baby/Disco Kid/Belle Jean/When Will You Be Mine/Angel Baby/Keep On Dancing/Once Upon A Star/Let's Go/Marlina/My Teenage Heart/Rock And Roll Honeymoon/Hey! Beautiful Dreamer PERSONNEL Les McKeown (v), Alan Longmuir (g), Derek Longmuir (d), Eric Faulkner (g), Stuart 'Woody' Wood (d)

The Seventies were big on absurdity. The Rollers, brainchild of self-proclaimed svengali Tam Paton, were unlikely teeny-bop sensations: Scotland's answer to The Osmonds. With their dodgy haircuts, scarves, tartan and too-short trousers, they somehow became scream 'n' dream fodder to a generation of girls. By the time their limp Four Seasons cover **Bye Bye Baby** became their first Number 1, the attendant hysteria was akin to Beatlemania. The equally soppy *Give A Little Love* and the marginally gutsier **Money Honey** were also enormous. This was their second chart-topping album, and before long the public's affections had moved on. The band, less than innocent behind the façade, split acrimoniously.

The lyrics and the singing of them are possibly tepid, the sentiments expressed blindly naive and sickly sentimental, the delivery as soggy as a week old pudding. And as for the actual playing. Well let's say that any given five of the Rollers' legions of fans could probably do as well. **Brian Harrigan, April 1975**

Once Upon A Time

ARTIST Donna Summer **RELEASE DATE** November 1977 (UK & US) **LABEL** Casablanca (UK & US) **PRODUCER** Giorgio Moroder, Pete Bellotte **UK CHART** peak/weeks 24/13 **US CHART** peak/weeks 26/58 **TRACK LISTING** Once Upon A Time/And Faster To Nowhere/Fairy Tale High/Say Something Nice/Now I Need You/Working The Midnight Shift/Queen For A Day/If You've Got It Flaunt It/Man Like You/Sweet Romance/Once Upon A Time/Dance Into My Life/Rumour Has It/I Love You/Happily Ever After/Once Upon A Time **PERSONNEL** Donna Summer (v), session musicians

Donna Summer was the biggest solo star to emerge during the disco era. She was also the most artistically ambitious. **Once Upon A Time**, produced by Italian electro-pop pioneer Giorgio Moroder and his sidekick Pete Bellotte, was the first disco concept LP, a grandiose double-album statement of intent, featuring all-original compositions penned by Summer and the Moroder-Bellotte team. **Once Upon A Time** presented Summer as fairytale princess on a Cinderella-like journey from slave labour (*Working The Midnight Shift*) to true romance (*Happily Ever After*). Meanwhile, Moroder and Bellotte crafted a lush, panoramic, metronomic soundscape against which Summer sighed her way to orgasmic nirvana. Manufactured in Germany by Americans and Italians, this was Eurodisco at its finest.

Once Upon A Time

ARTIST Simple Minds **RELEASE DATE** November 1985 (UK & US) **LABEL** Virgin (UK)/A&M (US) **PRODUCER** Jimmy Levine, Bob Clearmountain **UK CHART** peak/weeks 1/83 **US CHART** peak/weeks 10/42 **TRACK LISTING** Once Upon A Time/All The Things She Said/Ghost Dancing/Alive And Kicking/ Oh Jungleland / I Wish You Were Here / Sanctify Yourself / Come A Long Way **PERSONNEL** Charles Burchill (g), Michael McNeil (k), Jim Kerr (v), Mel Gaynor (d), John Giblin (b)

With the help of producers Jimmy Levine and Bob Clearmountain,

Simple Minds contrived a big-rock sound that was perfectly suited to America's FM radio. Like the hugely successful soundtrack smash from *The Breakfast Club*, ***Don't You Forget About Me***, **Once Upon A Time** was far removed from the Eurocentric atmospheres of their earlier albums, although the public didn't mind, turning **Alive And Kicking**, **Sanctify Yourself** and **All The Things She Said** into sizeable hits.

Once Upon A Time isn't as hollow as the promised miracles preceding it. On the contrary, it signals a reawakened interest in a world outside their wallets. But big is still the operative word, the 3Ms – monumental, mass, messianic – constitute the governing aesthetics… Biba Kopf, NME, October 1985

One Nation Under A Groove

ARTIST Funkadelic **RELEASE DATE** December 1978 (UK) **LABEL** Warner Bros. (UK & US) **PRODUCER** George Clinton **UK CHART** peak/weeks 56/5 **US CHART** peak/weeks 16/22 **TRACK LISTING** One Nation Under A Groove/ Groovallegiance/Who Says A Funk Band Can't Play Rock?!/ Promentalshit backwashpsychosis Enema Squad (The Doodoo Chasers)/Into You/Cholly (Funk Getting Ready To Roll)/Lunchmeataphobia (Think! It Ain't Illegal Yet!)/ P.E. Squad/Doodoo Chasers ('Going All-The-Way-Off' Instrumental Version)/ Maggot Brain **PERSONNEL** Gary Shider (g), Mike 'Kidd Funkadelic' Hampton (g), Bobby Lewis (bj), Bernie 'DaVinci' Worrell (k, sy), Walter 'Junie' Morrison (k, sy), Tyrone Lambkin (d, pc), W. Bootsy Collins (d, pc), Jerome Brailey (d, pc), Larry Fratangelo (d, pc), Cordell 'Boogie' Mosson (b), Rodney 'Skeet' Curtis (b), William 'Bootsy' Collins (b), Funkadelic Blamgusta Vocaloids: Raymond (Stingray) Davis, Lynn Mabry, Ron Ford, Dawn Silva, Debbie Wright, Gary 'Dowop' Shider,

By the time **One Nation Under a Groove** was released there was little difference between Funkadelic and George Clinton's other outfit, Parliament. Indeed, one suspects the reason why Funkadelic got a million-seller might have had something to do with record company pressure, for the title track could just as easily have been released by Parliament. What is not in dispute is the anthemic qualities of the tracks and the spirit embodied in the delightfully titled ***Who Says A Funk Band Can't Play Rock?!*** If you ever wondered where Prince got his inspiration, listen to this album.

It is a thin line between this cheering activisim and cabaret, and Funkadelic do step over it occasionally. The rhythm and the logic is entirely their own, an internal participatory join-the-dots. There are no superficial messages. There may be no 'messages' at all. **Ian Penman, NME, December 1978**

One Of These Nights

ARTIST Eagles **RELEASE DATE** July 1975 (UK) **LABEL** Asylum (UK & US) **PRODUCER** Bill Szymczyk **UK CHART** peak/weeks 8/40 **US CHART** peak/weeks 1/56 **TRACK LISTING** One Of These Nights/Too Many Hands/Hollywood Waltz/Journey Of The Sorcerer/Lyin' Eyes/Take It To The Limit/Visions/After The Thrill Is Gone/I Wish You Peace **PERSONNEL** Glen Fry (g, v), Bernie Leadon (g, v), Randy Meisner (b, v), Don Henley (d, v)

Amazingly for such a quintessentially American band, the Eagles recorded their first two albums in London. This, their fourth, was the one they brought back home to top the US chart for the first time – and even managed a songwriting credit for Ronald Reagan's daughter, Patti Davis, at the time a paramour of guitarist Bernie Leadon. That was for *I Wish You Peace* – but the big one was *Take It To The Limit*, an emotion-soaked ballad that gave Randy Meisner a rare lead vocal.

… the Eagles are such a rising force – definitely undervalued in Britain – that it's an album impossible to ignore. Perhaps the problem is that it lacks obvious classics… while a couple of tunes… could have been sacrificed for something more solid. **Melody Maker, July 1975**

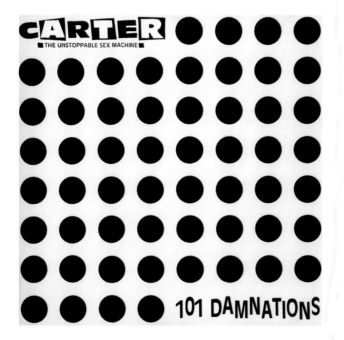

101 Damnations

ARTIST Carter-The Unstoppable Sex Machine **RELEASE DATE** January 1990 **LABEL** Big Cat **PRODUCER** Simon Painter **UK CHART** peak/weeks 29/6 **US CHART** peak/weeks - **TRACK LISTING** The Road To Domestos/Everytime A Churchbell Rings/Twenty Four Minutes From Tulse Hill/An All American National Sport/Sheriff Fatman/The Taking Of Peckham/Crimestoppers A' Go Go/Good Grief Carlie Brown/Midnight On The Murder Mile/A Perfect Day To Drop The Bomb/G.I.Blues **PERSONNEL** Jim Bob and Fruitbat (v), Rob Sheridan (p)

A sort of working-class retort to the Pet Shop Boys, Carter U.S.M. (as they soon came to be known) made indie dance-pop before it was moved to 'alternative' acts. Defiantly anti-glamorous, the duo's punning polemic won them acclaim and brickbats in equal measures. Their love/hate of south London was evident in *24 Minutes From Tulse Hill* and *The Taking Of Peckham 1-2-3*. Later they were to broaden their sound and decline into voguish popularity, but at this time it seemed only bullets could stop them.

This is Carter getting it right, using their mix of two guitars/tape machine and a peppering of samples to the full. It's weighted with a constant stream of clever touches, a sensible line in cynicism and a streak of humour. **NME, December 1990**

The Only Ones

ARTIST The Only Ones **RELEASE DATE** June 1978 (UK)/May 1978 (US) **LABEL** CBS (UK)/Columbia (US) **PRODUCER** Robert Ash **UK CHART** peak/weeks 56/1 **US CHART** peak/weeks 0/0 **TRACK LISTING** Whole Of The Law/Another Girl, Another Planet/Breaking Down/City Of Fun/Beast/Creature Of Doom/It's The Truth/Language Problem/No Peace For The Wicked/Immortal Story **PERSONNEL** Gordon Edwards, Mick Gallagher (k), Koulla Kakoulli (v), Mike Kellin (d), Alan Mair (b), Peter Perrett (g, v), John Perry (g, k), Raphael And Friends (hn)

A couple of years older than their contemporaries, The Only Ones owned all their own equipment, financed their debut single themselves and negotiated with the majors at their leisure. In mid 1977 they finally succumbed to CBS – maybe because of singer Peter Perrett's big hero Bob Dylan. Perrett's languid vocals and world-weary lyrics were propelled by a thundering rhythm section and coloured by the Coltrane-fuelled guitar licks of John Perry. Despite the initial failure of *Another Girl Another Planet* to take off as a single (which it did some 15 years later!), this is their most satisfying, most focused collection, unsullied by the drugs and disillusionment that characterized their demise.

I rate The Only Ones as one of the most stimulating and original bands around. That word has been rarely taxed of late, but if ever its application was justifiable, it is here and now.... **Ian Birch, Melody Maker, May 1978**

The Orb's Adventures Beyond The Ultraworld

ARTIST The Orb **RELEASE DATE** April 1991 (UK)/November 1991 (US) **LABEL** Big Life (UK)/Mercury (US) **PRODUCER** Youth, Dr Alex Patterson, Steve Hillage, Eddie Manasseh, Andy Falconer, Thomas Fehlmann, Baku, Jimi Cauty **UK CHART** peak/weeks 29/5 **US CHART** peak/weeks – **TRACK LISTING** Little Fluffy Clouds/Earth (Gaia)/Supernova At The End Of The Universe/Back Side Of The Moon/Spanish Castles In Space/Perpetual Dream/Into The Fourth Dimension/Outlands/Star 6 & 7 8 9/A Huge Ever Growing Pulsating Brain That Rules From The Centre Of The Ultraworld: Live Mix Mk 10 **PERSONNEL** Alex Paterson (sy, k) with Jim Cauty

Originally planned as a triple album – the third disc came out as **Aubrey Mixes: The Ultraworld Excursions** – The Orb's debut release was nevertheless hugely ambitious and, despite being immediately deleted by the Big Life label, gave them both a reputation and a chart debut. Music paper critics were put into flotation tanks to sample the music, whose highlight was a new version of their 1989 single *A Huge Ever-Growing Pulsating Brain...* – sampling Minnie Riperton's *Loving You*.

This is cosmic rock, for all its contemporary house-y-trappings. This music is an aural version of the visual pun that climaxes '2001 A Space Odyssey (a planet sized foetus)' **Simon Reynolds, Melody Maker, April 1991**

Otis Blue

ARTIST Otis Redding **RELEASE DATE** February 1966 (UK)/October 1965 (US) **LABEL** Atlantic (UK & US) **PRODUCER** Stax Staff **UK CHART** peak / weeks 6/21 **US CHART** peak / weeks 75/34 **TRACK LISTING** Ole Man Trouble / Respect / Change Gonna Come / Down In The Valley / Loving You Too Long / Shake / My Girl / Wonderful World / Rock Me Baby/(I Can't Get No) Satisfaction/You Don't Miss Your Water **PERSONNEL** Otis Redding (v), Booker T. Jones (k), Donald 'Duck' Dunn (b), Al Jackson Jr (d), session musicians

Alongside Sam Cooke, Otis Redding is the epitome of what a male soul singer should be, able to switch effortlessly from song to song, irrespective of style, and still make it sound like the sweetness thing this side of Tate and Lyle. Few singers could have breathed undreamed-of soul and real feeling into a song such as The Rolling Stones' *Satisfaction*, but here Redding manages it with ease.

Otis Redding has virtually become a yardstick against which the elusive properties of 'soul' can be measured.... Not a milestone in soul music, just a milestone, period. The lessons it teaches have never been expressed more simply or with more telling eloquence. **Adam Sweeting, Melody Maker, December 1983**

Our Favourite Shop

ARTIST The Style Council **RELEASE DATE** June 1985 (UK) **LABEL** Polydor (UK & US) **PRODUCER** Peter Wilson **UK CHART** peak/weeks 2/38 **US CHART** peak/weeks – **TRACK LISTING** Homebreakers/All Gone Away/Come To Milton Keynes/Internationalists/A Stone's Throw Away/The Stand Up Comic's Instructions/Boy Who Cried Wolf/A Man Of Great Promise/Down In The Seine/The Lodgers/Luck/With Everything To Lose/Our Favourite Shop/Walls Come Tumbling Down. **PERSONNEL** Paul Weller (v, g), Mick Talbot (k), Steve White (d), plus various artists

After dissolving the Jam in 1982, Paul Weller used The Style Council as an opportunity to explore his every musical whim: soul, jazz, mood muzak, funk and pop. **Our Favourite Shop** was the most successful, both commercially and artistically, of Weller's post-Jam experiments. Released as **Internationalists** in America, it contained the Top 10 UK hit, **Walls Come Tumbling Down**, as well as **Come To Milton Keynes**, which proved Weller could still match keenly observed social commentary with knockout hooks.

Homebreakers, the opener, is the strongest song here, a brooding survey of economic blight and Tory callousness… D. C. Lee helps Talbot out on the vocals, and Weller even permits himself a well-judged blues and guitar solo. **Adam Sweeting, Melody Maker, May 1985**

Out Of Our Heads

ARTIST The Rolling Stones **RELEASE DATE** October 1965 (UK)/August 1965 (US) **LABEL** Decca (UK)/London (US) **PRODUCER** Andrew Loog Oldham **UK CHART** peak/weeks 2/24 **US CHART** peak/weeks 1/66 **TRACK LISTING** She Said Yeah/Mercy, Mercy/Hitch Hike/That's How Strong My Love Is/Good Times/Gotta Get Away/Talkin' 'Bout You/Cry To Me/Oh, Baby (We've Got A Good Thing Going)/Heart Of Stone/The Under Assistant West Coast Promotion Man/I'm Free **PERSONNEL** Mick Jagger (v, h), Keith Richard (rg), Brian Jones (lg), Bill Wyman (b), Charlie Watts (d)

Originally boasting some bizarre Andrew Loog Oldham sleeve notes about knocking over blind men and robbing them, this took a foolish but brave running jump at Don Covay's **Mercy Mercy**. It is best remembered as the album that yielded not only **The Last Time** but also one of the defining singles of the decade and of a generation in **(I Can't Get No) Satisfaction**. This expressed the horniness usually dignified as 'anger' which has motivated rock 'n' roll since its birth. Keith Richards mastered an unforgettable riff which has been replayed as many times as any in the canon, while Jagger spat out 'Can't you see I'm on a losing streak?' with great conviction.

Inside are 12 great tracks, crammed with Stones' sounds – double tracking, harmonicas, tambourines, organs, pianos and the distinctive wailing, shouting voice of Mick Jagger – number one selling point of the Rolling Stones. **Melody Maker, September 1965**

Out Of The Blue

ARTIST Electric Light Orchestra **RELEASE DATE** November 1977 **LABEL** Jett (UK)/United Artists (US) **PRODUCER** Jeff Lynne **UK CHART** peak/weeks 4/108 **US CHART** peak/weeks 4/58 **TRACK LISTING** Turn To Stone/It's Over/Sweet Talkin' Woman/Across The Border/Night In The City/Starlight/Jungle/Believe Me Now/Steppin' Out/Standin' In The Rain/Summer And Lightning/Mr Blue Sky/Sweet Is The Night/The Whale/Birmingham Blues/Wild West Hero **PERSONNEL** Roy Wood (c, v), Feff Lynne (v, g), Ben Beven (d, v), Richard Tandy (b, k, v), Bill Hunt (k, f, h), Wilf Gibson (v), Hugh McDowell (c), Andy Craig (c)

As Star Wars mania swept the world, the ELO stepped out into a laser light show from under a suspended spaceship. And **Out Of The Blue**, a double album that racked up an amazing four million in advance orders worldwide, was every bit as spectacular as the stage show – and impossible to escape in a year historians would claim was dominated by punk. If Jeff Lynne saw his outfit as The Beatles' descendants, then this was **Revolver** filtered through **I Am**

Electric Light Orchestra
Out of the Blue

The Walrus with just a dash of Luke Skywalker.

… the experimentation between orchestra and pop music had become somewhat watered down over the years, to the point where strings merely flavour the overall sound… it's a skilfully, often brilliantly, executed album that epitomises the true meaning of the much abused phrase 'pop sensibilities'. **Harry Doherty, Melody Maker, November 1977**

Out Of Time

ARTIST R.E.M. **RELEASE DATE** March 1991 (UK & US) **LABEL** Warner Bros. (UK & US) **PRODUCER** Scott Litt, R.E.M. **UK CHART** peak/weeks 1/136 **US CHART** peak/weeks 1/109 **TRACK LISTING** Radio Song/Losing My Religion/Low/Near Wild Heaven/Endgame/Shiny Happy People/Belong/Half A World Away/Texarkana/Country Feedback/Me In Honey **PERSONNEL** Michael Stipe (v), Peter Buck (g), Mike Mills (b), Bill Berry (d)

Never the most conventional of rock bands, R.E.M. moved even further from the mainstream with **Out Of Time** as Pete Buck experimented with different instruments rather than the band's trademark Rickenbacker guitar sound. But the acoustic result chimed in with the *Unplugged* era while focusing attention on Michael Stipe's warm voice. Released on Jack Kerouac's birthday, it would rack up an incredible seven Grammy nominations (winning three) and widen people's perceptions of the band immeasurably.

Many of the songs and all of the arrangements work hard to disrupt those elements of the REM sound that were threatening to turn into a cliche… this brooding departure offers them at their most reflective, challenging and intriguing. **Mark Cooper, Q, April 1991**

Outlandos D'Amour

ARTIST The Police **RELEASE DATE** April 1979 (UK)/Febuary 1979 (US) **LABEL** A&M (UK & US) **PRODUCER** The Police **UK CHART** peak/weeks 6/96 **US CHART** peak/weeks 23/63 **TRACK LISTING** Next To You/So Lonely/Roxanne/Hole In My Life/Peanuts/Can't Stand Losing You/Truth Hits Everybody/Born In The 50's/Be My Girl Sally/Masoko Tanga **PERSONNEL** Andy Summers (g), Stewart Copeland (d), Sting (b, v)

They're competent and detached craftsmen, hard working at staving off the army. The album's ten well designed songs are neat but strained…. The Police have no ambition and too much complacency. **Paul Morley, NME, November 1978**

Oxygene

ARTIST Jean-Michel Jarre **RELEASE DATE** July 1977 (UK & US) **LABEL** Polydor (UK & US) **PRODUCER** Jean Michel-Jarre **UK CHART** peak/weeks 2/24 **US CHART** peak/weeks 78/19 **TRACK LISTING** Oxygene (Parts 1-6) **PERSONNEL** Jean-Michel Jarre (sy, k)

French synthesizer wizard Jarre came from nowhere to reach Number 2 in the great year of punk with a concept work that set the tone for future successes. In truth, his dark good looks and film-star wife Charlotte Rampling were a great deal more interesting than a collection of keyboard noodlings reminiscent (to those with long memories) of Hot Butter's 1972 hit single *Popcorn*. Twenty years on he was revisiting the **Oxygene** theme in an effort to register his fifteenth UK chart album... this time, sadly, without La Rampling.

Oxygene *(French for oxygen, no less) is just another interminable cosmic cruise. The German spacers (Dream, Schulze et al) mapped this part of the electronic galaxy aeons ago... infuriatingly derivative. Explore its prime influences instead.* **Angus MacKinnon, NME, August 1977**

Pablo Honey

ARTIST Radiohead **RELEASE DATE** February 1993 (UK)/June 1993 (US) **LABEL** Parlophone (UK)/Capitol (US) **PRODUCER** Sean Slade, Chris Hufford, Paul Kolderie **UK CHART** peak/weeks 25/8 **US CHART** peak/weeks 32/ **TRACK LISTING** You/Creep/How Do You?/Stop Whispering/Thinking About You/Anyone Can Play Guitar/Ripcord/Vegetable/Prove Yourself/I Can't/Lurgee/Blow Out **PERSONNEL** Thom Yorke (v, g), Ed O'Brien (g, v), Jon Greenwood (g), Colin Greenwood (b), Phil Selway (d)

Radiohead's first album enjoyed the Cranberries effect – just as *Linger* had broken the Irish band across the Atlantic, so the loser anthem *Creep* became a belated US hit thanks to alternative radio and MTV, sending **Pablo Honey** gold. The album had already gone Top 30 in Britain but gained a new lease of life as the single hit Number 7, preparing the ground for *The Bends* to give them their breakthrough into the big league. If *Creep* is all you've heard, check *Anyone Can Play Guitar*, also the lead track of an early EP, to hear just how off-kilter they can get.

... a satisfying portion of this album gives out a very warm glow – and besides, it's a debut album, remember?... though it's hard to shake off a feeling of anticlimactic disappointment, that's probably our fault, not Radiohead's. They're getting there. **John Harris, NME, February 1993**

Parade

ARTIST Prince & The Revolution **RELEASE DATE** April 1986 (UK) **LABEL** Paisley Park (UK & US) **PRODUCER** Prince (UK & US) **UK CHART** peak/weeks 4/26 **US CHART** peak/weeks 3/28 **TRACK LISTING** Christopher Tracey's Parade/New Position/I Wonder U/Under The Cherry Moon/Girls And Boys/Life Can Be So Nice/Venus De Milo/Mountains/Do U Lie/Kiss/Anotherloverholdenyohead/Sometimes It Snows In April **PERSONNEL** Prince (Multi-Instrumental), Wendy Melvoin (g)

This album has plenty to delight and excite, not least his American Number 1 *Kiss*, later a UK hit for Welsh crooner Tom Jones. At the time Prince was probably at his most prolific, for in addition to the US top spot he had penned the Bangles' Number 2, **Manic Monday**. By the next album a new backing crew was in place, but it has seldom mattered who has backed Prince, for most of the material is his and his alone.

Parade *is a soft-porn paradise, a sensual sacrament... The first side's well weird, nursery rhyme songs subjected to sensory overload... And side two, if anything, is more illicit, more abandoned to delight.* **Steve Sutherland, Melody Maker, April 1986**

Paradise And Lunch

ARTIST Ry Cooder **RELEASE DATE** May 1974 (UK) **LABEL** Reprise (UK & US) **PRODUCER** – **UK CHART** peak/weeks – **US CHART** peak/weeks 167/6 **TRACK LISTING** Tamp 'Em Up Solid/Tatler/Married Man's A Fool/Jesus On The Mainline/It's All Over Now/Fool About A Cigarette-Feelin' Good/If Walls Could Talk/Mexican Divorce/Ditty Wa Ditty **PERSONNEL** Ry Cooder (v, g), session musicians

A gifted guitarist whose obsession with ethnic folk music has led him down a diversity of roads: some blind alleys, mostly panoramic, even historic. He loves to collaborate with guest stars: the career list of partners – from Taj Mahal to Captain Beefheart, from the Stones to Little Feat – is endless. Here he ropes in Earl Fatha Hines on *Ditty Wah Ditty*. This is his most accessible and well-produced album of the period, with Cooder learning when to stop fiddling or over cooking. He only took up the guitar after losing his left eye in an accident.

Professor Cooder's Bottleneck Academy presents Lesson Four in how to be laid-back without getting boring... It don't exactly howl for attention, but you can go ahead and do other things while you're listening to it, and every so often it'll assert itself. **Charles Shaar Murray, NME, June 1974**

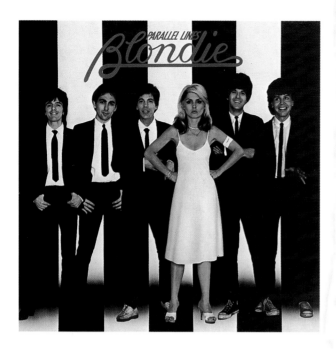

Parallel Lines

ARTIST Blondie RELEASE DATE September 1978 (UK) LABEL Chrysalis (UK & US) PRODUCER Mike Chapman UK CHART peak/weeks 1/105 US CHART peak/weeks 6/103 TRACK LISTING Hanging On The Telephone/One Way Or Another/Picture This/Fade Away And Radiate/Pretty Baby/I Know But I Don't Know/11:59/Will Anything Happen?/Sunday Girl/Heart Of Glass/I'm Gonna Love You Too/Just Go Away PERSONNEL Jimmy Destri (k), Frank Infante (g), Chris Stein (g), Nigel Harrison (b), Clem Burke (d), Deborah Harry (v)

One of THE great pop albums, it saw Debbie Harry and Chris Stein wising up to the rules of the global game and promptly slaughtering the opposition. With the band in cracking form – Clem Burke's drumming was mental, the others each contributed much – Blondie leapt from adrenalized and charmingly evocative rock rushes, such as *Hangin' On The Telephone* and *Picture This*, to slinky mid-tempo drawls like *Sunday Girl* to the frisky disco fusion *Heart Of Glass*. This was a world-wide Number 1, finally breaking them in America. The ideas, imagery and sheer pleasure of **Parallel Lines** were to be admired and mimicked for decades.

The new album is very definable, normal stuff… Everyone asks if we're selling out by going commercial, but I view it as a challenge to try to produce something that has mass appeal. **Chris Stein in an interview by Paul Morley, NME, September 1978**

Paranoid

ARTIST Black Sabbath RELEASE DATE September 1970 (UK)/Febuary 1971 (US) LABEL Vertigo (UK)/Warner Bros. (US) PRODUCER Rodger Bain UK CHART peak/weeks 1/27 US CHART peak/weeks 12/70 TRACK LISTING War Pigs/Paranoid/Planet Caravan/Iron Man/Electric Funeral/Hand Of Doom/Rat Salad/Fairies Wear Boots PERSONNEL Ozzy Ozborne (v), Tony Iommi (g), 'Geezer' Butler (b), Bill Ward (d)

Consolidating their position as metal monoliths of the early Seventies, Sabbath were also setting themselves up as alleged Satanists. The reality was eerier and certainly boozier, but Ozzy Osbourne did the reputation no harm by biting the head off a bat on stage and then having to be treated for rabies. The title song, with the ultra-fuzzy power chords courtesy of Iommi, and the preposterous yet somehow endearing lyric 'finished with my woman cos she couldn't help me with my mind' gave them a hoary

landmark hit. Their cartoon insanity was perceived as glamorous. *Iron Man* and *War Pigs*, both sludgy, stoned dirges, became live favourites.

A tight, punchy band who rely on menacing moods and a sense of impending doom for their effect, they rock as heavily as most wearers of the cross. **Chris Welch, Melody Maker, September 1970**

Paris 1919

ARTIST John Cale RELEASE DATE March 1973 (UK & US) LABEL CBS (UK)/Columbia (US) PRODUCER John Cale UK CHART peak/weeks 0/0 US CHART peak/weeks 0/0 TRACK LISTING Child's Christmas In Wales/Hanky Panky Nohow/The Endless Plain Of Fortune/Andalucia/Macbeth/Paris 1919/Graham Greene/Half Past France/Antartica Starts Here PERSONNEL John Cale (v, va, k, b, g), session musicians

After the demise of The Velvet Underground, Welshman Cale developed a curious baroque style for his patchy solo career. His arrangements and production techniques served as insights into Velvet analyses. This, his third, was one of his more song-based sets, with tasteful backing from Little Feat members and a sense of using the avant-garde to elevate rather than excavate. The track *Andalucia* can be cited as an example of the neurotic beauty he usually aimed for: this time it succumbed.

…the production is such perfection that few will listen closely to the words, hearing only the soothing, muted strings and politely funky rhythm section… Oh, John Cale, you'll probably never be famous, if only because reviewers like me can never do you justice. **R. W., Melody Maker, August 1973**

Parklife

ARTIST Blur RELEASE DATE April 1994 (UK & US) LABEL EMI (UK)/Food SBK (US) PRODUCER Stephen Street, Stephen Hauge, John Smith, Blur UK CHART peak/weeks 1/– US CHART peak/weeks – TRACK LISTING Girls And Boys/Tracy Jacks/End Of A Century/Park Life/Bank Holiday/Bad Head/The Debt Collector/Far Out/To The End/London Loves/Trouble In The Message Centre/Clover Over Dover/Magic America/Jubilee/This Is A Low/Lot 105. PERSONNEL Damon Albarn (v, k), Graham Coxon (g, s), Alex James (b), Dave Rowntree (d)

Blur, formerly known as Seymour, were art school drop-outs and

drinkers languishing in Indieville when their third album stopped the rot and shot them to international super stardom. The single **Girls And Boys**, with the charismatic and self-confident vocalist Damon Albarn's inquisitive lyrics propelling a killer chorus, was largely responsible. Actor Phil Daniels, a friend of Albarn's, chipped in with the narration of the title song, which also became a chant-along pub 'n' club anthem. Blur were now credible style icons – it was hip to be Brit again – and scream-inducing teeny-bop messiahs. They cleaned up at the Brit Awards in 1995.

*Songs echoing Eighties synth pop (**Girls and Boys**), Ray Davies (**Tracy Jacks**), as well as the Walker Brothers and even music hall sing-alongs make **Parklife** a carny ride through the theme park of classic Brit Pop. Teen dream cute and insufferably gifted…* **The Year In Records 1994, Rolling Stone, December 1994**

Paul's Boutique

ARTIST The Beastie Boys **RELEASE DATE** August 1989 (UK)/July 1989 (US) **LABEL** Capitol (UK & US) **PRODUCER** The Beastie Boys **UK CHART** peak/weeks 44/2 **US CHART** peak/weeks 14/ **TRACK LISTING** To All The Girls/Shake Your Rump/Johnny Ryall/Egg Man/High Plains Drifter/The Sound Of Science/3-Minute Rule/Hey Ladies/5-Piece Chicken Dinner/Looking Down The Barrel Of A Gun/Car Thief/What Comes Around/Shadrach/Ask For Janice/B-Boy Bouillabaisse Medley:-A Year And A Day-Hello Brookly-Dropping Names-Lay It On Me-Mike On The Mic-A.W.O.L. **PERSONNEL** 'MCA' Adam Yauch (v), 'MikeD' Mike Diamond (v), 'King Ad-Rock' Adam Horowitz (v), session musicians

A court case with Def Jam boss Rick Rubin meant three years had passed since the epochal **Licensed To Ill**: the Beasties had nearly blown it. **Paul's Boutique** astonished and bewildered people. More of the same it wasn't. With The Dust Brothers providing dense, complex sonic collages, the boys enticed us into a hedonistic city kid's world of trash, kitsch and TV subculture. Commercially, it stiffed, but any record that ripped off or layed into *The Old Testament, Clockwork Orange,* Isaac Newton and Ed Koch was a durable attention-grabber. For a cartoon, the Beasties were proving to have surprising depth.

Mellow? Mature? Listenable? You cannot be serious. What we're talking here is Maximum Snot… In other words they're still unlistenable and uncivilised in the best and most attractive sense of the words. The album is guaranteed free of all redeeming social merit. **Charles Shaar Murray, Q, August 1989**

Pearl

ARTIST Janis Joplin/Full Tilt Boogie **RELEASE DATE** January 1971 (UK & US) **LABEL** CBS 64188 (UK)/Columbia (US) **PRODUCER** Paul A. Rothchild **UK CHART** peak/weeks 50/1 **US CHART** peak/weeks 1/42 **TRACK LISTING** Move Over/Cry Baby/A Woman Left Lonely/Half Moon/Buried Alive In The Blues/My Baby/Me & Bobby McGee/Mercedez Benz/Trust Me/Get It While You Can **PERSONNEL** Janis Joplin (v), Brad Campbell (b), Clark Pierson (d), Ken Pearson (o), John Till (g), Richard Bell (p), Sandra Crouch (tm), Bobbie Hall (cg, bo), Bobby Womack (ag), Pearl (ag)

Death, say the cynics, can be a good career move, but Joplin's drug-fuelled demise as this album neared completion all but led to its abandonment. 'Everyone voted to finish as a monument to Janis's greatness,' said producer Paul Rothchild, 'so the record didn't die with her.' The result deserved US chart-topping status irrespective of the circumstances and spawned her first and only Number 1 single in Kris Kristofferson's **Me And Bobby McGee** – though many other tracks here equalled its intensity.

Pelican West

ARTIST Haircut 100 **RELEASE DATE** February 1982 (UK & US) **LABEL** Arista (UK & US) **PRODUCER** Bobby Sargeant **UK CHART** peak/weeks 2/34 **US CHART** peak/weeks 31/37 **TRACK LISTING** Favourite Shirts (Boy Meets Girl)/Love Plus One/Lemon Firebrigade/Marine Boy/Milk Film/Kingsize (You're My Little Steam Whistle)/Fantastic Day/Baked Bean/Snow Girl/Love's Got Me In Triangles/Surprise Me Again/Calling Captain Autumn **PERSONNEL** Nick Heywood (g, v), Mark (Ilford) Fox (pc), Blair Cunningham (d), Phil (Neville) Smith (s), Graham (Blythe) Jones (g), Les Nemes (b) with Dave Lord (t), Herschell Holder (t), Vince (Kenton) Sullivan (tb)

Nick Heyward and his fellow suburbanites from Beckenham found favour in the post punk music scene as the 'new Monkees', playing gigs at ski clubs in aran sweaters and toting big semi-acoustic guitars. **Pelican West**, the first of just two albums from the band, was kept from Number 1 only by Barbra Streisand, selling 300,000 in its first week. Eight months later singer and group parted company. Heyward did not feature on the second, more 'adult' album, where percussionist Fox did the vocals, but found brief solo fame with a similar brand of candy-floss pop.

Haircut 100 have a bright, honest spirit, without pretence – what you see is what you get. Nick Heyward has a way with songs, knows how to sing a hook. His great ones are really memorable…. **Richard Grabel, NME, August 1982**

Penthouse & Pavement

ARTIST Heaven 17 **RELEASE DATE** September 1981 (UK & US) **LABEL** Virgin (UK)/Arista (US) **PRODUCER** British Electric Foundation **UK CHART** peak/weeks 14/76 **US CHART** peak/weeks – **TRACK LISTING** (We Don't Need This) Fascist Groove Thang/Penthouse And Pavement/Play To Win/Soul Warfare/Geisha Boys And Temple Girls/The Height Of The Fighting/Song With No Name/We're Going To Live For A Very Long Time **PERSONNEL** Glenn Gregory (v), Ian Craig Marsh (sy, s, pc), Martyn Ware (sy, p, pc, bv), Josie James (v), Steve Travell (p), John Wilson (b, g, gsy), The Boys of Buddha (syh)

After abandoning the Human League, Marsh and Ware resurfaced under the British Electric Foundation banner and, with the addition of vocalist Gregory, became Heaven 17 whose carefully cultivated corporate image satirized the yuppie philosophy of the times. The cover painting depicted them as people with big ideas, a product to sell, and a business-like approach. And the product? – tight, intelligent dance music that exuded self-confidence. A fine start, but ultimately proved impossible to live up to.

'Well originally it was a satirical comment on the aspirations of the middle class to aspire to working class roots that they'd never had in the first place… the idea of it being a concept album is a load of rubbish, but there is some sort of theme running through it.' **From an interview by Ian Penman, NME, October 1981**

People

ARTIST Barbra Streisand **RELEASE DATE** October 1964 (UK & US) **LABEL** CBS (UK)/Columbia (US) **PRODUCER** Robert Mersey **UK CHART** peak/weeks – **US CHART** peak/weeks 1/84 **TRACK LISTING** Absent Minded Me/When In Rome/Fine And Dandy/Supper Time/Will He Like Me/How Does The Wine Taste/I'm All Smiles/Autumn/My Lord And Master/Love Is A Bore/Don't Like Goodbyes/People **PERSONNEL** Barbera Streisand (v), Peter Matz (arr, con), Raymond Ellis (arr, con), session musicians

With more gold and platinum albums than any post-War performer save Elvis Presley, Barbra Streisand was an anomaly in the rock era: a singer who did not write her own material, a throwback to the days when vocalists interpreted the songs of Gershwin, Rodgers & Hart and Cole Porter. **People**, her fifth LP, which includes the soundtrack to *Funny Girl*, was typical of her work during this period: all Tin Pan Alley-style tunes delivered with a mixture of bravado and vulnerability.

Here is an ordinary singer with, it is true, a reasonable voice, but one possessing that embarrassing Judy Garland technique of playing to the gallery, attacking the emotions and succeeding merely in making many people cringe at showbiz trickery. **Melody Maker, April 1963**

Pet Sounds

ARTIST Beach Boys **RELEASE DATE** May 1966 (UK) **LABEL** Capitol (UK & US) **PRODUCER** Brian Wilson **UK CHART** peak/weeks 2/39 **US CHART** peak/weeks 10/39 **TRACK LISTING** Wouldn't It Be Nice/You Still Believe In Me/That's Not Me/Don't Talk (Put Your Head On My Shoulder)/I'm Waiting For The Day/Let's Go Away For A While/Sloop John B/God Only Knows/I Know There's An Answer/Here Today/I Just Wasn't Made For These Times/Pet Sounds/Caroline No **PERSONNEL** Brian Wilson (b, k, v), Mike Love (v), Carl Wilson (g, v), Al Jardine (g, v), Dennis Wilson (d, v)

Hailed by many as the greatest album of all time, **Pet Sounds** was virtually constructed single-handedly by Brian Wilson while the rest of the group were on tour. Mike Love detested it, describing it as 'Brian's ego music', and blamed LSD. Indeed, despite critical acclaim, it sold only reasonably well, although the singles, particularly *God Only Knows*, did well. It was a journey through hope, to confusion and resigned despair: *I Just Wasn't Made For These Times*. The album became such a *cause célèbre* that it was re-issued as a four-CD train-spotter's delight with out-takes, stereo mix and all.

… breathtaking vocal-only performances… textures and colours hidden for more than thirty years. Beach Boys fanatics may also be comforted to hear the awful saxophone solo planned for **God Only Knows***, mercifully consigned to the wheelie bin of music history.* **Q magazine, December 1997**

Peter, Paul And Mary

ARTIST Peter, Paul And Mary **RELEASE DATE** January 1965 (UK)/1962 (US) **LABEL** Warner Bros. (UK & US) **PRODUCER** Albert Grossman **UK CHART** peak/weeks 18/1 **US CHART** peak/weeks 1/185 **TRACK LISTING** Early In The Morning/500 Miles/Sorrow/This Train/Bamboo/It's Raining/If I Had My Way/Cruel War/Lemon Tree/If I Had A Hammer/Autumn To May/Where Have All The Flowers Gone **PERSONNEL** Mary Travers (v), Peter Yarrow (g, v), Paul Stookey (v), session musicians

If truth be told, Peter, Paul and Mary should have been Paul, Mary and Peter – the way they cropped up in the stereo sound spectrum. That said, their debut album took an unusually long four weeks to complete with producer Albert Grossman (Dylan's manager-to-be and the man who brought the three protagonists together). It was initially a US chart-topper in the mono chart. Mono and stereo listings were amalgamated in August 1963, and the album returned to Number 1 two months later, a year to the week after it had first

made it to the top.

I asked Paul to comment on charges that the trio water down the old songs somewhat. He said that all folk songs were changed by time and individuals.... 'Suffice to say what Pete Seeger once said of contemporary folk music and the changing of old folk song: "Don't interfere with folk processes".' **Paul interviewed by Max Jones, Melody Maker, April 1964**

Physical Graffiti

ARTIST Led Zeppelin **RELEASE DATE** March 1975 (UK)/February 1975 (US) **LABEL** Swan Song (UK & US) **PRODUCER** Jimmy Page **UK CHART** peak/weeks 1/27 **US CHART** peak/weeks 1/41 **TRACK LISTING** Custard Pie/The Rover/In My Time Of Dying/Houses Of The Holy/Trampled Underfoot/Kashmir/In The Light/Bron-Y-Aur/Down By The Seaside/Ten Years Gone/Night Flight/The Wanton Song/Boogie With Stu/Black Country Woman/Sick Again **PERSONNEL** Robert Plant (v), Jimmy Page (g), John Paul Jones (b), John Bonham (d)

The first release on their own Swan Song label, **Physical Graffiti** was also Zeppelin's first double, its die-cut sleeve as elaborate as the 'spinning wheel' of **III**. They emerged from sessons at Headley Grange with one and a half albums worth of material: *Black Country Woman* and *The Rover* came from the 'Houses Of The Holy' sessions, *Bron-Y-Aur* Stomp from **III** and *Down By The Seaside*, *Night Flight* and *Boogie With Stu* from **IV**. Nevertheless, the collection has its own identity and, in the eastern-flavoured *Kashmir*, a key track in the Zeppelin canon.

Physical Graffiti *is confirmation that the band have lost none of their inspiration and ability, even if it did take them a long time to deliver. It's not the kind of music you play before breakfast unless you wake up in a particularly aggressive mood.* **Steve Clarke, NME, 1975**

Picture Book

ARTIST Simply Red **RELEASE DATE** October 1985 (UK)/April 1986 (US) **LABEL** Elektra (UK & US) **PRODUCER** Stewart Levine **UK CHART** peak/weeks 2/130 **US CHART** peak/weeks 16/60 **TRACK LISTING** Come To My Aid/Sad Old Red/Look At You Now/Heaven/Jericho/Money's Too Tight/Holding Back The Years/Red Box/No Direction/Picture Book **PERSONNEL** Mick Hucknall (v), Fritz McIntyre (k, v), Chris Joyce (d, pc), Tony Bowers (b), Sylvan (g), Tim Kellett (t)

Before his absorption into the mainstream Mick Hucknall was an ex-punk from Manchester whose first band, The Frantic Elevators, were about as far removed from MOR soul as it is possible to get. Simply Red – Hucknall plus assorted musicians – made their debut with **Picture Book**, a gritty work that includes a cover of The Valentine Brothers' **Money'$ Too Tight**, which revealed Hucknall's Stax/Motown roots, and a version of Talking Heads' **Heaven**, which drew a line back to the avant-funk explorations of the late Seventies. **Holding Back The Years**, Number 2 in the UK and Number 1 in the States, saw Hucknall scale Tim Buckley-esque vocal heights.

Hucknall has nothing but a five-point guide to soul boy culture, an off-the-peg style and sound you've heard before and better.... **Picture Book** *is soul by numbers and is as cliché ridden as the ugliest offspring of Gothic inter-breeding.* **Don Watson, NME, October 1985**

A Picture Of You

ARTIST Joe Brown **RELEASE DATE** September 1962 **LABEL** Pye (Golden Guinea) (UK) **PRODUCER** Pye Records (Sales) Ltd, London W1 **UK CHART** peak/weeks 3/39 **US CHART** peak/weeks – **TRACK LISTING** A Picture Of You/Lonely Island Pearl/A Lay-About's Lament/Stick Around/Talking Guitar/The Surrey With The Fringe On Top/The Switch/Goodluck And Goodbye/I'm Henery The Eighth I Am/Pop Corn/English Country Garden/Put On A Happy Face/What A Crazy World We're Living In **PERSONNEL** Joe Brown and The Bruvvers

The man with the perpetual cheeky grin once played lead guitar for Billy Fury, but soon had his own backing band, The Bruvvers (née The Spacemen). Gathering hits throughout the early Sixties, he learned to flavour his jaunty pop with a twist of country, and enjoyed a golden spell with the title single from this Top 3 album: **It Only Took A Minute**. America didn't take to him and then The Beatles happened, but the cheerful cockney moved into acting in stage musicals and television.

To commemorate his chart topping **Picture of You** *Pye Golden Guinea offers an album of the same title. Apart from a disastrous* **Surrey With The Fringe On Top**, *Joe is on top form.* **Melody Maker, September 1962**

Pictures At An Exhibition

ARTIST Emerson, Lake And Palmer **RELEASE DATE** December 1971 (UK &US) **LABEL** Island (UK)/Manticore (US) **PRODUCER** Greg Lake **UK CHART** peak/weeks 3/5 **US CHART** peak/weeks – **TRACK LISTING** Promenade/The Gnome/Promenade/The Sage/The Old Castle/Blues Variation/Promenade/The Curse Of Baba Yaga/The Hut Of Baba Yaga/The Great Gates Of Kiev **PERSONNEL** Keith Emerson (k), Greg Lake (b, v), Carl Palmer (d)

Pictures At An Exhibition was a re-working of Mussorgsky's classical composition, adapted by Keith Emerson for ELP'S musical resources; this version was recorded live at Newcastle's City Hall in March 1971, amidst variations on Mussorgsky's original the band also threw in a cover of the B. Bumble & The Stingers' song **Nut Rocker**, giving Emerson a chance to show off his frenetic keyboard skills. **Pictures** was later recorded live again, for a film released in March 1973, by which time the band were on the verge of sliding into full bombastic dinosaur mode.

If poor old Mussorgsky and Ravel can hear what Emerson, Lake and Palmer have done to their music ... speaking strictly as a fan of M&R and heretofore certified disdainer of EL & P, however, I can say that I listened to it twice tonight, beating my fists on the floor and laughing... **Lester Bangs, Rolling Stone, March 1972**

Pieces Of You

ARTIST Jewel **RELEASE DATE** February 1995 (US) **LABEL** Atlantic (UK & US) **PRODUCER** Ben Keith **UK CHART** peak/weeks -/- **US CHART** peak/weeks 25/31 **TRACK LISTING** Who Will Save Your Soul/Pieces Of You/Little Sister/Foolish Games/Near You Always/Painters/Morning Song/Adrian/I'm Sensitive/You Were Meant For Me/Don't/Daddy/Angel Standing By/Amen **PERSONNEL** Jewel (g, v, arr), Mark Howard (b), Tim Drummond (b), Robbie Buchanan (p), Oscar Butterworth (d), Charlotte Caffey (p, arr)

Born in Alaska with few luxuries (no TV, shower or running water), Jewel Kilcher moved to San Diego after graduating on a vocal scholarship and lived in a camper van. A coffee-shop gig got her spotted and before she knew it this album – recorded at Neil Young's studio – had sold three million plus, thanks to Top 10 hits **Who Will Save Your Soul** and **You Were Meant For Me**. Honesty and insight, combined with an octave-leaping voice reminiscent of Melanie, seemed to have struck a chord with Middle America....

Pills 'N' Thrills And Bellyaches

ARTIST Happy Mondays RELEASE DATE November 1990 (UK & US) LABEL Factory (UK)/Elektra (US) PRODUCER Paul Oakenfold UK CHART peak/weeks 4/28 US CHART peak/weeks 89/13 TRACK LISTING Kinky Afro/God's Cop/ Donovan/Gandbag's Funeral/Loose Fit/Dennis & Louis/Bob's Your Uncle/ Step On/Holiday/Harmony. PERSONNEL Shaun Ryder (v), Paul Ryder (b), Mark Day (g), Paul Davis (k), Gary 'Gaz' Whelan (d)

The so-called 'Madchester' explosion of drug-fuelled rock-dance fusion music reached its peak with this 1990 offering from Shaun Ryder and his crew. Nostalgic links were evident in *Donovan* – they later helped the Sixties star re-cut *Mellow Yellow* – while *Step On* retrod a John Kongos hit from 1971. But the innovative combination of Mark Day's guitar and Ryder's mumbling vocal style, the most distinctive to come out of the north since Mark E. Smith, made this a release to marvel at.

What's still great about the Mondays is that, in spite of outside attempts to make sensational 'sense' of them they remain too prickly and misshapen to get your head around too easily. **David Stubbs, Melody Maker, November 1990**

Pink Flag

ARTIST Wire RELEASE DATE November 1977 (UK) LABEL Harvest (UK & US) PRODUCER Mike Thorne UK CHART peak/weeks - US CHART peak/weeks – TRACK LISTING Reuters/Field Day For The Sundays/Three Girl Rhumba/Ex Lion Tamer/Lowdown/Start To Move/Brazil/It's So Obvious/Surgeon's Girl/ Pink Flag/The Commercial/Straight Line/106 Beats That/Mr Suit/ Strangle/ Fragile/Mannequin/Different To Me/Champs/Feeling Called Love/1 2 X U PERSONNEL B. Gilbert (g, v, sy), G. Lewis (b, v, sy), C. Newman (g, k), R. Gotobed (d)

Wire conformed to punk's minimalist aesthetic yet avoided the Neanderthal tendencies of their peers for a rather more intelligent approach. **Pink Flag** featured 21 tracks and clocked in at 37 minutes: brevity was as important to Wire as it was to, say, the Ramones. And yet the artily unintelligible lyrics and dense production marked Wire out as a sort of New Wave Roxy Music.

On this album the songs are closer to a sort of uncomfortable pop, as on French Film Blurred and the unnerving Sands In My Joints, which sounded particularly unconventional and avant garde at the time. **Tommy Udo, NME, July 1994**

Piper At The Gates Of Dawn

ARTIST Pink Floyd RELEASE DATE August 1967 (UK & US) LABEL Columbia (UK)/Tower (US) PRODUCER Norman Smith UK CHART peak/weeks 6/14 US CHART peak/weeks -/- TRACK LISTING Astronomy Domine/Lucifer Sam/Matilda Mother/Flaming/Pow R.Toc H./Take Up Thy Stethoscope And Walk/Interstellar Overdrive/The Gnome/Chapter 24/Scarecrow/Bike PERSONNEL Syd Barrett (v, g), Richard Wright (k), Roger Waters (b, v, pc), Nick Mason (d, pc)

One of the Floyd's biggest strengths was their questing spirit, fuelled by readily available amounts of LSD, and the long improvisatory *Astronomy Domine* and *Interstellar Overdrive* came to define the term 'space rock'. However Syd Barrett's pop songs were not to be overlooked: tunes like *Scarecrow* and *Gnome* caught the innocent spirit of the flower-power era, but it was *Bike* that suggested a stranger, more surreally humorous and psychotic mind just waiting to get out. The twin pressures of success and a spiralling acid habit soon proved too much for Barrett, who split for a short but celebrated solo career, while the remaining members of the Floyd turned corporate.

'… the human voice can't compete with Fender Telecasters and double drum kits. We're a very young group, not in age, but in experience. We're trying to solve problems that haven't existed before…' **Roger Waters from interview by Chris Welch, Melody Maker, August 1967**

Planet Rock: The Album

ARTIST Africa Bambaataa RELEASE DATE October 1993 (UK)/1986 (US) LABEL Tommy Boy (UK & US) PRODUCER Arthur Baker, Keith Le Blanc, John Robie, Skip Macdonald, Doug Wimbish, Leroy Evans UK CHART peak/weeks 8/2 US CHART peak/weeks 0/0 TRACK LISTING Planet Rock/Looking For The Perfect Boat/Renegades Of Funk/Frantic Situation/Who You Funkin' With?/Go Go Pop/They Made A Mistake PERSONNEL

For many, Afrika Bambaataa invented hip-hop, combining the James Brown school of soulful funk with the dispassionate techno plotting of Kraftwerk. A former DJ and leader of a gang known as The Black Spades, Bambaataa founded a dance group, Zulu Nation, and expressed strong political views. The album **Looking For The Perfect Beat** earned him the reputation as an 'electro-funk' godfather, while the single *Planet Rock*, produced by Arthur Baker, set the template for scratching and cross-cutting of rhythms. The album of the same name was a compilation of his seminal 12-inch releases. He remains a guru figure.

Plastic Letters

ARTIST Blondie RELEASE DATE April 1978 (UK)/Febuary 1978 (US) LABEL Chrysalis (UK & US) PRODUCER Richard Gottehrer UK CHART peak/weeks 10/54 US CHART peak/weeks 72/17 TRACK LISTING Fan Mail/Denis/ Bermuda Triangle Blues (Flight 45)/Youth Nabbed As Sniper/Contact in Red Square/(I'm Always Touched By Your) Presence Dear/I'm On E/I Didn't Have The Nerve To Say No/Love At The Pier/No Imagination/Kidnapper/Detroit 442/Cautious Lip. PERSONNEL Jimmy Destri (k), Frank Infante (g), Chris Stein (g), Nigel Harrison (b), Clem Burke (d), Deborah Harry (v)

Though the posters shrieked 'Blondie is a group!', the focal point by now was very much Debbie Harry, a punk-rock beauty queen with bags of smarts and attitude. Rescued from CBGBs squalor by a tremendous pop consciousness and La Harry's marketability, the band also boasted a natural musical dynamic, contorting all *genres* from trash rock to Motown. The cover of 'Randy and The Rainbows' *Denis* was the British breakthrough single; *Presence Dear* was even better. Numbers like *I Didn't Have The Nerve To Say No* hinted at Harry's hidden depths of personality. Cheap pop

that yielded limitless riches.

… if you have been foolish enough to swallow the two-bit publicity bait that Blondie are a simple, no frills pop band **Plastic Letters** *will give the kick of life you so desperately need.* **Harry Doherty, Melody Maker, February 1978**

Please Hammer Don't Hurt 'Em

ARTIST MC Hammer **RELEASE DATE** July 1990 (UK)/January (US) **LABEL** Capitol (UK & US) **PRODUCER** MC Hammer, Big Louis Burrell, Scott Folks **UK CHART** peak/weeks 8/59 **US CHART** peak/weeks 1/108 **TRACK LISTING** Here Comes The Hammer/U Can't Touch This/Have You Seen Her/Yo!! Sweetness/Help The Children/On Your Face/Dancin' Machine/Pray/Crime Story/She's Soft And Wet/Black Is Black/Let's Go Deeper/Work This **PERSONNEL** MC Hammer (v), James Early (bv), Felton Pilot (bv), Soft Touch (bv), Ho-Frat-Ho Sweet L.D. (bv), Too Big MC (bv), The Lone Mixer (bv), MC Hammer (bv)

Few chart-topping albums have been recorded on a mobile studio while the artist is on tour promoting its predecessor – but that is how rap star Stanley Kirk Burrell, alias MC Hammer, cut **Please Hammer Don't Hurt 'Em**. Its progress was fired by *U Can't Touch This*, a single based, as were most tracks here, on an existing soul classic, in this case Rick James' *Super Freak*. Capitol deleted the single to push the album, which spent 21 non-consecutive weeks on top of the US pop listing.

Hammer is an explosive live performer, sweating holes in his shirtless Armani suits, but he must spend all his creativity on-stage. In the studio he follows a lazy formula, interspersing concern with braggadocio, sexism with black pride. **Michael Corcoran, Rolling Stone, May 1990**

Please Please Me

ARTIST The Beatles **RELEASE DATE** March 1963 (UK & US) **LABEL** Parlophone (UK & US) **PRODUCER** George Martin **UK CHART** peak/weeks 1/70 **US CHART** peak/weeks – **TRACK LISTING** I Saw Her Standing There/Misery/Anna (Go To Him)/Chains/Boys/Ask Me Why/Please Please Me/Love Me Do/P.S I Love You/Baby It's You/Do You Want To Know A Secret/A Taste Of Honey/There's A Place/Twist And Shout **PERSONNEL** John Lennon (v, rg), Paul McCartney (v, g), George Harrison (v, lg), Ringo Starr (d)

'Groups with guitars are on the way out,' a Decca Records executive had said after cancelling a Beatles audition in 1961. In fact the fab four were to define the decade and exert a matchless influence on popular music and culture. Their debut album (14 tracks) was largely recorded in one 13-hour session. It mixed beat standards from their honed dynamic stage set, such as *Twist And Shout*, with their own naive but promising compositions. Three shows a night in their Hamburg residency had paid off: this was a lively, not to say speeding, band. Just the beginning.

Designed undoubtedly to be a best seller, this LP by our current top group is an insight into Merseyside Music. There is a relentless pressure which is a rare occurrence on British records. **Record Retailer, May 1963**

Pocket Full Of Kryptonite

ARTIST The Spin Doctors **RELEASE DATE** March 1993 (UK)/August 1992 (US) **LABEL** Epic (UK & US) **PRODUCER** Spin Doctors, Peter Denberg, Frankie La Rocka **UK CHART** peak/weeks 2/34 **US CHART** peak/weeks 3/115 **TRACK LISTING** Jimmy Olsen's Blues/What Time Is It/Little Miss Can't Be Wrong/Forty Or Fifty/Refrigerator Car/More Than She Knows/Two Princes/Off My Line/How Could You Want Him (When You Could Have Me?)/Shinbone Alley/Hard To Exist/Yo Mamas A Pajama/Sweet Widow/Stepped On A Crack **PERSONNEL** Aaron Camess (d, p, o, bv, cg), Mark White (b), Eric Schukman (g, v, p), Christopher Barron (v), John Popper (h, bv), John Bush (cg, tm)

A four-piece from New York, Spin Doctors blended rock with blues, added jazzy textures and funk-lite rhythms, and wrapped it up in a pop coating to wow the grunge hordes who needed light relief after the heavy-duty misery of Pearl Jam and Co. **Pocket Full Of Kryptonite** became a huge success (over three million sales) on the back of relentless plays on US college radio, an appearance on America's influential *Saturday Night Live* comedy show and three hit singles: *Little Miss Can't Be Wrong*, MTV favourite *Two Princes* and *Jimmy Olsen's Blues*.

Although it hangs together perfectly, the album has a strangely amoebic quality. No two tracks are particularly alike, and though they do sound as if they're being played by the same group, each demands to be judged on its own merits… this album is full of dynamite. **David Sinclair, Q, April 1993**

The Poet

ARTIST Bobby Womac **RELEASE DATE** June 1982 (UK)/January 1982 (US) **LABEL** Motown (UK)/Beverly Glen (US) **PRODUCER** Bobby Womack **UK CHART peak/weeks** - **US CHART peak/weeks** 169/13 **TRACK LISTING** So Many Sides To You/Lay Your Lovin' On Me/Secrets/Just My Imagination/Stand Up/Games/If You Think You're Lonely Now/Where Do We Go From Here **PERSONNEL** Bobby Womac (v), Roger Hawkins (d), Clayton Ivey (k), Jimmy Johnson (g), Barry Beckett (k) Truman Thomas (b)

A former sidekick of soul legend Sam Cooke and crony of Wilson Pickett, Bobby Womack's revolutionary wah-wah guitar effects would influence Jimi Hendrix, a style he later employed throughout Sly Stone's seminal **There's A Riot Goin' On**. **The Poet** saw Womack continue to develop well into his third decade as a soulful singer and dexterous musician. It was a triumph of gritty testifying and well-oiled craftsmanship.

… a subdued, even occasionally innocuous record which nevertheless shows a major talent opening out and taking the ballad form several leagues beyond the grasp of most of his in-Corporated contemporaries - and, of course, singing out his doggone poetic heart. **Barney Hoskins, NME, June 1982**

Poetic Champions Compose

ARTIST Van Morrison **RELEASE DATE** September 1987 (UK) **LABEL** Mercury (UK)/Warner Bros. (US) **PRODUCER** Van Morison **UK CHART peak/weeks** 26/6 **US CHART peak/weeks** 90/22 **TRACK LISTING** Spanish Steps/The Mystery/Queen Of The Slipstream/I Forgot That Love Existed/Sometimes I Feel Like A Motherless Child/Celtic Excavation/Someone Like You/Alan Watts Blues/Give Me My Rapture/Did Ye Get Healed?/Allow Me **PERSONNEL** Van Morrison (v, g, s)

Recorded in London with a set of new musicians after an announcement that he was retiring from touring, **Poetic Champions Compose** was conceived as a jazz album – 'but after three numbers I thought I should put some words in'. Arranger Fiachra Trench was very much involved in the creation of an album that slips in the traditional *Sometimes I Feel Like A Motherless Child* among the instrumentals and the spiritual question of *Did Ye Get Healed?*, a worthwhile addition to Morrison's Eighties canon.

Pop

ARTIST U2 **RELEASE DATE** March 1997 (US) **LABEL** Island (UK & US) **PRODUCER** Flood, Howie B, Steve Osbourne **UK CHART peak/weeks** – **US CHART peak/weeks** – **TRACK LISTING** Discotheque/Do You Feel Loved/Mofo/If God Will Send His Angels/Staring At The Sun/Last Night On Earth/Gone/Miami/The Playboy Mansion/If You Wear That Velvet Dress/Please/Wake Up Dead Man **PERSONNEL** Bono (v, g), The Edge (g, k, v), Adam Clayton (b), Larry Mullen (d, pc)

One could only applaud U2's transformation, over a decade and a half, from ultra-sincere rock zealots adhering steadfastly to the past, to the ultimate post-modern pop group with a keenly developed trash aesthetic and both eyes on the future. On **Pop**, the process was complete. Not only was dance remixer-techno artist Howie B. present on many tracks, but the first single from the album, *Discotheque*, featured U2 as Village People wannabes, all camp manoeuvres and kitsch regalia. Where U2 would go from here was anybody's guess.

Pop *is inspired to an exhilarating pitch of energetic invention despite the mood of troubled, unresolved quest that runs throughout. Or perhaps because of it, maybe for U2 it's still not the finding but the looking for.* **Mat Snow, Mojo, March 1997**

Pornography

ARTIST The Cure **RELEASE DATE** April 1982 (UK) **LABEL** Fiction (UK)/Sire (US) **PRODUCER** Phil Thornalley **UK CHART peak/weeks** 8/9 **US CHART peak/weeks** – **TRACK LISTING** One Hundred Years/A Short Term Effect/The Hanging Garden/Siamese Twins/The Figurehead/A Strange Day/Cold/Pornography **PERSONNEL** Robert Smith (v, g), Lol Tolhurst (k), Simon Galup (b), Porl Thompson (g), Borris Williams (d)

Described by some, for better or worse, as 'the quintessential Goth album', this revelled, or perhaps wallowed, in a mire of distorted guitars and doomy rhythms. Robert Smith's fatalistic yelps and mutterings ('It doesn't matter if we all die') served to hide the fact that the man actually had an ironic sense of humour, particularly about himself. Nevertheless this was where The Cure began to nurture one of the biggest and longest-lasting cults of the Eighties. Throughout Europe, they were to be the gurus of 'dark rock'. The personnel of the group was by now Smith plus whoever he had not fallen out with that month.

Presumably, this record wins its title because it portrays and parades its currency of exposed futility and utterly naked fear with so few distractions or adornments, and so little sense of shame. It really piles it on. **Dave Hill, NME, May 1982**

Post

ARTIST Björk **RELEASE DATE** June 1995 (UK & US) **LABEL** One Little Indian (UK)/Elektra (US) **PRODUCER** Nellee Hooper, Graham Massey, Björk **UK CHART peak/weeks** 2/- **US CHART peak/weeks** 32/20 **TRACK LISTING** Army Of Me/Hyper-Ballad/The Modern Things/It's Oh So Quiet/Enjoy/You've Been Flirting Again/Isobel/Possibly Maybe/I Miss You/Cover Me/Headphones **PERSONNEL** Marius De Vries (k), Paul Weller (k), Martin Virgo (k), Garry Hughes (k), Luis Jardim (b), Bruce Smith (d, pc), Jon Mallison (g), Corki Hale (hp), Jhelisa Anderson (bv), Oliver Lake (br), Gary Barnacle (br), Mike Mower (br), Björk (v, k)

More 'difficult' than her **Debut**, this barged more determinedly into club culture, investigating ambient and rave music, although it was the bizarre big-band belter *It's Oh So Quiet* which gave Björk a crossover Christmas hit. Fashion and pop mags alike adored her unique sense of style and chirpy features, although the thumping of a TV interviewer at Bangkok airport around this time, and a string of celebrity boyfriends, exploded the cliché of her cuddly impishness. The accompanying videos were state-of-the-art and stunning.

… the girl is a true original, an explosion of exuberance and sensuality in a cold climate… she has returned with a second album… as bold and beautiful as her first offering. Here is the same diversity of styles, the same dizzying gallery of voices, the same ingenious marriage of torching and technology… **Barney Hoskins, Mojo, June 1995**

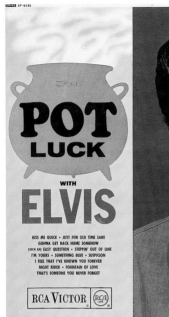

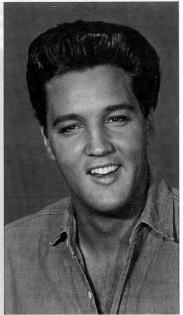

Pot Luck With Elvis

ARTIST Elvis Presley **RELEASE DATE** June 1962 (UK & US) **LABEL** RCA Victor (UK & US) **PRODUCER** Don Wardell **UK CHART** peak/weeks 1/25 **US CHART** peak/weeks 4/31 **TRACK LISTING** Kiss Me Quick/Just For Old Time's Sake/Fountain Of Love/Gonna Get Back Home Somehow/Such An Easy Question/Night Rider/Suspicion/Stepping Out Of Line/I Feel I've Known You Forever/That's Someone You Never Forget/Something Blue/I'm Yours **PERSONNEL** Elvis Presley (v), Floyd Gramer (p), Chet Atkins (g), Hank Garland (g), Boots Randolph (s), with Backing Singers The Jordanaires

By the time **Pot Luck** was released, Elvis was well on the way to being an all-round performer and albums were mere product – but it reached Number 4 nevertheless. Of the 12 songs contained on this album, eight were cut three months before release in Nashville, the other four dating from the previous year. **Steppin' Out Of Line** had originally been included in the *Blue Hawaii* soundtrack, but was dropped from the film to make an appearance here. In 1965, the Pomus and Shuman-composed **Night Rider** would be used in the Elvis film *Tickle Me*.

…right from the opening **Kiss Me Quick** *– where Elvis is in his most throbbing, urgent mood – to the final* **That's Someone You Never Forget**, *this album provides a real feast of beat and ballad.* **Melody Maker, July 1962**

Power, Corruption And Lies

ARTIST New Order **RELEASE DATE** May 1983 (UK & US) **LABEL** Factory (UK)/Streetwise (US) **PRODUCER** New Order **UK CHART** peak/weeks 4/29 **US CHART** peak/weeks – **TRACK LISTING** Your Silent Face/Ultraviolence/Ecstacy/Leave Me Alone/Age Of Consent/We All Stand/The Village/505/The Beach **PERSONNEL** Bernard Sumner (v, g), Peter Hook (b), Stephen Morris (d)

Though perhaps best remembered for their string of 12-inch singles that bestrode the mid Eighties, New Order's second album was the one that set out their stall with tracks like **Age Of Consent**, propelled by

Peter Hook's trademark bass riffs. Ironically they would not include singles on albums so **Blue Monday** was absent, a demo titled **505** taking its place – arguably, a wrong move.

… proof that New Order have arrived at an identity… The music… makes no pretentious claims for itself, nor does it labour after an impression of profundity. New Order are just getting on with it: simply, efficiently and enjoyably. **Paul Du Noyer, NME, May 1983**

The Predator

ARTIST Ice Cube **RELEASE DATE** December 1992 (US) **LABEL** Fourth & Broadway (UK)/Priority (US) **PRODUCER** Ice Cube **UK CHART** peak/weeks 73/1 **US CHART** peak/weeks 1/52 **TRACK LISTING** First Day Of School/When Will They Shoot/I'm Scared/Wicked/Now I Gotta Wet'cha/Predator/It Was A Good Day/We Had To Tear This Up/'Em/Dirty Mac/Don't Trust 'Em/Gangsta's Fairy Tale 2/Check Yo Self/Who Got The Camara?/ Integration/Say Hi To The Bad Guy **PERSONNEL** Ice Cube (rap)

It fell to O'Shea Jackson, alias Ice Cube, to register the very first rap album to top the *Billboard* pop Hot 100 when he displaced country superstar Garth Brooks in late 1992. But the US music trade magazine received scant thanks: the rapper used the title track to address them and other critics of his **Death Certificate** album. Released the previous year, it contained alleged racist lyrics which had attracted *Billboard*'s wrath.

… more glaring than the lack of mind-blowing songs is the absolute absence of introspection. Throughout **The Predator**, *Ice Cube's persona – his gangster lean – is so ancient it's creaky, so stagey you half expect someone to yell 'cut' at the end of each song.* **Danyel Smith, Rolling Stone, January 1993**

The Pretender

ARTIST Jackson Browne **RELEASE DATE** December 1976 (UK) **LABEL** Asylum (UK & US) **PRODUCER** Jon Landau **UK CHART** peak/weeks 26/5 **US CHART** peak/weeks 5/35 **TRACK LISTING** The Fuse/Your Bright Baby Blues/Linda Paloma/Here Come Those Tears Again/The Only Child/Daddy's Tune/Sleep's Dark And Silent Gate/The Pretender **PERSONNEL** Russell Kunkel (d), Leyland Sklar (b), Craig Doerge (p), David Lindley (g), Jim Gordon (d), Chuck Rainey (b), Roy Bittan (p), Jackson Browne (ag), Lowell George (g), Billy Payne (o, p), Luis F. Damian (g, v) Roberto Gutierrez (vl, bv) Arthur Gerst (hp, bv) Bob Glaub (b), Fred Tackett (G), John Hall (g), Mike Utley (o), Bonnie Raitt (v), Rosemary Butler (v), Jeff Porcaro (d), Albert Lee (g), Gary Coleman (pc), John David Souther (v), Don Henley (v) David Lindley (vl, g) David Nash

Browne's wife had committed suicide, so it's understandable that **The Pretender** was deeply introspective and often harrowing. Jon Landau, the producer behind prime Springsteen, gave it some

energy, and songs like **The Fuse** and the South of the Border-tinged **Linda Paloma** at least tried to find a light at the end of the tunnel. Usually, though, there was no light. The title song despairs at the inner thought processes of comfortable suburbia, but Bonnie Raitt and Rosemary Butler pipe in on the uncharacteristically bouncy **Here Come Those Tears Again**.

The Pretender *is a breakthrough – Browne has always had traces of cynicism in his writing, but about romance he has remained firm. Love can make a difference, all of his songs say.* **Dave Marsh, Rolling Stone, January 1971**

The Pretenders

ARTIST The Pretenders **RELEASE DATE** January 1980 (UK) **LABEL** Real (UK) / Sire (US) **PRODUCER** Chris Thomas, Nick Lowe **UK CHART** peak/ weeks 1 /35 **US CHART** peak/ weeks 9/78 **TRACK LISTING** Precious/The Phone Call/Up The Neck/ Tattooed Love Boys/Space Invader/The Wait/ Stop Your Sobbing /Kid/Private Life/Brass In Pocket/Lovers Of Today/ Mystery Achievement **PERSONNEL** Chrissie Hynde (v, g), Pete Farndon (b, v), James Honeyman Scott (g, k, v), Martin Chambers (d, v)

By combining a Sixties melodic sensibility with punk energy, expatriate American Chrissie Hynde created a debut album that stands up as a classic. The chart-topping **Brass In Pocket**, with its white-funk clichés, is hardly typical of the combination of soft-centred pop (**Kid**) and spiky rock (**Precious, Tattooed Love Boy**) that proved there was much more to Hynde and Co. than the Kinks cover that gave them their break. The follow-up just could not compare and two drug deaths broke the spell.

… If I've made the first side sound dispensable, it's more out of objective duty, because the second half alone is of such startling quality that the album is irresistible. Essential listening for the start of the Eighties… **Chris Brazier, Melody Maker, January 1980**

Pretty Hate Machine

ARTIST Nine Inch Nails **RELEASE DATE** October 1991 (UK)/November 1990 (US) **LABEL** MTV (UK)/Nothing Interscope (US) **PRODUCER** Trent Reznor, Adrian Sherwood, Keith Leblanc & John Fryer **UK CHART** peak/weeks - **US CHART** peak/weeks 75/113 **TRACK LISTING** Head Like A Hole/Terrible Lie/Down In It/Sanctified/Something I Can Never Have/Kinda I Want To/Sin/That's What I Get/The Only Time/Ringfinger. **PERSONNEL** Trent Reznor (v, g), James Wooley (k), Richard (g), Chris Vrenna (d)

When MTV took an interest in **Head Like A Hole**, the opening track of this album from Cleveland industrial rockers Nine Inch Nails, it had no idea what it was starting. The band, led by former classical pianist Trent Reznor, would pick up where Ministry had blazed a trail to bring noise and mayhem to the mainstream but, having expanded to a band and then shrinking back again to Reznor alone, the nihilism of tracks like **Something I Can Never Have** remained rarely plumbed as the decade progressed.

Nine Inch Nails are pretty much state of the art in 1991, at least in white musical terms… Reznor's panoramic vision is both admirably adventurous and yet accessible… Meanwhile Adrian Sherwood and Flood's co-production squeezes out sparks at every turn. **Martin Aston, Q, March 1991**

Pretzel Logic

ARTIST Steely Dan **RELEASE DATE** March 1974 (UK)/April 1974 (US) **LABEL** Probe SPBA 6282 **PRODUCER** – **UK CHART** peak/weeks 37/2 **US CHART** peak/weeks 8/- **TRACK LISTING** Rikki Don't Lose That Number/Night By Night/Any Major Dude/Barrytown/East St Louis Toodle Oo/Parker's Bad/Thru With Buzz/Pretzel Logic/With A Gun/Charlie Freak/Monkey In Your Soul **PERSONNEL** Donald Fagen (k, v), Walter Becker (b, v), David Palmer (v), Denny Dias (rg), Jeff Baxter (g), Jim Hodder (d)

On their third album Steely Dan's roots showed through: in the cover of Duke Ellington's *East St Louis Toodle-Oo* and the hard bop tribute to Charlie Parker, *Parker's Band*. **Pretzel Logic** was their most seamless collection of immaculately produced jazz-rock-pop yet. On **Night By Night** and **Any Major Dude Will Tell You**, they even ventured towards funk territory, while the deceptively pretty **Rikki Don't Lose That Number** provided the Dan with their biggest hit single to date.

They have soul and fire, but leave nothing to chance, with superb productions and songs…. **Melody Maker, April 1974**

Private Dancer

ARTIST Tina Turner **RELEASE DATE** June 1984 (UK & US) **LABEL** Capitol (UK & US) **PRODUCER** – **UK CHART** peak/weeks 2/147 **US CHART** peak/weeks 3/106 **TRACK LISTING** I Might Have Been Queen/What's Love Got To Do With It/Show Some Respect/I Can't Stand The Rain/Private Dancer/Let's Stay Together/Better Be Good To Me/Steel Claw/Help! **PERSONNEL** Tina Turner (v), session musicians

Tina Turner effectively started from scratch to rebuild a career that stretched back to the early Sixties, with the five-million selling **Private Dancer**. With its hi-tech production by the likes of Martyn Ware (of electro-poppers Heaven 17/B.E.F.), this was designer soul par excellence: Turner's hoarse vocals offset by the immaculate surfaces of the music. With worldwide smashes like **What's Love Got To Do With It?**, a cover of Al Green's **Let's Stay Together** and the title track, the album was virtually a Greatest Hits of the second part of Turner's career, as well as an opportunity for her to finally exorcise the demon of ex-husband Ike.

Tina Turner… blows through this brilliant album like a hundred-mile-an-hour hurricane. The production is all over the place… but Turner's indomitable wail holds the whole thing together from beginning to end. **The Year in Music and Entertainment 1984, Rolling Stone, 1984**

Procol Harum Live In Concert

ARTIST Procol Harum RELEASE DATE May 1972 (UK & US) LABEL Chrysalis (UK)/A&M (US) PRODUCER – UK CHART peak/weeks 48/1 US CHART peak/weeks 5/28 TRACK LISTING Conquistador/Whaling Stories/A Salty Dog/All This And More/In Hell 'Twas I/Glimpses of Nirvana/'Twas Teatime At The Circus/In The Autumn Of My Madness/I Know If I'd Been Wiser/Grand Finales PERSONNEL Gary Brooker (v, p), Chris Copping (k), Dave Ball (g), Barry J. Wilson (d), Alan Cartwright (b), Keith Reid (w), Edmonton Symphony Orchestra

In the land where Frampton came alive, Procol, who had topped bills over the Byrds and Santana, started it all by reprising their first four years of classic rock in concert on North American – well, Canadian – soil with the Edmonton Symphony Orchestra. The atmospheric, South American-flavoured *Conquistador*, originally tackled on their debut album, was a surprise hit single on both sides of the Atlantic, while the album gave them their US chart debut.

… this album departs from the simple funk of the others' pop patterns, and joins that small section of groups who make music and who owe more to notes than basic feeling. **M. P., Melody Maker, April 1972**

Protection

ARTIST Massive Attack RELEASE DATE September 1994 (UK & US) LABEL Wild Bunch Circa (UK)/Virgin (US) PRODUCER Nellee Hooper, Massive Attack UK CHART peak/weeks 14/- US CHART peak/weeks 0/0 TRACK LISTING Protection/Karmacoma/Three/Weather Storm/Spying Glass/Better Things/Eurochild/Sly/Heat Miser/Light My Fire PERSONNEL 3d (v), Mushroom (k), Daddy G (k)

Three years of appalling bad fortune – losing vocalist Shara Nelson, a disastrous US tour, having temporarily to abbreviate their name (to Massive) due to the Gulf War, management hassles, etc. – separated Massive Attack's critically acclaimed debut album **Blue Lines** and this follow-up. But the services of producer Nellee Hooper (part of the original Bristol posse, the Wild Bunch, which had spawned them), plus a trio of disparate yet talented singers in Tracy Thorn, Horace Andy and Nicolette successfully turned the tide. A dub version, **No Protection**, was helmed by Brixton's Mad Professor.

Cool, sexy stuff, it smoothly fuses dub, club and soul, grounding its grace in sampled hip-hop beats… **Protection** *lacks the focus of the masterful 1991 debut* **Blue Lines**. *But it lingers longer.* **Paul Evans, Rolling Stone, April 1995**

Psychocandy

ARTIST The Jesus And Mary Chain RELEASE DATE November 1985 (UK)/February 1986 (US) LABEL Blanco y Negro (UK)/Reprise (US) PRODUCER Jim Reid, William Reid UK CHART peak/weeks 31/10 US CHART peak/weeks 188/4 TRACK LISTING Just Like Honey/The Living End/Taste The Floor/Hardest Walk/Cut Dead/In A Hole/Taste Of Cindy/Never Understand/It's So Hard/Inside Me/Sowing Seeds/My Little Underground/You Trip Me Up/Something's Wrong PERSONNEL Jim Reid (v, g), Wiliam Reid (g, v), Murray Dalglish (d), Douglas Hart (b)

One of the classic 1980 debut albums, **Psychocandy** was the culmination of two years of amazing publicity, chaotic gigs of inordinately short length and apparent record company office

trashing. It lived up to the expectation with its multi-tracked guitars and sinister melodies. The departure of Bobby Gillespie would be weathered as the expatriate Scots continued to entrance and excite the capital. Critics could claim the music press and John Peel's patronage did much to boost the Chain's fortunes. Manager Alan McGee rated them among the great bands he had discovered.

… a great searing citadel of beauty whose wall of noise, once scaled, offers access to endless vistas of melody and emotion… what you really have to know is how this whole fits together, how it offers up itself as salvation for rock 'n' roll. **Andy Gill, October 1985**

Public Image Ltd

ARTIST Public Image RELEASE DATE December 1978 (UK) LABEL Virgin (UK)/Island (US) PRODUCER – UK CHART peak/weeks 22/11 US CHART peak/weeks 0/0 TRACK LISTING Theme/Religion I/Religion II/Annalisa/Public Image/Low Life/Attack/Fodderstompf PERSONNEL John Lydon (v), Keith Levene (g), Jah Wobble (b), Jim Walker (d)

This album, the first post-Sex Pistols statement by John Lydon (the former Johnny Rotten), was nearly credited to the Carnivorous Buttock Flies. But a change of heart and name led to this 'newspaper-clad' epic, which mixed songs like the single title track and **Low Life**, of their clear Pistols lineage, with more adventurous fare such as **Annalisa** and **Theme**. The experimentations of 1979's **Metal Box** developed yet further, but this debut proved there was post-Pistol life for the face of punk – and less than a year after the split.

… the record is all top and bottom and Rotten floats over the proceedings like he was a deejay talking against someone else's programme. My niggling complaint is that too often we, the listeners, are left out of PIL's introverted efforts. **Simon Frith, Melody Maker, December 1978**

Pump

ARTIST Aerosmith **RELEASE DATE** September 1989 (UK & US) **LABEL** Geffen (UK & US) **PRODUCER** Brian Fairbairn **UK CHART** peak/weeks 3/24 **US CHART** peak/weeks 5/110 **TRACK LISTING** Young Lust/F.I.N.E./Love In An Elevator/Monkey On My Back/Janie's Got A Gun/The Other Side/My Girl/Don't Get Mad Get Even/Voodoo Medicine Man/What It Takes **PERSONNEL** Joe Perry (g), Tom Hamilton (b), Steven Tyler (lv, k, bv), Joey Kramer (d), Brad Whitford (g)

A Grammy award winner, this was the album that catapulted Aerosmith to the zenith of their career, and their *genre*: the riffery-rockery was laced with smart hooks and tongue-in-cheek New Sexism humour. With Tyler having taken to the video medium like a duck to water, they found much hilarity in phrases like 'going down' as *Love In An Elevator* brought the band their first British hit. *Janie's Got A Gun* and *What It Takes* revealed a more complex nature, while the instrumentation gathered moss at every opportunity. Suddenly Aerosmith – survivors at the very least – were in on their own joke, and we warmed to them accordingly.

The pacing of **Pump** *practically guarantees that the listener's interest will never wane. Brief attention grabbers – snippets of hillbilly music, spoken segments, off beat instrumental side trips – are interspersed with song… Pump up the volume.* **Kim Neely, Rolling Stone, October 1989**

Purple

ARTIST Stone Temple Pilots **RELEASE DATE** June 1994 (UK)/May 1994 (US) **LABEL** Atlantic (UK & US) **PRODUCER** Brendan O'Brian **UK CHART** peak/weeks 10/– **US CHART** peak/weeks 1/64 **TRACK LISTING** Meatplow/Vasoline/Lounge Fly/Interstate Love Song/Still Remains/Pretty Penny/Silvergun Superman/Big Empty/Unglued/Army Ants/Kitchenware & Candybar!/Gracious Melodies. **PERSONNEL** Weiland (v), Dean DeLeo (g), Robert DeLeo (b), Eric Kretz (d)

Debuting at Number 1 and going triple platinum, **Purple** was one of the biggest selling albums of the grunge era. Although they denied any kinship with Pearl Jam, Soundgarden et al, Stone Temple Pilots did favour heavy Led Zep-style riffs, although they had a radio friendliness that had detractors labelling the band grunge lite. Mainman Scott Weiland's cocaine and heroin abuse

and subsequent admission to a rehab clinic did little to heighten STP's credibility.

What matters is the emotion, the passion. You can't get that from a f-in' synthesiser or a f-in' mini-Moog because the sound they make isn't organic. It's like masturbation against virtual masturbation. I'd like to try it, but that's all, you know what I mean. **Scott Weiland interviewed by Stefan de Batseiler, NME, June 1994**

Purple Rain - Music From The Motion Picture

ARTIST Prince **RELEASE DATE** July 1984 (UK & US) **LABEL** Warner Bros. (UK & US) **PRODUCER** Prince & The Revolution **UK CHART** peak/weeks 7/86 **US CHART** peak/weeks 1/72 **TRACK LISTING** Let's Go Crazy/Take Me With You/The Beautiful Ones/Computer Blue/Darling Nikki/When Doves Cry/I Would Die 4 U/Baby I'm A Star/Purple Rain **PERSONNEL** Prince (v), Wendy Melvion (g)

The success of **1999** made Prince the artist to watch and he delivered with **Purple Rain**. Although subsequently turned into a largely autobiographical film, the music stood the test of time far longer, for the driving force is to be found on such cuts as *Purple Rain*, *Let's Go Crazy* and *When Doves Cry* rather than anything cinematic. There were still the excesses – *Darling Nikki* concerning itself with public masturbation, but since no-one had ever tackled such issues perhaps Prince saw it as his duty to raise the matter.

There are some furious jams for sure (as in **Let's Go Crazy**)*, plus sultry funk (* **When Doves Cry**)*, whisper to a scream soul (* **The Beautiful Ones**) *and in the title track a tune that's commended to Willie Nelson to snazz up his next oldies snoozer… Essential listening.* **The year in music and entertainment 1984, Rolling Stone, 1984**

Pyromania

ARTIST Def Leppard **RELEASE DATE** March 1983 (UK) **LABEL** Vertigo (UK)/Mercury (US) **PRODUCER** Robert John 'Mutt' Range **UK CHART** peak/weeks 18/8 **US CHART** peak/weeks 2/116 **TRACK LISTING** Photograph/Too Late For Love/Comin' Under Fire/Foolin'/Die Hard The

Hunter/Rock! Rock! (Till You Drop)/Billy's Got A Gun/Action! Not Words/Stagefright/Rock Of Ages PERSONNEL Joe Elliot (lv), Steve 'Steamin' Clark (g), Phil Collen (g), Rick Savage (b), Rick Allen (d), Pete Williams (guitar backing tracks)

With ex-Girl guitarist Phil Collen replacing Pete Willis as recording sessions drew to a close, few guessed Sheffield's Def Leppard were on the verge of a breakthrough. But as **Photograph** took off in the US chart, they swapped a support slot with Billy Squier for headlining dates and by the time the *Pyromania Tour* ended in late 1983 they were million sellers four times over! Collen would play all the guitars on 1992's **Adrenalize** after the drink and drug-related death of guitar partner Steve Clark.

Def Leppard huff and they puff but they just can't blow the house down. Poor lambs – you feel you want to pat them on the head, give them a packet of liquorice allsorts and a few shillings for their trouble, and tell them you'll kill them if they ever show their larynxes round the house again. **Colin Irwin, Melody Maker, March 1983**

Q: Are We Not Men? A: We Are Devo!

ARTIST Devo RELEASE DATE September 1978 (UK & US) LABEL Virgin (UK)/Warner Bros. (US) PRODUCER Brian Eno UK CHART peak/weeks 12/7 US CHART peak/weeks 78/18 TRACK LISTING Uncontrollable Urge/Satisfaction (I Can't Get Me No)/Praying Hands/Space Junk/Mongoloid/Jocko Homo/Too Much Paranoias/Gut Feeling/(Slap Your Mummy)/Come Back Jonee/Sloppy (I Saw My Baby Gettin')/Shrivel Up PERSONNEL Bob Mothersbaugh (g, v), Bob Casale (g), Mark Mothersbaugh (sy), Jerry Casale (b), Alan Myers (d)

Having utilized slogan-happy indie label Stiff to give them their British break, *Akron*, Ohio natives Devo switched to Virgin for their LP debut. The first expression of their feelings about the 'de-evolution' (regression) of mankind would prove their UK peak in commercial terms. Their stock rose at home as success here waned. Unusually featuring two sets of brothers, Devo remained active in the late Eighties, but a new decade found Mark Mothersbaugh writing music for the children's cable TV series *Rugrats*. De-evolution?

Only a fanatic with seriously impaired hearing facilities would say that the Devo album was anything other than weak, insubstantial and insipid…. Live they invest those same songs with the power and dynamism they desperately lack on record… **Andy Gill, NME, December 1978**

The Queen Is Dead

ARTIST The Smiths RELEASE DATE June 1986 (UK & US) LABEL Rough Trade (UK)/Sire (US) PRODUCER Johnny Marr, Morrissey UK CHART peak/weeks 2/22 US CHART peak/weeks 70/37 TRACK LISTING Frankly Mr Shankly/I Know It's Over/Never Had No One Ever/Cemetery Gates/Big Mouth Strikes Again/Vicar In A Tutu/There Is A Light That Never Goes Out/Some Girls Are Bigger Than Others/The Queen Is Dead/The Boy With The Thorn In His Side. PERSONNEL Morrissey (v), Johnny Marr (g, h, md, p), Andy Rourke (b), Mike Joyce (d)

Widely regarded as their masterpiece, The Smiths' third album was a superb collection that ranged from savage riffing of the title track to exquisite beauty of **There Is A Light That Never Goes Out**, from the Ealing Comedy vignette of **Frankly Mr Shankly** to the self-indulgent confessionals of **I Know It's Over** and **Never Had No One Ever**, from the gentle narrative of **The Boy With The Thorn In His Side** to the surreal melodrama of **Vicar In A Tutu**.

The Queen Is Dead *will help bury the one-dimensional misery-guts attitude so beloved of the group's denigrators, while further displaying to all and sundry the simple fact that this is essentially music brimming with valorous intent.* **Nick Kent, Melody Maker, June 1986**

Quiet Riot

ARTIST Metal Health RELEASE DATE April 1983 (UK & US) LABEL Pasha (US) PRODUCER Spencer Proffer UK CHART peak/weeks 0/0 US CHART peak/weeks 1/81 TRACK LISTING Metal Health/Cum On Feel The Noise/Don't Wanna Let You Go/Slick Black Cadillac/Love's A Bitch/Breatless/Run For Cover/Battle Axe/Let's Get Crazy/Thunderbird PERSONNEL Franki Banali (d), Carlos Cavazo (g), Kevin DuBrow (bv), Rudy Srazo (b), Chuck Write (bv), Donna Slattery (bv)

Seventies glam-rockers Slade couldn't make a mark in America despite their UK success, which makes it all the more surprising that LA's Quiet Riot should make it with a very similar sound. Their cover of the Wolverhampton Wonders' **Cum On Feel The Noize** reached Number 5 Stateside and revived the band's career after original guitarist Randy Rhoads had left them for Ozzy Osbourne. He had been invited to guest on the closing track **Thunderbird** but died in a plane crash: the album was dedicated to his memory.

Radio

ARTIST L.L. Cool J RELEASE DATE February 1986 (UK)/January 1986 (US) LABEL Def Jam (UK)/Columbia (US) PRODUCER Rick Rubin UK CHART peak/weeks - US CHART peak/weeks 46/38 TRACK LISTING I Can't Live Without My Radio/You Can't Dance/Dear Yvette/I Can Give You More/Dangerous/Rock The Bells/I Need A Beat/That's A Lie/You'll Rock/I Want You PERSONNEL L.L. Cool J (v, rap), Nelson George (in)

What began as a novelty thanks to the likes of the Sugarhill Gang and Kurtis Blow became the dominating force within black music. Leading the way is undoubtedly L.L. Cool J (Ladies Love Cool James), who has enjoyed a successful career for over 10 years. While many of his peers were quick to court controversy with their lyrics, he remained remarkably consistent and quickly became something of a hero and role model to black youth. With production handled by Rick Rubin, **Radio** is as fine an example of rap music from the mid Eighties as you are likely to find.

Radio City

ARTIST Big Star **RELEASE DATE** Febuary 1974 (UK & US) **LABEL** Stax (UK)/Ardent (US) **PRODUCER** – **UK CHART** peak/weeks 0/0 **US CHART** peak/weeks 0/0 **TRACK LISTING** O, My Soul/Life Is White/Way Out West/What's Going On/You Got What You Deserve/Mod Lang/Back Of A Car/Daisy Glaze/She's A Mover/September Gurls/Morpha Too-Im In Love With A Girl. **PERSONNEL** Chris Bell (g, v), Andy Hummel (b), Jody Stephens (d), Alex Chilton (v)

Famously unlucky and undervalued in their time, Big Star – primarily the songwriting genius of Alex Chilton – became one of the hippest of cults. Dogged by record company errors, the Memphis group were mediocre live. Second string Chris Bell, also a fine pop craftsman, left early on. Yet the debut **#1 Record** and this, their second, fused order and chaos, tension and abandon in some deceptively complex three-minute jewels. *September Gurls* and *What's Going Ahn* sounded extraordinarily exciting, the former being one of the most effectively moving, effortlessly inspirational songs of all time. Countless young groups cite the Big Star legacy.

As a writer Chilton was patently unsuited to the starched collar conventions of straight pop. On this evidence he did not produce one totally memorable song until after the group collapsed, leaving him to fall into ruin. **Biba Kopf, NME, February 1987**

Ragged Glory

ARTIST Neil Young And Crazy Horse **RELEASE DATE** September 1990 (UK) **LABEL** Reprise (UK & US) **PRODUCER** David Briggs, Neil Young **UK CHART** peak/weeks 15/5 **US CHART** peak/weeks 31/- **TRACK LISTING** Country Home/White Line/F!#IN' Up/Over and Over/Love To Burn/Farmer John/Mansion On The Hill/Days That Used To Be/Love And Only Love/Mother Earth (Natural Anthem) **PERSONNEL** Neil Young (g, v), Frank 'Poncho' Sampedro (g, v), Billy Talbot (b, v), Ralph Molina (d, v)

Ragged Glory saw Neil Young reunited with old sparring partners Crazy Horse and, sure enough, it rocked with as much force as the work of Young the 20-something guitarslinger, evincing no loss of

power in the thrash and burn departments. In fact, Young is uniquely hip among his peers, responding to current trends without being swayed by them: his 1994 set, *Sleeps With Angels*, was spurred by the death of Nirvana's Kurt Cobain, while 1995's *Mirror Ball* was a collaboration with Nirvana's nemesis, Pearl Jam. **Ragged Glory** just about sums up Neil Young as as a supremely relevant singer-songwriter and guitarist.

You got a bit fed up a couple of months back, called your mates to your ranch and for a week or two you blasted your frustrations away by recording a bunch of old and new songs… you are, of course, Neil Young… **Ragged and glorious?** *Oh Yes.* **John Baldie, Q, October 1990**

Rain Dogs

ARTIST Tom Waits **RELEASE DATE** October 1985 (UK)/August 1985 (US) **LABEL** Island (UK & US) **PRODUCER** Tom Waits **UK CHART** peak/weeks 29/5 **US CHART** peak/weeks 181/7 **TRACK LISTING** Singapore/Clap Hands/Cemetry Polka/Jockey Full Of Bourbon/Tango Till They're Sore/Big Black Mariah/Diamonds And Gold/Hang Down Your Head/Time/Rain Dogs/Midtown/Ninth And Headpin/Gun Street Girl/Union Square/Blind Love/Walking Spanish/Downtown Train/Bride Of Rain Dog/Anywhere I Lay My Head **PERSONNEL** Tom Waits (v, p, ad)

Nominated as Album Of The Year by the *NME* (along with the Jesus And Mary Chain's **Psychocandy**), Tom Waits' eighth studio recording was the second in his experimental trilogy, after **Swordfishtrombones** and preceding **Frank's Wild Years**. Like its predecessor, **Rain Dogs** was a sprawling affair that seemed to encompass every American musical style of the twentieth century, although it did contain one song with a sufficiently conventional structure for Rod Stewart to have a hit with it: *Downtown Train*.

Waits' persona is so strong it has always threatened to imprison him in it… the lasting achievement of **Rain Dogs** *is that Waits has had to sacrifice none of his poetry in pursuit of new musical languages to meet its demand.* **Biba Kopf, NME, October 1985**

Raising Hell

ARTIST Run-D. M. C. **RELEASE DATE** July 1986 (UK)/June 1986 (US) **LABEL** London (UK)/Profile (US) **PRODUCER** Russell Simmons, Rick Rubin **UK CHART** peak/weeks 41/26 **US CHART** peak/weeks 3/71 **TRACK LISTING** Peter Piper/It's Tricky/My Adidas/Walk This Way/Is It Live/Perfection/Hit It Run/Raising Hell/You Be Illin'/Dumb Girl/Son Of Byford/Proud To Be Black **PERSONNEL** Jason Mizell aka 'Jam Master Jay' (v, k, pc), Joseph 'Run' Simmons (v), MC Darryl 'D' McDaniels (v), Sam Sever (dm), Daniel Shulman (b), Rick Ruben (g), Steve Tyler (v), Joe Perry (g)

The collaboration between rockers Aerosmith (or, at least, Joe Perry and Steven Tyler) and rappers Run D.M.C. on the seminal *Walk This Way* single helped propel rap into the mainstream and make it acceptable to legions of diehard guitarheads. Not surprisingly, the accompanying album, **Raising Hell**, was the most successful of its time, solidifying the image of the swaggering, street-tough rapper in Adidas sportswear, laces untied on his chunky trainers, massive gold chains around the neck. Fortunately, the music, all crunching beats and humorous self-aggrandizing, was just as memorable.

Raising Hell *scores both as a dance/noise fission, there to hotfoot fast reacting feet, and as a capsule of NY suburban Americana that satisfies desires for sassy back street culture that grates against mainstream homogeneity, while remaining impregnated with its flavour.* **Biba Kopf, NME, July 1986**

The Ramones

ARTIST Ramones **RELEASE DATE** July 1976 (UK)/May 1976 (US) **LABEL** Sire (UK & US) **PRODUCER** Craig Leon **UK CHART** peak/weeks – **US CHART** peak/weeks 111/18 **TRACK LISTING** Blitzkreig Bop/Beat On The Brat/Judy Is A Punk/I Wanna Be Your Boyfriend/Chain Saw/Now I Wanna Sniff Some Glue/I Don't Wanna Go Down To The Basement/Loudmouth/Havana Affair/Listen To My Heart/53rd & 3rd/Let's Dance/I Don't Wanna Walk Around With You/Today Your Love, Tomorrow The World **PERSONNEL** Joey Ramone (v), Johnny Ramone (g, v), Dee Dee Ramone (b, v), Tommy Ramone (d)

From the cover of four leather-jacketed blokes against a wall to the incessant beat and guitar buzzing like an angry wasp, **Ramones** defined the first US punk group so perfectly they need not have bothered with a follow-up. Few of the 14 tracks broke the two-minute barrier by much – some titles seemed longer than the songs themselves – while even **Now I Wanna Snif Some Glue** seemed too cartoony to be a serious call to solvent abuse. Fun, though.

The Ramones are authentic American primitives whose work has to be heard to be understood… In rock 'n' roll and matters of the heart, we should all hang on to a little amateurism. Let's hope these guys sell more records than Elton John has pennies. **Paul Nelson, Rolling Stone, July 1976**

Rapture

ARTIST Anita Baker **RELEASE DATE** May 1986 (UK) **LABEL** Elektra (UK & US) **PRODUCER** Michael J. Powell, Marti Sharron, Gary Skardina **UK CHART** peak/weeks 13/47 **US CHART** peak/weeks 11/157 **TRACK LISTING** Sweet Love/You Bring Me Love/Caught Up In The Rapture/Been So Long/Mystery/No One In The World/Same Ole Love/Watch Your Step **PERSONNEL** Anita Baker (v), session musicians

This sultry, sensuous set of soul ballads was a benchmark in modern R&B. Just as the more seductive side of the medium was being usurped by youthful, all but wanton aggression, Detroit-born Baker stumbled upon songs, co-written with pianist Michael Powell, which flew with grace and beauty. Her mature phrasing and gentle flourishes transported **Sweet Love** and **You Bring Me Joy** to a realm of lush romantic sexuality. A trace of gospel and jazz gilded the lily: caught up in the rapture of love, indeed.

Rapture *exudes an aura of dimmed lights and romantic introspection… an emotionally rich, subtly restrained suite of songs that merge elements of jazz and soul, with an emphasis on ballads.* **Rolling Stone, November 1989**

Rattle And Hum

ARTIST U2 **RELEASE DATE** October 1988 (UK & US) **LABEL** Island (UK & US) **PRODUCER** Jimmy Iovine **UK CHART** peak/weeks 1/54 **US CHART** peak/weeks 1/38 **TRACK LISTING** Helter Skelter/Van Diemen's Land/Desire/Hawkmoon 269/Angel Of Harlem/Love Rescue Me/When Love Comes To Town/Heartland/All Along The Watchtower/I Still Haven't Found What I'm Looking For/(Freedom For My People)/Pride (In The Name Of Love)/God Part II/(The Star Spangled Banner)/Bullet The Blue Sky/All I Want Is You **PERSONNEL** Bono (v), The Edge (g, k), Adam Clayton (b), Larry Mullen (d)

Rattle And Hum was the half-live, half-studio double LP set that accompanied the documentary of the same name. Featuring guest appearances from Bob Dylan (Bono's true predecessor in the Rock Messiah stakes) and blues man B. B. King, U2's seventh album was regarded by critics as the point where the band – and Bono in particular – started believing their own press about the 'superstar saviours of rock' and overstepped the mark. As a consequence, the

live rendition of **Pride** was bombastic, while the collaboration with B. B. King on **When Love Comes To Town** saw Bono over determined to express his passion and commitment.

U2 have found a new maturity by plunging their previously chaste muse into the twin maelstroms of American roots and human desire…. **Rattle and Hum** *throngs with the spirits of the Sixties and U2 fight hard to match their youthful urgency with the likes of Dylan, Hendrix and The Beatles.* **Mark Cooper, Q, November 1988**

Rattlesnakes

ARTIST Lloyd Cole And The Commotions **RELEASE DATE** October 1984 (UK & US) **LABEL** Polydor (UK)/Geffen (US) **PRODUCER** Paul Hardiman **UK CHART** peak/weeks 13/30 **US CHART** peak/weeks 0/0 **TRACK LISTING** Perfect Skin/Speedboat/Rattlesnakes/Down On Mission Street/Forest Fire/Charlotte Street/2cv/Four Flights Up/Patience/Are You Ready To Be Heartbroken? **PERSONNEL** Lloyd Cole (v, g), Neil Clark (g), Blair Cowan (k, v), Lawrence Donegan (b), Stephen Irvine (d)

Intelligent wordplay helped make Glasgow's Commotions an instant college success, but it was the consummate *Perfect Skin* single which hurled them into the hit parade. Cole was a visibly nervous front man: you saw him on *Top Of The Pops* and actually felt SORRY for him, but the Lou Reed/Tom Petty influence on the lean guitars covered his tremors. As a lyricist he inspired love and hate, daring to be halfway clever, or pretentious as some would have it. He also name dropped (Simone De Beauvoir, Eve Marie-Saint, Norman Mailer) rather too eagerly, but more substantial commercial success greeted the band when he eased up on this trait, consciously naming the next two albums **Easy Pieces** and **Mainstream**.

A record collection without this LP would be like a kitchen without tea. Would you dare to invite guests back without it?… The record plays like a film… Wild but sensitive! **Cath Carroll, NME, October 1984**

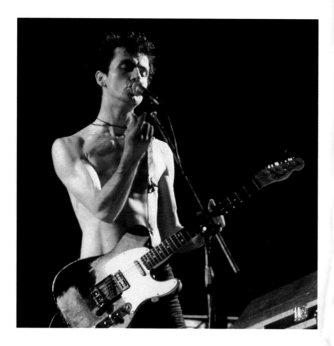

Rattus Norvegicus

ARTIST The Stranglers **RELEASE DATE** April 1977 (UK & US) **LABEL** United Artists (UK)/A&M (US) **PRODUCER** Martin Rushent **UK CHART** peak/weeks 4/34 **US CHART** peak/weeks 0/0 **TRACK LISTING** Sometimes/Goodbye Toulouse/London Lady/Princess Of The Streets/Hanging Around/Peaches/(Get A) Grip (On Yourself)/Ugly/Down In The Sewer/Falling- (b) Down in the sewer- (c) Trying to get out again- (d) Rats Rally **PERSONNEL** Hugh Cornwall (v, g), Jean-Jacques Burnel (b, v), Dave Greenfield (k), Jet Black (d)

The Stranglers were reviled by the hardline punks because of their ages (guitarist/vocalist Hugh Cornwall was born in 1949), their backgrounds (Cornwall was a former science teacher, bassist Jean-Jacques Burnel a history graduate), and their musical approach which, with its Sixties keyboard-dominated sound – a bit Doors And The Mysterians – hardly conformed to punk's Year Zero ethos. Nevertheless, they had the requisite menace and aggression and so **Rattus Norvegicus**, the debut album, propelled The Stranglers to the ranks of Most Successful New Wave Band, on the back of hits like *Hanging Around*, *Get A Grip On Yourself* and the misogynistic *Peaches*.

… *when we did talk about women on* **Ratus** *it was quite honest attitudinizing, really, of how some males consider women. I mean, one song referred to a woman as a piece of meat, but we weren't talking about the whole female gender.* **Jean Jacques Burnel in conversation with Chris Bohn, NME, August 1980**

The Raw & The Cooked

ARTIST Fine Young Cannibals **RELEASE DATE** February 1989 (UK & US) **LABEL** London (UK)/IRS (US) **PRODUCER** Fine Young Cannibals **UK CHART** peak/weeks 1/68 **US CHART** peak/weeks 1/63 **TRACK LISTING** She Drives Me Crazy/Good Thing/I'm Not The Man I Used To Be/I'm Not Satisfied/Tell Me What/Don't Look Back/It's OK (It's Alright)/Don't Let It Get You Down/As Hard As It Is/Ever Fallen In Love **PERSONNEL** Roland Gift (v), David Steele (k, b), Andy Cox (g)

When Birmingham ska-sters the Beat split asunder in 1982, few saw huge potential in the Fine Young Cannibals, critics placing their bets on General Public. But in the unknown Roland Gift FYC had located a frontman whose efforts dwarfed those of Ranking Roger and Dave Wakeling, the Beat's dual frontline who

transferred to GP. It took two albums for FYC to catch fire, but this first effort sired two US chart-topping singles in *She Drives Me Crazy* and *Good Thing*.

… *the band has reunited for* **The Raw And The Cooked**, *an album that far outshines the debut. On this soulful gem, the trio lose themselves in their new songs.* **Rolling Stone, 9 March 1989**

Raw Like Sushi

ARTIST Neneh Cherry **RELEASE DATE** June 1989 (UK) **LABEL** Circa (UK)/Virgin (US) **PRODUCER** Booga Bear **UK CHART** peak/weeks 2/42 **US CHART** peak/weeks 40/35 **TRACK LISTING** Buffalo Stance/Manchild/Kisses On The Wind/Inna City Mamma/The Next Generation/Love Ghetto/Heart/Phoney Ladies/Outré Risqué Locomotive/So Here I Come **PERSONNEL** Neneh Cherry (v)/Cameron (k)

Born in Stockholm, daughter of jazz legend Don Cherry, Neneh burst on to the London pop-dance scene with *Buffalo Stance*, which went Number 3 in Britain and Top 10 in America. Her chic-but-street image, frank outlook, and feisty yet seductive grooves made her a chart resident for the late Eighties. *Manchild* roped in strings on a Massive Attack collaboration, and Cherry stirred both respect and controversy when, heavily pregnant, she made a *Top Of The Pops* appearance clad in tight lycra. *Inna City Mama* accordingly addressed mother and child relationships with political undertones. She later enjoyed big hits with Youssou N'Dour, Cher and Chrissie Hynde.

Raw Like Sushi *is an artsy interpretation of current dance styles that recognises the music as todays most inventive and self-expressive form while attacking the social attitudes that commonly accompany it.* **Rob Tannenbaum, Rolling Stone, August 1989**

Raw Power

ARTIST Iggy Pop And The Stooges **RELEASE DATE** May 1973 (US & UK) **LABEL** CBS (UK)/Columbia (US) **PRODUCER** – **UK CHART** peak/weeks 44/2 **US CHART** peak/weeks 182/3 **TRACK LISTING** Search And Destroy/Gimme Danger/Hard To Beat/Penetration/Raw Power/I Need Somebody/Shake Appeal/Death Trip/Your Pretty Face Is Going To Hell **PERSONNEL** Iggy Pop (v), Ron Asheton (g), Dave Alexander (b), Scott Asheton (d), James Williamson (g)

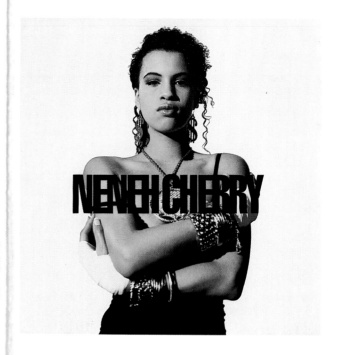

Produced by Iggy Pop and famously submerged in the mix after the event by David Bowie, **Raw Power** is still, for many, the greatest rock 'n' roll album ever made, in spite of – perhaps because of – the fact that Iggy and his Stooges were in the advanced stages of chemically induced schizophrenia. *Raw Power* sounds appropriately extreme, especially since its ultimate remix by Pop in 1997. *Search And Destroy*, *Your Pretty Face Is Going To Hell* and *Death Trip* are cataclysmic rockers, while on *Gimme Danger* and *I Need Somebody* Iggy croons like the ghost of Jim Morrison.

Released nearly 25 years ago, Raw Power, the Stooges' ultimate thuggish manifesto, was largely dismissed as degenerate Neanderthal trash. Now remixed… this definitive testament to the dumb geniuses of the mid-west remains defiantly untamed. **Paul Trynka, Mojo, May 1997**

The Real Thing

ARTIST Faith No More RELEASE DATE July 1989 (UK)/June 1989 (US) LABEL Slash London (UK)/Slash (US) PRODUCER Matt Wallace, Faith No More UK CHART peak/weeks 30/35 US CHART peak/weeks 11/60 TRACK LISTING From Out Of Nowhere/Epic/Falling To Pieces/Surprise! You're Dead!/Zombie Eaters/The Real Thing/Underwater Love/The Morning After/Woodpecker From Mars PERSONNEL Mike Patton (lv), Jim Martin (g), Billy Gould (b), Roddy Bottum (k), Mike 'Puffy' Bordin (d)

When 20-year-old dreadlocked singer Mike Patton replaced singer Chuck Moseley in 1988, the band he joined was in turmoil. Every member had walked out over a four-week period before Moseley got his cards. But he perservered and got down to writing the lyrics for what would be a landmark album: one that combined the Thrash Metal roots of the band with a melodic pop sensibility that attracted millions. Singles *Epic*, *From Out Of Nowhere* and *Falling To Pieces* thrust it ever higher and brought about a world tour that once again saw the band at each other's throats.

The Real Thing *is a real sleeper – a slow barrier with a disconcerting mix of elementary thunder thrash and art-pop complexity that doesn't catch fire until a few spins down the line.* **David Fricke, Rolling Stone, December 1989**

Really

ARTIST J. J. Cale RELEASE DATE January 1973 (UK)/December 1972 (US) LABEL A&M (UK)/Shelter (US) PRODUCER Audio Ashworth UK CHART peak/weeks - US CHART peak/weeks 92/11 TRACK LISTING Lies/Everything Will Be Alright/I'll Kiss The World Goodbye/Changes/Right Down Here/If You're Ever In Oklahoma/Ridin' Home/Going Down/Soulin'/Playin' In The Streets/Mo Jo/Louisiana Women PERSONNEL J.J. Cale (v, g, p)

The original 'unplugged' man, Oklahoman Cale was almost catatonically laid-back, yet his easy weary groove was to inspire bands as diverse as Dire Straits and Spiritualized. The success of an Eric Clapton cover of his *After Midnight* got him signed to fellow Tulsan Leon Russell's label, where he released several albums of flickering Southern country blues. **Really** also included his shuffling *Call Me The Breeze*, elsewhere pumped up by Lynyrd Skynyrd.

Reckless

ARTIST Bryan Adams RELEASE DATE March 1985 (UK)/November1984 (US) LABEL A&M (UK & US) PRODUCER Bryan Adams, Bob Clearmountain UK CHART peak/weeks 7/115 US CHART peak/weeks 1/83 TRACK LISTING One Night Love Affair/She's Only Happy When She's Dancing/Run To You/Heaven/Somebody/Summer Of '69/Kids Wanna Rock/It's Only Love/Long Gone/Ain't Gonna Cry PERSONNEL Bryan Adams (v, g), Jim Vallance (d, k, g, b)

Prior to the snowballing success of his Robin Hood theme ballad *(Everything I Do) I Do It For You*, Canadian singer/guitarist Adams had concentrated on earthy, no-frills rock. This radio-friendly work was his cross-over, thanks largely to Tina Turner's willingness to duet on *It's Only Love*, *Run To You* and *Heaven*, driven by Adams' gritty, if thin, vocals were also hits, as was the perennial stage favourite *Summer Of '69*. As Adams would have been nine years old in that golden season, it's debatable how authentic his nostalgic memories of the era, as described in the song, actually were. His obsession over the album's recording was, he said, 'brutal'.

… enough power-crunching guitar and drums to neatly occupy a hosehead demographic any rock Svengali would envy… elsewhere on this album, once his raspy tongue has scraped the platter clean, you realize how little brain food is in those lyrics. **The Year In Records 1985, Rolling Stone, December 1985**

Red

ARTIST Black Uhuru **RELEASE DATE** June 1981 (UK & US) **LABEL** Island (UK & US) **PRODUCER** Sly Dunbar, Robert Shakespeare **UK CHART** peak/weeks 28/13 **US CHART** peak/weeks 0/0 **TRACK LISTING** Youth Of Ellington/Sponji Reggae/Sistren/Journey/Utterance/Puff She Puff/Rockstone/Carbine **PERSONNEL** Sly Drumbar (d), Robert Basspeare (b), Sticky Thompson (pc), Rachie McLean (rg, lg), Mikey Chung (rg, lg), Robert Lyn (p), Keith Starling (p), Robert Shakespeare (p), Dougie Bryan (lg), Barry Reynolds (lg)

Arguably the greatest reggae session of the Eighties, Red arrived as interest in the *genre* enjoyed a revival thanks to some of the tangents sparked by the more imaginative punk rock acts. Founded in the mid Seventies, the ensemble went through several line-ups, peaking in the early Eighties with the charismatic, moody vocals of Michael Rose, many times acclaimed as the new Bob Marley. Sly and Robbie's shrewdly minimal rhythms shored up the inevitable militancy and suited the more hedonistic moments such as *Puff She Puff* and *Sponji Reggae*.

This music transcends categories, purely by its inventiveness and willingness to move people. It's rebel music with the joy of life in it. Optimistic but aware. Music to dance with and words to provoke. Paulo Newitt, Melody Maker, June 1981

Red Headed Stranger

ARTIST Willie Nelson **RELEASE DATE** July 1975 (UK & US) **LABEL** CBS (UK)/Columbia (US) **PRODUCER** Willie Nelson **UK CHART** peak/weeks – **US CHART** peak/weeks 28/43 **TRACK LISTING** Time Of The Preacher/I Couldn't Believe It/Time Of The Preacher Theme/Medley: Blue Rock, Montana, Red Headed Stranger/Red Headed Stranger/Blue Eyes Crying In The Rain/Just As I Am/Denver/O'er The Waves/Down Yonder/Can I Sleep In Your Arms/Remember Me/Hands On The Wheel/Bandera **PERSONNEL** Willie Nelson (v, g), Billy Gene English (d), Bucky Meadows (g), Bee Spears (b), Bobbie Nelson (p), session musicians

For an album recorded at a cost of $12,000 in a tiny studio in Garlan, Texas, **Red Headed Stranger** was surprisingly effective. Its arrangements (played by Nelson's touring band) were so sparse CBS chief Bruce Lundvall thought it was a demo, but the album's success, with **Blue Eyes Crying In The Rain** a US pop hit as well as country chart-topper, played its part in toppling the Nashville house of cards as outlaw music gained ground. The album told of a

preacher who killed his cheating wife and went riding in search of redemption.

Nelson, on this LP, ties precise, evocative lyrics to not quite remembered, never really forgotten folk melodies to create a similar effect, haunting yet utterly unsentimental.… **Paul Nelson, Rolling Stone, August 1975**

Red Octopus

ARTIST Jefferson Starship **RELEASE DATE** July 1975 (UK & US) **LABEL** Grunt RCA (UK & US) **PRODUCER** Jefferson Starship, Larry Cox **UK CHART** peak/weeks – **US CHART** peak/weeks 1/87 **TRACK LISTING** Fast Buck Freddie/Miracles/Git Fiddler/Al Garimasu/Sweeter Than Honey/Play On Love/Tumblin/I Want To See Another World/Sandalphon/There Will Be Love **PERSONNEL** Grace Slick (v), Marty Balin (v), Paul Kantner (g), Craig Chaquico (g), Papa John Creach (vl), David Freiberg (v), John Barbata (d, pc, cg), Pete Sears (b, k, v), Irv Cox (s), Bobbye Hall (pc, cg)

Including their earliest incarnation as the Airplane, Jefferson Starship had to wait 10 years and 14 albums to top the US chart – and in the last three months of 1975 **Red Octopus** enjoyed three brief spells at the top as the band toured to promote it. More commerical, its chart chances were boosted by Marty Balin's **Miracles**, edited from a seven-minute album track. Balin had recently rejoined to re-establish a legendary front line with Grace Slick and Paul Kantner: their success suggested they had lost none of their potency.

As it is, it sounds like a revue instead of a band… And with Grace's vocals now devoid of whatever subtlety they might have had, Marty's the only vocalist in the band. **Ed Ward, Rolling Stone, September 1975**

Regatta De Blanc

ARTIST The Police **RELEASE DATE** October 1979 (UK & US) **LABEL** A&M (UK & US) **PRODUCER** The Police, Nigel Gray **UK CHART** peak/weeks 1/74 **US CHART** peak/weeks 25/100 **TRACK LISTING** Message In A Bottle/Regatta De Blanc/It's Alright For You/Bring On The Night/Deathwish/Walking On The Moon/On Any Other Day/The Bed's Too Big Without You/Contact/The Everyone Stare/No Time This Time **PERSONNEL** Andy Summers (g), Stewart Copeland (d), Sting (b, v)

Touring constantly to promote their hits, The Police suffered second album syndrome: three Stewart Copeland songs (three too many), an earlier single B-side and the instrumental title track jammed from the **Can't Stand Losing You** riff berated its haste. Yet the highs were mighty: a pair of chart-topping singles and two more classics, **Bring On The Night**, which would title a Sting live album years later, and **The Bed's Too Big Without You**, a white reggae song so good Jamaican artists queued to cover it.

Throw in lyrics like 'I never noticed the size of my feet/Until I kicked you in the shin', a second album even better than the first, and you've got a band that's probably going to be around for a while. **Charles M. Young, Rolling Stone, December 1979**

Remain In Light

ARTIST Talking Heads **RELEASE DATE** October 1980 (UK & US) **LABEL** Sire (UK & US) **PRODUCER** Talking Heads, Brian Eno **UK CHART** peak/weeks 21/17 **US CHART** peak/weeks 19/27 **TRACK LISTING** The Great Curve/Crosseyed And Painless/Born Under Punches/Houses In Motion/Once In A Lifetime/Listening Wind/Seen And Not Seen/The Overlord **PERSONNEL** David Byrne (v, g), Tina Weymouth (b, v), Chris Frantz (d)

Even by Talking Heads' standards, **Remain In Light** offered a remarkable fusion of rock and funk. Augmented by a horn section and featuring a glittering array of extras from blue-eyed soul

pioneer Robert Palmer to Nona Hendryx of Labelle, Talking Heads' fourth album included their first British hit single, *Once In A Lifetime*. A video to accompany the single, starring David Byrne in trademark ultra-baggy suit, all flailing limbs and bug eyes, pushed the band even further into the public consciousness and helped to solidify their image as the acceptable face of experimental US art-pop.

These are songs in which the dreadful has already happened, in which disaster and alarm have an almost physical presence… The tears in the fabric of normality, previously hinted at are more vividly exposed. Byrne's writing has grown. **Allan Jones, Melody Maker, October 1980**

Reminiscing

ARTIST Buddy Holly **RELEASE DATE** April 1963 (UK)/Febuary 1963 (US) **LABEL** Coral (UK & US) **PRODUCER** Norman Petty **UK CHART** peak/weeks 2/31 **US CHART** peak/weeks 40/17 **TRACK LISTING** Reminiscing/Slippin' And Slidin'/Bo Diddley/Wait Till The Sun Shines Nellie/Baby, Won't You Come Out Tonight/Brown Eyed Handsome Man/Because I Love You/It's Not My Fault/I'm Gonna Set My Foot Down/Changing All Those Changes/Rock-A-Bye-Rock **PERSONNEL** Buddy Holly (v), The Fireballs

Parents Ella and Lawrence Holly wrote their personal approval from Lubbock, Texas, for this posthumous collection of songs from their late, great, four-years-dead son: 'A great young musical group called the Fireballs,' had been enlisted to overdub backing and this, said the Hollys, 'proved to be a very happy combination'. Alongside covers of Chuck Berry, Little Richard and Bo Diddley were five self-penned gems, but like many of those gone too soon the major part of Holly's legacy had already been heard.

Repeat Offender

ARTIST Richard Marx **RELEASE DATE** May 1989 (UK & US) **LABEL** Manhatten (UK & US) **PRODUCER** Richard Marx **UK CHART** peak/weeks 8/12 **US CHART** peak/weeks 1/66 **TRACK LISTING** Nothin' You Can Do About It/Satisfied/Angelia/Too Late To Say Goodbye/Right Here Waiting/Heart On The Line/Real World/If You Don't Want My Love/Wait For The Sunrise/Children Of The Night **PERSONNEL** Richard Marx (v), Joe Walsh (g), Prairie Prince (d), John Pierce (b), Michael Landall (g), Fee Waybill (v), Paulinko de Costa (pc)

He had already topped the US singles charts, but former Lionel Richie backing singer Richard Marx would not repeat the feat with a long-player until this, his second album. It contained two more Number 1 singles, the third *Right Here Waiting* a love letter in song to actress girlfriend Cynthia Rhodes on location in Africa. He had to be persuaded to release such a personal recording, but its arrival at the summit gave **Repeat Offender** the final push to displace Prince's so-successful *Batman* soundtrack.

*… **Repeat Offender** seems to have no real purpose: the rockers regurgitate an aesthetic that seemed tired when Marx was in high school,*

the ballads are bland… For all its merits, **Repeat Offender** *is recidivism at its worst.* **J. D. Considine, Rolling Stone, June 1989**

Repeat When Necessary

ARTIST Dave Edmunds **RELEASE DATE** June 1979 (UK)/August 1979 (US) **LABEL** Swansong (UK & US) **PRODUCER** Dave Edmunds, Nick Lowe **UK CHART** peak/weeks 39/12 **US CHART** peak/weeks 54/15 **TRACK LISTING** Girls Talk/Crawling From The Wreckage/Sweet Little Lisa/The Creature From The Black Lagoon/Home In My Hand/Take Me For A Little While/Queen Of Hearts/We Were Both Wrong/Bad Is Bad/Dynamite/Goodbye Mr Good Guy **PERSONNEL** Dave Edmunds (g, v, d, b)

While its sales performance was unremarkable, **Repeat When Necessary** represented the most satisfying half-hour of Dave Edmunds' three-decade recording career which began with *Love Sculpture* in 1968. Having topped the UK chart with the 1970's *I Hear You Knocking*, played the one-man band, and film-scored *Stardust*, the reclusive Welshman left the studio in the company of Rockpile (Nick Lowe, Terry Williams and Billy Bremner), adding his own interpretation to classic pop songs from Elvis Costello, Graham Parker and Huey Lewis and creating a bridge between old wave and new.

Revolver

ARTIST The Beatles **RELEASE DATE** August 1966 (UK & US) **LABEL** Parlophone (UK)/Capitol (US) **PRODUCER** George Martin **UK CHART** peak/weeks 1/34 **US CHART** peak/weeks 1/77 **TRACK LISTING** Taxman/Eleanor Rigby/I'm Only Sleeping/Love You Too/Here, There And Everywhere/Yellow Submarine/She Said She Said/Good Day Sunshine/And Your Bird Can Sing/For No One/Dr Robert/I Want To Tell You/Got To Get You Into My Life/Tomorrow Never Knows **PERSONNEL** John Lennon (v, rg), Paul McCartney (v, g), George Harrison (v, lg), Stu Sutcliffe (b), Ringo Starr (d)

With this album the band started to get strange: McCartney become a master craftsman, here dabbling with strings and horns, while Lennon opened up the doors of perception and brought back relatively upbeat tales from the drugged side. He laid a blueprint for the coming psychedelic boom, with *Tomorrow Never Knows* and *She Said She Said* – 'Listen to the colour of your dreams,' he urged. On this kaleidoscopic album could also be found poignant sociology – *Eleanor Rigby*, good humour –*Yellow Submarine*, *Good Day Sunshine*, and the underrated *For No One*. Harrison contributed three songs, including the snarling *Taxman*.

There are more ideas buzzing around in The Beatles heads than most of the pop world put together. A lot of them have been poured into **Revolver** *and the result is a veritable gold mine of ideas which the lesser fry will frantically scramble over.* **Melody Maker, July 1966.**

Rhythm Killers

ARTIST Sly And Robbie **RELEASE DATE** May 1987 (UK & US) **LABEL** Fouth & Broadway (UK)/Island (US) **PRODUCER** Bill Laswell **UK CHART** peak/weeks 35/5 **US CHART** peak/weeks – **TRACK LISTING** Fire/Boops (Here To Go)/Let's Rock/Yes, We Can (Can)/Rhythm Killer/Bank Job. **PERSONNEL** Shinehead (v), Benie Worrell (p), Sly Dunbar (pc, d), Robbie Shakespeare (b), Karl Berger (con, vp, st, arr), session musicians

Drummer Sly Dunbar and bassist Robbie Shakespeare, former sessioneers from Kingston, Jamaica, have long been regarded as the greatest rhythm section in any contemporary pop *genre*, let alone dance or reggae. *Rhythm Killers* was more than just an opportunity for two great dance technicians to show off, however. Produced by Bill Laswell and featuring P-Funkateer Bootsy Collins and dancehall toaster Shinehead, it ran the gamut of modern beat styles to create a truly satisfying whole.

There'll be people in ties nudging you in pubs and saying 'Ooh that Sly and Robbie, they're a good team aren't they?' as if pop should be played like a direct free kick. There's obviously a powerful partnership at the core of this record. **Paul Mathur, Melody Maker, May 1987**

Rickie Lee Jones

ARTIST Rickie Lee Jones **RELEASE DATE** June 1979 (UK)/April 1979 (US) **LABEL** Warner Bros. (UK & US) **PRODUCER** Lenny Waronker **UK CHART** peak/weeks 18/19 **US CHART** peak/weeks 3/36 **TRACK LISTING** Chuck E's In Love/On Saturday Afternoons In 1963/Night Train/Young Blood/Easy Money/The Last Chance Texaco/Danny's All-Star Joint/Coolsville/Weasel And The White Boys Cool/Company/After Hours (Twelve Bars Past Goodnight) **PERSONNEL** Rickie Lee Jones (v, g, k, pc, bv), Steve Gadd (d), Andy Newmark (d), Victor Feldman (d, k, pc), Mark Stevens (d, pc), Jeffrey Porcaro (d), Willie Weeks (fgb), Red Callender (b), Buzzy Feiten (g), Fred Tackett (g), Mac Rebennack (k), Fred Tackett (md), Neil Larson (k), Randy Kerber (k), Ralph Grierson (k), Randy Newman (sy), Tom Scott (hn), Chuck Findley (hn), session musicians

Ms Jones let her fingers do the walking to get this album up and running: a friend, Ivan Ulz, sung the song *Easy Money* over the phone to Little Feat leader Lowell George, who promptly cut it on his own debut solo album. Warners staff producer Ted Templeman and A&R man Lenny Waronker were intrigued, picked up her demo and signed her – and when *Chuck E* shot to Number 4 they had a hit-maker on their hands. Many of its songs had been written at the Tropicana Motel on Santa Monica Boulevard where Jones attracted the attention of another admirer, Tom Waits, in autumn 1977.

Every so often an album appears that is so unique in its perceptions and so passionate in its presentation that it carves out a new niche for itself in rock 'n' roll... Jones' music is full of raw rock edges, down beat swagger and dark colours. **Rolling Stone, December 1979**

Ricky

ARTIST Ricky Nelson **RELEASE DATE** January 1958 **LABEL** London Records (UK)/Imperial (US) **PRODUCER** – **UK CHART** peak/weeks · **US CHART** peak/weeks 1/33 **TRACK LISTING** Honeycomb/Bopin' The Blues/Be-Bop Baby/Have I Told You Lately That I Love You/Teenage Doll/If You Can't Rock Me/Stood Up/Whole Lotta Shakin' Goin' On/Baby, I'm Sorry/Am I Blue/I'm Confessin'/Your True Love/True Love/Waitin' In School **PERSONNEL** Ricky Nelson (v, g), Joe Maphis (g), session musicans

As his very first album hit the top of the US chart in January 1958, Ricky Nelson had the world at his feet. The King, Elvis Presley, was weeks away from army service, leaving the way clear for the young man who came to fame on his mum and dad's TV show to become the parentally approved alternative. As it turned out, though, the fortnight he spent on top of the pile would be as good as it got, and by the mid Sixties he would be re-inventing himself as a country star. His sons Matthew and Gunnar would follow in his chart

footsteps as Nelson.

*Ricky Nelson is an average rock singer, and on London, he gives two average rock tunes average treatment. It is all there – steel guitars, boo-de-boo choir, hand clapping, the lot. Best of the two titles is the medium tempo **Stood Up**.* Laurie Kemshaw, Melody Maker, February 1958

Rides Again

ARTIST James Gang **RELEASE DATE** October 1970 (UK)/July 1970 (US) **LABEL** Stateside (UK)/Bluesway (US) **PRODUCER** Bill Szymzyk **UK CHART** peak/weeks – **US CHART** peak/weeks 20/66 **TRACK LISTING** Funk 49/Ashton Park/Woman/The Bomber: (a) Closet Queen - (b) Cast Your Fate To The Wind/Tend My Garden/Garden Gate/There I Go Again/Thanks/Ashes The Rain And I **PERSONNEL** Joe Walsh (g, v), Tom Kriss (b, v), Jim Fox (d, v)

The James Gang's secret weapon was Joe Walsh, Anglophile singer-guitarist with a voice as nasal as his guitar was metallic. This, the second and best of the four albums he cut with the Cleveland-based Gang before heading on to paydirt with the Eagles via his own band, Barnstorm, featured the stand-outs *Tend My Garden* and *Ashes The Rain And I* (the latter with Jack Nitzsche-scored strings) from an acoustic-based second (vinyl) side. But the crowd pleaser was *Funk 49*, an archetypal Les Paul workout.

*From 1970, **Rides Again** enhanced The James Gang's reputation as they developed their mix of multi-harmonies in the Buffalo Springfield vein, alongside effective guitar arrangements.... Perhaps not one of the most touted US names from the late Sixties-early Seventies, The James Gang... nevertheless sound pretty damn fine.* **Dave Henderson, Q, March 1992**

Rio

ARTIST Duran Duran **RELEASE DATE** May 1982 (UK)/January 1983 (US) **LABEL** EMI (UK)/Capitol (US) **PRODUCER** Colin Thurston **UK CHART** peak/weeks 2/109 **US CHART** peak/weeks 6/129 **TRACK LISTING** Rio/My Own Way/Lonely In Your Nightmare/Hungry Like The Wolf/Hold Back The Rain/New Religion/Last Chance On The Stairway/Save A Prayer/The Chauffer **PERSONNEL** Simon LeBon (v), Andy Taylor (g), Nick Rhodes (k), John Taylor (b), Roger Taylor (d)

Shaking themselves free of the dreaded New Romantic tag, Duran Duran proved that they were more than just pretty faces with **Rio**, one of the period's finest pop collections. Although it narrowly

missed the coveted top spot, **Rio** spent two years in the UK album charts and spawned four hit singles, including *Save A Prayer*, a lush, haunting ballad which is arguably the band's finest moment. Bright, sharp, and supremely confident, **Rio** marked the point in Duran Duran's career where style and content were in perfect balance.

This is Duran Duran's second LP – another soft, seamless package of pop-dream, preferably for the very young and innocent. In its own blandly unambitious way, I guess, it's a perfect record. In other ways, it's as boring as hell. **Paul Du Noyer, NME, May 1982**

The Rise And Fall Of Ziggy Stardust And The Spiders From Mars

ARTIST David Bowie **RELEASE DATE** July 1972 (UK & US) **LABEL** RCA Victor (UK & US) **PRODUCER** David Bowie, Kenneth Scott **UK CHART** peak/weeks 5/106 **US CHART** peak/weeks 75/72 **TRACK LISTING** Five Years/Soul Love/Moonage Daydream/Starman/It Ain't Easy/Lady Stardust/Star/Hang On To Yourself/Ziggy Stardust/Suffragette City/Rock 'N' Roll Suicide **PERSONNEL** David Bowie (v, s, g), Mick Ronson (g, p, v), Trevor Bolder (b), Mick Woodmansey (d)

An album which neatly twisted the psyche of a generation, and of the rock form itself. Bowie's creation of a lurex 'n' lipstick, androgynously alien rock diva brought a new vitality and imagination to the arena. Making love with his ego, Ziggy soared and dived, preened and pouted, both a marvellous entity and a stirring, provocative comment on the (un)nature of fame. Bowie claimed glam-rock as his own, releasing the inhibitions of repressed Brits everywhere. 'Ziggy' retired after his 1973 tour – a classic rock 'n' roll suicide. Bowie's relentless intellect had moved on, and the notion of what a rock star could be was forever altered.

David Bowie has pulled off his complex task with consummate style… with all the wit and passion required to give it sufficient dimension and with a deep sense of humanity that regularly emerges… he hasn't sacrificed a bit of entertainment value for the sake of message. **Richard Cromelin, Rolling Stone, July 1972**

Risque

ARTIST Chic **RELEASE DATE** August 1979 (UK)/December 1977 (US) **LABEL** Atlantic (UK & US) **PRODUCER** Nile Rogers, Bernard Edwards **UK CHART** peak/weeks 29/12 **US CHART** peak/weeks 5/17 **TRACK LISTING** Good Times/A Warm Summer Night/My Feet Keep Dancing/My Forbidden Lover/Can't Stand To Love you/Will You Cry When Hear This Song/What About Me **PERSONNEL** Nile Rogers (g), Bernard Edwards (b), Tony Thompson (d), Alfa Anderson (v), Luci Martin (v)

The sensationally compelling and resonant interplay of Bernard Edwards' bass and Nile Rodgers' guitar bridged the gap between the snobbish rock audience and the burgeoning culture of dance and disco. So lean and tight were their rhythms that they have served as a blueprint for hits in rap and rock ever since. **Good Times** was a massive-seller and **My Feet Keep Dancing** flawless and addictive. **My Forbidden Lover** showed a more romantic side, as foreshadowed on C'est Chic's **At Last I Am Free**. Queen and The Sugarhill Gang were to borrow from **Good Times**. Rodgers went on to become one of the world's most consistently successful producers of name acts. Edwards tragically died in Japan in 1996.

While the album as a whole confirms Chic's status and development, there is the obvious possibility that a sound and an image so self-consciously fashionable may be doomed to swift rejection as tastes move on to something more chic still. **Melody Maker, August 1979**

The River

ARTIST Bruce Springsteen **RELEASE DATE** October 1980 (UK) **LABEL** CBS (UK)/Columbia (US) **PRODUCER** Bruce Springsteen, Steve Van Zandt, Jon Landau **UK CHART** peak/weeks 2/88 **US CHART** peak/weeks 1/108 **TRACK LISTING** The Ties That Bind/Sherry Darling/Jackson Cage/Two Hearts/Independence Day/Hungry Heart/Out In The Street/Crush On You/You Can Look (But You Better Not Touch)/I Wanna Marry You/The River/Point Blank/Cadillac Ranch/I'm A Rocker/Fade Away/Stolen Car/Ramrod/The Price You Pay/Drive All Night/Wreck On The High Way. **PERSONNEL** Bruce Springsteen (v, g), David Sancious & Danny Federici (k), Garry Tallent (b), Vini Lopez (d), Clarence Clemens (s)

The Number 1, two-million selling **The River** was no less uncompromising than its predecessor, but Springsteen's first double album did evince a shift back towards feel-good rock 'n' roll. Indeed, the upbeat single, *Hungry Heart*, went to the Top 5, a sign of the superstardom to come, while *I Want To Marry You* and *Cadillac Ranch* evince a temporary respite from the heavy atmosphere of **Darkness On The Edge Of Town**.

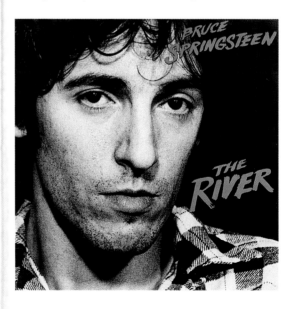

Rock 'n' Roll With The Modern Lovers

ARTIST Jonathan Richman And The Modern Lovers **RELEASE DATE** August 1977 (UK) **LABEL** Berserkley (UK) **PRODUCER** Matthew King Kaufman, Glen Kolotkin **UK CHART** peak/weeks 50/3 **US CHART** peak/weeks 0/0 **TRACK LISTING** Rockin' Shopping Center/Back In The U.S.A./Important In Your Life/New England/Lonely Financial Zone/Hi Dear/Abominable Snowman In The Market/Hey There Little Insect/Here Come The Martian Martians/Springtime/Amazing Grace **PERSONNEL** Leroy Radcliffe (v, g), Greg 'Curly' Keranen (b, v), David Robinson (d, v), Jonathan Richman (v, g)

The endearing Jonathan Richman and his acoustic **Modern Lovers** who, live, curried so much favour with massive UK audiences in 1977-1978, bore little resemblance to the driving rock band Richman had started in Beverley in northern Massachussetts years earlier. By the time hip emergent-indie Berserkley Records acquired and remixed the tapes as his debut album, Jonathan Richman was strumming a big acoustic and singing about Martians, whilst ex-members of his band were hitting the big time in the Talking Heads and the Cars. But this remains his finest darkest hour and contains the definitive Seventies cruising anthem, *Roadrunner*.

Rock And Rollin' With Fats Domino

ARTIST Fats Domino **RELEASE DATE** August 1956 (UK) **LABEL** London (UK)/Imperial (US) **PRODUCER** – **UK CHART** peak/weeks – **US CHART** peak/weeks 17/4 **TRACK LISTING** The Fat Man/Tired Of Crying Goin' Home/You Said You Love Me/Going To The River/Please Don't Leave Me/Rose Mary/All By Myself/Ain't That A Shame/Poor Me/Bo Weevil/Don't Blame It On Me **PERSONNEL** Fats Domino (v, p), Dave Bartholomew (t), Red Tyler (b), Earl Palmer (d)

Without a doubt, the year of 1957 belonged to easy-going New Orleans piano man Antoine 'Fats' Domino. In the wake of December 1956's mega hit *Blueberry Hill*, this, his first album, including the hit *Ain't That A Shame* followed the current **This Is Fats Domino!** album into the charts. As it did so, he finally relinquished hold on the US R&B top spot he had occupied for 22 straight weeks – no-one was going to push the Fat Man out of the way!

He seldom strays far from the melody but the tunes – with the exception of the odd popular standard or traditional – are all blues-rooted things of his own…. His fast numbers are never too fast and never frantic. **Max Jones, Melody Maker, April 1957**

Rock Bottom

ARTIST Robert Wyatt **RELEASE DATE** July 1974 (UK & US) **LABEL** Virgin (UK & US) **PRODUCER** Nick Mason **UK CHART** peak/weeks - **US CHART** peak/weeks – **TRACK LISTING** Sea Song/A Last Straw/Little Red Riding Hood Hit The Road/Alifib/Alife/Little Red Robin Hood Hit The Road **PERSONNEL** Richard Sinclair (v, k, d), Robert Wyatt (v, k, d), Hugh Hopper (b), Alfreda Benge (v), Laurie Allan (d), Mongezi Feza (t), Mike Oldfield (g), Ivor Cutler (v), Gary Windo (cl, v)

Former drummer with late Sixties jazz-rock psychedelicists The Soft Machine, Robert Wyatt fell from a window in the early Seventies, putting him in a wheelchair for the rest of his life. **Rock Bottom**, Wyatt's solo debut, was produced by fellow drum luminary, Pink Floyd's Nick Mason, and dealt with his accident via a series of alternately lovely and harrowing song experiments and tone poems that would later be dubbed 'oceanic rock', such were the free-flowing nature of the music and enveloping, 'underwater' ambience of the sound.

The most 'songful' album Wyatt has done in seven years… On keyboards he's progressing in leaps and bounds, sounding like a combination of Thelonious Monk, Dave Sinclair and Cecil Taylor at 16 rpm. **Melody Maker, September 1974**

Rock 'N' Roll Animal

ARTIST Lou Reed **RELEASE DATE** March 1974 (UK) **LABEL** RCA (UK & US) **PRODUCER** Steve Katz, Lou Reed **UK CHART** peak/weeks 26/1 **US CHART** peak/weeks 45/27 **TRACK LISTING** Intro/Sweet Jane/Heroin/White Light/White Heat/Lady Day/Rock 'N' Roll **PERSONNEL** Lou Reed (v), Dick Wagner (g), Ray Colcord (k), Pentti Glan (d), Prakash John (b), Steve Hunter (g)

The first of two live albums (the other being 1975's **Lou Reed Live**) to be extracted from Lou Reed's **Transformer** tour featuring a twin-guitar spearhead of Dick Wagner and Steve Hunter and showcasing his best known numbers from a then nascent solo career and his back pages fronting the Velvet Underground. In 1979 another live set, **Take No Prisoners,** appeared, which did less well, due perhaps to an irate Reed haranguing an unresponsive audience!

… dreaming and phantasmagoric… Reed… blends chilling description with the signal force of his imagination…. For the listener, Reed's strange alchemy of personality shackles him over to a sense of reality plunged in the depths of nightmare or delusion. **J. W., Melody Maker, March 1974**

Rock 'n' Roll Number 1

ARTIST Elvis Presley **RELEASE DATE** October 1956 (UK)/May 1956 (US) **LABEL** HMV (UK)/RCA (US) **PRODUCER** – **UK CHART** peak/weeks 4/9 **US CHART** peak/weeks – **TRACK LISTING** Blue Suede Shoes/I'm Counting On You/Money Honey/I Got A Sweetie (I Got A Woman)/One Sided Love Affair/I'm Gonna Sit Right Down And Cry Over You/Tryin' To Get To You/I Love You Because/Just Because/Blue Moon/I'll Never Let You Go/Tutti Frutti/Mystery Train/Lawdy Miss Clawdy/I'm Left, She's Gone/Shake Rattle And Roll **PERSONNEL** Elvis Presley (v, g), Scotty Moore (g), Bill Black (b), Floyd Cramer (p), Chet Atkins (g), Hank Garland (g), 'Boots' Randolph (s), Backing Vocals: The Jordanaires

While the follow-up **Number 2** duplicated its US counterpart **Elvis**, this first album from the 'King' to land on UK shores differed markedly from the Stateside debut **Elvis Presley** of seven months earlier. This was nevertheless an album which had a big impact on the forthcoming British beat generation. The single *Blue Suede Shoes* had already charted in the UK, Presley having vetoed its US release following a car crash involving author Carl Perkins, who had his own version out. HMV issued Elvis's British product till late 1957.

Unreservedly – the great rock album of the age. Whatever Elvis has done since, and what ever has been written or said, these classic performances ring down the years with cheering innocence and real excitement. **C. W., Melody Maker, May 1972**

Rocket To Russia

ARTIST Ramones **RELEASE DATE** December 1977 (UK)/November 1977 (US) **LABEL** Sire (UK & US) **PRODUCER** – **UK CHART** peak/weeks 60/2 **US CHART** peak/weeks 49/25 **TRACK LISTING** Cretin Hop/ Rockaway Beach/Here Today, Gone Tommorrow/ Locket Love/I Don't Care/Sheena Is A Punk Rocker/ We're A Happy Family/Teenage Lobotomy/ Do You Wanna Dance?/I Wanna Be Well/I Can't Give You Anything/Ramona/Surfin' Bird/Why Is It Always This Way **PERSONNEL** Joey Ramone (v), Johnny Ramone (g, v), Dee Dee Ramone (b, v), Tommy Ramone (d)

Their second release of 1977, punk's epochal year, found the Ramones back up against that brick wall which featured on the cover of their first album, but steadfastly refusing to progress in any way musically: that would come later with disastrous producer link-ups with Phil Spector and Graham Gouldman. For now, **Sheena Is A Punk Rocker** became a radio hit, updates of **Surfin' Bird** (the Trashment) and **Do You Wanna Dance** (Bobby Freeman) emphasized their links with a Brill Building past. Critical analysis almost impossible.

Rocket to Russia is the best American rock and roll of the year and possibly the funniest rock album ever made. Not that The Ramones are a joke – they're more worthwhile than almost anything that's more self-conscious... **Dave Marsh, Rolling Stone, December 1977**

Rocks

ARTIST Aerosmith **RELEASE DATE** June 1976 (UK)/April 1975 (US) **LABEL** CBS (UK)/Columbia (US) **PRODUCER** Jack Douglas, Aerosmith **UK CHART** peak/weeks – **US CHART** peak/weeks 3/53 **TRACK LISTING** Back In The Saddle/Last Child/Rats In The Cellar/Combination/Sick As A Dog/Nobody's Fault/Get The Lead Out/Lick And A Promise/Home Tonight **PERSONNEL** Joe Perry (g, v), Tom Hamilton (b), Steven Tyler (lv, k, b), Joey Kramer (d, pc), Brad Whitford (g)

A million seller in the States which made little or no impact here, this featured the hits **Back In The Saddle** and **Last Child** and a plethora of murky duelling guitar riffs. Hailed by Guns'N'Roses axeman Slash as 'the album that changed my life', it was a logical hedonistic extension of the Rolling Stones' ethos and music, with Joe Perry's sonic styling both anthemic and evocative. The blues had rarely sounded so white.

The material is **Rocks'** *major flaw: mostly pale remakes of their earlier hits.... Aerosmith may have their hard rock wings, but they won't truly fly until their inventiveness catches up with their fast maturing professionalism.* **John Milward, Rolling Stone, July 1976**

Roll With It

ARTIST Steve Winwood **RELEASE DATE** July 1988 **LABEL** Virgin (UK & US) **PRODUCER** Steve Winwood, Tom Lord Alge **UK CHART** peak/weeks 4/16 **US CHART** peak/weeks 1/45 **TRACK LISTING** Roll With It/Holding On/The Morning Side/Put On Your Dancing Shoes/Don't You Know What The Night Can Do?/Hearts On Fire/One More Morning/Shining Song **PERSONNEL** Steve Winwood (v, k), Willie Weeks (b), Andy Newmark (d), Reebop Kwaku Banu (cg)

Steve Winwood has always evinced his supreme mastery of black roots music. On his fifth solo album, however, he let his technique and sheer proficiency get the better of him, resulting in a rather bland collection of arid R&B – this was designer soul, or funk for XR3-driving Yuppies. Nevertheless, this double-platinum LP consolidated Winwood's reputation as the consummate professional, while the title track alone spent four weeks at the top of the American charts.

Roll With It, *the album, is the sound of Steve Winwood being boring... for about half of its length, the album shows that there's nothing fundamentally wrong with sitting back and going with the flow.* **Steve Pond, Rolling Stone, August 1988**

The Rolling Stones

ARTIST The Rolling Stones **RELEASE DATE** April 1964 (UK & US) **LABEL** Decca (UK)/London (US) **PRODUCER** – **UK CHART** peak/weeks 1/51 **US CHART** peak/weeks 11/35 **TRACK LISTING** Route 66/I Just Want To Make Love To You/Honest I Do/Mona (I Need You Baby)/Now I've Got A Witness/Little By Little/I'm A King Bee/Carol/Tell Me (You're Coming Back)/Can I Get A Witness/You Can Make It If You Try/Walking The Dog **PERSONNEL** Mick Jagger (v), Brian Jones (g), Keith Richards (g), Bill Wyman (b), Charlie Watts (d)

It's Rolling In For The Stones! The Rolling Stones continued their march to popularity this week as their first LP soared past the 170,000 mark and topped the album division of the hit parade. **Melody Maker, May 1964**

The Rolling Stones No. 2

ARTIST The Rolling Stones **RELEASE DATE** January 1965 (UK) **LABEL** Decca (UK)/London (US) **PRODUCER** Andrew Loog Oldham **UK CHART** peak/weeks 1/37 **US CHART** peak/weeks - **TRACK LISTING** Everybody Needs Somebody To Love/Down Home Girl/You Can't Catch Me/Time Is On My Side/What A Shame/Grown Up Wrong/Down The Road Apiece/Under The Boardwalk/ I Can't Be Satisfied/Pain In My Heart/Off The Hook/Suzie-Q **PERSONNEL** Mick Jagger (v, h), Keith Richard (rg), Brian Jones (lg), Bill Wyman (b), Charlie Watts (d)

As **Confessin' The Blues** and Berry's **Around And Around** show, the Stones were still mining the blues motherlode. But **Number Two** was their second straight Number 1 album. The sources had varied only slightly – rock 'n' roll, some soul – but the band were etching themselves on the public consciousness with the indelible image of long-haired sneering bad-boy rebels. Jagger was establishing himself as the master of lippy arrogance and strutting foppery, while Richards was revving up to give his own guitar riffs more of a spell in the spotlight.

Ropin' The Wind

ARTIST Garth Brooks **RELEASE DATE** February 1992 (UK)/September 1991 (US) **LABEL** Capitol (UK & US) **PRODUCER** Allen Reynolds **UK CHART** peak/weeks 41/2 **US CHART** peak/weeks 1/132 **TRACK LISTING** Against The Grain/Rodeo/What She's Doing Now/Burning Bridges/Papa Loved Mama/Shameless/Cold Shoulder/We Bury The Hatchet/In Lonesome Dove/River **PERSONNEL** Garth Brooks (v, b, g), Edgar Meyer (b), Booby Wood (k), Chris Levzinger (g), Mike Palmer (d, pc), session musicians

The first country album to go straight in at Number 1 in the *Billboard* pop chart, this made Brooks too big for Nashville. He branched out into various musical territories, without alienating his root fans. *The River* and *Lonesome Dove* were, for him, challenging and bold, and there was a Billy Joel cover in *Shameless*. Over six million copies were sold. Brooks invented 'stadium country': tripping about the stage with a radio mic. Whew! How loose could country get?

Brooks is clearly a child of his own time and familiar with the requirements of US radio… But apart from the pleasing melancholy of the trucker's lament Cold Shoulder, there isn't much here to suggest that Brooks's talent is the equal of his shrewdness. **David Hepworth, Q, March 1992**

Roxy Music

ARTIST Roxy Music **RELEASE DATE** July 1972 (UK & US) **LABEL** Island (UK)/Reprise (US) **PRODUCER** Pete Sinfield **UK CHART** peak/weeks 10/16 **US CHART** peak/weeks 81/7 **TRACK LISTING** Re-Make/Re-Model/Ladytron/If There Is Something/2 H.B./The Bob (Medley)/Chance Meeting/Would You Believe?/Sea Breezes/Bitters End **PERSONNEL** Bryan Ferry (v, p), Andrew Mackay (s, ob), Paul Thompson (d), Phil Manzanera (g), Graham Simpson (g), Bryan Eno (sy)

Retro-futurists and sophisticated primitivists, Roxy Music were arguably the first post-modern rock band, the first to mix and match sounds and styles from the previous two decades of pop. Roxy created something that, in music and manners, looked back at the Fifties while anticipating much of what was to come in the late Seventies (including the more garish and experimental members of the New Wave fraternity) and early Eighties ('a danceable solution to teenage revolution'). **Roxy Music**, the debut, introduced former art teacher Bryan Ferry as tormented lounge crooner, Brian Eno's intuitive, amateurish synthesizer effects, as well as Roxy's kitsch-glam aesthetic.

The Royal Scam

ARTIST Steely Dan **RELEASE DATE** May 1976 (UK & US) **LABEL** ABC. (UK & US) **PRODUCER** Gary Katz **UK CHART** peak/weeks 11/13 **US CHART** peak/weeks 15/29 **TRACK LISTING** Everything You Did/Haitian Divorce/Don't Take Me Alive/Kid Charlemagne/The Caves Of Altmina/The Royal Scam/Sign In Stranger/Green Earrings/The Fez **PERSONNEL** Donald Fagen (v, k), Walter Becker (b, v), session musicians

After a disappointing reaction to the intimate **Katy Lied**, most critics thought that Dan had lost their Steel – they responded with the sharp-edged **The Royal Scam** recorded with some of the best hired help money could buy. Becker and Fagan inspired some of the most passionate playing on any Steely Dan release, especially guitarist Larry Carlton's coruscating solos on **Don't Take Me Alive** and **Kid Charlemagne**, the latter's positively funky rhythm track recorded in one take by drummer Bernard Purdie and bassist Chuck Rainey. The arch-perfectionists knew that their invitees had nailed it.

Rubber Soul

ARTIST The Beatles **RELEASE DATE** November 1965 (UK & US) **LABEL** Parlophone (UK)/Capitol (US) **PRODUCER** George Martin **UK CHART** peak/weeks 1/42 **US CHART** peak/weeks 1/59 **TRACK LISTING** Drive My Car/Norwegian Wood/You Won't See Me/Nowhere Man/Think For Yourself/The Word/Michelle/What Goes On/Girl/I'm Looking Through You/In My Life/Wait/If I Needed Someone/Run For Your Life **PERSONNEL** John Lennon (v, rg), Paul McCartney (v, g), George Harrison (v, lg), Stu Sutcliffe (b), Ringo Starr (d)

Feeling challenged by Bob Dylan's **Subterranean Homesick Blues** and **Like A Rolling Stone**, The Beatles rose to the moment and produced an album of new maturity and depth, folk-rock in parts, curiously funky in others. Sung with sophistication, such ballads as **In My Life**, **Michelle** and **Norwegian Wood** were to reshuffle the canon. Harrison discovered the sitar for **Norwegian Wood**. Most consider this album to be the point at which The Beatles, creatively, went supernova….

Rubycon

ARTIST Tangerine Dream **RELEASE DATE** April 1975 (UK & US) **LABEL** Virgin (UK & US) **PRODUCER** Tangerine Dream **UK CHART** peak/weeks 12/14 **US CHART** peak/weeks – **TRACK LISTING** Rubycon-Part One/Rubycon-Part Two **PERSONNEL** Edgar Froese (g, sy, mln, o), Chris Franke (sy, o, p), Peter Baumann (o, sy, p)

German contemporaries of Kraftwerk, Tangerine Dream had almost as great an impact on the direction of ambient synthesizer pop as did Kraftwerk on rhythm-based electro-pop. Dismissed by many as purveyors of meandering synth noodles, their fans regard TD as seriously experimental sonic explorers. **Rubycon**, their highest charting British album, is as good a point of entry as any for fans of post-psychedelic cosmic soundscapes.

This new package of 23rd-century lounge schmaltz features exactly the same heady blend of electronic whooshes, whirls, hums, bleeps, whines, groans, sweeps and whistles that its predecessor did…. The album will retain your interest for a solid three minutes. **Alan Neister, Rolling Stone, September 1975**

Rum, Sodomy & The Lash

ARTIST The Pogues **RELEASE DATE** August 1985 (UK) **LABEL** Stiff (UK) **PRODUCER** Elvis Costello **UK CHART** peak/weeks 13/15 **US CHART** peak/weeks - **TRACK LISTING** The Sick Bed Of Cuchulainn/The Old Main Drag/Wild Cats Of Kilkenny/I'm A Man You Don't Meet Every Day/A Pair Of Brown Eyes/Sally Maclennane/Dirty Old Town/Jesse James/Navigator/Billy's Bones/The Gentleman Soldier/And The Band Played Waltzing Matilda **PERSONNEL** Shane MacGowan (g, v), Jem Finer (bj), James Fearnley (ad),

Caitlin O'Riordan (b), Andrew Ranken (d), Spider Stacey (w), Philip Chevron (g), Tommy Keane (pp), Henry Benagh (f), Dick Cuthell (hn)

This was the album, originally released on the Stiff label, that introduced the world to the throaty rasp of Shane MacGowan. Its title was taken from Winston Churchill's memorable description of life in the navy, while its unique content includes the classics *A Pair Of Brown Eyes* and *The Old Main Drag*, both perennial Pogues classics. Pushed to Number 13 by concerted music-press approval, this is of their best.

I can tire quickly of some of the Pogues' lachrymose balladry… A cheer, none the less, for Dick Cuthell's excellent horns and some poignant forays on the uillean pipes for Tommy Keane. **Adam Sweeting, Melody Maker, August 1985**

Rumour And Sigh

ARTIST Richard Thompson RELEASE DATE May 1991 (UK) LABEL Capitol ((UK & US) PRODUCER Mitchell Thompson UK CHART peak/weeks 32/3 US CHART peak/weeks – TRACK LISTING Read About Love/I Feel So Good/I Misunderstood/Grey Walls/You Dream Too Much/Why Must I Plead/1952 Vincent Black Lightning/Backlash Love Affair/Mystery Wind/Don't Sit On My Jimmy Shands/Keep Your Distance/Mother Knows Best/God Loves A Drunk/Psycho Street PERSONNEL Richard Thompson (g, md, hg), Richard Froom (p, ho, po, cha, ce, clv, eh), Jim Keltner (d), Mickey Curry (d), Alex Acuna (pc), Jerry Scheff (b), Simon Nicol (g), Phillip Pickett (sh, ctl, crh), John Kirkpatrick (ad), Aly Bain (fd), Clive Gregson (v), Christine Collister (v)

Richard Thompson moved label again, this time to Capitol, for his ninth solo album. Energized once more after 1988's patchy label debut, **Amnesia**, Thompson delivered a diverse collection that drew on rock, blues and balladry – there is even an attempt at a polka! Lyrically, **Rumour And Sigh** has no less broad a scope, ranging from the witty *Read About Love* to the bleak irony of *I Feel So Good* to superbly evocative narratives like *1952 Vincent Black Lightning* and *Mystery Wind*.

Thompson's concerns and approaches are probably too off-beat for acceptance in the bland pop world, so the redirection of **Rumour & Sigh** *may be an academic exercise sales wise… a hit album would be the long denied but richly deserved reward for an exemplary career.* **Ira Robbins, Rolling Stone, July 1991**

Rumours

ARTIST Fleetwood Mac RELEASE DATE February 1977 (UK) LABEL Warner Bros. (UK & US) PRODUCER Fleetwood Mac, Richard Dashut, Ken Caillat UK CHART peak/weeks 1/443 US CHART peak/weeks 1/130 TRACK LISTING Second Hand News/Dreams/Never Going Back Again/Don't Stop/Go Your Own Way/Songbird/The Chain/You Make Loving Fun/I Don't Want To Know/Oh Daddy/Gold Dust Woman PERSONNEL Jeremy Spencer (g, v), Peter Green (g, v), Mick Fleetwood (d), John McVie (b), Lindsey Buckingham (g, v), Stevie Nicks (v)

Only seven months divided *Fleetwood Mac's* seven days atop the US charts and its successor scoring the first of 31 non-consecutive weeks. It had taken the eponymous effort 58 weeks to climb to the exalted position, but **Rumours** had its own delayed reaction in the shape of *The Dance*, a semi-acoustic reworking by the reunited line-up 20 years after its 1977 recording.

Fleetwood Mac suddenly became a Californian pop group: instead of laborious blues and rock jams they started turning out bright little three minute singles with a hook in every chorus. **John Swanson, Rolling Stone, April 1977**

Running On Empty

ARTIST Jackson Browne RELEASE DATE January 1978 (UK) LABEL Asylum (UK & US) PRODUCER Jackson Browne UK CHART peak/weeks 26/5 US CHART peak/weeks 3/65 TRACK LISTING Running On Empty/The Road/Rosie/You Love The Thunder/Cocaine/Shaky Town/Love Needs A Heart/Nothing But Time/The Load-Out/Stay PERSONNEL Jackson Browne (g, p), David Lindley (fd, ls), Russel Kunkel (d), Leland Sklar (b), Craig Doerge (k), Danny Kortchmar (g), Doug Haywood (v), Rosemary Butler (v)

More casually pulled together and looser in feel than Browne's usual soul-searching earnestness, this live album did commit the cardinal sin of including songs about the hell that is life on the road, but ultimately he seemed to be saying he'd rather be on it than deal with emotional problems off it. It's perked up by *Stay*, a rousing take on the Maurice Williams song which, galvanized by his multi-instrumentalist David Lindley's impressive falsetto, gave him a rare, sizeable world-wide hit. With characteristic idealism he then threw himself into matters of liberal politics.

Running On Empty*… recreates the mood of a band on the road, on stage and off.… Life on the road is for the main part humdrum, and Browne fails to extract the colour that's needed to liven up a record of this curious existence.* **Colin Irwin, Melody Maker, December 1977**

Rust Never Sleeps

ARTIST Neil Young RELEASE DATE July 1979 (UK) LABEL Reprise (UK & US) PRODUCER Neil Young UK CHART peak/weeks 13/13 US CHART peak/weeks 8/- TRACK LISTING My My, Hey Hey (Out Of The Blue)/Thrasher/Ride My Llama/Pocahontes/Sail Away/Powder Finger/Welfare Mothers/Sedan Delivery/Hey Hey, My My (Into The Black) PERSONNEL Neil Young (v, g), Jim Messina (b)

A brilliant mid-career peak, **Rust Never Sleeps** offered clear evidence that Neil Young was not about to wither and die in the face of strong competition from punk's young turks. Split, as were his previous albums, between elegiac balladry and heads-down rockers, **Rust Never Sleeps** was more than just the paradigmatic late Seventies Young album – it featured some of his strongest ever material and his clearest statements of intent.

… unlike most of Youngs LPs, **Rust Never Sleeps** *is a deliberate grab bag of styles, from sensitive singer/songwriter seriousness to charming science fiction to country rock to an open embrace of the raw potency of rock.* **James Henke, Rolling Stone, December 1979**

Sailin' Shoes

ARTIST Little Feat RELEASE DATE May 1972 (UK) LABEL Warner Bros. (UK & US) PRODUCER Ted Templeman UK CHART peak/weeks – US CHART peak/weeks – TRACK LISTING Easy To Slip/Cold Cold Cold/Trouble/Tripe Face Boogie/Willin'/Apolitical Blues/Sailin' Shoes/Teenage Nervous Breakdown/Got No Shadow/Cat Fever/Texas Rose Cafe PERSONNEL Lowell George (v, g), Paul Barrere (lg), Bill Payne (k), Fred Tackett (g), Kenny Gradney (b), Richie Hayward (d), Sam Clayton (p)

By the early Seventies the once innovative West Coast sound had grown stale, but Little Feat were a proverbial beacon in its murk. Their eponymous debut had marked them as an innovative outfit but in singer/guitarist Lowell George, they had a leader who possessed both vision and serious songwriting skills. Obsessed with American truckers, seeing them as contemporary mythical heroes, he had penned a number of songs in celebration of their tough lifestyle, notably **Willin'**, and was at the zenith of his powers. A masterpiece right down to sleeve artist Neon Park's wicked pastiche of Fragonard's *The Swing*.

… when producer Ted Templeman showed **Sailin' Shoes** *album cover to Van Morrison he commented, 'How can you work with these guys? That's the most revolting thing I've ever seen in my whole life.' George said, 'I heard that and I said, "That's great. We're really onto something here."'* **Steve Moore, Rolling Stone, August 1973**

Sailor

ARTIST The Steve Miller Band RELEASE DATE Jan 1969 (UK)/October 1968 (US) LABEL Capitol (UK & US) PRODUCER The Steve Miller Band, Glyn Jones UK CHART peak/weeks – US CHART peak/weeks 24/17 TRACK LISTING Song For Our Ancestors/Dear Mary/My Friend/Living In The U.S.A./Quicksilver Girl/Lucky Man/Gangster Of Love/You're So Fine/Overdrive/Dime-A-Dance Romance PERSONNEL Steve Miller (v, g), James 'Curley' Cooke (g, v), Lonnie Turner (b, v), Tim Davis (d, v)

A bluesman from the Midwest, Miller married an underlying blues feel with some imaginative ideas on his second album. The slowly unfurling opening cut with its electronic keyboards and booming ship sirens recorded in San Francisco Bay was as atmospheric a soundscape as anything by the Floyd or early Dead, while the ecstatic, revved-up *Livin In The USA* revealed Miller's teenage Chicago roots. The band could also boast the ubiquitous West Coast vocal harmonies, as demonstrated on the paeon to Girl Freiburg, in *Quicksilver Girl*. And with Boz Scaggs aboard, throwing in a trio of his own silky funk-tinged tunes, **Sailor**

showcased an outfit at the very peak of its powers.

It is a pity that **Sailor** *is being promoted as a psychedelic item, because in contrast to the excess of that genre, this is in every sense of the word a musical album.* **Rolling Stone, November 1968**

St Dominic's Preview

ARTIST Van Morrison RELEASE DATE August 1972 LABEL Warner Bros. PRODUCER Van Morrison UK CHART peak/weeks 0/0 US CHART peak/weeks 15/6 TRACK LISTING Jackie Wilson Said/(I'm In Heaven When You Smile)/Gypsy/I Will Be There/Listen To The Lion/Saint Dominic's Preview/Redwood Tree/Almost Independence Day PERSONNEL Van Morrison (v, g, s), session musicians

After **Street Choir** and **Tupelo Hone**, two albums that left Van Morrison with 'a bad taste in my mouth', normal imperious service was resumed with this release. Two extended close-to-improvised songs, **Almost Independence Day** and **Listen To The Lion**, harking back to **Astral Weeks**, contrasted effectively with the Stax-y soul punch of *Jackie Wilson Said (I'm In Heaven When You Smile)*, a joyous tribute to the veteran singer that would later be covered by Dexy's Midnight Runners.

That album was kinda' rushed. Because of stupid things like studio time and stuff like that. But I thought it was a good shot, that album. There were a lot of good songs on it. **Van Morrison in interview with Ritchie Yorke, NME, February 1974**

St Louis To Liverpool

ARTIST Chuck Berry RELEASE DATE January 1965 LABEL Chess Records PRODUCER – UK CHART peak/weeks – US CHART peak/weeks – TRACK LISTING Little Marie/Our Little Rendezvous/No Particular Place To Go/You Two/Promised Land/You Never Can Tell/Go Bobby Soxer/Things I Used To Do/Night Beat/Liverpool Drive/Merry Christmas PERSONNEL Chuck Berry (v, g), Willie Dixon (b), Fred Below (d), Lafayette Leake (p)

Fresh out of two years in an Indiana jail on an immorality charge involving a teenage girl, Berry, who influenced The Beatles, Stones, Dylan, and anyone who ever strung three chords together, made one of rock 'n' roll's defining statements, 'cruisin' and playin' the radio'. **Promised Land**, **You Never Can Tell**, and **Nadine** are part of any would-be rocker's textbook. **No Particular Place To Go** captures the restless lusty *ennui* which so vitally informs the *genre*. The album roars through these as if an only partially chastened Berry feels maybe time isn't on his side, until the slow blues workout of **Night Beat** coaxes out a mellower side.

How do you feel just before you go on stage? 'I think a little about what can I do in the sense of what new gimmicks can I insert and generally new ways I can entertain. Not until I get up there do things really begin to flow…' **From an interview with Chuck Berry, Melody Maker, December 1972**

A Salty Dog

ARTIST Procol Harum RELEASE DATE 19th July 1969 (UK) LABEL Regal Zonophone (UK)/A&M (US) PRODUCER Matthew Fisher, Dave Knights UK CHART peak/weeks 27/2 US CHART peak/weeks 32/20 TRACK LISTING A Salty Dog/The Milk Of Human Kindness/Too Much Between Us/The Devil Came From Arkansas/Boredom/Juicy John Pink/Wreck Of The Hesperus/All This And More/Crucification Lane/Pilgrim's Progress PERSONNEL Gary Brooker (v, o), Ray Royer (g), Dave Knights (b), Bobby Harrison (d), Keith Reid (ly)

Having started recording at A&M in Los Angeles (only *Wreck Of The Hesperus* and a single B-side proved usable from those sessions), classic-rock specialists Harum headed home to the newly extended Abbey Road facilities – eight tracks, double the Pepper-

era technology – for their third album. Democracy meant Trower and Fisher enjoyed lead vocal outings, but Brooker's tracks were clearly the winners: the elegiac title track has been covered by artists as diverse as Billy Joel, Sarah Brightman and Marc Almond. The cover, incidentally, parodies a Players Navy Cut cigarette packet and was painted by lyricist Reid's girlfriend.

The songs have titles that read like paperback novels… Gary Brooker is extremely fond of descending chord structures and slow tempos and an atmosphere of resignation, and sadness, combined with a certain strength pervades all their work. **Melody Maker, July 1969**

Sandinista

ARTIST The Clash RELEASE DATE December 1980 (UK & US) LABEL CBS (UK)/Epic (US) PRODUCER The Clash UK CHART peak/weeks 19/9 US CHART peak/weeks 24/20 TRACK LISTING The Magnificent Seven/Hitsville U.K./ Junco Partner/Ivan Meets G.I. Joe/The Leader/Something About England/ Rebel Waltz/Look Here/The Crooked Beat/Somebody Got Murdered/One More Time/One More Dub/Lightning Strikes (Not Once But Twice)/Up In Heaven (Not Only Here)/Corner Soul/Let's Go Crazy/If Music Could Talk/The

Sound Of The Sinners/Police On My Back/Midnight Log/The Equaliser/The Call Up/Washington Bullets/Broadway/Lose This Skin/Charlie Don't Surf/Mensforth Hill/Junkie Slip/Kingston Advice/The Street Parade/ Version City/Living In Fame/Silicone On Sapphire/Version Pardner/Career Opportunities/Shepherds Delight PERSONNEL Mick Jones (g, v), Joe Strummer (v, rg), Paul Simonon (b, v), Topper Headon (d, pc)

Hubris maybe, but The Clash felt only a triple album could contain their flourishing ideas and ambition. It sold disappointingly, even though priced as a double, and perhaps over indulged their charming but flawed reggae dub stylings. The country hints and mock brass bands were only moderately winning, but the early stabs at rap 'n' roll yielded hits with **The Call-Up**, **The Magnificent Seven** and the ironic **Hitsville U.K.** Tellingly, the band's next, **Combat Rock** was more concise, mainstream, and their biggest seller.

Despite their conviction, slogans carry much more power if you can dance to them… **Sandinista** *strikes me as a sporadic, unyielding work. A sprawling statement which comes as a disappointment after the consistent excellence of last year's offering.* **Patrick Humphries, Melody Maker, December 1980**

Saturday Night Fever

ARTIST Bee Gees RELEASE DATE March 1978 (UK)/November 1977 (US) LABEL RSO (UK)/Polydor (US) PRODUCER Bee Gees UK CHART peak/weeks 1/ US CHART peak/weeks 1/120 TRACK LISTING Stayin' Alive/How Deep Is Your Love/Night Fever/More Than A Woman/If I Can't Have You/Fifth Of Beethoven/Manhattan Skyline/Calypso Breakdown/Night On Disco Mountain/Open Sesame/Jive Talking/You Should Be Dancing/Boogie Shoes/Salsaton/K-Jee/Disco Inferno PERSONNEL The Bee Gees (Barry, Maurice and Robin Gibb), Kool & The Gang, Tavares, The Tramps, Yvonne Elliman, Water Murphy, KC & The Sunshine Band, Ralph McDonald, David Shire.

The Bee Gees had enjoyed one spell as megastars with their lush, tearful ballads of 1967 to 1972 but seemed to have faded when, startlingly, they blazed back as purveyors of inspired mainstream disco. Their dress sense and facial hair, not to mention their supersonic falsettos, were often derided, but their songs for the John Travolta breakthrough movie were perfectly pitched. It was allegedly the year of punk rock, but this soundtrack album sold over 30 million copies worldwide and is remembered with intense affection to this day.

The Bee Gees' music, synthetic but compulsive, has best defined the trend, after years of solemn rock art, that has returned the art of dance, to pop music. **Michael Watts, Melody Maker, November 1979**

Say It Loud, I'm Black And I'm Proud

ARTIST James Brown **RELEASE DATE** April 1969 (UK)/March 1969 (US) **LABEL** Polydor (UK)/King (US) **PRODUCER** James Brown, Bud Hobgood **UK CHART** peak/weeks – **US CHART** peak/weeks 53/22 **TRACK LISTING** Say It Loud - I'm Black And I'm Proud (part 1)/Say It Loud - I'm Black And I'm Proud (part 2)/I Guess I'll Have To Cry, Cry, Cry/Goodbye My Love (part 1)/Goodbye My Love (part 2)/Shades Of Brown/Licking Stick/I Love You/Then You Can Tell Me Goodbye/Let Them Talk/Maybe I'll Understand/I'll Lose My Mind **PERSONNEL** James Brown (v), Bobby Byrd (o), Johnny Terry, Sylvester Keels, Nafloyd Scott etc. (g)

Brown was becoming more overt with his socio-political references, though it was as a creative artist that he made the best role model. The concept of 'black power' was still an argument-starter back then, and later hip-hop acts never fully appreciated how much Brown achieved for them. This was a mixed, if not brand-new, bag, with hedonistic whoops like *Licking Stick* to be found among the chest beating. As well as his raging vocals, Brown could contribute a nifty keyboard solo, whipping the band into ever more urgent fervour.

… *'the music has gotten so primitive…I do 95 per cent of the arranging myself, and it works itself out…I've always tried to go my own way. I think that I'm me and I become more "me" every day.'* **James Brown from an interview by Richard Williams, Melody Maker, August 1969**

School's Out

ARTIST Alice Cooper **RELEASE DATE** July 1972 (UK) **LABEL** Warner Bros. (UK & US) **PRODUCER** Bob Ezrin **UK CHART** peak/weeks 4/20 **US CHART** peak/weeks 2/32 **TRACK LISTING** School's Out/Alma Mater/Blue Turk/Grande Finale/Gutter Cat Vs The Jets/Luney Tune/My Stars/Public Animal **PERSONNEL** Alice Cooper (v), Glen Buxton (g), Michael Bruce (g, k), Dennis Dunaway (b), Neal Smith (d)

Vincent Furnier, son of a preacher, took his and his band's name from a ouija board, and took Seventies rock theatrics to a new, gross, level. With on-stage simulation of the killing of chickens and dolls, and the guillotining of Alice, they were schocky horror redeemed by some barnstorming, wirily anthemic songs. The title track of this heavy, pile driving album gave them a breakthrough hit, Number 1 in Britain, and made them the talking point of the moment: 'School's been blown to pieces…' Alice's sneering voice and darkly camp sense of humour made him a twisted sister of merciful tongue-in-cheek.

… *commitment and a palpable sense of self is above all what Alice Cooper lacks…. The music is more pictorial, plotted, broadly theatrical, ornate and convoluted than ever before, but the consequence is to undermine what this album pretends to be – a paean to teenage defiance.* **Ben Gerson, Rolling Stone, September 1972**

The Score

ARTIST The Fugees **RELEASE DATE** January 1996 (UK & US) **LABEL** Ruffhouse (Columbia) (UK & US) **PRODUCER** Diamond D, Handel Tucker, Salaam Remi, Wyclex Jerry 'Te Bass' Duplessis, Pras Prakazrel **UK CHART** peak/weeks 3/- **US CHART** peak/weeks 1/31 **TRACK LISTING** Red Intro/How Many Mics/Ready Or Not/Zealots/Beast/Fu-Gee-La/Family Business/Killing Me Softly/Score/Mask/Cowboys/No Woman, No Cry/Manifest Outro/Fu-Gee-La (Sly & Robbie Mix)/Fu-Gee-La (Refugee Camp Mix) **PERSONNEL** Lauryn 'L' Hill (v), Clef Jean (v, rap, g), Pras Prakazrel (rap), Sly Dunbar (d, dp, gst), Robbie Shakespeare (b, gst), session musicians

The New Jersey-based rap group's second album was written something in the style of a film soundtrack, mixing 13 tracks into one, seamless entity. The material was of a surprise too, with a number of cover versions mixed in among the originals. It is ironic that the original delivery of the cover versions was what made the album so accessible worldwide. If rap music had appeared to be losing its way, the Fugees at least tried to put it back on the right track.

Rap can be long on menace and short on sensuality, but the Fugees weave theirs around some beautiful hip-swaying R&B and mainstream pop melodicism. Dark and rich, it's a dense sonic tapestry, this album. The words pour out of it and cover you like honey. **Mojo, January 1997**

Scott

ARTIST Scott Walker **RELEASE DATE** September 1967 (UK & US) **LABEL** Philips (UK)/Smash (US) **PRODUCER** John Franz **UK CHART** peak/weeks 3/17 **US CHART** peak/weeks - **TRACK LISTING** Mathilde/Motague Terrace (In Blue)/Angelica/The Lady Came From Baltimore/When Joanna Loved Me/My Death/The Big Hurt/Such A Small Love/You're Gonna Hear From Me/Through A Long And Sleepless Night/Always Coming Back To You/Amsterdam **PERSONNEL** Scott Walker (v), Keith Altham (in), session musicians

Scott Walker was one of The Walker Brothers, who enjoyed a run of classy teen-bating hits in the mid Sixties. His quartet of late Sixties albums saw Walker take a different turn: though still powerfully orchestrated, **Scott** was suffused with a melancholy that must have baffled his scream-age fans. However, the mix of original material and interpretations of Jacques Brel, Tim Hardin and Weill/Mann songs sold very well, positing Walker as a latterday Sinatra-style torch crooner.

Strip away the carefully calculated mystique of Scott Walker, forget his sex-appeal good looks and what have you got? An average singer with pitch problems who can sing a ballad well, but who lacks the magic of the big league male singers… **Melody Maker, June 1969**

Scott 2

ARTIST Scott Walker **RELEASE DATE** April 1968 (UK) **LABEL** Philips (UK)/Smash (US) **PRODUCER** John Franz **UK CHART** peak/weeks 1/18 **US CHART** peak/weeks – **TRACK LISTING** Jackie/Best Of Both Worlds/Black Sheep Boy/The Amorous Humphrey Plugg/Next/The Girls From The Streets/Plastic Palace People/Wait Until Dark/The Girls And The Dogs/Windows Of The World/The Bridge/Come Next Spring **PERSONNEL** Scott Engel Walker (v, b, k)

Another eclectic mix, Walker's second solo effort (including Bacharach/David as well as Jacques Brel tunes) was his biggest seller and contained his first solo UK hit, *Jackie*. By now Walker was exploring the sort of themes, homosexuality, prostitution, the sleazy underbelly of love and romance, that would dominate his next two recordings, **Scott 3** and **Scott 4**, and would eventually prove too dark even for his adoring public.

Some people have the power to control the emotions of others – to bring them up or down, just by a word, gesture or in the case of Scott Walker, a song… it's his best album. **Chris Welch, Melody Maker, April 1968**

The Scream

ARTIST Siouxsie And The Banshees **RELEASE DATE** December 1978 (UK) **LABEL** Polydor (UK & US) **PRODUCER** Steve Lillywhite, Siouxsie And The Banshees (co-produced by) **UK CHART** peak/weeks 12/11 **US CHART** peak/weeks – **TRACK LISTING** Hong Kong Garden/Pure/Jigsaw Feeling/Overground/Carcass/Helter Skelter/Mirage Metal Postcard/Nicotine Stain/Suburban Relapse **PERSONNEL** Siouxsie Sioux (v), John McGeoch (g), Steve Severin (b), Budgie (d)

One of the Sex Pistols' infamous Bromley Contingent (she was present during the legendary Bill Grundy Incident), suburban girl Susan Dallion reinvented herself as Siouxsie Sioux before her twentieth birthday, just in time for an early incarnation of the Banshees (featuring Sid Vicious on drums) to debut at the 100 Club's 'Punk Festival'. Within two years, the Banshees had evolved way beyond the Luddite conventions of punk to create something exciting and new. **The Scream** was an audacious first foray. With its primal wailing, Teutonic rhythms and piercing, atonal guitars, it helped usher in the experimental post punk era.

'What we're trying to do with the music is what we're trying to do, not necessarily with the English language, but certainly with the rock lyric: just to tear it apart and put it all back together again in different pieces.' **Steve Severin in conversation with Paul Morley, NME, December 1978**

Screamadelica

ARTIST Primal Scream **RELEASE DATE** September 1991 (UK) **LABEL** Creation (UK)/Sire (US) **PRODUCER** Boys Own Productions, Hypnotone, Andrew Innes, The Orb, Jimmy Miller **UK CHART** peak/weeks 8/17 **US CHART** peak/weeks – **TRACK LISTING** Movin' On Up/Slip Inside This House/Don't Fight It, Feel It/Higher Than The Sun/Inner Flight/Come Together/Loaded/Damaged/I'm Comin' Down/Higher Than The Sun/Shine Like Stars **PERSONNEL** Bobby Gillespie (v), Robert Young (g), Andrew Innes (g), Henry Olsen (b), Tobay Toman (d)

The Primals finally hit gold when they embraced the emergent rave culture. Starting with their anthemic **Loaded** single produced by an as-yet unknown Andy Weatherall, the band explored the possibilities of what a marriage of classic rock moves and the ecstasy-fuelled house scene might create. They also allowed their abiding love of classic funk and dub to seep in – and the results

were startling. It was almost impossible to imagine an album that effortlessly segued from classic Stones-type rockers (deliberately produced by veteran Jimmy Miller) into whole vistas of acid house-type noise, but this they convincingly achieved to win the first Mercury Music Prize.

*Through the fog of this sometimes self-indulgent soundtrack to Nineties drug culture, only the excellent **Loaded** and the luxurious, languid **Higher Than The Sun** truly stand out.* **David Roberts, Q, October 1991**

Searching For The Young Soul Rebels

ARTIST Dexy's Midnight Runners **RELEASE DATE** July 1980 **LABEL** Parlophone **PRODUCER** Pete Wingfield **UK CHART** peak/weeks 6/10 **US CHART** peak/weeks - **TRACK LISTING** Burn It Down/Tell Me When My Light Turns Green/The Teams That Meet In Caffs/I'm Just Looking/Geno/Seven Day's Too Long/I Couldn't Help If I Tried/Thankfully Not Living In Yorkshire It Doesn't Apply/Keep It/Love Part One/There, There, My Dear **PERSONNEL** Kevin Rowland (v, g), Al Archer (g), Pete Williams (b), Pete Saunders (o), Andy Growcott (d), 'Big' Jimmy Patterson (tb), Steve 'Babyface' Spooner (as), Jeff 'J. B.' Blythe (ts)

Spurning the music press and communicating in paid-for ads, Kevin Rowland's eight strong team of donkey-jacketed, brass-reinforced desperados created a classic – and one that swam against the post punk tide. 2-Tone comparisons faded against the sheer power of **Dance Stance**, **There There My Dear** and the chart-topping **Geno**, homage to Sixties soulster Washington. Some said this prototype of Dexy's was modelled on De Niro's *Mean Streets*, and they acted mean by 'kidnapping' the master tapes in a contract row, but they had the musical muscle to back it up.

The outrageous theatricality of Rowland's vocals… setting out with a vision, looking back with joy and forward with uncertainty, and finishing purged and strengthened. **Phil McNeil, NME, July 1982**

Second Toughest In The Infants

ARTIST Underworld **RELEASE DATE** March 1996 (US) **LABEL** Junior Boy (UK)/Sire (US) **PRODUCER** Underworld **UK CHART** peak/weeks – **US CHART** peak/weeks – **TRACK LISTING** Juanita/Kiteless/To Dream Of Love/Banstyle-Sappys Curry/Confusion The Waitress/Rowla/Pearls Girl/Air Towel/Blueski/Stagger **PERSONNEL** Rick Smith (k,v), Karl Hyde (v,g), Alfie Thomas (g,v), Baz Allen (sy), Darren Emerson (k)

Two members of Underworld, Karl Hyde and Rick Smith, had already enjoyed a modicum of success with early Eighties synth-pop outfit Freur (whose **Doot Doot** was a minor novelty hit), before their re-emergence in the Nineties as forerunners of the new dance explosion that has enabled bands as diverse as The Prodigy and The Chemical Brothers to achieve mainstream recognition. **Second Toughest In The Infants** was the follow-up to 1994's **Dubnobasswithmyheadman** – hailed by *Melody Maker* as the most important LP since Primal Scream's **Screamadelica** – and, on the back of **Born Slippy** (as featured on the soundtrack to *Trainspotting*), asserted Underworld's position as true innovators in the field of left-field techno-dance pop.

Weirdly, the best thing about Emerson, Smith & Hyde isn't the music at all, but the lyrics… Mostly, though, it's music for aeroplanes and supermarkets. **Simon Price, Melody Maker, March 1996**

The Sensual World

ARTIST Kate Bush **RELEASE DATE** October 1989 (UK & US) **LABEL** EMI (UK)/Columbia (US) **PRODUCER** Kate Bush **UK CHART** peak/weeks 2/20 **US CHART** peak/weeks 43/26 **TRACK LISTING** The Sensual World/Love And Anger/The Fog/Reaching Out/Heads We're Dancing/Deeper Understanding/Between A Man And A Woman/Never Be Mine/Rocket's Tail/This Woman's Work/Walk Straight Down The Middle **PERSONNEL** Charlie Morgan (d), Del Palmer (b, pc, g), Davey Spilane (pp, w), Donal Lunny (bz), John Shehan (f), Stuart Elliot (d), John Giblin (b), Dave Gilmour (g), Paddy Bush (bv, md), Alan Murphy (g), Nigel Kennedy (v), Jonathan Williams (c), Alan Stivell (h), Mick Karn (b), Yanka Rupkhina (v), The Trio Bulgaria (v), Eberhard Weber (b), Kate Bush (v, p, k)

Weakened only by a couple of errors in judgement (songs about computers weren't a sound idea even back then), Bush's sixth was still tremendously involving and febrile. Probing into the gap between the genders, it couldn't help being robustly sexy, especially

on the hypnotic title track, which was another hit single. Bulgarian folk singers and a searing Dave Gilmour guitar solo elevated the show stopping *A Rocket's Tail*. Bush was still displaying more inspiration per song than most artists managed in an album. Whilst new female artists were about to make a challenge for her throne, they were going to have their work cut out.

The Sensual World *is a potent, heady collection that expresses a particularly feminine side of the sensual world.* **Sheila Rogers, Rolling Stone February 1990**

Sentimental Hygiene

ARTIST Warren Zevon **RELEASE DATE** June 1987 (UK & US) **LABEL** Virgin AM (UK & US) **PRODUCER** Niko Bolas, Andrew Slater, Richard Wachtel, Warren Zevon **UK CHART** peak/weeks 0/0 **US CHART** peak/weeks 63/18 **TRACK LISTING** Sentimental Hygiene/Boom Boom Mancini/The Factory/Trouble Waiting To Happen/Reconsider Me/Detox Mansion/Bad Karma/Even A Dog Can Shake Hands/The Heartache/Leave My Monkey Alone **PERSONNEL** Warren Zevon (v, p, g, ag, b, k), Bob Dylan (k), Don Henley (bv), Jennifer Warnes (bv), Neil Young (g), George Clinton (arr)

Backed by R.E.M.'s Peter Buck, Mike Mills and Bill Berry, and guest starring such luminaries as Bob Dylan, Neil Young and George Clinton, **Sentimental Hygiene** is the best album of the second half of Warren Zevon's much admired career. With typically merciless zeal, Zevon trained his critical eye on rehab culture on **Detox Mansion** and **Trouble Waiting To Happen**, taking no prisoners in the process.

With the tide changing in favour of singer-songwriters, he just might make it with this excellent fresh start. Instead of creeping back with a 'Hi! Remember me?' attitude, he thunders and pushes his way to the front as if he'd never been away. **Edwin Pouncey, NME, July 1987**

September Of My Years

ARTIST Frank Sinatra **RELEASE DATE** April 1965 (UK & US) **LABEL** Warner Bros. (UK & US) **PRODUCER** Sonny Burke **UK CHART** peak/weeks – **US CHART** peak/weeks 5/69 **TRACK LISTING** The September Of My Years/How Old Am I?/Don't Wait Too Long/It Gets Lonely Early/This Is All I Ask/Last Night When We Were Young/The Man In The Looking Glass/It Was A Very Good Year/When The Wind Was Green/Hello, Young Lovers/I See It Now/Once Upon A Time/September Song **PERSONNEL** Frank Sinatra (v), Orchestra arranged and conducted by Gordon Jenkins

In 1961, Frank Sinatra founded Reprise Records. Four years later he delivered his first classic for the label. **September Of My Years**, recorded on the eve of Sinatra's fiftieth birthday, had a suitably autumnal tone. Conductor/arranger Gordon Jenkins, with whom Sinatra first worked on **Where Are You?**, matched the gently symphonic splendour of his predecessors (Messrs Riddle and May) on a sequence of melancholy songs that addressed the anxieties of middle-aged former swingin' lovers everywhere. *It Was A Very Good Year*, a requiem for lost youth, remains one of Sinatra's most moving performances.

Gordon Jenkins works the magic behind the master who sets a deep mood and never loses it despite the rougher voice. **Melody Maker, August 1965**

Sgt Pepper's Lonely Hearts Club Band

ARTIST The Beatles **RELEASE DATE** June 1967 (UK & US) **LABEL** Parlophone (UK)/Capitol (US) **PRODUCER** George Martin **UK CHART** peak/weeks 1/148 **US CHART** peak/weeks 1/175 **TRACK LISTING** Sgt. Pepper's Lonely Hearts Club Band/A Little Help From My Friends/Lucy In The Sky With Diamonds/Getting Better/Fixing A Hole/She's Leaving Home/Being For The Benefit Of Mr Kite/Within You Without You/When I'm Sixty Four/Lovely Rita/Good Morning, Good Morning/Sgt. Pepper's Lonely Hearts Club Band (Reprise)/A Day In The Life **PERSONNEL** John Lennon (v, rg), Paul McCartney (v, g), George Harrison (v, lg), Ringo Starr (d)

Revered as arguably rock history's finest, a breathtaking whirl of wit, melody and innovative sound and structure, which has different nuances for every listener. It moulded popular music's previous heritage into brave new shapes and achieved, judged by McCartney's effort and drive, more by design than drug-addled accident. Lennon sang the monumental *A Day In The Life* with a tangible tremble. By now forced to withdraw to the studio – the level of their global fame had put an end to the relentless touring – the former mop tops emerged as *auteurs* and pioneering artists. **Sgt. Pepper** was, however, undoubtedly to blame for such horrors as progressive rock, rock opera, concept albums and, worst of all, **When I'm Sixty Four**.

It's not the greatest album ever made, as some people would have you believe. It's not even the best Beatles album. But it is the first example of recording technology being used as an instrument, and it does contain some good songs… **David Quantick, NME, October 1991**

Setting Sons

ARTIST The Jam **RELEASE DATE** November 1979 (UK & US) **LABEL** Polydor (UK & US) **PRODUCER** The Jam, Vic Coppersmith, Heaven **UK CHART** peak/weeks 4/19 **US CHART** peak/weeks 137/8 **TRACK LISTING** Girl On The Phone/Thick As Thieves/Private Hell/Little Boy Soldiers/Wasteland/Burning Sky/Smithers-Jones/Saturday's Kids/The Eton Rifles/Heat Wave **PERSONNEL** Paul Weller (v, g), Bruce Foxton (b), Rick Buckler (d)

The Jam's fourth album was the first to make any showing Stateside, though they would fail to scale the heights of their idols The Who in that market. Like the former Mods from Shepherds Bush, The Jam had come up with a solid concept. It mixed Paul Weller's vision of urban decay with the waning of the British empire – **Eton Rifles** was a prime slice that made the singles charts. To Townsend and Davies, add Weller.

… the album's success rests on its musical content, and the mark here is the band's ability to put together, at last, convincing soundtracks for their scenarios…. The Jam have never sounded better. **Paulo Hewitt, Melody Maker, November 1979**

Seventh Sojourn

ARTIST Moody Blues **RELEASE DATE** November 1972 (UK & US) **LABEL** Threshold Records (UK & US) **PRODUCER** Tony Clarke **UK CHART** peak/weeks 5/18 **US CHART** peak/weeks 1/44 **TRACK LISTING** Lost In A Lost World/New Horizons/For My Lady/Isn't Life Strange/You And Me/The Land Of Make-Believe/When You're A Free Man/I'm Just A Singer (In A Rock And Roll Band) **PERSONNEL** Justin Hayward (g, v), Mike Pinder (k), Ray Thomas (fl, h, v), John Lodge (b, v), Graeme Edge (d)

Ironically, the Moody Blues' seventh album was overshadowed by

the revival of an earlier classic, 1968's **Nights In White Satin**. The ballad charted afresh as a single, beating the current album's **Isn't Life Strange** and **I'm Just A Singer (In A Rock And Roll Band)**, but the album benefited from Moodies-mania by topping the US chart. There would follow a six-year recording gap as the band members followed individual careers.

It's predictable, and surely even the staunchest followers, even fanatics, hold out for some thing different. The surprise is that there are no surprises. This isn't so much a sojourn as a permanent residence. **A. M., Melody Maker, November 1972**

Seventh Son Of A Seventh Son

ARTIST Iron Maiden **RELEASE DATE** April 1988 (UK) **LABEL** EMI (UK)/Capitol (US) **PRODUCER** Martin Birch **UK CHART** peak/weeks 1/18 **US CHART** peak/weeks 12/23 **TRACK LISTING** Moonchild/Infinite Dreams/Can I Play With Madness/The Evil That Men Do/Seventh Son Of A Seventh Son/The Prophecy/The Clairvoyant/Only The Good Die Young **PERSONNEL** Bruce Dickinson (v), Dave Murray (lg), Adrian Smith (lg), Steve Harris (b), Clive Burr (d)

The endless cycle of album-tour-album had robbed Maiden of some of their ebullience by the time of this conceptual opus: the fifth from the same line-up, a band record. Critics were quick to slate, but four UK Top 10 singles and a 107,000 crowd pulled to Donington's 'Monsters Of Rock' combined with its chart-topping status to give them a well-deserved V for victory salute. Vocalist Bruce Dickinson was heard to say that this showed the way for heavy metal in the Nineties – few argued.

Iron Maiden can at least muster the odd exciting moment, almost in spite of themselves. It's obvious that the likes of Anthrax and Metallica owe a profound creative debt to the Maids. **John Tague, NME, April 1988**

The Shadows

ARTIST The Shadows RELEASE DATE September 1961 LABEL Columbia PRODUCER – UK CHART peak/weeks 1/57 US CHART peak/weeks - TRACK LISTING Shadoogie/Blue Star/Nivram/Baby My Heart/See You In My Drums/All My Sorrows/Stand Up And Say That!/Gonzales/Find Me In A Golden Street/Theme From A Filleted Place/That's My Desire/My Resistance Is Low/ Sleepwalk/Big Boy PERSONNEL Hank Marvin (lg), Bruce Welch (rg), Brian Bennett (d)

The debut album from Cliff Richard's backing troupe, having changed their name from The Drifters after the American R&B outfit objected. Their new moniker was courtesy of bassist Jet Harris, who felt they were in Richard's shadow. Although early hits such as *Apache* (later rapped up by The Sugar Hill Gang), *F.B.I.* and *Atlantis* sound like fairly innocuous instrumentals today, Hank Marvin became the role model and inspiration for a generation of guitarists.

The Shadows (Columbia) – first-ever album from Cliff Richard's famous accompanying group – must be regarded as a milestone in their career and a sizeable step toward a great future.... Solo guitar and rhythm work has now reached a truly professional standard... **Melody Maker, September 1961**

Shakey

ARTIST Shakin' Stevens RELEASE DATE 1981 (US) LABEL Epic (US) PRODUCER Mike Barrett UK CHART peak/weeks – US CHART peak/weeks – TRACK LISTING Mona Lisa/You Drive Me Crazy/Baby I'm Knockin'/It's Raining/Don't She Look Good/Green Door/Don't Bug Me/Baby/Don't Tell Me Your Troubles/I'm Going To Sit Right Down & Cry/This Time/Baby You're A Child/Don't Turn Your Back/Let Me Show You How/I'm Lookin' PERSONNEL Shakin' Stevens (v), Mike Barrett (v), session musicians

As Cliff Richard was to the early Sixties, so Shakin' Stevens was to the early Eighties: the anodyne Elvis, all turpentine quiff and trembling nether regions. Stevens was able to capitalize on Presley nostalgia in the wake of the King's death in 1977, with a slew of hits that made up in singalong accessibility what they lacked in raw sexuality.

... sparkling, polished and confident. Half of it written by Stevens himself, the material is predictably period in its inspiration... you know the results: formularised fun, bland and bouncy. **Paul Du Noyer, NME, November 1981**

She's So Unusual

ARTIST Cyndi Lauper RELEASE DATE January 1984 (UK)/December 1983 (US) LABEL Portrait (UK & US) PRODUCER Rick Chertoff UK CHART peak/weeks 16/32 US CHART peak/weeks 4/69 TRACK LISTING Money Changes Everything/Girls Just Want To Have Fun/When You Were Mine/Time After Time/She Bop/All Through The Night/Witness/I'll Kiss You/He's So Unusual/Yeah Yeah PERSONNEL Cyndi Lauper (v)

Few 30-year-olds make debut solo albums that sell five million in

the US alone – especially after being declared bankrupt. But New York-born Cynthia Anne Stephanie Lauper pulled it off, putting the financial and business complications of previous group Blue Angel behind her to craft a classic offbeat pop album ranging from the chart-topping ballad *Time After Time* to her infectiously danceable signature, *Girls Just Want To have Fun*, another of the four US Top 5 hits the album contained.

Cyndi Lauper's success story has to be the heart warmer of 1984. After going bankrupt with her former band, Blue Angel, Lauper struck multi-platinum with her debut solo album, **She's So Unusual***... she is one of the most vividly compelling female talents to emerge in the Eighties.* **The Year in Music and Entertainment 1984, Rolling Stone, 1984**

Sheet Music

ARTIST 10cc RELEASE DATE June 1974 (UK & US) LABEL UK-Decca (UK)/UK (US) PRODUCER 10cc UK CHART peak/weeks 9/24 US CHART peak/weeks 81/14 TRACK LISTING The Wall Street Shuffle/The Worst Band In The World/Hotel/Old Wild Men/Clockwork Creep/Silly Love/Somewhere In Hollywood/Baron Samedi/The Sacro-iliac/Oh Effendi PERSONNEL Eric Stewart (v, g, b), Lol Creme (v, g, k, b), Kevin Godley (d, v), Graham Gouldman (b, v)

The four members of 10cc had already proved themselves as members of Sixties outfits (Graham Gouldman had penned hits for, among others, The Hollies, Lol Creme and Kevin Godley who were in Frabjoy And The Runcible Spoon and Eric Stewart, a Mindbender), before all but Gouldman formed Hotlegs, who had an international smash in 1970 with *Neanderthal Man*. By 1974, with successful singles like *Rubber Bullets*, *The Dean And I* and *Donna* under their belts, 10cc were, along with Roxy Music, the most consistently inventive band in Britain. **Sheet Music**, 10cc's brilliant second album, proved their mastery both of the recording studio and of the ingenious three-minute pop song, as demonstrated by *The Wall Street Shuffle*, *Silly Love* and near hit, *The Worst Band In The World*.

What can you say about a record that fills you with such joy you wanna cry when it ends?... this one grips the heart of rock 'n' roll like nothing I've heard before... **C. I., Melody Maker, May 1974**

Sherry & 11 Others

ARTIST Frankie Valli & The Four Seasons **RELEASE DATE** October 1962 (UK & US) **LABEL** Veejay (US) **PRODUCER** Bob Crewe **UK CHART** peak/weeks – **US CHART** peak/weeks 6/27 **TRACK LISTING – PERSONNEL** Frankie Valli (lv)/Bob Gaudio (v, o)/Nick Massi (v, b)/Tommy Devito (v, g)

Well, you cannot fault the title for frankness! In the days when hit singles meant rushing out an album to coincide, the Vee Jay label was quick to pounce. This, the quartet's first album, was one of four issued in 1963 by the independent label which, having lost US rights to The Beatles, would lose the Seasons too after 1964's *Stay*, following a royalty dispute. Nevertheless, this is a quaint if dated example of the marriage of Italo-American doowop with amplified pop.

Four Seasons, who have hit the jackpot on both sides of the Atlantic with a belting vocal sound that is either liked or loathed, are featured.... The Album lives up to expectations with the quartet wailing on. **Melody Maker, June 1963**

Shoot Out The Lights

ARTIST Richard Thompson **RELEASE DATE** November 1982 (UK) **LABEL** Hannibal (UK & US) **PRODUCER** Joe Boyd **UK CHART** peak/weeks – **US CHART** peak/weeks 0/0 **TRACK LISTING** Man In Need/Walking On A Wire/Don't Renege On Your Love/Just The Motion/Shoot Out The Lights/Back Street Slide/Did She Jump Or Was She Pushed/Wall Of Death/ **PERSONNEL** Richard Thompson (v, g), Linda Peters/Pat Donaldson (b), Tim Donald (d), session musicians

After a decade or so, the Thompsons' marriage was falling apart. You can tell on **Shoot Out The Lights**. Most records that detail the break-up of a relationship, like Marvin Gaye's *Here, My Dear* for example, tell one side of the story. Here, both parties provide an account. The results – on self-explanatory titles such as *The Wall Of Death*, *Don't Renege On Our Love* and *Did She Jump Or Was She Pushed?* – are mesmerizing, while Richard's fluid and emotional guitar fills (Thompson is as revered for his playing as for his songwriting) heighten the compellingly bleak atmosphere.

SHEET MUSIC

Show Some Emotion

ARTIST Joan Armatrading **RELEASE DATE** October 1977 (UK & US) **LABEL** A&M (UK & US) **PRODUCER** Glyn Johns **UK CHART** peak/weeks 6/11 **US CHART** peak/weeks 52/21 **TRACK LISTING** Woncha Come On Home/Show Some Emotion/Warm Love/Never Is Too Late/Peace In Mind/Opportunity/Mama Mercy/Get In The Sun/Willow/Kissin' And A Huggin' **PERSONNEL** Joan Armatrading (g, v), session musicians

One of the most durable female singer-songwriters, Armatrading capitalized on the attention caught by the exquisite *Love And Affection* and her previous, eponymous album, by penning tender, frail love songs which gained backbone from her solid, Nina Simone-influenced vocal style. *Warm Love* and, particularly, *Willow* were beautifully crafted and confidently delivered. Younger artists such as Tasmin Archer and Tracy Chapman hailed this quiet opus as a major inspiration.

Siamese Dream

ARTIST The Smashing Pumpkins **RELEASE DATE** July 1993 (UK & US) **LABEL** Hut (UK)/Virgin (US) **PRODUCER** Butch Vig, Billy Corgan **UK CHART** peak/weeks 4/12 **US CHART** peak/weeks 10/89 **TRACK LISTING** Cherub Rock/ Quiet/ Today/ Hummer/ Rocket/ Disarm/ Soma Geek U.S.A./ Mayonnaise/Spaceboy/Silverfuck/Sweet Sweet/Luna **PERSONNEL** Billy Corgan (v, g), James Iha (g), D'Arcy (b, v), Jimmy Chamberlin (d)

Smashing Pumpkins ably filled the position of Grunge Icons left by Nirvana after the suicide of Kurt Cobain. A year before his death, however, the Pumpkins were still a cult waiting to be discovered. Their debut album, **Gish** (1990), had been produced by Nirvana knob-twiddler, Butch Vig, and he was invited back for **Siamese Dream**. *Nevermind Pt 2* it was not, though. Using mellotron, cello and violin to add atmosphere to Billy Corgan's unique wail and the band's pop hooks, this was rock with extra texture.

Their success derives from the eyebrow-raising ability to thrill. **Siamese Dream** *is something of a white-knuckle, roller coaster ride, leavened by moments of sometimes quite staggering beauty. Highlights are many.... This is big music indeed; fine music, certainly.* **John Aizlewood, Q, August 1993**

Sign O' The Times

ARTIST Prince **RELEASE DATE** March 1987 (UK) **LABEL** Paisley Park (UK & US) **PRODUCER** Prince **UK CHART** peak/weeks 4/32 **US CHART** peak/weeks 6/54 **TRACK LISTING** Sign O' The Times/Play In The Sunshine/Housequake/The Ballad Of Dorothy Parker/It/Starfish And Coffee/Slow Love/Hot Thing/Forever My Love/U Got The Look/If I was Your Girlfriend/Strange Relationship/I Could Never Take The Place Of Your Man/The Cross/It's Gonna Be A Beautiful Night/Adore **PERSONNEL** Prince (v, g), Fink, Leeds & Shelia E., Mico Weaver (g), Boni Boyer (k), Levi Steacher Jr (b), Cat Glover (v)

For many, the finest album Prince ever released and one of the most important of the last two decades. As ever it kicks off with one of the strongest cuts (the stunning title track) which sets the scene early on. But Prince, always unpredictable and full of surprises, included a duet with Sheena Easton that makes the TV-manufactured former pop singer sound remarkably funky, an abundance of musical styles and some of Prince's funkiest workouts for a while.

Prince undoubtedly holds the moment in pop; he's young, sickeningly talented and very productive.... At times it seems like he needs a controlling or navigating force to expurgate and give forms to the ever increasing areas that he covers. **Gavin Martin, April 1987**

The Sign

ARTIST Ace of Base **RELEASE DATE** April 1994 (UK)/December 1993 (US) **LABEL** Arista Records (US) **PRODUCER** – UK CHART peak/weeks - US CHART peak/weeks 1/102 **TRACK LISTING** All That She Wants/Don't Turn Around/Young And Proud/The Sign/Living In Danger/Dancer In A Daydream/Wheel Of Fortune/Waiting For Magic/Happy Nation/Voulez-Vous Danser/My Mind/All That She Wants (Banghra Version) **PERSONNEL** Jenny Berggren (v), Linn Berggren (v), Jonas 'Joker' Berggren (k), Ulf 'Buddha' Ekberg (k), John Ballard (v)

Referred to as 'the Nineties Abba' so often it must have set their teeth on edge, the dopily named purveyors of nondescript Euro-disco were a curious anachronism. The lyrics to their worldwide breakthrough hit **All that she wants is another baby** hinted at a darker, more probing side – illusory, alas. Generic beats and melodies and healthy Aryan looks made them favourites in dance halls and radio stations. The album's title song and the cod-reggae 'Don't Turn Around' kept the momentum up and karaoke clubs in business.

Simple Dreams

ARTIST Linda Ronstadt **RELEASE DATE** October 1977 (UK)/September 1977 (US) **LABEL** Elektra (UK)/Asylum (US) **PRODUCER** Peter Asher **UK CHART** peak/weeks 39/2 **US CHART** peak/weeks 1/147 **TRACK LISTING** It's So Easy/Carmelita/Simple Man, Simple Dream/Sorrow Lives Here/I Never Will Marry/Blue Bayou/Poor Poor Pitiful Me/Maybe I'm Right/Tumbling Dice/Old Paint **PERSONNEL** Linda Ronstadt (v)

On her ninth studio release, Linda Ronstadt confirmed her status as the premier interpreter of contemporary popular song, covering an audacious selection of material by artists as diverse as Dolly Parton – a heartbreaking rendition of **I Never Will Marry**, The Rolling Stones – risking sacrilege by attempting **Tumbling Dice**, Roy Orbison – a strident **Blue Bayou**, and Warren Zevon – the country girl turns wild child for **Carmelita** and **Poor Poor Pitiful Me**.

Siren

ARTIST Roxy Music **RELEASE DATE** November 1975 (UK) **LABEL** Island (UK)/Atco (US) **PRODUCER** Chris Thomas **UK CHART** peak/weeks 4/17 **US CHART** peak/weeks 50/20 **TRACK LISTING** Love Is The Drug/End Of The Line/Sentimental Fool/Whirlwind/She Sells/Could It Happen To Me?/Both Ends Burning/Nightingale/Just Another High **PERSONNEL** Bryan Ferry (v, k), Andrew Mackay (s, ob), Paul Thompson (d), Phil Manzanera (g), Edwin Jobson (k, sy, st), John Gustafson (b)

With **Siren**, Roxy Music became a bona fide international attraction on the back of the European hit **Love Is The Drug**. As a result, Bryan Ferry evolved into the jet-set superstar he so perfectly parodied on those early Roxy albums. **Siren** was the sleekest Roxy album yet, replacing savagery with an instrumental smoothness, although on tracks such as **Sentimental Fool** the band were still allying cool Euro-art soundscapes to Ferry's weary-decadent persona.

Siren suggests few possible escape routes from the impasse in which Ferry and Roxy currently find themselves… As another Roxy album Siren *is fine. But who wants that?* **Neil Spencer, NME, October 1975**

Sister Lovers

ARTIST Big Star **RELEASE DATE** November 1987/1978 (US) **LABEL** Aura (UK)/P.V.C (US) **PRODUCER** Jim Dickinson **UK CHART** peak/weeks – **US CHART** peak/weeks 0/0 **TRACK LISTING** Kizza Me/Thank You Friends/Big Black Car/Jesus Christ/Femme Fatale/O' Dana/Holocaust/Kangeroo/Stroke It Noel/For You/You Can't Have Me/Take Care/Nature Boy/Till The End Of The Day/Dream Lover/Downs/Whole Lotta Shakin' Goin On **PERSONNEL** Chris Bell (g), Andy Hummel (b), Jody Stephens (d)

With Chris Bell gone to be the cosmos, this was unofficially an Alex Chilton solo album. More haunting and poignant than its rockier predecessors, its stand-outs, the oddly elegiac **Holocaust** and **Kangaroo**, have often been eulogized and covered. The album was recorded in 1974, but didn't gain a release for four years – little wonder the gifted Chilton went through periods of depression and inactivity. Still, its sad seductive nature and many subsequent re-issues and critical rehabilitation have served to foster one of rock lore's most deserving 'neglected genius' myths.

These songs are unnerving in the extreme, Alex's choirboy voice – fragile at the best of times – sounds permanently on the edge of tears. **Bob Stanley, NME, November 1987**

The Six Wives Of Henry VIII

ARTIST Rick Wakeman **RELEASE DATE** February 1973 (UK & US) **LABEL** A&M (UK & US) **PRODUCER** Rick Wakeman **UK CHART** peak/weeks 7/22 **US CHART** peak/weeks 30/45 **TRACK LISTING** Catherine of Aragon/Anne of Cleeves/Catherine Howard/Jane Seymour/Anne Boleyn/Catherine Parr **PERSONNEL** Rick Wakeman (k), Bill Bruford (d), Steve Howe (g), Chris Squire (b), session musicians and members of Yes

Rick Wakeman (born Middlesex, 1949) was a member of Yes, along with ELP the leading exponents of progressive-classical (or pomp) rock. Wakeman, the only rival to Keith Emerson's title as undisputed master of the mellotron, recorded his solo debut, **The Six Wives Of Henry VIII**, while he and Yes were making **Close To The Edge**. The music was supposedly suggested by the lives and characters of Henry VIII's many spouses, but these six examples of often beautiful and melodic, meandering keyboard wizardry could have been about anyone or anything.

'I spent ages on the album, but I wanted it to be something special because I know whatever I do is a reflection on Yes... took it to A&M frightened out of my life because it's a concept album which is keyboard-oriented, without being keyboards heavy.' **From an interview with Mark Plummer, Melody Maker, December 1972**

The Sky Is Crying

ARTIST Stevie Ray Vaughan **RELEASE DATE** November 1991 (UK & US) **LABEL** Epic (UK & US) **PRODUCER** Double Trouble, Tommy Shannon, Chris Layton, Stevie Ray Vaughan, Jimmy Vaughan **UK CHART** peak/weeks – **US CHART** peak/weeks 10/48 **TRACK LISTING** Boot Hill/The Sky Is Crying/Empty Arms/Little Wing/Wham/May I Have A Talk With You/Chitlins Con Carne/So Excited/Life By The Drop **PERSONNEL** Stevie (v, g), Tommy Shannon (b), Chris 'Whipper' Layton (d)

One of the finest latterday exponents of blues-rock guitar, Stevie Ray Vaughan came to prominence in 1983 when, after a performance at the Montreaux Jazz Festival, he was invited to play on David Bowie's **Let's Dance** album. **The Sky Is Crying** was actually released posthumously: after a period of addiction to cocaine and alcohol, Vaughan had kicked his habits, only to die in a helicopter crash, following an on-stage jam at a Wisconsin theatre with his hero Eric Clapton. Particular highlights of this set of tracks recorded between 1984 and 1989 include a faithful rendition of Jimi Hendrix's **Little Wing**.

In contrast with generations of blues-rock pretenders Vaughan was obviously the real thing, an artist committed to probing the deepest emotions... there's so much prescience, passion and heart in these performances that it's harder than ever to believe Stevie's gone. **Don McLeese, Rolling Stone, November 1991**

Slade Alive

ARTIST Slade **RELEASE DATE** April 1972 (UK & US) **LABEL** Polydor (UK)/Cotillion (US) **PRODUCER** Chas Chandler **UK CHART** peak/weeks 2/58 **US CHART** peak/weeks 158/11 **TRACK LISTING** Hear Me Calling/In like A Shot From My Gun/Darling Be Home Soon/Know Who You Are/Keep On Rocking/Get Down With It/Born To Be Wild **PERSONNEL** Noddy Holder (v, g), Dave Hill (lg, v), Jimmy Lea (b, v), Don Powell (d)

Having metamorphosed from skinheaded, braced and DM-wearing bootboys to eccentrically coiffed, garishly kitted-out glam icons, this four-piece from Wolverhampton became arguably the leading lights of the glitter era. Despite their increasingly bizarre garb, Slade never lost their knack for crowd-pleasing, singalong anthems with the sort of working-class appeal that Oasis, to name but one, would pick up on. **Slade Alive!** captures the band at their brilliantly boneheaded best.

Kick out the jams and shake your ass till it hurts to this long awaited live offering from Slade. They've come up with the most exciting live album since The Who made Leeds University the top college gig in the North. It's a non-stop session of meaty rock. **C. C., Melody Maker, March 1972**

The Slider

ARTIST T. Rex **RELEASE DATE** July 1972 (UK)/September 1972 (US) **LABEL** EMI (UK)/Reprise (US) **PRODUCER** Toni Visconti **UK CHART** peak/weeks 4/18 **US CHART** peak/weeks 17/24 **TRACK LISTING** Metal Guru/Mystic Lady/Rock On/The Slider/Baby Boomerang/Spaceball Ricochet/Buick MacKane/ Telegram Sam/Rabbit Fighter/Baby Strange/Ballrooms Of Mars/Chariot Choogle/Main Man **PERSONNEL** Marc Bolan (v, g), Steve Peregrine Took (bo, v)

On the back of two Number 1 singles, **Metal Guru** and **Telegram Sam**, **The Slider** sold 100,000 copies in four days, unleashing new levels of T.Rexstasy in Britain and, to a lesser extent, America, where it charted higher than any other T.Rex LP, reaching Number 17. Although Bolan's lyrics made as little sense as ever (*Spaceball Ricochet*, indeed), and despite the fact that the band's music displayed little progression from their trademark glitter boogie, **The Slider** is a defining artefact of the age.

T. Rex/Marc Bolan have cranked out... something so new as to be downright outrageous and scary and yet something so familiar, a hybrid of the Chuck Berry rock & raunch grafted to the most monolithic, surreal of Beatle orchestrations. **Stephen Davis, Rolling Stone, October 1972**

Slippery When Wet

ARTIST Bon Jovi **RELEASE DATE** September 1986 **LABEL** Vertigo (UK)/Mercury (US) **PRODUCER** Bruce Fairbairn **UK CHART** peak/weeks 6/109 **US CHART** peak/weeks 1/94 **TRACK LISTING** Let It Rock/You Give Love A Bad Name/Livin' On A Prayer/Social Disease/Wanted Dead Or Alive/Raise Your Hands/Without Love/I'd Die For You/Never Say Goodbye/Wild In The Streets **PERSONNEL** Jon Bon Jovi (v), Richie Sambora (g), David Bryan (k), Alec John Such (b), Tico Torres (d)

Fastening melody and hooks to the heavy metal format, Jon Bon Jovi and his New Jersey buddies shifted an implausible 17 million copies of this album. They rocked bad enough for the boys; they looked good enough for the girls. Tough but sensitive was the pitch. The high vocals could grate on your nerves, but in **Livin' On A Prayer** and **You Give Love A Bad Name** they showed a nice line in song structure and no shortage of guitar power.

... The Jovis hit the 230-date tour conveyor belt, Jon hit the steroids to keep going and they barrelled into the Nineties seemingly oblivious of the Reaganomical and cultural shifts around them. **Roger Morton, NME, April 1996**

Slow Dazzle

ARTIST John Cale **RELEASE DATE** April 1975 **LABEL** Island **PRODUCER** John Cale **UK CHART** peak/weeks – **US CHART** peak/weeks - **TRACK LISTING** Mr Wilson/Taking It All Away/Dirty Ass Rock 'N' Roll/Darling I Need You/Rollaroll/Heartbreak Hotel/Ski Patrol/I'm Not The Loving Kind/Guts/The Jeweller **PERSONNEL** John Cale (v, va, k, b, g), Eno (sy), Phill Manzanera (g), Archie Leggat (b), Fred Smith (d), Judy Nylon (v)

Cale initially perceived this as the second part of a trilogy (preceded by **Fear**, followed by **Helen Of Troy**). In *Dirtyass Rock 'n' Roll* he claimed to have seen the punk-rock revolution coming a mile off. There seems some justification for his declaration when you listen to the spooky, epic, and highly radical treatment of Elvis' *Heartbreak Hotel* contained herein. With its rough-edged, abstract approach and grandiose yet almost comic irreverence, it seems to call into question the purpose of Cale's guitar and piano arrangements, as does the album. Challenging, and often chilling.

… it's generally a collection of highly rhythmic, melodically direct and homogeneously organised songs, which aren't put under the constraint of Art… this is intelligent, attractive music… **M. W., Melody Maker, April 1975**

Slowhand

ARTIST Eric Clapton **RELEASE DATE** November 1977 (UK & US) **LABEL** RSO (UK & US) **PRODUCER** Glyn Johns **UK CHART** peak/weeks 23/13 **US CHART** peak/weeks 2/74 **TRACK LISTING** Cocaine/Wonderful Tonight/Lay Down Sally/Next Time You See Her/We're All The Way/The Core/May You Never/Mean Old Frisco/Peaches And Diesel **PERSONNEL** Eric Clapton (g, v), Dick Sims (k), Marcy Levy (v), Carl Raddle (b), Yvonne Elliman (v), George Terry (g), Jamie Oldaker (d, pc), Mel Collins (s)

Drawing on the strengths of J.J.Cale's *Cocaine*, Clapton returned to form, if also to easy listening, with an album whose title may or may not have inspired the sexual innuendo of The Pointer Sisters hit of the same name. Forsaking the star cameos of recent records (Bob Dylan, Ronnie Wood and Robbie Robertson had featured on his previous LP), Clapton kicked back and eked out a gentler groove, showcasing his song writing talents in the process. *Wonderful Tonight*, a romantic ballad with a simple yet telling lead motif, became a standard. **Mean Old Frisco** showed he could still trade licks with the best of them, though, to his evident pleasure, this was no longer his sole selling point.

Clapton has learned the lesson he's been striving for all these years. He is in touch with the horrible moral power and long suffering self-righteousness that is the essence of the blues. And that knowledge gives him the power to stand up and be himself. **John Swanson, Rolling Stone, December 1977**

Smiley Smile

ARTIST The Beach Boys **RELEASE DATE** November 1967/September 1967 (US) **LABEL** Capitol (UK)/Brother (US) **PRODUCER** The Beach Boys **UK CHART** peak/weeks 9/8 **US CHART** peak/weeks 41/21 **TRACK LISTING** Heroes And Villans/Vegetables/Fall Breaks And Back To Winter (W. Woodpecker Symphony)/She's Goin' Bald/Little Pad/Good Vibrations/With Me Tonight/ Wind Chimes/Gettin' Hungry/Wonderful/Whistle In **PERSONNEL** Brian Wilson (b, k, v), Mike Love (v), Carl Wilson (g, v), Al Jardine (g, v), Dennis Wilson (d, v)

After **Pet Sounds** Brian Wilson grew obsessive and sought to top even that masterpiece, despite a daily diet of paranoia and drugs. The pressure nixed the intended 'Smile' album, but some of the sessions made it on to this next best thing. Production was credited to the whole band. Still, album sales couldn't match their singles hits. **Good Vibrations**, which cost £50,000 to record, is generally regarded as the group's zenith, both creatively and commercially. *Heroes And Villains*, co-written by Wilson and Van Dyke Parks, was yet another lofty 'pocket symphony'.

… the record was really just an exercise in…um, well how does 'do-it-yourself acid casualty doo-wop' sound? **Smiley Smile**, *see, must still rate as about the all-time strangest album ever to be released by a major rock band.* **Nick Kent, NME, June 1975**

The Smiths

ARTIST The Smiths **RELEASE DATE** February 1984 (UK & US) **LABEL** Rough Trade (UK)/Sire (US) **PRODUCER** John Porter **UK CHART** peak/weeks 2/33 **US CHART** peak/weeks 150/11 **TRACK LISTING** Reel Around The Fountain/You've Got Everything Now/Miserable Lie/Pretty Girls Make Graves/The Hand That Rocks The Cradle/Still Ill/Hand In Glove/What Difference Does It Make?/I Don't Owe You Anything/Suffer Little Children/ **PERSONNEL** Morrisey (v), Johnny Marr (g, h, md), Andy Rourke (b), Mike Joyce (d)

With Johnny Marr's chiming Byrds-ian guitar and the Wildean wit of front-fop Stephen Patrick Morrissey, The Smiths were a blast of fresh air when they first appeared with the single, *Hand In Glove*, in summer 1983. On tracks such as *Miserable Lie* and *Still Ill*, Morrissey invented a persona that was unique in rock: not sexual, not bisexual, but asexual. Unlike, say, Mick Jagger, here was a boy who most definitely could not get satisfaction. Elevating miserabilism to new heights (depths?) as Marr created rich textures with his 12-string, The Smiths' debut album changed British rock for ever. The Stone Roses, Oasis, Suede – they all started here.

*The music on **The Smiths** is simple, guitar-dominated rock. No synthesizers. No fancy production. The only thing that stops it being ready for American radio is Morrissey's voice… an often droning monotone that can be irritating.* **James Henke, Rolling Stones, June 1984**

Snow Goose

ARTIST Camel **RELEASE DATE** July 1975 (UK & US) **LABEL** Decca (UK)/Janus (US) **PRODUCER** David Hitchcock **UK CHART peak/weeks** – **US CHART peak/weeks** 162/5 **TRACK LISTING** The great marsh-Rhayander-Rhayander goes to town-Sanctuary-Fritha-The snow goose-Friendship-Migration-Rhayander alone/Flight of the snow goose-Preparation-Dunkirk-Epitaph-Fritha alone-LaPrincess Perdue-The great marsh **PERSONNEL** Peter Bardens (k, v), Andy Latimer (v, g), Doug Ferguson (b), Andy Ward (d)

Seventies prog-rock ensemble Camel were initially hindered by confusion with Peter Frampton's band of the same name. Never averse to the epic, or epic solo, this was actually one of their sparser works, and such a success that they were soon performing alongside the London Symphony Orchestra. *Rhayader* was voted the highlight by their fans. This definitive 'concept album' was based on Paul Gallico's children's stories: Gallico wasn't impressed and sued for copyright infringement.

… now at last comes to light the idea that has gripped them for over a year, a musical suite inspired by a short but beautiful story of Paul Gallico's… they interpret with vigour the airy freedom and contentment of a wild creature… **C. W., Melody Maker, May 1975**

So

ARTIST Peter Gabriel **RELEASE DATE** May 1986 (UK & US) **LABEL** Virgin (UK)/Geffen (US) **PRODUCER** Peter Gabriel, Daniel Lanois **UK CHART peak/weeks** 1/76 **US CHART peak/weeks** 2/93 **TRACK LISTING** Red Rain/Sledgehammer/Don't Give Up/That Voice Again/In Your Eyes/Mercy Street/Big Time/We Do What Were Told. **PERSONNEL** Peter Gabriel (v, k), Tony Levin (b), Steve Hunter (g), Larry Fast (k), Jimmy Maelen (pc), Alan Schwartzberg (d), Robert Fripp (g); featuring musical guests Laurie Anderson, P. P. Arnold, Kate Bush, Stewart Copeland, Jim Kerr, Nile Rodgers, Richard Tee (p)

Anthemic, emotional, and with all the commitment we have come to expect, **So** confirmed Peter Gabriel as a star of truly international proportions. *Sledgehammer*, *Red Rain*, *Big Time* and the haunting *Don't Give Up* gave Gabriel his best run of success in the singles charts, accompanied as they were by some memorable videos. There is less reliance on ethnic forms here than on the preceding and following albums, but you will rarely find better musicianship, or more attention to detail, and the end result is both distinctive and compelling.

*Both **Red Rain** and **Mercy Street** find the artiste waxing devotional, the former via a thundering rhythm track and impassioned vocals, the latter cunningly assembled from an array of instrumental parts which are used to explore the implications of some overtly religious imagery.* **Adam Sweeting, Melody Maker, May 1986**

So Tonight That I Might See

ARTIST Mazzy Star **RELEASE DATE** October 1993 (UK & US) **LABEL** Capitol (UK & US) **PRODUCER** – **UK CHART peak/weeks** 68/1 **US CHART peak/weeks** 36/ **TRACK LISTING** Fade Into You/Bells Ring/Mary Of Silence/Five String Serenade/Blue Light/She' My Baby/Unreflected/Wasted/Into Dust/So Tonight That I Might See **PERSONNEL** Hope Sandoval (v, g), David Roback (g)

Mazzy Star arose from the ashes of Opal and girl duo Going Home, combining a dark-hued lyricism and droning, guitar-led psychedelia with elements of blues and folk. Capitol signed them after the 1990s She Hangs Brightly and this strong second LP followed. Highlights included *Six String Serenade* by Arthur Lee of Love fame – Roback was due to produce an abortive solo album – and the gorgeous *Fade Into You*, all acoustic and slide guitars with Hope's languorous voice, which became an unlikely US hit. The LP's sales soared and Lee even received a gold disc for his part in the duo's dizzy ascent.

The Soft Machine

ARTIST The Soft Machine **RELEASE DATE** December 1968 **LABEL** Probe **PRODUCER** Chas Chandler **UK CHART peak/weeks** - **US CHART peak/weeks** 16/9 **TRACK LISTING** Hope For Happiness/Joy For A Toy/Hope For Happiness (Reprise)/Why Am I So Short?/So Boot If At All/A Certain Kind/Save Yourself/Priscilla/Lullabye Letter/We Did It Again/Plus Belle Qu'Une Poubelle/Why Are We Sleeping/Box 25-4 Lid. **PERSONNEL** Mike Ratledge (k), David Allen (g), Kevin Ayers (b, v), Robert Wyatt (v, d)

Straight outta Canterbury they came, named after a William Burroughs novel, and featuring the uniquely whispery vocals of drummer Robert Wyatt before the accident that put him in a wheelchair for the rest of his life. Fusing rock, jazz and classical, Soft Machine were masters of the epic, multipartite composition, all free-form improvisation and complex structures. The debut album, **The Soft Machine**, recorded and mixed in New York, set the pattern for future releases, with Kevin Ayers' unorthodox approach to pop battling it out with keyboardist Mike Ratledge's avant harmonics.

Sold Out

ARTIST The Kingston Trio **RELEASE DATE** April 1960 (UK & US) **LABEL** Capitol (UK & US) **PRODUCER** – **UK CHART** peak/weeks – **US CHART** peak/weeks 1/73 **TRACK LISTING** El Matador/The Mountains O'Mourne/Don't Cry Katie/Medley: Tanga Tika and Toerau/With Her Head Tucked Underneath Her Arm/Carrier Pigeon/Bimini/Raspberries, Strawberries/Mangwani Mpulele/With You My Johnny/The Hunter/Farewell Adelita **PERSONNEL** Dave Guard, Nick Reynolds, Bob Shane

The bandwagon rolled on for the Kingston Trio when **Sold Out** was released in March 1960. Despite the fact this was their sixth album in two years, the American public's taste for the Trio's carefully crafted brand of close harmony singing and acoustic backing that passed for popular folk music nearly 40 years ago was undiminished. It was their third consecutive Number 1 album. A remarkably hardworking group who toured regularly and were particularly popular on the college circuit, they were a major live act and released several in-concert albums.

The Trio, surely a group who will be written into musical history, present a collection of numbers they have heard and enjoyed, and it is guaranteed so will thousands of their admirers. **Melody Maker, October 1959**

Solid Air

ARTIST John Martyn **RELEASE DATE** February 1973 (UK & US) **LABEL** Island (UK & US) **PRODUCER** Simon Nichol **UK CHART** peak/weeks – **US CHART** peak/weeks – **TRACK LISTING** Over The Hill/Don't Want To Know/I'd Rather Be The Devil/Go Down Easy/Dreams By The Sea/May You Never/The Man In The Station/Easy Blues/Solid Air. **PERSONNEL** John Martyn (v, ag, g, h, k), Danny Thompson (db), Richard Thompson (g), Dave Pegg (b), Neemoi Acqaye, Tristan Fry (pc), John 'Rabbit' Bundrick (k), Sue Draheim (vl)

Despite critical plaudits and albums produced by hip Midas Joe Boyd, by the early Seventies Scottish folkie John Martyn had still to reap major success. **Solid Air** brought together his key influences: from John Coltrane and Weather Report to the Celtic style of folk circuit veterans like Alex Campbell, and enduring tunes such as the title track dedicated to Nick Drake and the easy roll of **May You Never** later covered by Clapton. With some fine backing musicians and imbued by his wonderfully bluesy, smokey vocals, the album established Martyn as a first-class singer-songwriter.

'I'm much more interested,' he says *'in the sound and in tone than in agility and precision. Using my voice as tone is as important – perhaps more important – than singing. On the guitar I'd rather hear one note played with soul than a whole lot from which I personally can't discern much emotion.'* **From an interview with Chris Salewicz, NME, December 1977**

Some Girls

ARTIST The Rolling Stones **RELEASE DATE** June 1978 (UK & US) **LABEL** Rolling Stones (UK & US) **PRODUCER** Mick Jagger, Keith Richards **UK CHART** peak/weeks 2/25 **US CHART** peak/weeks 1/82 **TRACK LISTING** Miss You/When The Whip Comes Down/Just My Imagination/Some Girls/Lies/Far Away Eyes/Respectable/Before They make Me Run/Beast Of Burden/Shattered **PERSONNEL** Mick Jagger (v, h), Keith Richard (rg), Brian Jones (lg), Bill Wyman (b), Charlie Watts (d)

The Stones finally discovered a self-awareness beyond narcissism, cunningly opting out of the punk wars with the mysteriously likeable hash disco of **Miss You**. Mick Taylor had left and Ronnie Wood arrived: within seconds it seemed as if he had lived there his whole life (in his head, he had). **Before They Make Me Run** was one of Keith's more convincing vocals, and **Beast Of Burden** was an alarmingly beautiful song, both sensitive and vulnerable. **Far Away Eyes** was a dotty country pastiche, and there was even a tender take on The Temptations' **Just My Imagination**. In America **Some Girls** somehow became the best-selling Stones album at the time.

The Stones' attempt to stop what is a rot… this reversion to basics isn't entirely successful, either, though it certainly helps to create a healthier, brighter atmosphere than was to be found on… **Black and Blue. Chris Brazier, Melody Maker, June 1978**

Something Anything?

ARTIST Todd Rundgren **RELEASE DATE** February 1972 (UK & US) **LABEL** Bearsville (UK & US) **PRODUCER** Todd Rundgren **UK CHART** peak/weeks – **US CHART** peak/weeks 29/48 **TRACK LISTING** I Saw The Light/It Wouldn't Have Made Any Difference/Wolfman Jack/Cold Morning Light/It Takes Two To Tango (This Is For The Girls)/Sweeter Memories/Breathless/The Night The Carousel Burnt Down/Saving Grace/Marlene/Song Of The Viking/I Went To The Mirror/Black Maria/One More Day (No Word)/Couldn't I Just Tell You/Torch Song/Little Red Lights/'Baby Needs A New Pair Of Snakeskin Boots'/Overture – My Roots/Dust In The Wind/Piss Aaron/Hello. It's Me/Some Folks Is Even Whiter Than Me/You Left Me Sore **PERSONNEL** Todd Rundgren (v), session musicians

For his third solo album, and first double, virtuoso whiz-kid Rundgren produced, arranged, engineered, wrote and played all the instruments on three of the four sides, while the fourth, a 'mini-operetta', featured guest musicians. The artist's only gold-selling

LP, **Something Anything?** was a phenomenal set that showed how accomplished the artist formerly known as Runt was, in areas as diverse as Motown pastiche, Philly soul, power pop, heavy metal, guitar pyrotechnics and synthesized noise.

Todd Rundgren is going to be big.... He's absorbed just about every popular music influence of the past decade, chewed it over, distilled and digested it and the result can be heard on this double set, his third album but only his first released here. **G. B., Melody Maker, April 1972**

Something Else

ARTIST The Kinks RELEASE DATE March 1968 (UK & US) LABEL Pye (UK)/Reprise (US) PRODUCER The Kinks UK CHART peak/weeks – US CHART peak/weeks 153/2 TRACK LISTING David Watts/Death Of A Clown/Two Sisters/No Return/Harry Rag/ Tin Soldier Man\Situation Vacant/Love Me Till The Sun Shines/Lazy Old Sun/Afternoon Tea/Funny Face/End Of The Season/Waterloo Sunset PERSONNEL Ray Davies (v, g), Dave Davies (g, v), Peter Quaife (b), with session drummers

If **Face To Face** marked the beginning of Ray Davies' preoccupation with Englishness, the following year's **Something Else** concerned itself with little else. As many of his contemporaries immersed themselves in psychedelia, Davies rejected studio trickery and relied instead on his talents as a songwriter. The result is a masterpiece, a series of eloquent observations that reaches its zenith with the superb *Waterloo Sunset*, but which also includes the original version of the Jam hit *David Watts* and a rare Dave Davies composition, *Death Of A Clown*.

Comic lunacy by the brothers Davies, Pete Quaife and Mick Avory, mixed with pathos and gentle understanding into a gallery of brilliant musical portraits... the material Ray Davies feeds them reveals a depth of thought that commands respect. **Melody Maker, September 1967**

Something For Everybody

ARTIST Elvis Presley RELEASE DATE July 1961 (UK & US) LABEL RCA Victor (UK & US) PRODUCER – UK CHART peak/weeks 2/- US CHART peak/weeks 1/25 TRACK LISTING There's Always Me/Give Me The Right/It's A Sin/Sentimental Me/Starting Today/Gently/I'm Comin Home/In Your Arms/Put The Blame On Me/Judy/I Want You With Me/I Slipped, I Stumbled, I Fell PERSONNEL Elvis Presley (v, g), The Jordanaires (v), session musicians

The title is revealing: ordinarily, the album release of 1961 would have been the soundtrack of *Wild In The Country*, pairing Elvis with Tuesday Weld, but the film was conceived as that rarity: an Elvis movie without songs. That idea was quickly discarded, but no soundtrack record could be made with just four numbers. One, *I Slipped, I Stumbled, I Fell*, made it on to this album, which nevertheless topped the US chart some three months later.

Songs For Swingin' Lovers!

ARTIST Frank Sinatra RELEASE DATE November 1958 (UK)/October 1955 (US) LABEL Capitol (UK)/Mobile Fidelity (US) PRODUCER Voyle Gilmore UK CHART peak/weeks – US CHART peak/weeks 2/50 TRACK LISTING You Make Me Feel So Young/It Happened In Monterey/You're Getting To Be A Habit With Me/You Brought A New Kind Of Love To Me/Too Marvelous For Words/I've Got You Under My Skin/I Thought About You/Old Devil Moon/Pennies From Heaven/Love Is Here To Stay/We'll Be Together Again/Makin' Whoopee/Swingin' Down The Lane/Anything Goes/How About You? PERSONNEL Frank Sinatra (v), orchestra arranged and conducted by Nelson Riddle

Sinatra's Fifties albums for Capitol veered between collections of saloon bar crooning and sophisticated swing tunes, and **Songs For Swingin' Lovers!** is the best known of the latter. Conducted by Nelson Riddle, songs such as *Pennies From Heaven*, *Anything Goes* and *I've Got You Under My Skin* aren't just standards, they are paradigms of the form.

Songs From The Big Chair

ARTIST Tears For Fears RELEASE DATE March 1985 (UK & US) LABEL Mercury (UK & US) PRODUCER Chris Hughes UK CHART peak/weeks 2/81 US CHART peak/weeks 1/83 TRACK LISTING Shout/The Working Hour/Everybody Wants To Rule The World/Mothers Talk/I Believe/Broken/Head Over Heels/Listen PERSONNEL Roland Orzabal (v, g), Curt Smith (v, b), John Baker (v, g), Steve Buck (k, fl), Andy Marsden (d)

Tears For Fears were a teen-zine friendly duo from Bath who peddled angst and alienation yet made it palatable to the *Smash Hits* generation. Taking their name from Arhur Janov's book on primal scream therapy, TFF enjoyed immediate success with the synthesized gloom of **Mad World** and **Pale Shelter**. Three years later, **Songs From The Big Chair** evinced a more mature Curt Smith and Roland Orzabal. The anthemic **Shout** and the layered arrangements of the lush, inspirational **Everybody Wants To Rule The World** became massive worldwide hits, and helped the album sell eight million copies.

This is the band that drowns you in buttermilk jets and gobbets of it, pouring in via repetitious sax fills, gluggy-arty vocals and buckets of bad memories of pomp rock throughout the years. **Rolling Stone, December 1985**

Songs In The Key Of Life

ARTIST Stevie Wonder **RELEASE DATE** October 1976 (UK)/September 1976 (US) **LABEL** Tamla Motown (UK)/Motown (US) **PRODUCER** Stevie Wonder **UK CHART** peak/weeks 2/54 **US CHART** peak/weeks 1/80 **TRACK LISTING** Love's In Need Of Love Today/Have A Talk With God/Village Ghetto Land/Confusion/Sir Duke/I Wish/Knocks Me Off My Feet/Pastime Paradise/Summer Soft/Ordinary Pain/Isn't She Lovely/Joy Inside My Tears/Black Man/Ngiculela - Es Una Historia- I Am Singing/If It's Magic/As/Another Star **PERSONNEL** Stevie Wonder (v)

A *tour de force*, **Songs In The Key Of Life** was a sprawling double album set, plus a four-song EP, that displayed a bewildering array of styles, even for the musically promiscuous Wonder. The singles, from the joyously jazzy Ellington celebration *Sir Duke* to the delightful though slightly mawkish tribute to a newborn child, *Isn't She Lovely*, continued Wonder's unbroken run of hits. As for the rest of the LP, it sounds like an index of possibilities for today's musicians, black or white – in fact, in 1995 rapper Coolio took *Pastime Paradise* and turned it into the multi-million selling *Gangsta's Paradise*.

My immediate impression of **Songs In The Key Of Life** *is that the album has none of the pinched, over-wrought, over-refined quality one might expect from material that's been coddled and polished over a period of two years.* **Vince Aletti, Rolling Stone, December 1976**

Songs Of Faith And Destruction

ARTIST Depeche Mode **RELEASE DATE** April 1994 (UK & US) **LABEL** Mute (UK)/Sire (US) **PRODUCER** Depeche Mode, Flood **UK CHART** peak/weeks 1/13 **US CHART** peak/weeks 1/29 **TRACK LISTING** I Feel You/Walking In My Shoes/Condemnation/Mercy In You/Judas/In Your Room/Get Right With Me/Rush/One Caress/Higher Love **PERSONNEL** Bazil Meade (v), Hilda Cambell (v), Samantha Smith (v)

From Basildon to *Billboard*, the Mode confounded the critics by vaulting back to the top after a three-year break, converting their cult following to a US Number 1 thanks to a heavy metal first single *I Feel You*. Gospel choirs and strings also made appearances

as the band deliberately rang the changes, intent on not duplicating their previous peak, 1990's **Violator**. In doing so and sacrificing their keyboard-based sound of old they broadened their appeal, even though radio shunned the result. Alternative was in, and the Essex boys were alternative.

The album drips with the wine and wafer of religious conceit in the services of rumpy-pumpy… the old Mode martial electronic style is only used on **Rush***… For the rest, this constitutes a resolute continuation of the mature experimental pop principles of* **Violator***…* **Andy Gill, Q, April 1993**

The Songs Of Leonard Cohen

ARTIST Leonard Cohen **RELEASE DATE** March 1968 (UK & US) **LABEL** CBS (UK)/Columbia (US) **PRODUCER** John Simon **UK CHART** peak/weeks 13/17 **US CHART** peak/weeks 83/14 **TRACK LISTING** Suzanne\Master Song\Winter Lady/The Stranger Song/Sisters Of Mercy/So Long, Marianne/Hey, That's No Way To Say Goodbye/Stories Of The Street/Teachers/One Of Us Cannot Be Wrong **PERSONNEL** Leonard Cohen (v, g), session musicians

Perhaps THE despairing Sixties singer/songwriter of choice, Cohen, a Canadian, had first enjoyed, or experienced, success as a poet and novelist. This accounted for his debut album's strong emphasis on lyrical content, and for the 1966 novel *Beautiful Losers*. Arriving on the back of a memorable 1967 *Newport Folk Festival* show, his romantic, quasi-religious imagery and mumbled lack of vocal technique made him a durable cult. Much of this album was used on the soundtrack of Robert Altman's *McCabe And Mrs. Miller*. **Sisters Of Mercy** and **So Long Marianne** have influenced many other artists.

Soro

ARTIST Salif Keita **RELEASE DATE** December 1987 **LABEL** Island (UK)/Mango (US) **PRODUCER** Ibrahim Silla, Francois Breant **UK CHART** peak/weeks 0/0 **US CHART** peak/weeks 0/0 **TRACK LISTING** Wamba/Soro (Afriki)/Souareba/Sina (Soumbouya)/Cono/Sanni Kegniba **PERSONNEL** Salif Keita (v), Ousmane Kouyate (g), session musicians

Named after a talisman designed to protect a house from evil spirits, **Soro** was Malian Salif Keita's first album for three years since moving to Paris and, issued by Stern's, brought his unique high-pitched vocal style to a whole new audience. His band was a supergroup from Cameroon and the Antilles and this, combined with 48-track studio technology, made for a classic that set a new standard and inspired imitators like Kasse Mady. It earned Keita a recording contract with Island's Mango subsidiary.

The word 'classic' is prone to wild misuse, but here is one occasion when it can be confidently applied…. Both as a personal achievement and a boost for African and 'world' music, **Soro** *represents a significant step forward.* **Chris Stapleton, Q, October 1987**

The Soul Album

ARTIST Otis Redding **RELEASE DATE** July 1966 (UK) April 1966 (US) **LABEL** Atlantic (UK)/Volt (US) **PRODUCER** – **UK CHART** peak/weeks 22/9 **US CHART** peak/weeks 54/29 **TRACK LISTING** Just One More Day/It's Grooving/Cigarettes And Coffee/Chain Gang/Nobody Knows You (When You're Down And Out)/Good To Me/Baby Scratch My Back/Treat Her Right/Everybody Makes A Mistake/Any Ole Way/634-5789 **PERSONNEL** Otis Redding (v), session musicians

Whether it is Sam Cooke's perennial favourite *Chain Gang*, or *Cigarettes And Coffee* or *Nobody Knows You (When You're Down and Out)*, everything on this album was given the five-star Otis treatment, ably supported by the cast of hundreds at Stax.

There is also one major reason why Otis attained such heights, for while many of the star performers at Motown were despatched to Las Vegas and made to record cabaret standards, Otis never lost sight of his audience and their needs.

Redding's voice seems to have lost a little of it's conviction – which came over so well on **Otis Blue**... *a good record, but the material is slightly dull and both Redding and his sidemen obviously need more jumping sounds to get working on.* **Melody Maker, August 1966**

Soul Dressing

ARTIST Booker T. & The MG's RELEASE DATE March 1964 LABEL Stax PRODUCER – UK CHART peak/weeks - US CHART peak/weeks 0/0 TRACK LISTING Soul Dressing/Tic-Tac-Toe/Big Train/Jellybread/Aw' Mercy/ Outrage/Night Owl Walk/Chinese Checkers/Home Grown/Mercy Mercy/ Plum Nellie/Can't Be Still PERSONNEL Booker T. Jones (k), Steve Crooper (g), Lewis Steinberg (b), Donald 'Duck' Dunn (b), Al Jackson Jr (d)

As backing band for Otis Redding and many of Stax's soul legends, Booker's boys honed their unshowy art. To many their musicianship, the essence of Memphis soul, affirms the truth of the adage 'less is more'. This second album, which followed **Green Onions**, was tight, efficient and razor-sharp. The rhythm guitar technique of Steve Cropper was the very antithesis of the era's masturbatory doodling, while bassist Dunn and drummer Jackson each invariably featured in any poll of all-time best. If anything, Booker's organ flourishes threatened the cool, jerk-free economy.

It certainly has a lot more fire than its predecessor, and if you haven't already got it, go and get a copy right now.... The rhythm section never fails to swing and it's a too much album. **Melody Maker, January 1967**

The Soul Of A Bell

ARTIST William Bell RELEASE DATE 1967 LABEL Stax Records PRODUCER – UK CHART peak/weeks – US CHART peak/weeks 0/0 TRACK LISTING Everybody Loves A Winner/You Don't Miss Your Water/Do Right Man/I've Been Loving You Too Long (To Stop Now)/Nothing Takes The Place Of You/Then You Can Tell Me Goodbye/Eloise (Hang On In There)/Any Other Way/It's Happening All Over/Never Like This Before/You're Such A Sweet Thang PERSONNEL William Bell, Booker T. Jones

One of the mainstays of legendary soul label Stax Records, Bell's subtle vocals never fell into histrionics or over emoting. This may be why he has never been granted the acclaim of other soul giants, but it has also been responsible for some beautifully expressive, slow-burning music. Born in Memphis, he embraced elements of country and gospel. His debut album included **You Don't Miss Your Water**, which many consider a *genre*-defining classic, and which The Byrds covered on **Sweetheart Of The Rodeo** The ascendancy of the more forthright Otis Redding hindered his progress, but a decade later Bell, who often co-wrote with Booker T., hit a million seller with *Trying To Love Two*.

Sound Effects

ARTIST Jam RELEASE DATE December 1980 (UK)/November 1980 (US) LABEL Polydor (UK & US) PRODUCER Vic Coppersmith-Heaven. the Jam UK CHART peak/weeks 2/19 US CHART peak/weeks 72/11 TRACK LISTING Pretty Green/Monday/But I'm Different Now/Set The House Ablaze/Start!/That's Entertainment/Dream Time/Man In The Corner Shop/Music For The Last Couple/Boy About Town/Scrape Away PERSONNEL Paul Weller (v, g), Bruce Foxton (b), Rick Buckler (d)

After reaching Numbers 6 and 4, another chart-topping performance by band and fans had been anticipated for the Jam's fifth album, but Abba's **Super Trouper** barred the way. Though as

far from Eurovision fodder as you could get, the album was stunningly eclectic, and would finish top of music press readers' polls for 1981. Brass bolstered **Boy About Town** while the acoustic **That's Entertainment** charted as an import single, having not been considered commercial enough for UK release. That's how good this was.

[Weller] has proved his ability at articulating the frustrations which form a sad foundation for this society.... It's an album notably clear of self indulgence with Weller's integrity coming across as fervently as **Auld Lang Syne** *in Trafalgar Square on New Year's Eve.* **Patrick Humphries, Melody Maker, November 1980**

Southern Accents

ARTIST Tom Petty & The Heartbreakers RELEASE DATE April 1985 (UK & US) LABEL MCA Records (UK)/Backstreet (US) PRODUCER Tom Petty, Jimmy Iovine, Mike Campbell, David A. Stewart, Robbie Robertson UK CHART peak/weeks 23/6 US CHART peak/weeks 7/32 TRACK LISTING Rebels/It Ain't Nothin' To Me/Don't Come Around Here No More/Southern Accents/ Make It Better (Forget About Me)/Spike/Dogs On The Run/Mary's New Car/The Best Of Everything PERSONNEL Tom Petty (v, g), Mike Campbell (g), Howard Epstein (b), Benmont Tench (k), Stan Lynch (d)

Eight years on from his first album with the Heartbreakers, Petty varied the formula with guest musicians and producers including Eurythmics' Dave Stewart and ex-Band guitarist Robbie Robertson. UK chart success, sporadic at best, was still not improved despite the vogueish Stewart's involvement, but the video for the Stewart co-penned **Don't Come Around Here No More** (an Alice in Wonderland fantasy) won an MTV award. After a live album, Petty's desire to experiment would see him join the Wilburys, then go solo.

Sure, this Confederate flag business is a bit dubious... but the sheer sonic crunch, slap and tickle of Tom Petty singing over his Heartbreakers covers a host of thematic sins. **The Year In Records 1985, Rolling Stone, December 1985**

The Southern Harmony And Musical Companion

ARTIST Black Crowes RELEASE DATE May 1992 (UK)/March 1990 (US) LABEL Def America (UK & US) PRODUCER Black Crowes, George Drakoulias UK CHART peak/weeks 2/7 US CHART peak/weeks 4/165 TRACK LISTING Sting Me/Remedy/Thorn In My Pride/Bad Luck Blue Eyes Goodbye/Sometime Salvation/Hotel Illness/Black Moon Creeping/No Speak, No Slave/My Morning Song/Time Will Tell PERSONNEL Chris Robinson (v), Rich Robinson (g), Jeff Cease (g), Johnny Colt (b), Steve Gorman (d)

Atlanta, Georgia rockers the Black Crowes lived and breathed old-school rock 'n' roll, idolizing bands like the Stones, Faces and Free, and emulating them in look, sound and 'rebel' attitude. Endless touring schedules and the gritty debut *Shake Your Money Maker* saw them gain snowballing success in America. Their retro rumblings were second nature to them by the time this album emerged, which was recorded in 10 days between gigs. This was long enough to employ gospel backing vocalists, trot through Bob Marley's *Time Will Tell*, and swagger impressively through their own numbers like *Hotel Illness* and *Remedy*, where Chris Robinson sang with derivative but emotive blues conviction.

A mixture of God-fearing gospel, bare-knuckled blues and solid tried and tested rock 'n' roll blues that brings to mind such masterworks as Big Star's Sister Lovers *and the Stones'* Exile On Main Street! **Edwin Pounce, NME, May 1992**

Specials

ARTIST The Specials RELEASE DATE November 1979 (UK & US) LABEL 2-Tone-Chrysalis (UK)/Chrysalis (US) PRODUCER Elvis Costello UK CHART peak/weeks 4/45 US CHART peak/weeks 84/21 TRACK LISTING A Message To You Rudy/Do The Dog/It's Up To You/Nite Club/Doesn't Make It Alright/Concrete Jungle/Too Hot/Monkey Man/(Dawning Of A) New Era/Blank Expression/Stupid Marriage/Too Much Too Young/Little Bitch/You're Wondering Now PERSONNEL Jerry Dammers (k), Terry Hall (v), Neville Staples (v, p), Lynval Golding (g), Roddy Radiation (g), Sir Horace Gentleman (b), John Bradbury (d)

Produced by Elvis Costello, **Specials** was a high point of Britain's 2-Tone scene: a rough mixture of punk energy, ska rhythms and socially conscious lyrics. A multi-ethnic conglomerate that embodied the punky-reggae party ethos of the late Seventies, The Specials were led by ideas man Jerry Dammers and featured Terry Hall on sardonic lead vocals, with assistance from Neville Staples and Lynval Golding (the latter three went on to form the successful Fun Boy Three). The Specials' debut album includes the hits, *Gangsters* and *A Message To You, Rudy*.

Spice

ARTIST Spice Girls RELEASE DATE 1996 (UK & US) LABEL Virgin (UK & US) PRODUCER Andy Bradfield, Richard Stannard, Matt Rowe, Absolute UK CHART peak/weeks – US CHART peak/weeks – TRACK LISTING Wannabe/Say You'll Be There/2 Become 1/Love Thing/Last Time Lover/Mama/Who Do You Think You Are/Something Kinda Funny/If You Can't Dance PERSONNEL Emma (v), Geri (v), Mel B. (v), Mel C. (v), Victoria (v), session musicians

Spice is a veritable trove of Number 1 hits: *Wannabe, Say You'll Be There, 2 Become 1*, the double A-side *Mama/Who Do You Think You Are...* Not bad for a debut. The rest is hardly filler, either, from the sassy New Jill Swing of *Love Thing* to the slick Eighties groove of *Last Time Lover* to the Chic-inspired *Something Kinda Funny*. A bunch of five typical girls next door, Spice Girls were also probably the most significant UK export to the US market since The Beatles.

Spice Girls with their crayon simple Girl power self sufficiency ('Don't wanna know about that love thing'), are infinitely more useful than anything to come out of the indie sector... **Simon Price, Melody Maker, November 1996**

The Spinners

ARTIST The Spinners RELEASE DATE July 1973 LABEL Atlantic Records (UK & US) PRODUCER Thom Bell UK CHART peak/weeks – US CHART peak/weeks 14/28 TRACK LISTING Just Can't Get You Out Of My Mind/Just You & Me Baby/Don't Let The Green Grass Fool You/I Could Never (Repay Your Love)/I'll Be Around/One Of A Kind/We Belong Together/Ghetto Child/How Could I Let You Get Away/Could It Be I'm Falling In Love PERSONNEL Bill Henderson, Bob Smith (v), Bob Babbit, Ronald Baker (b), Leroy Bell, Bobby 'Electronic' El, Ronald Chambers (g), Andrew Smith, Earl Young (d), session musicians

Philly soul giants the Spinners (always known as Detroit Spinners in the UK) had been recording for 10 years before they released their first great LP. Produced, arranged and conducted by Thom Bell, whose multi-layered symphonic approach to soul marks him out as the black Bacharach, **The Spinners** contains four singles: *I'll Be Around, One Of A Kind [Love Affair], Could It Be I'm Falling In Love* and *Ghetto Child* which have gone on to achieve classic status. With its generous share of material by Bell and Linda Creed (responsible for many of the Stylistics' hits), and Phillipe Wynne's conversational tenor, **The Spinners** is a superb collection

of dance tunes and ballads.

The Spinners don't scream and moan… their style is more reminiscent of the Fifties' crooners than the graceful pyrotechnics of Aretha Franklin. Yet in the past year they have been involved in some emotionally powerful and delicate pop music. **Russell Gersten, May 1973**

Spirit Of Eden

ARTIST Talk Talk **RELEASE DATE** September 1988 (UK) **LABEL** Parlophone (UK)/EMI America (US) **PRODUCER** Mark Hollis, Tim Friese-Greene **UK CHART** peak/weeks 8/21 **US CHART** peak/weeks 0/0 **TRACK LISTING** The Rainbow/Eden/Desire/Inheritance/I Believe In You/Wealth **PERSONNEL** Mark Hollis (v, p, g), Simon Bremner (k), Paul Webb (b, v), Lee Harris (d), session musicians

Talk Talk effected one of the most dramatic musical changes in recent times after turning their back on the concise melodics of their first incarnation – riding on the coat-tails of the New Romantic movement – and becoming arch experimentalists instead. **Spirit Of Eden** is more like an ambient suite than an album of pop songs, the six tracks flowing from one to the next with nary a thought for the pop market place. Recorded in a disused church, **Spirit Of Eden** is appropriately sepulchral in tone, bearing the influence of Eno's mid Seventies soundscapes, or even Miles Davis' **A Kind Of Blue.**

Spirit of Eden is a call and a bid to return to nature…. It's organic and feels wholesome and its purity is more of a political statement than Hollis probably knows because … it's an act against the artificial contradictions pop willingly and lazily imposes upon itself. **Steve Sutherland, Melody Maker, September 1988**

Spirits Having Flown

ARTIST Bee Gees **RELEASE DATE** February 1979 (UK & US) **LABEL** RSO (UK & US) **PRODUCER** Bee Gees, Karl Richardson, Albhy Galuten **UK CHART** peak/weeks 1/33 **US CHART** peak/weeks 1/55 **TRACK LISTING** Search, Find/Stop (Think Again)/Living Together/I'm Satisfied/Until/Tragedy/Too Much Heaven/Love You Inside Out/Reaching Out/Spirits (Having Flown)/Until. **PERSONNEL** Barry Gibb (g, v), Robin Gibb (v), Maurice Gibb (b, v), the Bee Gees Band: Dennis Bryon (d), Blue Weaver (p, sy), Alan Kendall (g), guest musicians: Gary Brown (s), Harold Cowart (b), Joe Lala (pc), Herbie Mann (fl), George Terry (g), Daniel Ben Zebulon (pc), Boneroo and Chicago Horns

Following up the **Saturday Night Fever** monster with aplomb and common sense, the Gibb brothers laced the kitsch dance grooves with genuine emotion. *Tragedy* was the instant number one, but *Too Much Heaven* has survived as a classic ballad. Conventional wisdom has the Bee Gees down as a camp circus act to be fondly endured: in reality, they have written more blindingly moving songs over the years than most more credible heroes. One day they will be duly canonized.

… the Bee Gees did what they had to do and put out more songs in **Fever** *vein, with somewhat advanced musical and lyrical content. Give this to anybody: Mom, Pop, brother, lover, teacher, insurance salesman – a safe bet and a satisfying one.* **Jann Wenner, Rolling Stones, December 1979**

Spooky

ARTIST Lush **RELEASE DATE** Febuary 1992 (UK) **LABEL** 4ad (UK)/4ad-Reprise (US) **PRODUCER** – **UK CHART** peak/weeks 7/3 **US CHART** peak/weeks - **TRACK LISTING** Stray/Nothing Natural/Tiny Smiles/Covert/Ocean/For Love/Superblast/Untogether/Fantasy/Take/Laura/Monochrome. **PERSONNEL** Miki Berenyi (v, g), Emma Anderson (g, v), Steve Rippon (b), Chris Acland (d)

Band name and album title are completely appropriate. **Spooky** is a journey into the subconscious minds of Miki and Emma, the group's main songwriters. Combining textured arrangements, intense structures and evocative vocal performances, it managed neatly to avoid the cod-Celt territory of Clannad or Enya and the crassness of goth. **Spooky** is an able demonstration of Lush's unique vision and masterful grasp of instrumentation. Unfortunately, the sound never connected with a mainstream market, prompting their change to a more commercial Brit-pop sound.

…their debut is not the much-anticipated box of musical fireworks…. One-dimensional to an irritatingly conformist degree, Lush's antiseptic, ethereal earbath is an unfathomably fashionable Nineties throwback to the prissy world of cobwebbed prog-rockers like Renaissance. **Paul Davies, Q, February 1992**

Sports

ARTIST Huey Lewis & The News **RELEASE DATE** September 1983 **LABEL** Chrysalis (UK & US) **PRODUCER** Huey Lewis And The News **UK CHART** peak/weeks 23/24 **US CHART** peak/weeks 1/158 **TRACK LISTING** The Heart Of Rock & Roll/Heart And Soul/Bad Is Bad/I Want A New Drug/Walking On A Thin Line/Finally Found A Home/If This Is It/You Crack Me Up/Honky Tonk Blues **PERSONNEL** Huey Lewis (v, h), Mario Cipollina (b), Johnny Colla (v, s, g), Bill Gibson (d, v, p), Chris Hayes (lg, v), Sean Hopper (k, v)

Until **Sports**, Huey Lewis was best known for fronting country-rock cult band Clover, who had backed Elvis Costello on his first album… while Lewis was on holiday! 1984 was the year for him to reap the rewards, his band teaming synthesizers and drum machines with rockabilly guitars and blues harmonica to create a strangely satisfying mix. *I Want A New Drug*, with its sequenced bass, was later ruled to have inspired Ray Parker Jr's *Ghostbusters* theme and a settlement reached, but the doo-wop harmonies of *If This Is It*, another of five hit singles, was arguably more impressive.

Huey Lewis sailed right up the pop mainstream this year, buoyed by a few all-purpose rock ditties… it may seem mean-spirited to dismiss them as MTV fodder. **Kurt Loder, Rolling Stone, December 1984**

Squeezing Out Sparks

ARTIST Graham Parker **RELEASE DATE** April 1979 (UK)/March 1979 (US) **LABEL** Vertigo (UK)/Arista (US) **PRODUCER** Jack Nitzsche **UK CHART** peak/weeks 18/8 **US CHART** peak/weeks 40/24 **TRACK LISTING** Discovering Japan/Local Girls/Nobody Hurts You/You Can't Be Too Strong/Passion Is No Ordinary Word/Saturday Nite Is Dead/Love Gets You Twisted/Protection/Waiting For The UFOs/Don't Get Excited **PERSONNEL** Graham Parker (v, rg), Brinsley Schwarz (g, bv), Martin Belmont (rg, bv), Bob Andrews (k, bv), Steve Goulding (d, bv), Andrew Bodnar (b)

Parker was considered by many to be a British Dylan wannabe – but he was far from disgraced in 1979 when he appeared on the same bill as the master at Blackbushe Airport in England. The same year saw his US Top 40 debut with this album, having dubbed himself 'The best-kept secret in the west'. No longer, as stunning songs like *Discovering Japan* put him beyond comparisons. As his star faded in Britain he made the US his home: this album was the key.

Stand By Your Man

ARTIST Tammy Wynette **RELEASE DATE** 1968 (US) **LABEL** Epic (UK & US) **PRODUCER** Billy Sherrill, Barry Feldman **UK CHART** peak/weeks 13/7 **US CHART** peak/weeks 43/21 **TRACK LISTING** Stand By Your Man/It's My Way/Forever Yours/I Stand Enough/It Keeps Slipping My Mind/My Arms Stay Open Late/I've Learned/Cry, Cry Again/Joey/If I Were A Little Girl/Don't Make Me Go To School. **PERSONNEL** Tammy Wynette (v, g), session musicians

The self-styled First Lady of Country, Tammy Wynette enjoyed 17 country Number 1s between 1967 and 1979, the most famous of which, **Stand By Your Man**, became the biggest selling single ever by a female country singer and remains a *genre* archetype. The album contained a slew of lovelorn melodramas that displayed Wynette's contradictory tough-yet-conciliatory persona.

'She has the rare ability to charge a lyric with meaning, to create some personal statement even from weepies which would doubtless make most people wince.' **From interview by Robert Partridge, Melody Maker, April 1975**

Stand!

ARTIST Sly And The Family Stone **RELEASE DATE** June 1969 (UK)/April 1969 (US) **LABEL** Direction (UK)/Epic (US) **PRODUCER** Sly Stone **UK CHART** peak/weeks – **US CHART** peak/weeks 13/102 **TRACK LISTING** Stand!/Don't Call Me Nigger, Whitey/I Want To Take You Higher/Somebody's Watching You/Sing A Simple Song/Everyday People/Sex Machine/You Can Make It If You Try **PERSONNEL** Sly Stone (v, k, g), Freddie Stone (g), Cynthia Robinson (t), Jerry Martini (s), Rosemary Stone (v, p), Larry Graham (b), Greg Errico (d)

Without Sly And The Family Stone, there would have been no Prince, black pop would have been less colourful and experimental, and rap might never have existed. **Stand!**, Sly and Co's fourth album in two years, was a mixture of psychedelic soul – *Everyday People*, joyous horn-drenched dance – *I Want To Take You Higher*, throbbing instrumental jams – *Sex Machine*, and dark, politicized funk – **Don't Call Me Nigger, Whitey**. Brilliant.

Wide mixture of influences from Afro to R&B and West Indian rhythms. Some exciting moments but lacks cohesion. **Melody Maker, August 1969**

Stanley Road

ARTIST Paul Weller **RELEASE DATE** May 1995 **LABEL** Go Disc's (UK) London (US) **PRODUCER** Brendan Lynch, Paul Weller **UK CHART** peak/weeks 1/- **US CHART** peak/weeks 0/0 **TRACK LISTING** The Changingman/Porcelain Goods/I Walk On Gilded Splinters/You Do Something To Me/Woodcutter's Son/Time Passes/Stanley Road/Broken Stones/Out Of The Sinking/Pink On White Walls/Whirlpool's End/Wings Of Speed **PERSONNEL** Paul Weller (v, g), Mick Talbot (k), Steve White (d), plus various guests

By the release of **Stanley Road** Paul Weller was once again considered the finest songwriter of his generation, to the extent that music magazines were competing to put him on the front cover. **Stanley Road** caught the mood of the moment. With bands like Oasis making conventional songwriterly virtues acceptable again, and with Noel Gallagher's patronage, it became the sound of the mid to late Nineties – a bit like the mid to late Sixties variety, all lengthy jam sessions (a nod to Weller's beloved Traffic) and soulful vocals.

Stanley Road *develops and even betters the liberated rock style of his previous solo albums, and now that he's no longer issuing calls-to-arms, his stand-out tracks like* **Porcelain Gods** *and* **Whirlpool's End** *are more thoughtful than anything he's ever done.* **Paul Du Noyer, Mojo, June 1995**

Star

ARTIST Belly **RELEASE DATE** January 1993 **LABEL** 47A.D. (UK)/Sire (US) **PRODUCER** – **UK CHART** peak/weeks 2/12 **US CHART** peak/weeks 59/28 **TRACK LISTING** Someone To Die For/Angel/Dusted/Every Word/Gepetto/Witch/Slow Dog/Low Red Moon/Feed The Tree/Full Moon, Empty Heart/White Belly/Untogether/Star/Sad Dress/Stay **PERSONNEL** Tanya Donnelly (v, g), Fred Abong (b), Chris Gorman (d), Thomas Gorman (g)

After some years happily playing second fiddle to her half sister Kristin Hersh in Throwing Muses, and then a brief spell with Kim Deal in The Breeders, Tanya Donnelly formed her own outlet. Belly retained some of the complex dynamics of The Muses but weren't afraid to soar with poppy enthusiasm. Donnelly's vocals moved impressively from sweet cooing to snarling sass, and when *Feed The Tree* became a hit the band transcended college cultdom and press favouritism. **Star** went gold in America and gained two Grammy nominations, which suggests some of the darker lyrical concerns had passed over heads. **Star** didn't so much twinkle as burn.

On Star, *Belly's debut, Donelly and her mates render a haunting avant-folk-rock sound that provides sonic and psychic space for Donelly's surreal meditations on birth, mortality and sexual longing…* **Kevin Ransom, Rolling Stone, April 1993**

Starchild

ARTIST Teena Marie **RELEASE DATE** December 1984 (US) **LABEL** Epic (US) **PRODUCER** Teena Marie/Larkin Arnold **UK CHART** peak/weeks – **US CHART** peak/weeks 31/35 **TRACK LISTING** Lovergirl/Help Youngblood Get To The Freaky Party/Out On A Limb/Alibi/Jammim/Starchild/We've Got To Stop (Meeting Like This)/My Dear Mr Gaye/Light **PERSONNEL** Teena Marie (v, k, g, d), Darren Carmichael, Randy Kerber, Walter Afanasieff (k), Paulinho Da Costa (pc), Nathan East, James Jamerson Jr (b), Dan Huff (g), Ernie Watts (sax)

Protégé of superfreak Rick James and true dance *auteur*, Teena Marie wrote, arranged and produced several albums and hits (*Behind The Groove, I'm A Sucker For Your Love, I Need Your Lovin'*) for Motown which established her as the queen of white disco before the emergence of Madonna. **Starchild** saw Marie relocate to Epic, where she was allowed free rein. Displaying the full range of her abilities, from the up-tempo strut of *Lovergirl* (her biggest single) to the erotic yearning of her Marvin Gaye tribute, *My Dear Mr Gaye*, **Starchild** reveals a rare and underrated talent.

Starring Sammy Davis Jr

ARTIST Sammy Davis Jr **RELEASE DATE** May 1955 (UK & US) **LABEL** Brunswick Records **PRODUCER** – **UK CHART** peak/weeks – **US CHART** peak/weeks 1/27 **TRACK LISTING** Lonesome Road/Hey There/And This Is My Beloved/September Song/Because Of You/Easy To Love/Glad To Be Unhappy/Stan' Up An' Fight/My Funny Valentine/Spoken For/Birth Of The Blues **PERSONNEL** Sammy Davis Jr (v), with orchestral support directed by Morty Stevens, Sy Oliver and Joseph Gershenson with Sam Taylor featuring on tenor sax on September Song

Essentially a showbiz entertainer, Davis was legendary for his on-stage pizzazz and panache rather than his recorded output. His first hit was in 1954 with *Hey There*. He lost an eye in a traffic accident the same year. He took to hanging out with the Rat Pack, and as a swinging Vegas buddy to Frank Sinatra and Dean Martin found himself drawn to movies and comedy as much as to singing. Still, his live recordings crackle with confident charisma. His Sixties ballads, especially *I've Gotta Be Me*, gave him a chart presence, and in 1972 he grabbed an unexpected Number 1 with the cheesy *Candyman*.

My major complaint about Sammy Davis Jr is that he too often sounds as though he is overtaxing his voice. But devotees will find no faults with **Starring Sammy Davis Jr. Laurie Hernshaw, Melody Maker, January 1961**

Stars

ARTIST Simply Red **RELEASE DATE** October 1991 (UK & US) **LABEL** East West (UK & US) **PRODUCER** Levine **UK CHART** peak/weeks 1/101 **US CHART** peak/weeks 76/43 **TRACK LISTING** Something Got Me Started/Stars/Thrill Me/Your Mirror/She's Got It Bad/For Your Babies/Model/How Could It Fall/Freedom/Wonderland **PERSONNEL** Mick Hucknell (v), Sylvan Richardson (g), Fritz Mcintyre (k), Tony Bowers (b), Chris Joyce (d), Tim Kellett (h)

Mick Hucknall moved into the superstar category with Simply Red's fourth album, one of the biggest sellers of the decade. Their

most polished, jazzily sophisticated work to date, **Stars** outsold everyone else in Britain in 1991, including U2 and Michael Jackson. Ironically for such a glossy Transatlantic slick funk sound, **Stars** failed to set the US charts on fire, stalling at Number 76.

Starsailor

ARTIST Tim Buckley **RELEASE DATE** January 1971 (UK)/1970 (US) **LABEL** Straight (UK & US) **PRODUCER** Tim Buckley **UK CHART** peak/weeks 0/0 **US CHART** peak/weeks 0/0 **TRACK LISTING** Come Here Woman/I Woke Up/Monterey/Moulin Rouge/Song To The Siren/Jungle Fire/Starsailor/The Healing Festival/Down By The Borderline **PERSONNEL** John Balkin (b), Lee Underwood (g, p, o), Buzz Gardner (t, h), Mary Baker (ty), Tim Buckley (g, v), Bunk Gardner (af, ts)

Arriving hot on the heels of the **Blue Afternoon** and **Lorca** albums, **Starsailor** witnessed the evolution of Buckley from folky troubadour to avant-garde jazz dabbler. It turned off many of his fans, with Mother Of Invention man Bunk Gardner's sax and flute input particularly irksome. Buckley sang with unbearable existential anguish of nature and landscapes, but you can tell more personal affairs and intimate tortures were on his mind and hanging heavy on his heart. Either unlistenable or unmissable: have a go if you think you're hard enough.

Buckley… stripped away nearly all of the regulation folk-rock jangle and post-Pepper art-pop trimmings of his earlier work… a poignant example of how far one songwriter was willing to go in search of a greater, purer form of musical expression. **David Fricke, Rolling Stone, December 1989**

Starting Over

ARTIST The Raspberries **RELEASE DATE** February 1975 (UK)/1974 (US) **LABEL** Capitol (UK & US) **PRODUCER** Jimmy Lenner **UK CHART** peak/weeks – **US CHART** peak/weeks 143/6 **TRACK LISTING** Overnight Sensation/Play On/Party's Over/I Don't Know What I Want/Rose Coloured Glasses/All Through The Night/Cruisin' Music/I Can Hardly Believe You're Mine/Cry/Hands On You/Starting Over. **PERSONNEL** Eric Carmen (sy, g, p, k, v), Wally Bryson (g, v), Jeff Hutton (k), Michael McBride (d), Scott McCarl (b, g, v)

Cleveland-based Anglophile rockers led by multi-instrumentalist Eric Carmen had their tough and tender sides, but were marketed by their label as teen fodder. By the time that band proved you could make power pop pay the Rasps had quit, dispirited – but not until this fourth and last album had proved their potential. The single *Overnight Sensation (Hit Record)* encapsulated their hopes and dreams. In 1996 British indie RPM put this on CD with its predecessor *Side 3* as part of their summation of the band's catalogue.

Owing a huge debt to Townshend and The Beatles they nevertheless maintain a distinctive approach, so that although they're copyists it's done with real feeling for the original style. **Max Bell, NME, February 1975**

Station To Station

ARTIST David Bowie **RELEASE DATE** February 1976 (UK & US) **LABEL** RCA (UK & US) **PRODUCER** David Bowie, Harry Maslin **UK CHART** peak/weeks 5/16 **US CHART** peak/weeks 3/32 **TRACK LISTING** Station To Station/Golden Years/ Word On A Wing/TVC15/Stay/Wild Is The Wind **PERSONNEL** David Bowie (v)

A halfway house between the white soul of **Young Americans** and the blanched anti-soul of the Eno trilogy, this drew heavily on Bowie's adopted thin white duke persona, inspired by his part in the Nicolas Roeg film *The Man Who Fell To Earth*. It's a cold record, enlivened in spells by Bowie's gliding vocals, which pep up the odd

structure of the 11-minute title track. *Golden Years* had a genuine swing to it, if *TVC15* did not. *Stay* was propelled by Carlos Alomar's stunning visceral guitar stabs, while the love songs *Word On A Wing* and *Wild Is The Wind* were spine-tinglingly sensitive.

… I must say that I find **Station To Station** *to be not only the most important recorded statement Bowie has ever made, but also one of the most significant albums released in the last five years.* **A.J., Melody Maker, January 1976**

Stephen Stills

ARTIST Stephen Stills **RELEASE DATE** December 1970 (UK & US) **LABEL** Atlantic (UK & US) **PRODUCER** Bill Halverson, Stephen Stills **UK CHART** peak/weeks 30/1 **US CHART** peak/weeks 3/39 **TRACK LISTING** Love The One You're With/Do For The Others/Church (Part Of Someone)/Old Times, Good Times/Go Backhome/Sit Yourself Down/To A Flame/Black Queen/Cheroke/We Are Not Helpless **PERSONNEL** Stephen Stills (v, g), Stephen Fromholtz (g), Paul Harris (k), Dallas Taylor (d), Calvin Samuels (b)

Featuring a galaxy of *Woodstock*-era superstars – Eric Clapton, David Crosby, Graham Nash, John Sebastian, Rita Coolidge and Jimi Hendrix (who OD'd during its recording, thus earning him a

dedication on the sleeve) – the debut album from the former Buffalo Springfield and Crosby, Stills & Nash guitarist/vocalist was a highly promising collection of acoustic and electric folk-tinged pop-rock. The gently relentless harmony-driven *Love The One You're With* was a big hit single.

Stephen Stills has a lot to say… but not enough to make **Stills** *a successful album… his arranging and recording approach tends to obscure whatever life and intimacy his songs and basic performances might originally have possessed.* **Bud Scoppa, Rolling Stone, August 1975**

Stereo 35/MM

ARTIST Enoch Light **RELEASE DATE** October 1961 (UK & US) **LABEL** Command (US) **PRODUCER** Enoch Light **UK CHART** peak/weeks – **US CHART** peak/weeks 1/57 **TRACK LISTING** – **PERSONNEL** Enoch Light (con, arr) plus orchestra

Having proved that stereo was the sound of things to come with his 1960 chart-topper **Persuasive Percussion**, Enoch Light took a new technological tack the following year by recording an orchestral concert not on normal magnetic tape but 35mm film, believing it offered improved sound quality when compared with its narrower, slower audio counterpart. The result was a second US Number 1, capturing the acoustics of New York's famed Carnegie Hall to perfection with a crack 60-piece orchestra in full flight.

Steve McQueen

ARTIST Prefab Sprout **RELEASE DATE** June 1985 (UK & US) **LABEL** Kitchenware (UK)/Epic (US) **PRODUCER** Thomas Dolby **UK CHART** peak/weeks 21/35 **US CHART** peak/weeks 178/5 **TRACK LISTING** Faron Young/When Love Breaks Down/ Appetite/Hallelujah/Goodbye Lucille (Johnny, Johnny)/ Moving The River/ Bonny/When The Angles/ Desire As/Horsin' Around/Blueberry Pies **PERSONNEL** Paddy McAloon, Wendy Smith (v, g), Martin McAloon (b), Neil Conti (d)

Americans will know the Sprout's second album as **Two Wheels Good**, relatives of the late actor having requested a change. But with new drummer Neil Conti and producer Thomas Dolby, singer-song-writer Paddy McAloon had completed a dream team, and having recorded this in less than a month cut another album, **Protest Songs**, straight away, though their label held up release until 1989. McAloon's fascination with America, reflected

by the album title, *Faron Young* and the Marvin Gaye tribute *When The Angels*, would surface anew in 1988.

McAlloon's slightly unbalanced humour surfaces with startling results on more than one occasion and the lacing of cute, carefully crafted pop with liberal streaks of genuine eccentricity contribute to a largely absorbing set of tracks. **Colin Irwin, Melody Maker, June 1985**

Sticky Fingers

ARTIST The Rolling Stones RELEASE DATE May 1971 (US & UK) LABEL Rolling Stones (US & UK) PRODUCER Jimmy Miller UK CHART peak/weeks 1/25 US CHART peak/weeks 1/62 TRACK LISTING Brown Sugar/Sway/Wild Horses/ Can't You Hear Me Knocking?/You Gotta Move/Bitch/I Got The Blues/Sister Morphine/Dead Flowers/Moonlight Mile PERSONNEL Mick Jagger (v, h), Keith Richard (rg), Brian Jones (lg), Bill Wyman (b), Charlie Watts (d)

Although strictly a hotch-potch of odds and sods from sessions of the previous two years, any album which includes **Brown Sugar** (which surprisingly only reached Number 2 in the UK), Marianne Faithfull's **Sister Morphine** and the lilting, lovely **Wild Horses**, is doing more than filling the racks. **I Got The Blues** didn't ring true, and the attempted jazziness of **Can't You Hear Me Knockin'** was sloppy. The first release on their own label, its cover was also to add to their mythology: designed by Andy Warhol, it zipped and unzipped, its poor taste matched by the cartoon of Jagger's mouth which subsequently became the band's universally recognized logo.

The only thing in **Sticky Fingers** *I don't have to do with is* **Moonlight Mile**, *'cause I wasn't there when they did it. It was great to hear that because I was very out of it by the end of the album and it was like listening, really listening.* **Keith Richards interviewed by Robert Greenfield, Rolling Stone, August 1971**

Still Crazy After All These Years

ARTIST Paul Simon RELEASE DATE October 1975 (UK & US) LABEL CBS (UK)/Columbia (US) PRODUCER Paul Simon, Phil Ramone UK CHART peak/weeks 6/31 US CHART peak/weeks 1/3 TRACK LISTING Still Crazy After All These Years/My Little Town/I Do It For Your Love/50 Ways To Leave Your Lover/Night Game/Gone At Last/Some Folks' Lives Roll Easy/Have A Good Time/You're Kind/Silent Eyes PERSONNEL Paul Simon (v), session musicians

Simon's third album, a Grammy Award winner, was less guitar and more piano-oriented than its predecessor; as a result the tone is more serious and sombre: appropriate for a record about the collapse of Simon's first marriage – **50 Ways To Leave Your Lover**, a US Number 1 single, is the best-known track. **Still Crazy…** also featured Art Garfunkel on **My Little Town** (who also placed the song on his own **Breakaway** LP), their first collaboration since

the **Bridge Over Troubled Water** album.

Still Crazy *is a return to the bleakness of Simon's first post-Garfunkel solo album. It seems that the occasional ebullience and optimism of* **Rhymin' Simon** *had been no more than a papering over the cracks; the mood of the new album is one of unrelieved isolation.* **Bob Woffinden, NME, October 1975**

Stone Gon'

ARTIST Barry White RELEASE DATE March 1974/1973 (US) LABEL Pye (UK)/20th Century (US) PRODUCER Barry White UK CHART peak/weeks 18/17 US CHART peak/weeks 20/37 TRACK LISTING – PERSONNEL Barry White (p, v, arr), Gene Page (arr), session musicians

To many, Barry White was the populist soulman of the Seventies whose deep bass growl and strings-drenched invitations to sex were little more than seduction soundtracks for aspiring lovemen and bored housewives. In fact, White was a superb writer, arranger and orchestrator whose grandiose self-penned, self-produced albums marked him out as a black Spector. **Stone Gon'** was a near faultless collection, featuring two classic up-tempo singles: **Honey Please, Can't Ya See** and **Never Never Gonna Give You Up**, and three epically lavish, slow-burning ballads.

Barry's music is 'love music', soothing and sweeet, but its also party music… It is the dinner music of tomorrow, today, exceeding all boundaries and categorization, for Barry has learnt that in versatility there is longevity…. **Patrick and Barbara Salvo, Melody Maker, April 1975**

The Stone Roses

ARTIST The Stone Roses RELEASE DATE 13th May 1989 (UK)/April 1989 (US) LABEL Silvertone (UK & US) PRODUCER John Leckie UK CHART peak/weeks 19/48 US CHART peak/weeks 86/26 TRACK LISTING I Wanna Be Adored/She Bangs The Drums/Waterfall/Don't Stop/Bye Bye Badman/Elizabeth My Dear/(Song For My) Sugar Spun Sister/Made Of Stone/This Is The One/I Am The Resurrection PERSONNEL Reni (d, bv), Gary Mounfield (b), John Squire (g), Ian Brown (v)

Manchester could do no wrong during the Eighties. First, New Order, then The Smiths, and finally, the most lionized band of the decade – The Stone Roses. Their debut, voted second-best LP of all time by NME, was released amid furious hype and excitement. With its blend of winsome Byrds-like melodies and an arrogance verging on narcissism – the titles, **I Wanna Be Adored** and **I Am The Resurrection**, said it all – **The Stone Roses** rehabilitated guitar-based pop for a generation then being seduced by the alternative universe that was the dance scene.

The writing of singer Ian Brown and guitarist John Squire is not always equal to the Roses' sound and mettle. But in fad-driven Britain, where psychedelia isn't an attitude so much as a marketing tool, The Stone Roses are blooming Technicolor. **David Fricke, Rolling Stone, December 1989**

The Stooges

ARTIST The Stooges **RELEASE DATE** August 1969 (US) **LABEL** Elektra (UK & US) **PRODUCER** John Cale **UK CHART** peak/weeks – **US CHART** peak/weeks 106/11 **TRACK LISTING** I Wanna Be Your Dog/We Will Fall/No Fun/Real Cool Time/Ann/Not Right/Little Doll **PERSONNEL** Iggy Pop (v), Ron Ashton (g), Dave Alexander (b), Scott Asheton (d)

The Stooges, along with The New York Dolls and fellow Detroit rockers MC5, pretty much kickstarted punk. Produced by the Velvet Underground's John Cale (the whiz at the controls of two other pre-punk *pièces de résistance*, Patti Smith's **Horses** and Jonathan Richman's **Modern Lovers**), **The Stooges** anticipated the mix of numbing boredom (**1969**), rage (**Not Right**) and nihilism (**No Fun**) of the punk Class of '76 and slacker Class of '91. There was sex as degradation (**I Wanna Be Your Dog**), too. Only **Ann** offered any respite. The rest was noise as antidote to *ennui*, noise as confrontation, noise as narcotic. The Sixties – literally, metaphorically – stopped here.

Storyville

ARTIST Robbie Robertson **RELEASE DATE** October 1991 (UK)/September 1991 (US) **LABEL** Geffen (UK & US) **PRODUCER** Robbie Robertson, Stephen Hague, Gary Gersh **UK CHART** peak/weeks 30/2 **US CHART** peak/weeks 69/10 **TRACK LISTING** Night Parade/Hold Back The Dawn/Go Back To Your Woods/Soap Box Preacher/Day Of Reckoning/Burning For You/What About Now/Shake This Town/Breaking The Rules/Resurrection/Sign Of The Rainbow **PERSONNEL** Warren Bell (ss), Duane Van Paulin (tr), Stacey Cole (t), Amadee Castenell (ts), Fred Kemp (ts), Carl A. Blouin (bs), Anthony Dagradi (ss), Brian Graber (t), Mark Isham (t, fh), Ken Kulger (tr), Richard Mitchell (ts), Dan Higgins (as, fl), John J. Mitchell (cl), Robbie Robertson (v)

Though it lacked a big hit single, unlike its predecessor with **Somewhere Down The Crazy River**, ex-Band guitarist Robbie Robertson's second effort was considerably more satisfying. He followed former boss Bob Dylan down to New Orleans where he revived his career with 1989's **Oh Mercy**, which mixed that city's gospel and R&B into his mature rock. **What About Now**, a duet with Aaron Neville who, as with Dylan, added backing with his Brothers, was not a success. Robertson retreated into making music for the small screen.

… an imaginative and spiritual journey, with New Orleans as its inspiration… stories about faith and faithlessness, about losing the world and saving your soul. It is a mature and masterful work. **Anthony De Curtis, Rolling Stone, October 1991**

Straight Outta Compton

ARTIST NWA **RELEASE DATE** 30 September 1989 (UK)/August 1989 (US) **LABEL** Fourth and Broadway (UK)/Ruthless (US) **PRODUCER** Easy-E/Dr Dre/Yella **UK CHART** peak/weeks 41/4 **US CHART** peak/weeks 37/81 **TRACK LISTING** Straight Outta Compton/F The Police/Gangsta Gangsta/If It Ain't Ruff/Parental Discreation Iz Advised/8 ball (Remix)/Something Like That/Express Yourself/Compton's In The House (Remix)/I Ain't That 1/Dopeman (Remix)/Quiet On The Set/Something To Dance To **PERSONNEL** Eric 'Easy-E' Wright (v), Lorenzo 'M.C. Ren' Patterson (v), Andre 'Dr Dre' Young (v), O'Shea 'Ice Cube' Jackson (v), DJ Antoine 'Yella' Carraby(tt)

Ten years later, the reputation of Niggaz With Attitude still rests fairly and squarely on the incendiary first three tracks of this album. The venom packed by the title track, **F The Police** and **Gangsta Gangsta** was so frightening the FBI apparently tried to stop the record being distributed. But too many egos in the band caused Ice Cube to split the dream team and the rest is history. Many followed in their black-clad footsteps, but this remains a rap landmark.

… quote from Ice Cube, 'The N.W.A. attitude is that we don't give a f, we don't care about the media or the police, about parents or community leaders. We're doing exactly what we're doing for the kids, the people who have experienced and seen and heard the same things we have.' **Melody Maker, August 1989**

Stranded

ARTIST Roxy Music **RELEASE DATE** December 1973 (UK & US) **LABEL** Island (UK)/Atco (US) **PRODUCER** Chris Thomas **UK CHART** peak/weeks 1/17 **US CHART** peak/weeks 186/4 **TRACK LISTING** Street Life/Just Like You/Amazona/Psalm/Serenade/A Song For Europe/Mother Of Pearl/Sunset **PERSONNEL** Bryan Ferry (v, k), Andrew Mackay (s, ob), Paul Thompson (d), Phil Manzanera (g), Edwin Jobson (k, sy, st), John Gustafson (b)

With Brian Eno's departure there were fewer sonic experiments, allowing Bryan Ferry to relax into his role as *ennui*-laden Chairman of the Bored. If, as Eno said after he split, **Stranded** lacked 'insanity', it more than made up for it in the neon oboe and sax of Andy Mackay and new boy Eddie Jobson's violin and keyboard embellishments. **Street Life** became the big hit off the LP, **A Song For Europe** plumbed new depths of exquisite melancholy, while the first part of **Mother Of Pearl** had all the energy of punk.

Stranded *is a classic, the album Roxy have been aiming at for 2 years – and the long awaited firm ground for the group's fans to stand on, even if some of the subtleties of the earlier approach have had to go in order to get there.* **Ian MacDonald, NME, November 1973**

Strange Days

ARTIST Doors **RELEASE DATE** December 1967 (UK)/April 1967 (US) **LABEL** Elektra (UK & US) **PRODUCER** Paul A. Rothchild **UK CHART** peak/weeks 0/0 **US CHART** peak/weeks 3/63 **TRACK LISTING** Strange Days/You're Lost Little Girl/Love Me Two Times/Unhappy Girl/Horse Latitudes/Moonlight Drive/People Are Strange/My Eyes Have Seen You/I Can't See Your Face In My Mind/When The Music's Over **PERSONNEL** Jim Morrison (v), Ray Manzarek (mba, k), Robby Krieger (g), John Densmore (d)

Now on their second album and becoming familiar with studio technology, the Doors experimented with sound effects, like the eerie white noise that shaped Jim's harrowing spoken-word **Horse Latitudes**. Overall, the record continued the preoccupation with

the darker side of West Coast acid culture. The band's strengths were indisputable: *Love Me Two Times* showed they could deliver a three-minute pop tune, while **When The Music's Over** became its fulcrum in the same way *The End* had for **The Doors**.

Their whole album, individual songs and especially the final track are constructed in the five parts of a tragedy. Like Greek drama, you know when the music's over because there is catharsis. **Rolling Stone, November 1967**

The Stranger

ARTIST Billy Joel RELEASE DATE March 1978 (UK)/October 1977 (US) LABEL CBS (UK)/Columbia (US) PRODUCER Phil Ramone UK CHART peak/weeks 25/40 US CHART peak/weeks 9/70 TRACK LISTING Movin' Out (Anthony's Song)/The Stranger/Just The Way You Are/Scenes From An Italian Restaurant/Vienna/Only The Good Die Young/She's Always A Woman/Get It Right The First Time/Everybody Has A Dream PERSONNEL Billy Joel (v), session musicians

After two albums in the lower reaches of the US Top 40, it was time for Billy Joel to make the break – and **The Stranger** did just that, rising to Number 2 during an impressive 70-week US chart stay. The slushy and much covered (200+ versions) single *Just The Way You Are* proved a millstone he later tried to shake off – Linda Ronstadt and Phoebe Snow had persuaded him to include it – but **The Stranger** would go on to become the label's second biggest seller ever behind **Bridge Over Troubled Water**.

The imagery and melodies of **The Stranger**, *more than often than not work… We don't expect subtlety or understatement from him and, indeed, his lyrics can be as smart assed as ever.* **Ira Mayer, Rolling Stone, December 1977**

Stranger In Town

ARTIST Bob Seger RELEASE DATE May 1978 (UK & US) LABEL Capitol (UK & US) PRODUCER Bob Segar UK CHART peak/weeks 31/6 US CHART peak/weeks 4/110 TRACK LISTING Hollywood Nights/Still The Same/Old Time Rock & Roll/Till It Shines/Feel Like A Number/Ain't Got No Money/We've Got Tonite/Brave Strangers/The Famous Final Scene

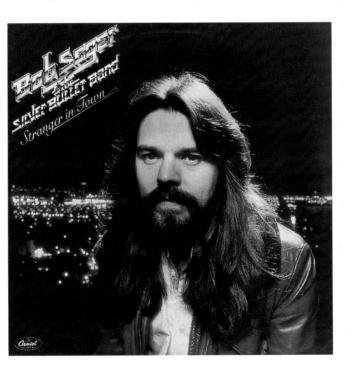

PERSONNEL Bob Seger (v), Drew Abbott (g), Robyn Robbins (k), Alto Reed (s), Chris Campbell (b), Charlie Allen Martin (d)

On his follow-up to the five million selling **Night Moves**, Seger was the accomplished rocker, having mastered everything from Springsteen-ish blue-collar bluster (**Hollywood Nights**) to sensitive ballads (**We've Got Tonight**). Evincing the influence of every great American rocker, from Chuck Berry to Bob Dylan to John Fogerty, Seger, along with the Eagles, epitomized pre-punk Seventies US rock.

… whilst the up-tempo, straight ahead rockers are fine as ever… it's within his ability to write truthfully and frankly about emotional situations normally dealt with so flippantly that Seger's future seems assured. **Andy Gill, NME, May 1978**

Street Survivors

ARTIST Lynyrd Skynyrd RELEASE DATE October 1977 (UK)/May 1977 (US) LABEL MCA (UK & US) PRODUCER Jimmy Johnson, Rodney Mills, Tim Smith UK CHART peak/weeks 13/4 US CHART peak/weeks 5/34 TRACK LISTING What's Your Name/That Smell/One More Time/I Know A Little/You Got That Right/I Never Dreamed/Honky Tonk Night Time Man/Ain't No Good Life PERSONNEL Ronnie Van Zant (v), Gary Rossington, Allen Collins, Steve Gaines (g), Leon Wilkeson (b, v), Artimus Pyle (d), Billy Powell (k)

Had it not been for events a week after release, this album would be recalled as Skynyrd's most cohesive since **Second Helping** three years earlier. It contained three classics in *You Got That Right*, **That Smell** and **What's Your Name**, while the appearance of Merle Haggard's **Honky Tonk Night Time Man** hinted at future directions: singer Johnny Van Zant was about to cut an album with Haggard and Waylon Jennings. As it was, the band's decimation in an air crash would render the fire-ringed cover art (replaced on later pressings) one of rock's great ironies.

The death of any musician, is, of course, a sad event, yet it's even more tragic when he's on the way up… their best album yet and one which proved that they had finally grown out of southern boogie into solid, entertaining and skilful rock… **Michael Oldfield, Melody Maker, October 1977**

String Along

ARTIST The Kingston Trio RELEASE DATE August 1960 (UK & US) LABEL World Record Club PRODUCER Voyle Gilmore UK CHART peak/weeks – US CHART peak/weeks 1/60 TRACK LISTING Bad Man's Blunder/The Escape Of Old John Webb/When I Was Young/Leave My Woman Alone/This Mornin', This Evenin', So Soon/Everglades/Buddy Better Get On Down The Line/South Wind/Who's Gonna Hold Her Hand/To Morrow/Colorado Trail/The Tattooed Lady PERSONNEL Dave Guard, Nick Reynolds, Bob Shane (v)

By August 1960, when the trio released their seventh album, the formula was becoming a little predictable. This was the fourth Number 1 album on the trot and it spawned two chart singles, *Everglades* and *Bad Man's Blunder*. Neither record made it into the Top 30, however, and none of their subsequent albums made top spot. The strains were starting to show within the group, with founder Dave Guard becoming more detached until he was replaced by John Stewart nine months later. It was, nevertheless, one of their best albums, with a higher than usual proportion of new material.

The Kingston Trio wind their expert way through a variety of folksy songs – wistful, mournful, dramatic some may be – but the Trio interlock their engaging vocalising with two bongos and a guitar, which give a sure touch of authority. **Melody Maker, March 1961**

Suede

ARTIST Suede RELEASE DATE April 1993 (UK & US) LABEL Nude-Sony (UK)/Sony (US) PRODUCER Ed Buller UK CHART peak/weeks 1/16 US CHART peak/weeks 0/0 TRACK LISTING So Young/Animal Nitrate/She's Not Dead/Moving/Pantomime Horse/The Downers/Sleeping Pills/Breakdown/Metal Micky/Animal Lover/The Next Life PERSONNEL Brett Anderson (v), Bernard Butler (g), Mat Osman (b), Simon Gilbert (d)

Although they had been gigging for several years, Suede seemed to arrive fully formed with their debut album, **Suede**, which went gold within days and eventually won the prestigious Mercury Prize Award. Containing **So Young**, **Animal Nitrate**, **The Drowners**, **Metal Mickey** and at least four other could-have-been hits, **Suede** was exactly how you imagined a band reared on glam-era Bowie and early-period Smiths might sound: elegant, decadent and electric.

Suede announced a changing of the guard in British music, powerfully confirming it with a debut album, **Suede***, of formidable grace and authority.... If Suede has done anything to deserve the mark down tag of glam, it has been introducing post-acid-house generation to pelvic posturing.* **Steve Daly, Rolling Stone, May 1993**

Suicide

ARTIST Suicide RELEASE DATE November 1977 (UK) LABEL Bronze (UK)/Red Star (US) PRODUCER Ric Ocasek/Marty Thau UK CHART peak/weeks – US CHART peak/weeks – TRACK LISTING Ghost Rider/Rocket U.S.A./Cheree/Frankie Teardrops/Johnny/Girl/Che PERSONNEL Alan Vega (v), Martine Rev (k, p)

Hailing from New York's bohemian performing art's scene of the early Seventies, Suicide – the man with the French heartthrob looks, Alan Vega, and Bowery hoodlum type, Martin Rev – provided the blueprint for every synthesizer duo of the Eighties, from Cabaret Voltaire to Soft Cell to Bronski Beat to Erasure. With its relentless barrage of mimimalist electronic beats, **Suicide** was also the prototype for the industrial bands of the Nineties such as Nine Inch Nails and Ministry.

Suicide are the Seeds of the Seventies.... Monotony is where it's at more than ever these days, and this record is such fine monotony that it shows up the rest of the wallpaper music around for what it is... **Lester Bangs, NME, January 1978**

Sulk

ARTIST The Associates RELEASE DATE June 1982 (UK) LABEL WEA (UK & US) PRODUCER Billy MacKenzie, Alan Rankine, Mike Hedges UK CHART peak/weeks 10/20 US CHART peak/weeks 0/0 TRACK LISTING It's Better This Way/Party Fears Two/Club Country/Love Hangover/18 Carat Love Affair/Arrogance Gave Him Up/No/Skipping/White Car In Germany/Gloomy Sunday/The Associate PERSONNEL Billy MacKenzie (v), Alan Rankine (k)

Billy Mackenzie's tragic death in 1997 led to a near hagiographic rehabilitation of his early Eighties work. Along with **The Affectionate Punch**, the Warners debut **Sulk** was belatedly hailed as a work of epic genius. It didn't do too badly with the critics upon its release either. Spawning three hit singles, it launched the difficult Edinburgh duo into the glam-pop slipstream of such acts as Soft Cell and ABC, while Mackenzie's far-reaching, Bowie-boosted voice drew comparisons with everyone from Maria Callas to Russell Mael. The breakthrough hit **Party Fears Two** was about an undesirable pair of gatecrashers Billy had literally bumped into at college.

... the **Sulk** *songs dramatize futility, failure, malice and weakness with such piercing lack of embarrassment, such pulverizing dedication, the whole thing often 'threatens' to tumble up and over into comedy and beyond... into a new type of beauty and idiocy.* **Paul Morley, NME, May 1982**

Sum And Substance

ARTIST The Mission RELEASE DATE Febuary 1994 LABEL Vertigo (UK)/Mercury (US) PRODUCER – UK CHART peak/weeks 49/ US CHART peak/weeks – TRACK LISTING Never Again/Hands Across The Ocean/Shades Of Green/Like A Child Again/Into The Blue/Deliverance/Tower Of Strength/Butterfly On A Wheel/Kingdom Come/Beyond The Pale/Severina/Stay With Me/Wasteland/Garden of Delight/Like A Hurricane/Serpent's Kiss/Sour Puss/Afterglow PERSONNEL Wayne Hussy (g, v), Simon Hinkler (g), Craig Adams (b), Mick Brown (d)

Having spun off from Gothic supergroup Sisters Of Mercy (they fought Andrew Eldritch for the name), the Mission found their own voice in 1986 with **God's Own Medicine. Sum And Substance**, released eight years later, marked the end of a commercial and creative streak, with bassist Craig Adams, the hub of the operation, and with guitarist Wayne Hussey – departing shortly after to join The Cult. Future albums would be on their own Equator label, but Goth had long since subsided and the band, who survived that, seemed to have little left in their creative locker.

Summer Holiday

ARTIST Cliff Richard **RELEASE DATE** January 1963 **LABEL** Columbia **PRODUCER** Norrie Paramor **UK CHART** peak/weeks 1/36 **US CHART** peak/weeks – **TRACK LISTING** Seven Days To A Holiday/Summer Holiday/Let Us Take You For A Ride/Les Girls/Round And Round/Foot Tapper/Stranger In Town/Orlando's Mime/Bachelor Boy/A Swingin' Affair/Really Waltzing/All At Once/Dancing Shoes/Yugoslav Wedding/The Next Time/Big News **PERSONNEL** Cliff Richard (v), Jet Harris (b), Hank B. Marvin (lg), Bruce Welch (rg), Tony Meehan (d)

The soundtrack for Cliff's fourth feature film included 11 songs performed with The Shadows, three by The Shadows alone and two by the ABS Orchestra. The singles *The Next Time* and *Bachelor Boy* were released as a double A-side, but the latter was clearly more popular. Radio Luxembourg received 4,000 entries in a competition to guess which side would go higher in the charts. Compared with Elvis's latest *Girls Girls Girls*, Cliff came out on top.

Sunflower

ARTIST Beach Boys **RELEASE DATE** December 1970 (UK)/September 1970 (US) **LABEL** Stateside (UK)/Brother/Reprise (US) **PRODUCER** The Beach Boys **UK CHART** peak/weeks 29/6 **US CHART** peak/weeks 151/4 **TRACK LISTING** Cottonfields/Slip On Through/This Whole World/Add Some Music To Your Day/Deirdre/Got To Know The Woman/It's About Time/Tears In The Morning/All I Wanna Do/Forever/Our Sweet Love/At My Window/Cool, Cool, Water **PERSONNEL** Brian Wilson (b, k, v), Mike Love (v), Carl Wilson (g, v), Al Jardine (g, v), Dennis Wilson (d, v)

Their twenty-first album in seven years, the Beach Boys weren't exactly masters of supply and demand. They'd left Capitol for the Warners label, which somewhat revived their fortunes. In New York, whilst fearing ridicule, they were greeted ecstatically by a Grateful Dead audience. **Sunflower** was one of their more conservative albums, in that it featured sweet, accessible songs that steered clear of their sometimes indulgent waffle. Warners must have been delighted.

After a long period of recovery, mediocrity, and general disaster, the Beach Boys have finally produced an album that can stand with **Pet Sounds** *… It is decadent fluff – but brilliant fluff. The Beach Boys are plastic madmen, rock geniuses.* **Jim Miller, Rolling Stone, October 1970**

Sunshine Superman

ARTIST Donovan **RELEASE DATE** July 1967 (UK & US) **LABEL** Pye (UK)/Epic (US) **PRODUCER** Mickie Most **UK CHART** peak/weeks 25/7 **US CHART** peak/weeks 11/29 **TRACK LISTING** Sunshine Superman/Legend Of A Girl Child Linda/The Observation/Guinevere/Celeste/Writer In The Sun/Season Of The Witch/Hampstead Incident/Sand Foam/Young Girl Blues/Three Kingfishers/Bert's Blues **PERSONNEL** Donovan (w, v, g, ag), with arrangements by John Cameron

Breaking the mould of Donovan Leitc's earlier protest-singer image and introducing him to an even wider audience, **Sunshine Superman** kicks off with one of his best-loved hits, the title track with its wonderfully ebullient rhythms courtesy of Spike Heatley and Tony Carr and given shape by Jimmy Page's lead guitar riff. It had been written for John Lennon and Paul McCartney with whom Don would later collaborate, albeit uncredited, on their *Yellow Submarine* song. **Sunshine Superman** heralded 1967's Summer of Love and the impending flower-power culture with its use of sitar.

… the album which bridged the gap between the **Sensitivity Edition Dylan** *and* **Floricultural Ambassador** *phases of his career and which verified him as a truly distinctive singer and composer, flying several aerial miles ahead of most of his 1967 contemporaries.* **Al Clark, NME, January 1975**

Super Trouper

ARTIST Abba **RELEASE DATE** November 1980 (UK)/December 1980 (US) **LABEL** Epic (UK)/Atlantic (US) **PRODUCER** Benny Anderson & Björn Ulvaeus **UK CHART** peak/weeks 1/43 **US CHART** peak/weeks 17/38 **TRACK LISTING** Super Trouper/The Winner Takes All/On And On And On/Andante, Andante/Ma And I/Happy New Year/Our Last Summer/The Piper/Lay All Your Love On Me/The Way Old Friends Do **PERSONNEL** Benny Anderson (k, sy, v), Björn Ulvaeus (g, v), Agnetha Fältskog (v), Frida Lyngstad (v)

It is a little-known fact that the working title for *I Have A Dream* was 'Under My Armpit'. While the Swedish demi-gods may have admitted to a sense of humour after the event, there was scant trace of it at the time. On this album there were the first faint signs of internal distress – symptoms of 'taking-themselves-too-seriously': **Super Trouper** was a self-pitying melodrama, though the smash single *The Winner Takes It All* was poignant and pertinent. Björn and Benny drowned the songs in with synths, whilst Agnetha and Frida sang with something dangerously close to emotion.

Yes, Abba are a marketing exercise… They are – at least in places – sickly. But as long as they go on churning out such high quality pop I'm prepared to turn one blind eye at least. **Lyden Barber, Melody Maker, November 1980**

Superfly

ARTIST Curtis Mayfield RELEASE DATE March 1973 (UK)/August 1972 (US) LABEL Buddah (UK)/Curtom (US) PRODUCER Curtis Mayfield UK CHART peak/ weeks 26/2 US CHART peak/weeks 1/46 TRACK LISTING Little Child Running Wild/Freddie's Dead/ Give Me Your Love/No Thing On Me (Coccaine Song)/ Superfly / Pusherman / Junkie Chase / Eddie You Should Know/Think PERSONNEL Curtis Mayfield (v, g, k) and live band

The classic blaxploitation movie *Shaft* spawned a host of imitators, as did Isaac Hayes' hit soundtrack. But few were as finely crafted as Curtis Mayfield's first film-related effort which topped the US chart for a month and spun off his first million-selling single, *Freddie's Dead*. He had been inspired by the screenplay, but felt the resulting film was something of an 'infomercial' for cocaine, so worked against that with his lyrics to undercut the glamour and point the finger at the real villain – the Pusherman.

Superfly is not only a superior, imaginative soundtrack, but fine funky music as well and the best of Curtis Mayfield's four albums since he left the Impressions. **Bob Donat, Rolling Stone, November 1972**

Superunknown

ARTIST Soundgarden RELEASE DATE March 1994 (UK) LABEL A&M (UK & US) PRODUCER Michael Beinhorn, Soundgarden UK CHART peak/weeks 4/ US CHART peak/weeks 1/75 TRACK LISTING Let Me Drown/My Wave/ Fell On Black Days/Mailman/Superunknown/Head Down/Black Hole Sun/ Spoonman/Limo Wreck/The Day I Tried To Live/Kickstand/Fresh Tendrils/ 4th Of July/Half/Like Suicide/She Likes Surprises PERSONNEL Chris Cornell (v, g), Kim Thavil (g), Ben Shepherd (b, v), Matt Cameron (d, pc)

One of the key acts from the Seattle scene, and one of the first to sign to Sub Pop (early home to Nirvana), Soundgarden were arguably the heaviest of all the grunge bands, too heavy for mass consumption. That is, until their fourth album, **Superunknown**, by which time the world had caught up with them and, thanks to Pearl Jam, Smashing Pumpkins and Nirvana, grown accustomed to their dense rock sound. **Superunknown** debuted at Number 1, helped somewhat by the relentless MTV rotation of the **Black Hole Sun** single, which suggested Soundgarden were no one-trick ponies and could pen a pretty psych-pop ditty with the best of them.

It's metal to be sure, but there's light and shade, thrills and spills and the constant nagging suggestion that Cornell, Kim Thayil, Ben Shepherd and Matt Cameron, grunge's losers, have transformed themselves into as close as matters to great. **John Aizlewood, Q, April 1994**

The Supremes A Go Go

ARTIST The Supremes RELEASE DATE December 1966 (UK)/September 1966 (US) LABEL Tamla Motown (UK)/Motown (US) PRODUCER – UK CHART peak/weeks 15/21 US CHART peak/weeks 1/60 TRACK LISTING Love Is Like An Itching In My Heart/This Old Heart Of Mine (Is Weak For You)/You Can't Hurry Love/Shake Me, Wake Me (When It's Over)/Baby I Need Your Loving/ These Boots Are Made For Walking/I Can't Help Myself/Get Ready/Put Yourself In My Place/Money (That's What I Want)/Come And Get These Memories/Hang On Sloopy PERSONNEL Diana Ross (lv), Florance Ballard (v), Mary Wilson (v)

The most successful female act of the Sixties, The Supremes racked up 12 Number 1 singles and launched the international career of Diana Ross. **The Supremes A Go Go**, the girls' sixth LP, not only featured strong individual material, it also hinted that, like The Beatles and the Beach Boys, Motown's bosses knew the long-player held the key to prolonged success. The only Supremes album apart from compilations to spend more than a week on top of the charts, **The Supremes A Go Go** was an excellent collection of lavishly arranged dance-pop.

Yeah! A continuity LP – continues to swing with that hypnotic low in the bar from the first track to the last – a sort of blanket Tamla sound, and the glorious voice of Diana Ross insinuates through every track… **Melody Maker, December 1987**

Surf's Up

ARTIST The Beach Boys RELEASE DATE November 1971 (UK)/August 1971 (US) LABEL Stateside (UK)/Brother-Reprise (US) PRODUCER – UK CHART peak/weeks 15/6 US CHART peak/weeks 29/17 TRACK LISTING Don't Go Near The Water/Long Promised Road/Take A Load Off Your Feet/Disney Girls (1957)/Student Demonstration Time/Feel Flows/Lookin' At Tomorrow (A Welfare Time)/A Day In The Life Of A Tree/'Til I Die/Surf's Up PERSONNEL Brian Wilson (b, k, v), Mike Love (v), Carl Wilson (g, v), Al Jardine (g, v), Dennis Wilson (d, v)

The title suite, a collaboration between Brian Wilson and Van Dyke Parks, was originally composed for the lost and legendary 'Smile' opus, but **Surf's Up** also showcased the writing talents of the less mythologized members of the group, Mike Love and Al Jardine, who wrote **Don't Go Near The Water**, and Carl Wilson, who penned **Long Promised Land** and **Feel Flows**. The album's title was poignantly ironic. Brian was searching for something else when the simple, innocent era (the Sixties notion of 'revolution') was on the verge of passing.

It is, without doubt, the most complete pop album ever released, capturing, as it does, the Beach Boys at their creative peak, when their social conscience was aroused, filtering through the inspired vocal arrangements… **Harry Doherty, Melody Maker, February 1980**

Surfer Rose

ARTIST The Pixies RELEASE DATE March 1988 LABEL 4-A.D PRODUCER Steve Albini UK CHART peak/weeks 0/0 US CHART peak/weeks - TRACK LISTING Bone Machine/Break My Body/Something Against You/Broken Face/Gigantic/River Euphrates/Where Is My Mind?/Cactus/Tony's Theme/Oh My Golly!/Vamos/I'm Amazed/Brick Is Red PERSONNEL Black Francis (v, g), Jerry Santigo (lg), Kim Deal (b, v), Dave Lovering (d)

A full healthy appreciation of The Pixies is entirely dependent upon a terribly, terribly good sense of humour. Any attempt to locate their muse would flounder face-down in a pool of warm beer, sweat and semen. So laugh with the devil basically. **Chris Roberts, Melody Maker, March 1988**

Surrealistic Pillow

ARTIST Jefferson Airplane **RELEASE DATE** September 1967 (UK)/Febuary 1967 (US) **LABEL** RCA (UK & US) **PRODUCER** Rick Jarrard **UK CHART** peak/weeks – **US CHART** peak/weeks 3/56 **TRACK LISTING** She Has Funny Cars/Somebody To Love/My Best Friend/Today/Comin' Back To Me/3/5 Of A Mile In 10 Seconds/D.C.B.A.-25/How Do you Feel/Embryonic Journey/White Rabbit/ Plastic Fantastic Lover **PERSONNEL** Grace Slick (v), Marty Balin (v), Paul Kantner (g), Jorma Kaukonen (g), Jack Casady (b), Spencer Dryden (d)

Ostensibly handled by a straight staff producer, Rick Jarrard, the Airplane's second album was guided spiritually by the Dead's Jerry Garcia who flew down from 'Frisco in time for the album's second night of sessions. It was he who, describing the material on the LP to singer Marty Balin as 'surrealistic as a pillow', gave the record its legendary name. Slick had brought with her two of the Society's strongest tunes, **Somebody To Love** and **White Rabbit** – and as singles they subsequently launched the Airplane as THE psychedelic San Francisco band.

'We don't really make singles,' replied Spencer. *'On the last album we talked for four weeks trying to decide what to use as a single… we are really an album group. We like to sell singles because they get to more people but I don't think the band depends on that.'* **Spencer Dryden (drummer) interview by Tony Wilson, Melody Maker, September 1968**

Suspending Disbelief

ARTIST Jimmy Webb **RELEASE DATE** – **LABEL** – **PRODUCER** Linda Ronstadt, George Massenberg **UK CHART** peak/weeks – **US CHART** peak/weeks – **TRACK LISTING** Too Young To Die/I Don't Know How To Love You Anymore/Elvis And Me/It Won't Bring Her Back/Sandy Cove/Friends To Burn/What Does A Woman See In A Man/Postcard From Paris/Just Like Always/Adios/I Will Arise **PERSONNEL** Jimmy Webb (lv, ep, ap, sy), Dean Parks (g, ag), Russ Kunkel (d, pc), Leland Sklar (b)

Hits such as **Wichita Lineman, By The Time I Get To Phoenix, Up, Up And Away, MacArthur Park** and **Galveston** made songwriter Jimmy Webb a millionaire by the time he was 21. That was in the late Sixties. He spent the Seventies producing artists as diverse as Art Garfunkel, Lowell George and Cher, while intermittently recording his own albums, to little acclaim or public interest. **Suspending Disbelief** followed a prolonged absence but, for once, was greeted with some enthusiasm by a generation reared on Webb's exquisite compositions. Rawer and grittier than his famous tunes, the confessional nature of these 11 new songs, rendered with quavery emotion by the lost boy of pop himself, made for poignant listening.

Suspending Disbelief *is a powerful meditation on mortality and middle life that drifts in and out of autobiography. Alternating between styles as diverse as L.A. rock, country pop, show tunes and the lush romanticism of his trademark ballads.* **John McAlley, Rolling Stone, October 1993**

Sweet Baby James

ARTIST James Taylor **RELEASE DATE** November 1970 (UK)/March 1970 (US) **LABEL** Warner (UK & US) **PRODUCER** Bill Lazerus **UK CHART** peak/weeks 7/53 **US CHART** peak/weeks 3/102 **TRACK LISTING** Sweet Baby James/Lo And Behold/Sunny Skies/Steamroller/Country Road/Oh, Susannah/Fire And Rain/Blossom/Anywhere Like Heaven/Oh Baby, Don't You Loose Your Lip On Me/Suite For 20G **PERSONNEL** JamesTaylor (v, g), session musicians

The archetypal sensitive singer-songwriter of the early Seventies, James Taylor, along with Joni Mitchell, Carole King and Neil Young, made popular the acoustic, autobiographical style of

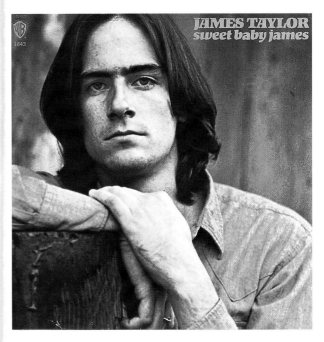

melodic confessionals that served as aural balm for shattered souls following the death of the hippy dream at Altamont. **Sweet Baby James**, Taylor's fourth album, fused folk, jazz and blues influences into a seamless pop whole that caught the mood of a generation. Hits like **Fire And Rain** were perfect for the adult tastes of the then burgeoning FM radio.

James is not a great blues singer – or country singer. But somehow, the English chap with an adapted American accent (for rock and roll purposes), has made an extremely enjoyable album… While not exactly country music it could be described as Green Belt Rock. **C.W., Melody Maker, April 1970**

Sweet Dreams

ARTIST Eurythmics **RELEASE DATE** February 1983 (UK)/March 1983 (US) **LABEL** RCA (UK & US) **PRODUCER** Dave Stewart, A. Williams **UK CHART** peak/weeks 3/60 **US CHART** peak/weeks 15/59 **TRACK LISTING** Love Is A Stranger/I've Got An Angel/'Wrap It Up'/I Could Give You A Mirror/The Walk/Sweet Dreams Are Made Of This/Jennifer/This Is The House/Somebody Told Me/This City Never Sleeps **PERSONNEL** Annie Lennox (v), Dave Stewart (k, g)

After a string of flop singles and a non-commercial debut album, ex-Tourists Dave Stewart and Annie Lennox made a shockingly sudden breakthrough in early 1983. The key was the hit single title track and, more especially, its innovative video in which the pair's highly contrasting visual appeal was given full rein backed by a musical mix of electro rhythms, memorable melodies and challenging lyrics. But in truth it was the video that sold the single that sold the album.

This is a leisurely, entirely pleasant album with a few morbid edges but fewer traces of those sacharine sentiments which have marred Lennox and Stewart's music in the past. It explores the facades and banalities of Romance Today far more honestly and interestingly than say ABC. **Cynthia Rose, NME, February 1983**

A Swingin' Affair!

ARTIST Frank Sinatra **RELEASE DATE** May 1957 (UK & US) **LABEL** Capitol (UK & US) **PRODUCER** – **UK CHART** peak/weeks 0/0 **US CHART** peak/weeks 2/36 **TRACK LISTING** Night And Day/I Wish I Were In Love Again/I Got Plenty O' Nuttin'/I Guess I'll have To Change My Plan/Nice Work If You Can Get It/Stars Fell On Alabama/No One Ever Tells You/I Won't Dance/The Lonesome Road/At Long Last Love/You'd Be So Nice To Come Home To/I Got It Bad And That Ain't Good/From This Moment On/If I Had You/Oh! Look At Me Now **PERSONNEL** Frank Sinatra (v), orchestra arranged and conducted by Nelson Riddle

The same year as the towering angst of **Where Are You?** came **A Swingin' Affair!**, another fine example of Sinatra's schizoid impulses, all sassy and smooth where its successor was anxious and tense. Although it failed to chart in the UK, it wowed the Americans, who were captivated by the immaculate choice of material (Gershwin, Rodgers/Hart, Duke Ellington) and Sinatra's peerless phrasing.

Sinatra has come up with another real winner – And as I have said before, I prefer him in a swingin' mood… It all adds up to two words: artistry and talent. **Laurie Hernshaw, Melody Maker, September 1957**

Swordfishtrombones

ARTIST Tom Waits **RELEASE DATE** October 1983 (UK) **LABEL** Island (UK & US) **PRODUCER** Tom Waits **UK CHART** peak/weeks 62/3 **US CHART** peak/weeks 167/7 **TRACK LISTING** Underground/Shore Leave/Dave The Butcher/Johnsburg, Illinois/16 Shells From A Thirty-Ought-Six/Town With No Cheer/In The Neighbourhood/Just Another Sucker On The Vine/Frank's Wild Years/Swordfishtrombones/Down, Down, Down/Soldier's Things/Gin Soaked Boy/Trouble's Braids/Rainbirds **PERSONNEL** Tom Waits (v, p, a)

Tom Waits started out as a relatively traditional singer-songwriter with a penchant for after-hours cocktail muzak and a latterday lounge crooner persona. By **Swordfishtrombones** he was outdoing Captain Beefheart with his gravelly growl and experimental fusion of Dixieland jazz, free-form squonking, blues, ragtime and folk.

Swordfishtrombones – *a risk taken, a conglomeration of differences, of an altogether different Tom Waits…. He recognises the profound strangeness in the clear speech of folk music and his words assume an organic, jumbled life of their own: sounds as places, places as sound.* **Ian Penman, NME, September 1983**

Synchronicity

ARTIST The Police **RELEASE DATE** June 1983 (UK) **LABEL** A&M (UK & US) **PRODUCER** Hugh Padgham, The Police **UK CHART** peak/weeks 1/74 **US CHART** peak/weeks 1/17 **TRACK LISTING** Synchronicity I/Walking In Your Footsteps/O My God/Mother/Miss Gradenko/Synchronicity II/Every Breath You Take/King Of Pain/Wrapped Around Your Finger/Tea In The Sahara **PERSONNEL** Andy Summers (g), Stewart Copeland (d), Sting (b, v)

Having started life in 1977 as old stagers jumping on the new-wave bandwagon, The Police ended it five albums later as unashamed classic rockers in The Who mould. Compositionally it was Sting's show – the other two's contributions, **Miss Gradenko** and **Mother**, show why. But though **Murder By Numbers** was bumped off to languish in B-side status, Sting's other masterpiece, **Every Breath You Take**, which hit the top again in a 1997 Puff Daddy cover, was well-nigh perfect. A good point to quit.

Sting's eyes are secretly murderous. He smiles with a mouth that looks like its about to bite the head off a baby doll. There are five songs that suggest he is working out a perplexed and vexed persona through his pop music, and the result is fascinating. **Richard Cole, NME, June 1983**

Talking Book

ARTIST Stevie Wonder **RELEASE DATE** January 1973 (UK)/November 1972 (US) **LABEL** Tamla Motown (UK & US) **PRODUCER** Stevie Wonder **UK CHART** peak/weeks 16/48 **US CHART** peak/weeks 1/109 **TRACK LISTING** You Are The Sunshine Of My Life/Maybe Your Baby/You And I (We Can Conquer The World)/Tuesday Heartbreak/You've Got It Bad Girl/Superstition/Big Brother/Blame It On The Sun/Lookin' For Another Pure Love/I Believe (When I Fall In Love It Will Be Forever) **PERSONNEL** With Scott Edwards (b), Daniel Ben Zebulon (cg), Gloria Barley (bv), Lani Groves (bv), Jim Gilstrap (bv), Ray Parker Jr (g), Jeff Beck (lg), Buzzy Feton (lg), Loris Harvin (bv), Shirley Brewer (bv), Debra Wilson (bv), Trevor Laurence (s), Steve Madaio (t), Denise Williams (bv), Dave Sanbourne (as)

Wonder's 1972 support slot with The Rolling Stones helped him become the biggest crossover artist of the early Seventies. It also helped the first two singles from **Talking Book** – *Superstition* (written for Jeff Beck) and *You Are The Sunshine Of My Life* reach Number 1. Of course, it didn't do any harm that **Talking Book** featured a dazzling range of brilliant material: the sinuous funk of **Superstition** to the exuberant pop of **Tuesday Heartbreak** to the unabashed romanticism of **I Believe (When I Fall In Love It Will Be Forever)**.

'People ask me what soul is, but all people have soul. Soul is what you feel and you have what you feel. So anybody can have soul and you can call it whatever you want.' **Interview with Nick Jones, Melody Maker, October 1967**

Talking Heads 77

ARTIST Talking Heads **RELEASE DATE** February 1978 (UK)/September 1977 (US) **LABEL** Sire (UK & US) **PRODUCER** Tony Bongiovi, Lance Quinn, Talking Heads **UK CHART** peak/weeks 60/1 **US CHART** peak/weeks 97/6 **TRACK LISTING** Uh-Oh, Love Comes To Town/New Feeling/Tentative Decisions/Happy Day/Who Is It?/No Compassion/The Book I Read/Don't Worry About The Government/First Week-Last Week…Carefree/Psycho Killer/Pulled Up **PERSONNEL** Martina Weymouth (b), Jerry Harrison (g, k, v), David Byrne (g, v), Chris Frantz (d)

Of all the bands to emerge from New York's seminal CBGBs art-punk scene (Television, Ramones, Blondie, Richard Hell & The

Voidoids), Talking Heads were the most obviously 'intelligent': three members having attended the Rhode Island School Of Design in the early Seventies. **Talking Heads 77** was an ingenious debut, the herky-jerky, stop-start rhythms and the wayward lyrical preoccupations of mainman David Byrne indicating that here was a band who not only read books (unusual for the punk era), but also knew their pop history. Tracks like **Don't Worry About The Government** and especially the band's signature tune, **Psycho Killer**, evince a past absorbing everything from rock 'n' roll to funk to bubblegum.

… the words are often cutesy and obscure, and sometimes simplistic, seldom achieving an ideal balance. And then, despite the general bounciness, the music throughout is very self-contained, its clever but cold formality suggesting rational control, but unbridled emotion. **Chris Brazier, Melody Maker, October 1977**

Tapestry

ARTIST Carole King RELEASE DATE July 1971 (UK)/October 1970 (US) LABEL A&M (UK)/Ode (US) PRODUCER Lou Adler UK CHART peak/weeks 4/90 US CHART peak/weeks 1/302 TRACK LISTING I Feel The Earth Move/So Far Away/It's Too Late/Home Again/Beautiful/Way Over Yonder/You've Got A Friend/Where You Lead/Will You Love Me Tomorrow?/Smackwater Jack/Tapestry/(You Make Me Feel Like) A Natural Woman PERSONNEL Carole King (v), Russ Kunkel (d), Danny 'Kootch' Kortchmar (g), Charles Larkey (b), James Taylor (g, v)

Perhaps the ultimate singer-songwriter album, **Tapestry** confirmed Carole King's successful switch from Brill Building writer-by-numbers to sensitive bedsit bard. She was assisted in the transition by James Taylor, and the pair worked concurrently on his **Mud Slide Slim And The Blue Horizon** album which, released in 1971, would spawn a Number 1 single in Taylor's version of a **Tapestry** track, **You've Got A Friend**. King did likewise with **It's Too Late**, while the parent album spent a record (for a female singer) 302 weeks on the *Billboard* listing.

It is an album of surpassing personal intimacy and musical accomplishment and a work infused with a sense of artistic purpose. **Jon Landau, Rolling Stone, April 1971**

Tattoo You

ARTIST The Rolling Stones RELEASE DATE September 1981 (UK & US) LABEL Rolling Stones (UK & US) PRODUCER – UK CHART peak/weeks 2/29 US CHART peak/weeks 1/9 TRACK LISTING Start Me Up/Hang Fire/Slave/Little T&A/Black Limousine/Neighbours/Worried About You/Tops/Heaven/No Use In Crying/Waiting On A Friend PERSONNEL Mick Jagger (v, h), Keith Richard (rg), Brian Jones (lg), Bill Wyman (b), Charlie Watts (d)

As the Stones' prestige and voguishness faded, they could still trot out the odd glimmer of lazy genius and this was a patchily stunning work. The first half rocked effectively enough, but it was during the second half that the band excelled themselves. Finding a new way to cruise through ballads, they sounded genuinely soulful and almost ethereal on **Heaven**, **Worried About You** and the hit **Waiting On A Friend**. Number 1 in America for over two months, it was trailed by the **Start Me Up** single, which had a spring in its step and perhaps their last great riff to grab the groin.

Over the years the Stones have gone from a scream to a whisper… They've proved in the past they could do it and they go a considerable way towards proving it here, but the cracks are showing, and they widen with age. **Patrick Humphries, Melody Maker, September 1981**

Tea For The Tillerman

ARTIST Cat Stevens RELEASE DATE November 1970 (UK)/February 1971 (US) LABEL Island (UK)/A&M (US) PRODUCER Paul Samwell-Smith UK CHART peak/weeks 20/39 US CHART peak/weeks 8/79 TRACK LISTING Where Do The Children Play/Hard Headed Woman/Wild World/Sad Lisa/Miles From Nowhere/But I Might Die Tonight/Longer Boats/Into White/On The Road To Find Out/Father And Son/Tea For The Tillerman PERSONNEL Cat Stevens (v), Alun Davies (g), John Ryan (b), Harvey Burns (d), with string arrangments by Del Newman

Cat Stevens' transition from folk-pop teen idol to serious singer-songwriter occurred after he contracted tuberculosis in 1968, forcing him to take a sabbatical. On his return, he hit the Top 10 with **Lady D'Arbanville**. But it was the childlike narratives of **Tea For The Tillerman**, his fifth album, that really catapulted Stevens to international stardom, on the back of hits like **Wild World**.

This is the kind of album which is hard to put down but equally as hard to get excited about… like his last one, this is pleasant, relaxed and tasteful… excellent though it is… it lacks energy and tension. **A. L., Melody Maker, November 1970**

Technique

ARTIST New Order **RELEASE DATE** February 1989 (UK)/1989 **LABEL** Factory (UK)/Quest (US) **PRODUCER** New Order, Stephen Hague **UK CHART** peak/weeks 1/14 **US CHART** peak/weeks 32/28 **TRACK LISTING** Fine Time/All The Way/Love Less/Round & Round/Guilty Partner/Run/Mr Disco/ Vanishing Point/Dream Attack **PERSONNEL** Bernard Sumner (v, g), Peter Hook (b), Syephen Morris (d)

Balearic beats loomed large in New Order's fifth album since rising from the ashes of Joy Division. The new optimism and back-to-basics approach engendered by the Ibiza sessions put all talk of splits on the back burner for another year and resulted in the England football anthem *World In Motion* (not included here), which was surely as far as they could move from their doom-laden roots.

Technique never quite lives up to the sum of its considerable parts and suggests a band who have replaced some of its old edge with a new-found competence…Elsewhere New Order make anthems for people who like to dance with their headaches intact, a valuable and very British occupation. **Mark Cooper, Q, February 1989**

Teenage Head

ARTIST The Flamin' Groovies **RELEASE DATE** 1971 **LABEL** Karma Sutra **PRODUCER** – **UK CHART** peak/weeks - **US CHART** peak/weeks – **TRACK LISTING** Teenage Head/Whiskey Women/Yesterday's Numbers 32:20/High Flyin' Baby/City Lights/Have You Seen My Baby/Evil Hearted Ada/Doctor Boogie/Rumble/Shakin' All Over/That'll Be The Day/Round And Round/Going Out Theme **PERSONNEL** Rob Looney (v), Cyril Jordan (lg), Tim Lynch (rg), George Alexander (b), Danny Mihm (d)

Taking their cue from the (original Charlatans), San Francisco's Flamin' Groovies, like the MC5 and the Stooges, kept the spirit of rock 'n' roll alive in the early Seventies when pretence and indulgence threatened to capsize the already-sinking ship. **Flamingo** and its successor **Teenage Head** were part of a handful of records that opened the way for what was to become punk. Sadly they invited Dave Edmunds to produce their next album, **Shake Some Action**, and its air of classicism flipped them into the realms of power pop from which they never returned.

I always knew the Flamin' Groovies had in them… I tell ya, the fun's a-poppin' all over this album. It has the power to pull you into the never-ending party that follows the Flamin' Groovies around. **Greg Shaw, Rolling Stone, May 1971**

Temple Of Low Men

ARTIST Crowded House **RELEASE DATE** July 1988 **LABEL** Capitol (UK & US) **PRODUCER** Mitchel Froom **UK CHART** peak/weeks – **US CHART** peak/weeks 40/19 **TRACK LISTING** I Feel Possessed/Kill Eye/Into Temptation/Mansion In The Slums/When You Come/Never Be The Same/Love This life/Sister Madly/In The Lowlands/Better Be Home Soon **PERSONNEL** Neil Finn (lv, g), Paul Hester (d, v), Nick Seymour (b, v), Tim Finn (v), Richard Thompson (g), Alex Acuna (pc), Heart Attack (h), Mitchell Froom (k)

After the Split Enz break-up in 1985 Neil Finn formed a band who laboured under the names The Mullanes and then Largest Living Things before calling themselves Crowded House, after their living conditions. A multi-million selling debut album was reassuring, but this, their second, fared less well, and induced another temporary split. It was not as hit based as its predecessor (which had included *Don't Dream It's Over*), but Finn's craftsmanship had not gone astray. He was exploring darker avenues on songs like **Into Temptation** and **Better Be Home Soon**. Richard Thompson guested.

Temple Of Low Men *is entirely devoid of virtue. It's like getting wet sick tipped into your ear, listen to it gurgle about for a bit, before*

tipping itself out of the other ear for want of something a bit more interesting to do. **John Wilde, Melody Maker, July 1988**

The Temptations Sing Smokey

ARTIST The Temptations **RELEASE DATE** October 1965 (UK)/March 1965 (US) **LABEL** Tamala Motown (UK)/Gordy (US) **PRODUCER** – **UK CHART** peak/weeks 0/0 **US CHART** peak/weeks 35/26 **TRACK LISTING** The Way You Do The Things You Do/Baby, Baby I Need You/You'd Lose A Precious Love/My Girl/It's Growing/Who's Loving You/What Love Has Joined Together/What's So Good 'Bout Saying Goodbye **PERSONNEL** Eddie Kendricks (lv), Paul Williams (v), Melvin Franklin (v), Otis Williams (v), Eldridge Bryant (v)

The Temptations Sing Smokey is that rarity: a non-hits collection from Sixties Motown that is more than just a few singles plus a load of filler. *Baby, Baby I Need You* evinces the doo-wop roots of this most revered of Motown's all-male harmony groups who could boast no fewer than three lead singers: Eddie Kendricks, David Ruffin and Paul Williams. And *My Girl* was the giant hit that introduced The Temptations' alternately gruff and smooth vocals, and their lush orchestral R&B, to the world.

Tamla's five Temptations pay tribute to the fantastic songwriting, composing, record producing, Bill 'Smokey' Robinson, leader of another Tamla singing team, The Miracles… The harmonious singing is sheer delight, but these Motown males ooze such smoothness and coolness it can get dull. **Melody Maker, October 1965**

Ten

ARTIST Pearl Jam **RELEASE DATE** Febuary 1992 (UK)/December 1991 (US) **LABEL** Epic (UK & US) **PRODUCER** Pearl Jam, Rick Parashar **UK CHART** peak/weeks 18/53 **US CHART** peak/weeks 2/248 **TRACK LISTING** Once/Even Flow/Alive/Why Go/Black/Jeremy/Oceans/Porch/Garden/Deep/Release **PERSONNEL** Dave (d), Jeff (b), Eddie Vedder (v), Mike (lg), Stone (g), Rick Parashar (p, o, pc), Walter Gray (c)

To name a debut album after the basketball jersey number of your hero, Mookie Blaylock, can be considered perverse but, by selling over five million copies and only being denied the top spot by Billy Ray Cyrus, Pearl Jam's first effort more than distinguished itself. *Jeremy*, the tale of a bullied schoolkid who killed himself in front of his tormentors was controversial enough, with several other

10cc The Original Soundtrack

ARTIST 10cc **RELEASE DATE** March 1975 (UK)/April 1995 (US) **LABEL** Mercury (UK & US) **PRODUCER** 10cc **UK CHART** peak/weeks 4/40 **US CHART** peak/weeks 15/25 **TRACK LISTING** Une Nuit A Paris Part 1-One Night In Paris, Part 2-The Same Night In Paris, Part 3-Later The Same Night In Paris/I'm Not In Love/Blackmail/The Second Sitting For The Last Supper/Brand New Day/Flying Junk/Life Is A Minestrone/The Film Of My Love **PERSONNEL** Eric Stewart (v, g, b), Lol Creme (v, g, k, b), Kevin Godley (d, v), Graham Gouldman (b, v)

10cc's third long-player was a far darker affair than its predecessor. Covering such bleak subject matter as drug pushers in *Flying Junk* and the porn industry in *Blackmail*, **The Original Soundtrack** emphasised 10cc's rapier wit. There are few better examples of sophisticated, intelligent Seventies pop than this. The Mancunian studiocrats surpassed themselves on the global hit, *I'm Not In Love*, all multi-tracked harmonies and sumptuous atmospherics. And the three-part, eight-minute *Une Nuit A Paris* anticipated the baroque 'n' roll of Queen's *Bohemian Rhapsody*.

… once they scuttle into Strawberry Studios and get stuck into their composing, arranging, producing, engineering, overdubbing, compressing, mixing and so on and so forth, they mess your mind around a treat… The playing is superb throughout but the production and engineering are exemplary. **Charles Shaar Murray, NME, March 1975**

That's The Way Of The World

ARTIST Earth, Wind & Fire **RELEASE DATE** April 1975 (UK)/March 1975 (US) **LABEL** CBS (UK)/Columbia (US) **PRODUCER** – **UK CHART** peak/weeks - **US CHART** peak/weeks 1/55 **TRACK LISTING** Shinning Star/That's The Way Of The World/Happy Feelin'/All About Love/Yearnin' Learnin'/ Reasons/Africano/See The Light **PERSONNEL** Maurice White (v, d, p (k), Verdine White (v, b), Philip Bailey (v, c, p), Larry Dunn (p, s), Al McKay (g), Fred White (d), Ralph Johnson (d), Johnny Graham (g), Andrew Woolfolk (t, s)

Three years after Curtis Mayfield had topped the US chart with the soundtrack to Sig Shore's 'blaxploitation' classic **Superfly**, Earth Wind & Fire did likewise with the eponymous soundtrack to Shore's latest production which became their sixth album and first chart-topper. The band's music was so inspiring that the film was retitled after one of the songs, though its plot, which starred EW&F as a hopeful young band and Harvey Keitel as the A&R talent scout that discovered them, was nothing to write home about.

The album is a joy to listen to, while the actual playing itself is of the highest quality… Earth, Wind And Fire actually do play a brand of soul and jazz that is as eclectic as the press office at CBS would have us believe. **Chas De Whalley, NME, October 1975**

songs reflecting singer-lyricist Eddie Vedder's troubled youth. Kurt Cobain attacked the band as 'corporate', but 1992 saw **Ten** outselling Nirvana's **Nevermind**. Classic rock in the Hendrix mould.

Pearl Jam's debut finally gets a UK release and all the hoo-hah has been no word of a lie… Pearl Jam are a socially aware, riff-heavy monster re-designing the embarrassment of metal decades gone, while still cranking it up to 11. **Dave Henderson, Q, March 1992**

Ten Summoner's Tales

ARTIST Sting **RELEASE DATE** March 1993 (UK & US) **LABEL** A&M (UK & US) **PRODUCER** Sting, Hugh Padgham **UK CHART** peak/weeks 2/42 **US CHART** peak/weeks 2/68 **TRACK LISTING** Prologue (If I Ever Lose My Faith In You)/Love Is Stronger Than Justice (The Magnificent Seven)/Fields Of Gold/Heavy Cloud No Rain/She's Too Good For Me/Seven Days/Saint Augustine In Hell/It's Probably Me/Everybody Laughed But You/Shape Of My Heart/Something The Boy Said/Epilogue (Nothing 'Bout Me) **PERSONNEL** Sting (v, b), session musicians

With a reputation for pretentiousness since he disbanded the Police, Sting delivered a relatively straightforward set of pop-rock tunes on **Ten Summoner's Tales**, his fourth studio album proper. Abandoning the jazzy complexity of his 1987 LP, **Nothing Like The Sun**, and the sombre meditations of 1991's **The Soul Cages** (overshadowed by the death of his father), here Sting did what he's best at: writing accessible, melodic contemporary music such as *If I Ever Lose My Faith In You*.

… both uncompromised and relaxed… it neither chases trends, attempts to break new ground nor strains for Major Statements. It's ambitions are modest – to entertain you, of all things – and for that reason, its successes are all the more pleasing. **Anthony De Curtis, Rolling Stone, March 1993**

There Goes Rhymin' Simon

ARTIST Paul Simon RELEASE DATE May 1973 LABEL CBS (UK)/Columbia (US) PRODUCER Paul Simon UK CHART peak/weeks 4/22 US CHART peak/weeks 2/48 TRACK LISTING Kodachrome/Tenderness/Take Me To The Mardi Gras/Something So Right/One Man's Ceiling Is Another Man's Floor/American Tune/Was A Sunny Day/Learn How To Fall/St. Judy's Comet/Loves Me Like A Rock PERSONNEL Paul Simon (g), David Hood (b), Roger Hawkins (d), The Dixie Hummingbirds (v)

His eponymous debut solo album (1965's **The Paul Simon Songbook** was only released in the UK) from 1972 hinted at the World Music to come on **Gracelands**, but the follow-up, **There Goes Rhymin' Simon**, was more rooted in Simon's homeland and the music he grew up listening to, drawing on gospel with *Loves Me Like A Rock*, New Orleans jazz with *Take Me To The Mardi Gras*, and American prayer with *American Tune*.

Undoubtedly a good album, hard to criticise. It works better than his first – and shows a progression that frequently re-states much of his musical background. **Tony Stewart, NME, May 1973**

There's A Riot Going On

ARTIST Sly And The Family Stone RELEASE DATE Feb 1972 (UK)/November 1971 (US) LABEL Epic (UK & US) PRODUCER Sly Stone UK CHART peak/weeks 31/2 US CHART peak/weeks 1/31 TRACK LISTING Luv 'N' Haight/Just Like A Baby/Poet/Family Affair/Africa Talks To You 'The Asphalt Jungle'/Brave & Strong/(You Caught Me) Smilin'/Time/Spaced/Cowboy/Runnin' Away/Thank You For Talkin' To Me Africa PERSONNEL Sly Stone (v, k, g), Freddie Stone (g), Cynthia Robinson (t), Jerry Martini (s), Rosemary Stone (v, p), Larry Graham (b), Greg Errico (d)

If **Don't Call Me Nigger, Whitey** hinted at the dark side of Sly Stone's muse, **There's A Riot Goin' On** was more explicit – it is one of the bleakest albums ever made, dance or otherwise. A brutal rejection of the optimism both of the Family and of the hippy dream, it shows a beleaguered Stone attempting to deal with, in radical style, the problems of the black community, while simultaneously addressing the pitfalls of fame. Caked in cocaine, **Riot** is also one of the most stoned LPs of all time.

… one of the most drugged sounding albums yet to be released. In effect Sly was saying, 'you've made me a star and maybe I don't want to be one – what are you going to do about it?' **John Ingham, NME, May 1973**

These Foolish Things

ARTIST Bryan Ferry RELEASE DATE November 1973 LABEL Island (UK)/Atco (US) PRODUCER Bryan Ferry, John Porter, John Punter. UK CHART peak/ weeks 5/42 US CHART peak/weeks 0/0 TRACK LISTING A Hard Rain's Gonna Fall/River Of Salt/Don't Ever Change/Piece Of My Heart/Baby I Don't Care/ It's My Party/Don't Worry Baby/Sympathy For The Devil/Tracks Of My Tears/ You Won't See Me/I Love How You Love Me/Loving You Is Sweeter Than Ever/These Foolish Things PERSONNEL Bryan Ferry (v), session musicians

Bizarre that someone as avant-garde as Ferry in his role as frontman of Roxy Music should have been so determinedly retro in his parallel solo career. This, his second groupless effort, packed with cover versions and standards, saw him adopt the lounge-lizard persona many now associate with him rather than the military style he was affecting with Roxy – and when three Royal Albert Hall concerts saw him backed by group and orchestra in evening dress the writing was on the wall. The man was bigger than the group and from the late Seventies on Ferry/Roxy would be more or less interchangeable.

Self-indulgence is no crime if it works for its author, but this is an undistinguished record except in its conceit. **M. W., Melody Maker, September 1973**

Third Stage

ARTIST Boston RELEASE DATE October 1986 (UK)/November 1986 (US) LABEL MCA (UK & US) PRODUCER – UK CHART peak/weeks 37/11 US CHART peak/ weeks 1/50 TRACK LISTING Amanda/We're Ready/The Launch: Countdown-Ignition-Third Stage Separation/Cool The Engines/My Destination/A New World/To Be A Man/I Think I Like It/Can'tcha Say (You Believe In Me)/Still In Love/Hollyann. PERSONNEL Brad Delp (v, g), Tom Scholz (g, k, v), Barry Goudreau (g), Fran Sheenan (b), Sib Hashian (d), Gary Phil (g), Jim Masdea (d)

Boston are most remembered for the 1976 AOR hit **More Than A Feeling**, which heavily influenced Nirvana's anthem **Smells Like Teen Spirit**. By the mid-Eighties, however, the perfectionism of guitarist and producer Tom Scholz was in danger of leaving them in limbo. It had been eight years since their second album, **Don't Look Back**, but **Third Stage** topped the charts and yielded hits in **Amanda** and **We're Ready**. It was not as classic a work as their self-titled debut, but the obsessive focus of Scholz and Brad Delp's multilayered voice pleased a patient nation of fans.

… although he says there is, 'nothing to surpass the feeling of playing on-stage in a band like this one,' he may be rock's most reluctant star: after spending the better part of the last decade fighting with band mates, managers… Scholz has decided that he wants Boston to be a platform for philanthropic and social causes. **From an interview with Fred Goodman, Rolling Stone, October 1988**

13 songs

ARTIST Fugazi RELEASE DATE April 1990 LABEL Dischord (US) PRODUCER Fugazi/John Loder/Ted Niceley UK CHART peak/weeks – US CHART peak/weeks 0/0 TRACK LISTING Waiting Room/Bulldog Front/ Badmouth/Burning/Give Me The Cure/Suggestion/Blue Man/Margin Walker/And The Same/Burning Too/Provisional/Lockdown/Promises PERSONNEL Ian MacKaye (v, g), Guy Picciotto (v), Edward Janney (g), session musicians

These US hardcore heroes have turned their albums into six-figure sellers on their own Dischord label by persistent touring, keeping ticket prices low, permitting entrance to all ages and a refusal to play the corporate game. This, their LP debut, was technically a compilation album comprising the previously issued 12-inch singles **Fugazi** and **Margin Walker**. It has since been followed by an equally uncompromising series of releases more or less once every two years from the same line-up, but still remains a potent manifesto.

Fugazi are a breath of fresh air, a slap in the face for a music scene that is so conceited, so lazy and so jaded… Fugazi are a live grenade of raw power. **John Robb, Melody Maker, October 1991**

This Is Big Audio Dynamite

ARTIST Big Audio Dynamite RELEASE DATE November 1985 LABEL CBS (UK)/Columbia (US) PRODUCER Mick Jones UK CHART peak/weeks – US CHART peak/weeks 103/35 TRACK LISTING Medicine Show/Sony/E=Mc2/The Bottom Line/Sudden Impact/Stone Thames/B.A.D/A Party PERSONNEL Mick Jones (v, g), Don Letts (v), Dan Donovan (k), Leo Williams (b), Greg Roberts (d)

Mick Jones' West London beatbox-rock posse promised great things with this post Clash debut. Fractionally ahead of its time in welding standard guitar riffs to electro hip-hop and vocals which came within a whisker of rap, it also embraced a love of reggae's space and the capital's metropolitan pace. Don Letts was more than equipped to whip up a word-of-mouth club vibe and some snappy visuals, and this was debatably the first album by a mostly white British act to utilize sampling. **E=MC2** was a faultless single, but later agit-pop sloganeering and a reunion with Joe Strummer led to decline, Jones' pneumonia, and a split.

An occasionally engaging mess which consists of eight dub-singed middle eights stretched at times to transparency… Letts adds soundtracks; scratches and snatches of film dialogue which often come in handy as matchsticks for keeping tired ears open… sad, not bad. **John McCready, NME, November 1985**

This Nation's Saving Grace

ARTIST The Fall RELEASE DATE September 1985 LABEL Beggars Banquet (UK)/P.V.C (US) PRODUCER John Leckie UK CHART peak/weeks 54/2 US CHART peak/weeks 0/0 TRACK LISTING Mansion/Bombast/Barmy/What You Need/Spoilt Victorian Child/L.A./Gut Of The Quantifier/My New Hose/Paint Work/I Am Damo Suzuki/To Nkroachment: Yarbles PERSONNEL Stephen Hanley (b), Karl Burns (d), Brix Smith (lg, v), Simon Rogers (k, ag, b), Mark E. Smith (v, vl, g), Craig Scawlow (rg)

A triumphantly complex collection of songs which, though sometimes presenting a slightly diluted version of Mark E. Smith's vision, sound all the better for it. While the angular riffs and repetitive, mesmeric drones are present and correct, they're tempered by the presence of American guitarist Brix Smith. Her dominant pop sensibilities rub off some of the more awkward corners, resulting in a satisfyingly quirky but accessible album, with odd moments of ambiguous beauty. God forbid, you can even whistle some of the tunes.

The hip priest has taken his place as purveyor of the NOW sound. He is the lord of the new church, the man they couldn't hang, and she looks on, watching as they dance for him, laughing as they shout for him, and Mark shouts 'Yarbles'. The party's not over yet. So never mind the yarbles, here's the Fall. **The Legendary Stud Brothers, Melody Maker, September 1985**

This Year's Model

ARTIST Elvis Costello RELEASE DATE April 1978 LABEL Radar (UK)/Columbia (US) PRODUCER Nick Lowe UK CHART peak/weeks 4/14 US CHART peak/weeks 30/17 TRACK LISTING No Action/This Year's Girl/The Beat/Pump It Up/Little Triggers/You Belong To Me/Hand In Hand/(I Don't Want To Go To) Chelsea/Lip Service/Living In Paradise/Lipstick/Vogue/Night Rally PERSONNEL Elvis Costello (v, g) The Shamrocks (backing band), John McFee (g), Alex Call (g, v), Sean Hopper (k), John Ciambotti (b), Michael Shine (d)

Costello here joined forces with The Attractions for the first time, and found a sympathetic producer and ally in Nick Lowe. The band gave him visceral power and Lowe's textures. **Radio Radio** was an attack which, predictably, the airwaves read as an embrace. **Pump It Up** and (**I Don't Want To Go To) Chelsea** were hits and demonstrated that literacy and wit could play a part in the prevailing heads-down musical landscape. **Lipstick Vogue**, driven by astounding drums, was sexy despite itself.

This Year's Model… *is an achievement so comprehensive, so inspired, that it exhausts superlatives. It promotes its author to the foremost ranks of contemporary rock writers.* **Allan Jones, Melody Maker, March 1978**

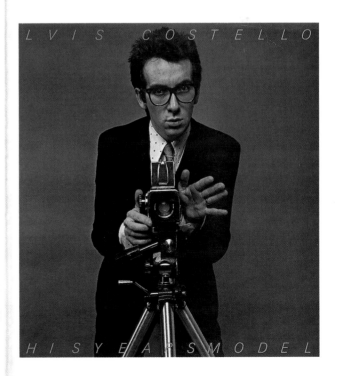

3 Feet High And Rising

ARTIST De La Soul RELEASE DATE March 1989 LABEL Big Life (UK)/Tommy Boy (US) PRODUCER Prince Paul, De La Soul UK CHART peak/weeks 13/57 US CHART peak/weeks 24/29 TRACK LISTING Intro/The Magic Number/ Change In Speak/Cool Breeze On The Rocks/Can U Keep A Secret/Jenifa Taught Me (Derwin's Revenge)/Ghetto Thang/Transmitting Live From Mars/ Eye Know/Take It Off/A Little Bit Of Soap/Tread Water/Say No Go/Do As De La Does/Plug Tunin' (Last Chance To Comprehend)/De La Orgee/Buddy (With Jungle Brothers and Q-Tip from A Tribe Called Quest)/Description/Me Myself And I/This Is A Recording 4 Living In A Full Time Era (L.I.F.E.)/I Can Do Anything (Delacratic)/D.A.I.S.Y. Age/Potholes In My Lawn PERSONNEL Posdnuos (v), Trugoy the Dove (v), P.A. Pasemaster Mase (v)

Inspired by the funky surrealism of Parliament and Funkadelic, the trio known as De La Soul came as welcome relief from rap's relentless aggression and macho posturing. Lacing hip-hop beats with their own reinvention of 'flower power', their debut album was a massive success, brimming with mellow vibes, clever textures, inscrutable in-joke references and feel-good energy. *The Daisy Age* was their creation and their kingdom. Sadly the sampling of a Sixties Turtles hit *Happy Together* initiated a lengthy and awkward law suit. Was it this that led to 1991's follow-up bearing the title *De La Soul Is Dead*? It seems these creative cartoons can't be kept down for long…

Welcome to the first psychedelic hip-hop record.… One of the most original rap records ever to come down the pile, the inventive, playful 3 Feet High And Rising *stands staid rap conventions on their def ear.* **Michael Azerrad, Rolling Stone, March 1989**

3+3

ARTIST The Isley Brothers RELEASE DATE November 1973 (UK)/September 1973 (US) LABEL Epic (UK)/T-Neck (US) PRODUCER R. Isley, O. Isley, R. Isley UK CHART peak/weeks - US CHART peak/weeks 8/37 TRACK LISTING That Lady/Don't Let Me Be Lonely Tonight/If You Were There/You Walk Your Way/Listen To The Music/What It Comes Down To/Sunshine (Go Away Today)/Summer Breeze/The Highways Of My Life PERSONNEL Ernie Isley (g, ag, pc), Marvin Isley (b), Chris Jasper (p, cl), Rocky (cg), Truman Thomas (o), George Moreland (d)

Around as a vocal group since the early Fifties, Ronald, Rudolph and O'Kelly Isley drafted in new blood for a new decade in the shape of younger brothers Ernie and Marvin and keyboardist Chris

Jasper – hence the '3+3' title. The reward was a Number 8 US album that went gold, as did the lead single *That Lady* featuring Ernie's searing, Hendrix-inspired guitar. The rock-funk mix continued through *Live It Up* until they topped the pop pile with *The Heat Is On* – but this was the breakthrough.

The mark of a great group is not always the ability to write their own material. More often it is their interpretative ability.… Their own writing is still as powerful as ever. Their arrangements are still precise, their production still critically toned to each song. **G. B., Melody Maker, November 1973**

Thriller

ARTIST Michael Jackson RELEASE DATE December 1982 LABEL Epic (UK & US) PRODUCER Quincy Jones UK CHART peak/weeks 1/173 US CHART peak/ weeks 1/122 TRACK LISTING Wanna Be Startin' Somethin'/Baby Be Mine/The Girl Is Mine (with Paul McCartney)/Thriller/Beat It/Billie Jean/Human Nature/P.Y.T. (Pretty Young Thing)/The Lady In My Life PERSONNEL Michael Jackson (v), Paul McCartney (v), session musicians

The facts are impressive enough: the biggest selling album in the world, with sales in excess of 48 million. Yet of far greater importance were the accompanying videos, all of which took the medium to new heights and broke down MTVs reluctance to air black videos. The success of **Thriller** confirmed Jackson's emergence as the key player within black music; it was also amazing to have broken down the barriers on the airwaves, a result eagerly capitalized upon by the likes of Prince. Who would have thought it all possible when the album was preceded by something as twee as **The Girl Is Mine**?

'm sure that, with the success of his last record, Jackson could have persuaded his record company to let him record with a herd of elephants. And the overall feeling that comes from **Thriller** *is that of a barely developed artist being given too much control.* **Gavin Martin, December 1982**

Timeless

ARTIST Goldie **RELEASE DATE** July 1995 **LABEL** ffrr (UK)/London (US) **PRODUCER** – **UK CHART** peak/weeks 7/- **US CHART** peak/weeks 0/0 **TRACK LISTING** Timeless/Saint Angel/State Of Mind/This Is A Bad/Sea Of Tears/Jah The Seventh/State Of Rage/Still Life/Angel/Adrift/Kemistry/You & Me **PERSONNEL** Goldie (v), with Metalheadz

After a Stateside spell promoting hip-hop, former Walsall graffiti artist Goldie came to public attention as one of the architects of Jungle, paralleling Massive Attack in his juxtaposition of reggae, orchestral and rock elements. Billed as **Goldie Presents Metalheadz**, this was the album that put it all together, blazing a trail for Roni Size and others to follow, yet few could approach his sheer eclecticism: **Sea Of Tears** was inspired by jazz-rock guitarist Pat Metheny. He'd go on briefly to squire Bjork – no more an odd combination than some of the musical elements here.

Timeless *is a relentlessly awesome compendium of the hardest, fastest, most pulse-racing, shocking, inventive, most sophisticated and finely wrought modernistic music you'll hear anywhere right now, as state of the art as* **Terminator V***.* **David Stubbs, Melody Maker, July 1995**

The Times They Are A-Changin'

ARTIST Bob Dylan **RELEASE DATE** July 1964 (UK)/March 1964 (US) **LABEL** CBS (UK)/Columbia (US) **PRODUCER** Tom Wilson **UK CHART** peak/weeks 4/20 **US CHART** peak/weeks 20/21 **TRACK LISTING** The Times They Are A-Changin'/Ballad Of Hollis Brown/With God On Our Side/One Too Many Mornings/North Country Blues/Only A Pawn In Their Game/Boots Of Spanish Leather/When The Ship Comes In/The Lonesome Death Of Hattie Carroll/Restless Farewell **PERSONNEL** Bob Dylan (v, g, h)

Having established his protest credentials with the likes of **Blowin' In The Wind** and **Talking John Birch Society Blues** Dylan nailed his colours to the mast with this album. Though his most topical effort, it now seems comparatively dated – and the likes of **One Too Many Mornings** and **Restless Farewell** indicated he was ready to move on. His next release, **Another Side Of**, would marry the solo vocal/piano/guitar approach with better songs, though the autobiographical **North Country Blues** about his upbringing in Minnesota is an often-overlooked gem.

To The Extreme

ARTIST Vanilla Ice **RELEASE DATE** September 1990 **LABEL** SBK (US) **PRODUCER** – **UK CHART** peak/weeks 4/20 **US CHART** peak/weeks 1/67 **TRACK LISTING** Dancin'/Go Ill/Havin' A Roni/Hooked/I Love You/Ice Cold/Ice, Ice Baby/Ice Is Workin' It/It's A Party/Life Is A Fantasy/Rasta Man/Stop That Train **PERSONNEL** Robert Van Winkle 'Vanilla Ice' (rap)

Vanilla Ice was a one-album-wonder who, for a brief period in late 1990, dominated the charts. Only the second ever white rapper to reach Number 1 (after the Beastie Boys), Vanilla Ice's sudden rise to prominence came with a rapped-up steal of the bassline from Queen and David Bowie's 1981 collaboration, **Under Pressure**. The attendant LP stayed at pole position for 16 weeks, shifting over seven million units, but it wasn't long before the hip-hop clothes horse with a penchant for self-mythologizing (he had to invent a violent gangsta past to appease the cred-conscious rap community) disappeared as quickly as he came.

The album consists of recycled electrosound, the fusion of weedy melodies and irritatingly tinny beats… The ryhmes are equally lame, totally lacking in substance… and delivered with the competence of a hippo on a trapeze. **Push, Melody Maker, December 1990**

Together Alone

ARTIST Crowded House **RELEASE DATE** October 1993 **LABEL** Capitol (UK & US) **PRODUCER** Micheal Froom **UK CHART** peak/weeks 4/10 **US CHART** peak/weeks 73/7 **TRACK LISTING** Kare Kare/In My Command/Nails In My Feet/Black and White Boy/Fingers Of Love/Pineapple Head/Locked Out/Private Universe/Walking On The Spot/Distant Sun/Catherine Wheels/Skin Feeling/Together Alone **PERSONNEL** Eddie Rayner (k), Noel Crombie (pc), Geoffrey Hales (pc), Tim Finn (bv), Sharon Finn (bv), Dror Erez (ad)

Recording in Kare Kare, a remote coastal area of New Zealand, and incorporating into their sound such elements as Maori choirs, brass bands and ethnic drummers, Crowded House somehow came up with their biggest seller yet. Produced by the unlikely combination of Bob Clearmountain and Youth, it gave us another glut of hit singles, such as **Nails In My Feet** and **Distant Sun**, and was only kept off the top spot by a revived Meatloaf. **Locked Out** introduced a harder, heavier guitar-driven sound. To top all this, The Finn brothers were the same year awarded the O.B.E. for services to New Zealand music.

On Together Alone, *Crowded Houses' fourth album, the lurking melancholy has come out of the shadows and moved into the foreground. The guitars are still intricately interwoven; they ring and echo. Pretty alluring sounds are still juxtaposed with ugly scenes…* **Christian Wright, Rolling Stone, April 1994**

Tommy

ARTIST The Who **RELEASE DATE** May 1969 **LABEL** Track (UK)/ Decca (US) **PRODUCER** Kit Lambert **UK CHART** peak/weeks 2/9 **US CHART** peak/weeks 4/126 **TRACK LISTING** Overture/It's A Boy/1921/Amazing Journey/Sparks/The Hawker/Christmas/Cousin Kevin/The Acid Queen/Underture/Do You Think It's Alright/Fiddle About/Pinball Wizard/There's A Doctor/Go To The Mirror!/Tommy Can You Hear Me?/Smash The Mirror/Sensation/Miracle Cure/Sally Simpson/I'm Free/Welcome/Tommy's Holiday Camp (C)/We're Not Gonna Take It **PERSONNEL** Roger Daltry (v), Pete Townsend (g, v), John Entwistle (b, v), Keith Moon (d, v repl.)

The first rock opera, *Tommy* not only became a monstrously successful movie about a deaf, dumb and blind boy (the ultimate alienated outsider for a generation coming to terms with a new decade and a new sense of hopelessness after the 'failure' of *Woodstock*), it established The Who as an international proposition and Pete Townshend as a serious rock songwriter on a par with the likes of Lennon and Dylan. And on **Pinball Wizard** and **See Me, Feel Me**, he reasserted his primacy over the melodic power-pop form, bringing a classical elegance to the *genre*.

The finished product is remarkable for the way it coheres musically as well as textually. Townshend builds his songs on simple patterns which hark back to the very beginnings of rock and roll, but the result invariably has a freshness which is The Who's birthright. **R. W., Melody Maker, January 1970**

Tonight's The Night

ARTIST Neil Young RELEASE DATE July 1975 LABEL Warner Bros. (UK)/Reprise (US) PRODUCER David Briggs & Neil Young UK CHART peak/weeks 48/1 US CHART peak/weeks 25/ TRACK LISTING Tonight's The Night/Speakin' Out/ World On A String/Borrowed Tune/Come On Baby/Let's Go Downtown/ Mellow My Mind/Roll Another Number/Albuquerque/New Mama/Lookout Joe/Tired Eyes/Tonight's The Night PERSONNEL Neil Young (v, g) Jim Messina (b), session men etc.

Inspired, if that is the word, by the drug-related deaths of Crazy Horse's Danny Whitten and Crosby, Stills, Nash & Young roadie, Bruce Berry, **Tonight's The Night** is widely hailed as one of the bleakest, most depressing records ever made: an expression of suicidal despair that ranks way down there with Lou Reed's **Berlin** and Big Star's **Sister Lovers** in the annals of chilling rock catharsis. **Tonight's The Night** made it clear, if proof were needed, that Neil Young was here for the long haul, warts and all.

Tonight's the Night… announced Neil Young's emergence from confused agonizing – about rock 'n' roll, America, Life and so on – into a creative spate which makes even Prince look like a slacker. **Phil Sutcliffe, Q, August 1993**

Too-Rye-Ay

ARTIST Dexy's Midnight Runners RELEASE DATE August 1982 (UK)/April 1983 (US) LABEL Mercury (UK & US) PRODUCER – UK CHART peak/weeks 2/46 US CHART peak/weeks 14/24 TRACK LISTING The Celtic Soul Brothers/Let's Make This Precious/All In All (This One Last Wild Waltz)/Jackie Wilson Said (I'm In Heaven When You Smile)/Old/Plan B/I'll Show You/Liars A To E/Until I Believe In My Soul/Come On Eileen PERSONNEL Kevin Rowland (v, g), Al Archer (g), Pete Williams (b), Pete Saunders (o), Andy Growcott (d), 'Big' Jimmy Patterson (tb), Steve 'Babyface' Spooner (as), Jeff 'J. B.'Blythe (ts)

As Kevin Rowland dropped the donkey jackets for gipsy chic, he exchanged R&B horns for folky strings, but still the public loved him! The 90-degree change in direction was, he confesed in the Nineties, inspired by his former lieutenant, Al Archer, who had left the picture by the time **Too-Rye-Ay** hit the charts. But though a second re-invention for *Don't Stand Me Down*, which brought shirts, suits and ties into the picture, proved too much for their fans, the lilting sounds of **Come On Eileen** and a charming cover of Van Morrison's *Jackie Wilson Said* gave this album legs.

Like **Young Soul Rebels**, *Too-Rye-Ay is also a journey through catharsis, albeit of a less intense kind. The confusion of old and new, the lyrical cross-references and recurring themes… all serve to lose you within this world, so that the overall emotional framework becomes more important than any individual song.* **Phil McNeill, NME, July 1982**

Toys In The Attic

ARTIST Aerosmith RELEASE DATE July 1975 (UK)/April 1975 (US) LABEL CBS (UK)/Columbia (US) PRODUCER Jack Douglas UK CHART peak/weeks – US CHART peak/weeks 11/128 TRACK LISTING Toys In The Attic/Uncle Salty/Adam's Apple/Walk This Way/Big Ten Inch Record/Sweet Emotion/No More No More/Round And Round/You See Me Crying PERSONNEL Tom Hamilton (b, g), Joey Kramer (d, pc), Joe Perry (lg, rg, bv, pc), Steven Tyler (v), hm (pc), Brad Whitford (rg, lg), orchestra conducted by Michael Maineiri

The durable Aerosmith, who reputedly only ever 'wanted to be the biggest thing that walked the planet', put 'Stones clones' accusations to rest – although singer Steven Tyler boasts the most Jaggeresque mouth this side of Jagger – with a sleaze rock classic brimming with energy and not averse to tunes. R.E.M. were much later to cover the title track, and **Walk This Way** was translated into a rap 'n' roll standard in 1986 by Run DMC (thus resuscitating Areosmith's own declining legend). Deeply influential and famously ribald, the band were touring the USA vigorously at the time, but not elsewhere, quipping: 'We were afraid to go through customs.'

There's nothing especially new about Aerosmith's music, no revelations of a new dawn, or sign of unmitigated genius at work. There is however an indefinable rightness about their brand of rocking, a cool confidence that is no mere flashiness. **Chris Welch, Melody Maker, June 1975**

TRACY CHAPMAN

Tracy Chapman

ARTIST Tracy Chapman RELEASE DATE April 1988 LABEL Elektra (UK & US) PRODUCER David Kershenbaum UK CHART peak/weeks 1/75 US CHART peak/weeks 1/61 TRACK LISTING Talkin' Bout A Revolution/Fast Car/Across The Lines/Behind The Wall/Baby Can I Hold You/Mountains 'O Things/She's Got Her Ticket/Why?/For My Lover/If Not Now…/For You PERSONNEL Tracy Chapman (v, ag), Jack Holder (g, o), Larry Klein (b), Denny Fongheiser (d)

A Sixties throwback, Ohio-born Chapman sang, strummed, and made brief but biting political statements. This debut album emerged just prior to her appearance at the Nelson Mandela tribute concert at Wembley, which was watched by a massive television audience and made her flavour of the year, though it was not repeated. While **Talkin' Bout A Revolution** was self-typecasting, the global hit **Fast Car** revealed a deft songwriting ability and lyrical suss.

She writes strong songs, not in the earth-moving, finger-pointing sense, but in a personal open-soul style. Production wise it tends to stray towards niceville, hence the Suzanne/Joni slurs, but like Vega and Mitchell she's able to rise above the mellowness and pierce the hearts with her pain. **Len Brown, NME, December 1988**

Traffic

ARTIST Traffic RELEASE DATE October 1968 (UK)/November 1968 (US) LABEL Island (UK)/United Artist (US) PRODUCER Jimmy Miller UK CHART peak/weeks 9/8 US CHART peak/weeks 17/26 TRACK LISTING You Can All Join In/ Pearly Queen/Don't Be Sad/Who Knows What Tomorrow May Bring/ Feelin' Alright?/Vagabond Virgin/Forty Thousand Headmen/Cryin' To Be Heard/No Time To Live/Means To An End PERSONNEL Dave Mason (h, lv, g, ag, b, o), Steve Winwood (lg, b, lv, o, p, hd), Chris Wood (ts, fl, ss, d, pc), Dave Mason (lv, ag, h, g, b, o), Jim Capaldi (d, pc, lv)

The conflict between Winwood and his jazzy pretensions and the poppier sensibilities of co-founder Dave Mason led to the latter's departure during recording of their second, eponymous album. **Traffic** does, however, contain some of Mason's strongest material, such as the insistent *Feelin' Alright?*, later recorded by Joe Cocker and vocal group Three Dog Night. The absence of the whimsical million seller, *Hole In My Shoe*, emphasized the band's serious intentions.

Trans-Europe Express

ARTIST Kraftwerk RELEASE DATE April 1977 LABEL Capitol (UK & US) PRODUCER Ralf Hütter & Florien Schneider UK CHART peak/weeks 49/7 US CHART peak/weeks 119/10 TRACK LISTING Europe Endless/The Hall of Mirrors/Showroom Dummies/Trans-Europe Express/Metal on Metal/Franz Schubert/Endless Endless PERSONNEL Ralf Hütter (v, e), Florien Schneider (v, e), Karl Bartos (ep), Wolfgang Flur (ep)

Having inspired David Bowie's Berlin soundscapes, Kraftwerk were entitled to drop his name on their 1977 release, recorded at their Kling Klang studios. Returning to the transport theme of their commercial breakthrough, **Autobahn**, they created an album that would only chart in Britain in 1982 after the surprise success of **The Model**, but it was influential enough to be sampled incessantly in the Eighties, most notably Afrika Bambaataa's **Planet Rock**.

Synthesizers, or electronic waves, are an androgynous medium, more so than playing the guitar… We have been playing synthesizers for 16 years. **In interview, NME, January 1987**

Transformer

ARTIST Lou Reed RELEASE DATE 21st April 1973 LABEL RCA (UK & US) PRODUCER David Bowie, Mick Ronson UK CHART peak/weeks 13/25 US CHART peak/weeks 29/31 TRACK LISTING Vicious/Andy's Chest/Perfect Day/Hangin' 'Round/Walk On The Wild Side/Make Up/Satellite Of Love/ Wagon Wheel/New York Telephone Conversation/I'm So Free/Goodnight Ladies PERSONNEL Lou Reed (v, g), David Bowie (bv), Mick Ronson (bv, g, p, rc), The Thunder Thighs (bv), Klaus Voorman (b), Herbie Flowers (b, ta, dbb), John Halzey (d), Barry Desouza (d), Ritchie Dharma (d), Ronnie Ross (bs)

When Lou Reed left The Velvet Underground they weren't the legends they are today, so he (like Mott the Hoople) was glad of a leg-up from the currently chart-storming David Bowie. This focused on the street-smarts apparent on Reed's solo debut and sugar-coated them with melody, as with **Walk On The Wild Side** (which even got the phrase 'giving head' on to the radio) and **Perfect Day**, a song that became a hit 25 years later in a bizarre all-star BBC-sponsored version.

'I don't think **Transformer** *is a decadent album. Singing about hustlers and gay people isn't decadent, is it? Singing about violence isn't decadent. The only song that I'd put in that category would be* **New York Conversation**.*'* Lou Reed interview with Nick Kent, NME, April 1973

Treasure

ARTIST The Cocteau Twins RELEASE DATE November 1984 LABEL 4-A.D. (UK)/ Reprise (US) PRODUCER Cocteau Twins UK CHART peak/weeks 29/8 US CHART peak/weeks 0/0 TRACK LISTING Ivo/Lorelei/Beatrix/ Persephone/ Pandora/Amelia/Aloysius/Cicely/Otterley/Domino PERSONNEL Elizabeth Fraser (v), Robin Guthrie (g, k), Will Heggie (b)

With **Treasure**, the Cocteau's bold and originally over-reaching experimentation dovetailed with structured emotion to produce an album that helped to define not just the trio but also their then label and an entire indie era. The first to prompt reviews bearing the phrase 'sonic cathedrals', Liz, Robin and Will were themselves personable and self-deprecating. Yet Guthrie's inspired layers of dreamy guitars and Liz's breathtaking voice still possess the magic to jolt you from musical *ennui*. Lorelei and Domino were just two ports of call on an astounding aural journey, though perhaps naming the first track after the boss of their record company was a tad creepy.

There is indeed an air of twee-ness about these Cocteau Twins, which would be cloying except that their music can rise above it, sometimes to realms of genuine magnificence… there's something that haunts – something more than most music does. **Paul Du Noyer, NME, November 1984**

The Trinity Sessions

ARTIST Cowboy Junkies RELEASE DATE January 1988 LABEL Latent PRODUCER – UK CHART peak/weeks - US CHART peak/weeks 26/29 TRACK LISTING Mining For Gold/Misguided Angel/Blue Moon Revisited/I Don't Get In/I'm So Lonesome I Could Cry/To Love Is To Bury/200 More Miles Dreaming My Dreams With You/Working On A Building/Sweet Jane/Postcard Blues/Walking After Midnight PERSONNEL Michael Timmins (g), Margo Timmins (v), Peter Timmins (d), Alan Anton (B)

Recorded for $500 in an abandoned Toronto church, with one microphone, this oozed with a mournful, eerie atmosphere. Margo Timmins sang with hypnotic languor, and her brother Michael showed the beginnings of major songwriting gifts. Meanwhile their interpretations of others' nuggets, worked through on their debut **Whites Off Earth Now!**, were so special that Lou Reed described their minimal, plaintive **Sweet Jane** as the best version of the song he'd heard. Hank Williams's **I'm So Lonesome I Could Cry** and Patsy Cline's **Walking After Midnight** were similarly onomatopoeic. These sessions may have invented country-trance. They sold a quarter of a million, mainly by word of mouth and press response.

Their trump card is definitely the quiet intensity of Margo Timmins' vocals which carry the album. Not quite so compelling are the Junkie's 'developing' songwriting skills... a harmless, rootsy cabaret entertainment, well stocked with 'slow numbers' for when the world music dance party decides to take a breather. **Robert Sandall, Q, April 1989**

Triumph

ARTIST The Jacksons RELEASE DATE October 1980 (UK & US) LABEL Epic (UK & US) PRODUCER The Jacksons UK CHART peak/weeks 13/16 US CHART peak/weeks 10/29 TRACK LISTING Can You Feel It/Lovely One/State of Shock/Your Ways/Everybody/Heartbreak Hotel/Time Waits For No One/Walk Right Now/Give It Up/Wondering Who PERSONNEL Michael Jackson (lv), Jackie Jackson (v), Tito Jackson (v), Jermaine Jackson (v), Marlon Jackson (v)

Michael Jackson has frequently cast a long shadow over the efforts of his siblings: while their work for Motown is often recalled, albums get overlooked – which is a pity, for **Triumph** is worthy of more than a passing glance. The Michael influence was very much in evidence, extending to the video for **Can You Feel It**, which arrived too late to support the single in the UK; but L.A. radio station KIQQ surely went over the top by playing **State Of Shock** (featuring guest vocalist Mick Jagger) for 22 continuous hours!

The album doesn't have a weak track on it and the Jackson writing, producing and performing combines to make as strong, exciting and satisfying a pop record as you're likely to get before Christmas. Its title is no exaggeration. **Geoff Brown, Melody Maker, October 1980**

Trout Mask Replica

ARTIST Captain Beefheart RELEASE DATE November 1969 LABEL Straight (UK & US) PRODUCER Captain Beefheart UK CHART peak/weeks 21/1 US CHART peak/weeks 0/0 TRACK LISTING Frownland/The Dust Blows Forward 'N Dust Blows Back/Dachau Blues/Ella Guru/Hair Pie: Bake/Moonlight On Vermont/Hair Pie: Bake 2/Pena/Well/When Big Joan Sets Up/Fallin' Ditch/Sugar 'N' Spikes/Ant Man Be/Pachuco Cadaver/Bill's Corpse/Sweet Sweet Bulbs/Neon Meate Dream Of An Octafish/China Pig/My Human Gets Me Blues/Dali's Car/Orange Claw Hammer/Wild Life/She's Too Much For My Mirror/Hobo Chang Ba/The Blimp (Mousetrap Replica)/Steal Softly Thru Snow/Old Fart At Play/Veteran's Day Poppy PERSONNEL Captain Beefheart (b), Don Van Vliet, (v, h, g, wi inst.), Alex St. Clair (g), Doug Moon (g), Jerry Handley (b), Paul Blakely (d)

Zappa-produced, this is a 28-track double and an avant-garde milestone. Musically it's hysterically inventive, simultaneously embracing ordered blues and chaotic jazz-based improvisation.

Mistakes can clearly be heard, though whether they are mistakes remains disputable, and The Captain's voice is ludicrously high in the mix. Very weird, it was described by Lester Bangs as 'a whole new universe... a landscape of guitars which hit me like a bomb.' *Dali's Car* later lent its name to an Eighties band featuring Peter Murphy and Mick Karn, but even that was possibly the least peculiar thing about Beefheart's best.

The entire double-album... was conceived, written, and recorded in just eight and a half hours, according to Beefheart.... 'I really wonder about mixing. I don't like the idea of it. **Trout Mask Replica** *has a natural sound – as natural as you can get from amplifiers.'* **Captain Beefheart in interview with Richard Williams, Melody Maker, November 1969**

Truckin' With Albert Collins

ARTIST Albert Collins RELEASE DATE 1969 LABEL Blue Thumb PRODUCER Billy Hall UK CHART peak/weeks – US CHART peak/weeks 0/0 TRACK LISTING – PERSONNEL Albert Collins (g, v, cp), Big Tiny (ts), Henry Hayes (as), Herbert Henderson (d), Bill Johnson (b), Frank Mitchell (t), Pete Welding (in)

A seminal blues guitarist, hailed as one of the world's best, by Hendrix among many, he went by many nicknames or lordly titles: the master of the Telecaster, the Houston twister and the Razorblade amongst them. The band Canned Heat sought him out and helped bring him some of the popularity his cool sharp style merited. This technique is evident all over this glacial album of instrumentals. He later worked on some scorching collaborations with fellow blues giants old and young, and revealed a sumptuous ability as a knowing blues vocalist.

True

ARTIST Spandau Ballet RELEASE DATE March 1983 (UK)/May 1983 (US) LABEL Chrysalis (UK & US) PRODUCER – UK CHART peak/weeks 1/- US CHART peak/weeks 19/37 TRACK LISTING Pleasure/Communication/Code Of Love/Gold/Lifeline/Heaven Is A Secret/Foundation/True PERSONNEL Tony Hadley (v, sn), Gary Kemp (k, g), Steve Norman (s, g), Martin Kemp (b), John Keeble (d)

Spandau Ballet started life as heroes of London's underground club scene, although with early electro hits like **To Cut A Long Story Short** and **The Freeze**, they soon left behind their original cult audience. Their big single from 1981, **Chant Number One**, was a seminal chunk of white funk, but by **True** Spandau had moved even further towards the mainstream. Featuring the hits **Gold**, **Communication** and the title track – their first UK Number 1 – **True** was a successful collection of blue-eyed pop-dance.

Well the truth is that it's extremely easy to listen to... and even easier to forget. They really shoud date-stamp these things, perfectly disposable product for the greedy, slobbering jaws for runaway consumer society. Not to be eaten after March 5. **Steve Lake, Melody Maker, February 1983**

True Blue

ARTIST Madonna **RELEASE DATE** July 1986 **LABEL** Sire (UK & US) **PRODUCER** Madonna, Patrick Leonard, Stephen Bray **UK CHART** peak/weeks 1/81 **US CHART** peak/weeks 1/82 **TRACK LISTING** Papa Don't Preach/Open Your Heart/White Heat/Live To Tell/Where's The Party/True Blue/La Isla Bonita/Jimmy Jimmy/Love Makes The World Go Round **PERSONNEL** Madonna (v), session musicians

Two men, Patrick Leonard and Steve Bray, arguably played as big a part in this album as Madonna herself, co-writing songs and producing the result with her. Leonard, best known for his work with the Jacksons, became a father during the sessions – ironic, since the album's controversial opening track *Papa Don't Preach* posed Madonna in the role of a single mother. Its UK Number 1 title track, her third, gave her a share of the record with Sandie Shaw for a female artist, *La Isla Bonita* making it hers alone.

What Warhol captured about Monroe was not her personality (except in negative) but the sheer iconic power of her image, and it's that status that Madonna aspires to. Music is the medium, but stardom is the message (and the massage). **Don Watson, NME, July 1986**

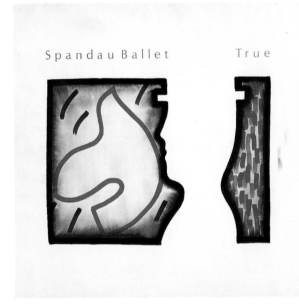

Truth And Beauty

ARTIST Ian McNabb **RELEASE DATE** June 1993 **LABEL** This Way Up **PRODUCER** – **UK CHART** peak/weeks 51/- **US CHART** peak/weeks – **TRACK LISTING** (I Go) My Own Way/These Are The Days/Great Dreams Of Heaven/Truth And Beauty/I'm Game/If Love Was Like Guitars/Story Of My Life/That's Why I Believe/Trip With Me/Make Love To You/Presence Of The One **PERSONNEL** Ian Mcnab (v, g, k)

Merseyside singer-songwriter McNabb split his band the Icicle Works after they failed to crack the big time. This, his first solo album, which took three post-band years to emerge, was an undeniably impressive collection of timeless, guitar-based songs including the single *Great Dreams Of Heaven*. Though it charmed critics, sales disappointed Epic, the major label he had signed the Icicles to just before their split, so he found more congenial indie-label surroundings to regain his momentum with the subsequent *Head Like A Rock* and *Merseybeast*, the former a blaring, band-backed effort inspired by Neil Young and using his musicians.

'If love was like guitars' Ian McNabb sang on his last album, **Truth and Beauty**, *'We'd all be stars.' He was for a while… McNabb made a solo album full of stirring guitars… paid for it himself…* **CUT, July 1984**

Tubular Bells

ARTIST Mike Oldfield **RELEASE DATE** May 1973 (UK)/November 1973 (US) **LABEL** Virgin (UK & US) **PRODUCER** – **UK CHART** peak/weeks 1/271 **US CHART** peak/weeks 3/45 **TRACK LISTING** Tubular Bells (Side 1)/Tubular Bells (Side 2) **PERSONNEL** Mike Oldfield with: Jon Field (fl), Sally Oldfield (v), Mundy Ellis (v), Steve Broughton (d), Lindsay Cooper (dbb)

Without the former Kevin Ayers guitarist, Virgin boss Richard Branson would not have had a record company, let alone an airline! What's more, he realized it: when the reclusive multi-instrumentalist proved unwilling to tour to promote his UK chart-topping opus, Branson dangled the keys to his sports car in front of him – an incentive Oldfield apparently found irresistible! Excerpts were later used in the horror movie *The Exorcist*, leading to a surprise US Top 10 single.

I first heard this album in the home of a disk jockey who feels **Tubular Bells** *will be a lasting work of the rock era. I cannot see into 2000, but… in the land of should be, it is already a gold album.* **Paul Gambaccini, Rolling Stone, November 1973**

Tuesday Night Music Club

ARTIST Sheryl Crow **RELEASE DATE** October 1993 **LABEL** A&M (UK & US) **PRODUCER** Bill Bottrell **UK CHART** peak/weeks 68/ **US CHART** peak/weeks 3/100 **TRACK LISTING** Run, Baby, Run/Leaving Las Vegas/Strong Enough/Can't Cry Anymore/Solidify/The Na-Na Song/No One Said It Would Be Easy/What I Can Do For You/All I Wanna Do/We Do What We Can/I Shall Believe **PERSONNEL** Sheryl Crow (v, p, g), Bill Bottrell (g, sp), Kevin Gilbert (d), David Baerwald (g), Dan Schwartz (b), Brian Macleod (d), David Ricketts (b)

How different things might have been for this 'overnight' success story: already aged 30, her debut album was scrapped, at great expense to A&M, after she deemed it 'too perfect'. With a new producer and musician friends she initiated Tuesday evening get-togethers doubling as jam sessions which resulted in the laid-back mannerisms of this release. Global hit and Grammy-winner *All I Wanna Do* boasted an ingratiating hook uncharacteristic of her better songs but did its job by winning two further Grammys. Lacing her acoustic rock with light funk flirtations Crow's crisp voice and unaffected good looks gave her the populist appeal such fine songs as *Run Baby Run* and *Leaving Las Vegas* demanded.

'I'm a well-rounded musician,' Crow says, 'but I don't do any one thing well. In a way, that's been good because I think that if you become too adept at something, you can lose touch with your sense of spontaneity… When we made **Tuesday Night Music Club**, *the rule was that everyone had to play unfamiliar instruments.'* **From an interview with Elysa Gardner, Rolling Stone, December 1994**

Tunnel Of Love

ARTIST Bruce Springsteen RELEASE DATE October 1987 LABEL CBS (UK)/Columbia (US) PRODUCER Bruce Springsteen, Jon Landou, Chuck Plotkin UK CHART peak/weeks 1/33 US CHART peak/weeks 1/45 TRACK LISTING Ain't Got You/Tougher Than The Rest/All That Heaven Will Allow/Spare Parts/Cautious Man/Walk Like A Man/Tunnel Of Love/Two Faces/Brilliant Disguise/One Step Up/When You're Alone/Valentine's Day PERSONNEL Bruce Springsteen (v, g), David Sancious (k), Danny Federici (k), Garry Tallent (b), Vini Lopez (d), Clarence Clemens (S), Steve Van Zandt (lg)

In a now characteristic *volte-face*, Springsteen rejected the vote-winning formula of **Born In The USA** for the darker, moodier textures of **Tunnel Of Love**. Here, Springsteen shifted his gaze from the streets of America's heartland to the blue-collar homes themselves, an analysis of the private wars that take place every day between married couples (his relationship with his wife, model Julianne Phillips, was disintegrating at the time).

There is too much purpose behind **Tunnel Of Love** *to treat it as anything but various expressions of moral dilemma…. The songs are monuments to struggle and dissatisfaction, attempts to flesh out and activate what broods inactive inside us all.* **Steve Sutherland, Melody Maker, October 1987**

The Twang's The Thang

ARTIST Duane Eddy His 'Twangy' Guitar And The Rebels RELEASE DATE April 1960 (UK)/January 1960 (US) LABEL London (UK)/Jamie (US) PRODUCER Lester Sill, Lee Hazlewood UK CHART peak/weeks 2/25 US CHART peak/weeks 18/24 TRACK LISTING My Blue Heaven/Tiger Love And Turnip Greens/The Last Minute Of Innocence/Route No 1/You Are My Sunshine/St Louis Blues/Night Train To Memphis/The Battle/Trambone/Blueberry Hill/Rebel Walk/Easy PERSONNEL Jim Horn (s, fl), Larry Knechtel (p), Al Casey (b), Don Owens and Corky Casey (rg), Jimmy Troxel (d), E.V. Freeman Singers (v), Ben Domotto (Rebel Yells), DUANE EDDY (Twangy Guitar)

It was his trademark: the word 'twang' appears in half a dozen titles of Duane Eddy Albums, and the 'Twangy' guitar sound, perfected on his beloved red Gretsch Chet Atkins 6120, likewise dominated single hits like **Rebel Rouse** and **Peter Gunn** and influenced the likes of Hank Marvin and George Harrison. **The Twang's The Thang** maintained the formula developed by Eddy and his producer Lee Hazelwood – a bassy, bluesy guitar riff, a dollop of sax and a liberal peppering of good ol' rebel yells.

Twelve Dreams Of Dr Sardonicus

ARTIST Spirit RELEASE DATE Febuary 1971 (UK)/December 1970 (US) LABEL Epic (UK & US) PRODUCER – UK CHART peak/weeks – US CHART peak/weeks 63/14 TRACK LISTING Nothing To Hide/Nature's Way/Animal Zoo/Love Has Found A Way/Why Can't I Be Free/Mr Skin/Space Child/When I Touch You/Sweet Worm/Life Has Just Begun/Morning Will Come/Soldier PERSONNEL Randy California (g, v), Jay Ferguson (v), John Locke (k), Mark Andes (b), Ed Cassidy (d)

After three albums' worth of psychedelic jazz-blues-rock-folk eclecticism, Spirit released what is widely considered their masterpiece. A West Coast band quite unlike any other, Spirit were led by the charismatic Randy California (who died in 1997, aged 45) and his famously bald stepfather, Ed Cassidy, on drums. **Twelve Dreams…** demonstrates their supreme mastery of pop's myriad styles: from the cool jazz of **Love Has Found A Way** to the freakily vari-speed **Soldier** to the horn-driven rock of **Mr Skin** to Spirit's theme song, the gentle eco-ballad, **Nature's Way**.

… to bad mouth this LP on account of its shortcomings is like chastising the child for watering the rhubarb but forgetting to buy the bacon… A blockbuster of a record. **Nick Tosches, Rolling Stone, March 1971**

12 songs

ARTIST Randy Newman RELEASE DATE April 1970 LABEL Reprise (UK & US) PRODUCER – UK CHART peak/weeks – US CHART peak/weeks – TRACK LISTING Have You Seen My Baby?/Let's Burn The Cornfield/Mama Told Me Not To Come/Tickle Me/I'll Be Home/So Long Dad/Living Without You/Last Night I Had A Dream/I Think Its Going To Rain Today/Lover's Prayer/Maybe I'm Doing It Wrong/Yellow Man/Old Kentucky Home/Davy The Fat Boy/Lonely At The Top PERSONNEL Randy Newman (v, p)

Master of irony Randy Newman hit his stride with this, his second album which featured another giant of American music Ry Cooder on guitar. *Arrivistes* will recognize **Mama Told Me Not To Come**, taken to the top by Three Dog Night months after this album's release, but other songs were less commercial: rape, suicide, inbreeding were all covered in a deceptively genial style, not unlike his early idol Fats Domino – who would return the compliment by covering **Have You Seen My Baby**.

12 Songs *is the announcement of the full emergence of a leading innovator in rock 'n' roll; hopefully, with the release of this album, Randy Newman will no longer have to worry about being misunderstood.* **Bruce Grimes, Rolling Stone, April 1970**

Two Sevens Clash

ARTIST Culture RELEASE DATE 1978 LABEL Shanachie PRODUCER – UK CHART peak/weeks – US CHART peak/weeks – TRACK LISTING Get Ready To Ride The Lion To Zion/Black Starliner Must Come/Jah Pretty Face/See Them A-Come/Natty Dread Taking Over/Talking Over/Calling Rasta Far 1/I'm Alone In The Wilderness/Private Days/Two Sevens Clash/I'm Not Ashamed PERSONNEL Kenneth Lloyd Dayes (v), Sly Dunbar (d), Lennox Gordon, Eric Lamont (g), Lloyd Parks, Robbie Shakespeare (b), Errol Nelson, Franklyn Waul (k), session musicians

Singer Joseph Hill's poeticism and diversity and some complex yet concise rhythms made Culture an instant essential to the reggae world. Chanting and brooding, against racial oppression and acclaiming the joys of his Rastafarian beliefs, Hill's harmonies with Albert Walker and Kenneth Dayes served as a template for all his later work. Jamaica had rarely if ever known a more influential work. *Fussing And Fighting* became the song most identified with the Kingston ghetto peace movement of that year and the next; but **Two Sevens Clash** had tunes too, and some super-tight arrangements. And, of course, Hill's gigantic versatile voice.

Culture have emerged as something not unlike the 1977 reggae sensation. Fittingly so, considering the trio have been as responsible as any… in establishing the year in the calendar… It's dread! **Penny Reel, NME, September 1977**

Tyranny And Mutation

ARTIST Blue Öyster Cult RELEASE DATE March 1973 LABEL CBS (UK)/Columbia (US) PRODUCER Murray Krugman & Sandy Pearlman UK CHART peak/weeks – US CHART peak/weeks 122/13 TRACK LISTING The Black/The Red & The Black/O.D.'d On Life Itself/Hot Rails To Hell/7 Screaming Diz-Busters/The Red/Baby Ice Dog/Wings Wetted Down/Teen Archer/Mistress Of The Salmon/Salt (Quicklime Girl) PERSONNEL Eric Bloom (v, g), Buck Dharma (lg, v), Allen Lanier (rg, k), Joe Bouchard (b, v), Albert Bouchard (d, v)

With ambitions beyond heavy metal's generally empty posturing, B.O.C. sought to bring real weight to their handling of Hell's Angel biker imagery and *Altamont* references. They wanted a one-way ticket to darkness and oblivion, sure, but they wanted to say brainy bookish things along the ride (guitarist/keyboardist Allan Lanier was then courting one Patti Smith). Studiously tight but wantonly loud, their second album accordingly mixed full-on hedonism and bleak narcotic languor. Donald Roeser's guitar flew. At this time B.O.C. hadn't lapsed into self-parody; they did not yet fear the reaper.

The music is unswervingly heavy in the best punk rock traditions. Their speciality is to rip through songs at such a pace that the listener has hardly time to gather his wits together… the result is one hell of an album. **M. O., Melody Maker, May 1974**

UF Orb

ARTIST The Orb RELEASE DATE July 1992 LABEL Big Life (UK)/Mercury (US) PRODUCER – UK CHART peak/weeks 1/ US CHART peak/weeks – TRACK LISTING O.O.B.E./U.F. Orb/Blue Room/Towers Of Dub/Close Encounters/Majestic/Sticky End PERSONNEL Dr Alex Paterson (sy, k), Jim Cauty (sy, k)

With a typically mobile bassline supplied by Jah Wobble, the near 40-minute track, *Blue Room*, dominates the Orb's second album. It was released as a single and created pop history as the longest

ever chart entry. The album was no less sensational: an ambient triple vinyl effort from an underground act that topped not only the indie but the national charts. The third vinyl disc, featuring a Brixton Academy performance from 1991, was available for CD buyers with an accompanying video: *Beyond The Ultraworld: Patterns And Textures.*

The magnificent 12-minute **Towers of Dub** *is the main attraction here, with its ticking rhythm urged on by an insistent bass, while a bluesy mouth organ and waves of gentle melodic electronics and effects are woven in and out.* **Ian Cranna, Q, August 1992**

Uncle Meat

ARTIST Frank Zappa RELEASE DATE September 1969 LABEL Transatlantic UK)/Bizarre/Straight (US) PRODUCER Herb Cohen UK CHART peak/weeks – US CHART peak/weeks – TRACK LISTING Uncle Meat/The Voice Of Cheese/Nine Types Of Industrial Pollution/Zolar Czakl/Dog Breath In The Year Of The Plague/The Legend Of The Variations/Louie Louie/The Dog Breath Variations/Sleeping In A Jar/Our Bizarre Relationship/The Uncle Meat Variations/Electric Aunt Jemima/Prelude To King Kong/God Bless America/A Pound For A Brown On The Bus/Ian Underwood Whips It Out/Mr Green Genes/We Can Shoot You/If We'd All Been Living In California/The Air/Project X/Cruising For Burgers/Uncle Meat Film Excerpt Part II/King Kong Itself/King Kong II/King Kong III/King Kong IV/King Kong V/King Kong VI/PERSONNEL Frank Zappa (g, v), Ray Collins (v), Elliott Ingber (g), Roy Estrada (b), Jim Black (d)

Satirist, modern classical composer, doo-wop *aficionado* and straight rock 'n' roller, Frank Zappa was master of many trades, able to leap from complex Stravinsky and Stockhausen-inspired symphonic collages to pure pop, often within a single tune. **Uncle Meat** was a sprawling double album soundtrack to a film that was never completed, featuring 31 song bites full of snatched conversations, instrumental passages, jazz fusioneering and focused melodies that demonstrated Zappa's bewilderingly versatile approach.

A double volume set of madness, absurdity, serious music, rock and roll, electronics… it remains exciting, weird and basically entertaining… they are obviously fine musicians and it is well worth the effort to try and understand them. **Melody Maker, June 1969**

Under A Blood Red Sky

ARTIST U2 **RELEASE DATE** February 1983 (UK & US) **LABEL** Island (UK & US) **PRODUCER** Jimmy Levine **UK CHART** peak/weeks 2/203 **US CHART** peak/weeks 28/- **TRACK LISTING** Gloria/11 O'Clock Tick Tock/I Will Follow/Party Girl/Sunday Bloody Sunday/New Year's Day/'40'/The Electric Co **PERSONNEL** Bono (v), The Edge (g, k), Adam Clayton (b), Larry Mullen (d)

Red Rocks Amphitheater, a natural bowl nestling between sandstone cliffs 12 miles west of Denver, has proved a tough venue on occasion. The Beatles suffered from altitude sickness and in July 1971 Colorado police were forced to use tear gas to quell an unruly Jethro Tull audience. In June 1983 U2 were confronted by a torrential downpour, but played on despite the conditions to record for posterity the majestic power of the band in performance, including **Sunday Bloody Sunday** off the album **War**, a highlight of their set for many years. The result: a most successful live album.

Under The Pink

ARTIST Tori Amos **RELEASE DATE** Febuary 1994 **LABEL** Atlantic Records (UK)/Eastwest (US) **PRODUCER** – **UK CHART** peak/weeks 1/- **US CHART** peak/weeks 12/35 **TRACK LISTING** Pretty Good Year/God/Bells For Her/Past The Mission/Baker Baker/The Wrong Band/The Waitress/Cornflake Girl/Icicle/Cloud On My Tongue/Space Dog/Yes, Anastasia **PERSONNEL** Tori Amos (v,p)

Amos showed scant regard for commercialism with this abstract opus, which took the emotional bloodletting of **Little Earthquakes** into more mystical terrain. While **Cornflake Girl** was jaunty enough and nodded at Kate Bush, the bulk of the record was harrowingly emotional and full of striking imagery. Not many artists can call a song **God** and keep your attention on the serious side of laughter. Unlike Bush, Amos put herself through marathon world tours. Truly kinky and fascinatingly oddball, she seemed, in this album, to establish a unique style.

Perfect for listeners who regard their own overblown emotion as opera; she's the anal retentive's demon fantasy. And her work… captures a beauty that's disturbing, private, and almost too intimate to reveal. **The Year In Records 1994, Rolling Stone, December 1994**

The Undertones

ARTIST The Undertones **RELEASE DATE** May 1979 (UK)/January 1980 (US) **LABEL** Sire (UK & US) **PRODUCER** – **UK CHART** peak/weeks 13/21 **US CHART** peak/weeks 154/7 **TRACK LISTING** Family Entertainment/Girl's Don't Like It/Male Model/I Gotta Getta/Wrong Way/Jump Boys/Here Comes The Summer/Billy's Third/Jimmy Jimmy/True Confessions/(She's A) Runaround/I Know A Girl/Listening In **PERSONNEL** Feargal Sharkey (v), John O'Neill (g),

Damien 'Dee' O'Neill (g), Michael Bradley (b), Billy Doherty (d)

Northern Ireland's Undertones were defiant primitivists. Like America's Ramones or Manchester's Buzzcocks, they used punk as an opportunity to reassert the simple pleasures of short, sharp melodic songs played fast on bass, guitar and drums. **The Undertones** revealed the band's back-to-basics approach, while tracks such as **Jimmy Jimmy**, **Here Comes The Summer** and **Teenage Kicks** explored such time-honoured pop themes as infatuation and adolescent romance, all topped off with Feargal Sharkey's affecting warble.

They play perfect timeless pop as natural as you or I pull on our socks… they are naive, but they know. The Undertones are better than others. **Paul Morley, NME, May 1979**

The Unforgettable Fire

ARTIST U2 **RELEASE DATE** October 1984 **LABEL** Island (UK & US) **PRODUCER** Eno, Lanois **UK CHART** peak/weeks 1/130 **US CHART** peak/weeks 12/132 **TRACK LISTING** A Sort Of Homecoming/Pride (In The Name Of Love)/Wire/The Unforgettable Fire/Promenade/4th Of July/Bad/Indian Summer Sky/Elvis Presley And America/MLK **PERSONNEL** Bono (v), The Edge (g), Adam Clayton (b), Larry Mullen Jr (d)

The first of U2's studio collaborations with Brian Eno, **The Unforgettable Fire** had a far wider range of sounds, and the band certainly benefited from the subtler atmospherics. The album also marked the beginning of Bono's lyrical preoccupation with the USA: **(Pride) In The Name Of Love**, their first American Top 40 hit, was a celebration of civil rights leader Martin Luther King, while the instrumental **4th Of July** was self-explanatory. Just after the LP's release and following their defining performance at *Live Aid*, U2 were named Band Of The Eighties by *Rolling Stone* magazine.

… there is a panoramic soundscape, multiple textures, subtle shifts in emphasis. In parts U2 are scarcely recognisable. String and synth arrangements abound… Set against **Boy***, I don't say it's their best album yet, but it sounds like music worth spending some months getting to know.* **Paul Du Noyer, NME, October 1984**

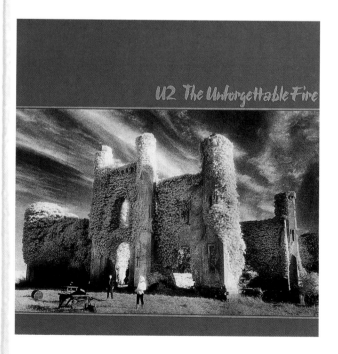

U2 The Unforgettable Fire

Unhalfbricking

ARTIST Fairport Convention RELEASE DATE August 1969 LABEL Island (UK & US) PRODUCER Joe Boyd, Simon, Fairport Witchseason Productions Ltd UK CHART peak/weeks 12/8 US CHART peak/weeks 0/0 TRACK LISTING Genesis Hall/Si Tu Dois Partir/Autopsy/A Sailor's Life/Cajun Woman/Who Knows Where The Time Goes/Percy's Song/Million Dollar Bash PERSONNEL Sandy Denny (v), Ashley Hutchings (b), Martin Lamble (d), Simon Nicol (g), Richard Thompson (g) with Dave Swarbrick (f, md), Trevor Lucas (tg), Marc Ellington (v), Ian Matthews (v)

Folk-rock's first supergroup was never more packed with disparate talents than in this third album. To Denny, Thompson and the soon-to-depart Matthews was added folk's superstar fiddler Dave Swarbrick, who made his presence felt on the seminal *A Sailor's Life*, the combination of folk, jazz and rock truly unique. Added to Denny's best ever ballad, **Who Knows Where The Time Goes**, and the band's only hit, a wacky French version of Dylan's *If You Gotta Go*, there was something for everyone.

Those who want to get moved are directed… to **Unhalfbricking** *which has Fairport Convention at its best… buy the album immediately… we can only hope that they've only just begun to make our musical world that much better.* **John Mendelsohn, Rolling Stone, June 1970**

Unknown Pleasures

ARTIST Joy Division RELEASE DATE August 1980 LABEL Factory PRODUCER Martin Hannett UK CHART peak/weeks 71/1 US CHART peak/weeks - TRACK LISTING Disorder/Day Of The Lords/Candidate/Insight/New Dawn Fades/She's Lost Control/Shadowplay/Wilderness/Interzone/I Remember Nothing PERSONNEL Ian Curtis (v), Bernard Albrecht (g), Peter Hook (b), Stephen Morris (d)

'The ultimate Eighties hard-rock group: eloquent, introspective, hysterical' was how Factory Records publicized Joy Division in June 1979 – and producer Hannett lived up to the tag, adding smashing glass and eerie elevator sounds to a drum-heavy mix that captured the sound and spirit of the economically depressed late Seventies. Label boss Tony Wilson had invested his life savings, and that looked a sound move, but singer Curtis's suicide within a year on the eve of a US tour overshadowed everything achieved here.

Unknown Pleasures *is a brave bullet in a danceable dream; brilliantly, a record of place – of one particular city, Manchester:… it is contended that* **Unknown Pleasures**, *in defining reaction and adjustment to place so accurately, makes the specific general, the particular a paradigm.* **Jon Savage, Melody Maker, July 1979**

Unleashed In The East

ARTIST Judas Priest RELEASE DATE September 1979 LABEL CBS (UK)/ Columbia (US) PRODUCER Tom Allom, Judas Priest UK CHART peak/weeks 10/8 US CHART peak/weeks 70/11 TRACK LISTING Exciter/Running Wild/ Sinner/Ripper/The Green Manalishi (With The Two-Pronged Crown)/ Diamonds And Rust/Victim Of Changes/Genocide/Tyrant PERSONNEL Bob Halford (lv), K. K. Downing (lg), Glenn Tipton (lg), Ian Hill (b), Dave Holland (d)

Following seven years after the mould-maker, Deep Purple's **Made In Japan**, the Priest notched their first UK Top 10 album by, as HM mag *Kerrang!* put it, 'revisiting their earlier career highlights – but playing them louder!' A bone-crunching cover of Fleetwood Mac's classic *Green Manalishi* was a bonus. After this album had attracted US attention, they broke through to the Top 40 with the following year's **British Steel** and became one of British metal's most successful exports – albeit eventually without singer Halford.

Violence is the message of Judas Priest's **Unleashed In The East**, *an excellent representation of the bands on-stage capabilities. Recorded*

in the land of the rising sun… it is happily free from the disrupting sound of fanatical Nipponese teenagers. **Steve Gett, Melody Maker, September 1979**

Unplugged

ARTIST Eric Clapton RELEASE DATE September 1992 LABEL Duck Warner (UK)/Warner Bros. (US) PRODUCER Russ Titelman UK CHART peak/weeks 2/67 US CHART peak/weeks 1/137 TRACK LISTING Sign/Before You Accuse Me/Hey Hey/Tears In Heaven/Lonely Stranger/Nobody Knows You When You're Down And Out/Layla/Running On Faith/Walkin' Blues/Alberta/San Francisco Bay Blues/Malted Milk/Old Love/Rollin' and Tumblin' PERSONNEL Eric Clapton (g, v), Ray Cooper (pc), Nathan East (b, bv), Steve Ferrone (d), Chuck Leavell (k), Andy Fairweather Low (g), Katie Kissoon (bv), Tessa Niles (bv)

Six Grammys and seven million sales in America greeted this work, which wasn't the first in MTV's *Unplugged* series but did establish the formula. Suddenly acoustic-based music was semi-fashionable again. Clapton rediscovered a fresh simplicity and directness in his blues-based material, and, importantly, a heart. It was doubtless galvanized by **Tears In Heaven**, an enormous single inspired, sadly, by the death of his five-year-old son, Conor, in 1991. He'd fallen from a window of a New York apartment belonging to his mother. While this song was terribly poignant, the new interpretation of *Layla* expressed almost an equal depth of emotion.

The album's accessibility and sense of fun will probably bring a sneer to the lips of the bluesier-than-thou brigade – someone even plays a kazoo during San Francisco Bay Blues – but it's undoubtedly Clapton's most enjoyable album for years. **Colin Shearman, Q, September 1992**

Urban Dancefloor Guerrilla

ARTIST P Funk All Stars RELEASE DATE 1983 LABEL CBS (UK)/Columbia (US) PRODUCER George Clinton, Various UK CHART peak/weeks 0/0 US CHART peak/weeks – TRACK LISTING Generator Pop/Acupuncture/One Of Those Summers/Catch A Keeper/Pumpin' It Up/Copy Cat/Hydraulic Pump/Pumpin' It Up (Reprise) PERSONNEL George Clinton (v), Gary Shider (g), Sly Stone, Bootsy Collins

By the end of the Seventies George Clinton had once again lost the rights to record under either the Parliament or Funkadelic monikers and was forced to re-invent himself. This album is the ideal link between Clinton's better moments with Parliament and Funkadelic and his later solo work. Indeed, despite the pressures building up – contractual disagreements, tax bills and cocaine addiction – Clinton remained creative and came up with an album that is still revered.

That bass, lurching, flowing, parks its ass on the groove, and rides it like a bucking bronco. Many aspects of Clinton's musical vision has been stolen by others, but nobody sounds like this. **Simon Witter, NME, March 1984**

Use Your Illusion I

ARTIST Guns 'N' Roses RELEASE DATE September 1991 LABEL Geffen (UK & US) PRODUCER Mike Clink, Guns 'N' Roses UK CHART peak/weeks 2/81 US CHART peak/weeks 2/108 TRACK LISTING Right Next Door To Hell/Dust N' Bones/Live And Let Die/Don't Cry (Original)/Perfect Crime/You Ain't The First/Bad Obsession/Back Off Bitch/Double Talkin' Jive/November Rain/The Garden/Garden Of Eden/Don't Damn Me/Bad Apples/Dead Horse/Coma PERSONNEL Steven Adler (d), Slash (lg, rg, ag), Duff 'Rose' McKagan (b, v), Izzy Stradlin (rg, lg, v, pc), W. Axl Rose (v, sy, pc)

Releasing two albums simultaneously – and doubles at that – confirmed Guns 'N'Roses hard-won reputation as rock renegades. It was the more obviously rocky **Use Your Illusion II** that took the honours sales-wise in Britain and the US, though its reflective predecessor spawned big hits in **Don't Cry** and **November Rain**, the latter with its memorable video of singer Axl Rose 'marrying' then girlfriend Stephanie Seymour. G'N'R's musical marriage of attitude and ability had won the day, though a 1993 follow-up of covers suggested they had written themselves out.

*The Gunners' anything-worth-doing-is-worth- overdoing spirit is a bracing slap at the reigning fascism of studio perfection. For better or worse **Illusion I** also mirrors the turmoil in **Teenage Wasteland**, one nation under a grudge.* **David Fricke, Rolling Stone, October 1991**

Utopia

ARTIST Todd Rundgren RELEASE DATE December 1974 LABEL Bearsville (UK & US) PRODUCER – UK CHART peak/weeks – US CHART peak/weeks 34/ TRACK LISTING Utopia (Theme)/Freak Parade/Freedom Fighter/The Ikon PERSONNEL Todd Rundgren (v), Mark Klingman (k), Ralph Shukett (k), Roger Powell (sy), John Siegler (b), John Wilcox (d), Kevin Elliman (per)

Utopia were a suitably democratic bunch of like-minded musicians, although Todd remained sole writer. **Todd Rundgren's Utopia** was their debut, future releases simply attributed to Utopia. Todd had already been in a group in the late Sixties: the Anglophile mod-rockers, Nazz. But Utopia were no ordinary band: this was Rundgren in full post-acid visionary-messiah mode, creating music designed to represent the complex workings of his brain – dizzyingly intricate, by turns ambient-like and furiously electronic, proving, if nothing else, that half-hour-long segments of brainiac cosmic prog-rock can be funky.

… an irresistible album of technical brilliance, lyrical and vocal inventiveness, melodic beauty and hair raising lead guitar… there isn't a song that's a moment too long, an emotional pitch that falters, or a departure point that leads to nowhere. **Susan Hill, Melody Maker, January 1980**

Van Halen

ARTIST Van Halen RELEASE DATE April 1978 (UK)/June 1978 (US) LABEL Warner Bros. (UK & US) PRODUCER Ted Templeton UK CHART peak/weeks 34/11 US CHART peak/weeks 19/169 TRACK LISTING You Really Got Me/Jamie's Cryin'/On Fire/Runnin' With The Devil/I'm The One/Ain't Talkin' 'Bout Love/Little Dreamer/Feel Your Love Tonight/Atomic Punk/Eruption/Ice Cream Man PERSONNEL David Roth (v), Edward Van Halen (g), Alex Van Halen (d), Michael Anthony (b)

Van Halen picked up the baton from Kiss as premier American heavy metal band. In fact, it was Kiss's frontman, Gene Simmons, who financed some of Van Halen's early demos. Although it would prove to be their lowest ever charting album, **The Night We Fell In Love**, the debut, eventually sold over six million copies and introduced the two secrets of the band's success: singer David Lee Roth, all bouffant hair, shiny white teeth and macho *braggadocio*

(albeit the caricature-ish, ironic variety), and guitarist Eddie Van Halen, whose dazzling technique exerted almost as much influence on subsequent generations as did the likes of Clapton, Beck and Page on early Seventies guitarslingers.

For it's all there in abundance: screaming guitar solos, thundering riffs, pounding rhythm section and tough vocals. An outstanding and thoroughly recommended (but only to the converted) debut. **Michael Oldfield, Melody Maker, June 1978**

Vauxhall And I

ARTIST Morrissey **RELEASE DATE** March 26th 1994 (UK & US) **LABEL** Parlophone (UK)/Sire (US) **PRODUCER** Steve Lillywhite **UK CHART** peak/weeks 1/28 **US CHART** peak/weeks 18/10 **TRACK LISTING** Now My Heart Is Full/Spring-Hilled Jimmy/Billy Budd/Hold Onto Your Friends/The More You Ignore Me, The Closer I Get/Why Don't You Find Out For Yourself/I Am Hated For Loving/Lifeguard Sleeping, Girl Drowning/Used To Be A Sweet Boy/The Lazy Sunbathers/Speedway **PERSONNEL** Steven P. Morrissey (v), Steven Street (g, b), Andrew Paresi (d), Vini Reilly (g, k)

The second solo chart-topper of Morrissey's career came with his sixth album, though compilation and live sets had postponed the day. It was named after a south London district known for a gay drag bar and campness was evident in *Billy Budd* and *Spring Heel Jim*. Elsewhere producer Lillywhite provided the perfect setting for the former Smiths singer's sometimes delicate, sometimes stinging songs. This was the nearest he had come to the mainstream.

Vauxhall and I *rises effortlessly to the top. It could be Morrissey's best album…. The lyrical tone … is, while predictably melodramatic and self-pitying, more resigned and even peaceful…. Thank heavens he's come around to making exceptional, unique music again.* **Andrew Collins, Q, April 1994**

Velvet Underground

ARTIST The Velvet Underground **RELEASE DATE** MAY 1969 (UK)/March 1969 (US) **LABEL** MGM (UK & US) **PRODUCER** – **UK CHART** peak/weeks 47/4 **US CHART** peak/weeks 197/2 **TRACK LISTING** Candy Says…/What Goes On/Some Kinda Love/Pale Blue Eyes/Jesus/Beginning To See The Light/I'm Set Free/That's The Story Of My Life/The Murder Mystery/After Hours **PERSONNEL** Lou Reed (v, g), Sterling Morrison (b, g), John Cale (b, k, via, v), Nico (v), Maureen Tucker (b, g)

Discovered by pop art pioneer Andy Warhol (whose name appears on the sleeve), New York's The Velvet Underground sold few records at the time but are regarded by many today as the most influential band of the Sixties after The Beatles and the Stones. **The Velvet Underground And Nico** was an extraordinary debut, more so considering it was released at the height of Flower Power: these were no peace and love anthems. Rather, singer-songwriter Lou Reed entered all sorts of urban 'no-go' areas – decadence, addiction, fetishism – while multi-instrumentalist John Cale added new colours to rock's palette and Nico offered a strangely sensual Teutonic murmur.

45 minutes of drugs, death, grunge production, atonality and sick melody. **From Waiting For The Man** *to* **All Tomorrow's Parties,** *this is anti-hippie New York art hate and as such has no peer.* **Stuart Bailie, NME, May 1992**

Velvet Underground And Nico

ARTIST The Velvet Underground **RELEASE DATE** October 1967 (UK)/December 1966 (US) **LABEL** Verve (UK & US) **PRODUCER** Andy Warhol **UK CHART** peak/weeks - **US CHART** peak/weeks 171/13 **TRACK LISTING** I'm Waiting For The Man/Candy Says/Run, Run, Run/White Light/White Heat/All Tomorrow's Parties/Sunday Morning/I Heard Her Call My Name/Femme Fatale/Heroin/Here She Comes Now/There She Goes Again/Sister Ray/ Venus In Furs/European Son/Pale Blue Eyes/Black Angel's Death Song/ Beginning To See The Light **PERSONNEL** Lou Reed (vg), Sterling Morrison (bg), John Cale (b, k, v, via), Nico (v), Maureen Tucker (d)

After the deluge of noise that was **White Light/White Heat**, The Velvet Underground's third album (the first to follow John Cale's departure) offered some respite in *Candy Says*, *Pale Blue Eyes* and *Jesus*: the sort of gentle, almost hymn-like songs that Spiritualized, to name but one contemporary band, have based a career around. However, because of who they were (and the drugs they took and the company they kept), the Velvets' 'gospel rock' seemed no less disturbing than their droning trance-rock, of which there were two shining examples here: *Beginning To See The Light* and *What Goes On* – punk prototypes both.

It is almost impossible to think of The Velvet Underground in the past tense… I can hear them almost everywhere these days, and have done for years. **Allan Jones, Melody Maker, May 1986**

Venus And Mars

ARTIST Wings **RELEASE DATE** June 1975 (UK & US) **LABEL** Apple (UK)/Capitol (US) **PRODUCER** Paul McCartney **UK CHART** peak/weeks 1/29 **US CHART** peak/weeks 1/77 **TRACK LISTING** Venus And Mars Rock Show/Love In A Sing/You Gave Me The Answer/Magneto And Titanium Man/Letting Go/Venus And Mars (Reprise)/Spirits Of Ancient Egypt/Medicine Jar/Call Me Back Again/Listen To What The Man Said/Treat Her Gentle-Lonely Old People/Crossroads Theme/Zoogang/My Carnival/Lunch Box-Odd Socks **PERSONNEL** Paul McCartney (v, b ,g,) Linda McCartney (bv, k, p) Denny Seiwell (d, v) Denny Laine (g, v)

Another set of well-crafted studio confections, Paul McCartney's sixth post-Beatles album was a less than perfect concept LP, but it did contain enough classy pop, like the effortlessly melodic hit single, *Listen To What The Man Said*, to keep those detractors who believed McCartney's gifts had deserted him at bay. The version of Tony Hatch's *Crossroads* theme veered close to MOR, however, and hinted at the easy-listening mediocrities to come.

… this is a thoroughly enjoyable album, with a loose thread running through pieces… a pervading mood of cosmic exploration, contrasting waves of pressure and release are hinted at and revealed in songs of love and imagery. **Chris Welch, Melody Maker, May 1975**

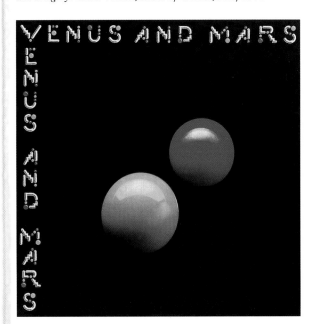

Village Green Preservation Society

ARTIST The Kinks RELEASE DATE July 1968 (UK & US) LABEL PYE Records Ltd (UK)/Reprise (US) PRODUCER – UK CHART peak/weeks – US CHART peak/weeks – TRACK LISTING The Village Green Preservation Society/Do You Remember Walter/Picture Book/Johnny Thunder/Last Of The Steam-Powered Trains/Big Sky/Sitting By The Riverside/Animal Farm/Village Green/Starstruck/Phonominal Cat/All Of My Friends Were There/Wicked Annabella/Monica/People Take Pictures Of Each Other PERSONNEL Michael Charles Avory (d), Peter Alexander Greenlaw Quaife (b), David Russell Gordon Davies (v, g), Raymond Douglas Davies (g, k, v)

While his peers embraced the emergent hippy culture, Ray Davies remained anchored in his north London roots, his songs celebrating holidays, the pub, football – themes he expanded in 1968 into the first of many Kinks concept albums. **Preservation Society** harked back to a pre Great War golden age, explored through fantastic characters like the Phenomenal Cat, Johnny Thunder and Wicked Annabella. Though it contained some of his best songs, Pye failed to promote it seriously. In retrospect it did much to establish Ray's longevity as a songwriter, and in ensuing years (especially post Brit-pop) it came to be regarded as one of the touchstones of British rock.

When we made **Village Green Preservation Society** *everybody, even people around us, said, 'This is good. This is a departure.' But it was not heavy, and everything was heavy at that time. So it just got lost.* **Ray Davies interviewed by Phil McNeil, NME, April 1977**

Violator

ARTIST Depeche Mode RELEASE DATE March 1990 LABEL Mute (UK)/Sire (US) PRODUCER Flood UK CHART peak/weeks 2/30 US CHART peak/weeks 7/74 TRACK LISTING World In My Eyes/Sweetest Perfection/Personal Jesus/Halo/Waiting For The Night/Enjoy The Silence/Policy Of Truth/Blue Dress/Clean PERSONNEL Dave Gahan (v), Marin Gore (sy), Andy Fletcher (bsy), Alan Wilder (sy)

Few would have predicted that Depeche Mode, formed as a rinky-dink synthesizer trio in 1980, would still be going strong in 1990, still less that they would be US megastars. *Enjoy The Silence*, a Number 4 single Stateside, was the catalyst, and the album from which it was plucked exceeded two million sales in the US alone. A signing session at a LA record shop saw five fans treated for injuries as thousands flocked to pay homage. Back home, **Violator** entered the chart at Number 2 despite the absence of such hysteria.

Violator is Depeche Mode's most mature work, less bound by the adolescent fascination with demi-monde decadence that dominates earlier albums… It's also their most effective LP at working mainstream rock forms into their machine pop. **Q, January 1991**

Virgin Fugs

ARTIST The Fugs RELEASE DATE January 1965 LABEL Broadside PRODUCER – UK CHART peak/weeks - US CHART peak/weeks 0/0 TRACK LISTING We're The Fugs/New Amphetamine Shriek/Saran Wrap/The Ten Commandments/Hallucination Horrors/I Command The House Of The Devil/C.I.A. Man/Coco Cola Douche/My Bed Is Getting Crowded/Coca Rocka/I Saw The Best Of My Generation Rot PERSONNEL Ed Sanders (v, g), Tuli Kupferberg (v, pc), Ken Weaver (d, v), Peter Stampfel (g, b, v), Steve Weber (g), Vinny Leary (g, b), John Anderson (b), Pete Kearney (g)

The great political agitators of American pop, the Fugs were formed on New York's Lower East Side by Tuli Kupferberg, Ed Sanders and Ken Weaver. Their aim was to subvert: there were no serious ambitions to become rock stars in any conventional sense. Written and conceived in the summer of 1966 at the Players Theatre in Greenwich Village, **Virgin Fugs** was their last for ESP and caught the band in full satirical tilt, prefacing work by the like-minded Mothers of Invention by several months. After a *faux pas* with Atlantic they would sign a more lucrative deal with Reprise, who released their next album only after it had been OK'd by Frank Sinatra!

Not for the suburban market. Hardly virtuoso musicians, the Fugs are frequently bawdy, often funny and occasionally hit their satirical targets plumb on the nose. **Melody Maker, July 1969**

Vision Thing

ARTIST Sisters Of Mercy RELEASE DATE October 1990 (UK & US) LABEL Merciful-WEA (UK)/Elektra (US) PRODUCER Andrew Eldritch UK CHART peak/weeks 11/4 US CHART peak/weeks 136/23 TRACK LISTING Vision Thing/Ribbons/Destination Boulevard/Something Fast/When You Don't See Me/Doctor Jeep/More/I Was Wrong PERSONNEL Andrew Eldritch (v, dm), Tony James (b, v), Andreas Bruhn (g), Tim Bricheno (g), Maggie Reilly (bv, gst), John Perry (g, gst)

By the release of this, the third LP by The Sisters Of Mercy (who were named after a song by the Lord of Darkness himself, Leonard Cohen), Patricia Morrison of The Gun Club had left, having assisted Andrew Eldritch on their neo-Wagnerian masterpiece,

1987's **Floodland** (featuring production bombast courtesy of Jim 'Meatloaf' Steinman). **Vision Thing** was the band's rockiest effort to date, due in part to to the arrival of Tony James, formerly of Generation X and Sigue Sigue Sputnik.

The question being asked is not whether this record is going to be crap, but how crap… Ugh, ugh, ugh! This sounds suspiciously like a record made for US radio. Dreadfully disappointing. **Steven Wells, NME, October 1990**

Viva Hate

ARTIST Morrisey RELEASE DATE March 1988 (UK & US) LABEL HMV (UK)/SIRE (US) PRODUCER Stephen Street UK CHART peak/weeks 1/20 US CHART peak/weeks 48/20 TRACK LISTING Alsation Cousin/Little Man/What Now?/Everyday Is Like Sunday/Bengali In Platforms/Angel, Angel, Down We Go Together/Late Night, Maudlin Street/Suedehead/Break Up The Family/ The Ordinary Boys/I Don't Mind If You Forget Me/Dial-A-Cliche/Margaret On The Guillotine PERSONNEL Morrisey (v), Stephen Street (b, g), Vini Reilly (g, k), Andrew Paresi (d), John Metcalfe (va), Fenella Barton (vl), Mark Davies (c), Richard Koster (vl), Robert Woodland (c), Rachel Maguire (c)

The Smiths singer equalled his band's best by topping the chart first time out. His studio team included Durutti Column guitarist Vini Reilly (in place of long-time cohort Johnny Marr) and producer Stephen Street, while the Number 5 single *Suedehead* (titled after a violent 1971 novel by Richard Allen on skinhead culture) would revive EMI's long-defunct HMV label. The year of 1988 ended with a one-off last Smiths gig in Wolverhampton, but the success of **Viva Hate** had ensured a solo future.

Volunteers

ARTIST Jefferson Airplane RELEASE DATE March 1970 (UK)/November 1969 (US) LABEL RCA (UK & US) PRODUCER – UK CHART peak/weeks 34/1 US CHART peak/weeks 13/44 TRACK LISTING We Can Be Together/Good Shepherd/The Farm/Hey Fredrick/Turn My Life Down/Wooden Ships/Eskimo Blue Day/A Song For All Seasons/Meadowlands/Volunteers PERSONNEL Grace Slick (v), Marty Balin (v), Paul Kantner (g), Jorma Kaukonen (g), Jack Casady (b), Spencer Dryden (d)

Volunteers was rumoured to be the iconoclastic album many hoped the Airplane would finally make – after all they had played at almost all the major tribal gatherings in the late Sixties, from the *Human Be-In* to *Woodstock*, and had constantly been a thorn in the side of the Nixon regime. But the dynamics within the band had shifted considerably, and **Volunteers** never quite lived up to everyone's expectations. The title track – a rousing call to revolutionary arms – rang hollow in the fall-out from the *Altamont* fiasco and on the way the Airplane had become overtly rich and elite. It was left to *Wooden Ships*, a Crosby/Stills/Kantner epic, to give the album its one sublime moment.

I happen to think that the Jefferson Airplane, on the basis of what they have done on **Bathing at Baxter's** *and now* **Volunteers** *are musical pioneers… soon we'll be seeing the emergence of a whole new brand of 'serious rock'.* **Ed Ward, Rolling Stone, February 1970**

Voulez Vous

ARTIST Abba RELEASE DATE 19th May 1979 (UK)/July 1979 (US) LABEL Epic (UK)/Atlantic (US) PRODUCER Benny Anderson & Björn Ulvaeus UK CHART peak/weeks 1/43 US CHART peak/weeks 19/27 TRACK LISTING As Good As New/Voulez-Vous/I Have A Dream/Angel Eyes/The King Has Lost His Crown/Does Your Mother Know/If It Wasn't For The Nights/ Chiquitta/ Lovers/Kisses Of Fire PERSONNEL Benny Anderson (k, sy, v), Björn Ulvaeus (g, v), Agnetha Fältskog (v), Frida Lyngstad (v)

The Swedes were profoundly influenced by the Bee Gees' hits from **Saturday Night Fever**: Benny later confessed that they took this

perhaps a little too far on **Voulez-Vous**, which glistened with disco rhythms. The title track and *Angel Eyes* (also, confusingly, the title of a distinct hit for Roxy Music at the same time), made for a fitfully funky double A-side. By contrast, the boys' disastrous ***Does Your Mother Know*** was an out-of-character leering rock clumper, and *Chiquitta* was mushy pomp-pop. Remarkably, both this and their next, **Super Trouper**, spent exactly 43 weeks in the British album chart.

What we have on this album is not Abba attempting to be crass and stupid, as you could be excused for imagining, but post-Bjorn, Agnetha marriage-break-up Abba trying to be sophisticated. **Tony Parsons, NME, May 1979**

Vs

ARTIST Pearl Jam RELEASE DATE October 1993 (UK & US) LABEL Epic (UK & US) PRODUCER Brendan O'Brien, Pearl Jam UK CHART peak/weeks 2/10 US CHART peak/weeks 1/67 TRACK LISTING Go/Animal/Daughter/Glorified G/Dissident/W.M.A./Blood/Rearview Mirror/Rats/Elderly Woman Behind The Counter In A Small Town/Leash/Indifference PERSONNEL Jeff Ament (b, v), Stone Gossard (g, v), Eddie Vedder (v), Mike McCready (g), Dave Abbruzzese (d)

Alongside Nirvana, Pearl Jam were the leaders of the West Coast grunge wave and, like their contemporaries, they found it difficult to live with the price fame would exact. The title, abbreviated from 'Five Against One' (a lyric from the song *Animal*), combined with the cover picture of a goat looking through a containing fence, hinted of a feeling of pressure on them, and singer/lyricist Eddie Vedder reflected this in his lyrics. Even though they decided not to release videos for the album, it entered the US chart at the top. Pearl Jam would continue to be prisoners of their own success.

… the g-word in Pearl Jam's sound isn't grunge but groove. Rhythm. Pulse. The beat. That's what lives at the beast of **Vs** *– not Eddie Vedder's singing or Mike McCready's guitar solos, but the way those elements lock into the momentum generated by the rhythm section.* **J. D. Considine, Rolling Stone, December 1993**

Waiting For The Sun

ARTIST Doors RELEASE DATE September 1968 (UK)/August 1968 (US) LABEL Elektra (UK & US) PRODUCER Paul A. Rothchild UK CHART peak/weeks 16/10 US CHART peak/weeks 1/41 TRACK LISTING Hello, I Love You/Love Street/Not To Touch The Earth/Summer's Almost Gone/Wintertime Love/The Unknown Soldier/Spanish Caravan/My Wild Love/We Could Be So Good Together/Yes, The River Knows/Five To One PERSONNEL Jim Morrison (v), Ray Manzarek (k), Robby Krieger (g), John Densmore (d), with Douglas Lubahn, Kerry Magness and Leroy Vinegar (b)

As life had become one long round of national promo tours there was little opportunity to break in new material and, with Morrison already on the slippery slope to self-destruction, tensions began to develop. **Waiting For The Sun** was patchy and indecisive compared to its two illustrious predecessors: 'fillers' like **Yes The River Knows** appeared next to more traditional Doors fare, such as the flamenco-styled **Spanish Caravan** and the closing track **Five To One**. Ultimately, the album begged the question as to whether the band could survive.

The Waking Hour

ARTIST Del Amitri RELEASE DATE February 1990 (UK)/March 1990 LABEL A&M (UK & US) PRODUCER Mark Freegard, Hugh Jones, Gil Norton UK CHART peak/weeks 6/44 US CHART peak/weeks 95/19 TRACK LISTING Kiss This Thing Goodbye/Opposite View/Move Away Jimmy Blue/Stone Cold Sober/You're Gone/When I Want You/This Side Of The Morning/Empty/Hatful Of Rain/Nothing Ever Happens PERSONNEL Mick Slaven (g), Andy Alston (k), Robert Cairns (vl), Blair Cowan (ad), Stephen Irvine (d), Julian Dawson (h), James O'Malley (b), Caroline Levelle (c), Will Mowat (k), Justin Currie (v, b, ag), Iain Harvie (g), Bryan Tolland (d, pc)

Having false started as faux-indies on Chrysalis's pseudo-independent Big Star label, Scots guitar-rockers Del Amitri got back to basics, reduced themselves to a duo and four years of listening to Faces albums later re-emerged with this collection of pre-worn classics, as comfortable as an old pair of 501s. Irony of ironies, the hit was **Nothing Ever Happens**, an atypical folksong in **Streets Of London** vein they've moved ever rockwards to disown. But there is nothing on this album to be ashamed of as songwriter Justin Currie hits form.

Spiking rumours of their untimely demise with arrogant disdain, Del

Amitri's major label debut is a sleek belter of a record... Criss-crossing deftly between a spiky, angular British guitar pop and American country-flavoured rock, Justin Currie's vividly scripted songs conjure up a cascading flood of resonant images. **Paul Davies, Q, August 1989**

A Walk Across The Rooftops

ARTIST The Blue Nile RELEASE DATE May 1984 (UK)/1985 (US) LABEL Linn-Virgin (UK)/A&M (US) PRODUCER Blue Nile UK CHART peak/weeks 80/2 US CHART peak/weeks 0/0 TRACK LISTING A Walk Across The Rooftops/Tinseltown In The Rain/From Rags To Riches/Stay/Easter Parade/Heatwave/Automobile Noise PERSONNEL Paul Buchanan (v, g, sy), Paul Joseph Moore (k, sy), Robert Bell (b, sy)

The Glasgow trio's brittle and beautiful debut was just the start of what's become a 15-year enigma. Economically recorded and sonically slight, it somehow evoked impossible worlds of romance and breathed new life into love-song clichés. Paul Buchanan's gift of a voice seemed to express yearning and joy and grief with every simple swerve and shudder. The title song and **Tinseltown In The Rain** demonstrated the group's facility with layers of imagery. **Stay** was a marvellous introductory single. It took them five years to follow this up, but in that gap the mystique grew and the mesmeric magic of this music won further word-of-mouth converts.

A Walk Across The Rooftops *is a sneaky album. The music slips between the cracks, an effortless flow of acoustic and electronic sounds with many a hook in the curiously murky mix.... This shimmering music is not difficult, just sophisticated.* **Tim Holmes, Rolling Stone, September 1985**

Walking Wounded

ARTIST Everything But The Girl **RELEASE DATE** May 1996 (UK)/June 1996 (US) **LABEL** Blanco Y Negro (UK)/Atlantic (US) **PRODUCER** Ben Watt, Spring Heel **UK CHART** peak/weeks – **US CHART** peak/weeks 37/16 **TRACK LISTING** Before Today/Wrong/Single/The Heart Remains A Child/Walking Wounded/Flipside/Big Deal/Mirrorball/Good Cop Bad Cop/Wrong/Walking Wounded (Omni Trio Remix) **PERSONNEL** Tracey Thorn (v), Ben Watt (sy, ag, v), Howie B. and Spring Heel Jack

Having lucked out in the hit single stakes when Todd Terry remixed **Missing** from their **Amplified Heart** album, the label-less EBTG suddenly found themselves in a great bargaining position. Signing to Virgin, they rushed out a new release that took its musical cues from drum and bass, and found themselves just as hot as in their heyday a decade previously. Bedsitter images for the rave generation.

Walking Wounded *is a near faultless comeback… A testimony to the strength of collaboration, the possibility of rejuvenation, and the universal preoccupation with the heart and its related organs due south.* **Glyn Brown, Mojo, June 1996**

The Wall

ARTIST Pink Floyd **RELEASE DATE** December 1979 (UK & US) **LABEL** Harvest (UK)/Columbia (US) **PRODUCER** David Gilmour, Bob Ezrin, Roger Waters **UK CHART** peak/weeks 3/51 **US CHART** peak/weeks 1/15 **TRACK LISTING** In The Flesh/The Thin Ice/The Happiest Days Of Our Lives/Another Brick In The Wall (part 2)/Mother/Goodbye Blue Sky/Empty Spaces/Young Lust/One Of My Turns/Don't Leave Me Now/Another Brick In The Wall (part 3)/Goodbye Cruel World/Hey You/Is There Anybody Out There?/Nobody Home/Vera/Comfortably Numb/The Show Must Go On/Run Like Hell/Waiting For The Worms/Stop/The Trial/Outside The World **PERSONNEL** Roger Waters (v, b), Rick Wright (k), David Gilmour (v, g), Nick Mason (d)

When a possibly punk-fixated audience member spat at Roger Waters, it started a train of thought about an audience's relationship with a group that led to **The Wall**. Live performance of the double album was accompanied by the building of a wall across the stage, which would eventually be demolished. The album would become a film, with Bob Geldof as Pink, a character who becomes the symbol of society's oppression of the individual, but this would not be as successful. Waters, by now an ex-Floyd member, staged the album live in the shadow of the Berlin Wall in 1990.

The Wall *is an extraordinary record. I'm not sure whether it's brilliant or terrible, but I find it utterly compelling. Despite the inevitable expensive production it can't be dismissed as comfortable easy listening… Pink Floyd are still relevant, still important, and above all, still thinking.* **Chris Brazier, Melody Maker, December 1979**

Walls & Bridges

ARTIST John Lennon **RELEASE DATE** October 1974 (UK & US) **LABEL** Apple (UK & US) **PRODUCER** John Lennon **UK CHART** peak/weeks 6/10 **US CHART** peak/weeks 1/35 **TRACK LISTING** Going Down On Love/Whatever Gets You Thru The Night/Old Dirt Road/What You Got/Bless You/Scared/£9 Dream/Surprise, Surprise (Sweet Bird Of Paradox)/Steel And Glass/Beef Jerky/Nobody Loves You (When You're Down And Out)/Ya Ya **PERSONNEL** John Lennon (g, v), Julian Lennon (d), Jim Keltner (d), Klaus Voorman (b), Jesse Ed Davis (lg), Ken Ascher and Nicky Hopkins (keyboards), Elton John (bv)(p), Harry Nilsson (bv)

Recorded during his infamous 'lost weekend' in LA, **Walls & Bridges** said more about Lennon's personal suffering than any album since his first. His music always worked best when it revealed most about himself and here the pain of separation from Yoko surfaced in **Down On Love** and **Nobody Loves You (When You're Down And Ou)**, while **Scared** was a stark admission of insecurity. In spite of this, **Walls & Bridges** includes **Whatever Gets You Thru The Night**, a cracking rocker, and the ethereal **£9 Dream**: both deservedly success ful singles.

The playing is faultless, if a trifle pedestrian, and the production is as smooth and silky as any discerning hi-fi buff could want…. The songs are mostly a drag, and worse, most of them are solidly rooted in Lennonlore of old. **Charles Shaar Murray, NME, October 1974.**

War

ARTIST U2 **RELEASE DATE** February 1983 (UK & US) **LABEL** Island (UK & US) **PRODUCER** Steve Lillywhite, except The Refugee produced by Bill Whelan **UK CHART** peak/weeks 1/147 **US CHART** peak/weeks 12/179 **TRACK LISTING** Sunday Bloody Sunday/Seconds/New Year's Day/Like A Song…/Drowning Man/The Refugee/Two Hearts Beat As One/Red Light/Surrender/'40' **PERSONNEL** Bono (V), The Edge (g), Adam Clayton (b), Larry Mullen Jr (d)

While Britain was in thrall to the glamour and escapism of synthi-pop, along came U2 with their passion for rock in its basest, purest form. **War**, U2's third album, was their breakthrough set, including three classics: **Sunday Bloody Sunday**, **New Year's Day** and **Two Hearts Beat As One** – the latter two being hits. Their first two albums, **Boy** and **October**, introduced the four young men from Dublin with more than sex and drugs on their mind. **War** emphasized their conviction, with Bono's yearning voice and The Edge's soaring guitar heightening the charged socio-political atmosphere. **War** provided U2's first step on the road to global domination.

War *fails as must all such projects that no doubt have their germination in some genuinely noble sentiment, the very idea of a socially engaged pop group remaining for ever a contradiction in terms.* **Steve Lake, Melody Maker, February 1983**

The War Of The Worlds

ARTIST Jeff Wayne RELEASE DATE July 1978 (UK & US) LABEL CBS (UK)/Columbia (US) PRODUCER Jerry Wayne UK CHART peak/weeks 5/232 US CHART peak/weeks – TRACK LISTING The Coming Of The Martians/The Eve Of The War/Horsell Common And The Heat Ray/The Artillery Man And The Fighting Machine/The Earth Under The Martians/The Red Weed And Parson Nathaniel/The Artillery Man And Dead London/Dead London/Epilogue PERSONNEL Chris Spedding (g), Jo Partridge (g, v), Herbie Flowers (b), Barry Morgan (d), Ray Cooper (pc), Barry Da Souza (pc), Roy Jones (pc), Ken 'Prof' Freeman (k, sy), Jeff Wayne (k), Jerry Wayne (v), Richard Burton (v), Julie Covington (v), David Essex (v), Justin Hayward (v), Phil Lynott (v), Jo Partridge (v), Chris Thompson (v), Billy Lawrie (v), Gary Osbourne (v), Paul Vigrass (v), Charles Dubin (v), Jerry Wayne (v)

Jeff Wayne was best known as CBS in-house producer in the early Seventies and the man who helped elevate David Essex from star of *Godspell* to mainstream chart contender via **Rock On** and **Gonna Make You A Star**. **War Of The Worlds** was the most ambitious concept album since Pete Townshend's double whammy of **Tommy** and **Quadrophenia**. Essentially a cod-rock version of the classic H. G. Wells novel, it featured narration by Richard Burton and provided Moody Blue Justin Hayward with the worldwide hit, *Forever Autumn*. A mooted live-action stage version has yet to see the light of day 20 years after the album's release.

Warehouse: Songs And Stories

ARTIST Husker Du RELEASE DATE February 1987 (UK)/January 1987 (US) LABEL Warner Bros. (UK & US) PRODUCER – UK CHART peak/weeks 72/1 US CHART peak/weeks 117/10 TRACK LISTING These Important Years/Charity, Chastity, Prudence And Hope/Standing In The Rain/Back From Somewhere/Ice Cold Ice/You're A Soldier/Could You Be The One?/Too Much Spice/Friend, You've Got To Fall/Visionary/She Floated Away/Bed Of Nails/Tell You Why Tomorrow/It's Not Peculiar/Actual Condition/No Reservations/Turn It Around/She's A Woman (And Now He Is A Man)/Up In The Air/You Can Live At Home PERSONNEL Bob Mould (v, g, k, pc), Grant Hart (d, k, pc), Greg Norton (b)

After debuting on Warner Brothers with **Candy Apple Grey**, an album that lowered the frantic pace of previous efforts to the distress of some fans, Husker Du turned in the second double set of their career in **Warehouse: Songs And Stories**. But Grant Hart would leave the band the year after release, his drug problems having combined with management hassles to undermine the classic partnership with fellow songwriter Bob Mould. This was both a varied and consistent swansong incorporating elements of jazz and acid-rock among the pop and punk.

I have a couple of tricks I like to stick with, essentially trying to build tension within a song. I don't like to throw the knockout punch right away… I think it's a pretty happy record. The feel I get from it is very upbeat. **Bob Mould interview by David Fricke, Melody Maker, January 1987**

Warren Zevon

ARTIST Warren Zevon RELEASE DATE June 1976 LABEL Asylum (UK & US) PRODUCER Jackson Browne UK CHART peak/weeks 0/0 US CHART peak/weeks 189/2 TRACK LISTING Frank And Jesse James/Mama Couldn't Be Persuaded/Backs Turned Looking Down The Path/Hasten Down The Wind/Poor Poor Pitiful Me/The French Inhaler/Mohammed's Radio/I'll Sleep When I'm Dead/Carmelita/Join Me In L.A./Desperados Under The Eaves PERSONNEL Warren Zevon (v, p), Lindsey Buckingham (gst), Stevie Nicks (gst), Bonnie Raitt (gst), session musicians

Along with the more critically lauded Randy Newman, Warren Zevon was the preeminent black-humoured songwriter of the Seventies and Eighties with a penchant for highlighting America's dark underbelly, and lampooning the pretensions of the L.A. lifestyle. Although he had already recorded an album with scam-merchant Kim Fowley in 1969, the now deleted **Wanted Dead Or Alive**, his debut album proper was **Warren Zevon**, wherein the songwriter tilted at sadomasochism on *Poor Poor Pitiful Me*, bravely covered by Linda Ronstadt, and the California dream on *I'll Sleep When I'm Dead*.

Welcome to Wimp Central. Zevon and Souther have, with their respective albums, just promoted themselves to premier positions in the Drip Rock league…. Zevon has a strictly minimal talent as a songwriter, and his use of imagery… is imprecise and unimaginative. **Melody Maker, July 1976**

Water From The Wells Of Home

ARTIST Johnny Cash RELEASE DATE December 1988 (UK & US) LABEL Mercury (UK & US) PRODUCER – UK CHART peak/weeks 0/0 US CHART peak/weeks 0/0 TRACK LISTING As Long As I Live/Ballad Of A Teenage Queen/Last Of The Drifters/Where Did We Go Right/Call Me The Breeze/The Ole Wheel/Sweeter Than The Flowers/Ballad Of Robb MacDunn/New Moon Over Jamaica PERSONNEL Johnny Cash (v) with: Rosanne Cash, John Cash, Hank Williams Jr, Paul McCartney, Emmylou Harris, Waylon Jennings and the Everlys

A mere 32 years on from his first hit single, Cash had forged a highly creative alliance with producer Jack Clement. This proudly glowering album is sentimental without soppiness, macho without boneheadedness. With telling reverential contributions from Paul McCartney and Emmylou Harris, it confirmed that Cash had become a symbol for all that's durable, misguided or otherwise, about America and its myths.

Watermark

ARTIST Enya RELEASE DATE October 1988 (UK)/March 1989 (US) LABEL WEA WX (UK)/Geffen (US) PRODUCER Nicky Ryan UK CHART peak/weeks 5/87 US CHART peak/weeks 25/39 TRACK LISTING Watermark/Cursum Perficio/On Your Shore/Storms In Africa/Exile/Miss Clare Remembers/Orinoco Flow/Evening Falls/River/The Longships/Na Laetha Geal M'Oige/Storms In Africa (part 2) PERSONNEL Enya (v, k, pc)

Donegal-born Eithne (Enya) Ní Bhraonaín enjoyed worldwide acclaim with the release of **Watermark**, a debut album of ambient compositions utilizing multivocal and keyboard recording

techniques. Remixed under the influence of painkillers with the former Clannad keyboardist's leg in plaster following an altercation with a flight of stairs, it features a breathtaking display of Enya's talents as vocalist and arranger, the catchy UK Number 1 single *Orinoco Flow* proving the highlight.

We Are Family

ARTIST Sister Sledge RELEASE DATE May 1979 LABEL Atlantic PRODUCER Bernard Edwards, Nile Rodgers UK CHART peak/weeks 7/39 US CHART peak/weeks 3/93 TRACK LISTING He's The Greatest Dancer/Lost In Music/Somebody Loves Me/Thinking Of You/We Are Family/Easier To Love/You're A Friend To Me/One More Time PERSONNEL Kathie Sledge (v), Debbie Sledge (v), Kim Sledge (v), Joni Sledge (v), Alfa Anderson (bv), Norma Jean Wright (bv), David Lasley (bv), Diva Gray (bv), Luther Vandross (bv), Nile Rodgers (g), Bernard Edwards (b), Tony Thompson (d), Robert Sabino (p), Andy Schwarz (p), Raymond Jones (fdg), Robert Savino (ctte), Sammy Figueroa (pc)

Chic's Bernard Edwards and Nile Rodgers were unstoppable between 1978 and 1980. Not only did they write, produce, arrange, sing and perform on four Chic albums, they also found time to resuscitate the careers of several other artists, among them Diana Ross, Blondie's Debbie Harry, Carly Simon, French group Sheila & B Devotion and Sister Sledge. **We Are Family** was one of two Sister Sledge albums to receive Chic's midas touch (**Love Somebody Today** was released in 1980), and it amounts to a virtual greatest hits, including such disco classics as *He's The Greatest Dancer*, *Lost In Music*, *Thinking Of You* and the epic title track, all of which feature the late Bernard Edwards' sublime basslines, Nile Rodgers' choppy guitar patterns and the duo's peerless melodies.

The Sisters Sledge… provide the vocals and very seductive they are

too. There's no question, though, about who's really in charge… 'produced by Bernard Edwards and Nile Rodgers for CHIC Organisations Ltd'. **Bob Edmunds, NME, April 1979**

We Can Make It

ARTIST Peters And Lee RELEASE DATE June 1973 LABEL Philips PRODUCER – UK CHART peak/weeks 1/55 US CHART peak/weeks – TRACK LISTING – PERSONNEL –

The combination of a blind Cockney pub pianist and a blonde ex-dancer was as unlikely as the title track's Number 1 success, sandwiched between chart-toppers from Slade and Gary Glitter – such was the power of TV's *Opportunity Knocks* talent show which gave them their passport to fame and fortune. The undemanding ballad-heavy MOR fare was lushly orchestrated by Johnny Franz, who had worked with the Walker Brothers, and this album was rich reward for the pair's three years in clubs and stage shows.

We're An American Band

ARTIST Grand Funk Railroad RELEASE DATE August 1973 (UK)/July 1973 (US) LABEL Capitol Records (UK & US) PRODUCER Todd Rundgren UK CHART peak/weeks – US CHART peak/weeks 2/35 TRACK LISTING We're An American Band/Stop/Lookin' Back/Black Lycurice/The Railroad/Ain't Got Nobody/Walk Like A Man/Loneliest Rider PERSONNEL Mark Farner (v, g), Craig Frost (k), Mel Schacher (b), Donald Brewer (d)

Hated by critics and ignored by radio, Grand Funk found success by constant roadwork, setting attendance records as they notched up a record 10 consecutive platinum albums. This, their ninth release, was first to be produced by studio *wonderkind* Rundgren and boasted their long-awaited debut Top 20 single – and a Number 1 at that – in the title track, which they cheekily pressed in gold vinyl! Maybe shortening their name (they dropped the Railroad after splitting from long-time manager Terry Knight) did the trick.

Man of the match is definitely producer Todd Rundgren. He's tightened up the Grand Funk sound enormously and even got them writing pretty tunes… Grand Funk have finally lived up to their name. **M. O., Melody Maker, October 1973**

We're Only In It For The Money

ARTIST Mothers Of Invention **RELEASE DATE** July 1968 (UK)/January 1968 (US) **LABEL** Bizarre Productions (UK)/Verve/MGM (US) **PRODUCER** Frank Zappa **UK CHART** peak/weeks 32/5 **US CHART** peak/weeks 30/19 **TRACK LISTING** Are You Hung Up?/Who Needs The Peace Corps?/Concentration Moon/Mom & Dad/Bow The Daddy/Harry, You're A Beast/What's The Ugliest Part Of Your Body?/Absolutely Free/Flower Punk/Nasal Retentive Calliope Music/Let's Make The Water Turn Black/The Idiot Bastard Son/It's His Voice On The Radio/Take Your Clothes Off When You Dance/What's The Ugliest Part Of Your Body (Reprise)/Mother People/The Chrome Plated Megaphone Of Destiny **PERSONNEL** Frank Zappa (g, v), Ray Collins (v), Jim 'Motorhead' Sherwood (g), Don Preston (k), Roy Estrada (b), Bunk Gardner (s), Jimmy Carl Black (d)

From its cover lampooning the iconic **Sgt. Pepper** (its release was delayed as The Beatles' lawyers kicked up a stink), the Mothers' third album continued to present music at odds with the Sixties norm. Few targets went unscathed as hippies, psychedelia and flower power got a good kicking. The month after release they were invited to play at the US record industry's annual dinner, where they served up the same recipe live, to much discomfiture.

… beneath the outrage and revulsion which Zappa sets out to create in his public posturing is an acute musical intelligence… this album reveals the real strength of Zappa and the Mothers as brilliant satirists and commentators on the American way of life… **Bob Houston, Melody Maker, June 1968**

WELCOME TO THE
PLEASUREDOME

Welcome To The Pleasure Dome

ARTIST Frankie Goes To Hollywood **RELEASE DATE** November 1984 (UK & US) **LABEL** Island (UK & US) **PRODUCER** Trevor Horn **UK CHART** peak/weeks 1/58 **US CHART** peak/weeks 33/41 **TRACK LISTING** Well…/The World Is My Oyster/Snatch Of Fury/Welcome To The Pleasure Dome/Relax/War/Two Tribes/Ferry/Born To Run/San Jose/Wish The Lads Were Here (inc.'Ballard of 32')/Black Night White Light/The Only Star In Heaven/The Power Of Love/Bang… **PERSONNEL** Holly Johnson (v), Paul Rutherford (v), Brian 'Nasher' Nash (g), Mark O'Toole (b), Peter 'Ged' Gill (d)

Two things were the making of Frankie: Radio 1 DJ Mike Read's decision to abort gay love song *Relax* in mid play for reasons of

'good taste', and producer Trevor Horn, who turned what was a cult sound into this widescreen creation. Blockheads Norman Watt-Roy and Charley Charles supplied the rhythmic base uncredited, while Horn and vocalist Holly Johnson added the icing. This double album, spawning a record four UK Number 1s, was the one to be seen with: the 'Frankie Says' T-shirt was optional.

It's that elegant gelling of slogans which Frankie have substituted for songwriting, leaving the girder structure of brash, pumping heart chords which the musician Horne can weave his wonders around…. By next week I'll be tired of it but today this 'play' is funny, sharp and gorgeous. **Richard Cook, NME, November 1984**

Weld

ARTIST Neil Young And Crazy Horse **RELEASE DATE** November 1991 (UK & US) **LABEL** Reprise (UK & US) **PRODUCER** Neil Young, David Briggs, Billy Talbot **UK CHART** peak/weeks 20/3 **US CHART** peak/weeks 154/– **TRACK LISTING** Hey Hey, My My (Into The Black), Crime In The City/Blowin' In The Wind/Welfare Mothers/Love To Burn/Cinnamon Girl/Mansion On The Hill/F!#IN' Up/Cortez The Killer/Powderfinger/Love And Only Love/Rockin' In The Free World/Like A Hurricane/Farmer John/Tonight's The Night/Roll Another Number **PERSONNEL** Ralph Molina (d, v), Billy Talbot (b, v), Frank (Poncho) Sampedro (g, v), Neil Young (g, v)

Brutal and uncompromising: these were watchwords for Neil Young's career throughout the Seventies and Eighties. For him to then come up with something as howlingly unapologetic as the 34 minutes and 58 seconds of feedback and guitar detonations that comprised side three of this triple LP set (titled **Arc**) spoke volumes about the man's sheer nerve and determination to do what he pleases, when he pleases, and never mind the consequences. The two indirectly socio-political **Weld** CDs, recorded live as America began strafing Bhagdad during the Gulf War, presented the grunge kids as defiant a statement as did **Rust Never Sleeps** at the height of punk.

Young and Crazy Horse hit the road just as Bush set out to liberate the Kuwaiti oil fields, and Young's own mixed feelings about war, honour, imperialism and the mounting casualties in America's own back alleys were vividly and angrily summed up in his set list. **The Year In Records 1991, Rolling Stone, December 1991**

What Now, My Love

ARTIST Herb Alpert And The Tijuana Brass **RELEASE DATE** April 1966 **LABEL** Pye (UK)/A&M (US) **PRODUCER** Herb Alpert **UK CHART** peak/weeks 18/17 **US CHART** peak/weeks 1/129 **TRACK LISTING** Brasilia/Cantina Blue/Five Minutes More/Freckles/If I Were A Rich Man/It Was A Very Good Year/Magic Trumpet/Memories of Madrid/Plucky/Shadow Of Your Smile/So What's New?/What Now, My Love **PERSONNEL** Herb Alpert (v), session musicians

As a trumpeter, Alpert had worked with Jan And Dean before bullishly forging a solo career with his south-of-the-border easy listening. He formed A&M Records and enjoyed a stream of hit singles and albums. Sixty-six's **What Now, My Love** didn't boast as dubiously exotic a cover as its predecessor **Whipped Cream And Other Delights**, but, coming hot on the heels of the smash *Taste Of Honey*, it was equally epochal. After 1968's *This Guy's In Love With You*, he stopped recording, rising again to an Indian summer in the late Seventies. His record company's annual turnover was $200 million when he sold it in 1989.

'When we formed the group, I was also very concerned to create a happy band as well as a good one. All the musicians… have a piece of Tijuana Brass, and in the time we've been together we've become a very closely knit group.' **In interview, Melody Maker, March 1966**

What Up, Dog?

ARTIST Was (Not Was) **RELEASE DATE** April 1988 (UK)/October 1988 (US) **LABEL** Fontana (UK)/Chrysalis (US) **PRODUCER** David Bates **UK CHART** peak/weeks 47/6 **US CHART** peak/weeks 43/– **TRACK LISTING** Somewhere In America/Spy In The House Of Love/Out Come The Freaks/Earth To Doris/Love Can Be Bad Luck/Boy's Gone Crazy/11 Miles An Hour/What Up Dog?/Anything Can Happen/Robot Girl/Wedding Vows In Vegas/Anytime Lisa/Walk The Dinosaur/I Can't Turn You Loose/Shadow And Jimmy/Dad I'm In Jail **PERSONNEL** Don 'Rope Drink' (b, k, g, md), David 'Michigan-Boy Snake' (fl, k, h, v), Sweet Pea Atkinson (lv), Sir Harry Bowens (lv), Frank Sinatra Jr (v), Luis Resto (k), John Van Tongeren (k), Al Kooper (k), Amp Fiddler (k), Martin Phillips (k), Aaron Zigman (k), Daniel Schroeger (k), Vic Emmerson (k), Robin Smith (k), Paul Wickens (k), Randy Jacobs (g), Bruce Nazarian (g), Paul Jackson Jr (g), Steve Salas (g), Dan Huff (g), Marcus Miller (b), Neil Steubenhaus (b), John Patitucci (b)

David Weiss and Don Fagenson were the Steely Dan of the Eighties: two studio-centric musicians who allied barbed, witty lyrics to immaculately arranged, and expertly played, pop-rock, soul-funk and R&B. Their eponymous debut on Ze Records placed them at the forefront of the radical dance faction, but it attracted only a cult following. By **What's Up, Dog?**, they were collaborating with Frank Sinatra Jr and Elvis Costello and contriving successful melodic funk hits such as *Spy In The House Of Love* and *Walk The Dinosaur*.

So what will become of Was (Not Was)? Is **What Up Dog?** *another outstanding and intelligent album that no one will hear? Probably, The voice of disenchantment and real longing is one rarely heard on the radio.* **Fred Goodman, Rolling Stone, October 1988**

What's Going On

ARTIST Marvin Gaye **RELEASE DATE** June 1971 **LABEL** Tamla Motwon (UK)/Tamla (US) **PRODUCER** – **UK CHART** peak/weeks 0/0 **US CHART** peak/weeks 6/53 **TRACK LISTING** What's Going On/What's Happening Brother/Flyin' High (In The Friendly Sky)/Save The Children/God Is Love/Mercy, Mercy Me (The Ecology)/Right On/Wholly Holy/Inner City Blues (Make Me Wanna Holler) **PERSONNEL** Marvin Gaye (v), session musicians

Berry Gordy (founder and then owner of Motown) refused to release this at first, thinking the public would not be interested in a concept album, especially one of such dark subject matter. It was Gordy, rather than Gaye, who was proved wrong, for the public

loved the new Marvin – freed from the restraints of Motown's formula to explore poverty, the Vietnam war, discrimination and other political issues. Following its success, others at Motown, like Stevie Wonder, quickly followed suit. Marvin, having shaken up the boardroom, moved on – to the bedroom theme!

… Gaye does emerge as a man of integrity with a deep love of life and God… the album improves with every hearing. Gaye produced and co-wrote all the songs, and plays piano. **A.L., Melody Maker, October 1971**

(What's The Story) Morning Glory?

ARTIST Oasis **RELEASE DATE** October 1995 (UK & US) **LABEL** Creation (UK)/Sony (US) **PRODUCER** Owen Morris & Noel Gallagher **UK CHART** peak/weeks 1/72 **US CHART** peak/weeks 4/50 **TRACK LISTING** Hello/Roll With It/Wonderwall/Don't Look Back In Anger/Hey Now!/Some Might Say/Cast No Shadow/She's Electric/Morning Glory/Champagne Supernova **PERSONNEL** Liam Gallagher (v), Noel Gallagher (lg, v, p, m, b), Paul Arthurs (rg, m, p), Paul McGuigan (b), Alan White (d, pc)

Oasis topped the record sales of their debut album when their label claimed 350,000 sales of **Morning Glory** in seven days, gaining revenge for Brit-pop rivals Blur's cheek in beating *Roll With It* to the Number 1 singles spot. Opener *Hello* tipped the hat to Gary Glitter, *Wonderwall* (in its title, at least) to George Harrison – but the whole was undeniably Oasis. Bassist Guigsy temporarily stood down as the band promoted it, fazed by the pressures of fame, but would be back in harness as 1996 opened with the chart-topping *Don't Look Back In Anger*, the third single to be lifted from a classic album.

And again Noel has proved himself a rich resource of songcraft… What burns brightest on this album, though, is its self-belief. There is the invincible force of its tunes, Liam's insistent whine and the band's supple laddish stomp. **Paul Du Noyer, Mojo, October 1995**

Whatever

ARTIST Aimee Mann **RELEASE DATE** September 1993 (UK & US) **LABEL** Imago (UK & US) **PRODUCER** Jon Brion, Aimee Mann, Michael Hausman **UK CHART** peak/weeks 39/1 **US CHART** peak/weeks 127/4 **TRACK LISTING** I Should've Known/Fifty Years After The Fair/4th Of July/Could've Been Anyone/Put Me On Top/Stupid Thing/Say Anything/Jacob Marley's Chain/Mr Harris/I Could Hurt You Now/I Know There's A Word/I've Had It/Way Back When **PERSONNEL** Aimee Man (v, g), Michael Hausman (bd, d, cg), Buddy Judge (v), Mike Breaux (bsn), Jon Brion (g, p, o, b, h)

The first solo album from the Boston-born singer-songwriter delivered on the promise shown when working within the group format of Til Tuesday, and with three years of enforced silence due to record company politics she had plenty of songs to choose from. Sadly, Imago, the label which issued this, promptly disintegrated, leaving her and label-mate Paula Cole, another promising US singer, to go through the process of disentanglement again. Happily she repeated the pure-pop punch of this debut with 1995's *I'm With Stupid*.

… strong, vulnerable, believable… simple arrangements make maximum use of minimum resources, with subtle acoustic and electric textures intertwining like Virginia creeper gone rampant. **Johnny Black, Q, September 1993**

Wheels Of Fire

ARTIST Cream **RELEASE DATE** August 1968 (UK)/July 1968 (US) **LABEL** Polydor (UK)/Atco (US) **PRODUCER** Felix Pappalardi by arrangement with Robert Stigwood **UK CHART** peak/weeks 3/26 **US CHART** peak/weeks 1/46 **TRACK LISTING** White Room/Sitting On Top Of The World/Passing The Time/As You Said/Pressed Rat And Warthog/Politician/Those Were The Days/Born Under A Bad Sign/Deserted Cities Of The Heart/Crossroads/ Spoonful/ Traintime/ Toad **PERSONNEL** Eric Clapton (g, v), Jack Bruce (b, v, h, c), Ginger Baker (d) with Felix Pappalardi (o, va, pc, t)

Playing a residency at New York's Fillmore West, Cream found the courage to match their undoubted musicianship and travelled new, improvised, aural paths. Half this double album was recorded live in San Francisco, including the Robert Johnson number *Crossroads*, which Clapton was to make his own. It is not free of indulgence: *Spoonful* was over 16 minutes. But Cream were using 'the song' as a platform, going off on jazz-blues trajectories of free-flowing imagination. The studio sides gave them a second Top 10 hit in Bruce's *White Room*, and included Albert King's *Born Under A Bad Sign*. Yet the band were threatening to split even before the album came out.

… they are fantastic performers and excellent musicians… only rarely do they have a good original song to work with, their standard procedure is to put a strong rhythm and chord structure behind it and sort of recite the lyrics…. The album will be a monster. **Jann Wenner, Rolling Stone, July 1968**

When A Man Loves A Woman

ARTIST Percy Sledge **RELEASE DATE** July 1966 (UK)/May 1966 (US) **LABEL** Atlantic (UK & US) **PRODUCER** – **UK CHART** peak/weeks 36/4 **US CHART** peak/weeks 37/21 **TRACK LISTING** When A Man Loves A Woman/My Adorable One/Put A Little Lovin' On Me/Love Me All The Way/When She Touches Me (Nothing Else Matters)/You're Pouring Water On A Drowning Man/Thief In The Night/You Fooled Me/Love Makes The World Go Round/Success/Love Me Like You Mean It **PERSONNEL** Percy Sledge (v), session musicians

Percy Sledge achieved international acclaim with the title track of his debut album, one of the most impassioned performances ever committed to vinyl and a Top 5 hit on both sides of the Atlantic. The album when it sprung was no one-hit wonder. A successful attempt to explore the interface between country and soul, it displayed Sledge's manfully tender vocals, often sounding on the verge of cracking up as the Muscle Shoals' sessioneers added Southern grit to Sledge's coarse paeans to love.

There is nothing mechanical about the tortuously honeyed Sledge vocals as he aches and glides through 16 songs… even if you already know these songs backwards, his voice still sounds remarkable. **NME, March 1987**

When The World Knows Your Name

ARTIST Deacon Blue **RELEASE DATE** April 1989 (UK & US) **LABEL** CBS (UK)/Columbia (US) **PRODUCER** Warne Livesey with Deacon Blue, David Kahne **UK CHART** peak/weeks 1/54 **US CHART** peak/weeks - **TRACK LISTING** Queen Of The New Year/Wages Day/Real Gone Kid/Love And Regret/Circus Lights/This Changing Light/Sad Loved Girl/Fergus Sings The Blues/The World Is Lit By Lightning/Silhoutte/One Hundred Things/Your Constant Heart/Orphans **PERSONNEL** Ricky Ross (v), Lorraine McIntosh (v), Graeme Kelling (g), James Prime (k) Ewan Vernal (b, k), Douglas Vipond (d, pc)

Former teacher Ricky Ross learned his lesson from the critical acclaim but slow sales of his band's debut, **Raintown**. The release of the follow-up was announced by two great singles *Real Gone Kid* (inspired by Lone Justice singer Maria McKee) and *Wages Day*. Hence the album crashed into the chart to the summit, displacing Madonna and confirming the Scots' arrival. They repeated the feat in 1994 with **Our Town**, the greatest hits package.

If only life were so intense, so larger-than-life!… **When The World Knows Your Name** *perhaps has fewer songs of the melodic order of the debut's* **Chocolate Girl** *and* **Loaded**, *but it makes up in sheer brass-neck and raucous sense of occasion.* **Mat Snow, Q, April 1989**

White Light/White Heat

ARTIST The Velvet Underground **RELEASE DATE** June 1968 (UK)/December 1967 (US) **LABEL** Verve (UK & US) **PRODUCER** Tom Wilson **UK CHART** peak/weeks - **US CHART** peak/weeks 199/2 **TRACK LISTING** White Light/White Heat/The Gift/Lady Godiva's Operation/Here She Comes Now/I Heard Her Call My Name/Sister Ray **PERSONNEL** Lou Reed (v, g, p), John Cale (v, ev, o, b), Sterling Morrison (v, g, b), Maureen Tucker (pc)

WHITE LIGHT/WHITE HEAT
THE VELVET UNDERGROUND

MGM

With former avant-garde classical music student John Cale on board, drummer Maureen Tucker's fondness for relentless pulse beats and Lou Reed's attraction to the dark side of life, it was inevitable that The Velvet Underground would create something startlingly different. **White Light/White Heat** is a landmark of interminable drones, wailing feedback and abrasive textures. No wonder it is said that everyone who ever heard The Velvets immediately went out and formed a band. The 17-minute *Sister Ray* has long been a favourite of garage acts with space to fill and noise on their minds.

Utterly pretentious, unbelievably monotonous. It even has one track taken up by a long bit of story telling. **Melody Maker, July 1968**

White On Blonde

ARTIST Texas RELEASE DATE 1997 (UK & US) LABEL Mercury (UK & US) PRODUCER Texas, Mike Hedges, Dave Stewart, Rae & Christian, The Boilerhouse Boys UK CHART peak/weeks – US CHART peak/weeks – TRACK LISTING 0.34/Say What You Want/Drawing Crazy Patterns/Halo/Put Your Arms Around Me/Insane/Black-Eyed Boy/Polo Mint City/White On Blonde/Postcard/0.28/Ticket To Lie/Good Advice/Breathless PERSONNEL Sharleen Spiteri (v), Ally McErlaine, Eddie Campbell, Richard Hynd, Johnny McElhone

With former Altered Images member Johnny McElhone on board, Texas had a bassist with a knack for perfectly formed, three-minute pop-soul nuggets. With the photogenic Sharleen Spiteri on board as singer and McElhone's co-writer, Texas couldn't fail. **White On Blonde** sold more than all of their three previous albums put together. The third single from the LP, **Black-Eyed Boy**, has been hailed as one of the singles of the decade, Spiteri's vocals redolent of the young Diana Ross. First single, *Say What You Want*, also owed a debt to old-school soul, being reminiscent of Marvin Gaye's *Sexual Healing* and Al Green's *Tired Of Being Alone*, which Texas covered in 1992.

The White Room

ARTIST KLF RELEASE DATE July 1989 (UK)/May 1989 (US) LABEL KLF (UK) Arista (US) PRODUCER – UK CHART peak/weeks 3/46 US CHART peak/weeks 39/50 TRACK LISTING What Time Is Love?/Make It Rain/3 A.M. Eternal/Church Of The KLF/Last Train To Transcentral/Build A Fire/The White Room/No More Tears PERSONNEL Bill Drummond, Jimmy Cauty

Having tried ambient music for size, Bill Drummond and Jimmy Cauty (who would later found the Orb) returned to dance-rock with a series of three singles, **What Time Is Love**, **3A.M. Eternal** and **Last Train To Transcentral** that restored their fortunes. **The White Room** compiled this so-called 'Stadium House Trilogy' and became a surprise chart-topper, as well as providing the name for a TV music programme.

In many ways, it's their most subtle, successful and dangerous musical mischief to date. 1991: What the f is going on? Love it. **Push, Melody Maker, March 1991**

Whitney Houston

ARTIST Whitney Houston RELEASE DATE December 1985 (UK)/March 1985 (US) LABEL Arista (UK & US) PRODUCER Jermaine Jackson, Kashif, Michael Masser, Narada Michael Walden UK CHART peak/weeks 2/119 US CHART peak/weeks 1/162 TRACK LISTING You Give Good Love/Thinking About You/Someone For Me/Saving All My Love For You/Nobody Loves Me Like You Do/How Will You Know/All At Once/Take Good Care Of My Heart/Greatest Love Of All/Hold Me PERSONNEL Whitney Houston (v), Jermaine Jackson (v)

Whitney Houston was one of six solo females to top the US album chart in 1986 – but none of her contemporaries, from Streisand to Sade, could boast three Number 1 singles from the record. The third Number 1 single, *Greatest Love Of All*, coincided with the album peaking in its fiftieth chart week and suggested the 23-year-old niece of Dionne Warwick would have an even brighter future

*.. there's not a single song among these 10 that completely showcases her gifts. You get more than a hint of her smooth power in **How Will I Know**, but **The Greatest Love Of All** is the track that builds most convincingly. With the right song and settings, she could be an earth-shaking performer.* **The Year In Records 1985, Rolling Stone, December 1985**

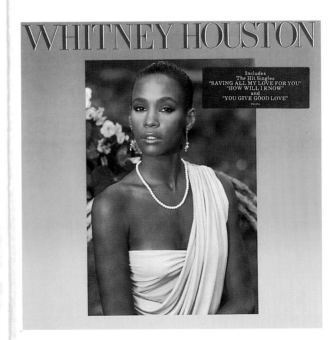

The Who Sell Out

ARTIST The Who RELEASE DATE January 1968 (UK & US)) LABEL Track (UK)/Decca (US) PRODUCER – UK CHART peak/weeks 13/11 US CHART peak/weeks 48/23 TRACK LISTING Armenian City In The Sky/Heinz Baked Beans/Mary-Anne With The Shakey Hands/Odorono/Tattoo/Our Love Was, Is/I Can See For Miles/I Can't Reach You/Medac/Silas Stingy/ Sunrise/ Tattoo/Real PERSONNEL Roger Daltrey (v), Pete Townsend (g, v), John Entwistle (b, v), Keith Moon (d, v)

Featuring mock advertisements and real jingles from offshore British pirate radio stations **The Who Sell Out** was a concept album to rank alongside **Sgt. Pepper**. In between the pop-art experiments, there were also some classic anthems, such as *I Can See For Miles*, a powerful rocker that showed off the individual brilliance of the band's three players, as well as Townshend, Daltrey and Entwistle's increasingly complex harmonies and mastery of the recording console.

The inclusion of Radio 1 commercials and station identification breaks make it somewhat of a period piece, but also give it a maniac speedy energy which more than compensates. Reportedly written in airport departure lounges and US whistle-stop hops. **Roy Carr, Charles Shaar Murray, NME, November 1973**

Who's Next

ARTIST The Who RELEASE DATE September 1971 (UK & US) LABEL Track (UK)/Decca (US) PRODUCER The Who Associate producer: Glyn Jones UK CHART peak/weeks 1/13 US CHART peak/weeks 4/41 TRACK LISTING Baba O'Riley/Bargain, Love Ain't For Keeping/My Wife/Song Is Over/Getting In Tune/Going Mobile/Behind Blue Eyes/Won't Get Fooled Again PERSONNEL Roger Daltrey (v), Keith Moon (d), John Entwistle (b, v, p), Pete Townsend (g, o, sy, v, p)

Regarded by many as The Who's masterpiece, **Who's Next** was superbly produced by the band with the help of Glyn Johns, who brought a crystalline clarity to the sound, whilst Pete Townshend employed the synthesizer to add a new dimension to The Who's trad-rock line-up – a cold, mechanical feel that offset the mad, slashing guitars. As for Townshend's writing, it was never better: *Baba O'Riley* was a terrific anthem, while **Won't Get Fooled Again** was the definitive Who song, with its enormous sound filling radio station playlists for years to come.

A nine-track album that contains at least four Who classics can't be all that bad. The trouble was that, by The Who's immaculate standards, the rest of the album was disposable. **Roy Carr, Charles Shaar Murray, NME, November 1973**

Wild Wood

ARTIST Paul Weller RELEASE DATE September 1993 (UK & US) LABEL Go! Discs (UK)/London (US) PRODUCER Brendan Lynch, Paul Weller UK CHART peak/weeks 2/15 US CHART peak/weeks – TRACK LISTING Sunflower/Can You Heal Us (Holy Man)/Wild Wood – Instrumental (pt.1)/All The Pictures On The Wall/Has My Fire Really Gone Out?/Country/5th Season/The Weaver – Instrumental (pt.2)/Foot Of The Mountain/Shadow Of The Sun – Holy Man (Reprise)/Moon On Your Pyjamas PERSONNEL Paul Weller (v, g)

After disbanding the Jam and achieving considerable success with The Style Council, it appeared that Paul Weller could do no wrong. His debut solo album was released to little fanfare, however, and it wasn't until the following year's **Wild Wood** that the full-scale rehabilitation of Paul Weller as Great British Institution began in earnest. **Wild Wood** eschewed the preachy politicizing of his two previous incarnations for an earnest soul-searching confessional style that proved he had finally come of age.

Wild Wood... *walks like a cat, but there are fences under which it*

will never squeeze. This is, after all, a man in his early thirties, fusing his perception of NOW! with ghosts of the past he'll never be able to lose... **Taylor Parkes, Melody Maker, September 1993**

The Wild, The Innocent And The E-Street Shuffle

ARTIST Bruce Springsteen RELEASE DATE February 1974 (UK)/November 1973 (US) LABEL CBS (UK)/Columbia (US) PRODUCER Mike Appel, Jim Cretecos UK CHART peak/weeks 0/0 US CHART peak/weeks 59/34 TRACK LISTING The E-Street Shuffle/4th Of July, Asbury Park (Sandy)/Kitty's Back/ Wild Billy's Circus Story/Incident On 57th Street/Rosalita (Come Out Tonight)/New York City Seranade PERSONNEL Bruce Springsteen (v, g), David Sancious (k), Danny Federici (k), Garry Tallent (b), Ernest Carter (d), Clarence Clemens (s)

Bruce Springsteen's debut album, **Greetings From Asbury Park, NJ** (1973), may have been released amid much hype about this 'new Dylan', yet it only sold around 30,000 copies initially. So, too, did the follow-up, **The Wild, The Innocent And The E-Street Shuffle**, until a now legendary review of a Springsteen concert by critic (and, later, Bruce's manager) Jon Landau exclaimed: 'I saw rock 'n' roll's future and its name is Bruce Springtseen.' This propelled the LP, with its far more successful blend of poetic street imagery and R&B-based rock than the debut, further towards the super league.

Bruce Springsteen has very little taste and no small endowment of pretentiousness, but when he pulls it off he comes on like a man who knows what he's doing at least part of the time. **Charles Shaar Murray, NME, February 1975**

Willy And The Poor Boys

ARTIST Creedence Clearwater Revival RELEASE DATE March 1970 (UK)/ December 1969 (US) LABEL Liberty (UK)/Fantasy (US) PRODUCER John Fogerty UK CHART peak/weeks 10/24 US CHART peak/weeks 3/60 TRACK LISTING Down On The Corner/It Came Out Of The Sky/Cotton Fields/Poorboy Shuffle/Feelin' Blue/Fortunate Son/Don't Look Now (It Ain't You Or Me)/The Midnight Special/Side Of The Road/Effigy PERSONNEL Doug Clifford (d), Stu Cook (b), John Dogerty (lg, v), Tom Fogerty (rg)

Creedence were 'the anti-**Sgt. Pepper**', spraying three minute pop nuggets around as if sprawling muso epics hadn't been discovered. Redneck and raw, they did slip a little politics into **Don't Look Now** and **Fortunate Son**, while residing down home through **Cotton Fields** and **Down On The Corner** – another hit. They were more 'down South' than most down South groups, also bringing a cheeky flair to Memphis soul grooves. And all this from John Fogerty, who later wrote **Rockin' All Over The World**, 'immortalized' by Status Quo.

Their music here crossbreeds rock 'n' roll with blues and country and the child is healthy and thriving. **B. D., Melody Maker, March 1970**

Wings At The Speed Of Sound

ARTIST Wings RELEASE DATE April 1976 LABEL EMI (UK)/Capitol (US) PRODUCER – UK CHART peak/weeks 2/35 US CHART peak/weeks 1/51 TRACK LISTING Let 'Em In/The Note You Never Wrote/She's My Baby/ Beware My Love/Wino Junko/Silly Love Songs/Cook Of The House/Time To Hide/Must Do Something About It/San Ferry Anne/Warm And Beautiful PERSONNEL Paul McCartney (v, g, b), Linda McCartney (k, bv, pc), Denny Seiwell (d, v), Denny Laine (g, v), Joe English (d)

The release of **Wings At The Speed Of Sound** coincided with Paul McCartney's first post-Beatles American tour, but suffered from his insistence on democracy: the contributions from the other Wings did the album few favours. And although **Silly Love Songs** and **Let 'Em In** both reached Number 2 in the UK, they highlighted McCartney's mawkish streak. The former, in particular, was aimed as an answer to critics who felt he had lost his edge. They may have had a point.

This is not an album that hits you with the sustained power of **Band On The Run** *or* **Venus And Mars***, but, as Linda says: 'It grows on yer!'* **Chris Welch, Melody Maker, March 1976**

Wish

ARTIST The Cure RELEASE DATE April 1992 (UK & US) LABEL Fiction (UK)/Elektra (US) PRODUCER The Cure, David M. Allen UK CHART peak/weeks 1/13 US CHART peak/weeks 2/26 TRACK LISTING Open/High/Apart/From The Edge Of The Deep Green Sea/Wendy Time/Doing The Unstuck/Friday I'm In Love/Trust/A Letter To Elise/Cut/To Wish Impossible Things/End PERSONNEL Robert Smith (v, b, k), Simon Gallup (b, k), Porl Thompson (g), Boris Williams (d, pc, g, b, k)

Here, The Cure brought a more engaging, diverse collection of songs than the easy clichés that dogged them might have allowed. *Friday I'm In Love*, a positively buoyant hit, won over sceptics. Its charm infected **Apart and Open**, and **Doing The Unstuck** sang, 'Kick out the gloom!' before, admittedly, advocating suicide. Elsewhere the customary low-blood sugar tempos were evident. Nevertheless it got a result, crashing straight into the American charts at Number 2. A decline followed, but for now millions were prepared to worship at the church of Robert Smith and his boys in black and dodgy make-up, even if it meant standing through 20 minutes of **A Forest** live.

Wish *turns out to contain several of the best things The Cure have done, as well as one or two items which they should be able to pull off in*

their sleep, and, by the sound of it, quite possibly did... this is not the perfect Cure album. **Q, May 1992**

Wish You Were Here

ARTIST Badfinger RELEASE DATE October 1974 (UK & US) LABEL Warner Bros. (UK & US) PRODUCER Chris Thomas UK CHART PEAK/WEEKS 0/0 US CHART PEAK/WEEKS 148/6 TRACK LISTING Just A Chance/You're So Fine/Got To Get Out Of Here/Know One Knows/Dennis/In The Meantime/Love Time/ Some Other Time/King Of The Load/Meanwhile Back At The Ranch – Should I Smoke PERSONNEL Joey Molland (lg, k, v), Tommy Evans (b, v), Pete Ham (g, v, p), Ron Griffiths (b, v), Mike Gibbons (d)

Badfinger were hounded by bad luck. Having left Apple for Warners only to encounter legal disputes between label and management, the Beatles-influenced blend of harmony, melody and slightly more aggressive guitar that composed this legendary album was withdrawn from sale, despite rave reviews, just weeks after release. Within a year Joey Molland quit and Pete Ham hanged himself. The irony remains that with producer Chris Thomas in all-conquering form, they'd made one of the great lost soft-rock LPs, full of yearning and passion and a sense of do or die.

'We were genuine, real hippies,' says Joey Molland of Badfinger... 'Not air heads, but hippies. We really believed in certain concepts; our reality was based on certain ideals. And it was a bit of a drag to find out that wasn't the real world.' **Parke Puterbaugh, Rolling Stone, August 1989**

With The Beatles

ARTIST The Beatles RELEASE DATE November 1963 LABEL Parlophone PRODUCER George Martin UK CHART peak/weeks 1/51 US CHART peak/weeks - TRACK LISTING It Won't Be Long/All I've Got To Do/All My Loving/Don't Bother Me/Little Child/Till There Was You/Please Mister Postman/Roll Over Beethoven/Hold Me Tight/You Really Got A Hold On Me/I Wanna Be Your Man/Devil In Her Heart/Not A Second Time/Money PERSONNEL Paul McCartney (v, g), John Lennon (v, g), George Harrisson (v, lg), Ringo Starr (d)

Britain's favourite group by miles and soon, after a punishing schedule, to be America's. They had coined the **Mersey Beat** sound, but were already stretching out. Chuck Berry's **Roll Over Beethoven** and Barrett Strong's **Money**, with Lennon's extraordinary voice, were inspired renditions, while **All My Loving** hinted at their mastery of the simple yet irresistible pop song. The album still crackles with ferocious momentum, despite the weird inclusion of the Broadway show tune **Till There Was You** from *The Music Man*.

A great album, with variety of tempo and a raw style that puts The Beatles unmistakably at the top of the beat tree. **Melody Maker, November 1963**

Wish You Were Here

ARTIST Pink Floyd RELEASE DATE September 1975 LABEL Harvest (UK) Columbia (US) PRODUCER – UK CHART peak/weeks 1/- US CHART peak/weeks 1/39 TRACK LISTING Shine On You Crazy Diamond (parts 1-5)/Welcome To The Machine/Have A Cigar/Wish You Were Here/Shine On You Crazy Diamond (Parts 6-9) PERSONNEL Roger Waters (v, b), Rick Wright (k), David Gilmour (v, g), Nick Mason (d), Stephane Grappelli (vl)

It took the Floyd two years to come up with something to equal **Dark Side Of The Moon**, nearly splitting in the process, and inevitably some critics felt it remained in its predecessor's shadow. The key track was the lengthy tribute to long-lost and spaced-out founder Syd Barrett, **Shine On You Crazy Diamond**, inspired by his visit to the recording studio, and graced with his replacement Dave Gilmour's best ever guitar, while Roy Harper guested on the lighter hearted song that bore his name.

A Wizard, A True Star

ARTIST Todd Rundren RELEASE DATE June 1973 LABEL Bearsville PRODUCER Todd Rundren UK CHART peak/weeks - US CHART peak/weeks 86/15 TRACK LISTING International Feel/Never Never Land/Tic Tic Tic It Wear Off/You Need Your Head/Rock And Roll Pussy/Dogfight Giggle/You Don't Have To Camp Around/Flamingo/Zen Archer/Just Another Onion Head-Da Da Dali/When The Shit Hits The Fan – Sunset Blvd/Le Feel Internacionale/Sometimes I Don't Know What To Feel/Does Anybody Love You?/I'm So Proud -Ooh Ooh Baby - La La Means I Love You - Cool Jerk/Is It My Name?/Just One Victory PERSONNEL Todd Rundren (lg, v, composer), session musicians

Described by Todd Rundgren at the time as his first 'stream-of-consciousness album', **A Wizard, A True Star** was a 60-minute fantasy ride through the more colourful recesses of the musician's imagination, newly warped by his experiments with acid. Side one saw Rundgren apply some amazing sonic effects to his usual immaculate melodics, while side two featured a medley of R&B covers – Todd sings The Impressions, The Delfonics and Smokey Robinson – that sounded like nothing so much as soul from outer space.

… this album runs for an hour, and finally determines that Rundgren is in fact for real, and not the charlatan that many thought he was… shows Rundgren as an ace producer, an energetic writer, and a singer with a pleasing amount of flair. **Melody Maker, July 1973**

With A Little Help From My Friends

ARTIST Joe Cocker RELEASE DATE May 1969 LABEL Regal Zono (UK)/A&M (US) PRODUCER – UK CHART peak/weeks 29/4 US CHART peak/weeks 35/37 TRACK LISTING Feeling Alright/Bye Bye Blackbird/Change In Louise/Marjorine/Just Like A Woman/Do I Still Figure In Your Life/Sandpaper Cadillac/Don't Let Me Be Misunderstood/With A Little Help From My Friends/I Shall Be Released PERSONNEL Joe Cocker (v), Henry McCulloch (g), Kenny Slade (d), Vernon Nash (p), Dave Green (b), session musicians

Throwing himself into the album's title, Sheffield blues-pop vocalist Cocker enlisted the assistance of such luminaries as Jimmy Page, Steve Winwood, Leon Russell and Albert Lee as he tried to build on the successes of his chart-topping Lennon/McCartney epic. He'd been building up for an authentic smash since his bizarre, face-crunching and arm-windmilling 'soul singer' mannerisms had wowed *Woodstock*. Russell's **Delta Lady** was also a hit, **Feelin' Alright** was a Traffic cover, **I Shall Be Released**' was Dylan's, but Cocker's sandpaper-and-glue voice made all these inimitably his own.

With A Little Help From My Friends, *(Reprise), a thundering good album with Joe's 'friends', including Jimmy Page, Stevie Winwood, Clem Cattini.* **Melody Maker, July 1969**

Woodface

ARTIST Crowded House **RELEASE DATE** July 1991 **LABEL** Capitol (UK & US) **PRODUCER** Mitchell Froom, Neil Finn **UK CHART** peak/weeks 6/56 **US CHART** peak/weeks 83/17 **TRACK LISTING** Chocolate Cake/It's Only Natural/Fall At Your Feet/Tall Trees/Weather With You/Whispers And Moans/Four Seasons In One Day/There Goes God/Fame Is/All I Ask/As Sure As I Am/Italian Plastic/She Goes On/How Will You Go **PERSONNEL** Paul Hester (d, v, k, pc), Nick Seymour (b, v), Neil Finn (g, v, k), Tim Finn (p, g, v), Rick Fataar (d, pc), Chris Wilson (h), Peter Bucknell (v), Vince Parsonage (va), Alex Acuna (pc), Geoffrey Hales (pc), Jack Mack (br), David Hidalgo (ad), Sharon Finn (bv), Mitchell Froom (k), Mark Hart (k), Stuart Ellison (k)

Tim Finn rejoined after the break-up following the disappointing response to **Temple of Low Men**, and the most successful New Zealand band of all time were back on track, joining the upbeat pop melodies of their first album to the more introspective soul-searching of the second. The Finns harmonized wonderfully, and saw the hit **Weather With You** fostering their first big British seller. **Fall At Your Feet** gave them another hit, but during the subsequent tour the brothers had another row, and Tim went solo yet again (enjoying a hit under his own name with **Persuasion**). Neil could console himself with the chart ascendancy of **It's Only Natural** and **Four Seasons In One Day**.

Neil & Tim Finn's gift for tune-smithery seem as seamlessly compatible as their creamy vocal harmonies. Crowded House's virtues lie with what is so often called 'classic' pop song… intricately layered melodies, bittersweet and wistful… or sardonic… **Q, July 1991**

Woodstock, The Album

ARTIST Various **RELEASE DATE** July 1970 (UK & US) **LABEL** Atlantic/Cotillion (UK & US) **PRODUCER** – **UK CHART** peak/weeks 35/19 **US CHART** peak/weeks 1/68 **TRACK LISTING** At The Hop/Coming Into Los Angeles/Dance To The Music (Medley)/Drug Store Truck Drivin' Man/Fish Cheer (Medley)/Freedom/Going Up The Country/I-Feel-Like-Im-A-Fixin-To-Die (medley)/I Had A Dream/I Want To Take You Higher (Medley)/Purple Haze (Medley)/Rainbows All Over Your Blues/Rock 'N' Soul Music/Sea Of Madness/Soul Sacrifice/Star Spangled Banner (Medley)/Suite: Judy Blue Eyes/We're Not Gonna Make It/With A Little Help From My Friends/Wooden Ships **PERSONNEL** Sha-Na-Na, Arlo Guthrie, Sly And The Family Stone, Joan Baez, Country Joe And The Fish, Richie Havens, Canned Heat, John Sebastian, Ten Years After, Butterfield Blues Band, Jimi Hendrix, Crosby, Stills Nash & Young, Santana, Jefferson Airplane, The Who, Joe Cocker

Half a million attended the (to many) defining moment of late Sixties peace and love. Three days long and very muddy, the hippie festival was 'stardust, golden' in Joni Mitchell's blissed-out view. Some reputations were made purely on their performances here, from Sha Na Na to Richie Havens. Not many Brits appeared, apart from The Who and Joe Cocker. Crosby, Stills and Nash emoted, Joan Baez pleaded, Jimi Hendrix freaked out through 13 minutes of **The Star-Spangled Banner** and **Purple Haze**. The dawning of the age of Aquarius or a lot of stoned twaddle, depending on your birth date.

The **Woodstock** *album is a new step forward in recorded entertainment. Not only is it the finest live album ever, but it summarizes as no album ever has or ever will the rock mania of the late Sixties.* **Ed Ward, July 1970**

Workbook

ARTIST Bob Mould **RELEASE DATE** May 1987 (UK)/April 1989 (US) **LABEL** Virgin (UK & US) **PRODUCER** Bob Mould **UK CHART** peak/weeks 0/0 **US CHART** peak/weeks 127/14 **TRACK LISTING** Compositions For The Young And The Old/Dreaming I Am/Heartbreak A Stranger/Lonely Afternoon/Poison Years/See A Little Light/Sinners And Their Repentences/ Sunspots/ Whichever Way The Wind Blows/Wishing Well/Brasilia Crossed With Trenton **PERSONNEL** Bob Mould (v, g, md, pc, lp, k), Anton Fier (d), Steve Haigler (pc), Tony Maimone (b), Jane Scarpentoni (c)

Anyone expecting **Husker Du** mark two from the group's former front man would have been disappointed… for the moment anyway. Though the follow-up, 1990's **Black Sheets Of Rain**, edged back towards the Minneapolis trio, presaging a full-time group return to thrash with **Sugar**, this altogether more reflective debut, recorded with the Pere Ubu rhythm section, underlined the melodic side of his work, with a cello and acoustic guitars prominent. Only **Whichever Way The Wind Blows** brought former glories to mind.

The autumnal feel of the music is an ideal match with Mould's ambitious lyrics…. The road to success and maturity can indeed be treacherous for anyone who ventures onto it, but **Workbook** *is proof that every once in a while, its worth it.* **David Browne, Rolling Stone, May 1989**

Workingman's Dead

ARTIST The Grateful Dead **RELEASE DATE** September 1970 (UK)/February 1967 (US) **LABEL** Warner Bros. (UK & US) **PRODUCER** Bob Matthews with Betty Cantor, The Grateful Dead **UK CHART** peak/weeks 69/2 **US CHART** peak/weeks 27/26 **TRACK LISTING** Uncle John's Band/High Time/Dire Wolf/New Speedway Boogie/Cumberland Blues/Black Peter/Easy Wind/Casey Jones **PERSONNEL** Jerry Garcia (lg), Bob Weir (rg), Ron 'Pigpen' McKernan (o, bv), Phil Lesh (b), Bill Kreutzmann (d)

Anyone who witnessed the Grateful Dead's sprawling, psychedelic, four-hour set at the *Hollywood Rock Festival* in Staffordshire three months earlier, their first live date outside the US, would perhaps have been bemused by this acoustic, countrified set that owed more to the likes of CSN&Y. Jerry Garcia brought in two members of his country spin-off group, New Riders of the Purple Sage, Marmaduke Dawson and David Nelson, and they helped shape a work which represented a real departure for the Dead.

Workingman's Dead *is an excellent album. It's a warming album. And most importantly, the Dead have finally produced a complete studio album. The songs stand up quite nicely right on their own merits, which are considerable.* **Andy Zwerling, Rolling Stone, July 1970**

World Clique

ARTIST Deee-Lite RELEASE DATE September 1990 LABEL Elektra PRODUCER – UK CHART peak/weeks 14/18 US CHART peak/weeks 20/41 TRACK LISTING Good Beat/Power Of love/Try Me On...I'm Very You/Smile On/What Is Love?/World Clique/E.S.P./Groove Is In The Heart/Who Was That?/Deep-Ending PERSONNEL Super DJ Dimitry Brill, Jungle DJ Towa 'Towa' Tei, Lady Miss Kier (v)

A dance trio made up of husband and wife Lady Miss Kier (Kier Kirby from Ohio) and Super DJ Dmitri Brill (from Kiev), together with Jungle DJ Towa 'Towa' Tei (from Tokyo). They scored a massive transatlantic hit with *Groove Is In The Heart*, sending this album into the Top 20 in its wake, but the novelty quickly wore off and Tei left after 1992's **Infinity Within**, replaced by Ani. Bottom end was provided by legendary bassist Bootsy Collins

... a deeper exploration of rhythms than seems to be expected these days, slotting in counteracting patterns to build a base strong enough to allow some genuine musical silliness to take place on top. That done, they know the difference between wit and self-indulgence. **Q, January 1991**

World Machine

ARTIST Level 42 RELEASE DATE November 1985 (UK)/March 1986 (US) LABEL Polydor (UK)/A&M (US) PRODUCER Wally Badarou & Level 42 UK CHART peak/weeks 3/72 US CHART peak/weeks 18/36 TRACK LISTING World Machine/Physical Presence/Something About You/Leaving Me Now/I Sleep On My Heart/It's Not The Same For Us/Good Man In A Storm/Coup D'Etat/Lying Still PERSONNEL Mark King (v, b), Phil Gould (d), Mike Lindup (k, v), Boon (g), Wally Badarou (sy, v), Gary Barnacle (s)

By reaching Number 3 and staying 72 weeks in the charts, bassman Mark King's funk machine from the Isle of Wight started a run of best-selling albums that generated massive sales, were played on radio and in discos alike yet failed to produce any great lyrical insight or musical *frisson*. Level 42 had been linked with labelmates Shakatak as music for geezers who drove round with fluffy dice hanging from their XR3's driving mirror – and nice as King undoubtedly was **World Machine** failed to shatter that perception.

If there was a Brit-trot-punk band that had half Level 42's glossy panther sheen – rippling hammer blow psychomotion, pellucid colourwax drawl – ahem, hard to describe qualities... no let's not pretend, no worthy drones will supplant these unaccountable elder gods. **Mark Sinker, NME, November 1985**

Wrecking Ball

ARTIST Emmylou Harris RELEASE DATE October 1995 LABEL Grapevine (UK)/Asylum (US) PRODUCER Daniel Lanois UK CHART peak/weeks 46/– US CHART peak/weeks 94/7 TRACK LISTING Where Will I Be/Goodbye/All My Tears/Wrecking Ball/Goin' Back To Harlan/Deeper Well/Every Grain Of Sand/Sweet Old World/May This Be Love/Orphan Girl/Blackhawk/Waltz Across Texas Tonight PERSONNEL Daniel Lanois (md, g, b, v, ag, pc), Brian Blade (d), Daryl Johnson (v, tt, k, bp, d, b), Larry Mullen Jr (d), Malcolm Burn (p, tm, o, sy, k, g), Tony Hall (b), Steve Earle (ag), Neil Young (v, h), Emmylou Harris (ag), Kufaru Mouton (pc), Lucinda Williams (ag), Richard Bennett (g), Kate McGarrigle (v), Anna McGarrigle (v)

After two decades in the solo spotlight, Emmylou was a very much known quantity until she linked with U2 producer Daniel Lanois and dramatically changed how people viewed her. Time-honoured classics like Dylan's *Every Grain Of Sand* plus pages from the Hendrix, Neil Young and Steve Earle songbooks came out sounding radically different, and her reward was a Grammy for Best Contemporary Folk Album. Forget the folk tag, it must have been the contemporary that pleased the 49-year-old most.

Harris floats in some nether-land amid Country, Rock and Folk. Her latest album turns this stylistic ambiguity into a shining virtue: **Wrecking Ball** *is a wrenching collection of songs that merges popular and historic styles like a Nineties rethink of The Band.* **Rolling Stone, February 1995**

The Yardbirds

ARTIST The Yardbirds **RELEASE DATE** July 1966 (UK) **LABEL** EMI **PRODUCER** Paul Samwell-Smith, Simon Napier Bell **UK CHART** peak/weeks 20/8 **US CHART** peak/weeks 52/– **TRACK LISTING** Lost Woman/Over, Under, Sideways, Down/The Nazz Are Blue/I Can't Make Your Way/Rack My Mind/Farewell/Hot House Of Omagararshid/Jeff's Boogie/He's Always There/Turn Into Earth/What Do You Want/Ever Since The World Began **PERSONNEL** Keith Relf (v, h), Eric Clapton (lg, v), Chris Dreja (rg), Paul Samwell Smith (b), Jim McCarty (d)

A lot of hard work and thought has gone into the production. Not all the ideas come off, maybe as a result of trying too hard. But that's never a crime, and the overall result is an interesting and often exciting album. **Melody Maker, July 1966**

The Yes Album

ARTIST Yes **RELEASE DATE** April 1971 (UK)/May 1971 (US) **LABEL** Atlantic (UK & US) **PRODUCER** Yes, Eddie Offord **UK CHART** peak/weeks 7/29 **US CHART** peak/weeks 40/– **TRACK LISTING** Yours To No Disgrace/The Clap/Starship Trooper: A. Life Seeker B. All Good People C. Wurm/I've Seen All Good People: A. Your Move B. All Good People/A Venture/Perpetual Change **PERSONNEL** John Anderson (v, pc), Chris Squire (b, v), Steve howe (g, ag, v), Tony Kaye (p, o, sy), Bill Bruford (d, pc)

Complex harmonies, neo-classical song-structures, Byzantine

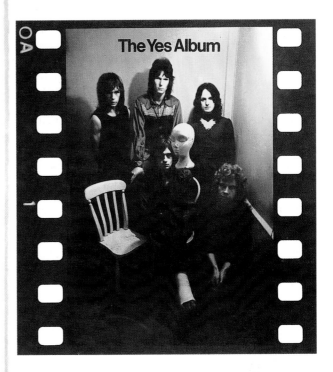

arrangements, overblown production, quasi-mystical lyrics, acid-tinged album sleeves, Yes were the apotheosis of that much maligned *genre*, progressive rock. **The Yes Album**, the band's third, was actually the quiet before the prog-rock storm. Before the arrival of Rick Wakeman's sonic arsenal, and with Jon Anderson's ethereal choirboy tenor singing a relatively unfussy series of melodies, it remains one of the period's more accessible, enjoyable moments.

As for vocals, Yes has an ear for harmony and takes full advantage of this asset. Squire and Howe supplement Anderson's delightful leads with harmonies in the upper register. Forget your inhibitions and take **The Yes Album** *home with you.* **John Koegal, Rolling Stone, July 1971**

You Can't Hide Your Love Forever

ARTIST Orange Juice **RELEASE DATE** March 1982 **LABEL** Polydor **PRODUCER** – **UK CHART** peak/weeks 21/6 **US CHART** peak/weeks – **TRACK LISTING** Tender Object/L.O.V.E./Falling And Laughing/Wan Light/Untitled Melody/Dying Day/Upwards And Onwards/Felicity/Three Cheers For Our Side/Intuition Told Me/Satellite City/In A Nutshell/Consolation Prize **PERSONNEL** Edwyn Collins (g, v), James Kirk (g, v), David McClymont (b, sy), Stephen Daly (d)

Having created a reputation on the independent Postcard label with a string of classic singles, Orange Juice took the corporate shilling to complete this, their first album. But mainman Edwyn Collins' recruitment of Malcolm Ross from label-mates Josef K saw James Kirk and Steven Daly quit to form their own band, Memphis. The music would become more competent and rhythmic but lose the simplicity and charm of the early work.

You Can't Hide Your Love Forever *is a surprisingly strong debut… Orange Juice are still imperfect, but on this LP, captured at their most disciplined, there's more fizz than flatness, and no sickly aftertaste. Just how Orange Juice should be.* **Leyla Sanai, NME, February 1982**

You Don't Mess Around With Jim

ARTIST Jim Croce RELEASE DATE April 1972 (UK & US) LABEL Vertigo (UK)/ABC (US) PRODUCER Terry Cashman, Tommy West UK CHART peak/weeks – US CHART peak/weeks 1/– TRACK LISTING You Don't Mess Around With Jim/Tomorrow's Gonna Be A Brighter Day/New York's Not My Home/Hard Time Losin' Man/Photographs And Memories/Walkin' Back To Georgia/Operator (That's Not The Way It Feels)/Time In A Bottle/Rapid Roy (The Stock Car Boy)/Box 10/A Long Time Ago/Hey Tomorrow PERSONNEL Jim Croce (rg, w, v), Maury Muehleisen (lg, bv), Gary Chester (d), Tommy West (k, b, bv), Joe Macho (b), Tommy West (b, bv), Jim Ryan (b), Ellie Greenwich (bv), Tasha Thomas (bv), Briggs, Digs and Slim (bv)

The laid-back Philadelphia singer-songwriter was starting to enjoy great crossover success when he was tragically killed in a plane crash in 1973. His posthumous hits were of a sentimental, balladic strain, but prior to his death such releases were countered by story songs and witty satirical vignettes of wry wordplay. The title track was just such a fun piece, and, along with the more sincere *Operator*, was a curious American hit. Croce never translated to the UK the swansongs *Time In A Bottle* and *I'll Have To Say I Love You In A Song* are probably the sweeter refrains for which he will be remembered, though he also wrote *Bad Bad Leroy Brown* for Frank Sinatra.

'I'm so into music,' he tells you smiling, looking cross-ways, *'because I can't get that serious about other things. I like meeting people on a music level… It's an opportunity to have a good time and to share the experience.'* **From an interview with Jacoba Atlas, Melody Maker, September 1972**

You Gotta Say Yes To Another Excess

ARTIST Yello RELEASE DATE May 1983 (UK & US) LABEL Stiff (UK)/Elektra (US) PRODUCER – UK CHART peak/weeks 65/2 US CHART peak/weeks – TRACK LISTING I Love You/Lost Again/No More Words/Crash Dance/Great Mission/You Gotta Say Yes To Another Excess/Swing/Heavy Whispers/Smile On You/Pumping Velvet/Salut Mayoumba PERSONNEL Dieter Meir (v, hn), Boris Blank (sy)

Along with America's Suicide and Germany's D.A.F., Yello are a pioneering electro-duo and forebears of the notion of ironic luxury as perpetrated by ABC, Pet Shop Boys, Erasure et al. **You Gotta Say Yes To Another Excess** was Yello's third album but the first to introduce the Swiss outfit's scientifically precise, frantic neuro-dance. Featuring millionaire gambler-cum-disco Dadaist Dieter Meier on lugubrious baritone, and Boris Blank the meticulous soundscape artist, tracks such as *Lost Again* and *I Love You* were lush, cinematic, all magisterial beats and sweeping arrangements, like a series of European travelogues with voiceovers from an LSD-deranged Tommy Cooper.

… like no album you've ever heard before, this one aims straight at the senses – and hits… their sound is like their vision: one where funny peculiar blends with funny ha-ha, and where we're left none the wiser but all the more disturbed. **Mark Brennan, NME, May 1983**

Young Americans

ARTIST David Bowie RELEASE DATE March 1975 (UK & US) LABEL RCA (UK & US) PRODUCER – UK CHART peak/weeks 2/12 US CHART peak/weeks 9/51 TRACK LISTING Young Americans/Win/Fascination/Right/Somebody Up There Likes Me/Across The Universe/Can You Hear Me/Fame PERSONNEL Dennis Davis (d), Andy Newmark (d), Emir Ksasen (b), Willy Weeks (b), Carlos Alomar (g), David Bowie (g, k, bv), John Lennon (g, bv), Earl Slick (g), Michael Garson (k), David Sanborn (s), Ralph McDonald (pc), Pablo Rosario (pc), Larry Washington (pc), Ava Cherry (bv), Robin Clark (bv), Jean Fineberg (bv), Anthony Hinton (bv), Jean Millington (bv), Warren Peace (bv), Diane Sumler (bv), Luther Vandross (bv)

Adapting to Philly soul like a fish to water, Bowie showcased his versatile vocal abilities on some alarmingly lush and beautiful songs. John Lennon co-wrote *Fame*, Bowie's first American Number 1. The title song proffered a novelist's eye for detail, while gentle numbers like *Win* and the tensely poised *Can You Hear Me* grew stronger through the years. An obese reading of *Across The Universe*, again with Lennon, was the only weak link on an album fascinated by funk and by itself. And the new clean-cut Bowie still knew how to hold a cigarette in a cover shot.

The Young Ones

ARTIST Cliff Richard RELEASE DATE December 1961 LABEL Columbia PRODUCER Norrie Paramor UK CHART peak/weeks 1/42 US CHART peak/weeks – TRACK LISTING Friday Night/Got A Funny Feeling/Peace Pipe/Nothing's Impossible/The Young Ones/All For One/No One For Me But Nicky/What D'You Know/We've Got A Show & Vaudeville Routine - Have A Smile For Everyone We Meet/Tinkle, Tinkle Tinkle/The Eccentric/Algy The Picadilly Johnny/Captain Ginjah/Joshuah/Where Did You Get That Hat?/What D'You Know We've Got A Show/Living Doll/When The Girl In Your Arms Is The Girl In Your Heart/Mambo/Just Dance (b) Mood Mambo/The Savage/We Say Yeah PERSONNEL Cliff Richard (v), Jet Harris (b), Hank B. Marvin (lg), Bruce Welch (rg), Tony Meehan (d)

Cliff's third film, released weeks after his twenty-first birthday, inspired reviews like, 'The best musical Britain has ever made – and the finest teenage screen entertainment produced for a long time anywhere.' The title track, released as a single, clocked up record advance sales of over a million, becoming only the fourth single to debut at Number 1 and, unsurprisingly, became his biggest seller to date; plans were already afoot for another film.

Younger Than Yesterday

ARTIST The Byrds RELEASE DATE April 1967 (UK)/March 1967 (US) LABEL CBS (UK)/Columbia (US) PRODUCER Gary Usher UK CHART peak/weeks 37/4 US CHART peak/weeks 24/24 TRACK LISTING So You Want To Be A Rock 'N' Roll Star/Have You Seen Her Face/C.T.A.-102/Renaissance Fair/Time

Between/Everybody's Been Burned/Thoughts And Words/Mind Gardens/My Back Pages/The Girl With No Name/Why PERSONNEL Roger McGuinn (g, v), Gene Clark (v, t), David Crosby (g, v), Chris Hillman (b, v), Michael Clarke (d)

This was the Byrds album where Chris Hillman dug his heels in, writing half the songs. Of these the ironic anthem *So You Want To Be A Rock 'N' Roll Star* as an unlikely, yet somehow inevitable hit, as was the spirited cover of Dylan's **My Back Pages**. The psychedelia was getting heavier, bringing in trumpets and sitars. This was to the cost of some of the younger fans, but endeared the group to the growing hippie underground.

… if you ignore this album you are not only foolish – but deaf! Naturally it surpasses all other Byrds works, being rich in sparkling ideas, the most incredible feeling, and what's more – beauty… The Byrds are beautiful – there's no other word for it. **Melody Maker, May 1967**

Your Arsenal

ARTIST Morrissey **RELEASE DATE** August 1992 **LABEL** HMV (UK)/Sire (US) **PRODUCER** Mick Ronson **UK CHART** peak/weeks 4/5 **US CHART** peak/weeks 21/14 **TRACK LISTING** You're Gonna Need Someone On Your Side/Glamorous Glue/We'll Let You Know/The National Front Disco/Certain People I Know/We Hate It When Our Friends Become Succesful/You're The One For Me, Fatty/Seaside, Yet Still Docked/I Know It's Gonna Happen Someday/Tomorrow **PERSONNEL** Morrissey (v), Stephen Street (g, b), Andrew Paresi (d), Vini Reilly (g, k), Bedders (b), Mark E. Nevin (g), Steve Heart (k), Seamus Beaghan (k), Nawazish Ali Khan (vl)

The shine was taken off Steven Morrissey's fourth solo album by the simultaneous appearance of **Best…I**, first of two compilations from his former band The Smiths whose Rough Trade catalogue had been acquired by Warner Brothers. It leap-frogged **Your Arsenal** to finish three places higher at the top of the pile, but this Mick Ronson production, with songs co-written with Marr substitute Alan Whyte, was, arguably, a superior product. Ronson's ex-boss Bowie would cover **Know It's Gonna Happen Someday**, while the album would form the basis of the following year's live **Beethoven Was Deaf**.

… it's as if Morrissey has finally dared to do what he's always really wanted: to merge his childhood rocking… with his own distinct lyricism. **Your Arsenal** *is his best solo work yet and easily stands comparison with the best of The Smiths.* **John Aizlewood, Q, September 1992**

Your Twist Party

ARTIST Chubby Checker **RELEASE DATE** January 1962 (UK)/December 1961 (US) **LABEL** Cameo Parkway (UK)/Parkway (US) **PRODUCER** – **UK CHART** peak/weeks – **US CHART** peak/weeks 2/67 **TRACK LISTING** Ballin' The Jack/Blueberry Hill/Hound Dog/The Hucklebuck/I Could Have Danced All Night/Let' Twist Again/Mexican Hat Twist/Mister Twister/Rock Around The Clock/The Twist/Twistin' USA/Whole Lotta Shakin' Goin' On **PERSONNEL** Chubby Checker (v), session musicians

The king of the twist, born Ernest Evans, a hunky Philadelphia boy, was given his name because of his resemblance to Fats Domino. It was **The Twist**, written by Hank Ballard and a Number 1 in both 1960 and 1961 (as well as a recurring hit every few years from then on) that made that name stick. He went on to initiate other dance crazes, such as **The Hucklebuck**, **The Limbo** and **The Fly**. He sold over 10 million records. In 1988 he duetted with The Fat Boys on a revival of **Let's Twist Again**, and a year after that Jive Bunny

sampled his hits for the UK chart-topper, **That's What I Like**.

'All dances are based on sex – and the Twist is no exception. When I thought it up, I looked for something that had sex appeal…I watched young kids back home swaying from the hips even when their legs were still.' **Interview with R. C., Melody Maker, December 1961**

Zen Arcade

ARTIST Husker Du **RELEASE DATE** September 1984 **LABEL** S.S.T. **PRODUCER** – **UK CHART** peak/weeks 0/0 **US CHART** peak/weeks – **TRACK LISTING** Something I Learned Today/Broken Home, Broken Heart/Never Talking To You Again/Chartered Trips/Dreams Reoccuring/Indecision Time/Hare Krishna/Beyond The Threshold/Pride/I'll Never Forget You/The Biggest Lie/What's Going On/Masochism World/Standing By The Sea/Somewhere/One Step At A Time/Pink Turns To Blue/Newest Industry/Monday Will Never Be The Same/Whatever/The Tooth Fairy And The Princess/Turn On The News/Reoccuring Dreams **PERSONNEL** Bob Mould (v, g, k, pc), Grant Hart (d, k, pc, v), Greg Norton (b)

The second album, give or take an EP, by this influential Minneapolis-based punk trio was a double set, telling the story of a boy who leaves home but finds life on his own more challenging than he had supposed, as in the overdose tale **Pink Turns To Blue**, only to find in the closing 14-minute **Recurring Dreams** that it had all been a nightmare. After two more albums Husker Du would leave indie roots behind, but the fragile democracy of songwriters Mould and Hart blew up and the group with it.

Zen Arcade *is probably the closest hardcore will ever get to an opera. A kind of thrash* **Quadrophenia**: *it traces a young buck's passage through a series of social and emotional wastelands.* **David Fricke, Rolling Stone, February 1985**

Zooropa

ARTIST U2 **RELEASE DATE** July 1993 (UK & US) **LABEL** Island (UK & US) **PRODUCER** Flood, Brian Eno, The Edge **UK CHART** peak/weeks 1/24 **US CHART** peak/weeks 1/40 **TRACK LISTING** Zooropa/Babyface/Numb/Lemon/Stay (Faraway, So Close!)/Daddy's Gonna Pay For Your Crashed Car/Some Days Are Better Than Others/The First Time/Dirty Day/The Wanderer **PERSONNEL** Bono (v), The Edge (g), Adam Clayton (b), Larry Mullen (d)

In the Nineties, U2 re-invented themselves admirably: where previously they offered the last word in serious, passionate rock, on **Zooropa** one could detect not just irony and a keen sense of humour but also a realization that for music to move forward, it must embrace contemporary developments. Hence, **Zooropa** features sampling, treated sounds and a shift away from the gritty rock textures of yore towards a cooler, more European ambience. The subsequent Zoo TV tour was a triumph for U2's new postmodern aesthetic.

Zooropa *is music that just insisted on getting made… sung with a sensual tenderness in line with current Bono-think about pulling your own poetry out of media saturation, surrendering your psyche to a million random, fragmentary messages until they begin to coalesce into some perverse new logic.* **Paul Du Noyer, Q, August 1993**

Index of Artists

Abba, 11, 17, 215, 237
ABC, 127
Abdul, Paula, 82
AC/DC, 21, 80, 102
Ace of Base, 198
Adam Ant And The Ants, 121
Adams, Bryan, 181
Aerosmith, 176, 187, 226
Africa Bambaataa, 170
Allman Brothers Band, 38, 66
Allman Brothers, The, 18
Alpert, Herb, And The Tijuana Brass, 242
America, 13
Amos, Tori, 129, 232
Anderson, Laurie, 29
Animals, The, 14
Anthrax, 18
Armatrading, Joan, 142, 197
Ash, 156
Asia, 17
Associates, The, 214
Augustus Pablo, 121
Average White Band, 20
Ayers, Kevin, 48
Aztec Camera, 102
B52's, The, 20
Babybird, 107
Bad Company, 23
Badfinger, 247
Baez, Joan, 115
Baker, Anita, 179
Band, The, 23, 123, 148
Barrett, Syd, 137
Bay City Rollers, The, 161
Beach Boys, The, 26, 168, 200, 215, 216
Beastie Boys, The, 128, 167
Beatles, The, 8, 26, 27, 97, 100, 126, 138, 171, 183, 188, 194, 248
Beautiful South, The, 44
Beck, 159
Beck, Jeff, 27
Bee Gees, The, 191, 207
Belafonte, Harry, 41
Bell, William, 205
Belly, 208
Bennett, Tony, 106
Berry, Chuck, 21, 190
Big Audio Dynamite, 223
Big Brother And The Holding Company, 43
Big Country, 51
Big Star, 178, 198
Björk, 55, 172

Black Crowes, 206
Black Flag, 52
Black Grape, 114
Black Sabbath, 30, 166
Black Uhuru, 182
Black, Mary, 20
Blades, Ruben, 40
Bland, Bobby, 64
Blind Faith, 31
Blondie, 66, 166, 170
Blood Sweat & Tears, 32
Blue Nile, 98, 238
Blue Öyster Cult, 231
Blur, 94, 166
Bon Jovi, 199
Boney M, 154
Boo Radleys, The, 90
Booker T. & The MG's, 205
Boston, 222
Bowie, David, 11, 58, 101, 105, 126, 132, 136, 140, 185, 210, 252
Boyz II Men, 49
Bragg, Billy, 22
Brooks, Garth, 43, 188
Brown, James, 130, 192
Brown, Joe, 169
Browne, Jackson, 114, 123, 173, 189
Buckley, Jeff, 93
Buckley, Tim, 92, 209
Buffalo Springfield, 39
Buffalo, Grant Lee, 87
Burning Spear, 64, 140
Bush, Kate, 104, 119, 194
Butthole Surfers, 41
Buzzcocks, 15, 134
Byrds, The, 77, 147, 158, 252
Caberet Voltaire, 47
Cale, J. J., 181
Cale, John, 166, 200
Camel, 201
Can, 86
Canned Heat, 132
Captain Beefheart & His Magic Band, 46, 61
Captain Beefheart, 228
Carey, Mariah, 140, 148
Carpenter, Mary Chapin, 48
Carpenters, The, 158
Carter-The Unstoppable Sex Machine, 163
Cash, Johnny, 116, 240
Cash, Rosanne, 112
Cassidy, David, 43
Chapman, Tracy, 226
Charles, Ray, 88, 144
Cheap Trick, 109
Checker, Chubby, 253
Chemical Brothers, The, 73

Cherry, Neneh, 180
Chic, 185
Chicago, 44
Christians, The, 45
Clapton, Eric, 82, 118, 200, 233
Clash, The, 45, 133, 191
Cliff, Jimmy, 97
Cocker, Joe, 248
Cocteau Twins, The, 99, 227
Cohen, Leonard, 108, 204
Cole, Lloyd, 62
Cole, Lloyd, And The Commotions, 179
Cole, Nat 'King', 134
Collins, Albert, 228
Collins, Judy, 77
Collins, Phil, 41, 74, 100, 156
Commander Cody And His Lost Planet Airmen, 104
Cooder, Ry, 44, 165
Cooper, Alice, 30, 192
Costello, Elvis, 32, 149, 223
Costello, Elvis, And The Attractions, 17, 89, 109
Cowboy Junkies, 228
Coyne, Kevin, 141
Cramps, The, 159
Cranberries, The, 71
Cream, 60, 92, 244,
Creedence Clearwater Revival, 50, 95, 247
Crickets, The, 44
Croce, Jim, 252
Crosby, David, 108
Crosby, Stills And Nash, 51
Crosby, Stills, Nash & Young, 56
Crow, Sheryl, 229
Crowded House, 220, 225, 249
Cult, The, 134
Culture Club, 47
Culture, 231
Cure, The, 59, 172, 247
Cypress Hill, 30
Damned, The, 53
Davis, Sammy Jr, 209
De La Soul, 224
Deacon Blue, 244
Deee-Lite, 250
Deep Purple, 56, 137, 138
Def Leppard, 105, 176
Del Amitri, 238
Delaney & Bonnie & Friends, 161
Delfonics, The, 56
Denny, Martin, 73
Denver, John, 21
Depeche Mode, 204, 236

Derek And The Dominos, 124
Devo, 177
Dexy's Midnight Runners, 193, 226
Dinosaur Jr, 95
Dion, Celine, 75
Dire Straits, 38, 59, 135, 139
Dodgy, 84
Dolby, Thomas, 92
Domino, Fats, 186
Donegan, Lonnie, 91
Donovan, 215
Doobie Brothers, The, 42
Doonican, Val, 136
Doors, The, 8, 63, 121, 146, 212, 238
Dr Dre, 45
Dr Feelgood, 63
Dr John, The Night Tripper, 95
Drake, Nick, 39, 78
Dubliners, The, 64
Duran Duran, 184
Dury, Ian And The Blockheads, 152
Dylan, Bob, 24, 31, 32, 38, 57, 84, 102, 116, 150, 160, 225
Eagles, The, 57, 104, 133, 162
Earle, Steve, And The Dukes, 49
Earth, Wind & Fire, 94, 221
Echo And The Bunnymen, 51
Eddy, Duane, His 'Twangy' Guitar And The Rebels, 230
Edmunds, Dave, 183
Elastica, 67
Electric Light Orchestra, 164
Emerson, Lake And Palmer, 169
En Vogue, 86
English Beat, 106
Eno, Brian, 15, 28, 100
Enoch Light, 210
Enya, 240
Eurythmics, 25, 217
Everly Brothers, The, 54, 113
Everything But The Girl, 21, 239
Faces, The, 157
Fagen, Donald, 155
Fairport Convention, 128, 233
Faith No More, 181
Faithfull, Marianne, 38
Fall, 96, 223
Family, 75, 148
Fanny Hill, 76

Ferry, Bryan, 222
5th Dimension, The, 10
Fine Young Cannibals, 180
Five Royals, 56
Flack, Roberta, 78
Flamin' Groovies, The, 220
Fleetwood Mac, 79, 144, 189
Flying Burrito Brothers, The, 90
Focus, 80
Fogerty, John, 43
Foreigner, 82
Frampton, Peter, 83
Frankie Goes To Hollywood, 242
Franklin, Aretha, 12, 16, 106
Free, 78, 83
Fugazi, 223
Fugees, The, 192
Fugs, The, 236
Funkadelic, 84, 162
Gabriel, Peter, 201
Gallagher, Rory, 131
Gang Of Four, 71
Garbage, 87
Garland, Judy, 118
Gaye, Marvin, 101, 127, 243
Genesis, 65, 122
Gentry, Bobbie, 159
Gerry & The Pacemakers, 105
Go-Betweens, The, 127
Go-Go's, 27
Goldie, 225
Gong, 80
Grand Funk Railroad, 241
Grateful Dead, The, 13, 131, 249
Green, Al, 28, 41
Griffith, Nanci, 124
Guns N' Roses, 15, 234
Guthrie, Arlo, 11
Haircut 100, 167
Hall And Oates, 8
Happy Mondays, 170
Harris, Emmylou, 68, 250
Harrison, George, 12
Harvey, P. J., 64
Hawkwind, 110
Hayes, Isaac, 103
Heart, 98
Heaven 17, 167
Hell, Richard, And The Void-Oids, 31
Hendrix, Jimi, 16
Henley, Don, 39, 70
Hiatt, John, 37
Hitchcock, Robyn, And The Egyptians, 68
Hole, 131

Holly, Buddy, 39, 183,
Hooker, John Lee, 98
Hootie & The Blowfish, 50
Horslips, 34
Housemartins, The, 132
Houston, Whitney, 245
Human League, 53
Husker Du, 240, 253
Ice Cube, 173
Ice T, 158
Ifield, Frank, 106
Impressions, The, 30
Incredible String Band, The, 96
Inspiral Carpets, 26
INXS, 119
Iron Maiden, 158, 195
Isaak, Chris, 99
Isley Brothers, The, 224
Jackson, Janet, 115
Jackson, Joe, 133
Jackson, Michael, 23, 53, 160, 224
Jacksons, The, 228
Jam, The, 12, 195, 205
James Gang, 184
James, 91
Jamiroquai, 70
Jane's Addiction, 157
Jarre, Jean-Michel, 165
Jefferson Airplane, 52, 217, 237
Jefferson Starship, 182
Jesus And Mary Chain, 54, 175
Jethro Tull, 15
Jewel, 169
Jimi Hendrix Experience, The, 20, 67
Joel, Billy, 77, 90, 213
John, Elton, 42, 62, 69, 93, 103
Johnson, Linton Kwesi, 81
Jones, Rickie Lee, 184
Jones, Tom, 57
Joplin, Janis /Full Tilt Boogie, 167
Journey, 71
Joy Division, 46, 233
Judas Priest, 233
Keita, Salif, 204
Killing Joke, 120
King Crimson, 110, 122
King, Albert, 35
King, B. B., 130
King, Carole, 219
Kingston Trio, The, 101, 138, 202, 213
Kinks, The, 74, 203, 236
Kiss, 12

KLF, 245
Knack, The, 89
Kraftwerk, 18, 139, 227
Kravitz, Lenny, 139
L.L. Cool J, 139, 177
L7, 37
La's, The, 122
Lang, k. d., 122
Lauper, Cyndi, 196
Led Zeppelin, 111, 125, 126, 168
Lemonheads, 113
Lennon, John, 63, 109, 143, 239
Lennon, John, And The Plastic Ono Band, 116
Lennox, Annie, 60
Level 42, 250
Leven, Jackie, 150
Lewis, Huey, & The News, 207
Lighthouse Family, The, 158
Lightning Seeds, The, 46
Lindisfarne, 80
Little Feat, 61, 76, 123, 190
Little Richard, 74, 101
Lofgren, Nils, 155
Los Lobos, 119
Love, 81
Lovett, Lyle, 117
Lush, 207
Lynyrd Skynyrd, 213
Madness, 137
Madonna, 27, 128, 229
Magazine, 49
Manic Street Preachers, The, 72, 88
Mann, Aimee, 244
Marie, Teena, 209
Marley, Bob, & The Wailers, 40, 43, 73, 129, 150
Martyn, John, 93, 202
Marx, Richard, 183
Massive Attack, 33, 175
Mathis, Johnny, 99
Mayall, John, 34
Mayfield, Curtis, 216
Mazzy Star, 201
MC Hammer, 171
MC5, 22
McCartney, Paul, 79, 141
McCartney, Paul, And Wings, 24
McColl, Kirsty, 121
McDonald, Country Joe (And The Fish), 67
McGarrigle, Kate & Anna, 84
McLean, Don, 13
McNabb, Ian, 229
Meat Loaf, 24

Mellencamp, John Cougar, 13
Men At Work, 40
Metal Health, 177
Metallica, 119, 143
Michael, George, 75, 161
Midler, Bette, 60
Midnight Oil, 59
Ministry, 122
Mission, The, 214
Mitchell, Joni, 33, 50, 100, 102
Moby Grape, 144
Monkees, The, 145
Moody Blues With The London Festival Orchestra..., 55
Moody Blues, The, 72, 195
Morissette, Alanis, 114
Morrison, Van, & The Chieftains, 112
Morrison, Van, 17, 19, 97, 114, 145, 172, 190
Morrissey, 235, 237, 253
Mothers Of Invention, 83, 242
Motorhead, 156
Mott The Hoople, 147
Mould, Bob, 249
Moyet, Alison, 11
Muldaur, Maria, 140
My Bloody Valentine, 135
Nazz, 151
Nelson, Ricky, 184
Nelson, Willie, 182
Nesmith, Mike, 14
New Order, 173, 220
New York Dolls, 153
Newman, Randy, 34, 92, 122, 230
Nilsson, 155
Nine Inch Nails, 174
Nirvana, 111, 152
NWA, 212
Nyro, Laura, 68
O'Connor, Sinead, 105
O'Hara, Mary Margaret, 144
O'Jays, The, 22
O'Sullivan, Gilbert, 23
Oasis, 25, 56, 243
Ocean Colour Scene, 146
Oldfield, Mike, 161, 229
Only Ones, The, 163
Orange Juice, 251
Orb, The, 163, 231
Orbison, Roy, 109
P Funk All Stars, 234
Parker, Graham, 207
Parliament, 146
Parsons, Gram, 95
Pearl Jam, 220, 237

Pentangle, 24
Pere Ubu, 65, 144
Pet Shop Boys, 9, 112
Peter, Paul And Mary, 110, 168,
Peters And Lee, 241
Petty, Tom, & The Heartbreakers, 52, 205
Petty, Tom, 85
Phair, Liz, 72
Pink Floyd, 14, 18, 54, 61, 170, 239, 248
Pixies, The, 36, 63, 216,
Pogues, The, 188
Police, The, 90, 164, 182, 218
Pop, Iggy, 108, 136
Pop, Iggy, And The Stooges, 180
Portishead, 65
Prefab Sprout, 117, 210
Presley, Elvis, 33, 69, 84, 87, 120, 136, 173, 186, 203
Pretenders, The, 174
Price, Alan, 29
Primal Scream, 193
Prince & The Revolution, 155, 165
Prince And The New Power Generation, 58
Prince, 176, 197
Prine, John, 116
Procol Harum, 175, 190
Prodigy, 76, 148
Public Enemy, 76, 113, 175
Pulp, 59
Queen, 120, 137, 154
Quick Silver Messenger Service, 96
R.E.M., 19, 61, 94, 148, 164,
Radiohead, 28, 160, 165
Raitt, Bonnie, 154
Ramones, The, 125, 179, 187
Raspberries, The, 209
Red Hot Chilli Peppers, 32
Redding, Otis, 61, 163, 204
Reed, Lou, 28, 153, 186, 227
Reeves, Jim, 8
REO Speedwagon, 102
Replacements, The, 126
Richard, Cliff, 46, 107, 129, 142, 215, 252
Richie, Lionel, 42
Richman, Jonathan, And The Modern Lovers, 186
Robertson, Robbie, 212
Robinson, Smokey, And The Miracles, 91
Rolling Stones, The, 9, 28, 29, 73, 90, 126, 164, 187, 202, 211, 219

Ronstadt, Linda, 98, 198
Ross, Diana, 58
Roxy Music, 19, 79, 81, 188, 198, 212
Run-D. M. C., 178
Rundgren, Todd, 75, 202, 234, 248
Sade, 58
Santana, 8, 134
Sayer, Leo, 70
Scaggs, Boz, 36
Searchers, The, 142
Sedaka, Neil, 124
Seekers, The, 48
Seger, Bob, & The Silver Bullet Band, 130
Seger, Bob, 213
Sex Pistols, The, 152
Shadows, The, 196
Shakin' Stevens, 196
Shamen, The, 35
Sherman, Allan, 150
Simon And Garfunkel, 34, 37
Simon, Carly, 156
Simon, Paul, 94, 211, 222
Simple Minds, 152, 162
Simply Red, 168, 209
Sinatra, Frank, 47, 48, 83, 110, 153, 194, 203, 218
Siouxsie And The Banshees, 193
Sister Sledge, 241
Sisters Of Mercy, 236
Size, Roni & Reprazent, 152
Slade, 199
Sledge, Percy, 244
Slits, 52
Sly And Robbie, 184
Sly And The Family Stone, 208, 222
Small Faces, The, 160
Smashing Pumpkins, The, 143, 197
Smith, Patti, 103
Smiths, The, 142, 177, 200
Snoop Doggy Dogg, 62
Soft Cell, 157
Soft Machine, The, 201
Sonic Youth, 55
Soul II Soul, 47
Soundgarden, 216
Spandau Ballet, 228
Sparks, 120
Specials, The, 206
Spector, Phil, 45
Spice Girls, 206
Spin Doctors, The, 171
Spinal Tap, 36
Spinners, The, 206
Spirit, 230

Spiritualized, 124
Springfield, Dusty, 66
Springsteen, Bruce, 34, 35, 54, 151, 185, 230, 246
Squeeze, 66
Stansfield, Lisa, 9
Steely Dan, 10, 42, 50, 88, 174, 188
Stereo MCs, The, 48
Steve Miller Band, The, 80, 190
Stevens, Cat, 219
Stewart, Rod, 18, 72, 88, 151, 154
Stills, Stephen, 210
Sting, 221
Stone Roses, The, 211
Stone Temple Pilots, 176
Stooges, The, 85, 212
Stranglers, The, 132, 180
Streisand, Barbra, 96, 135, 168
Style Council, The, 164
Suede, 62, 214
Suicide, 214
Summer, Donna, 23, 162
Super Furry Animals, 87
Supergrass, 106
Supertramp, 36, 51, 71
Supremes, The, 216
T. Rex, 67, 199
Talk Talk, 207
Talking Heads, 76, 146, 182, 218
Tangerine Dream, 188
Taylor, James, 217
Teardrop Explodes, 119
Tears For Fears, 203
Teenage Fanclub, 24
Television, 141
Temptations, The, 220
10CC, 196, 221
10,000 Maniacs, 110
Texas, 245
The The, 111
Them, 14
Thin Lizzy, 115
Thompson, Richard & Linda, 107
Thompson, Richard, 53, 189, 197
Toots And The Maytals, 86
Traffic, 115, 136, 147, 226
Tricky, 141
Trower, Robin, 37
Turner, Tina, 174
Tyrannosaurus Rex, 26, 150
U2, 9, 118, 172, 179, 232, 239, 253
Undertones, The, 232

Underworld, 194
Valli, Frankie & The Four Seasons, 197
Van Halen, 78, 234
Vandross, Luther, 154
Vanilla Ice, 225
Various, 249
Vaughan, Stevie Ray, 199
Velvet Underground, The, 131, 132, 235, 244
Verve, The, 157
Vincent, Gene, 33
Wailer, Bunny, 30
Waits, Tom, 178, 218
Wakeman, Rick, 199
Walker, Scott, 192
Was Not Was, 243
Waterboys, The, 78
Waters, Muddy, 96, 147
Wayne, Jeff, 240
Webb, Jimmy, 217
Weller, Paul, 208, 246
Wendy & Lisa, 85
Wham!, 138
White, Barry, 211
Who, The, 130, 142, 149, 225, 246
Williams, Andy 55
Wings, 235, 247
Winter, Johnny, 117
Winwood, Steve, 16, 187
Wire, 170
Wishbone Ash, 16
Womac, Bobby, 172
Wonder, Stevie, 112, 129, 149, 204, 218
World Party, 93
Wu-Tang Clan, 70
Wyatt, Robert, 186
Wynette, Tammy, 208
X Ray Spex, 89
X, 134
XTC, 64
Yardbirds, The, 251
Yello, 252
Yes, 251
Young, Neil, 10, 98, 190, 226
Young, Neil, And Crazy Horse, 72, 178, 242
Youssou N'Dour Et Le Super Etoile De Dakar, 109
Zappa, Frank, 104, 231
Zevon, Warren, 194, 240
Zombies, The, 159
ZZ Top, 68